THE COMPLETE STEP-BY-STEP GUIDE TO

CHESS &
BRIDGE

HOW TO PLAY • WINNING STRATEGIES • RULES • HISTORY

THE COMPLETE STEP-BY-STEP GUIDE TO

CHESS & BRIDGE

HOW TO PLAY • WINNING STRATEGIES • RULES • HISTORY

DAVID BIRD AND JOHN SAUNDERS

southwater

This edition is published by Southwater,
an imprint of Anness Publishing Ltd,
108 Great Russell Street,
London WC1B 3NA;
info@anness.com

www.southwaterbooks.com;
www.annesspublishing.com;
twitter: @Anness_Books

If you like the images in this book and would
like to investigate using them for publishing,
promotions or advertising, please visit our website
www.practicalpictures.com for more information.

A CIP catalogue record for this book
is available from the British Library.

Designed and produced for Anness Publishing by
The Bridgewater Book Company Ltd.

Publisher: Joanna Lorenz
Editorial Director: Helen Sudell
Editors: Rosie Gordon, Robin Pridy, Elizabeth Young
    and Felicity Forster
Designers: Jo Hill, Stuart Perry and Sylvia Tate
Production Controller: Ben Worley

CONTENTS

INTRODUCTION

Chess and bridge are both fascinating games to learn and play. Although they are quite different games, each with their own set of complex rules and strategies, they do share some similarities. They are both forward thinking and tactical games requiring intricate planning, careful strategy and forethought, experience and insight.

What is Chess?

A dictionary or an encyclopaedia will tell you that it is a game of skill played by two players taking turns to move pieces or figures on a chequered board. This is perfectly correct, and chess belongs to a vast family of other parlour games that people of all ages play. Like all such games, it has a number of rules to learn, and the primary aim of this book is to teach you these rules so that you can start playing. Let's begin by dispelling a myth: chess is not hard to learn or play. It might appear complicated at first sight, especially when you find that there are five different types of pieces on the board at the beginning of the game, all of which move in different ways.

Another question worth asking is 'Why chess?' Why should you play chess – rather than snakes and ladders? The reason is because chess is far more than 'a board game' in the sense that a Rolls-Royce is superior to 'a car'. Yes, chess is a board game, and many people learn it and play it as such all their lives. There is nothing wrong with that – in fact, it is one of its greatest virtues. However, chess can also be a game of depth, creativity and imagination, and it has fascinated millions of people for over 500 years. Unlike other board games, its mysteries have yet to be solved by the colossal computing power available in the 21st century, despite millions of dollars being expended in the attempt. Chess has not yet yielded all of its secrets.

Above: Many great chess players started playing at a very young age.

Left: The National Contract Bridge Championships in 1939, held at Asbury Park, New Jersey, USA. The jumbo playing cards are for the benefit of the kibitzers (watchers) who are sitting in a specially-built seating gallery. Players from left to right are Charles Goren, Oswald Jacoby, B.Jay Becker and John Crawford.

Left: Learning chess is a challenging but rewarding pastime, and one that can become a passion for many players.

Below: Most bridge players sort the cards in their hand so that all the cards in one suit are together, with the highest-ranking card on the left and the lowest-ranking on the right.

What is Bridge?

Bridge is a trick-taking card game of skill and chance, played by four players. It has been one of the world's most popular games for many years, and is well-respected as a strategic game that can be as competitive and technical or as fun and sociable as the players decide. A big attraction of the game is that it is played in partnership. You and your partner sit opposite each other at the card table, competing against two other players, also in partnership. However good you may be as a single player, you will not achieve very much without the co-operation of your partner, and a long-term bridge partnership in many ways resembles a marriage.

In bridge, the deal consists of two parts. First the four players, each looking only at their own hand of 13 cards, conduct an auction of ever ascending 'bids'. This will be fully explained in the text of the book but, for example, a player might bid 'one heart' to tell his partner that he holds an above average collection of high cards (aces, kings, queens and jacks) and that hearts is his longest suit and might therefore make a good trump suit. When a suit eventually becomes 'trumps', it is more powerful than the other three suits; a low trump will defeat even an ace in one of the other three suits. When the bidding comes to an end, one or other partnership will have set themselves a target for the second part of the proceedings: the play. For example, they may have said they will attempt to make ten tricks with spades as trumps. The play begins and that partnership must then try to make the target of ten tricks. The two defenders will do their best to prevent it. If you are new to the game and find this hard to follow, do not worry. Everything is clearly explained in the following chapters.

How to use this book

Divided into two easy-to-use sections, the first section, How to Play Chess, begins by looking at the history of chess, its origins and evolution through the Victorian era and how it has evolved into the game it is today. In this part of the book you will find simple, structured guidance on how each individual piece moves and, by working through the examples, it won't be long before you have mastered the basic elements of the game. Once you have learned the rules, the book also introduces some basic strategies and tactics to inspire you from the start. This will prepare you for your first few chessboard battles, and also provide a ready reference for the early phase of your chess-playing career. Before laying out the rules of the game, this book looks at the wider world of chess: its history, top players, celebrated aficionados and cultural significance. No other board game can compete with chess in terms of longevity. The codification of most sports and games only dates to the 1800s, but chess is more than 1,000 years old, and the rules, as played today, have remained completely unchanged for about 500 years. In this regard, it is one of the intellectual wonders of the world. There are records of matches by chess players from the 16th and 17th centuries, which demonstrate a highly sophisticated level of play. Nobody knows who made the final amendments to

the rules in the 15th century, but to have created a game that has remained unchanged for half a millennium is true genius.

Having absorbed something of the culture and history of the game and learned the basic rules, the next step is to learn how to win at chess. It is one thing to know how to play a game, and another to be able to win with any regularity. Winning isn't everything – but it's definitely important.

Above: Chess rules and strategies are clearly explained and many are illustrated with diagrams that show the chess positions involved in each move. From simple to complex, you will be guided through a wide variety of chess scenarios step by step.

Left: Having regular games of bridge is a great way to build up a close circle of friends who share the same passion.

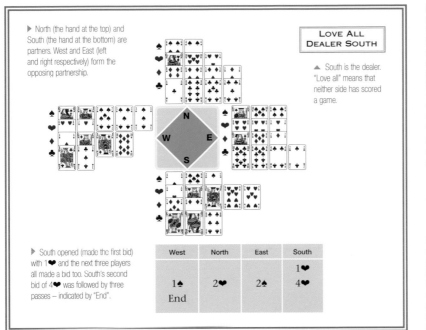

▶ North (the hand at the top) and South (the hand at the bottom) are partners. West and East (left and right respectively) form the opposing partnership.

LOVE ALL
DEALER SOUTH

▲ South is the dealer. "Love all" means that neither side has scored a game.

Left: An example of a typical hand diagram in the How to Play Bridge section of the book. The bidding, which takes place before the play, is shown in the green table at the bottom. All the basic bridge terms such as "bid", "tricks", "pass", "contract", "play the contract", "trumps", "defenders", "declarer", "dummy", are clearly explained in the section called Starting Out on pages 258–67.

▶ South opened (made the first bid) with 1♥ and the next three players all made a bid too. South's second bid of 4♥ was followed by three passes – indicated by "End".

West	North	East	South
			1♥
1♠	2♥	2♠	4♥
End			

Below: There are many different styles of chess pieces and boards available, from portable magnetic and mini travel sets to exquisite ones made of crystal, glass and marble. You can even find large-sized sets for outdoor play.

The second section, How to Play Bridge, looks at the history of contract bridge. It will explain the rules and teach you how to play the game competitively. An early section will explain the basics, such as tricks and trumps, assuming that you know nothing at all about the game. From then on, there are basic, intermediate and advanced sections on all three aspects of the game – bidding, dummy play and defence. Apart from instruction, there is also a summary of the history of bridge, from its original roots to the game we know today, and there is a brief look at some of the most famous players in the world, past and present, and the deals they have played.

Having access to a computer and the Internet, makes it very easy to play chess and bridge online, perhaps with players from the other side of the world. This aspect of play is also fully described.

There is a huge range of literature and learning aids available for both these games, and this book contains plenty of advice for further reading. A comprehensive and detailed glossary of all the terms used is included at the back of the book for reference. Practical advice is provided on the best way to practise and improve your chess and bridge games, and there are tips on how to take your first steps competitively.

HOW TO PLAY CHESS

Many board games have been invented over the centuries, but none have been as popular as chess, or have endured unchanged for so long. It is hugely rewarding to play, whether purely for fun or in high-level competitions.

THE HISTORY OF CHESS

Chess has one of the richest histories of all games or sports, in part due to its sheer antiquity. Something in the game has appealed to people of all ages and cultures, already spreading widely across Asia during the 6th and 7th centuries, and equally popular with the computer-game-playing teenagers of the 21st century. For at least the last 500 years, chess has been particularly popular among literate people who have often applied their skills to the task of writing about it, even to the point of recording each move of games they have played. Consequently, although its origins are somewhat obscure, chess has an extraordinarily well-documented history. At the beginning of the 21st century, chess is more popular than ever. It has been estimated that upwards of 600 million people in more than 120 countries know how to play chess.

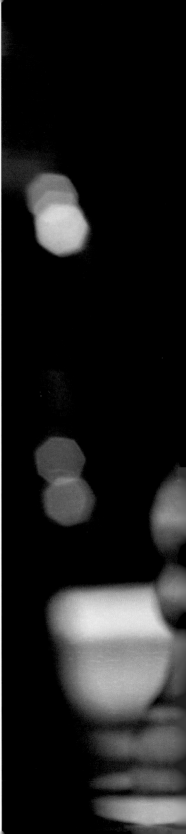

Right: As you will learn, the king is the most important piece on the chessboard. The object of the game is to checkmate the opponent's king.

THE EARLY HISTORY OF CHESS

The one thing we can say with great certainty about chess is that it is a very, very old game. It has been established that a forerunner of modern chess emerged well over 1,000 years ago, while the modern game, with the rules of the game as played today, came into being about 500 years ago.

Indian invention

Board games in general date from at least 6,000 years ago, but the first chess derivative emerged around AD600 in India. In one myth associated with a very early form of chess in India, the invention of the game is credited to a Hindu saint called Sissa, who was a Brahman at the court of a king. One day the Indian king (rajah) Balhait summoned Sissa and requested that he create a game based on mental skill and oppose the teaching of games in which mere chance decided the outcome by the throw of dice. The king also told Sissa that this new game should be designed to enhance the mental qualities required to analyse and

reason. The Brahman later returned to the court of the king with a board (*ashtapada*) consisting of 8 x 8 = 64 squares with rules that were strikingly similar to the ones we use today. The game he devised was called *chaturanga*, which is a Sanskrit military term meaning 'army composed of four members' – thought to be made up of chariots, foot soldiers, horses and elephants.

It is unclear whether *chaturanga* was a game in the sense in which we use the word today, and some chess historians believe that it actually derived from a divination ceremony. However, it was extremely similar to the game we now call chess: like the modern game, it was played on a 64-square board; the two players had 16 pieces each, with starting positions much as they are today; at least two of them (the knight and rook) moved exactly as those pieces do in modern chess; and the players took it in turns to make a move. *Chaturanga* later became known as 'chess'.

Above: *Xiang qi* is native to China and is commonly called Chinese chess. The earliest indications reveal the game was played as early as the 4th century BC in China.

Right: In medieval times the game of chess was played on the same type of board with the same pieces and basic rules as today. However, there were several variations concerning the movement of certain pieces.

Éfte es otro juego departido en á arvin. trebeios que an a seer en

se mismo toque pueto en la segun casa del cauallo blanco. e entrara el

Above: The 12th-century Muslim leader Saladin was said to be a very bad chess player, though a great war tactician. Here, he is depicted playing chess with his sister.

Chess travels east and west

The game then started its travels, in two directions. It travelled east to China, where it became known as *xiang qi*, or Chinese chess. This form is significantly different from the game as known in the West, but it has survived to the present day and remains very popular in China and other Asian countries.

The game also travelled west from India to Persia in the late 7th century AD, where it came to be known as *chatranj*. The rules were extremely similar to modern chess. Like today's game, the idea was to trap the king. It too proved hugely popular, spreading across the Arab world for 900 years. From Persia and the Arab countries, the game travelled farther west via the Mediterranean and North Africa, and also travelled via the European mainland to Russia and northern Europe by the 11th century, at the time of the Norman Conquest.

The game played in medieval Europe was very similar to the game played by the Persians 600 years earlier. The Crusades may also have played a part in the development of chess, and one myth has the 12th-century Muslim leader Saladin teaching the game to King Richard I of England, although legend also tells us that Saladin was a notoriously bad player. Popular tournaments were held throughout the Middle Ages as ways of solving disputes across Europe. During this period the complexity of the game meant it was played almost exclusively by the nobility.

THE GAME OF CHATRANJ

The Arabs reached a high level of skill in the game they called *chatranj*. They studied the theory of the game, developed a notation for recording games and composed problems for solving.

Above: Today's chess is based on a version of *chaturanga* that was played in India around the 7th century AD. It is believed that the Persians created a more modern version of the game, called *chatranj*.

The chessboard below shows a composition for which the solution in *chatranj* is exactly the same as it would be in modern chess. Black is to move first and checkmate White in five moves. Even a good chess player will find this puzzle tough to crack. But the most astonishing thing about this puzzle is its age: it was composed more than a 1,000 years ago.

Above: Black to play and mate in five moves.

THE BEGINNINGS OF MODERN CHESS

By the 11th century, chess was a well-known game throughout Europe, but it was still some time before the game turned into what we now recognize as chess. The ancient game seems to have gradually evolved into modern chess. Some of the rule changes were so specific that it is tempting to imagine them being made by one person, but nobody knows quite how this came about. Two of the pieces underwent a fundamental change in the way they were moved: the piece now known as a queen became the most powerful piece on the board after being one of the least useful, while the modern bishop also gained extra power after being little better than a pawn in terms of relative strength. These changes, together with a number of other smaller adjustments, were evidently the product of some very agile brains. They had the effect of making chess more dynamic and subtle; games could reach a quick conclusion, in a handful of moves if one of the players was unwary, but could also go to great lengths and require a great deal of patience.

Below: In the 11th century, the chess piece known as the queen became the most important piece on the board. Here is a 12th-century Italian queen, carved from ivory.

Guides to chess

Although there were still some regional variations and parts of the world where the old form of chess persisted, the revamped game quickly supplanted the old and spread through Spain and Italy. Soon expert chess players in Spain, Portugal and Italy were writing practical guides on how to play the game. The first one

FIRST WORLD CHAMPION

♛ ♝ ♞ ♚

Ruy López de Segura (c.1530–1580), more commonly known as Ruy López, is sometimes accorded the title of first unofficial world champion. He was a priest from Badajoz in Spain and wrote one of the best-known early works on chess in 1561, called *Book of the Liberal Invention and Art of the Game of Chess*. His book included advice on chess openings, one of which came to be known by his name and is still played in high-level chess to this day. In his book, Ruy López introduced the word 'gambit', which derives from an Italian word describing the act of tripping up an opponent in wrestling. It is an apt term: chess players invariably use the word 'gambit' to describe a chess opening in which a player allows the opponent to capture a pawn in order to gain time to pursue an attack or get a grip on the game.

was a book by a Catalan player named Francesc Vicent, published in Valencia in 1495. This was soon followed by more chess books, which had tips for starting and ending the game (known by modern chess players as 'openings' and 'endgames'), as well as chess puzzles (or problems). It is clear from the advice in these books that play was already of a high order, with some of the principles of modern chess strategy already in place. Top players in different parts of the world were becoming known to each other. Two Italians, Paolo Boi (1528–1598) and Giovanni Leonardo Di Bona da Cutri (1542–1587) made trips to Spain, during which time they met the leading Iberian chess player, Ruy López, and beat him. With these successes, chess supremacy passed from Spain to Italy.

Far left: The growing popularity of chess as a recreational activity can be seen in its depiction in the art and artefacts of the 15th, 16th and 17th centuries. Here, a game of chess is portrayed on a 17th-century French mirror frame.

Left: Carved from ivory and dating from the 11th century, this chess piece belongs to the 16-piece Charlemagne chess set. The set includes two kings, two queens, four elephants, four knights, three chariots and one foot soldier.

Below: This 15th-century French miniature depicts Lancelot and Guinevere playing a game of chess. Chess has often been associated with the 'game of love'.

CHESS IN THE PRE-VICTORIAN ERA

Since the 1600s, the basic rules of chess have remained the same. Although relatively few chess games were recorded until the late 18th century, records of early chess games allow meaningful comparisons to be made between the standard of modern chess today and the game as played 300 years ago. This is one of the most exciting aspects of the history of chess. Imagine if football experts had full-colour videos of 19th-century matches, with action-replay facilities, in order to see how the sport's originators played it (and to find out if they were good players). Chess players are fortunate to have this fascinating capability available to them.

Below: In the painting, *Still Life*, by Lubin Baugin (1612/13–1663) the box on the right is a chessboard with the pieces stored inside.

A fashionable game

By the 17th century, chess was firmly established as a fashionable board game throughout Europe, and a small number of leading players engaged in matches for high stakes. One such player was Gioacchino Greco (b.c.1600–1634), from Calabria, in Italy. Nicknamed 'the Calabrese' and credited (almost certainly erroneously) with inventing the Greco Counter Gambit, he played matches with rivals in Paris, London and Madrid, becoming famous for his flamboyant style of play. While in England, he sold his chess opening analyses (which purported to be records of his games) to supplement his income. Some of these manuscripts still exist. Much of Greco's chess analysis makes perfect sense today, although some of it consists of tricks that would be unlikely to snare a well-coached modern chess player.

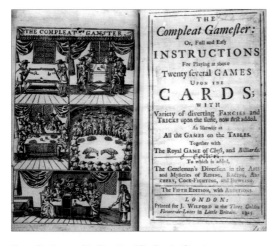

Above: The title page of the fifth edition of *The Compleat Gamester*, attributed to Charles Cotton (1630–1687). This book gave instructions on playing billiards, bowls, card games and chess.

In the 18th century, the proliferation of coffee houses coincided with the growing popularity of chess. As well as normal games between the clientele, these were also the venues for challenge matches between the best players of the era. Coffee houses tended to be upper-class establishments in the 1700s, but were frequented more by the middle classes in the 19th century.

So, how do early generations of players compare? The big difference between chess in the 21st century and in the 19th century (and before) is that we have the benefit of knowing what each successive generation has discovered about the game. Some of the strategies of early chess players seem naive to the modern chess master, particularly when it comes to the opening moves of a game. This part of the game has been studied in enormous detail by chess experts, with many books and computer databases published containing vast arrays of opening move possibilities. Dissemination of information on this scale only became possible relatively recently, although some chess masters of the Victorian era wrote substantial manuals on chess openings, and there were quite a number of chess periodicals and regular columns in newspapers. Some of the games show that chess of quite a high order was being played from the earliest days of the modern rules – the players were certainly accomplished enough to beat all the upper strata of modern competition chess players.

PHILIDOR

François-André Danican Philidor (1726–1795) is generally considered to be the best chess player of his era, and he was also a profound writer on the game. One of the most remarkable people of the 18th century, he was born into a musical family and grew up to become one of the leading French composers of his day. He made his living in the world of music but soon learned and fell in love with chess, which he played at the Café de la Régence, a celebrated chess haunt in Paris. He played with great skill, being one of the first people to master blindfold chess – in which one or both of the competitors plays without sight of the board and pieces (moves being communicated verbally). He could play more than one game at a time in this mode. Philidor spent time in the Netherlands and England, and made money teaching and displaying his chess skills while abroad. Once home in France, he concentrated more on his music and composed comic operas. After the French Revolution he moved to London, where he lived for the rest of his life. From the records of his games, it is evident that he was the greatest chess player of his age, and he far exceeded those before him. He remains as famous a name in the world of music as he is in chess.

Above: This portrait of François-André Danican Philidor was engraved by Augustus de Saint-Aubin in 1772.

CHESS IN THE VICTORIAN ERA

As happened with many other sports and games, the 19th century saw great developments in the organization and codification of chess. It had hitherto been played privately or in various meeting places but many chess clubs and associations sprang up during the 19th century. Chess also became the main attraction at other very notable venues, such as Simpson's Divan, a well-known cafe-restaurant on the Strand in London. Founded in 1820, it became a mecca for all the leading chess players of the Victorian era as well as those who would challenge them, and continued to be a leading chess centre into the early years of the 20th century. It is still a restaurant in the 21st century and retains its connection with chess: some chess relics are on display there.

Growth of chess clubs

Most of the countries of Europe, as well as North America and Australasia, had well-established clubs from about the middle of the 19th century. Most of them began to run formal competitions and club championships, and the concept of team chess was born. Clubs would line up a number of their best players and play the teams from other clubs, with normally one game played between each representative, and the best player of each team meeting that of the other (and so on, in descending order of strength). Although it was some time before a player came along to match Philidor in strength, there was a significant explosion in the strength of the top players from the 1820s. French players were generally

Above: *The Coffee Boiler*, a chalk lithograph made c.1840 by August Strixner, depicts the busy but convivial scene of a Viennese coffee house. The chess game in progress is watched with interest by the other customers.

Right: Though men dominated the game in this era, it was by no means a male preserve. Here, two Victorian women enjoy a game of chess.

reckoned to be the best during the early years of the 19th century, although this was often by reputation and hardly put to a rigorous test.

Technological developments

Progress in technology in the fields of publishing, travel and communication also contributed to the growing popularity of chess. The earliest periodical devoted to chess, *Le Palamède*, was first published in Paris in 1836 and it was quickly followed by chess magazines in Britain, Germany and elsewhere. As well as general articles on chess and reports of club activity, magazines contained game scores (i.e. transcriptions of the moves of games) from recent matches, which meant that players could learn from games played by stronger players and acquire intelligence about future rivals. These magazines proved very popular with club players and some had long runs. One, *British Chess Magazine*, has appeared every month from 1881 to the present day.

The invention of the telegraph made it possible for chess games to be played over vast distances. The first electric telegraph match was between Washington and Baltimore in 1844, linked by the first American telegraph line. In Britain in 1845, two leading players journeyed on the railway from London to Gosport, where they played a game via telegraph with some opponents back at the London terminus. By the end of the century it had become possible to play a transatlantic game via cable, the first successful one being played in 1896 between the British and Manhattan chess clubs.

A CHALLENGE TO THE FRENCH

♛ ♝ ♞ ♚

Alexandre Deschapelles (1780–1847) and Louis de la Bourdonnais (1795–1840) were leading habitués of the Café de la Régence, with the younger man gaining ascendancy over the older from about 1821. A challenge to French supremacy came from across the English Channel, and Bourdonnais played a vast match (consisting of 85 games) against an Ulsterman named Alexander McDonnell (1798–1835) over a period of four months in London in 1834. The Frenchman won the match, but the quality of the games was of a high standard, and the match fostered a taste for chess competition among the general public.

THE EARLY WORLD CHAMPIONS

Chess statisticians treat the 1886 match between the Austrian, US-resident player Wilhelm Steinitz, and the Polish chess master Johannes Zukertort as the first official championship of the world. Indeed, modern world chess champions are often accorded an ordinal number that connects them back to Steinitz, the winner of the match and the first world champion. However, it is appropriate to include some of Steinitz's predecessors in this section since, despite not holding an official title, they were nevertheless acclaimed as the greatest players of their respective eras.

Howard Staunton
After the death of Louis de la Bourdonnais in 1840, the best player in the world was unnofficially considered to be Pierre Saint-Amant (1800–1872). On a trip to London in 1843, Saint-Amant defeated a Shakespearean scholar and chess writer named Howard Staunton (1810–1874) in a short match. However, the defeated Englishman challenged him to a return match that took place over 21 games in front of large audiences at the Café de la Régence. This time Staunton won the match, and with it the unofficial title of the world's best player. To this day, Staunton is the nearest thing Britain has had to a world chess champion. Sadly, his win against Saint-Amant was his high-water mark, and his play thereafter was less impressive.

Staunton also forged a career as a chess writer and journalist, writing the famous *Chess Player's Handbook*, which his fame helped to sell as the main chess instructional manual of its time. In one of the earliest examples of sports sponsorship, he also gave his name as the registered trademark of the standard design of chess pieces, which are still used today.

Paul Morphy
The next major player of the 19th century was an American, Paul Morphy (1837–1884). Born in New Orleans and of Creole descent, Morphy was the first recognized chess prodigy, who became an exceptionally strong chess player as a boy. He took on the best players in New Orleans at the age of eight, and by the time he was 13 he could beat them all.

Below left: Howard Staunton (1810–1874) is still the only British player to have been considered the world's best chess player of his era. As well as a chess player, he was a Shakespearean scholar.

Below centre: Paul Charles Morphy (1837–1884) was considered to be the greatest player in the world in the 1850s. After qualifying as a lawyer, he travelled to Europe, seeking to play and defeat the top European chess masters.

Below right: Wilhelm Steinitz (1836–1900) was born in Prague, later settling in London. In 1888 he became a US citizen. He is regarded as the first official world chess champion, winning the title in a match with Johannes Zukertort in 1886, but he was probably the world's best player from 1866 until 1894, when he lost his title to Emanuel Lasker.

Photo, Bradshaw, Hastings.

E Lasker

Above: Emanuel Lasker (1868–1941) had a longer reign as world champion (1894–1921) than anyone before or since.

Right: Johannes Zukertort (1842–1888) lost to Wilhelm Steinitz in the first official world championship match, held in the USA in 1886. Born in Poland, he later moved to Berlin and finally settled in London. He excelled at blindfold chess (playing without sight of the board) and was able to play 16 games simultaneously in this fashion.

After completing his studies to become a lawyer, Morphy travelled to Europe to seek out and beat the top European chess masters. In 1858 he met several of them in matches and defeated them all, except that he was thwarted in his attempts to play a match against Staunton. It is almost certain that Morphy would have won had he played Staunton, since the Englishman was past his best by then.

Morphy was now considered the finest player in the world, but chose to concentrate on his legal career thereafter. Following Morphy's return to the USA, one of the players he had beaten in 1858, Adolf Anderssen, was for a time considered to be the best player in the world, but in 1866 he was beaten by Wilhelm Steinitz (1836–1900), originally from Prague but by now resident in London. From that time forward, Steinitz was generally considered to be the world's best player.

World chess champions

The formal title of world chess champion is generally recognized as dating from 1886, when Wilhelm Steinitz was challenged to a match by Johannes Zukertort. Steinitz, by now a US resident, won the match comfortably and is known formally as the first world chess champion. Finally, his proud record of 24 match victories came to an end in 1894 when he was defeated by a young German rival, Emanuel Lasker (1868–1941).

Lasker was a man of many parts, with a doctorate in mathematics and a strong ability in many other games. However, such was his skill at chess that he held the world championship title until 1921, when he lost it to a Cuban, José Raúl Capablanca (1888–1942). Capablanca, like Paul Morphy, was a child prodigy at chess who was seemingly able to play despite very little study or coaching in the strategy of the game.

GREAT 20TH-CENTURY PLAYERS

José Raúl Capablanca was perhaps the first true chess celebrity. A good-looking and well-educated man, he divided his time between acting as a diplomat for his native Cuba and working as a globe-trotting chess player. He lost few games during his time as champion and was widely expected to see off the challenge of Alexander Alekhine (1892–1945), an expatriate Russian player, when they met at a match in Buenos Aires in 1927. But the Russian succeeded in defeating the Cuban in a 34-game match, by six wins to three (with the other games drawn). Capablanca and Alekhine remained rivals throughout the interwar years, but all attempts to organize a rematch were spurned by the new champion, now a French citizen.

Alekhine met a number of other challengers and in 1935 faced a young Dutch schoolmaster named Max Euwe (1901–1981) whom nobody – least of all Alekhine – expected to give him much trouble. However, Euwe narrowly defeated Alekhine and became the world chess champion – the only true amateur player ever to do so. In 1937, Euwe granted Alekhine a return match and was well beaten.

Having regained his title, Alekhine remained world champion throughout World War II, during which chess activity more or less ceased. He died in 1946 just as plans were afoot to organize a match between him and a Soviet Russian challenger, Mikhail Botvinnik (1911–1995). Until this point, the organization of championship matches had been a private matter between champions and potential challengers, but with the hiatus caused by the champion Alekhine's death, the World Chess Federation (known as FIDE, the abbreviated form of its French name) stepped in to organize a match-tournament between the strongest players in the world. In 1948, a five-player tournament was held to fill the world champion title vacancy. Botvinnik triumphed ahead of Vasily Smyslov (USSR), Samuel Reshevsky (USA), Paul Keres (USSR) and Max Euwe (Netherlands).

Below: Mikhail Botvinnik (1911–1995) (seated, centre) was world champion 1948–1957, 1958–1960 and 1961–1963. Botvinnik lost some of his prime chess-playing years to World War II, but still reigned as world champion for 13 years after the war. He was the most influential Soviet chess player of his era, and helped guide the early careers of players such as Karpov and Kasparov. Here he is shown with the top young English players of the early 1980s.

Below: Samuel Reshevsky (1911–1992) was the most celebrated child prodigy in the world after World War I. Born in Poland, his family emigrated to the USA where he toured the country giving simultaneous displays. His fame as a chess player is reflected in this photograph, where he is seen playing with Charlie Chaplin in Hollywood.

World chess championship

From this point forward, FIDE took control of the world chess championship and instituted a regular cycle of qualifying competitions and title matches. The regulations were heavily influenced by the demands of the very powerful Soviet Chess Federation. Under the new regulations, the world champion had to defend his title against an official challenger every three years, retaining the title in the event of a drawn match and with the right to a rematch the following year should he lose his title. Botvinnik was to take full advantage of these clauses. In 1951 he met another Soviet grandmaster, David Bronstein (b. 1924), in the

championship final and the match was drawn. Botvinnik thus retained his title, as he did in 1954 when he drew with Vasily Smyslov (b. 1921). In 1957 Smyslov beat Botvinnik to take the title but lost it back in the regulation return match in 1958. Botvinnik lost the title to a brilliant young Latvian, Mikhail Tal (1936–1992), who became the youngest-ever world champion in 1960. But Botvinnik once again regained the title in 1961. In 1963, Botvinnik played and lost to an Armenian, Tigran Petrosian, but by this time the rematch clause had been rescinded, and Botvinnik decided to retire from championship chess. Despite his variable results as champion, Botvinnik was universally admired for his ability to work out a method to revenge himself on each challenger in turn. He became one of the greatest-ever chess coaches, and played a significant role in the development of future champions Anatoly Karpov and Garry Kasparov.

Tigran Petrosian (1929–1984) was to be champion for six years. He defended his title successfully in 1966 against Boris Spassky (b. 1937) but lost it in another match against the same opponent in 1969.

Left: Alexander Alekhine (1892–1946) was Russian by birth but settled in France in the 1920s. He was world champion from 1927 to 1935 and from 1937 to his death, in 1946. The vacant title was not held again until 1948, when Botvinnik won a five-player match-tournament.

Below: Mikhail Tal (1936–1992) was born in Riga, Latvia. Despite long bouts of very poor health, he was one of the most spectacular and successful chess players in history.

Below left: José Raúl Capablanca (1888–1942) was born in Cuba. A child prodigy, his ability at chess seemed effortless. He won the world championship in 1921.

BOBBY FISCHER

Although chess had been popular in the USA since the days of Morphy, and a number of gold medal successes were achieved in team events between the wars, the game had never been high profile, and financial support always remained scanty. This was the chess culture into which Bobby (Robert James) Fischer was born in Chicago on 9 March 1943. Brought up in Brooklyn by his mother, who was a divorcee, he was introduced to chess at the age of six and soon became completely absorbed in the game. However, although Bobby Fischer was very good, it was to be some years before his exceptional ability became fully apparent and he was to meet his rival Boris Spassky, a Russian, in the world championship.

Chess had been popular in Russia since the 19th century, but under the Soviet regime its value as a propaganda tool for demonstrating the country's cultural and intellectual superiority was recognized. Following World War II, the Soviet Chess Federation had virtually become a government department, with a handsome budget and large numbers of chess players receiving stipends as players, coaches and administrators. No other country put anywhere near as many resources or as much professional expertise into the game, and therefore it was hardly surprising that the Soviet Union had achieved total domination of championship-level chess.

Fischer's success

The year 1957 was to be Fischer's *annus mirabilis*. First he won the US Junior Championship, then tied first in the US Open and finally he won the US (closed) Championship ahead of all the country's top grandmasters. Fischer's success in the 1957/8 US Championship qualified him for the World Championship inter-zonal tournament, held in Yugoslavia in August 1958. This was a massive event, where 21 of the world's top players would meet each other over the course of more than a month. Against all expectation, Fischer finished fifth and qualified for the final rung on the world championship qualification ladder. This success not only brought him the title of youngest-ever grandmaster, but also international fame.

Below: Bobby Fischer (right) at the Siegen Chess Olympiad in 1970. He became the most famous chess player in history when he won the right to challenge Boris Spassky for the world championship. In 1972 he was the first Western player to win the title since the 1930s, but he never defended his title and became a recluse.

THE WORLD CHESS CHAMPIONSHIP

Above: After becoming world champion in 1972, Bobby Fischer (right) disappeared from the chess scene and played no competitive games for 20 years. However, in 1992, he played another match with his former rival Boris Spassky in Yugoslavia. This was billed by the organizers as 'the world chess championship', but in reality chess had moved on, and the two players would no longer have been serious candidates for the real chess title, by then held by Garry Kasparov.

Left: A large crowd tries to catch a glimpse of Bobby Fischer playing world champion Boris Spassky in the 1970 Siegen Olympiad. Spassky won this game and never lost a game to Fischer until they met in the 1972 world championship match in Reykjavik.

In 1959, Fischer played in an eight-man World Championship Candidates' tournament to decide who would go on to challenge the world champion. Unfortunately, he was still too raw to get the better of a group of top Soviet grandmasters who stood between him and the pinnacle, and he finished fifth. He went on to challenge again in 1962 but once again found himself thwarted by a group of Soviet grandmasters in a Candidates' competition. This time he made accusations that they were colluding among themselves. Many years later, after the collapse of the Soviet Union, some of them admitted that he had actually been right.

Although the championship system was changed to match-play to avoid group collusion, it was not until 1970 that Fischer again competed for the championship. Once again, he had an easy win at the inter-zonal stage, and in 1971 he won three qualifying matches with flying colours. Two opponents,

Taimanov and Larsen, were summarily beaten 6–0 (such whitewashes were practically unprecedented) and then the former world champion Petrosian was also well beaten in a match in Buenos Aires. Fischer reached 20 games unbeaten in this match; this was the longest winning run in the history of chess.

This qualified Fischer to face Spassky in 1972. The match became a symbol of the Cold War between the West and the Soviet bloc, and Fischer's reputation for out-spokenness and prickliness with the press only added to its mystery. The world's press watched closely as Fischer first showed reluctance to journey to the match venue, Reykjavik, and then defaulted the second game after a disaster in the first. The odds were that Fischer would once again withdraw and Spassky would retain his title without a fight. However, Fischer came back, played the third game and won it. This was his first-ever win against Spassky and he soon took the lead and won the match.

ANATOLY KARPOV

Anatoly Karpov was born on 23 May 1951 in Zlatoust in the former Soviet Union and learned to play chess at the age of four. In 1974, this young star of Soviet chess had made such remarkable progress that he won the right to challenge Bobby Fischer for the world crown.

Bobby Fischer's conquest of the world chess championship in 1972 ushered in a new age for chess in the West. The game received a massive boost from his title success, with many Western countries, such as the UK, enjoying a chess boom on the back of increased sponsorship. This later translated into the development of a group of professional grandmasters who were able to play on equal terms against Soviet players. However, Fischer himself never played a single game as world champion. Despite some large offers of sponsorship, he could not be tempted back to the board. In 1975 he was due to meet his first official challenger but he failed to meet the deadline set for agreeing terms to the match, after finding fault with all manner of conditions laid down for it.

Karpov versus Fischer

The World Chess Federation believed that they had no option other than to strip Fischer of the title and award it without a fight to his challenger, Anatoly Karpov. The loss of the world title in 1972 had been a major blow to the prestige of the Soviet chess establishment, but even before Spassky had lost the title, Karpov had emerged as the outstanding candidate to win it back. He had won the World Junior Championship in 1969 and had qualified to meet Fischer in 1974 via a series of tough matches against top players, including the former champion Boris Spassky and the formidable Soviet star Viktor Korchnoi (b. 1931). Chastened by the defeat of their champion in 1972, the Soviet Chess Federation put all its considerable resources behind Karpov to ensure that the title was regained with all speed.

Having won the title without playing Fischer, Karpov was left with the unenviable task of proving himself to a chess world that was at first slightly sceptical of his right to the title. This he did highly

Above: Viktor Korchnoi (b. 1931) is believed by many to be the strongest chess player never to become world champion. After defecting from the Soviet Union in 1976, he played two bitterly hostile title matches with Anatoly Karpov, but lost them both.

Right: Anatoly Karpov (b. 1951) became world champion by default in 1975 when Bobby Fischer failed to defend his title. He held the title until 1985 when he lost it after a match with Garry Kasparov. He later regained the World Chess Federation version of the title in 1993.

Above: Here, Karpov is seen contemplating a move while competing in the 1981 World Chess Championships held in Merano, Italy. Karpov would go on to win the match, easily defeating rival Viktor Korchnoi, 11–7, in what became known as the 'Massacre of Merano.' Three years earlier, the two had also played for the title – a match that Korchnoi had come close to winning.

effectively by playing regularly in major tournaments and winning a long string of first prizes, something that few of his predecessors as world champions had been able to do.

Karpov versus Korchnoi

In 1978 Karpov faced his first challenger for the world title. Once again he faced Viktor Korchnoi, whom he had beaten in the final eliminator in 1974. But since that time, Korchnoi had defected from the Soviet Union and become a highly vocal critic of its regime, which had prevented other members of his family from joining him in the West.

Once again a chess match caught the world's attention, more because of its fraught political background than the chess moves played on the board.

It was a longer match than normal. Most post-war matches had been the best of 24 games, but this one was to be won by the first player to win six games. As many top-level chess games end in draws, this meant that the match was to last somewhat longer. Karpov reached a score of five wins to two, but then visibly tired and lost three out of the next four. However, with both players needing a single win for victory, Korchnoi tried too hard in the next game and lost. Karpov had retained his title.

Karpov continued to win many first prizes in tournaments during the next three years and, in 1981, his challenger was once again to be Viktor Korchnoi. However, Karpov was by now in his prime (aged 30) while his opponent was rather past his, and Karpov won comfortably.

Karpov continued to effectively dominate the chess world throughout the 1980s, but he soon came up against a young and determined challenger, also from the Soviet Union, who would prove to be his nemesis: Garry Kasparov.

GARRY KASPAROV

Garry Kimovich Kasparov (b. 1963 in Baku, Azerbaijan) was from a very different generation and background from Anatoly Karpov. His name at birth was Harry Weinstein, but after his father's death he was given a Russified version of his mother's family name, Kasparian. Like Karpov, he was soon picked out by the highly efficient Soviet talent-spotting network and placed under the wing of former champion Mikhail Botvinnik. In 1978 Kasparov finished eighth in the Soviet Championship, indicating that he was probably as good as Fischer had been at the same age. He officially became a grandmaster in 1980 when he also won the world junior championship.

Kasporov versus Karpov

In 1981 Kasparov won the Soviet Championship and a number of other major tournaments, and it was already apparent that he would soon challenge Karpov. In 1983/4 he qualified as Karpov's official challenger. Once again the match winner would be the first to six wins. However, it was to be the last time that such an open-ended match was tried. The match started in September 1984 and Karpov's experience told as he progressed to four wins to zero by the ninth game. However, Kasparov managed to dig his heels in at this point. A run of 17 draws followed. Karpov then won his fifth game, so needed just one to retain his title. But Kasparov held on, won his first game and, after more draws, won two more games. The score stood at five wins to Karpov and three to Kasparov, after five months' play. At this point, the president of the World Chess Federation controversially decided to declare the match void, proposing another match between the two (but limited by the number of games) for later in the year. Thus, the most protracted match in chess history was left unfinished, with both contestants claiming that the annulment had unfairly favoured their rival.

Karpov duly defended his title against Kasparov in September 1985. By this time Kasparov had become much stronger and he managed to win the

Above: The controversial breakaway chess title match between English grandmaster Nigel Short and Kasparov in 1993.

Left: Garry Kasparov (left), in animated discussion with Peter Leko (b. 1979). Both were child prodigies. Leko qualified as a grandmaster aged 14. He has yet to win the world championship, although he drew a title match with Vladimir Kramnik in 2004.

championship. But this was by no means the end of the Karpov–Kasparov story. Karpov was entitled to a return match, which took place in 1986. Kasparov also won this match, although only by one point.

Karpov won the right to challenge Kasparov yet again in 1987. Karpov needed only a draw from the last game to regain his title, but the younger man then won one of the most exciting chess games in history to clinch a win, and tie the match, thus retaining his title. The fifth and last Karpov–Kasparov match took place in 1990, and Kasparov won again, finally setting the seal on the greatest and closest chess rivalry in history (in 144 championship games, Kasparov won 21 to Karpov's 19).

The breakaway match

In 1993 Kasparov played a title match against the English grandmaster Nigel Short. It caused great acrimony in the chess world because the two players had broken away from the World Chess Federation and held the match under the auspices of a newly formed organization called the Professional Chess Association (PCA). Kasparov won the match quite easily, but he was stripped of his official title. However, such was Kasparov's personal prestige that his breakaway version of the title was generally recognized by the chess world at large.

Like Karpov, Kasparov went on to win many first prizes in major chess tournaments throughout the world, defending his title in 1995 and 2000 in privately sponsored matches. In 2000 he met a young Russian prodigy, Vladimir Kramnik (b. 1975) and, surprisingly, lost a close match. But Kasparov remained the dominant figure in the chess world into the 21st century, heading the world rankings until his retirement in 2005.

CHESS STARS OF THE 21ST CENTURY

Kasparov remained top of the official rating list until his retirement in April 2005, and it was to be nearly a decade before a similarly dominant figure emerged in world chess, in the shape of the Norwegian player Magnus Carlsen.

Between 1993 and 2004 the World Chess Federation ran the world championship system on a knock-out basis, with 128 players contesting two-game mini-matches with 'rapidplay' and 'blitz' deciders in the event of a tie. This meant that chance played a bigger part than it had in the traditional long-distance match format. After Kasparov forfeited the official title in 1993, Anatoly Karpov came back to regain it and hold it until 1999, when it was won in Las Vegas by Russian grandmaster Alexander Khalifman (b. 1966). Khalifman was ranked only 45th in the world at the time, when FIDE ratings (a more reliable guide) to the strength of the top players indicated that the best players in the

world were Garry Kasparov, Vladimir Kramnik and the Indian grandmaster Viswanathan Anand (b. 1969). However, the following year Anand duly won the world knock-out championship, to add a degree of credibility to the new championship system.

The next world knock-out championship in 2002 featured an all-Ukrainian final between the country's leading player, Vasyl Ivanchuk (b. 1969), and the much younger and inexperienced Ruslan Ponomariov (b. 1983). However, it was a triumph for youth over experience as the 19-year-old beat his older rival to become, at 19, the youngest-ever world chess champion. In 2004, the world knock-out championship was held in Libya, and the final contested by Michael Adams (b. 1971) of England and Rustam Kasimdzhanov (b. 1979) of Uzbekistan. The Englishman came close to success, but in the end the Uzbeki player triumphed.

Right: Viswanathan Anand (b. 1969) challenged Garry Kasparov's world title unsuccessfully in 1995, but won the World Chess Federation version of the title in 2000. Subsequently one of the highest-ranked players ever, he became the undisputed world champion in 2007, holding off several challengers before being defeated by Magnus Carlsen in 2013.

Below: Vladimir Kramnik (b. 1975) is interviewed by the press after an exhibition game against David Howell (b. 1990) in 2002. Kramnik beat Garry Kasparov to become the world match-play champion in 2000. In 2006 he became the first undisputed world chess champion since 1993, before losing the title in 2007.

Above: Veselin Topalov (b. 1975) won the official 2005 world championship tournament held in Argentina. In July 2006 he was the top-ranked chess player in the world but lost his world title reunification match to Vladimir Kramnik in October of that year. He challenged Viswanathan Anand in 2010 but was defeated.

Above: Magnus Carlsen (b. 1990, Norway) became undisputed world champion in 2013 by defeating Viswanathan Anand in the Indian's home city of Chennai. During the course of 2014 Carlsen set a new world-best rating of 2882, and retained his title in a return match against Anand in Sochi, Russia.

The knock-out formula had still not won the hearts of the chess public, so the format was switched to an all-play-all tournament basis in 2005, when Veselin Topalov of Bulgaria won the title in San Luís, Argentina.

The world match-play champion Vladimir Kramnik did not take part in any of the above events. After winning his version of the title from Kasparov in 2000, he defended it successfully in 2004. Though unofficial, Kramnik's match-based version of the title was still favoured by a significant proportion of the chess public. The schism in the championship system was finally healed in 2006 when Veselin Topalov met Kramnik in a 12-game match in Elista, Kalmykia. A close and highly controversial match ended with a four-game tie-break which went in favour of Kramnik, who thus became the first undisputed world champion for 13 years.

The World Chess Federation switched back to a tournament basis for the 2007 world championship, which was held in Mexico City. Reigning champion Kramnik took part, but the tournament was won by Viswanathan Anand of India, thus becoming champion. The following year he dispelled any further misgivings about the legitimacy of his title by defeating Kramnik in a match. He remains the only world champion ever to have won the championship title in all three formats (knock-out, tournament and match).

Viswanathan Anand went on to defend his title in matches against Veselin Topalov of Bulgaria in 2010 and Boris Gelfand of Israel in 2012. In 2013 he was defeated by Magnus Carlsen of Norway in his home city of Chennai. Carlsen, the younger man by 21 years, and significantly higher than the champion on the world rating list, was the hot favourite, and won by three wins to zero, with seven draws. In 2014 Carlsen again defeated Viswanathan Anand, this time by three wins to one, with seven draws. Magnus Carlsen is proving to be as dominant as Fischer, Karpov and Kasparov before him, and no clear rival has yet emerged.

GREAT WOMEN CHESS PLAYERS

To date, only one woman chess player – Judit Polgar – has reached the top ten in the chess rankings. The fundamental reason for women's inferior results is that fewer than one in ten competition players is female. In 2006, of the 50,000+ chess players registered by the World Chess Federation as active in international competitions worldwide, only 3,000 were female. By 2015, despite a large increase in the numbers of registered competition players worldwide (200,000), the proportion of female players had only increased to 9.5 per cent (19,000). It is perhaps to do with the cultural background of chess, with clubs being more male-oriented and the game traditionally being played in male-only schools. More simply, it may be that the game appeals to men more than women.

The first female chess star

Vera Menchik (1906–1944) was the first woman chess player to make a significant impact on the game. Born in Moscow to a Czech father and English mother, she won the first women's world championship in 1927. She won all the women's world championship events held before the war. Although less successful in mixed events, she enjoyed notable one-off victories in games against leading players. She beat the future world champion, Max Euwe, twice in the early 1930s. Sadly, she died during an air raid in England in 1944.

Above: Judit Polgar (b. 1976) is universally regarded as the finest woman chess player of all time. In 2002 she won a rapid chess game against Kasparov. She was for a time the youngest player ever to qualify as a grandmaster (at 15), beating Bobby Fischer's record.

Below: Vera Menchik (1906–1944) was born in Moscow, the daughter of a Czech father and an English mother. Along with her mother and sister, she died in a bombing raid in England. She was easily the best woman player from 1927 to her death.

Right: The world's highest ever rated female player Judit Polgar (b. 1976) plays world champion Viswanathan Anand.

Right: Former women's world champions Susan (formerly Zsusza) Polgar and Xie Jun playing in 2004. Susan Polgar (b. 1969) was the first woman to qualify for the grandmaster title, and was world champion from 1996 to 1999. Xie Jun (b. 1970) reigned as champion from 1991 to 1996, and again from 1999 to 2001.

Above: Hou Yifan (b. 1994) became a grandmaster at a younger age than either Bobby Fischer or Judit Polgar. She became the youngest ever women's world champion at the age of 16 in 2010, and has held the title twice (2010–2012 and 2013–2015).

Soviet dominance broken by China

After World War II, Soviet women players dominated the women's world championship competitions for many years. The most notable was Nona Gaprindashvili (b. 1941), who won the title in 1962 and held it until 1978 when she was dethroned by Maia Chiburdanidze (b. 1961). Both champions came from the Soviet republic of Georgia, which developed a particularly rich tradition of women's chess at that time.

The Soviet Union enjoyed an unbroken series of successes in women's chess competitions until the 1980s, when their dominance was broken by China, the world's most populous country. China had only started to take an interest in the Western form of chess in the 1970s, and concentrated on the women's game. Their first success came in 1991 when Xie Jun (b. 1970) beat Chiburdanidze to take the women's world championship title.

The Polgar sisters

Meanwhile, in Budapest, three young sisters were being brought up to play the game by a chess-playing father. Laszlo Polgar and his wife Klara educated their three daughters at home, and included advanced chess coaching among their academic studies. All three girls became very strong players at an early age. The eldest,

Zsuzsa (now Susan) Polgar (b. 1969), became the world under-16 champion aged 12, was the first woman to qualify for the grandmaster title (in 1991), and went on to take the world title from Xie Jun in 1996. The second sister, Sofia Polgar (b. 1974), also competed successfully in mixed chess events.

The third sister, Judit Polgar (b. 1976), is universally acclaimed as the strongest woman chess player in history. She eschewed women-only events, preferring to hone her talents in company with the world's top players. She achieved the title of grandmaster in 1991, breaking Bobby Fischer's age record. In 2008 she reached a peak world ranking of eighth in the world (men and women) and took part in the eight-player world championship tournament held in 2005.

Hou Yifan

Judit Polgar retired from competition in 2014, but her various records and peak performances are now being challenged by the Chinese player Hou Yifan (b. 1994), who became a grandmaster aged 14 years, 6 months – ten months younger than Polgar. In 2015 Hou Yifan became the first female player to have a higher rating than Judit Polgar for 25 years, and is now within reach of Polgar's peak rating and ranking. Though Hou Yifan is the current women's world champion, with few credible challengers amongst women players she seems likely to relinquish it and follow Judit Polgar's lead by competing exclusively against leading male players.

CHESS PRODIGIES

Chess is like music and mathematics in that it can be learnt and mastered at a remarkably young age. Among major chess figures, Morphy, Capablanca, Fischer, Karpov and Kasparov were all demonstrating exceptional chess ability before the age of ten. Morphy is reputed to have learnt the game simply from watching his father and uncle at the age of eight, and by nine was able to beat the best players in New Orleans. A similar story is told of Capablanca. Fischer also played exceptionally good chess before the age of ten, though the sophisticated opposition he met in New York in the early 1950s was such that eye-catching successes took a little longer to achieve. Karpov and Kasparov reached a similar level (known as 'first category' in the old Soviet ranking system) at the ages of ten and nine respectively.

The first chess prodigy

Samuel Reshevsky (1911–92) was the first player to receive wide publicity for his exploits as a chess prodigy. Born to a Jewish family in Poland, his prowess soon won him attention, and he toured the country giving simultaneous exhibitions at the age of six, during which he would win the majority of his games against 20 or more adult players. He settled with his family in the USA at the age of nine, and then went on two years of exhibition tours. From the age of 12 he concentrated on school for a number of years before returning to chess. Although one of the very best players in the world from 1935 to the late 1960s, he never became world champion, lacking the level of support that Soviet rivals enjoyed during that period.

Below: Samuel Reshevsky, the chess prodigy, at the age of six. Here he is pictured at one of his simultaneous exhibitions, which astounded the chess world.

Below: Sergey Karyakin (b. 1990) was the youngest player ever to qualify for the chess grandmaster title – he was 12 years and 7 months when he did so in 2002. Here he is playing at the 2003 annual Hastings International Tournament in the UK.

Nigel Short

The emergence of child prodigies sometimes coincides with the flowering of chess interest in a given country. The Fischer–Spassky match caused a chess boom around the world, particularly in the United Kingdom, where the most notable chess prodigy was Nigel Short (b. 1965). He defeated world title contender Viktor Korchnoi in a simultaneous exhibition when only ten. At the age of 12, he competed in the 1977 British Championship, during which he won a game against Jonathan Penrose, who still holds the record for winning the most British Championship titles. Short went on to defeat former world champion Anatoly Karpov in a match on his way to challenging Garry Kasparov for the title in 1993.

Breaking records

Since the 1990s, the age at which a player has qualified for the grandmaster title has become the yardstick by which the achievements of young players have been judged. Fischer became a grandmaster at 15 and his record stood until 1991, when it was broken by the Hungarian player Judit Polgar. Since then, the record has been broken several more times, although the inflationary effect of the rating system used has made it significantly easier to qualify as a grandmaster since Fischer's day. Another Hungarian, Peter Leko (b. 1979), became the first 14-year-old to qualify as a grandmaster in 1994, the Chinese player Bu Xiangzhi (b. 1985) became a grandmaster at 13 in 1998, and the Ukrainian player Sergey Karyakin (b. 1990) became the first pre-teen grandmaster, at the age of 12 years and 7 months, in 2002.

Above: Hou Yifan (right) was born in 1994 and, following the retirement of Judit Polgar, is the strongest woman player of the 21st century. She became a grandmaster at the age of 14, and women's world champion at 16. She is ranked in the top 60 players in the world of both sexes.

Female prodigies

Judit Polgar was the first female child prodigy, but her record as the youngest female grandmaster was broken by the Chinese player Hou Yifan (b. 1994) in 2008.

Magnus Carlsen

The 2015 world champion Magnus Carlsen was taught to play chess at the age of five but showed little interest in the game until he was eight, when he won his first junior tournament. Within a year he was studying the game seriously, and he qualified for the grandmaster title aged 13 years, 4 months. He became the highest rated player in the world at the age of 19 years, 1 month in 2009, and world champion four years later.

Left: China played its own version of chess for many hundreds of years but is now becoming very interested in 'Western chess'. The girl on the left of the front row is Hou Yifan (b. 1994), one of the greatest players of the 21st century. Pictured here is the entire squad of junior players that the Chinese Chess Federation sent to the World Junior Championships in Halkidiki, Greece, in 2003.

CHESS IN LITERATURE

One of the first-ever books to be printed in English was a book on a chess theme. It was William Caxton's 1474 edition of *Game and Playe of the Chesse*, a translation of a series of morality stories, with a chess allegory written by Jacopo da Cessole, a Dominican monk of the late 13th and early 14th centuries who liked to use chess as the theme of his sermons. It was by no means the first allegory along these lines: a long 14th-century romantic poem titled *Les Échecs Amoureux* (*Chess of Love*) had been translated into English around 1412 and had been much imitated.

William Shakespeare seems to have had some fondness for the game of chess and used it in the context of a cosy flirtation in *The Tempest*. Two lovers are shown on stage playing chess, with Miranda making the teasing accusation that Ferdinand was 'playing [her] false'.

Chess is prominent in *Tales from the Arabian Nights* and Lewis Carroll's *Through the Looking Glass*. In the latter the chess pieces come to life when Alice goes through the mirror (the author, however, displays his ignorance of the game by referring to rooks as 'castles').

Chess as a novel theme

One of the first works of literature with a major chess theme was Vladimir Nabokov's 1929 novel *The Defence*. It tells the story of a brilliant but troubled chess professional called Luzhin and his obsession with the game at the expense of real life. The novel was made into a film titled *The Luzhin Defence* in 2000 in the USA; it starred John Turturro as the chess genius, and depicted tournament chess (as played in the 1920s) in a vivid and compelling way. Nabokov himself was a keen chess player, with a particular interest in composing chess problems.

Another novel with a story woven around chess was Stefan Zweig's *The Royal Game*, which he wrote in 1942. In it, the world chess champion (improbably, an idiot-savant) plays chess games with fellow passengers on a boat voyage from Europe to South America, and with one particular passenger who survived solitary confinement by the Nazis by playing chess matches entirely in his head. As in *The Luzhin Defence*, chess is seen as a very alienating preoccupation, a view that is not very popular in the chess-playing world.

Left: 'The Chess Players', one of the classic Sir John Tenniel illustrations for *Through the Looking Glass* by Lewis Carroll (1832–1898). This particular illustration shows a king and queen conversing while a bishop sits on a boulder reading a newspaper. Behind them stands a pawn, arms akimbo, and a pair of marching rooks, presumably on sentry duty. To the rear, a group of knights and bishops socialize.

Above: This 19th-century painting by Lucy Madox Brown depicts the chess game that takes place in *The Tempest*. Chess was a popular pastime in Shakespeare's day. Indeed, Queen Elizabeth I was said to enjoy playing it.

Intrigue, suspense and poetry

Mystery writers have been fond of weaving chess into their plots. Although these are often contrived and bear little relation to real-life competitive chess, they can be very entertaining. One notable example is *The Flanders Panel* by Arturo Perez Reverte, where the meaning of a hidden inscription on a 500-year-old artwork turns out to be a chess puzzle that contains the clue to a murder. Ian Fleming also incorporated a scene depicting championship chess into his 1957 James Bond book *From Russia With Love*, which appeared in the movie of the same name.

Chess also appears in poetry, from *The Rubaiyat of Omar Khayyam* to the poems of Ezra Pound and more modern poets. The second part of T.S. Eliot's 1922 work *The Waste Land* is headed 'A Game of Chess', although anyone expecting significant chess content is to be disappointed. There is none, as the line mentioning it was supposedly removed, at the request of Eliot's wife. It is also possible that Eliot is alluding to a satirical play of the same name by the Jacobean playwright Thomas Middleton, which used chess and chess pieces in an allegory on Anglo-Spanish politics in the 1620s.

Above: Sean Connery in the film version of Ian Fleming's book, *From Russia With Love*. The game played in the film replicates a Spassky–Bronstein game that took place in Leningrad in 1960.

CAÏSSA

♛ ♝ ♞ ♚

Chess enjoys its very own muse or goddess, named Caïssa (pronounced *Ky-eéssa*). She originated as a nymph in a 1763 poem by Sir William Jones (1746–1794), who is famous as the founder of comparative linguistics. In the poem, Mars persuades the god of sport to invent chess as a way of softening the heart of the nymph towards him. Although the original poem is not widely known in the chess world, Caïssa's name is familiar to all keen players, some of whom occasionally attribute their success to 'Caïssa smiling on them'.

CHESS IN FILM

Film-makers have found many creative ways to exploit chess in films and on the small screen. Although chess has rarely been the central theme of a major film, the game lends itself to being used in depicting various themes, both positive and negative. The earliest film with a significant chess content was *Chess Fever* (1925), a delightful short Soviet comedy about a young man obsessed with the game to the detriment of his relationship with his fiancée. This silent movie contained real footage of a major chess tournament taking place at the time in Moscow. In fact, the then world chess champion at the time, José Raúl Capablanca, played a short scene in the film and was given star billing in order to popularize it. The film is much beloved of chess buffs as it contains the only extant moving images of some early chess legends, including Capablanca and the long-time US champion Frank Marshall.

Chess-playing film stars

One big-screen icon, Humphrey Bogart, was himself a very good chess player and was instrumental in seeing that his favourite game be used to good effect in his films. Bogart's most famous film was *Casablanca* (1942), in which his character is first seen sitting alone at a chessboard. The basis of this scene was actually Bogart's own suggestion to the director, Michael Curtiz, and his meticulous care in getting the scene right is demonstrated by the position on the board in the scene, which was one of Bogart's favourite starting positions in his own games. This was not the only time in Bogart's film career that his character was introduced as he played chess – the same device was used in *Knock on Any Door* (1949).

Many other movie stars and directors have been chess players. John Wayne was a keen player and often played Marlene Dietrich during breaks in shooting. Charlie Chaplin was keen on chess, and a photo from the 1920s showed him playing against the then child prodigy Sammy Reshevsky when the future grandmaster was in California.

Chess is probably most often exploited as a metaphor for scheming and conflict, but it has also been used in the context of seduction. Probably the most famous example was in *The Thomas Crown Affair*

Top: As suggested by Bogart himself, Peter Lorre and Humphrey Bogart play a game of chess in a scene from *Casablanca* (1942).

Above: Humphrey Bogart and Susan Perry play chess in a scene from the 1949 film *Knock on Any Door.*

Right: Humphrey Bogart's position in *Casablanca*, which also happened to be one of the actor's own favourite starting positions.

(1968), in which Steve McQueen's millionaire-turned-bank-robber character plays chess with an attractive insurance investigator played by Faye Dunaway. There are three games in one: boy woos girl, cop chases robber, and the chess game itself, which ends when McQueen (in a lost position) says to Dunaway: 'Let's play something else.' The chess moves in the game were based on a real game played in Vienna in 1898. The scene has been rated highly in various polls to decide the most memorable moments in films, including fourth place in a poll of the 'sexiest sexless movie scene'.

Real-life connections

Perhaps the best-known film of recent years with chess content was *Searching for Bobby Fischer* (1993), also known as *Innocent Moves*. This was based on the book of the same name by Fred Waitzkin, which documented his real-life son Josh's early career as a young American chess prodigy, the family pressures it involved and the rivalry between child chess players and their equally competitive parents. Bobby Fischer appears in documentary footage shown over the opening credits. The 'search' is purely metaphorical and refers to the pinnacle of chess achievement to which every ambitious player aspires.

Chess plays a key part in the film *Harry Potter and the Philosopher's Stone*. Harry Potter and his schoolfriend Ron Weasley enjoy playing what they call Wizard Chess. The rules of the game are as in real-life chess except that the pieces on the board are animated and enact battles when captures are made. Ron's chess prowess proves to be a key element in the film's climax.

Left: A celebrated moment from *The Thomas Crown Affair* (1968), in which Steve McQueen plays a match against Faye Dunaway.

Below: A scene from *Searching for Bobby Fischer* (titled *Innocent Moves* in the UK): the boy who wants to emulate Bobby Fischer plays against a chess hustler in the local park.

CHESS IN ART

Since medieval times, chess has always been a popular subject for the visual arts. Paintings of a man and a woman playing chess have been used to symbolize courtship, while the pieces themselves also make suitable subjects for inclusion in still-life depictions. Among great artists who have used chess as a theme in their work are Delacroix, Magritte, Matisse, Sargent and Ernst.

Early medieval art

Chess and chess playing has also been depicted in mosaics, tapestries and murals from the early medieval period, and seems to have been a favourite subject from the time when secular subjects became acceptable.

One example is a frieze in the Cappella Palatina in Palermo, Sicily, which shows two people playing chess. The chapel forms part of a Norman palace built by Roger II, the Norman king of Sicily, in the middle part of the 12th century. Much of the painting is believed to have been done by Islamic artists, and the chess scene shows two turbaned figures engaged in playing on a standard 8 x 8 chessboard.

Another beautiful chess representation is *The Chess Players* by the Italian Renaissance painter Liberale da Verona (*c*.1445–1530). It is a painted panel from a

Below: *Arabs Playing Chess* (*c*.1847–1849) by the artist Eugène Delacroix (1798–1863) is one of his classic paintings.

Above: *The Chess Game*, a 15th-century painting by the Italian female painter, Sofonisba Anguissola. An idealized landscape provides the backdrop to two sisters playing chess, watched by their younger sister. The game was one of the few considered sufficiently refined for young women.

Above: This image entitled "Playing Chess in a Castle Garden", is taken from the *c.*1400 manuscript *Li Livres du Graunt Caam* (*Travels of Marco Polo*). The miniature is by the artist Johannes and his school.

larger work and is now housed in the Metropolitan Museum of Art, New York. It shows a group of young men watching a young couple playing chess. Another good example of such a scene is Lukas van Leyden's 1508 work *A Game of Chess*. Once again, a crowd of spectators are watching the game as a young woman makes her move (on a chessboard with rather more than eight files, for some reason). Such scenes were also very popular with much later artists, a good example being John Singer Sargent's *The Chess Game* (1907).

Modern art

Many modern artists have also been attracted to chess as a subject. Matisse's 1928 work *Femme à côté d'un échiquier* shows a woman lying asleep on a couch with a chessboard beside her. Chessboard patterns have particularly attracted abstract painters. One example is Paul Klee's *Super Chess* (1937), which shows a patchwork chessboard with figurative chess pieces, rather like diagram representations in chess books.

Probably the most famous artist to take chess as a regular subject was the French surrealist painter and sculptor Marcel Duchamp (1887–1968). As well as being a famous artist, Duchamp was a chess master

who played well enough to be selected to represent France in international competitions in the 1920s and 1930s. So obsessed was he with the game that his wife grew frustrated and one night glued all his chess pieces to his board while he slept. They were divorced soon after.

Duchamp's Cubist work *The Chess Players* (1910) is one example of the overlap between his two passions, as is his design for a pocket chess set (1943), which was practical as well as artistic. His evident love for playing chess was also turned into photographic art, including the famous 1963 Julian Wasser photograph showing Duchamp engrossed in a game of chess and apparently oblivious to the charms of the nude female player on the other side of the board. The photograph was taken at the Pasadena Museum of Art and shows artistic works by Duchamp in the background.

A number of major art exhibitions have been devoted to chess themes. One such was *The Art of Chess* exhibition that ran at the Gilbert Gallery in London, in 2003. The exhibition concentrated on artistic interpretation of the chess pieces and board, with striking chess set designs by modern artists including Damien Hirst, Jake and Dinos Chapman, and Paul McCarthy placed beside designs by 20th-century artists such as Duchamp, Man Ray, Max Ernst, Alexander Calder and Yoko Ono.

CHESS SET DESIGNS

Chess set designs have varied enormously over the centuries. They can be broadly divided into two types: pieces designed to be used for practical play, and pieces that are primarily for show. As far as the first group is concerned, the pieces are primarily game tokens, with key design factors being that the different pieces should be easily distinguishable and comfortable to handle as well as stable and sturdy. Aesthetic design is a secondary factor, particularly when it comes to organized competitive chess, but clarity and elegance can still be an important adjunct to the enjoyment of the game. These factors can also be important when it comes to ornamental chess pieces, but usually it is the visual impression of the pieces that forms the primary consideration.

The Lewis chessmen

Probably the best-known ancient chessmen in existence are the Lewis chessmen, 67 of which were acquired by the British Museum in London and another 11 by the National Museum of Antiquities in Edinburgh, Scotland. Made of walrus ivory, their exact age is not known and has not so far been scientifically verified. They are of a 12th-century Viking design, but this does not preclude the possibility that they were made several centuries later. In 1831 they were found hidden in an underground structure on the Isle of Lewis in the Outer Hebrides, Scotland. The chessmen differ from conventional modern chess piece designs in that they are human representations, with facial expressions, weapons, helmets and crowns, except for the pawns, which have been said to resemble gravestones. All the six different chess pieces are represented among the 78 pieces and it is most likely that they came from at least seven different chess sets originally.

Arab influence

The fame and appeal of the Lewis pieces lies in their striking appearance, their completeness and the fact that they are unquestionably chessmen. There are other artefacts, surviving in smaller numbers, which pre-date them and which may also be chess pieces. In 1972 archaeologists in Uzbekistan discovered two small animal figures dating back to the 2nd century AD that are thought to be chess pieces. A better-attested chessman is a carved ivory Arab king that dates to the 8th or 9th century AD. Many other early medieval chess pieces show Arab influence in their design, with walrus ivory, whalebone and, later, rock crystal being favoured materials for their construction.

Right: Chess had travelled to northern Europe by the 11th century. These are nine ivory chess pieces that form part of the Lewis Chessmen (dating from around c.1150–1200) from a collection of 78 found at Uig on the Isle of Lewis in the Outer Hebrides, Scotland.

Below: For a time in the 7th century, chess was banned for Muslims, and the abstract shape of these pieces reflects Islamic concern over the carving of images.

Left: One of Napoleon's chess sets, which he used while in exile on St Helena. The chessmen were prized by the Emperor and have been much copied since. Contemporaries of the emperor reported that he was an enthusiastic but, ultimately, weak chess player.

Below: There are many variants of chess across the world, including Indian, Chinese and Thai chess. In this, Thai chess, not only are all the pieces different (except for the knight) but the squares are all the same colour, rather than chequered.

Change in style

Prior to the 16th century, chess set designs tended towards the ornate and representational, but towards the end of that century, designs gravitated towards the simpler, symbolic designs that have been familiar for the past 100 years.

Chess set design has often reflected the architectural style of the times, and chess pieces once again became richly ornate in the 17th and 18th centuries. Indian and Chinese sets were made and imported into Europe, with ivory becoming a favourite material for their construction, often beautifully carved into the most delicate designs. It became fashionable to style the white and black pieces as rival armies. Chinese-made sets showed the Chinese army facing the Mongols, Indian sets showed opposing armies from the time of the Indian Mutiny, while European manufacturers chose Napoleonic War themes. Chess sets were even made in ceramic pottery by the famous English Wedgwood factory.

For all the exotic and elaborate designs of chess sets through many centuries, pieces used for practical play tended to be less ornate and less representational. Even so, there was no hint of true standardization in design until the 19th century, when the advent of chess salons and clubs meant that cheaper sets were needed in large quantities.

MODERN CHESS SET DESIGNS

As chess became more popular and widespread as an organized competitive game in the 19th century, there came a need for more functional chess sets with a standard design. For the first half of the century, the favoured design in the UK was the so-called Saint George chess set, which was broadly based on the type of designs on ivory Indian chess sets, but in wood. They were relatively easy to turn on a lathe, hence cheaper. In comparison with chess sets used today, they tended to be slimmer where the main body of the piece connected to the base, and featured two or three rings, similar to ruffs, between upper parts and base. In some designs, bishops were slightly similar to pawns and even queens.

In France the favoured design was the Régence chess set, named after the famous chess venue, the Café de la Régence, in Paris. A number of other designs (for example the so-called English Barleycorn and the central European Selenus) existed side by side with the Saint George and the Régence, but the pieces of all of these designs were perhaps too tall and unstable for their intended purpose, and players sometimes had difficulty in recognizing the pieces when using an unfamiliar set.

The Staunton pattern

Clearly, what was required for practical play was a standardized design, so that players from all parts of the world would be readily able to recognize the pieces and not be handicapped by unfamiliarity with the style of chessmen with which they were required to play. In the 1840s, the game-making company John Jaques of London came up with a new design based on existing styles but flavoured with the neo-classicist fashion that influenced the architecture and culture of the times. Responsibility for the design is often attributed to Nathaniel Cook, who registered it in 1849, but it may actually have been his brother-in-law, John Jaques, the owner of the company, who drew up the new designs. Much thought had gone into the redesign. The rings above the base had been pruned back to one and replaced (in the case of the bishop, queen and king) with some smaller, neater rings below the mitre, coronet and crown. The bases had been made more sturdy, and weighted down with a small slug of lead. The knights were particularly beautiful, having been modelled on the horse's head sculpture from the Elgin marbles (the collection of Parthenon friezes in the

Above: An elegantly designed modern chess set, in gold and walnut, based on the Staunton pattern. Though the design has become the only officially accepted standard, the board and pieces can be made of various materials. Wooden pieces are typically used in competitive play.

Above: This board and set are made to a standard wooden Staunton design but equipped with electronic sensors that detect moves played and transmit them (via cables or wireless) to a computer. The moves can be redirected on to the Internet, allowing top-level chess games to be watched by thousands.

British Museum). The last touch of genius on the part of the manufacturers of the redesigned pieces was to get the best-known chess player in the world, Howard Staunton, to lend his name to the new pattern. As a reward, he was paid a percentage for every set sold. This sort of sports-celebrity endorsement is routine today when it comes to the marketing of golf or tennis equipment, but was quite revolutionary for its time.

The Staunton pattern (as it came to be known) was immediately successful and has passed the test of time. Today it is the official – and only recognized – pattern for chess sets used in chess competitions played under the auspices of the World Chess Federation. It allows for some flexibility of design. In eastern Europe, some of the minor decorative elements of the pieces can vary, but there is rarely any difficulty in adapting the eye to such slight readjustments. No restrictions concerning materials to be used are included in the Staunton pattern, but the best-quality sets tend to be made from boxwood and ebony. In modern chess competitions, where the large amount of equipment required makes storage and transportation a major issue, the pieces are often made from plastic and are less heavy than the traditional design.

Above: A modern de luxe wooden Staunton-pattern chess set. The board is made of tiger ebony and maple wood. The black pieces are also made of ebony and heavily weighted with lead inserts in the bases to give them a substantial feel.

Below: In the Staunton set, the design of the knight is based on a horse's head on the Parthenon frieze, which forms part of the Elgin Marbles. The work of the Athenian sculptor Phidias, the marbles were taken to the UK in 1806 by Thomas Bruce, 7th Lord of Elgin.

How to Play: The Basics

This chapter explains the basic rules of chess, right from the beginning. It assumes that you have absolutely no prior knowledge of the game. It covers the layout of the chessboard, the moves of the pieces, chess notation, basic terminology, and also a few basic principles of strategy to help you get started. Once you have read this chapter, you will have some insight into chess and will know enough to enjoy your first few games. It is essential to follow the chapter in the given order, as it is important to make sure that you understand each element that is introduced before moving on to the next one. The first rule of chess is that it requires two people to play, so while you are reading this chapter you ought to consider who your first opponent is going to be. It is a good idea to find someone who can help show you the ropes, which makes learning the game even more enjoyable.

Right: The pawn is the least powerful piece on the chessboard – but the appreciation of its merits is the hallmark of a strong chess player.

THE CHESSBOARD

Chess is played on a square board marked out with 64 smaller squares in an 8 x 8 grid in alternating light and dark colours, and is identical to the board used for English draughts (or American checkers). The light-coloured squares are most often cream or white, and the dark squares can be black, brown or green, but chess players always refer to them as white squares and black squares, regardless of their physical colour.

Which way up?
It is important to set the board up the right way around at the start of the game. The two players sit opposite each other and both players should see a white square in the corner of the board nearest their right hand. If you are an English speaker, it is easy to remember the rule, as it rhymes – white on the right.

Finding your way around
There are three important ways of referring to squares on a chessboard. A column of eight squares running across the board between where the two players sit is called a file, shown vertically in the diagram. There are eight files. Ranks are the eight horizontal equivalents, rather like the ranks of soldiers in a battle – very apt, because chess is a war game.

Chess players also talk about diagonals. These straight lines of squares of the same colour, touching corner to corner, are of varying lengths. For instance,

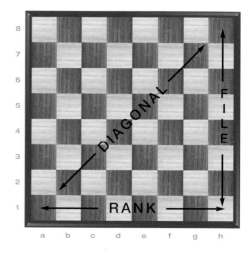

Above: The horizontal squares running across the board are called ranks; the squares going up and down are called files. A diagonal is a straight line of same-coloured squares running obliquely across the board, which can be of varying lengths.

the line of eight squares between a1 and h8 is a diagonal, as is the line of two squares from h7 to g8. If you look at the diagram opposite, you will see how this works.

The diagram below shows the chessboard with the chessmen (more commonly referred to as pieces) on it, in their starting positions. There are two players in a game of chess, one having what are called the white pieces, and the other having the black pieces. As you can see in the diagram below, both players start with 16 pieces. As with the squares, the physical colour of the pieces is not relevant: chess players are effectively colour blind, and the player with the white pieces is simply referred to as White, and his or her opponent as Black.

The two-dimensional diagram shown below represents the board and chess pieces as set up at the beginning of the game, as if we were looking down upon it vertically. You can probably see that each player starts with pieces of six different types in various quantities: on the next page you will learn what each piece is called, but for now the important thing is to make sure you have the board the right way around.

Below: A chessboard with pieces ready to play. Each square has a unique name, which is defined by its file and rank (1-8 and a-h). These co-ordinates are shown around the edges of the diagram. Square h1 is always a white square when the board is set up.

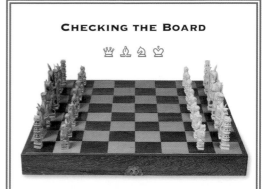

CHECKING THE BOARD

Above: A board with the pieces positioned incorrectly.

Next time you are watching a film or TV programme in which the characters are shown playing chess, look carefully to see if they have the chessboard the right way round (remember – *white on the right* as you sit facing the board). If you think about it, you have a one in two chance of getting it right (or wrong) if you put the board down without regard to its orientation. But you'll be amazed at how often they get it wrong in films and on TV – around eight times out of ten!

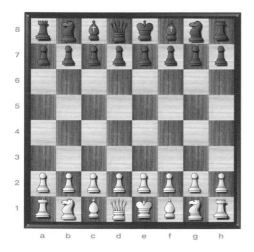

Left: Chess is played by millions of people all around the world. It is as much a game as a part of refined culture, a symbol of intellect, logic and raw skill. It can be enjoyed by people of all ages and played at different levels of skill, competence and experience.

Right: World Champion grandmaster Garry Kasparov with the chess pieces in position at the start of a game. Kasparov announced that he would be retiring from serious competitive chess in March 2005, but would continue to play events for fun.

THE CHESS PIECES

There are six different types of pieces (or chessmen) used in a game of chess – pawn, rook, knight, bishop, queen and king. It is important to recognize what each piece looks like, both in real life on a three-dimensional chessboard, and on the printed page (such as in this book).

It is noticeable from the illustration below that the pieces vary in size. The king is usually the biggest piece, and the pawn invariably the smallest. This corresponds to their relative values in the game, but this is not true of all the pieces. We will discover later that the rook – which is physically shorter than a bishop or knight – is actually a more valuable piece than either of them.

| King | Queen | Bishop | Knight | Rook | Pawn |

The king

The diagram shows the two kings (white and black) on their starting positions in a game of chess. The king is usually the tallest piece in the set, by a small margin relative to the queen, but readily distinguishable by the small cross on top of the crown. The king is the most important piece on the chessboard, and translates as king in virtually all languages (for example, *könig* in German and *roi* in French). Most importantly, the result of a game of chess is decided by the fate of the king. When a king has been trapped, or in chess terms 'checkmated', by the opposition pieces and cannot escape, the game is lost and ends immediately.

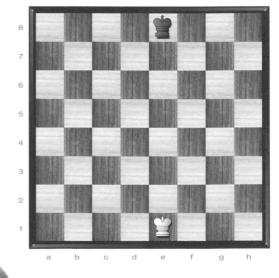

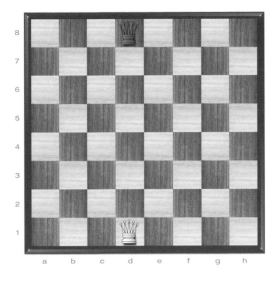

The queen

The diagram shows the two queens on their starting squares, beside their respective kings. The queen is distinguishable from the king by the five prongs of the coronet (and absence of a cross); it is slightly shorter, but taller than all the other pieces. The queen is the most powerful piece on the chessboard in modern chess, but this was not always the case: at one time it was the most limited. That fact is reflected by a less august title by which it is known in many languages (e.g. *dame* in French, or *dama* in Spanish, although it is *regina* in Italian). It is important to remember that the two queens stand on squares of their own colour at the beginning of the game.

The bishop

There are four bishops on the board at the start of the game, split between the two players. They are placed on the c-file and f-file, flanking the squares occupied by the king and queen. They are called 'bishops' in the English-speaking world because the upper part of the piece is thought to resemble a bishop's mitre, but English is alone in making this association. In some cultures, the piece is thought to resemble a jester's cap – for example, in French, it is referred to as *le fou* – 'the jester', and in German it is called *läufe,* meaning 'courier'. Bishops in chess sets from eastern Europe can be a little disconcerting: the small round globe on top of the mitre is often the opposite colour to the colour of the piece – a black bishop will have a white globe at the top and vice versa.

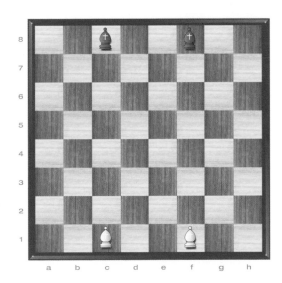

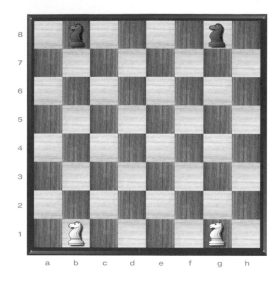

Below: The pieces are lined up at the start of a game, ready to do battle. The knights are placed on squares b1, g1, b8 and g8.

The knight

Each player has two knights at the start of the game. The name is not entirely apt: as you can see, they look rather more like horses than riders. Competition chess players sometimes jocularly refer to the knight as 'horse', and in many languages this piece is indeed called a horse (for example, *caballo* in Spanish). The Germans, however, call it a *springer* which, as you might expect, means 'jumper' or 'leaper'. This name has more to do with the way the chess piece is moved (it does not move along straight lines as do the other pieces). The standard design of the knight is modelled on a horse as it appears in the frieze of the Parthenon.

The rook

Each player has two rooks in the starting position, and they are placed in the four corners of the board. Chess-playing beginners are often tempted to call this piece 'a castle' because it looks rather like the tower and battlements of a medieval castle, and perhaps also because they have heard the chess word castling. But experienced chess players never call it a castle, even in jest. In English it is always called a rook. This has nothing to do with the crow-like bird of the same name: it comes originally from Sanskrit *ratha* and a Persian/Arabic word *rukh*, both meaning 'chariot'. Other languages, however, make the connection with its appearance and call it a 'tower' (French *tour*, Spanish *torre*, German *turm*).

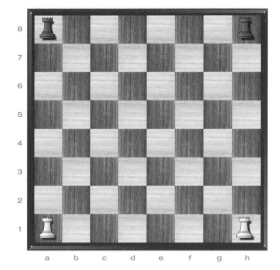

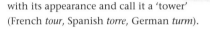

The pawn

Each player starts the game with eight pawns, placed as shown in the diagram on the rank in front of the rest of the pieces. The name derives from the Latin for 'foot' and an old French word for 'foot soldier', which gives a true indication of the pawn's status as the lowest ranking chessman in a player's army. The pawn is also the smallest piece on the chessboard, so it is usually easy to distinguish it from the other pieces by reference to its size, though in some designs it can look rather like the bishop. Despite its limitations, the rules relating to the pawn are slightly more complicated than those of the other pieces – so we will be considering how it moves after introducing the rules relating to the moves of the other pieces.

THE BISHOP

On a single turn or move, the bishop can be moved any number of vacant squares along the diagonal on which it stands. It can capture enemy pieces that stand in its way. The nearer it is to the centre of the board, the greater will be its scope in different directions.

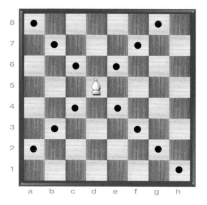

The bishop in the above diagram can be played to any of the 13 squares marked with a black dot. You should note that all of these squares are white: because they only move diagonally, bishops are restricted to squares of one colour. The white bishop in the diagram can be referred to as a white-squared bishop because it is only capable of visiting one of the 32 white squares on the chessboard.

The players start the game with two bishops each, one of which stands on a white square and the other on a black square. Thus, one of the bishops can visit the white squares, and the other the black squares. Between the two of them, if placed in the middle of the board, they can control 26 squares.

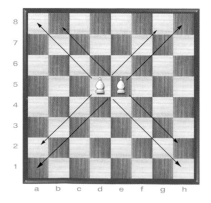

Bishops cannot jump over other pieces of either colour. If there is a piece of the same colour (i.e. a piece belonging to the same player) along the diagonal, it can go no further.

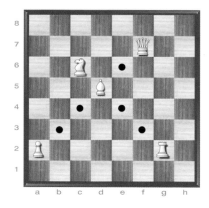

In the diagram above, the bishop can go to any one of the five squares marked by black dots, but cannot jump over or displace any of its own pieces.

Generally speaking, it is a good idea to give the pieces plenty of scope for action. The more squares a piece has access to, the more useful it will be in the game. Bishops are particularly susceptible to becoming blocked in by their own side's pawns.

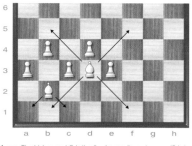

Above: The bishop on b2 is 'bad', whereas its partner on d3 is 'good'.

The part diagram, above, shows examples of a well-placed and a poorly placed bishop. The white bishop on the b2 shown here has only two moves in this position and, even if it moves to the c1 square, its further scope will remain limited by the white pawn on e3. Chess players would refer to this as a 'bad' bishop. However, the bishop on d3 is much better placed: it is unrestricted by the pawns, with plenty of scope for forward movement, and is therefore a 'good' bishop.

Capturing other pieces

A bishop cannot jump over an enemy piece either, but (with the exception of the king) it can capture (or take) it. When a piece is captured, it plays no further part in the game: it is removed from the board and replaced by the piece that effects the capture.

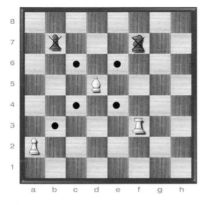

In the diagram above, with White's turn to move, as well as playing to any one of the five marked squares, the white bishop can capture on the squares marked with crosses: the black pawn on the b7 square or the black knight on the f7 square. The bishop in the diagram thus has seven legal moves: five ordinary moves and two captures. If White takes the black knight with the bishop, the position after the capture would be as follows:

One curiosity: because bishops only move on squares of one colour, it means that white-squared bishops and black-squared bishops never cross each other's path.

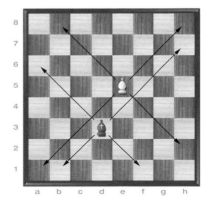

In the diagram above, the white bishop can only move to black squares and the black bishop only to white squares. These references to white and black in different contexts can cause confusion, hence chess players tend to refer to the white bishop on e5 as a 'dark-squared bishop' and the black bishop on d3 as a 'light-squared bishop'. Note that neither of these can ever capture the other.

The above diagram shows enemy bishops of the same (square) colour. If it is White to play, White can take the bishop on d4 with the bishop on b2. Similarly, if it is Black to play, Black can take the b2 bishop with the bishop on d4.

THE ROOK

On a single move, the rook can be moved any number of squares along the file or rank on which it stands. As we will see, this gives it great strength, especially when it is supported by a second rook that stands either on the same rank or the same file.

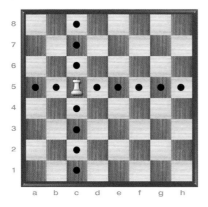

The rook in the above diagram can be played to any of the 14 squares marked with a black dot. Note that, unlike the bishop, the rook is not restricted to squares of one colour. Hence, it has the potential to visit all 64 squares on the chessboard and, if there are no other pieces in the way, it can reach any square in a maximum of two moves. For this reason, it is a particularly powerful and valuable piece.

The players start the game with two rooks each, which stand in the four corner squares of the board. Like bishops, rooks need to be given plenty of scope in order to exploit their power, and they are also susceptible to being hemmed in by their own army. This is noticeable right from the beginning of the game, when they are restricted by the line of pawns ahead of them, particularly the one immediately ahead of it on the file. This problem often takes time to

Above: Start position: the rook on a1 has no moves.

resolve itself, and rooks tend to enter the main battle rather later than the other pieces.

Rooks often benefit from a reduction in the overall forces, particularly when some of the pawns have disappeared from the board. An open file is one on which there are no pawns, and they make particularly good paths for rooks to travel in order to attack or infiltrate the enemy camp. They are much less happy on closed files, where their scope is restricted.

Above: The rook is on a closed file and restricted by the white pawn.

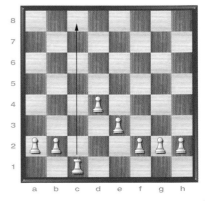

Above: The rook is on an open file and can advance into enemy territory.

Capturing other pieces

The rook can capture enemy pieces along both files and ranks.

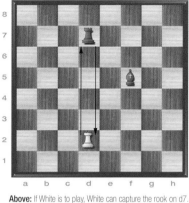

Above: If White is to play, White can capture the rook on d7.
If Black is to play, Black can take the rook on d2.

In the diagram above, the rooks attack each other. If it is White's turn, White can play rook on d2 to d7, removing the black rook from that square. Conversely, if it is Black's move, Black can take the white rook on d2 with the rook on d7. Notice that, if it is White's move and White captures the rook on d7, Black can then take the white rook with the bishop on f5. This move is referred to as a 'recapture'.

Below: In this position, the white rook on d4 is able to move along the open rank and capture the bishop on h4.

ATTACKING AND DEFENDING

♕ ♗ ♘ ♔

Here is another example of chess terminology: in the diagram to the left, it would be said that the black bishop is 'defending' the black rook. In other words, it would have the option to recapture any piece that captured the black rook. Incidentally, chess players also talk in terms of 'attacking' or 'defending' specific squares. Usually it is defending when referring to squares adjacent to its main forces and attacking for squares in or near the enemy camp, but the meaning is the same. For example, in the diagram, the black bishop attacks the empty square at c2. If White moves a piece there, it is liable to capture.

Recapture

Generally speaking, it is a good idea to capture enemy pieces, as it depletes the opponent's forces, and bigger armies tend to prevail. Captures are often answered by a recapture. This is slightly misleading terminology, as a piece never reappears on the board after being captured. It simply refers to the immediate capture of a piece that has just taken another man. Where equivalent pieces are captured on consecutive moves, it is called an 'exchange' or 'swap'.

THE QUEEN

On a single move, the queen can be moved any number of squares along the file, rank or diagonal on which it stands. This makes it very versatile and thus the focus of many winning attacks, though, as we shall see, this very strength brings certain drawbacks.

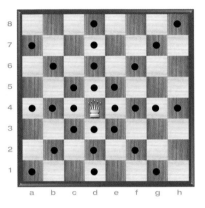

Located in the middle of the board (above), the queen can reach no fewer than 27 squares (represented here by the black dots). Thus, it combines the functions of the bishop and the rook, and is considerably more powerful than either of those pieces. In fact, it is potentially the strongest piece on the chessboard, with fast access to any square on the board.

At the beginning of the game, the two players have one queen each. Queens cannot jump over their own (or the opponent's) pieces any more than bishops and rooks can, but such is their manoeuvrability that it is less common for them to be hemmed in.

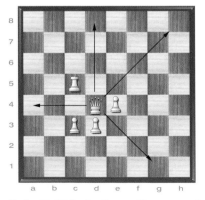

Above: Despite some restriction, the white queen still has some scope for action.

Capturing other pieces

The queen captures exactly as it moves – along a file, rank or diagonal.

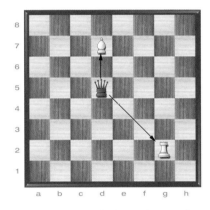

In the diagram above, Black attacks (i.e. threatens to capture) both the white rook and the white bishop. Note that neither of the white pieces is attacking the black queen – the bishop is as powerless along the file as the rook is along the diagonal. This double attack by a single piece against two or more enemy pieces is called a 'fork'. Double attacks are often hard to defend against – often it is a case of defending or moving away the most valuable of the two pieces and leaving the other to its fate. Here, White could move the rook away from attack by playing it to the g7 square, which simultaneously defends the bishop. An alternative is to play the bishop to h3 to defend the attacked rook. In either case, this would almost certainly discourage Black from capturing, since the more valuable queen would be lost in exchange for a rook or bishop. This is known as an 'unfavourable exchange'.

Paradoxically, the queen's superiority in value can be its Achilles' heel. It is less expendable than its colleagues. As we have seen above, it is often possible to defend a piece from capture (i.e. threaten recapture), but it is rarely appropriate to defend a queen in this way (except from capture by another queen). Usually the queen is simply too valuable to be defended from

capture by inferior pieces and its owner will have to move it away from the attack.

Above: The queen is the most powerful piece on the chessboard. This queen has the choice of capturing any one of four black pieces on the next turn.

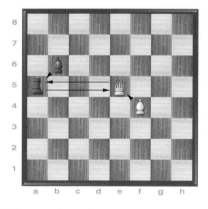

In the diagram above, the queen and rook are attacking each other, with both being defended by a bishop. If it is Black's move, Black would capture the queen in exchange for the rook. This is known as a 'favourable exchange'. However, if it is White's move, it would be highly unlikely to take the rook and lose the queen. In this instance, the best idea would be to move the queen to a safe square.

USING THE QUEEN WITH CARE

Beginners are often infatuated by the power of the queen and tend to move it repeatedly from a very early stage in the game. However, strong chess players usually prefer to deploy (or 'develop') their less valuable pieces first and rarely embark on solo escapades with the queen. It is true that the queen can often get behind enemy lines quicker than other pieces, but it can equally easily become trapped there. Like other pieces, the queen works best in co-ordination with the other pieces. Also, beginners often get discouraged or depressed if queens are exchanged (i.e. both players' queens have been captured) at an early stage in the game. There is no need to worry in this situation, since it is the same for both players and it is still perfectly possible to win a game without queens.

THE KNIGHT

The knight can be moved to one of the nearest squares to that on which it stands, but not on the same rank, file or diagonal. Its move may sound somewhat complicated when expressed in words, but it becomes more clear when shown graphically.

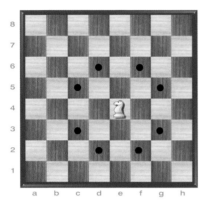

The knight in the diagram above can be played to any one of the squares with the black dots. This move is perhaps less intuitive than those of other chess pieces that move along visible lines of squares on the board, and thus can be slightly trickier to remember. For the purpose of visualization, some players prefer to think of the move as an 'L'-shape: the knight moves two squares along a rank or file and then one square at a right angle.

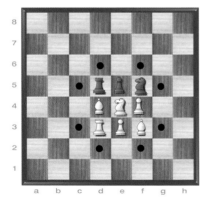

Another key difference between the knight and other pieces is that it can jump over other pieces (of either colour). In the diagram above, the white knight can be played to any of the eight marked squares, just as if the surrounding pieces were not there. However, it is possible for the knight to be blocked in by its own side's pieces if they are placed on one of these target squares.

Capturing other pieces

Knights use the same move to make captures.

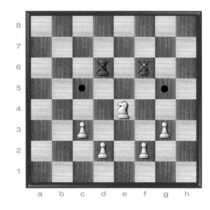

In the diagram above, the white knight cannot play a backwards move (since its target squares are occupied by pawns), but it has two moves (to empty squares

---

PRACTISE THE KNIGHT MOVE

♕ ♗ ♘ ♔

Look again at the diagram showing knight paths across the board. There are several possible paths other than those shown that would get the knights to their destinations in the same number of moves, but none would get them there any quicker. Because the knight move is counter-intuitive, it is a good idea to practise moving it around the board. First, try to find alternative ways to get the knight from a1 to h8 in six moves. Try some other paths: for instance, it might surprise you to find that it takes four moves to get a knight from a1 to b2 – the adjacent square on the diagonal.

with black dots) as well as two possible captures (of the black rook or black bishop).

The knight is the only piece with a move that the queen cannot emulate. This makes it especially useful in playing deadly forks.

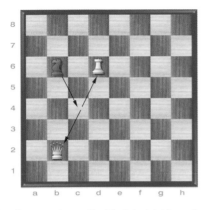

In the diagram above, the black knight is under attack from the white queen and the white rook. However, it can turn the tables on the attacking pieces by moving to c4, where it will attack both queen and rook at the same time. In all likelihood, the queen would then have to move away, leaving the rook to be captured by the knight.

Despite its unique powers, the knight is generally reckoned to be less valuable than the bishop and considerably less powerful than the rook or queen. Compared to a queen, rook or bishop, it lacks

manoeuvrability and takes too many moves to cross the board. It also lacks options when situated on the edge (or in the corner) of the board.

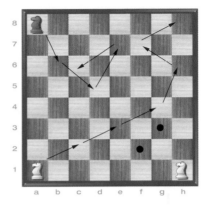

In the diagram above, the white knight shown on h1 has only two possible moves: to f2 or g3. As for the white knight on a1, it would take no fewer than six moves to reach h8, the square at the end of the diagonal. And should the black knight on a8 need to reach the c6 square (which is only two squares away on the diagonal) it would take four knight moves to get there. However, unlike the bishop, the knight has the potential to visit every square on the board.

Below: The knight knows no barriers. Unlike other chess pieces, it can jump over any piece, of either colour. Here, with White to play, the white knight on d4 can capture the black queen on e6.

THE PAWN

The pawn is the most limited piece on the chessboard in terms of its power and value, but the way it makes moves and captures is a little more complex than the other pieces. It is worth spending time mastering the way the pawn moves as good pawn play is often a key factor in success at chess.

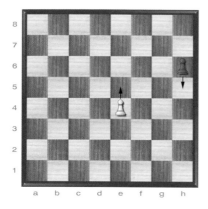

The diagram above shows the basic move of the pawn: one square forward to the square immediately in front of it, so long as that square is unoccupied. White (to play) can play the pawn from e4 to e5. If it is Black to move, the pawn can be played from h6 to h5. The pawn is different from all the other moves in that it never moves backwards. For this reason the decision to move a pawn is highly committal.

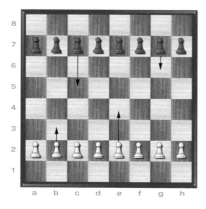

Players start the game with eight pawns each, arrayed along the rank immediately in front of their other pieces. On its first turn, a pawn may move either one square or two squares forward (provided both of those squares are unoccupied). Thus, in the diagram above,

the pawn on e2 may move either to e3 or to e4 (as indicated by the arrow) and if it is Black's move, the pawn on c7 may move forward to c6 or c5.

A pawn's forward trajectory can quickly become blocked, often by an opposing pawn. A common example, as shown below, occurs right at the beginning of the game.

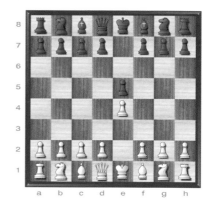

The position above frequently appears on the chessboard after the players have made just one move each. White starts the game by moving a pawn from e2 to e4, and Black replies by moving a pawn from e7 to e5. These two pawns effectively immobilize each other, and neither pawn can make any further moves until such time as the situation changes around them. Often one or both of them will be attacked and captured and play no further part in the game. Immobility leads to vulnerability, and is one of the key limiting factors that makes the pawn the least-powerful chess piece.

However, it is easy to overlook one of the cardinal virtues of the humble pawn – its value (in conjunction with its colleagues) as a strong protective barrier against attack. The line of eight pawns across the board provides a front line of defence for the more valuable pieces that stand behind it. But sometimes a pawn barrier can be a disadvantage, restricting the scope of a player who wants files, ranks or diagonals to be open so that the opponent can be attacked with queens,

rooks and bishops. Advanced chess players always take care over the arrangement of their pawns – what is known as the pawn structure – having both defence and attack in mind.

Capturing other pieces

Unlike other pieces, a pawn moves differently when it captures compared to when it makes a move to an unoccupied square – a pawn may capture a piece that is one square ahead of it diagonally on an adjacent file.

In the diagram above, the white pawn on c4 may capture either the pawn on b5 or the rook on d5. If it is Black's turn, the pawn on h6 may capture the white knight on g5, or the black pawn on b5 may take the white pawn on c4. Note that, if it is White's turn, White may not play the pawn on c4 one square forward because the path is blocked by the pawn on c5.

A stout defender

We have already seen how the mighty queen often has to run away quickly when it is attacked. The pawn, however, has no such problems. So long as it is defended, it can usually just stand its ground. This is just as well, because it cannot run as fast or as far away as the other pieces.

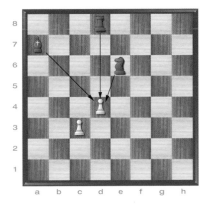

In the above diagram, the white pawn on d4 appears to be under a withering attack from all three of Black's pieces. However, White need not be concerned. The d4 pawn is defended by the pawn on c3. Should Black capture the d4 pawn with knight, bishop or rook, the capturing piece would be captured by the pawn on c3. This is an unfavourable exchange, even though Black could capture the second pawn on the following turn. Two pawns are usually worth less than one knight, bishop or rook.

THE PAWN: SPECIAL MOVES

Though it may seem a very ordinary piece, it is true to say that the humble pawn has some surprises up its sleeve. First, unlike any other piece, it has the potential to upgrade itself to a queen, rook, bishop or knight. Second, in a special circumstance it has a unique way of capturing opposing pawns.

Promotion

We now know that the pawn is the least-valuable piece on the board, but this condition is not necessarily permanent. Should a pawn succeed in advancing all the way to the other side of the board, something magical happens – it is 'promoted'. This means that it changes from being a pawn to a queen, rook, bishop or knight of the same colour. The player chooses which of these four pieces it becomes. As the queen is the most powerful piece on the board, normally the player chooses to exchange the pawn for a queen.

Here's how it happens:

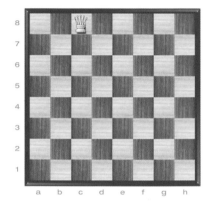

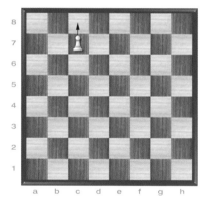

In the diagram above, White plays the pawn from c7 to c8. Now the player must choose whether to promote the pawn to a queen, rook, bishop or knight. Let us say that White chooses to promote to a queen (the most usual). The white pawn on c8 is then replaced with a white queen.

What had previously been one of the weakest pieces on the board has become one of the most powerful, with the potential to help win the game. Lowly it may be, but the further it advances up the board, provided it is defended against capture, the more of a threat each pawn becomes, especially in the later stages of a game.

White now has a queen on c8 and that completes the turn to move. This new white queen has all the powers of White's original queen. It is perfectly permissible for White to have two queens on the board – or even nine, in the unlikely event that all eight pawns are promoted to queens, and the original queen is still on the board. This is extremely unusual in practice, but two queens of the same colour are occasionally seen, or more rarely, an extra rook, bishop or knight.

NOT ENOUGH PIECES!

Pawn promotion sometimes brings about a small practical problem: most chess sets only contain those pieces that are used to start the game, so it is sometimes necessary to find another small object that can be used to betoken a second queen or a third rook, bishop or knight. Often, a captured rook is used and turned upside down to show it is being used as a second queen. The important thing is to agree with your opponent what you are doing and ensure that you both know what the substitute token is.

En passant

We have already seen how pawns can make captures, but there is one special capturing move that pawns can make in specific circumstances. The pawn can capture an opposing pawn *en passant* if it attacks a square crossed by the opposing pawn which has crossed that square in one move from its original square. This capture can only be made on the move immediately following the opposing pawn's advance.

The *en passant* rule is, understandably, one which beginners find quite hard to remember. Let us see how it works in practice.

In the first partial diagram, the white pawn stands on its original square, a2, while the black pawn stands on b4. It is White's turn to move, and the white pawn is moved two squares forward to a4 as it is entitled to do on the first move of any pawn. The second partial diagram shows the position after White's move. Black can capture this pawn *en passant* because it has crossed a square (a3) that is attacked by the black pawn. So, on the next move, Black takes the white pawn off the board and puts his own pawn on a3, producing the position in the third partial diagram. If Black were to make any other move instead, he would forfeit the right to make this *en passant* capture on a subsequent move.

Effectively, the pawn captures its opposite number as if it had moved only one square forward. Note that this is the only situation in chess in which a capturing piece is placed on a square other than the one on which the captured piece stood previously.

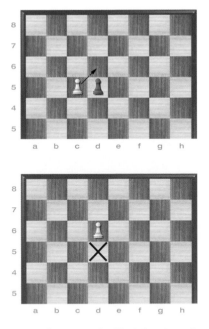

Above is another example. Black has just played the pawn from d7 to d5. On the next move only, White has the right to capture this pawn *en passant,* using the pawn standing on c5, as if the black pawn had only travelled as far as d6. White plays his pawn diagonally to d6 and simultaneously removes the black pawn on d5 from the board (marked with a cross in the partial diagram).

THE KING

Although it is able to move in any direction along the file, rank or diagonal on which it stands, the king can only move one square at a time. This limited mobility makes it a particularly vulnerable piece, especially when either the opposing queen or the opposing rooks are still on the board.

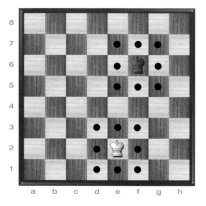

The diagram above shows the possible squares to which the white and black king can move. Hence, the king moves rather like a queen, but its range is more restricted.

Capturing other pieces

The king can capture enemy pieces that stand within its moving range.

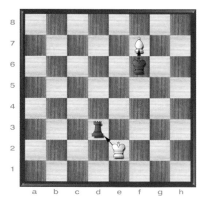

However, the king cannot be captured like other chess pieces, nor can it be placed or left on a square which is attacked by an opposing piece. It is the most important piece on the board – the fate of the king decides the game.

Checking the king

There are pieces, other than the king, that are liable to capture by the opposing force. Although it is usual to try to stop the opponent capturing valuable pieces, it is permissible under the rules to leave pieces where they can be captured or even to move a piece to a square where it can be taken immediately. However, it is against the rules of chess to play a move that allows a king to be captured on the next turn. An attacked king is said to be 'in check'.

A king can be attacked (or checked) by any opposing piece except for the opposing king. Kings are not permitted to stand on adjacent squares.

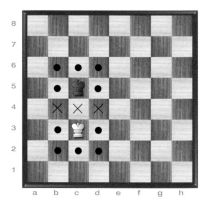

In the diagram above, neither king can move to any of the squares marked with a cross. Thus, kings can never attack each other, although they can restrict each other's scope for movement considerably.

A player whose king is in check (attacked by an opposing piece) must make a move on the next turn which escapes the check. There are three possible ways to escape check: capture the checking piece; move the king away from check; interpose a piece between your king and the checking piece.

If there is no legal move that achieves any of these options, the game ends and the player unable to escape check is said to be 'checkmated' (or 'in checkmate'). The first option is to capture the checking piece.

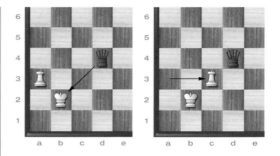

In the above diagram, the black rook attacks the white king, which is in check. On the next turn, White must move to escape the check. The best move would be to capture the rook with the white bishop. This escapes the check and gains valuable material for White.

A second way to escape a check is simply to move the king away from the attack. This could be achieved in the above diagram by moving the king to an adjacent file, as it is being attacked along the file by the rook. Here is another example.

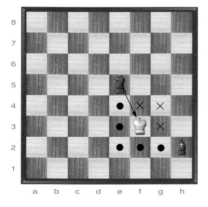

The white king on f3 is in check from the black knight on e5. White cannot capture the knight because the knight is not attacked by any white pieces. So White must move the king away from check. There are eight squares around the king but three of them are controlled by black pieces. The king can move to any of the five squares marked with a dot, but not to one of the three squares marked with a cross. The g4 square is also attacked by the knight, while the f4 and g3 squares are both attacked by the black bishop.

The final way to escape check, as long as the attacking piece is not a knight, is to block the check. This is where the player places a piece between the king and the attacking piece to block the check.

In the first partial diagram above, Black has played the queen to d4 to check White's king. White can reply, as shown in the second partial diagram above, by playing the rook on a3 to c3, thereby blocking the queen's attack on the king.

No legal move

Positions where the king has no legal moves are not necessarily a cause for alarm. Take, for example, the situation shown in the diagram below.

With White to play, the king has no legal moves. It cannot displace one of its own pieces and cannot go to any of the squares along the g-file because they are attacked by the black rook. However, the king is not directly attacked and White can proceed with a move of the bishop. Had the piece on h4 been, say, a protected black pawn rather than one of White's own pieces, the situation would then, as we will see later, have been very different.

SPECIAL FORMS OF CHECK

Checking the king can be a very useful weapon in a game of chess as it forces the opponent to defend the attack on the king immediately rather than indulging in some offensive action of his own. Some forms of check are more useful than others, having a potentially lethal impact.

Discovered check

One particular type of check that can often be devastating in its effect is the 'discovered' check. This is a move that uncovers an attack by another piece on the opponent's king.

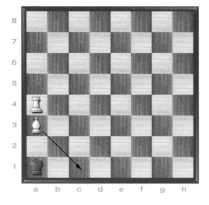

In the diagram above, Black's king is not attacked. The rook is on the same file, but it is blocked by its own bishop on a3. However, if, for example, White plays his bishop to c1, it will reveal (or 'discover') a check by the rook against the king on a1.

Discovered attacks often can be truly devastating, as shown below.

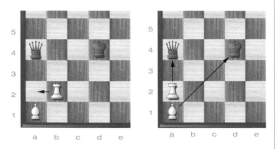

In the first partial diagram above, Black's king is not attacked by the bishop because its scope along the diagonal is blocked by the rook. However, when White plays the rook to a2 (see the second partial diagram),

it discovers check by the bishop against the black king. Black must escape the check on the next turn. The bishop cannot be captured (notice how the rook blocks the queen's attack on the bishop). There is no way to block the check, so Black will be obliged to move the king. On the following move, White will be free to capture the black queen with the rook.

Double check

Another form of check that can be very strong is the 'double check'. This is an extension of the discovered check except that the moved piece as well as the unblocked piece gives check to the king, shown below.

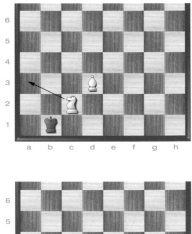

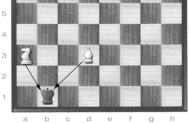

From the first partial diagram above, White plays the knight to the a3 square. From there, the knight checks the king on b1 and also reveals an attack on the king from the bishop on d3.

It is sometimes possible, as shown below, to escape from a double check by capturing (if the king stands on an adjacent square to one of the two checking pieces), but it is never possible to block a double check.

White could play the bishop to b2, which would be double check from the rook (along the file) and the bishop (along the diagonal). But it would not be very clever, because Black could simply capture the bishop with the king, simultaneously capturing one checking piece and moving away from the attack of the other. However, a better-executed double check can offer immunity from capture or blocking attempts to the attacking side. The double-attacked king is usually reduced to moving away from the attack, often at the expense of a lot of damage elsewhere on the board.

One key difference between the above example and the following one is that the two pieces involved in delivering the double check that follows are at some distance from the enemy king. This means that neither

piece can be captured, since the king remains in check from the piece that remains.

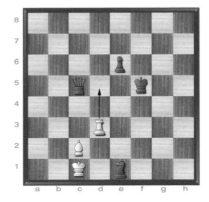

On the face of things in the diagram above, White is not doing particularly well, with fewer pieces and both rook and bishop under threat. But there is the option of moving the rook to d5, which is a double check.

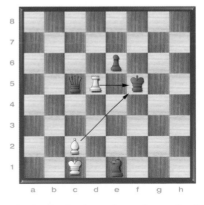

The rook checks the king along the rank while the bishop checks the king along the diagonal. Black must make a move to escape both checks, and cannot capture the rook (although it is attacked by both queen and pawn), or block by playing the pawn to e5, because neither move would do anything to escape the bishop check. Similarly, Black cannot capture the bishop (also attacked twice, by queen and knight) or block (by playing the knight to d3) because the king would still be under attack from the rook. Black's only option is a king move (to f6, f4 or g4). Whatever Black does, on the following move, White could capture the queen with the rook and gain a major advantage.

CHECKMATE

A player whose king is in check must escape the check on the next turn. He can do this either by capturing a checking piece, blocking the check or by moving the king to a square where it is not attacked. If the player is unable to achieve any of those three things and the king has no escape, the game ends immediately. It is checkmate, and the player whose king is thus trapped has lost.

The diagram below shows an example of a queen giving checkmate.

The white queen has just moved to e7 and attacks the black king. Black cannot capture the queen because the e7 square is adjacent to the white king on f6, so the white king effectively defends the queen. There is no blocking possibility, and the four contiguous squares to which the king could otherwise move are also attacked by the white queen. Black's king is attacked and there is no escape. It is checkmate and the game ends immediately in favour of White.

It is worth noting that a piece cannot give checkmate to a king without some help from other pieces – of either colour. In the diagram on the left, the queen is supported by its own king. If the king were further away from the action, it could not defend the queen, and Black could capture the queen with the king, thus preventing checkmate.

There are also occasions when a player's own pieces contribute to their own defeat. The position below demonstrates that a player's own pieces can sometimes prove to be a liability.

White, to move, plays the white rook to the a8 square. This gives check along the rank to the king on g8.

Below: In this scenario, White will play the rook to a8 and checkmate the black king on a4.

Black is obliged to escape check. The white rook cannot be captured, and the king cannot move away from the rank on which it is situated because it is impeded by the row of three pawns in front of it. The only option to continue the game is to block the check by playing the black rook to d8, as shown above.

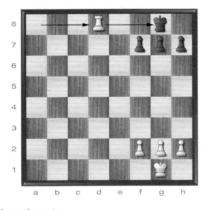

Back-rank mate

White simply takes the rook on d8 with its own rook. Now Black has the same problem with the king. It has no good move, still being imprisoned by its own pawns. The black rook has disappeared from the board. There is no longer any escape: it is checkmate, and White wins the game. This particular example is called a 'back-rank mate' because the king is trapped on its own back (starting) rank. The sequence of moves in this example might be referred to as 'mate in two', meaning that White plays two moves to achieve checkmate. To avoid the calamity of a back-rank check, it is often prudent to move the pawns one square forward so that the king can escape a back-rank check.

The diagrams below show another less common example of a king being hampered by its own pieces.

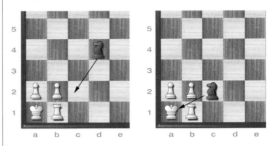

Black, to move, plays the knight to the c2 square, attacking the white king on a1. White cannot capture the knight, nor can the check be blocked (attacks from knights can never be blocked because they have the power to jump over intervening pieces). The king cannot be moved because it is entirely surrounded by pieces of the same colour. It cannot escape, so is mated. Game over!

The pawn is the humblest of pieces, but on occasion it can deliver mate as effectively as any of its more powerful colleagues, as shown below.

White, to play, moves the pawn from e4 to e5. Pawns give check diagonally, just as they capture, so this move attacks the black king on f6. The pawn cannot be captured by the black king because it is defended by the white king. In addition to this, Black's king cannot retreat because all the retreat squares are occupied by its own pieces. It cannot go to f5 or g5 because they are next to the white king, and it cannot go to g6 because that square is threatened by the pawn on h5. It has no moves and thus has been mated by the pawn on e5.

MORE CHECKMATES

We have seen two examples of checkmate being achieved via surprise ambushes from lone pieces (pages 68–69), but these are exceptional and require negligence from the opponent in deploying their forces. In normal circumstances, a player's pieces must work together to force checkmate and end the game.

All the pieces on the chessboard, except for the king, are liable to capture, and it is possible for all the pieces on the board to disappear, leaving only kings on the board. A king on its own cannot checkmate another, so the game ends immediately as a draw.

If one side has a single queen or rook left, checkmate can be achieved with some help from the king. Below are typical examples of a queen giving checkmate.

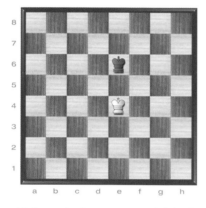

In both of the above diagrams, it can be seen that the white queen gives checkmate but with significant support from the white king. In the first diagram, the white king defends the queen from capture and in the second, it prevents the black king from moving away from the file on which it is attacked. A rook can effect a similar checkmate to the second queen.

As shown below, the rook attacks the king along the file and the white king prevents the black king from escaping the attack via the squares b1, b2 or b3.

A lone bishop or knight cannot force checkmate against a lone king, even if the defender played the worst moves possible. So a position with bishop and king against king, or knight and king against king, is a draw. A lone pawn, however, can win against a lone king if it can be promoted to a queen or rook.

In the above example, White is left with just a pawn to accompany the king. But there is nothing to stop the pawn racing through to promote to a queen. This can be accomplished in five moves (count the arrows – the pawn can move forward two squares on its first move). Black's king is too far away from the action to stop it. In five moves it can only get as far as the c-file, so White will promote the pawn to a queen and, with just a modicum of skill thereafter, win the game.

Combining forces

Two pieces in tandem can work very well together, particularly a queen and rook. Two rooks are equally effective, being able in just a few moves to checkmate the opponent's king without any support of their own. The process is illustrated below and, as you can see, is relatively simple.

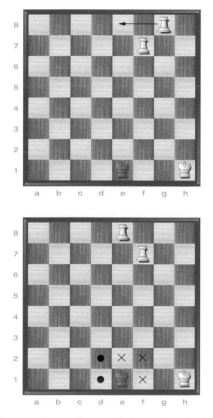

White starts by moving a rook from g8 to e8, checking the black king on e1. The king's only option is to move to a square on the d-file as all the squares on the e-file and f-file are attacked by the rooks.

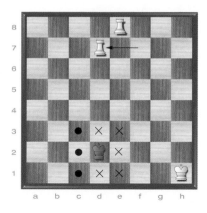

White now moves his other rook to d7, bringing about much the same situation, except that Black can now only move to a square on the c-file. But White can continue alternating moves with the rooks to push the black king to the edge of the board.

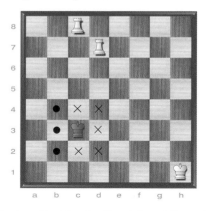

Black plays the king to c3 and the white rook goes to c8. The black king must go to the b-file and the white rook on d7 goes to b7, now forcing Black to the a-file. White now plays the c8 rook to a8 and it is checkmate.

This series of five moves by White is designed to push Black to the edge of the board. It is common for a king to meet its end at the side of the board because it is thus deprived of three escape squares which it would otherwise have access to.

In some positions it is possible for the king to get close to the rooks so that they cannot checkmate quite so easily, but the technique then is to move the rooks to a distance, but at the same time keeping the king boxed-in, nearest the edge of the board.

STALEMATE

We have already seen that – when neither side has sufficient material to deliver checkmate – not all chess games end in a decisive result. Another draw possibility in chess is stalemate. Stalemate occurs when a player has no legal move, but the king is not attacked. The game ends immediately as a draw.

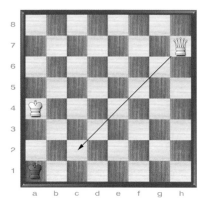

In the above position, White might be tempted to play the queen to c2 in order to prepare checkmate in a couple of moves. The snag is that this deprives the king of any moves at all, although the king is not directly attacked. So it is stalemate, and a rather lucky draw for Black. Instead of moving the queen to c2, it would be a similar mistake for White to move the king to a3 or b3, as this would also deprive Black of any legal moves and create a stalemate position.

It is always worth making sure that the opponent has a legal move or two at their disposal when rounding up a king. Below is an amusing trick that allows White to escape with a draw.

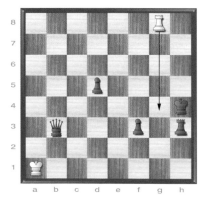

White's position (below left) looks miserable, but there is a way out of his problems. The white king cannot move, but it is not stalemate because there is still a rook on the board which can (and indeed must) be moved. The rook can move to g4 and give check to the black king on h4. The rook is undefended and the black king can simply capture – but if it does, White no longer has a legal move and the game ends in stalemate.

Perpetual check

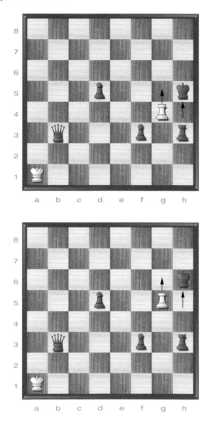

If Black avoids the capture and instead plays the king to h5, White carries on with the plan and plays the rook to g5, giving check again. It is the same situation as before: if the white rook is captured, the game ends immediately in stalemate. Black can continue to move the king up and down the h-file and White will follow with a rook check in the hope that Black will capture.

In fact, this process will continue ad infinitum and there is no way for Black to break the sequence. This is known as 'perpetual check' and, when Black gets fed up trying to win, the game will be agreed a draw. In a formal competitive game, where the players keep a record of the moves, a player can claim a draw when the same position on the board has occurred (or is about to occur) three times.

The fact that stalemate constitutes a draw in circumstances where one player has such a large material advantage might seem rather unfair but it is a fact of chess. It is perhaps seen to be fairer in situations where the difference in material is much smaller.

In the position above right, White can play the king into the corner and sit tight. If Black advances the pawn to a2, it is stalemate because the white king has no legal move. In fact, it makes no difference whatever Black does in reply to the king moving to the a1 square. White can simply move the king backwards and forwards from b1 to a1. Black cannot force the white king out of the corner and will eventually have to give up and agree a draw.

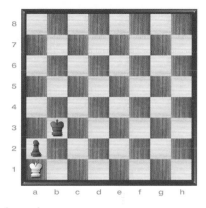

Offering a draw

In tournament chess, chess players often agree draws when there are still several pieces on the board. The protocol is to make a move and ask: 'Would you like a draw?'

The player offered a draw may decide at their leisure whether to accept the draw (usually by proffering a handshake) or by continuing the game (by making a move and, optionally, replying verbally). Once a further move has been made, the draw offer is deemed to have lapsed.

Right: Vladimir Kramnik (left) waits for reigning world champion Garry Kasparov to make his move at the World Chess Championship at Hammersmith, London, UK, on 31 October 2000.

CASTLING

The only time in a game of chess when a player is allowed to move two pieces on the same turn is called castling. This is a special move involving the king and a rook of the same colour. The mechanics of the move are very simple. However there are a number of provisos that need to be understood first.

A player is only allowed to castle when both king and rook are on their original squares and have not moved previously in the game. There must be no pieces of either colour between the king and rook. And the king must not be attacked on its original square, its target square or any intervening squares between the two.

Above, the king and rook are on their original squares. Castling is effected by first moving the king two squares to the right (to g1 in the case of White) and the rook two squares to the left (to f1 in the case of White). After the moves are completed, the board looks like this:

This is called 'kingside' castling, because it involves the rook that stands on the king's side of the board at the

beginning of the game (the files lettered from e to h). A player can also castle with the rook that stands on the queen's side of the board (the files lettered from a to d). Below is an example of queenside castling.

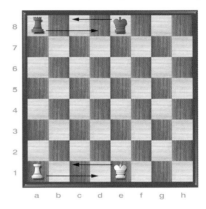

First, the king is moved two squares to the left (to c1, in the case of the white king) and then the rook is moved three squares to the right (to d1 in the case of the white rook), as seen below:

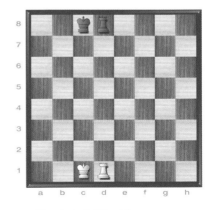

When castling is not allowed
Castling is only allowed if the pieces involved have not yet been moved in the game (even if they have returned to their original squares after moving). Here are some examples where a player may not castle:

Above, White may not castle because the king is in check from the knight on d3. Should the knight subsequently move to a square from where it did not attack the d1 square, castling would be possible.

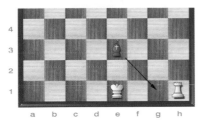

In the above position, White may not castle because the king would land on a square attacked by the black bishop. If the black bishop moves away and leaves g1 unattacked, castling would become permissible.

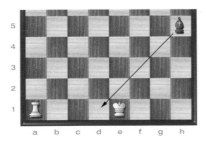

Above, White may not castle – it would mean the king passing over a square attacked by the black bishop. Note that an attack on a rook or a square over which a rook passes is not a bar to castling.

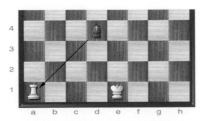

Below left, the rook on a1 is attacked by the bishop, but it is permissible for White to castle, by moving the king to c1 and the rook to d1.

In the above example, assuming that White has not previously moved the king or either rook, White can legally castle on either side of the board. So White castles kingside (as shown by the arrows).

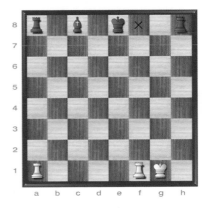

Above is the position after White has castled. Can Black now castle? Answer: no, because there is a bishop in the way on the queenside, while on the kingside the white rook is attacking the square f8, over which the black king would need to pass.

Note that, when castling, the king should always be moved before the rook. In formal competitive chess, a player touching the rook first would not be allowed to castle but must make a move with the touched rook.

MORE RULES AND CONVENTIONS

As well as the basic rules of the pieces, chess has several conventions that are traditionally respected. If you're playing informally with a friend you may well choose to ignore these, but anyone wishing to take part in serious matches must learn them until their observance becomes second nature.

Touch-piece-move rule

You now know the rules for moving the chess pieces. If a player whose turn it is to move touches one or more of his own pieces, then he is obliged to move the first piece touched that can be moved. If the piece or pieces touched belong to the opponent, then he must capture the first piece touched that can be captured. Having moved a piece to a square, the actual move is not complete until the player releases the piece. If he still has a hand on the piece, he is committed to moving the piece (because it has been touched), but can move it somewhere else.

In practice, it is not a good idea to make moves tentatively. Some inexperienced players make a move and leave a finger on the piece while they perform a last-minute check to see if the move is alright. Strong players never do this. Leaving your hand on a piece (or hovering over the piece with your hand) can partially obscure the opponent's view of the board (and is

arguably poor manners); and visible indecision encourages the opponent psychologically. Good chess players make their moves with precision and panache, giving an impression of brisk efficiency and confidence. Another rule with which many chess players are unfamiliar: the laws of the game stipulate that a move may be made with one hand only.

In informal chess games between friends, strict application of what is called the 'touch-piece-move' rule is often relaxed, with players requesting and being allowed 'take-backs' when they realize that they have done something silly. However, a take-back is never allowed in a chess competition and, if it is done too often in informal play, it can lead to a sloppy or lazy approach to the game. It is good practice to adhere to the touch-piece-move rule even in informal games.

Below: It is customary to centralize all the pieces on their squares before starting play. World champion Vladimir Kramnik adjusts his pieces before a big game against Grandmaster Peter Leko at a tournament in Germany.

No-talking rule

In formal competitions, chess players rarely talk at the board. One exception to this is to offer a draw. This should be done verbally, immediately after making a move. If you offer a draw without making a move, the opponent can ask to see a move before they decide whether to accept or not. After you have moved, they may choose to accept, politely refuse or simply continue play without saying anything. It is conventional to accept a draw by offering a handshake. Having made a draw offer and had it refused, it is bad form to make further draw offers unless the position on the board changes markedly.

Another exception to the no-talking convention is that you may decide that your position is so bad that it is time to give up. You are permitted to resign the game in these circumstances, either by saying: 'I resign', toppling over your king or perhaps by offering a handshake. It is usually clear from the context of the game whether the handshake denotes a resignation or a draw acceptance – but there have occasionally been misunderstandings. Having said that chess players do not talk during play, it is perfectly normal to exchange small talk or offer to buy refreshments, provided it does not disturb the opponent or neighbouring players.

Right: Leading Dutch player Tea Bosboom-Lanchava moves her queen in a tournament in London.

Below: White's bare king is up against a large army of black pieces, so White decides to resign – signified by toppling over the white king.

THE 50-MOVE RULE

One obscure rule that is rarely invoked is the 50-move rule. If 50 consecutive moves are played by each player without a single pawn move or any capture, either player can claim a draw. In practice, the players would need to be keeping score of the moves in order to make such a claim, so it does not arise in informal play.

RELATIVE VALUES OF THE PIECES

We now know, in general terms, that the queen is more valuable than the other chessmen, and that the pawn is the least valuable piece on the board. We also know that the point of the game is to checkmate the opponent's king. But in order to bring about a checkmate it is generally true that the side with the most valuable force of pieces will have an advantage in achieving the goal of checkmate.

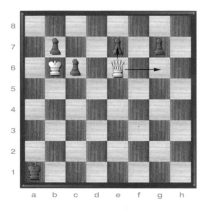

The most valuable force is not the same as the largest force. In the position above, White has only two pieces to Black's five. But White has a very powerful queen and Black only has four pawns that are a long way from promotion. On the first move, the white queen can capture the black pawn on e7, and it will then be threatening to capture the pawns on b7 and g7, and the remaining pawn will also disappear in a further move or two. White will then soon be in a position to checkmate the lone black king using the queen supported by the white king.

Above: Although the least powerful piece, the pawn is unique in that it is capable of promotion. When promoted, it can be exchanged for a queen, rook, bishop or knight.

Thus it can be seen that the white queen's relative value is much greater than that of the four black pawns. This is a simple example, but things can become more complicated if there is a greater variety of pieces in different configurations on either side.

Above, White and Black have the same number of pieces, but everything depends on their relative value – and whose turn it is to move. White has a bishop and knight and one pawn, which is more valuable than three pawns. However, with Black to play, everything changes. Black can advance the pawn on e2 to e1 and promote it to a queen, as shown below.

| 9 | 5 | 3 | 3 | 1 |

Above: Each of the pieces is assigned a points value but this is only a general rule of thumb. The true value varies in accordance with the specific position on the board.

The points system

Now Black has a queen and two pawns to White's bishop, knight and one pawn. It is not so easy to quantify the value of the two forces, but chess players have devised a handy rule of thumb that can be used to estimate the difference in relative value of a position. Each chess piece is assigned a relative value in points, these being:

Queen = 9
Rook = 5
Bishop = 3
Knight = 3
Pawn = 1

The king is not assigned a points value because its value is effectively infinite, and because there is always one king of each colour on the board, so their values cancel each other out. Similarly, there is no need to tot up the values of those pieces that both players have in common (so in the previous diagram we may discount White's pawn and one of Black's pawns as being of equal value). We are only concerned with the differences between the two opposing forces. Therefore, the differences between the two sides are White's bishop and knight (if you add it up that's 3 + 3 = 6 points) compared with Black's queen and pawn (that's 9 + 1 = 10 points). This equates to a difference in relative value of four points in favour of Black.

Above: Try adding up the points value of the pieces of each side. It should come to 11 points for White and 10 points for Black. So White stands a better chance because he has a material advantage of one point.

As far as beginner play goes, a difference of one point may not be terribly significant, but a difference of three or four points is starting to get dangerous for the player with the lower point count. This suggests that the position illustrated opposite is very good for Black. A number of other factors, such as the advanced white pawn on a6, swings the pendulum back slightly towards White. But the overall assessment would still favour Black.

THE STARTING POSITION

We have explored how individual pieces work in isolation, or in situations where there are much-reduced forces on the board, but these situations occur well into the game, after some pieces have been captured. Now it is time to learn how a chess game begins, with both sides having their full set of pieces on their starting squares.

This is the starting position for a game.

In two-dimensional diagrams of chess positions in books and magazines, it is usual to show the board from White's point of view, with the white pieces at the bottom of the diagram (with the pawns moving up the page) and the black pieces at the top of the diagram (with the pawns moving down the page). When looking at a diagram (or indeed a chessboard), it is particularly important to be clear which way the pawns can move, since they can only move in one direction – forwards. Chess players sit behind their forces (as do modern army commanders) and move their pawns towards the enemy.

The positions of the pieces have to be memorized, with particular attention to the king and queen. Remember that, as players look at the board, they should see a white square in the right-hand corner ('white on the right') and that both queens stand on their own colour square (i.e. white queen on a white square, black queen on a black square). It is usually easy enough to distinguish the pieces in a chess set. The king and queen might appear a little similar, but the king in a conventionally designed Staunton pattern set has a small cross on the top, compared to a coronet on the queen. Chess players use the terms kingside and queenside in reference to the two halves of the board on which the king and queen sit in the starting position. The dividing line in the adjacent diagram does not actually appear on a real chessboard – it is to show the conceptual division of the board.

Below: The two armies face each other across the board, ready to do battle. Each king stands on its opposite colour square, with the corner square to its right being white.

Above: Play usually starts with a pawn move (though knight moves are possible). Here White (who always starts) plays a pawn from e2 to e4. This is probably the commonest first move.

Making the first moves

The game starts with White making a move. White always moves first. This confers a small advantage, rather like the advantage of serving first in tennis, but it is not significant at the beginner or elementary level of the game. When playing a series of informal games, chess players normally turn the board round after each game and take turns to have White. In competition chess, the same applies: as far as possible, players are given White and Black in alternate rounds in order to even up the chances. In every other respect, the two sides are level.

White has to make a move. This is mandatory: it is not possible to 'pass' as in some other games. How many options are there? The king, queen, rooks and bishops are currently hemmed in by the rank of pawns ahead of them and cannot move. The knights however are able to hop over other pieces. The two knights have two possible moves each. The eight pawns also have two possible moves each: either one or two squares forward. So, in total, White has 20 possible moves to start the game. The adjacent diagram shows White's 20 first move options.

After White has moved, it is Black's turn, with exactly the same possible options with the black pieces. This means that the possible number of positions after White and Black have made just one move each is 20 x 20 = 400 positions: a very big number, considering that the game has only just begun. This should give you an inkling of the number of chess positions that become possible after a few more moves, or after the 30 to 50 moves played in most games of chess. It is, quite simply, colossal and goes a long way to explaining why every possible chess move has yet to be explored by human or computer.

STANDARD NOTATION

The diagram on the previous page showing all 20 of White's first-move options was rather cluttered, but there is a much simpler way to record and communicate chess games than using a diagram for every move played. This is called chess notation. This book uses standard notation, also commonly known as algebraic notation because of the cross-reference system used to identify the squares.

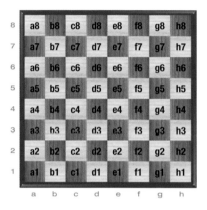

Each file is lettered, from a to h, while the ranks are numbered 1 to 8. Consequently, each square on the chessboard has a unique grid reference, from a1 to h8. Note that the letters denoting files always appear in *lower* case.

Each piece is assigned a capital letter. In English, this is as follows:

K	KING
Q	QUEEN
R	ROOK
B	BISHOP
N	KNIGHT (K is already used for the king)

No letter is assigned to the pawn – if no capital letter appears in the move code, then it can be assumed that the move is made by a pawn.

Recording chess moves

In standard notation, a chess move is recorded by giving the capital letter denoting the piece used (except in the case of a pawn) and the coordinate of the square to which it is moved. Hence, 'Qe4' signifies 'the queen moves to the e4 square', 'Rc7' that 'the rook goes to the

c7 square', 'c7' that 'the pawn goes to the c7 square', etc. Note that there is no need to record whether it is a white or black piece being moved. White and Black make alternate moves, so this can be deduced from the sequence of the moves, and usually from the layout on the page. Let's see a simple example, from the starting position, numbering the moves in pairs as we go.

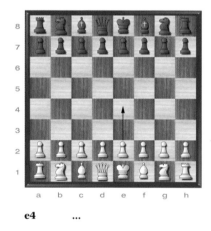

1   e4   ...

LEARN AS YOU PLAY

♛ ♝ ♞ ♚

Don't worry too much about the notation just yet, or try to memorize where all the squares are on the grid. You'll most certainly pick it up as you go along, and you can always come back to this section of the book for reference if you are unsure. Many people learn chess from other people, rather than from a book, and enjoy playing chess all their lives without even knowing that such a thing as chess notation exists. However, it is undoubtedly an advantage to be 'chess literate', so that you can consult written sources of chess information in order to improve your game.

This means that White starts the game by moving a pawn that can go to the e4 square. Only one pawn can do this – the one sitting on e2. So that pawn moves from e2 to e4.

1   **...**   **Nf6**

Now it is Black's turn, as shown above. Notice that the move is indented to the right after three dots to show that we are talking about Black's move. The code Nf6 means 'knight to the f6 square'. Only one of Black's two knights has the possibility of making this move – the one on g8. So it means 'knight on g8 moves to f6'.

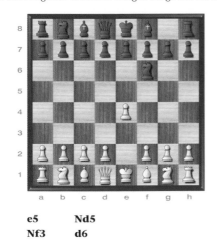

2   **e5**   **Nd5**
3   **Nf3**   **d6**

We have noted two more pairs of moves now. White's moves are those shown in the left-hand column and Black's are in the right. After making these moves, the position of both players pieces will be as in the following diagram.

As you can probably see, White is about to capture the pawn on d6 with the white pawn on e5. This is signified by an 'x' in the notation below. Additionally, for clarity in the case of a pawn capture, an extra small letter signifies the original file in addition to the destination file. Thus:

4   **exd6**   **...**

White moved the pawn on e5 (hence 'e'), made a capture ('x') and put the pawn down on d6.

continues on the next page ➜

Black then captures the pawn on d6 with the queen.

4   ...   Qxd6

5   Bb5+   ...

White plays the bishop to the b5 square. This move gives check to the black king, signified by the '+' character after the move notation.

5   ...   Kd8

Black moves the king to the d8 square. Now White decides to castle.

6   0-0   ...

Notice the special notation used for castling: 0-0. For castling queenside, the notation would be 0-0-0. Let's move the game on a couple of moves.

6   ...   Nd7
7   d4   ...

EQUIPMENT

♛ ♝ ♞ ♚

Although the rest of the book will contain plenty of diagrams for guidance, there will not be diagrams to show every position as games and sequences of moves are explained. It is therefore a good idea to play through the moves on a chessboard as you read the book. If you don't already own one, now is the time to acquire a full-sized chess set. It is best to use a wooden or plastic set that is as close as possible to the design of the pieces shown on this page. It does not have to be expensive – a plastic set with a board is generally very inexpensive. Two more important factors in choosing a set are: it should be easy to distinguish one type of piece from another, and the pieces should be in proportion to the board. Big pieces on a tiny board are as bad as small pieces on a big board. Look for a set with a king height of about 9cm (3½in) and a board with squares of about 5cm x 5cm (2in x 2in).

Now the board looks like this.

On the next move, Black intends to move the knight on d7 to f6. But notice that both black knights can go to that square in this position, so it is necessary to distinguish between them. It is no good referring to the file on which they are standing because they are both on the d-file. But one is on rank 7 and the other on rank 5 (normally we would say 'the seventh rank and the fifth rank'). So we distinguish by referring to the rank, thus:

7   ...   N7f6

Simple and unambiguous. This means that the knight on the seventh rank goes to f6. Had Black moved the other knight to this position the notation would instead be N5f6.

Now, White wants to reply by moving the knight that is currently on b1 to d2. Again, there is an ambiguity, so it is no good just putting 'Nd2'. One way to solve the problem would be to make a reference to the rank, as with Black's 7th move, i.e. 8 N1d2. In fact, standard notation prefers to make a reference to a file rather than a rank, where both are possible. So the correct notation is:

8   Nbd2   ...

This means 'White's knight currently on the b-file is moved to the d2 square'. To reiterate, where two identical pieces could move to the same square, indicate the file from which the correct piece is to be moved. If both are on the same file, indicate the rank instead. The following diagram, top right, shows how the board looks after the pair of knight moves made above.

That is as far as we are going with this game (which, incidentally, contains some rather poor moves). It contains nearly all the standard notation that you will need to read and understand chess moves, both in this book and in most other chess literature.

Other codes and symbols

Here is a summary of the various codes and symbols used as part of standard notation, including some not yet discussed:

0-0	CASTLES KINGSIDE
0-0-0	CASTLES QUEENSIDE
+	CHECK
#	CHECKMATE
x	(CAPTURES)
1-0	WHITE WINS (OR BLACK RESIGNS)
0-1	BLACK WINS (OR WHITE RESIGNS)
½-½	GAME DRAWN
!	GOOD MOVE
!!	BRILLIANT MOVE
?	BAD MOVE
??	AWFUL MOVE (chess players often use the word 'blunder')

STRATEGY 1: THE PIN

We already know that the king cannot expose itself to an attack by an enemy piece. The same rule applies to any piece that is currently blocking an attack on its own side's king. It is not permitted to move away and, in doing so, expose the king to attack. This position is known as a 'pin'.

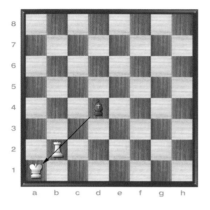

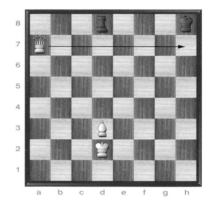

In the diagram above, with White to play, the rook is not allowed to move away because that would put the white king in check to the bishop on d4. White would have to play either Kb1 or Ka2, i.e. move the king to the b1 or a2 squares. The white rook is said to be 'pinned' to the king.

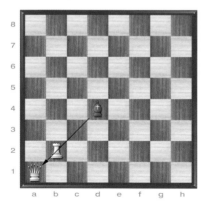

The above diagram shows another example of a pin. Here, the bishop is pinning the rook against the queen. That does not mean that the rook is forbidden to move in this case. It can be moved if White wants to, but it means that a more valuable piece (the queen) might be captured by the bishop, which is usually a very bad idea.

Above, it is White to play. The white bishop is pinned against the king by the black rook on d8. But White doesn't care because he can play Qh7 mate. The white queen moves to the h7 square next to the black king, where it is protected by the white bishop on d3 and cannot be captured by Black – checkmate: White wins. 'Not so fast,' protests Black. 'The bishop on d3 is pinned, so it doesn't really defend the queen!' Good try – but in fact it really is checkmate. Black cannot take the queen with the king because it would mean exposing the king to attack by the bishop. Although the bishop has no legal move, it still prevents the king from moving to any of the squares which it controls. A pin can be very useful in negating the power of a defending piece.

Only bishops, rooks and queens can effect pins. Kings and pawns only move one square at a time, while knights can jump over intervening pieces. In terms of vulnerability, all pieces other than the king can be pinned. One dangerous pin to look out for is where the queen moves one square diagonally from its starting square to the square in front of the king on its original square (i.e. Qe2 for White or Qe7 for Black). Beginners' queens often fall victim to an enemy rook pin played to the open e-file.

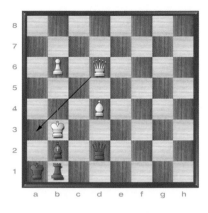

White can play Qa3 mate, i.e. queen to the a3 square, checkmate. Black has no king move, or blocking move, available. At first sight it looks like Black could reply Bxa3 (bishop takes the queen on a3), but in fact, the black bishop is pinned against the king by the white bishop on d4, so that move is illegal. The white bishop prevents the black bishop from performing this vital defensive function.

Countering a pin

If one of your pieces is pinned, it can often be a good idea to break the pin.

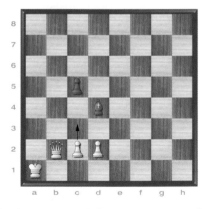

In the above position, White's queen is pinned against the king. Of course, queens can move along diagonals as well as bishops, so White has the option of capturing the bishop on d4. However, the bishop is stoutly defended by a pawn on c5, so it would be a bad exchange for White – the loss of the queen (9 points) for the bishop (3 points), making a deficit of 6 points. But there is another simple way to break the pin.

White can play c3 – i.e. move a pawn from c2 to c3 – and suddenly it is the black bishop that must take evasive action.

Another way to counter a pin is to play a cross-pin.

Here, with White to play, White's queen is pinned by the black bishop (which is defended by the black knight). However, White can reply Be3! (white bishop to the e3 square, a good move) and now the black bishop cannot take the queen because it is pinned against the black king. Black can play Bxe3 (capturing the e3 bishop), but then White plays dxe3 (pawn on d2 takes the bishop on e3), which is a level exchange. White's problems are solved.

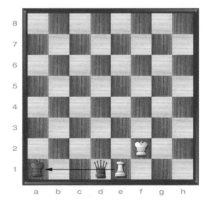

Above: The rook pins the queen against the king on a1. The black queen cannot move away from the first rank.

STRATEGY 2: THE FORK

Where a piece threatens more than one enemy piece at the same time, it is called a fork. All chess pieces are capable of doing this. The knight is particularly deadly at performing forks because its move is unique and higher value pieces such as queens and rooks cannot return fire when attacked by a knight.

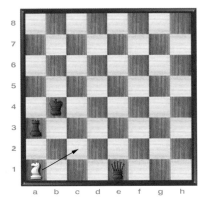

Here, the knight is attacked by both queen and rook, but, with White to move, it hits back with tremendous force (Nc2+!!) that is, knight to c2, giving check to the king on b4. This is a very good move.

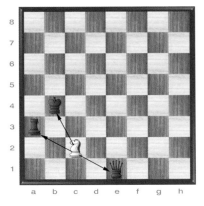

It is a scene of devastation: the king is in check, and the queen and rook are also attacked by the knight. All three pieces are said to be forked. Black would have to deal with the check and the only solution would be to move the king. Next move, White would be free to play Nxe1 – i.e. knight captures the piece on the e1 square, which is the queen. Here, a lower-value piece proves more powerful and the notion of the relative value of pieces is turned on its head.

Pawns are also capable of forking pieces. Below, White can play c3, forking queen and rook.

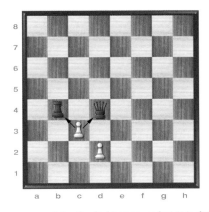

The queen can take the forking pawn but it is defended by another pawn on d2 and it would cost Black the queen. Black could also take the pawn on d2 – 1...Qxd2 – but then the game would proceed 2 cxb4 (the pawn on c3 takes the rook on b4) Qxb4 (the queen takes the pawn on b4). The body count after this little skirmish would show White to have lost two pawns (1 + 1 = 2 points) while Black would have lost a rook (5 points). White would therefore be three points better off in material terms – the equivalent of capturing a bishop or knight: a highly successful operation.

Above: The knight will move to d5, where it will fork four of Black's pieces. The black king is in check and will have to move. Then White will have the choice of three pieces to capture.

Chess players usually only refer to a simultaneous attack as a fork when the move leads to some sort of advantage for the player making the move.

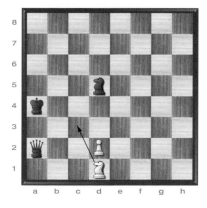

In this position, White can play 1 Nc3+, which attacks the king, queen and knight simultaneously. But there is no particular virtue in the move because Black can play 1...Nxc3 – the black knight captures the knight on c3 – and the attack has been rebuffed. After White recaptures with 2 dxc3 (pawn takes the black knight on c3), all that has happened is that White and Black have exchanged knights. Therefore, no advantage accrues to either side.

Countering a fork

Having your pieces forked need not be the end of the world. In the following position, Black has two satisfactory ways to counter a fork.

White has played 1 Qc2 and is simultaneously attacking the rook on b3 and the knight on c4. Both black pieces are undefended so Black has to do something about the safety of both pieces in only one move. There are three common ways to meet an attack on a piece – move it somewhere safe, block the attack or defend it with another piece. Black cannot block here but can run away with one piece and defend the other in one go. Black can either play 1...Na5 (knight to a5, which defends the rook on b3) or 1...Rb4 (rook to b4, where it defends the knight on c4).

STRATEGY 3: THE SKEWER

A 'skewer' is a lot like a pin, as both can only be achieved by pieces that can move more than one square along lines (files, ranks and diagonals). The difference with a skewer is that the more valuable piece is the one caught in the direct line of fire, with the lesser value one behind it usually being the ultimate casualty.

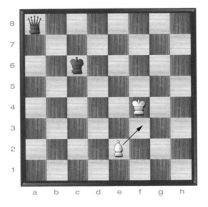

White plays Bf3+ – bishop to f3, check. Black has to move the king out of check, and on the following move White plays Bxa8 – bishop takes the queen on the a8 square. The move Bf3+ is called a skewer.

Skewers can only be achieved by pieces that move more than one square at a time along files, ranks and diagonals. Here is an example of a rook skewer:

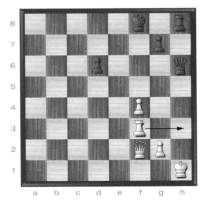

White is in check from the black queen. 1 Kg1?? – king to g1 – would be a dreadful mistake. Black would reply 1...Qh1# – queen to h1, checkmate. The queen is defended by the rook on h8 and the white king has no escape squares. However, White can play a blocking move instead.

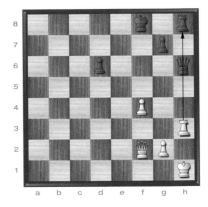

1 Rh3!! (rook to h3) is an excellent move. It skewers the rook on h8. The rook on h3 directly menaces the queen. The queen cannot sensibly play 1...Qxh3+ – capturing the rook on h3 with the queen – because the rook is defended by the pawn on g2. But it is equally disastrous if the queen is moved away from the h-file with, for example, the move 1...Qf6. White would play 2 Rxh8+ – the white rook captures the undefended rook on h8 – giving check to the black king as shown below.

If we make a small adjustment to this example – relocating the black pawn that was on g7 to the f6 square, it makes a big difference to the outcome.

Above: The bishop skewers the queen. If the queen moves, the bishop will be able to capture the black rook further down the diagonal.

White again plays 1 Rh3 to block the check (and avoid checkmate), but this time it is not really a skewer. Black can safely play 1...Qg7 – queen to the g7 square – to accomplish the two-fold purpose of getting the queen away from the rook's attack and providing a defender for the rook on h8. White plays 2 Rxh8+ – rook takes rook on h8 with check – but Black can then play 2...Qxh8+ – queen recaptures the rook on h8. The outcome is a simple exchange of rooks.

A pin, a fork and a skewer – in one

Occasionally you may get the chance to play a move that is a pin, fork and skewer at the same time:

Let's do a quick point count of this position. First, discount all pieces that the two players have in common, or where the piece values are identical (i.e. bishops and knights, which are both worth 3 points): two pawns, one pair of knights and one knight for bishop. That leaves White with a bishop/knight and two pawns (3 + 1 + 1 = 5 points) for Black's two rooks

(5 x 2 = 10 points). So Black is way ahead of the game. However, White can play the move 1 Bxe5!! – bishop takes the pawn on e5. It is an excellent move.

The bishop on e5 pins the knight against the king on h8, forks the two rooks on c3 and d6 and skewers the knight on b8. Black must try and capture as much material for one of the rooks as possible. In this position, the best move is 1...Rcxd3 – rook on c3 takes the pawn on d3 (note that it is necessary to include the original file identifier here, because both rooks can legally capture on d3). White plays 2 exd3. If we tot up the points, we find that White has bishop/knight and two pawns (3 + 1 + 1 = 5 points) against Black's rook (5 points). In theory this indicates a level position, but White still has the pin and skewer in place and is much better placed to win.

STRATEGY 4: PASSED PAWNS

If there is one thing that distinguishes a good chess player from a poor one, it is a deep respect for the pawn. While weaker players know that the pawn is the lowest rank in the chess army, they often fail to appreciate how useful and powerful it can be in many chessboard situations.

It is true that, at the beginning of the game, the pawn is the least valuable piece, but its value can grow as its path to the promotion square begins to clear. One pawn with more potential than most is a passed pawn. This is how a pawn is known when it faces no enemy pawn on the same file, or adjacent files, ahead of it. Its journey to promotion can only be stopped by higher-value enemy pieces. If a pawn becomes passed while there are still many pieces on the board, it is unlikely to be too dangerous, but as pieces disappear from the board and the endgame begins, a passed pawn can become much more dangerous.

Above: All the pawns shown here have a clear run to the eighth rank. In the context of a game they are said to have be 'passed' pawns.

2 Bf1 and next move can advance the a-pawn to a6. After that Black would probably have to give up the bishop to stop the pawn from 'queening' (i.e. reaching the a8 square where it would become a queen).

The two highlighted pawns in this position are both passed pawns. Note that the white pawn on f4 and the black pawn on g6 are not passed pawns because they are on adjacent squares; each can therefore potentially capture the other should it advance up the board.

A check on the relative values of the pieces possessed by both sides reveals that the position is equal as regards material. In reality, the situation is more complex. White's passed pawn on a5 is rather more menacing than Black's pawn on h5. True, both are blockaded by pieces (the black bishop and the white king), so neither can advance as yet. However, White has an advantage of being able to force Black to give ground. For example, 1 Bg2, and now if Black moves the bishop, e.g. 1...Bc8, then White can play

The position is equal as regards material, but in a game between good chess players White would almost certainly go on to win because of the advantage conferred by the powerful passed pawn on a5. By contrast, Black's passed pawn on h5 is being kept securely at bay by White's king and the pawn on f4.

Two connected passed pawns, well advanced up the board, can be as powerful as a queen.

Black has two connected passed pawns on a3 and b4. If it is White's turn to play here, it would be an easy win with 1 Rxb4 – rook takes the pawn on b4 – when 1...a2 – pawn to a2 – loses after 2 Ra4, and White will gobble up the pawn, or the queen on the next move if Black plays 2...a1Q+ (note that, when a pawn is promoted, the capital letter denoting the piece it becomes is appended to the notation).

However, it is a very different story if it is Black's turn to move in the above position. Black plays 1...a2, threatening to queen next move. White has to stop that with 2 Ra8, but then Black plays 2...b3, defending the a2 pawn.

White cannot stop one of the pawns from becoming a queen. If White plays 4 Rxa2?, Black replies with 4...b1Q+, making a new queen and forking the king and the rook on a2.

White has a large material advantage (rook = 5, two pawns = 2), but the horrible truth is that White should now lose with best play. If White tries 3 Ra3 to attack the b3 pawn, Black simply plays 3...b2!

Right: No black pawn can block the progress of White's pawn on b4. As such it poses a serious threat to Black, the black king being tied to obstructing its progress.

SIMPLE OPENING STRATEGY

The opening moves of a game of chess have a strategy all of their own. The basic idea is to make a general advance in the direction of the enemy forces but in a controlled manner. Below are a number of general principles that will help you to select the right piece to move and the right place to move it to.

We have already had a look at the start position in chess, and seen that White has 20 possible moves from the starting position.

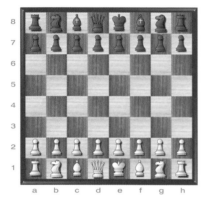

Of those 20 moves, four are highly regarded and regularly played by professional chess players, another three or four are also reasonable (but not played so often), and the rest are regarded as unorthodox and unproductive. However, none of them actually loses outright.

Occupying the centre

We are not going to deal with any specific opening moves in this section, but will instead concentrate on a few general principles to get things started. First, the initial 10 or 15 moves of a chess game are referred to as 'the opening'. There are a very large number of openings that have been worked out by chess players over the centuries. Very few of them, even the most ancient, have been totally disproved (or refuted), although some have better reputations than others. The selection of an opening is often a matter of taste, based on whether a player prefers an attacking or a more restrained game.

One general principle is that players should try to occupy the centre. By the centre, chess players mean the four squares in the middle of the board that tend to be the focus of the battle in its early stages.

One way for White to do this in the initial position is to advance either the e-pawn or d-pawn. For example, 1 e4:

The pawn on e4 effectively occupies one of the central squares. Note that it is usually just as useful to control the centre as it is to occupy it – in other words, to put pieces on squares from which they can capture enemy pieces that land on a central square.

Top right: Following the general principle of mobilizing pieces during the opening, White here develops the knight on b1 to d2, from where it exerts pressure on the centre.

Far right: Black here pushes his pawn from c7 to c6, defending the pawn on d5 which, in turn, occupies and contests the centre.

Mobilizing pieces

Another general principle is that it is a good idea to mobilize the pieces. This is often referred to as 'development'. The idea is that you should try to 'develop' pieces to squares where they have more scope, or can exert pressure against the enemy pieces. Notice that the initial move 1 e4 helps to achieve this objective. It frees the bishop on f1, and the queen on d1, to develop via the f1–a6 and d1–h5 diagonals.

Another general principle is that you should, as far as possible, make the minimum moves by each piece in the opening. Try to make one move only with each piece during the development stage. This should not be treated as a hard-and-fast principle – there are plenty of exceptions – but it is important not to waste time in mobilizing the pieces.

It is usually prudent to mobilize lower-value pieces in preference to higher values in the early stages. It is usually better to move knights and bishops into the fray before queens and rooks. It is also a little easier for knights and bishops to find space to move while the two armies are at full strength. It can be quite hard to find good vantage points to exploit the full power of queens and rooks while there are still eight well-defended pawns strung across the board. Rooks, in

particular, benefit from exchanges of pawns, which can result in open files on which to operate.

Never advance up the board with your king in the early stages of a game. The king is too valuable to be risked in this way. It is better for the king to stay on its home rank, and usually a good idea to make use of the special castling move, tucking the king away in a safe corner, preferably with a row of three or four unmoved pawns in front of it.

One simple, general principle is: after every move of the opponent, ask yourself: 'Is there a threat?'

HOW TO AVOID EARLY DISASTERS

The well-known chess saying 'all the mistakes are there, waiting to be made' does not just apply to beginners – grandmasters also make mistakes. All beginners can expect to make quite a few errors during their first games. Below are a few pitfalls to avoid. More positively, it is also possible to make use of this knowledge to snare an unwary opponent. A game of chess will usually last from 30 to 50 moves, but it can also be over in no time. Just two moves apiece is all it takes in the following extreme case. This is often referred to as Fool's Mate.

1   f3?

White starts the game by moving a pawn from f2 to f3. The question mark after the notation indicates that it is regarded as a bad move. On f3, the pawn blocks the entry into the game of the knight at g1. More significantly, in view of what follows, it also exposes the king to a potential attack on the diagonal from e1 to h4.

1   ...   e5

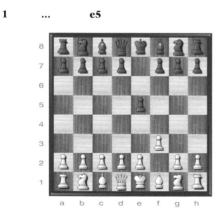

Black replies by moving a pawn from e7 to e5. The move provides scope for Black's queen and bishop (on f8) to make an early entry into the game.

2   g4??

The two question marks signify that this is a big mistake.

2   ...   Qh4 mate

The queen on h4 gives check to the king along the e1–h4 diagonal. One way to get out of check is to capture the checking piece, but that is not possible here. Another way of escaping check is to move the king out of the way but the only available square (f2) is also attacked by the queen. The third way to get out of check is to block with another piece but none of White's pieces can go to f2 or g3. So in fact it is checkmate. That is a drastic example of how quickly a chess game can finish. Next, we follow a game that was played in a junior match in the 1970s.

1 e4

This was a much better first move for White. The pawn has some control of the central squares and has opened the way for bishop and queen to enter the fray.

1 ... Nh6?

This was not a very good first move by Black. This knight has no impact on the central squares and will not control many squares from the edge of the board.

2 d4

Since Black has made no attempt to contest the centre, White decides to occupy another important square with a pawn, and also give scope for his dark-squared bishop (on c1) to join the fray.

2 ... f6??

3 Bxh6!

White cleverly made a mental connection with Fool's mate. It is not exactly the same scenario, since the move 3 Qh5+ does not lead to checkmate - Black could reply by blocking the check with 3...g6 and survive. However, White has a simple combination which makes a quick finish possible.

3 ... gxh6?

Black could avoid checkmate by playing another move (rather than recapturing the bishop) but the loss of the knight would probably be fatal anyway.

4 Qh5 mate

The checking piece cannot be captured, the king has no move and no piece can block the check. It is important to note the similarity with the checkmate produced in Fool's mate. One of the important aspects in learning chess is the ability to recognize patterns and learn from previous experience.

ANOTHER EARLY DISASTER

The next example of a disastrous chess move is often referred to as 'Scholar's mate'. This is not intended as a complimentary name. An early 17th-century chess author dubbed it this because of its rather childish lack of subtlety. Perhaps it would be better to name it 'Schoolkid's mate'.

1   e4   e5

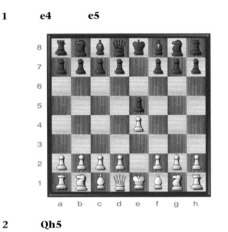

2   Qh5

This early sally by the queen is regarded as an inferior move. Though it is not positively disastrous, it is certainly not recommended. In the long run, other moves will yield better results.

2   ...   Nc6

A sensible move, defending the e5 pawn from capture by the white queen. The famous world chess champion Garry Kasparov once played this move so it comes with the highest recommendation. He was playing an exhibition game against the equally famous German tennis star, Boris Becker, at the time.

3   Bc4

Here Boris Becker opted for 3 Qf3. A surprisingly timid move for such a great serve and volley tennis player, and one that violated the opening principle of not moving the same piece twice without good reason. Of course he soon lost. The move Bc4 contains a powerful if crude threat. It is important to study the position for a moment to make sure you can see what is coming. Thousands of rookie players have failed to do so and as a result have suffered the humiliation of early defeat.

3   ...   d6??

Disaster.

4   Qxf7 mate

The queen is defended by the bishop on c4 so the queen cannot be captured. The black king cannot move or block the check, so it is checkmate. In the starting position of a game of chess, the f7 square is one of the weakest points in Black's structure – as the f2 square is in White's – and it is usually a good idea to keep a special eye open for summary attacks in this area. Such vulnerability tends to arise after 1 e4 e5 where White plays either Bc4 or Qh5, or Black plays Bc5 or Qh4. Examine the danger to your f7 (or f2) square to make sure you have enough defence from a summary attack.

Let's look at the diagram position again after 3 Bc4.

Suppose that Black played instead ...

3   ...   g6

A very sensible move which blocks the threat of checkmate and also attacks White's queen. White must retreat this piece.

4   Qf3

Now, having beaten off the threat of checkmate, Black seeks to harass White's retreating queen further ...

OPENING TRAPS

♛ ♝ ♞ ♚

It can be tempting to play for traps in the opening but this is a bad habit to get into and the long-term effect on your chess will not be good. It is much better to play conservatively in the opening stages of the game and only seek to play tactically when most of your pieces are in open play. You should not assume that your opponent is a poor player. Your choice of moves should be as objective as possible, based on the assumption that your opponent will find the best reply. So the best advice is: develop your pieces first, and only then play for checkmate if the chance arises.

---

4   ...   Nd4??

Black decides to pursue his plan of harassing the white queen. A better move is 4...Nf6, which gets another piece into play as well as blocking the threat along the f-file.

5   Qxf7 mate

Black hadn't noticed that White's move Qf3 had renewed the threat of checkmate. One reason for the popularity of this little trap among beginners is that you get two checkmate tricks for the price of one. If your opponent avoids the first one, he might fall for the second.

In real life, no one but the most unwary or inexperienced chess player would fall for a well-known trap of this sort. Though there are many other opening traps, in practice few games end in such short order. But these early disasters serve to illustrate just how quickly a chess position can become critical. Almost from the start of the game, it is good practice to have a quick look in the vicinity of both kings – to see if danger threatens, or perhaps if a sudden knock-out can be administered to the opposition king.

OPENING 1: THE GIUOCO PIANO

Most regularly used chess openings have names, and some are centuries old. One such is the Giuoco Piano, which means 'quiet game' in Italian. Also sometimes called 'the Italian Opening', it suits players who prefer a restrained game. It also conforms to most of the principles referred to in the previous section.

The Giuoco Piano has several different variations, or different ways to proceed after a few moves have been played. We will look at a variation (or line) that is known as the Giuoco Pianissimo ('very quiet game').

	White	Black
1	e4	e5

White has moved a pawn to e4 and Black has replied symmetrically. Both moves seek to occupy a central square and control an adjacent central square.

2	Nf3	...

This move develops a piece, exerting some pressure on central squares (d4 and e5) and posing a direct threat: to play Nxe5 and capture Black's pawn on e5.

2	...	Nc6

Black noticed that White was threatening to capture the e5 pawn. So the first priority was to address the threat, which Black has done by defending the e5 pawn with the knight. It is also a useful developing move in its own right, increasing Black's control over what happens on the central square at d4.

3	Bc4	...

White develops the bishop to a useful square. From c4, the bishop adds to White's control over the d5 square and looks farther along the diagonal at the pawn on f7. It does not threaten to take it because the pawn is adequately defended by the king on e8, but note that this threat could come in handy later.

3 ... Bc5

Black's move is similar to White's last move. It develops the bishop, on a strong post along the a7–g1 diagonal.

4 d3 d6

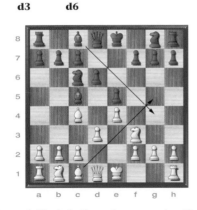

White and Black both make moves to d3 and d6 respectively. The moves were made to free the bishops on the marked diagonals.

5 Nc3 Nf6

One more knight move from each side has brought about a totally symmetrical set-up. Now White, deciding it is time to tuck the white king away somewhere safe, castles kingside.

6 0-0 ...

The king goes from e1 to g1, and the rook comes round from h1 to f1.

6 ... Bg4

Black decides to break the symmetry and play the bishop to g4, where it pins the f3 knight against the queen on d1. Black could have played 6...0-0, or perhaps a move such as 6...h6 (to prevent a pin by a bishop on g5, as Black has just played). The choice of moves here is largely a matter of taste.

Both sides have now completed more than half their development. There now remains the more complicated matter of how to get the queens and the rooks into the fray. The opening phase is coming to an end and the players are about to embark on the 'middlegame'.

OPENING 2: QUEEN'S GAMBIT

The word 'gambit' is used in everyday conversation to mean an attempt to do something with an element of trickery involved. In chess it means an opening in which a pawn sacrifice is offered in order to gain an advantage. The opening called the Queen's Gambit is so named, not because it involves sacrificing a queen but because a queenside pawn is offered to Black in order to speed up White's development.

Here are the opening moves of the Queen's Gambit, which is another well-respected opening.

1   d4   d5

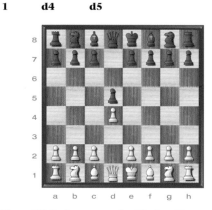

Here, White has opened with the d2 pawn – often called **t**he queen's pawn because it stands on the same file as the queen. Many other openings, collectively referred to as queen's pawn openings, also start with the move d4. The e2 pawn is called the king's pawn and the family of chess openings that begin with 1 e4 are called king's pawn openings. As in the Giuoco Piano, Black mimics White's opening and plays the queen's pawn two squares forward.

2   c4   ...

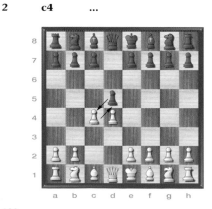

The diagram below shows the move that gives the Queen's Gambit opening its name. It offers the c4 pawn (which is one of White's queenside pawns) as a small sacrifice, mainly to undermine the control of the centre enjoyed by Black's d5 pawn if it makes the capture on c4. Here, Black has to decide whether to capture the c4 pawn or not – or, to use the correct chess term, whether to accept or decline the gambit. Both options are perfectly respectable but we are going to look at what might happen if Black decides to accept the gambit.

2   ...   dxc4

The Queen's Gambit Accepted

Black takes the pawn, which White cannot immediately recapture. This variation is called the Queen's Gambit Accepted. If White were desperate to restore the material balance, 3 Qa4+ could be played, forking the king on e8 and the pawn on c4, and White could make sure of winning back the white pawn. But White is in no great hurry to recapture the pawn since Black will find it hard to defend in the long run. So White develops a knight, and Black does the same. White and Black play to control some central squares with their next pair of moves. White has a little more control over the centre, because the white d4 pawn still stands there.

3   Nf3   Nf6

4   e3   e6

Once again there is similarity between the two players' pawn moves. Both are played to give the f1 and f8 bishops some scope in order to castle kingside, but note that the moves restrict the scope of the other bishops.

5   Bxc4   ...

After a few simple developing moves, White has managed to recoup the sacrificed pawn. The material is now even, but White might feel that the prominent d4 pawn gives slightly better control in the centre. The game proceeds.

5   ...   c5

The last move challenges White's control of the centre. White has no need to panic as the d4 pawn is adequately defended.

6   0-0   cxd4
7   exd4   Nc6
8   Nc3   Be7

Both players have concentrated on their development. Two pawns have been exchanged and this has resulted in some files opening up for later exploitation by rooks. The position is roughly equal.

OPENING 3: THE COLLE OPENING

The Colle Opening (or Colle System) is named after a 20th-century Belgian chess expert. Many openings are named after famous players, or after countries where the particular opening was first played. This is another tried and trusted system for beginning a chess game. Like the Queen's Gambit, it is a queen's pawn opening.

1	d4	d5
2	Nf3	Nf6

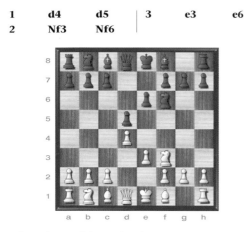

White diverged from the Queen's Gambit on move two, preferring the development of the knight to f3 to the pawn move c4. So far, Black has followed White's lead. Play in the Colle Opening is based on solidity, emphasizing the strength of the pawn structure.

4	Bd3	c5

White might now be tempted to play a check with 5 Bb5+. It is not exactly a mistake, but is not very useful. Black can easily parry by interposing a knight or bishop on d7 or c6. It offends against a general principle of the opening – keeping the number of moves with the same piece to a minimum.

3	e3	e6

The bishop has already moved once and achieves nothing of value by moving a second time here.

5	c3	...

White aims to reinforce the pawn on d4. Rather than taking the initiative, the strategy in the Colle Opening is more circumspect and reactive.

5	...	Nc6	6	Nbd2	...

White moves the knight that is on b1 to d2 (the other knight could have gone there as well – hence the extra file identifier in the notation). White continues with development, but the knight move to d2 actually blocks the c1 bishop's entry into the game. One snag is that it leaves White in a rather cramped position.

6 ... Bd6 | 7 0-0 0-0

Here, White could keep the position closed, but let's see what happens if some pawns are exchanged.

8 dxc5 Bxc5 | 9 e4 ...

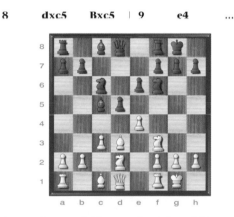

A second move of this pawn, but it is useful in creating scope for the c1 bishop.

9 ... Qc7

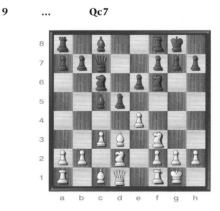

The black queen wants to prevent the advance of the e4 pawn to e5, and also has in mind some exploitation of the b8–h2 diagonal.

10 Qe2 Bd6 | 11 Re1 Ng4

Black hopes to play something like 12...Bxh2+ 13 Nxh2?? (bad move) Qxh2+ 14 Kf1 Qh1# – checkmate!

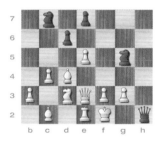

The above position shows Black's idea.

12 h3 ...

If 12...Bh2+? 13 Kh1! and White is quite safe. The Colle Opening is a playable opening for a beginner.

WINNING MATERIAL

Although the main goal in chess is to checkmate the opponent, stampeding all your pieces in the direction of the opponent's king is rarely successful as a winning strategy. Attacking the king can be effective (as we shall soon see), but many more games of chess are settled by one player gaining a material advantage, after which the process of winning the game becomes relatively straightforward.

In elementary chess, it happens quite often that players gain material simply because the opponent overlooks a threat to take a piece, or actually puts one on a square which is attacked.

This position is complicated. White has one pawn fewer than his opponent. He can capture the f7 pawn with the knight on g5 (which will be defended by the bishop on c4), or capture the pawn on e5. White also has to consider Black's threat to play Nxc2 – knight takes the pawn on c2 – which forks the queen on e3 and the rook on a1. Instead, White becomes confused and tries to pin the knight on d4 against the queen on d7.

1   Rad1??   ...

White plays the rook on a1 to d1, but has overlooked the fact that Black's bishop on g4 attacks the d1 square. Chess players call this putting a piece *en prise* (a French expression: literally 'in take'). The bishop is worth less than the rook, so the exchange is favourable to Black. Winning a rook in exchange for a bishop or knight is often referred to as 'winning the exchange'. After winning a rook for such a piece, players refer to themselves as being 'the exchange up'.

1   ...   Bxd1
2   Nxd1   ...

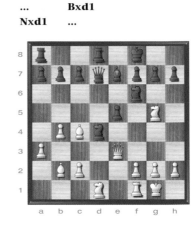

Counting the difference in material, Black has a rook and pawn (5 + 1 = 6) compared to White's bishop (3 points). Black is, in the language of chess, 'the exchange and a pawn up'. This in itself should be good enough to win in the long run, although with plenty of pieces still left on the board, White can play on in hope.

There are still opportunities for counter-play, which may just possibly enable White to recoup some of the lost material, perhaps winning the exchange in turn later in the game. If Black is a strong player though, this is less likely.

Setting a trap

Rather than simply waiting for the opponent to overlook a threat, a player can set a trap. It is often useful to bait the trap with a pawn.

In this position, it is Black to move. Black notices that the pawn on d4 is only defended once, by the knight on f3. However, Black also notices that the pawn is being attacked twice, with the knight on c6 and the queen on b6. That means that Black can play 1...Nxd4 – knight takes the pawn on d4 – White replies 2 Nxd4 – knight on f3 captures the knight on d4 – and then Black plays 2...Qxd4 – the black queen captures the knight on d4. After those three moves, the players will have exchanged knights but Black will have gained a pawn. However, there is a snag...

It is now White's turn to move. White can play the move 3 Bb5+!! – an excellent move of the bishop to b5, giving check to the king on e8. Black has only calculated the sequence of moves up to and including the recapture of the knight on d4 but has failed to spot what follows.

Now Black has to deal with the threat to the king, but the bishop move has also uncovered an attack on the queen on d4 from White's queen on d1. After Black has countered the check, White will capture the queen – Qxd4 – and, in material terms, White will be a whole queen up. That is pretty much game over. Going back to the original position, we can see that Black fell into a big trap when he played 1...Nxd4.

Above: The pawn here is in the process of taking the queen. Humble it may be, but a pawn, like any other piece, can win material, in this case capturing Black's queen.

SIMPLE MIDDLEGAME STRATEGY

The phase of the game after each player has moved most of their pieces (not including the pawns) at least once, and the two armies are at close quarters with each other, is called the middlegame. This is the part of the game where players can deploy all their tactical tricks – pins, forks, attacks on the king, etc – while most of the pieces are on the board. It is a fascinating part of the overall game, and vital to master.

The aim in this phase of the game is to outplay the opponent and gain a material advantage or to attack and give checkmate directly. Not all games reach an endgame, which is the phase of the game when there are somewhat fewer pieces (other than pawns) on the board and the strategy changes.

Scope and mobility

One fundamental of middlegame strategy is to find scope and mobility for pieces that move along lines. This often means open files for rooks and queens, and long diagonals for bishops and queens.

The above diagram is of a typical middlegame position. Most of the pieces have made one developing move, except for the rooks.

No immediate tactical tricks suggest themselves and it is time to consider longer-term strategy. The rooks are not well placed at the moment, still boxed in by their own pawns. White wants to find open lines for the two white rooks. One possibility is 1 Rac1, putting pressure on the semi-open file. The c-file is semi-open because there is only an enemy pawn on it.

By playing 1 Rac1, White threatens to capture the c7 pawn by 2 Qxc7. Black could then capture the queen with 2...Qxc7 and White would then take the black queen with 3 Rxc7 and be a pawn up.

After 1 Rac1, Black might have to think about defending the c7 pawn with a rook, or could try 1...Rfb8 – rook on f8 moves to b8, which is a semi-open file from Black's point of view. If White captures the c7 pawn now, Black exchanges queens as before and then captures on b2 with the black rook. That position would be even.

Another possibility on the first move is 1 Rfe1. The e-file is an open file (as is the d-file): there are no pawns on it. You might not think that the e-file looks very open, because there is a queen and a bishop of each colour standing on it at the moment. The description

Above: A typically complex situation in the middle game. With the centre closed, both players jostle for position, each looking for some move or tactical combination that will help them seize the initiative.

is more to do with its potential than the actuality. After 1 Rfe1, White has a beady eye on the black queen that stands on the same file. If Black is unwary, things can soon happen on the open file. For example...

1	**Rfe1**	**Rab8?**
2	**Bc4**	...

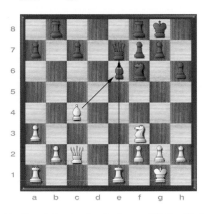

The situation is beginning to favour White. Notice that White has uncovered a pin along the e-file. The bishop on e6 cannot move because it would expose the queen to capture by the rook on e1. Black now tries to solve these problems by playing a pin in reply.

2	...	**Qc5??**

Black now pins the white bishop with the white queen. If, for instance, White were to play 3 Bxe6??, Black could triumphantly capture the undefended queen on c2 with the black queen. However, Black has overlooked a vicious tactical blow (or combination), one that turns the position on its head and renders the

pin superfluous. White's combination is not immediately apparent. In two moves, White can win a bishop or even capture the black queen.

3	**Rxe6!!**	...

White unexpectedly captures the bishop on e6 with the rook, although it is apparently well defended by the pawn on f7.

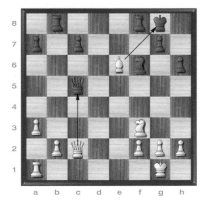

3	...	**fxe6**
4	**Bxe6+**	...

The point of White's combination (the player's series of tactical moves) is revealed. The bishop has captured the pawn on e6 with check, simultaneously uncovering an attack on the black queen by the white queen on c2. Black will have to move the black king, after which the black queen will be lost.

MORE ABOUT THE MIDDLEGAME

Just as rooks thrive on open files, bishops can be lethal on long diagonals, since it is in these positions that they command the maximum squares. Knights, by contrast, are at their most dangerous when placed deep in enemy territory on a square where it is hard for your opponent to dislodge them.

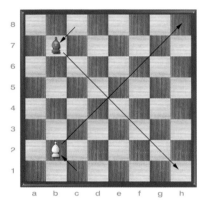

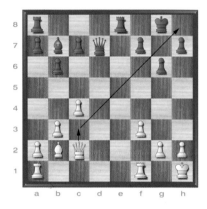

The diagram above shows that bishops which have moved from their original squares (c1 and c8 respectively) are now positioned on long diagonals. However, they can easily become blocked, as seen below, particularly by enemy and friendly pawns.

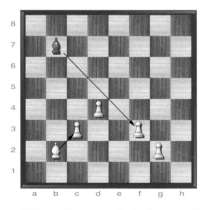

The two bishops above have limited scope. The white bishop is stuck behind its own pawns and is not playing much part in the game. The black bishop is attacking the pawn on f3, but it is solidly defended by a fellow pawn on g2. Unfortunately, while the pawns stay put, the bishops will not have much influence on the game. Should White push the pawn on g2 forward, however, the situation for Black's bishop would be very different.

In this position, the material is level, but White's bishop has complete control of the a1–h8 diagonal, compared with its rather restricted opposite number. If it is White to move, White plays 1 Qc3! – and Black is suddenly in a desperate situation.

The threat is to play Qg7 or Qh8, both of which are checkmate. If Black tries to run away with 1...Kf8, White plays 2 Qg7+ Ke7 3 Bf6+ Ke6 4 Rae1+ Kd6 5 Rd1+, skewering the queen on d7. Black could try 1...f6, but after 2 Qxf6, White will soon drive the black king out into the open where it will be gunned down by the white rooks: and all the trouble stems from the powerful bishop on b2. Even with Black to move in the above position, Black will be hard put to mount a defence to the threats along the long diagonal.

Outposts

Knights are not interested in open lines and diagonals, but they often become more powerful when located on 'outposts'. An outpost in chess is a square in or near the enemy camp (the opponent's side), where a piece is well defended and hard to dislodge. In particular, it usually refers to a square that cannot be attacked by an enemy pawn. With this, much depends on the pawn structure. If this is still fluid (i.e. able and likely to change), then any outpost will almost certainly be temporary. If they are fixed, however, it's a different matter.

Above: If you find yourself without an obvious plan in the middlegame, start by thinking about which is your worst-placed piece and then see if there is a way that you can improve its position or scope. This might involve moving a different piece to give it more room for manoeuvre.

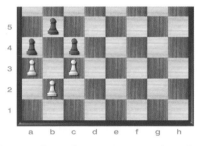

The diagram above shows a situation where the pawns have become locked. The two b-pawns can still move, but, if they advance, they would be captured immediately. For example if White plays 1 b3, the pawn can be captured either by 1…axb3 or 1…cxb3. If the b-pawn advances two squares – i.e. 1 b4 – exactly the same capture could be made because of the *en passant* rule – 1…axb3 – when the black pawn on a4 goes to b3, capturing the white pawn on b4 as if it had only moved to b3. 1…cxb3 *en passant* would also be possible if White played 1 b4.

So the pawns are locked. However, the pawn structure creates a possible outpost for Black on b3. Were Black to locate a knight there, it would be

strongly defended and hard to drive away. The b4 square would similarly be an outpost for White, except that it is one rank further away from the enemy side of the board and likely to be less threatening to Black.

In the position (above), which is level on material, the white knight can occupy the outpost on e6. From there it can never be evicted by an enemy pawn, or anything else of equal or lower value, since Black's bishop only moves on dark squares. It is also well supported by a pawn on d5. So the move 1 Ne6 is a very good choice here, giving White much the better game. Although the black bishop is also well dug in on c5, White would have the future option of exchanging it with his knight should the bishop prove dangerous.

ATTACKING THE KING

So far in this book, we have seen how to improve the position gradually and learned a 'materialistic' approach to winning a chess game. In this context, the term 'materialistic' means trying to accumulate a material advantage with a view to converting it into a long-term checkmate. However, in some positions, it can be appropriate to dispense with this cautious policy and mount a direct attack on the king.

Mounting a direct attack on the king requires fine judgement and precise calculation. Before embarking on such an approach, you must (a) have calculated that the coming series of moves (or combination) leads to a certain checkmate; or (b) that the enemy king will be so exposed to immediate attack from a sufficient number of your pieces that it cannot hope to escape checkmate (or surrendering too much material to escape it).

In such positions, it becomes possible to disregard the relative values of the pieces. Here are some factors to look for when assessing the chances of a direct mating attack. Is the opposing king exposed? If it is not protected by a row of pawns, or is situated towards the middle of the board, it may be vulnerable to a mating

attack. Are there fewer defending pieces in the vicinity of the opposing king compared to your attacking army? Sometimes, when an important enemy piece is left stranded too far away from the action (chess players sometimes borrow football parlance and refer to such a piece as 'offside'), it can be a good reason to take direct action against the king.

The Greek gift sacrifice

Sometimes a king can be forced out into the open via a sacrifice (that is, deliberately surrendering a piece for one of lesser value or even for no material at all, with a view to gaining more material in the long term, establishing a winning attack or securing a swift checkmate). One such sacrifice is so common that it has a name: the Greek gift (the name derives from the Greek legend of the wooden horse that contained an invading army, unwittingly taken into the city of Troy by its inhabitants). In chess, a Greek gift is the sacrifice of a bishop on h7 (if played by White) in front of a castled king.

In this position, the material is level, but White has better scope for the pieces. Black's king looks secure

Left: White plays Bxh7, the Greek gift sacrifice, surrendering his bishop to drive Black's king out into the open.

from the point of view of the row of pawns in front of it, but otherwise it is quite hard to cover a possible attack. White, to play, could try 1 Ng5 to create a double attack on the vulnerable h7 pawn. This is quite good, but Black can perhaps defend with 1...g6, which blocks the scope of the bishop on d3. However, White spots a chance to unleash the Greek gift sacrifice and plays 1 Bxh7+!

Black now has two options: to accept the sacrifice with 1...Kxh7, or to decline it with 1...Kh8. If Black declines the sacrifice, playing 1...Kh8, White will follow up with 2 Ng5 and then, after Black's next move, 3 Qh5 will threaten mate on h7. Black could try something like 2...f6 and, following 3 Qh5, play 3...fxg5, but after 4 Bg6+ there is no escape for Black's king. If Black plays 1...Kxh7, White will follow up with 2 Ng5+.

If Black retreats with 2...Kg8, White plays 3 Qh5, threatening checkmate with Qh7 on the next move. In fact this is virtually the end, as Black has to surrender the queen for the knight on g5 to avoid checkmate – with a

queen for bishop and knight (that's 9 points for 3 + 3 = 6), White will be winning. If Black plays 2...Kg6, it is not so straightforward, but after 3 Qd3+, the black king is exposed to a withering attack from the white pieces.

Here is an example line: 3...f5 (blocking the attack) 4 exf6+ (the e5 pawn takes the f5 pawn *en passant*) Kxf6 5 Qf3+ Ke7 (Black tries to defend the rook on f8, which would otherwise be skewered) 6 Re1+ Kd6 7 Qxf8+.

The game has turned into a rout. White is now material up and still attacking the king. If Black plays 7...Kc7, White wins material with 8 Rxe8 Qf6 9 Bf4+ d6 10 Ne6+ Kd7 11 Qg8 when Black has lost a rook and a pawn, while if 7...Kxd5, White plays 8 Nc3+ Kc6 9 Rxe8 and Black's exposed king will not last long. The Greek gift sacrifice is a lovely way to finish a game.

DEFENDING THE KING

A good strategy when it comes to defending the king in the opening or middlegame is to castle. The idea of castling is to relocate the king to a position where it will not get embroiled in the hand-to-hand fighting in the middlegame. Indeed, the middlegame is usually the province of the major pieces (queens and rooks), minor pieces (bishops and knights) and the pawns.

In practice, it is not usually wise to castle to a side of the board where the pawn cover has disappeared or where the enemy forces have built up in a menacing fashion. The king prefers a quiet sector where it can ride out the storm, perhaps joining the fray later when the forces on the board have reduced down to a pair of minor pieces and some pawns on each side.

As well as pawns, the king may need defensive help from at least one piece.

The position in the above diagram is identical to the first one on the previous page used to demonstrate a direct attack on the king, but with two differences – the white pawn on e5 and the black pawn on d7 have been removed. This makes a big difference to the black king's defensive possibilities.

If White were now to attempt a direct attack on the black king with 1 Bxh7+, the chances of success would be slim. Black captures 1...Kxh7 and after 2 Ng5+, retreats with 2...Kg8. If now 3 Qh5, Black can now play 3...Nf6!, attacking the queen and, more importantly, defending against the threat of Qh7 mate.

Black has solved all his problems, and has a material advantage of bishop for one pawn. Looking again at the position at the top of the page, we can see that the row of pawns in front of the king is still an important defensive barrier, but that the potential of the knight on e8 to come to f6 to bolster the defence of the black king makes all the difference in resisting the Greek gift sacrifice.

The diagram above shows a typical castled king set up, with a knight on f3 providing a double defence to the h2 pawn. It is often a good idea to consider the king's safety before making a move, and perhaps count the defenders to the pawn barrier in front of the king. In the diagram below left, we can see that the f2 pawn is defended by rook and king, and h2 by knight and king. The g2 pawn is the weakest point in this particular set-up, because it is only defended by the king. An attack could come down the g-file in the shape of a rook or queen, and could be supported by (for example) a knight on f4.

The diagram (right) shows a very similar configuration, except that the g-pawn has advanced to g3. The f2 and h2 pawns are defended exactly as they were in the previous example, but now White is better defended against an attack down the g-file because the g3 pawn is doubly defended by the pawns on the adjoining flanks. However, there are also potential disadvantages to this set-up. Black could locate a piece on h3, for example a queen or a bishop. If Black could also generate a threat along the a8–h1 diagonal, the undefended knight could be driven away from f3 and black could threaten a checkmate on g2.

Both the above examples show castled kings that are likely to be reasonably safe in many positions – and both are certainly better than having a totally exposed

king – but the truth is that no king can ever be totally impregnable, no matter how defensive the set-up. It depends entirely on the specific position on the board. When playing against an unwary defender, creative attacking players can always unlock the key to the defence.

Below: The king needs plenty of defenders around it to ensure its safety in the middlegame. In the endgame, when the two armies are much reduced, it can be a good time to bring the king out of hiding and use it to attack.

PAWN WEAKNESS

Although it is true to say that all pawns start the game having an equal value to each other, individual pawns can become weaker than others if they become separated from their colleagues, stuck in front of each other (as the result of a capture), or become blocked on a square where they cannot be supported by a fellow pawn.

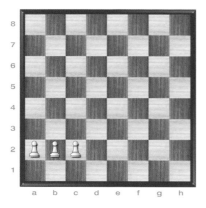

Above, these three pawns are undefended, but if attacked from the front they can at least move into a defended position. For example, if a rook further up the b-file were to attack the pawn on b2, it could advance to b3 where it would be adequately defended by its colleagues on a2 and c2. Similarly, if the a2 pawn were to be attacked by a rook along the a-file, it could advance to a3 and be defended by the pawn on b2.

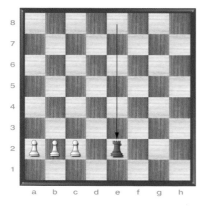

The above situation is more problematic for the pawns. If an enemy rook reaches the second rank (or the seventh rank from its original rank), it can be highly effective in threatening to capture a line of pawns on their original squares. If the c2 pawn moves out of the

way, Black can capture the b2 pawn that stands beyond it. For this reason, a rook on the seventh (as it is known) can be a potent attacking weapon in chess.

Doubled pawns

After captures, it is possible for pawns to become 'doubled', i.e. two pawns of the same colour on the same file.

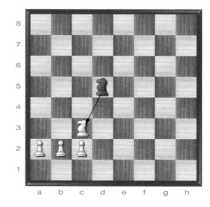

In this position, Black (to play) can capture the knight on c3, and White can recapture with the b2 pawn, thus: 1...Nxc3 2 bxc3.

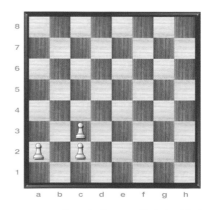

The pawns on c2 and c3 are called doubled pawns. Note that the pawn on c3 impedes the progress of the pawn on c2. Note also that they are now incapable of defending each other from capture. In fact, all three pawns shown in the diagram above are now incapable of defending each other (unless, for example, one of them has a later opportunity to effect a capture and thus move to the b-file). For this reason, double pawns are usually considered a weakness. The only incidental advantage that could accrue from pawns being doubled is that it can open a file to allow major pieces to advance upon the enemy or attack an important square on the other side of the board.

In this diagram, with White to play, a quick count shows that the material situation is exactly equal. However, Black has a pair of doubled pawns on c7 and c6. It may later be possible to effect an exchange so that they can be undoubled but it is not easy to achieve. Meanwhile, on the other side of the board, four white pawns face three black pawns. There is a serious danger that, after three pawns have been exchanged, White may be left with one passed pawn that could even promote to a queen one day. This is all very long-term strategy, but gives some idea of the problems that can accrue from doubled pawns.

Backward pawns

In the next diagram, the pawn on b2 is what's known as a 'backward' pawn. It is called this because it lags behind the adjacent pawns and cannot easily advance. If it goes to b3, either black pawn can capture – and if it goes straight to b4, they can still capture it, *en passant* (on the first move after the move b4 is played), so it does not have a rosy future. Another aspect to this position is that the two black pawns are effectively tying up three of their adversaries. If the material were

equal – and let's suppose the third black pawn were somewhere on the kingside, Black could be considered to be virtually a pawn up. As things stand, the pawn on b2 would hardly count for the usual one point attributed to a pawn.

WEAK PAWNS DROP OFF

Chess players are fond of saying that 'weak pawns drop off' – and few pawns are as weak as backward pawns. In the diagram below, the pawn on b2 is a backward pawn. It is performing a small service (defending the a3 pawn) but otherwise is particularly vulnerable because it cannot move without falling victim to a capture (*en passant* or otherwise) on b3. The bishop on d4 menaces it and there is nothing to be done. Once it falls, the blockaded a3 pawn will soon follow.

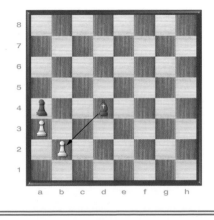

PAWN STRENGTHS

We have already seen that the strongest pawn is what we call a passed pawn – and that the one thing better than a passed pawn is two passed pawns, preferably connected. Now we consider what we need to do to transform an ordinary pawn (or pawns) into the extra-special passed variety.

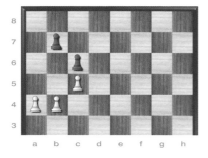

In the above position, it is clear that White has an extra pawn, so the basic strategy here might be to exchange two pairs of pawns so that White's one remaining pawn will become a passed pawn and eventually advance to the queening square. The extra pawn seems to be the a-pawn, so there may be a temptation to advance it one square towards promotion – 1 a5.

However, this is an error here if the objective is to create a single passed pawn. After 1 a5, White cannot advance either the a-pawn or b-pawn without loss. The correct move to start with would be 1 b5, offering a pawn exchange. Were Black to play anything other than an exchange of pawns (let's assume the presence of kings somewhere remote from this action), White could play 2 bxc6, forcing 2...bxc6, at which point the a-pawn is a passed pawn with nothing between it and the queening square.

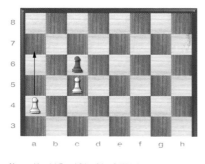

Above: After 1 b5 and 2 bxc6 bxc6, White's a-pawn is unimpeded.

If Black replies to 1 b5 with 1...cxb5 2 axb5, we reach this position:

Now White can create a passed pawn next move with 3 c6 and, after the exchange of pawns, White will have a passed pawn on c6.

Creating unstoppable passed pawns

Exceptionally, it can be possible to create an unstoppable passed pawn, even though equal numbers of pawns confront each other.

In the above diagram, White is to play. On the face of it, things look equal, with level material and three pawns apiece apparently blocking each others' path to their respective queening squares. However, there are two points to note about this position: (a) White's pawns are much nearer to their queening squares; and (b) if White can create a passed pawn quickly, Black's king will be too far away from the action to stop the passed pawn. White can now force a black pawn through to become a queen at the price of giving up (or sacrificing) the other two (a very small price to pay for a new queen). White plays 1 b6!.

The b-pawn can be captured by either the a-pawn or the c-pawn. Black has to capture because otherwise the white b-pawn will itself capture one of the two pawns and promote on the next move. Let's say Black plays 1...cxb6. White replies 2 a6!.

Black, who now has doubled b-pawns, is again confronted with two possible captures. If Black takes the c5 pawn with 2...bxc5, it is easy to see that White will reply 3 axb7 and promote to a queen on the next move. In order to slow White's progress Black tries 2...bxa6. White plays 3 c6!.

Something extraordinary has now happened. White has sacrificed two pawns in order to gain one passed pawn on c6. This pawn can no longer be stopped from queening in two more moves. Black cannot get across to stop it with the king, and Black's own pawns are still five moves from queening. The new queen will mop up the three pawns very quickly and win the game.

Note that it makes no difference if, on move one, Black decides to capture the b6 pawn with his a-pawn. Thus, 1 b6 axb6, and now White plays the same trick, this time with the c-pawn: 2 c6!.

This is a mirror image of the problems that Black had in the other line of play. If Black plays 2...bxc6, then White plays 3 a6! – and once again wins easily. In both cases there is absolutely nothing Black can do to prevent the creation of a passed pawn and, in consequence, certain defeat. Take time to learn the techniques shown here; they will serve you well.

PIECES WORKING TOGETHER

We have seen various middlegame stratagems in isolation, but here is an opportunity to see how they all fit together in a real competition chess game played between strong amateur players. We are only going to look at the middle part of the game, concentrating on a remarkable combination found by Black.

A combination is a planned tactical sequence of moves. In this example, Black sees about seven moves ahead, by which we mean pairs of moves, one each by White and Black. Non-chess players are sometimes interested in the number of moves that chess players can see ahead. The answer is that it varies, depending on the complexity of the position. Sometimes it is possible to see as many as ten moves ahead, or even more; at other times, two moves ahead is difficult to evaluate. Black is to move. The material is level, with two pairs of pawns

having been exchanged. A couple of captures are possible (1...Bxa4 and 1...Nxd3) but only lead to level exchanges. Note how well defended the pieces and pawns are. The only undefended pawn on the board is Black's pawn on d6, but it is not currently vulnerable to capture.

In this position, Black conceives an idea that starts with a sacrifice that opens up a file, involves an exchange of knight for bishop to open up a long diagonal, a skewer leading to another exchange, and finally a decisive exploitation of a possible pin along the a7–g1 diagonal. This is quite a lot to see ahead. It may seem totally beyond you at first, but don't despair: it's not as hard as it sounds. The key thing is to keep in mind the tactical manoeuvres mentioned above and look for ways you can engineer them. Try to understand the logical sequence of the following combination.

| 1 | ... | Nxd5! |

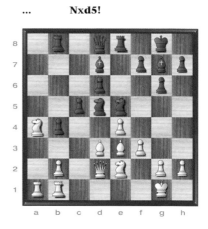

Black sacrifices a knight for a pawn. It takes a while before the reason for this becomes clear, but the general idea is to open the e-file (after White plays 2 exd5) and also give the bishop on g7 some scope along the a1–h8 long diagonal.

| 2 | exd5 | Nxd3 |
| 3 | Qxd3 | Bb5 |

Strictly speaking, this is not a skewer (because it simply leads to the exchange of the b5 bishop for the e2 knight), but the ultimate effect is equally devastating. It should already be becoming clearer that Black's pieces (the two bishops and the e8 rook) have open lines of attack, while White's pieces are slightly 'offside'. In particular, the knight on a4 is poorly posted. Although it is defended by the rook on a1, it has no squares to go to from a4. Knights on the edge of the board are usually less effective than when they are placed somewhere nearer the middle of the board. White now has to move the white queen away from the attack of the black bishop.

| 4 | Qd2 | Bxe2 | 5 | Qxe2 | ... |

This is the position that Black foresaw when 1...Nxd5 was played. Black spotted the very powerful pin on the bishop on e3 against the queen on e2. This made the bishop very vulnerable. In fact, Black could have exploited this immediately by playing 5...Bd4,

---

ANOTHER EXAMPLE

Here, we can see how four pieces can work together to defend each other.

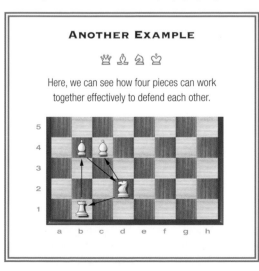

---

which would win the bishop on e3 – but Black found something more powerful still.

| 5 | ... | Rxe3! |

Black captures the bishop, which means that the material balance has swung in favour of Black, who is now a pawn up. White, who by this point is struggling to survive, should probably have run away now with the queen, but dared instead to capture the undefended rook.

| 6 | Qxe3 | Bd4! |

Black pins the queen against the king. White captured the bishop with the white queen, which was immediately taken off by the pawn on c5. This left Black with queen and pawn (9 + 1 = 10) for rook and knight (5 + 3 = 8) – two points down on material, and with a lost position. Though the result is not a foregone conclusion in a game between beginners, Black was soon able to convert the extra material into a win.

THE ENDGAME: SUFFICIENT MATERIAL

The term 'endgame' refers to the final phase of a game after many of the pieces have disappeared from the board. It is worth noting that not all chess games reach a true endgame: many conclude with a checkmate in the middlegame when there are still many pieces on the board.

Sometimes there are so few pieces on the board that checkmate cannot be achieved. Such a game can be abandoned as a draw. In competition chess, the arbiter would declare the game a draw. The most obvious is bare king versus bare king.

As it is not possible for one king to checkmate another, the game is a draw.

The same applies if one player has only one bishop or one knight left with the king. On their own they cannot effect a mate, so the game is drawn.

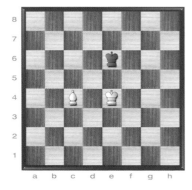

Above, Black has to move out of check, but White cannot force checkmate whatever Black plays. As for knights, a player cannot even force checkmate with two knights and king versus a king.

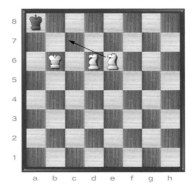

Despite Black's apparent entrapment in the corner, White cannot force checkmate. 1 Nc7+ Kb8 2 Na6+ Ka8 and now any move of the knight on d6 would result in stalemate. It is possible for Black to be checkmated but only by incompetent defence.

A single rook or queen with a king is sufficient material to force checkmate, and it is also possible to checkmate with two bishops, or with one bishop and one knight. A single pawn with a king is sufficient material to win, but only if it is possible to promote the pawn to a queen or rook. Positions tend to be drawn if the king of the player with the extra pawn is behind the pawn, and the defending king is able to stop the king supporting the pawn from in front. A typical example appears below. It shows optimum play by both players.

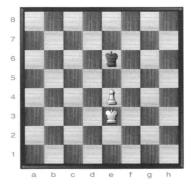

1   Kd4   Kd6!

White's first move aims to outflank the black king, get to d5 and then shepherd the pawn through. Black must confront the white king with his own king.

2   e5+   Ke6   3   Ke4   Kd7

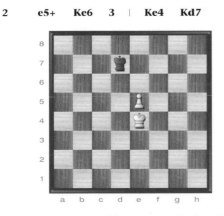

Black has to give ground but it is not critical at this stage.

4   Kd5   Ke7!

Black must stop the white king from getting in front of the white pawn, so Black has to play the king to e7.

5   e6   ...

Black must play his king back to e8 to get the draw.

5   ...   Ke8! | 7   e7+   Ke8
6   Kd6   Kd8

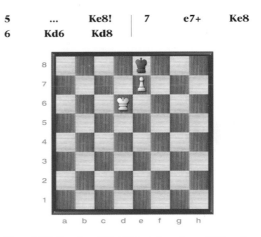

Now, if White plays 8 Ke6 it is stalemate and if he plays anything else, Black takes the e7 pawn. So it is a draw. However, going back to the previous diagram, if Black plays 5...Kd8??, this is what happens.

5   ...   Kd8??
6   Kd6   Ke8
7   e7   ...

We have reached the same position as above but with a different player to move. Now it is Black's turn. He must play 7...Kf7, allowing 8 Kd7 and White promotes the pawn on the following move. So this time Black loses.

SIMPLE ENDGAME STRATEGY

One very important thing about endgame strategy is that the king becomes a fighting piece. After keeping out of the battle for much of the middlegame, the king emerges to play an important role in the game once the two armies have become depleted. This is particularly true in endgames with pawns and no other pieces (or king and pawn endgames). The king should head towards the centre of the action, getting involved in the creation of passed pawns or standing in the way of enemy pawns as they advance towards the queening square.

In the case of king and pawn versus king: if the attacking king can get in front of a single pawn, then it can often steer it home to promotion.

Here the move 1 e5? would be a bad move, allowing Black to draw with best play. Instead, White can win by getting the black king in front of the pawn. Let's first consider the *wrong* way to proceed.

1   Kd5?   Kd7!

Now White cannot make progress. If the king moves to one side, Black can move his king in the same direction, which means he will be once again confronting the king. White cannot gain ground.

From the original diagram, White should play thus:

1   Ke5!   ...

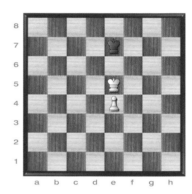

The kings oppose each other along the same file, but Black is obliged to move. In chess parlance, White is said to 'have the opposition', meaning that the player to move has to give ground with the king. Whichever way the king goes, White can gain ground with his own king.

| **1** | **...** | **Kd7** | **3** | **e5** | **Kf8** |
| **2** | **Kf6!** | **Ke8** | | | |

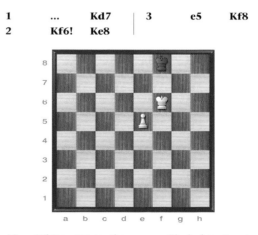

After White moves the pawn, Black has to give more ground.

4	e6!	Ke8
5	e7	...

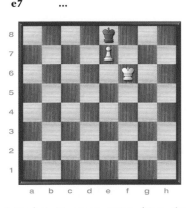

Black now has to move away from the pawn's queening square.

5	...	Kd7
6	Kf7	Kd6
7	e8Q	...

White has duly queened the pawn and now has to win a queen and king versus king endgame. The strategy is fairly straightforward. The king needs to be corralled towards the edge of the board with the queen, using the king as necessary. Once there, it can be checkmated quite easily.

7	...	Kd5

Black tries to make things a bit more difficult by getting as near to the centre of the board as possible. This is the best defensive tactic when left with a bare king in the endgame.

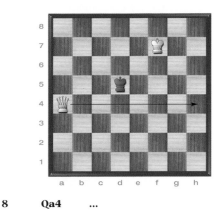

8	Qa4	...

Queen and pawn endgames can be like sheepdog trials! The queen ('dog') boxes off the king's escape routes, pushing it in the direction of its own king ('shepherd').

8	...	Ke5	10	Qb5	...
9	Qc4	Kd6			

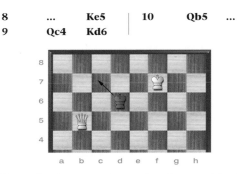

To avoid stalemate, make sure that the opposition king always has at least one legal move available.

10	...	Kc7	12	Kd6	Kd8
11	Ke7	Kc8			

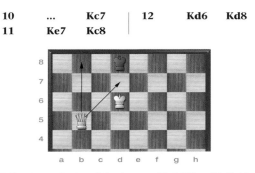

White has a choice of checkmates: 13 Qd7# or 13 Qb8#.

MORE ENDGAME STRATEGY

Checkmating with the rook and the king against the opponent's king is similar to the checkmating technique using the queen and the king but it takes just a little bit longer to effect. Using the same example as previously, but this time promoting the pawn to a rook, we reach this position.

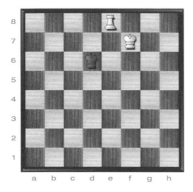

Once again the defensive technique for Black will be to stay as close to the centre of the board for as long as possible.

1	...	Kd5	4	Rd8+	Ke4
2	Rc8	Kd6	5	Rd6	...
3	Kf6	Kd5			

It is still not entirely clear where White's strategy is leading, but White is gradually limiting the black king's scope.

| 5 | ... | Kf4 | 7 | Kf5 | Ke3 |
| 6 | Rd4+ | Kf3 | | | |

The defending king in a rook endgame as compared with a queen endgame has the advantage that it can approach the rook on a diagonal and harass it to some extent. However, the rook can keep it cut off just as easily as a queen along ranks and files.

| 8 | Rd6 | Kf3 | 9 | Rd3+ | ... |

The white rook and attacking white king work together to herd the black king towards the edge of the board.

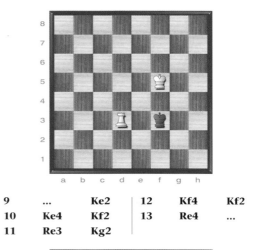

9	...	Ke2	12	Kf4	Kf2
10	Ke4	Kf2	13	Re4	...
11	Re3	Kg2			

Using the 'opposition' concept, White plays a move with the rook so that Black has to cede ground.

| 13 | ... | Kg2 | 14 | Re2+ | ... |

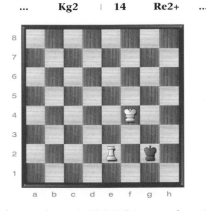

If Black now plays 14...Kh3, White can play a 'pass' move with the white rook, e.g. 15 Rd2, and Black has to play 15 Kh4, allowing 16 Rh2# – checkmate. Black can last two moves longer as follows.

14	...	Kf1		17	Kg3	Kg1
15	Kf3	Kg1		18	Ra1#	
16	Ra2	Kh1				

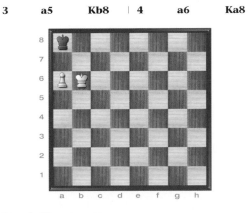

King and Rook Pawn Endings

In king and pawn endgames, we have seen how it can often be possible to force through a pawn to promotion when the attacking king gets in front of the pawn to support its advance. However, there is no forced win in the case of a-pawns or h-pawns (which chess players refer to as rook pawns because they stand in front of rooks in the starting position) as long as the defending king has access to the potential queening square – and sometimes even when it doesn't.

This position is drawn whatever White tries.

| 1 | Ka6 | Kb8 | | 2 | Kb6 | Ka8 |

Black simply shuffles the king between a8 and b8.

| 3 | a5 | Kb8 | | 4 | a6 | Ka8 |

Now 5 a7 is stalemate.

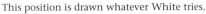

In the example above, Black plays Kc7 and then back to c8. The white king is boxed in on a7 and a8. It is a draw.

GENERAL TIPS ABOUT PLAY

It is important to know the general etiquette and rules of chess. For example, what happens if you have a lapse of concentration and inadvertently make an illegal move? What do you do if a piece not quite on its square keeps catching your eye and distracting you? In both cases there is a formal procedure to follow.

Illegal moves

During the first few games you play, you can expect to make the occasional illegal move. If you or your opponent (or, in a formal chess competition, the arbiter) notices the illegality, the rule is that you should return to the position immediately before the illegality occurred and the player making the illegal move replace it with a legal one. However, the 'touch-piece-move' rule applies.

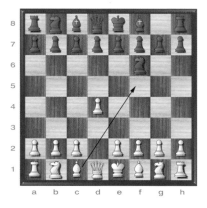

Let's suppose White has a complete aberration in this position and moves the bishop on c1 to f5. This is an illegal move. Either now or after a few moves, one of the players realizes that an illegal move has been played. The correct procedure would be for the position in the diagram be set up again and that White, having touched the bishop, is obliged to make a move with it. So White has five legal moves with the c1 bishop to choose from. Should an illegal move not be spotted until several moves after it was made, the original position before that move should be reinstated. It can be difficult if the move is not spotted immediately.

In the above position, Black tries to play the move 1...Bg4. This is illegal because his king is in check. Therefore, Black has to retract the bishop move and replace it with a move that gets out of check. If possible, Black is also obliged to move the bishop that has already been touched. As it happens, the move 1...Bd7 is possible with the bishop, to block the check, so that is the only legal move in this position. Rather luckily for Black, it is also a good move.

Right: Black tries to advance the rook-pawn but White calls a halt. Black's king is in check from the queen on b2 so, although the pawn has been touched, the king has to be moved instead in order to escape the check.

Black, to play, is oblivious to the check against the black king and tries to play 1...Qd6. This is illegal and must be replaced with a legal move, with the piece that was originally touched, if possible. Unfortunately for Black, the move 1...Qd7 is the only legal move using the touched queen. It must be played and no doubt White will capture the luckless queen.

In this position, White has just played the terrible move 1 Bb5+. In reply, Black plays the equally terrible 1...dxe4. But, luckily for Black, it is also illegal: Black is in check. When obliged to replace this with something legal, Black finds that no legal move of the touched d-pawn is possible to escape check. The touch-piece-move obligation becomes void, and Black is free to play any legal move to get out of check. Black finally notices that Black can improve on the previous try and plays 1...axb5!, winning the bishop. It may seem rather arbitrary that some illegal moves are positively rewarded while others harshly punished – but, as in life, crime on the chessboard can sometimes pay.

Above: The white queen overlaps two squares, which is potentially misleading. Either player on their turn can reposition the piece, but they must advise their opponent first.

Even in informal games, it is a good idea to observe the rule about the touching of pieces, so as to get into a good habit of thinking carefully before making decisions. In formal competitions, even among schoolchildren, the rule is strictly enforced. Note that it does not apply if you accidentally touch a piece, or knock a piece over.

Repositioning

Occasionally the situation arises when the pieces are not neatly set up on the board. For example, in making a move, a player may have put a piece on the border between two squares. This can sometimes make it difficult to know which square a piece is actually on. In such circumstances – so long as it is your turn to move – you should advise your opponent that you are going to adjust the positioning of a piece. You are then free to go ahead and reposition the piece without penalty. Chess players often do this by using the French phrase *J'adoube*, which means 'I adjust'.

135

BEYOND THE BASICS

If you have read and absorbed everything in the previous chapter, you should now know enough to be able to play an enjoyable game of chess with your friends, read a chess book or article, or play through a published chess game, and understand what is going on. If not, it would be a good idea to play some games and perhaps read a newspaper column about chess before reading any further, to gain a bit of experience before embarking on this last lap of your journey. At this stage, you may find that you lose more games than you win. Don't worry. Now you are going to learn not just how to play, but how to win. One of the most enjoyable and rewarding ways to achieve chess prowess is by looking at games played by world champions. We shall be looking at some of their masterpieces in this chapter.

Right: After the queen, the rook is the second most powerful piece on the chessboard. Although called the 'rook' in English, it is known as the 'tower' in French, German and Spanish.

PLAY BETTER CHESS

Now that we are through the basic rules of the game, the order in which you read this book is less significant. In fact, now is a very good time to browse later pages of the book that deal with expanding your horizons and choosing chess-playing software, or a chess computer. As the man in the street said to the lady who asked him 'How do I get to the Carnegie Hall?' – 'You gotta practise!' It is simply not possible to transmit the benefit of regular practice via the pages of a book. Playing and studying must go in tandem.

Digital opponents

Ideally, you need to be playing someone who is a bit further advanced than you are, but not too much. Playing a much stronger player would not be sensible in terms of competition or encouragement, although he or she might be persuaded to treat it as a tutorial and show you where you are going wrong. Computer software, or Internet play, is a good idea from the point of view of convenience, but it is inadvisable to play too often against computers. For one thing, playing with an inanimate (or remote) opponent is a bit lonely and unsociable. For another, bear in mind that the latest chess software programs play chess of a phenomenally high standard.

There are many inexpensive software programs available for purchase that are more than capable of holding their own with the world chess champion in a quick game, so they will be vastly too good for you and me. But don't be discouraged, because it is still interesting trying to figure out how the computer wins. Further, it is a wonderful experience when you play your first human opponent after a long series of depressing digital defeats – and you see this person make a mistake.

Below: Ten-year-olds play chess during their school chess lesson, in Stroebeck, Germany. Stroebeck has the only school in Germany where chess is a compulsory subject for every student. The tradition of playing chess at the school is nearly 200 years old.

Above: Chess is not only a game for all ages but is also one you can play almost anywhere, enjoying hours of fun in doing so. It can be very beneficial to play with a more advanced player – you may not win but you will learn more about the game.

Right: It may look small but modern-day software is so advanced that even a hand-held chess computer such as this can beat most players with ease. Even great chess masters have been beaten by today's computer software.

One peculiar advantage of chess software – that it does not snigger when it wins – is sometimes cited, but this is not strictly true. Be warned, some PC-based chess software is programmed to give verbal commentary during play. This usually consists of desperate attempts at humour and is valueless. It is advisable to find out how to switch off your computer's sound facilities during play.

Principle number one: there are no principles

Now that we have progressed beyond the basic rules and general principles of the game, here is another rule of thumb that is worth absorbing – be sceptical of general principles. That includes any such principles you may read in this book. General principles exist for guidance, but should not be slavishly adhered to. Much of the aesthetic beauty in chess occurs when general principles are turned on their head; for example, a position where a pawn is more valuable than a queen. General principles always have to be weighed against a pragmatic and objective assessment of the actual position on the board. The ability to judge when general principles do not apply comes with experience and is the essence of chess wisdom. But it is a good idea to follow your instincts in playing moves right from the start. Your judgement may be wrong, but the resultant defeat will teach you a valuable lesson.

Time is a key factor in chess. Competition chess is played with clocks, but in informal chess you have as long as you like to think about your moves. However, it is usually a mistake to spend too long over these in your first games of chess – 20 or 30 seconds is plenty.

INTERMEDIATE OPENING STRATEGY

Although the keynote to many chess openings is the occupation of the centre, it can be just as useful to control the centre from a distance. Generally speaking, many of the openings that involve occupation of the centre were developed before the 20th century but, since then, chess masters have developed a more pragmatic approach to opening play. Here are various strategies for opening the game.

Previously, chess experts could be very dogmatic about the 'right' way to play the opening, but nowadays leading players often take the view that whatever seems to work in practice is good. Here is an example:

1	d4	Nf6
2	c4	g6
3	Nc3	Bg7
4	e4	d6
5	Nf3	0-0

If we survey the position, we can see that White has fully occupied the centre with pawns, and is controlling the d5 and e5 squares. Black, on the other hand, has sat back and apparently given White free rein in the centre.

You might conclude that this is a poor opening for Black. In fact, it is regarded as a very respectable one, and has been played by stellar players such as Bobby Fischer and Garry Kasparov. The reason is that, on the basis of many thousands of games played in this opening, White has never been able to prove that this central control necessarily leads to a tangible advantage. Black's pieces are set up rather passively, but there is no obvious way for White's pawns to advance, or for White's pieces to reach squares, such that an attack on the king or other advantage will accrue.

This opening is called the 'King's Indian Defence'. The word 'Indian' in this context is an allusion to the old Indian form of the game, where the pieces were characteristically positioned as in the part-diagram below, with the knight on f6 and the pawn moved to g6 to allow the bishop to come to g7. The 'King' component of the name indicates that the 'Indian' configuration is on the kingside of the board.

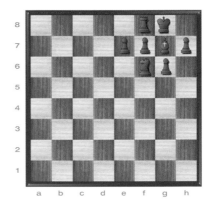

When a bishop is moved one square from its original position to one of the board's long diagonals (a1–h8 or h1–a8) in this way, it is referred to as a *fianchetto* (this term is used as a noun or verb). This is an Italian word meaning 'little flank'. There is a large family of openings in which one or both of the players *fianchetto* bishops – these are sometimes referred to as 'flank openings'.

Black's underlying strategy in this opening is to allow White to dominate the centre but then to launch a counter-attack from the flank. The black pawns are held in reserve, waiting for the right moment to strike. For White, the temptation is to push forward too far until a seemingly impregnable centre becomes overstretched. In some variations, Black probes on the queenside, starting with the pawn thrust c5. More often, Black looks to move the knight on f6 to e8 or h5, paving the way for f5 and a pawn storm if White castles kingside. Defence, in this position, can very swiftly turn into attack. Returning to the game position, one possible continuation could be as follows:

6   Be2   Nbd7

7   0-0   e5

8   d5   ...

The important thing to note here is that the central pawns are locked together, which rather restricts the movement of the major and minor pieces. This is referred to as a 'closed position'. Such positions usually require a long sequence of patient and subtle manoeuvring in order to open the position up for tactical action. As such, this sort of opening is not very suitable for play between beginners and elementary players. It is better to start with openings that allow more scope for the pieces, in order to learn and practise tactical chess. For now, it is enough to know that such openings exist, and that Black's passive-looking

---

QUEEN'S INDIAN DEFENCE

There is also an opening called the 'Queen's Indian Defence'. In it, Black *fianchettoes* a bishop on the queenside. Typical opening moves are:

1	d4	Nf6
2	c4	e6
3	Nf3	b6
4	g3	Bb7
5	Bg2	Be7

Note that both White and Black have *fianchettoed* a bishop (White on g2 and Black on b7).

---

opening strategy is by no means mistaken. However, looking again at the diagram after 8 d5, it is worth considering what Black's plan might be in this position. One idea is to play 8...Nc5, which attacks the white pawn on e4. After White defends it (with a move such as 9 Qc2), it would then be a good idea to play 9...a5, which prevents White from playing 10 b4 to chase the knight back to its previous position. Another idea for Black in this sort of position is to drop the f6 knight back with 8...Ne8, and follow up with 9...f5 to undermine the white pawn on e4.

THE RUY LÓPEZ

Perhaps the most famous of chess openings is the one that is named after the famous Spanish chess-playing priest Ruy López de Segura (*c*.1530–1580), who was one of the best players of his time and the author of an early book on the game. The opening is also sometimes referred to as 'The Spanish Game'.

The initial moves that give this opening its name are as follows:

1	e4	e5
2	Nf3	Nc6
3	Bb5	...

The last move played, 3 Bb5, is the signature move of the Ruy López opening. White threatens to capture the knight on c6 (4 Bxc6), thus removing the only defender of the pawn on e5 and allowing its capture with 5 Nxe5.

However, over the course of several hundred years, chess players have worked out that this threat is superficial. Black can usually recapture a pawn if White follows through with this rather crude threat. So, Black often plays a move designed to attack the bishop or to encourage it to capture the knight anyway.

3	...	a6

This is by no means the only move for Black in this position. Other possibilities are 3...Nf6, 3...f5, 3...Bc5, 3...d6 and 3...Nd4. All of these moves are respectable and lead to quite different positions from those that generally occur after 3...a6. It is important to know that chess openings are multi-layered – there are openings within openings (known as variations) – and

some of these variations have quite different sub-variations. It is not necessary to know all the variations and sub-variations in order to play an opening, but it is important to keep an open mind when your opponent appears to depart from what you might have read in books. Just because a move is unorthodox, it doesn't mean it is bad.

4	Ba4	...

This is the most common continuation in competitive chess. But some players prefer to capture on c6: 4 Bxc6 dxc6. Now it is a good idea to develop normally, with a move such as 5 0-0. However, it is a waste of time to play 5 Nxe5? because Black replies 5...Qd4, simultaneously attacking the knight and the pawn on e4. After White moves the knight, Black can recapture the pawn with 6...Qxe4+ and the position is equal. White, having the first move, should strive for something a little better than equality from the opening.

4	...	Nf6

5   0-0   ...

This time it is White's turn to allow the capture of a pawn. Once again, Black can take it or leave it: both variations are regarded as respectable.

5   ...   Be7

Black continues with a quiet, developing move. But 5...Nxe4 is perfectly playable. Then there follows something like 6 d4 b5 7 Bb3 d5 8 dxe5 Be6 9 c3 Bc5, when the material is level and both players have some open lines for their pieces. This is a good line for elementary and intermediate level players to try out.

6   Re1   b5
7   Bb3   d6

8   c3   0-0

9   h3   Na5
10   Bc2   c5
11   d4   ...

Quite a complex position has arisen, with pawns challenging each other in the centre. The position can become closed (if White soon opts to play d5, for example). If there is a major pawn exchange, the game can open up for the bishops and rooks to become active.

The possibilities and complexities of the Ruy López opening have fascinated chess players for many hundreds of years, and it has also been one of the most fashionable openings in top competition. One of its attractions is that it suits elementary level play as well as it does top grandmaster play. The ideas behind the opening are fairly easy to grasp and conform to most general principles. From White's point of view it offers a slight and enduring edge, while from Black's point of view it is solid and contests the centre of the board in a positive manner.

THE SICILIAN DEFENCE

Until perhaps 50 years ago, the most common reply to White's first move of 1 e4 was 1...e5, but in the modern era, the move 1...c5 has become more common. This is the move that gives the name to the 'Sicilian Defence' (often shortened to 'The Sicilian'). The name of the defence is taken from the homeland of a 17th-century player named Pietro Carrera, who first mentioned it in his chess writings. It was known and appreciated several centuries ago, but only really came into its own in the 20th century.

1   e4   c5

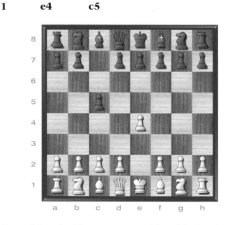

One of the significant aspects of 1...c5 is that it avoids the symmetry that can follow after 1...e5. The pawn on c5 controls the d4 square just as a pawn on e5 would do, but leaves the central situation slightly more flexible.

2   Nf3   ...

This is by far the most common second move for White, just as it is against 1...e5. It is a good developing move. However, there are other reasonable options for White. One is 2 Nc3, often followed by g3 and Bg2. This is known as the 'Closed Sicilian', as play tends to be cagey after the pawns become locked. Another option is 2 c3, where White plans to advance 3 d4 and, if the pawn is captured (3...cxd4), replace it with another pawn (4 cxd4) in order to have a pair of pawns occupying the centre.

One of the attractions of the Sicilian for both colours is the sheer multiplicity of options available. After 2 Nf3, the Sicilian Defence subdivides into three major variations that themselves subdivide further into many different sub-variations. There is only room here to give a flavour of the possibilities, which will be

perfectly sufficient to play elementary chess. At the higher levels of the game, it becomes important to know some opening theory in depth, but at the lower levels it is not necessary to spend time memorizing specific lines.

2   ...   Nc6

2...d6 and 2...e6 are very common and equally reasonable alternatives. In fact, 2...d6 is the most common move of all in this position. A common continuation is 3 d4 cxd4 4 Nxd4 Nf6 5 Nc3 g6 6 Be3 Bg7 7 f3 0-0 8 Qd2 Nc6 9 Bc4 Bd7 10 0-0-0.

This variation is known as the 'Sicilian Dragon' because it is thought that Black's piece configuration is similar in aspect to the constellation Draco. Let's look at how the game might progress after the move 2...Nc6.

3   d4

White could play 3 Bb5 (as in the Ruy López), but the n next move is the most common, seeking to open lines and uncover attacking possibilities. But, if Black then played 3...a6, 4 Ba4?? would be a blunder: 4...b5 5 Bb3 c4 and the bishop is lost.

3	...	cxd4
4	Nxd4	Nf6

5	Nc3	d6
6	Bg5	e6

It might appear that Black is playing slightly more passively than White. It is true that White has slightly more space (or freedom to manoeuvre) but the two black pawns on d6 and e6 still control important centre squares.

7	Qd2	Be7

White now decides to castle queenside, but this is not obligatory. 8 f4 is also possible. 8 Be2 may be not so good because Black could play 8...Nxe4 9 Nxe4 Bxg5 10 Nxg5 Nxd4 11 Qxd4 Qxg5 12 Qxd6 Bd7 13 Bf3 0-0-0 when the position may slightly favour Black.

Right: Geographical map of Sicily by Pietro da Cortona. Homeland of the 17th-century player Pietro Carrera, the region gives its name to the Sicilian Defence, which Carrera was the first to mention in his writings.

8	0-0-0	0-0

This position is roughly equal but imbalanced because the players have castled on opposite sides of the board. This can be very significant in the middlegame. With the white king tucked away safely on the queenside, White can attack the black king on the kingside by advancing the pawns there without danger to his own However, Black can do the same thing – attack the white king on the queenside by advancing pawns, thus a6, b5 and then b4 to attack the knight on c3.

THE NIMZO-INDIAN DEFENCE

The name of the 'Nimzo-Indian Defence' (or 'Nimzowitsch-Indian Defence') is partly a tribute to a great chess player, and partly a misnomer. The Latvian player Aron Nimzowitsch (1886–1935) was one of the greatest-ever chess theorists and also a very fine player, being a close rival of the world champions of the 1920s and 1930s, José Raúl Capablanca and Alexander Alekhine. In 1925 he wrote a highly influential book on chess for advanced players, entitled *My System*, in which he exploded a few myths about chess strategy and set out his own pragmatic ideas for playing the game. Nimzowitsch was also an opening theorist of some renown.

The Nimzo-Indian defence, which we are going to look at here, was pioneered by Nimzowitsch. The 'Indian' component of the name is actually not correct because the opening does not involve a *fianchetto* (as in the King's Indian Defence).

| 1 | d4 | Nf6 |
| 2 | c4 | e6 |

Instead of playing 2...g6 and moving the bishop to g7, Black decides to use the bishop on the a3–f8 diagonal.

| 3 | Nc3 | |

If, instead, White plays 3 Nf3, play can develop down different lines. For example, Black could play 3...Bb4+, which is the starting point for what is known as the

'Bogo-Indian Defence' (partly named after another famous between-wars player from Ukraine called Efim Bogoljubow), when White often replies with 4 Bd2 Qe7 5 g3 Nc6 6 Bg2 Bxd2+ 7 Nbxd2 and a fairly even position results. Another possibility is 3...b6 4 g3 which, as we have already seen, are the starting moves of what is known as the Queen's Indian Defence.

3   ...   Bb4

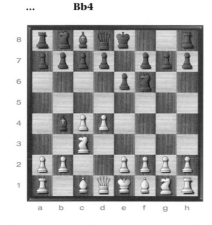

The above position is the starting point for the Nimzo-Indian Defence. Black's bishop pins the knight to the king, so White cannot continue with 4 e4? because Black could simply capture with 4...Nxe4.

4   e3   ...

A slightly passive-looking move, but it is the most common move at this point. Other possibilities are 4 Bg5, 4 Nf3 or 4 a3, provoking the bishop to capture or retreat. 4 Qc2 is also possible and has the slight plus point that it allows the queen to recapture (after 4...Bxc3+) and avoid the doubling of the pawns. This is largely a matter of taste. The line with 4 Qc2 is known as the 'Classical variation', as it was the most popular line when the Nimzo-Indian was first played in the early part of the 20th century.

4   ...   0–0

Black could capture on c3 with 4...Bxc3+, but there is no hurry to play this. It would be a more or less equal

exchange: the small advantage of doubling White's pawns (on c3 and c4) would perhaps be outweighed by the loss of the (slightly more valuable) bishop for White's knight.

5   Bd3   d5

Black's move is designed to stop White playing the advance e4. Note that Black often plays 5...c5 here when play can follow 6 Nf3 d5 – reaching the same position as appears in the main line. This is a simple example of an opening transposition. The order in which the moves are played is sometimes not significant. However, there are other possibilities. For example, after 5...c5 6 Nf3 Nc6 7 0-0 d6 8 Qc2 Bxc3 9 bxc3 e5, play moves along very different lines.

6   Nf3   c5
7   0–0   Nc6

A number of pawn captures are now possible, but would result in a straightforward recapture.

Both sides have succeeded in developing most of their pieces, and both kings are tucked away on safe squares. This is a perfectly playable position for both colours. The only problem – and this applies to both sides – lies in how to develop the bishops that are currently still on their original squares.

FLANK OPENINGS

All the openings examined so far involved either 1 e4 or 1 d4 on White's first move. Neither of these moves is obligatory, and there are other respectable ways of starting a chess game. These are known collectively as 'flank openings', as they do not involve a move of a central pawn on the first turn.

The first move 1 c4 begins what is known as the 'English Opening', so called because it was first championed by the great English player Howard Staunton, who used it in his 1843 match against the French player St Amant. We have already seen that 1...c5 (the Sicilian Defence) is a good move for Black against 1 e4, so it stands to reason that 1 c4 should be reasonable for White.

Despite Staunton's example, this opening was infrequently used until the mid-20th century, when it was taken up by top Soviet players such as world champions Botvinnik and Smyslov. Today, although still not played as frequently as 1 e4 or 1 d4, it retains a good reputation.

1	c4	e5

1...Nf6 is seen more frequently, with Black inviting White to transpose into the Nimzo-Indian or King's Indian after 2 d4. Another frequent response is 1...c5, where Black often strives to play symmetrically for a number of moves (e.g. 2 Nf3 Nf6 3 Nc3 Nc6 4 g3 g6 5 Bg2 Bg7 6 0-0 0-0, etc).

2	Nc3	Nf6
3	Nf3	...

3 g3 is another frequently played move when play can continue 3...d5 4 cxd5 Nxd5 5 Bg2.

3	...	Nc6
4	g3	d5
5	cxd5	Nxd5
6	Bg2	...

Note how similar this is to the Sicilian Defence, but with the colours the other way round. In fact, it is sometimes known as the 'Reversed Sicilian Defence'. It can be a little hazardous for Black to play openings designed for White because, if you think about it, White will always have an extra move by virtue of having started the game. However, in this specific line, it is not a problem. The downside of choosing a Black-style set-up if you have White is that such positions tend to be slightly more passive than can be achieved by playing conventional opening variations. Notice, for example, in the above diagram, White's rather limited control of the centre. Again, this tends to be a matter of taste, but if you like to play attacking chess from the beginning, you may find yourself temperamentally unsuited to playing flank openings.

Another flank opening starts with 1 Nf3, which is known as the 'Réti Opening', after Czech player Richard Réti (1889–1929), who, like Nimzowitsch, contributed radically new ideas to chess strategy after

| 2 | ... | d5 |
| 3 | Bg2 | c6 |

3...c5 is perfectly playable, but 3...c6 is ultra-solid, with a view to blighting the g2 bishop's prospects on the long diagonal.

4	0–0	Bg4
5	d3	Nbd7
6	Nbd2	...

The above set of moves seems to restrict the scope of the c1 bishop, but White is concentrating on supporting a pawn advance such as e4 or c4 with this knight.

| 6 | ... | e5 |
| 7 | e4 | ... |

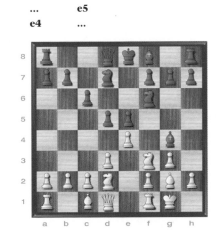

This is a very solid set-up for White, but is perhaps a little cagey and passive.

Above: Mikhail Botvinnik, seen playing in the 1961/62 Hastings International Congress. He played at the traditional British Christmas/New Year event three times, winning first prize in 1961/62 and 1966/67, playing 1 c4 in most of his White games.

World War I. In practice, 1 Nf3 and 1 c4 overlap to a considerable degree and often transpose.

| 1 | Nf3 | Nf6 |

The temptation to mimic White's opening moves is always strong, but there are other possibilities, such as 1...d5, 1...c5 (after which 2 c4 transposes to the Sicilian Defence) or 1...g6.

| 2 | g3 | ... |

2 d4 transposes into a standard Queen's pawn opening, or perhaps the Queen's Gambit (once White plays c4). 2 c4 transposes into the English Opening.

THINKING AHEAD AND CALCULATING 1

Strong chess players are often asked how far ahead they can see when calculating a move. The rather unsatisfying answer usually given is that it depends on the position. In fact, much depends on the complexity of the situation, with an extreme example of a simple one shown below.

Here, with White to play, a strong player would not calculate but simply count moves. Can the white pawn reach a8 before the black king arrives to stop it? White counts squares – a4 (the pawn moves two squares on its first turn), a5, a6, a7 and a8 = five. But the black king can only reach the b-file in five moves so it cannot catch the pawn. Thus the pawn queens. However, if it is Black to move, the king reaches b7 after the pawn gets to a7, saving the day and securing a draw with best play.

In the above position, White, to play, has a very much better position. One simple idea here is to win a pawn.

| 1 | Nxg3 | hxg3 |
| 2 | Qxg3 | Bf6! |

White is a pawn up, but Black's last move has secured the defence of the g7 pawn and the knight on e5.

It is likely that White might win at some point, but there is a long way to go. However, White has a much better move in the initial position.

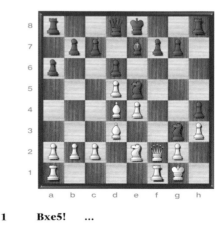

| 1 | Bxe5! | ... |

White has removed Black's only defender of the key f7 square, but it involves sacrificing the rook on f1.

1	...	Nxf1
2	Rxf1	dxe5

In the game from which this was taken, Black played 2...f6, but that left Black at a material disadvantage of bishop and knight for the rook. White's well-placed minor pieces soon made short work of Black.

3	Qxf7+	Kd7
4	Qe6+	Ke8
5	Qxe5	...

White has a knight and two pawns for a rook, so in material terms, it is level. However, Black's king remains exposed, the g7 pawn is under threat and White's two minor pieces will soon swing into action. It is very definitely better for White.

Sometimes, even in a complex position, it is sufficient to calculate just a couple of moves to be satisfied that a big advantage will accrue.

White, to play, has a big advantage because the black king is very exposed. A move such as 1 Qf5 would put further pressure on the king, but there is something immediately decisive.

1	Nxd5+!	...

A fork with check, which also discovers an attack on the queen on c7.

1	...	Nxd5

Not a bad defensive move. Black captures the checking piece and also manages to provide a defender for the queen. 2 Qxc7 Nxc7 3 Rxc7 would leave White a pawn up in a good position – but there is something very much better than this.

2	Qe4+!	...

After this check, White will capture on c7 with the rook, winning easily. For example, 2...Kd8 3 Rxc7 Kxc7 and now White plays 4 Bxd5 after which he has a queen and pawn in return for a rook – a huge material advantage. If Black tries 2...Qe5 White can capture with the knight, 3 Nxe5, and White will have a material advantage of queen and pawn for knight. Having satisfied themselves that the moves 1 Nxd5+ Nxd5 2 Qe4+ would lead to a huge material advantage, most strong players playing White would soon make the move. That said, having made up their mind to play the move, they would probably go through their analysis two or three times to make sure they hadn't missed anything. This is particularly important when you are playing a complex sacrifice.

THINKING AHEAD AND CALCULATING 2

We have looked at some examples where careful calculation of the next few moves has brought rewards in terms of a cut-and-dried tactical solution. In some positions there may be one move that is markedly better than all the others (e.g. a move that leads to checkmate, material advantage, or simply a recapture or a logical developing move); but in many others, it may not be so clear-cut and it will be necessary to consider your options.

Before doing any thinking, it is necessary to look at the board and run through the options. For example, you may want to start by looking at the move you want to play. Does it work? If you are happy that it does work, should you play it right away? No – wait – have another look around to see if there is something better or more clear-cut. But first make a careful mental note of the move you think is good. If there is a snag to the move, try and concentrate on why it doesn't work. The basic idea behind the move may be promising. Perhaps you can play another move that will allow the idea to work perfectly a move or two later.

White, to play, notices that Black's king has no legal move, but that the intended checkmating move R1e6 currently fails because Black can reply Nxe6. However, that thought leads to another: the black knight is effectively tied to the defence of the e6 square so it is not really defending the b5 pawn.

1   Bxb5!   ...

Now if 1...Nxb5, White simply answers 2 R1e6 mate.

1   ...   Rxd5

This looks like a good answer, but White has another trick to play.

2   Bc4!   ...

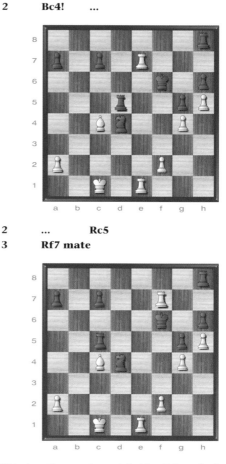

2   ...   Rc5
3   Rf7 mate

This is rather a piquant finish. Although the black rook pins the bishop against White's king, the bishop still effectively defends the rook on f7 and helps it to checkmate. Black didn't have to move the rook on move 2, but any other move would have cost the exchange (i.e. rook for a minor piece).

Left: Black is about to play the knight to c2, bringing about a 'smothered mate'. This term describes the situation where a king is completely hemmed in by its own pieces and cannot move out of check from a knight.

White, to play, looks around the board and decides that everything is defended and all is well.

1	Rd2??	f3!

Black's last move threatens mate (with Qxg2) and the capture of the white queen. There is no alternative other than to capture the pawn with the queen (the g2 pawn is pinned).

2	Qxf3	Rxc4

Black has won a bishop for a pawn. The 2...f3 move is called a 'deflecting sacrifice' because it forced the queen away from the defence of the bishop. Another way of looking at this is to say that the white queen was overloaded. It wasn't able to defend the bishop and also guard against the f3 move at the same time.

Instinct versus learning

Players often experience a dilemma when choosing between a move that looks impressive and another that looks like the sort of thing they have seen in textbooks. The most sensible course is to calculate as objectively as you can and play the move that makes the most sense. If you are still confused after a lot of thinking, play the instinctive selection. Even if it is wrong, you may learn something from what happens.

It is often worth spending the last moments doing some last-minute checking before you make a move. Ask yourself: 'Have I overlooked an obvious capture of one of my men?' Or: 'Have I missed an obvious chance to capture one of my opponent's pieces?' It doesn't take long to review each piece in turn and examine capturing possibilities. It is also a good idea to cast an eye over any obvious threats from your opponent.

PLANNING

It is always a good idea to have a plan. Obviously, the long-term plan is to deliver checkmate, but it is good to have something more achievable, particularly in simple positions where there are fewer tactical possibilities to calculate. A plan does not have to be too grandiose. It might consist of redeploying your worst-posted piece, improving the scope of a blocked-in bishop or ensuring a weak or backward pawn is supported.

Material is level (above) with Black to play. In general terms, it might be argued that, with bishop for knight and with Black having doubled pawns on g7 and g6, White stands better. However, in this specific situation, the doubled pawn on g6 is acting as a barrier to the white bishop and to any chance of a viable kingside attack.

Black has no immediate tactical possibilities in this position, and there are no serious threats to guard against. So it is necessary to think of a constructive plan. One idea here would be to play the knight to d5 to attack the pawn on c3. However, it seems more sensible to do something useful with the rook on f8, which is Black's worst-placed piece. It can only go to e8, where it would be not much better than on f8, so Black creates space for it to find a better square.

1   ...   Rd7!

Now Black will have the choice of playing the f8 rook to c8 or d8 next move.

2   Bf1   ...

This retreat looks passive, but is actually quite sensible. White gets ready to challenge rooks on the d-file, should Black now play Rfd8.

2   ...   Nd5

Black could have played Rfd8 or Rfc8 here, both of which look just as good.

3   Re4   Rc8

Black now has three pieces menacing the pawn on c3.

4   Rd4   ...

White sets a trap. If 4...Nxc3, White can play 5 Rxd7 Qxd7 6 Rxc3, winning a piece.

4 ... a6

This is a waiting move that also restricts the scope of White's bishop. There follows a series of cagey moves, during which the two players hope to exploit any inaccurate moves that may occur. The position is still roughly level, but Black starts to pressurize the weaknesses in White's position.

5	Qd3	Rcd8
6	Qf3	Rc8
7	Bg2	Qe5

8 Re4 Qg5 | 9 Ree1? ...

White starts to go wrong. 9 Rc2 looks a safer move.

9 ... Rdc7

Black may even have been able to play 9...Nxb4 here, since 10 cxb4 allows 10...Rxc1. However, the move played is also good.

10 h4 Qd2

It is a little risky placing the queen here, but the black queen can escape to a safe square if attacked.

11 Red1 Qb2

There is still a long way to go in the game, but this position can be seen as the culmination of Black's short-term plan initiated with 1...Rd7. Black has managed to bring no fewer than four pieces to bear on the weak pawn on c3 and will soon win it by force.

Most people playing the white side in this position would find it rather depressing and probably fold very quickly. But a grandmaster (or a powerful computer) could still put up a tough defence: 12 Rb1, and if 12...Qxc3 13 Qd3. Black is a pawn up, but White now has some counterplay against the knight on d5. For example, 13...Qxd3 14 Rxd3 Rc1+ 15 Rxc1 Rxc1+ 16 Kh2 Rc4 17 Bxd5 exd5 18 Rxd5 Rxb4. Although Black remains a pawn up, it could be hard to force a win.

ATTACKING CHESS

By the term 'attacking chess', chess players usually mean that play involves a direct attack on the opponent's king. This is by no means the only way to play a game of chess. Many chess players engage in 'percentage chess', which involves players paying closer attention to the material situation or to the safety of their army than to the ultimate aim of checkmating the opponent. However, attacking players enjoy the excitement of a checkmating attack and tailor their play to that end.

The first prerequisite of attacking chess is a suitable choice of opening. Not all openings are equally well suited for attacking chess. But the openings often preferred by elementary players (such as the Giuoco Piano or the Ruy López) can be a good choice for someone who enjoys attacking chess. They tend to provide more open lines, so that you can gain swift access to the opponent's king.

The downside to attacking chess is that it is easy to go wrong in a tactical melee. The result becomes something of a lottery. Consequently, a strong player will often prefer percentage chess against a weaker opponent, seeking to exploit their extra skill without excess risk. But it can be a good idea for a weaker player to indulge in attacking play against a stronger opponent, as the more complicated the position, the more chance that luck will play a part.

Here is a game between two junior players, showing how a game can get out of control very quickly and lead to a swift denouement.

| 1 | e4 | e5 |
| 2 | Nf3 | Nc6 |

Probably the commonest opening moves in all forms of chess – both professional and amateur.

| 3 | Bc4 | Nf6 |

Black's last move is the starting position of the 'Two Knights' Defence'. This opening is ideal for players of either colour who enjoy attacking chess. There are plenty of aggressive possibilities for both colours.

| 4 | Ng5 | ... |

White starts the fun going with the very crude threat of 5 Bxf7+ or 5 Nxf7, forking queen and rook. It is a good move. Instead, White could play 4 d4, which is aggressive, or 4 d3, which would be the choice of a more cautious player. 4 Nc3 is also possible, but then Black could try 4...Nxe4 and, if 5 Nxe4 d5, could win back the piece.

4	...	d5

Black sensibly blocks the threat to the f7 pawn. It is by no means the only move available to Black. Some very aggressive Black players prefer 4...Bc5. This is a sacrifice, allowing a capture on f7. White can probably get away with either capture (5 Bxf7+ or 5 Nxf7), but Black often gets a powerful counterattack against the white king.

5	exd5	Nxd5?

This looks like a routine recapture, but it is regarded as a poor move by chess experts. White will get a big attack. Instead, Black normally plays 5...Na5 to molest the c4 bishop. Play continues 6 Bb5+ c6 7 dxc6 bxc6 8 Be2 h6 9 Nf3 e4 10 Ne5 Bd6. White is a pawn up, but is being relentlessly harried by Black. The result is that White is poorly developed. A strong player for White could hope to survive Black's counterattack, but a weaker one would be likely to go under.

Looking at the position above, it is not obvious why Black's last move is an error. It cannot be explained by reference to 'general principles'. Chess players over the centuries have worked out a very strong continuation for White in this position, and it is necessary to know this before playing the Two Knights' Defence.

6	d4	...

An even more aggressive, but perhaps overly risky, alternative is 6 Nxf7, sacrificing a knight for a direct attack on the black king. Play can continue 6...Kxf7 7 Qf3+ Ke6 (the only move to defend the knight on d5) 8 Nc3 Ncb4 9 Qe4. White has a strong grip on the game and it will be hard for Black to withstand the threats with the black king so exposed.

6	...	exd4
7	0–0	...

continues on the next page ➔

Position after 7 0–0

Taking stock of the above position, it can be seen that Black has an extra pawn, but that White has considerable compensation in terms of better development. Black is still a couple of moves away from being able to castle on the kingside, while White is about to play Re1+ and perhaps bring the white queen to f3, where it would threaten both Qxf7 mate and Qxd5, winning a piece. White played d4 earlier in order to open up the e-file for the rook to give check. There is quite a lot for Black to cope with.

7   ...   Bd6?
8   Nxf7   ...

In fact, White could simply have taken the knight on d5 that had been left undefended by Black's hurry to develop pieces. But White's attacking instincts are right, and this move commences a fierce attack against Black's king.

8   ...   Kxf7
9   Bxd5+   Ke8

A poor choice. Black should invite the exchange of the powerful c4 bishop with 9...Be6. On e8, the king will be exposed to a check on the e-file.

10   Qf3   ...

Both players are finding it hard to sift through the many options available in this open position. 10 Re1+ Ne7 11 Qh5+ g6 12 Qh4 would work out as a stronger option for White.

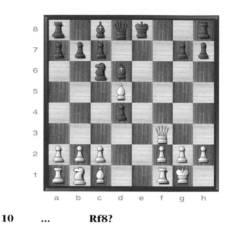

10   ...   Rf8?

10...Ne5 is a more resilient move, blocking the e-file and keeping a defence on f7 as well as attacking the white queen. Even so, after 11 Re1 Qe7, followed by the surprising retreat 12 Qd1, White's powerful pin on the e-file leaves Black with major problems to solve. The knight on e5 is in great danger of White playing f4 to win it.

11   Qh5+   ...

White is trying to weaken the squares around Black's king and also to pick up the pawn on h7.

11   ...   g6

The move 11...Kd7 is answered by 12 Qg4+ Ke8 13 Re1+ Ne5 14 Qxg7, and White still has a strong attack.

12   Bxc6+   ...

If White plays 12 Qxh7, Black can reply with 12...Bxh2+ 13 Qxh2 Qxd5, which means Black has at least some chance of saving the game.

Instead, White simplifies the position. Although this means relinquishing the dangerous white-squared bishop, it has done its job, helping to puncture holes in Black's position. At best, Black is saddled now with doubled pawns on the c-file, but the black king is horribly exposed in the centre of the rank and vulnerable to a direct attack.

12	...	bxc6

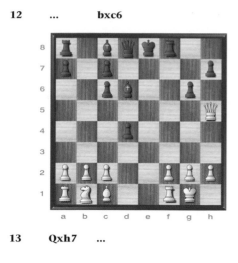

13	Qxh7	...

Not the best move. 13 Re1+ is hard to meet: 13...Be7 14 Qxh7 Qd6 15 Bh6 leaves Black in a hole.

13	...	g5?

After this, the game is over. 13...Qf6 gives Black a chance of holding the position together, although White stands better.

14	Qg6+	...

Once again, White misses the most decisive move to end the game. After 14 Re1+, it is clear that Black cannot move the king but has to interpose a piece to escape check. But after 14...Be7, White simply plays 15 Bxg5 and Black has run out of good defences. If 15...Rf7 16 Qg8+ Rf8 17 Qg6+, then White will capture the bishop on e7 next move.

14	...	Rf7

14...Kd7 is a better move, but still loses after 15 Bxg5 when White is a comfortable two pawns up with a strong attack.

15	Bxg5	Qd7

If Black blocks the attack on the queen with 15...Be7, White pins the bishop with 16 Re1 and it will soon be captured.

16	Re1+	Kf8

Black is now at White's mercy. In fact there is a mate in three moves here. Can you see it?

17	Bh6+	Rg7

There is no choice.

18	Re8+!	...

An attractive rook sacrifice to force checkmate.

18	...	Qxe8
19	Qxg7 mate	

This is a good example of aggressive chess. It is noticeable in the final position that White has not moved the queenside rook or knight. That is a little unusual. It is normally better to ensure that the majority of the pieces are in play before launching such an attack.

THE SACRIFICE

We have already seen some examples of sacrifices at various stages of a game. For example, a gambit is a pawn sacrifice that occurs during the opening stages of a game. This particular sacrifice is designed to gain momentum for an attack while the opponent expends valuable time rounding up the pawn. On the previous page, White finished with a rook sacrifice in order to create a mating finish.

The sacrifice is an important part of attacking chess. Very often, it is an inducement to the opponent to move a piece away from an important defensive role, or to allow lines to be opened up for an attack. Here is an interesting example of a pawn sacrifice being used to open the position up to an attack. Playing White was the leading English woman player, Harriet Hunt.

| 1 | e4 | c6 |

This is the first move of the 'Caro-Kann Defence', named after two 19th-century players. It is a good opening for Black, albeit slightly more sedate than the uncompromising Sicilian Defence.

| 2 | d4 | d5 |

The basic idea of the Caro-Kann Defence is for the c6 pawn to support the pawn on d5, so that if it is captured, Black can recapture with the pawn.

3	e5	Bf5
4	Nf3	e6
5	Be2	c5

Black seeks to open up the position. If this is not done, then White will have more room to manoeuvre, and Black's set-up will remain rather cramped. The disadvantage of opening up the position is that it gives White scope for her pieces.

6	Be3	Nd7
7	0–0	Ne7
8	c4	...

White seeks to open the position still further. White has developed a little quicker than Black. Notice that Black used two moves to move the c-pawn, first to c6 and then to c5.

| 8 | ... | dxc4 |
| 9 | Na3 | ... |

White could recapture on c4 immediately with 9 Bxc4, but prefers to play another developing move since the c4 pawn cannot be defended in any case.

| 9 | ... | cxd4? |

This looks like an error. Black should play 9...Nd5 with a view to playing Be7 and then 0–0. Black needs to get the black king to safety.

10   Nxc4!   ...

White avoids a mechanical recapturing move on d4, but instead plays something else first. This is sometimes referred to as an *intermezzo* move – an 'in-between' move used to improve the position before making an obvious recapture. White's move is also a sacrifice because Black can now play 10...dxe3, winning a bishop for a pawn.

10   ...   Nc6

Had Black played the greedy 10...dxe3, White's next move would have come as a shock – 11 Nd6 checkmate! The black king is surrounded and cannot escape. This is a nice example of a smothered mate.

11   Nxd4!   ...

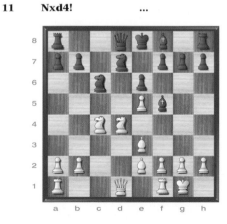

This move offers another sacrifice. Both of Black's knights are threatening the e5 pawn and it is only defended by White's knight on c4.

11   ...   Ndxe5?

Black accepts the sacrifice, but it would have been better to decline with 11...Nxd4 12 Qxd4 Bc5 13 Nd6+ Bxd6 14 Qxd6, although White still has a better position because the black king is stranded on a central file.

12   Nxe5   Nxe5
13   Bb5+   ...

13...Ke7 14 Nxf5+ exf5 15 Qa4 leaves the black king at the mercy of White's pieces.

13   ...   Nd7
14   Nxf5   exf5

15   Re1   Black resigns

Resignation may seem premature, but Black has no hope of salvation here. White threatens a lethal discovered check 16 Bg5+. If 15...Be7, 16 Bc5 will win the bishop on e7.

QUEEN SACRIFICES

If you play chess on a regular basis – and that is the only way to improve – you will become used to playing (or see your opponent playing) pawn sacrifices. But a queen sacrifice is not something that comes along every day. They are regarded as aesthetically pleasing, perhaps akin to a 'hole in one' in golf. Nevertheless, it is worth knowing about some queen sacrifice themes that can occasionally be exploited in practical play.

Here is a very famous example played by Legall de Kermeur (1702–1792), whose other claim to fame was as the chess teacher of Philidor at the Café de la Régence in Paris. It occurs in the early stages of the game and is worth remembering.

Legall–St Brie, Paris 1750
1	e4	e5
2	Nf3	d6

These are the first moves of the opening known as 'Philidor's Defence', although it was first played and analysed long before the famous Frenchman's birth. Although solid enough, this defence has the disadvantage of restricting the development of Black's f8 bishop. This will have significant consequences.

3	Bc4	Bg4

One debatable principle of chess that is often quoted states that 'knights should be developed before bishops'. That is far from being a hard-and-fast principle, and 3...Nf6 would be poor here after 4 Ng5, when Black's only reasonable option is to waste a move playing 4...d5, having already played 2...d6. Black should probably play 3...Be7 and then Nf6 on the next move, when Ng5 can be answered by 0-0.

4	Nc3	g6?

Here, Monsieur Legall played a move so beautiful and surprising that the whole sequence has been known by his name ever since.

5	Nxe5!!	...

The white knight had seemingly been pinned against the queen by the bishop on g4, but Legall had seen further into the position. This is a fine example of an occasion when a strong chess player ignores the principles of the game to indulge in a piece of individual brilliance.

5	...	Bxd1

Black was not obliged to accept the sacrifice and could have continued with 5...Be6 6 Bxe6 fxe6 7 Nf3 when Black would have been only one pawn down. Legall's brilliant move would have been no less impressive for that.

6	Bxf7+	Ke7

The only move.

7   Nd5 mate

Black's king has been fatally encircled by White's three minor pieces.

Philidor's legacy

This example of a queen sacrifice occurs with surprising regularity – 'Philidor's Legacy' is named after Legall's distinguished protégé, although there is no extant example of him using it in play.

White, to play, appears to be in some trouble, being the exchange down (i.e. knight for rook). However White can force mate in four moves.

1   Nf7+   Kg8

1...Rxf7 allows 2 Qd8+, and it will be checkmate on the back rank in two more moves after the queen and rook have been interposed and captured. In similar positions in practical chess (rather than our composed example), it is often possible to make this Rxf7 capture without being mated on the back rank, so the defending player may be able to survive at the cost of the exchange.

2   Nh6+   ...

Double check means Black must move the king again.

2   ...   Kh8
3   Qg8+!!   ...

A stunning coup. Note how the knight on h6 defends the queen on g8, forcing Black's next move.

3   ...   Rxg8
4   Nf7 mate

A beautiful smothered mate. This attractive concept is almost as old as modern chess itself: it was first recorded in 1497 in the writings of the Spanish chess player and writer Luís Ramírez Lucena.

CONSTRUCTIVE DEFENCE

As in most games and sports, nobody likes to have to defend. This aversion is reflected in the titles of chess books, where the word 'attack' or 'attacking' heavily outnumbers 'defence' or 'defensive', and also in chess puzzles, where the objective is nearly always to win rather than to escape with an ingeniously achieved draw.

At the highest level of chess, draws outnumber decisive results, and a grandmaster's defensive technique is as important as his or her attacking prowess. Good defensive skills can turn likely losses into draws, or, even into wins, if opponents overplay their hand.

The main barrier to good defence is the psychological one. Players become depressed playing a difficult position and tend to make more mistakes. The best idea is to adopt some sort of plan – perhaps to put up a long and dogged resistance in the hope that your opponent goes wrong, or perhaps to throw all your remaining pieces at your opponent's king in the hope of a surprise checkmate.

If you are material down, remember that there are some endgames to aim for where the player with more material cannot win by force. If, for example, your opponent has an extra bishop, and both sides have some pawns, you should aim to exchange all the pawns off to reach the endgame of king and bishop versus king, which is a draw. The same applies to king and knight versus king – it is a draw. Even two knights and king are not enough to force checkmate against a bare king.

Below is an example of a combination leading to a forced draw.

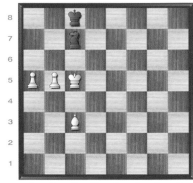

Black is to play. The position looks hopeless. White has two connected passed pawns and there is every prospect that at least one of the pawns will be promoted in due course, after which the win will be simple. However, armed with a little knowledge of the endgame, Black found a way to draw:

1   ...   Nxb5!

On a very surprising move, Black gives up the knight for one of the pawns, but White still has the a-pawn.

2   Kxb5   Kb8

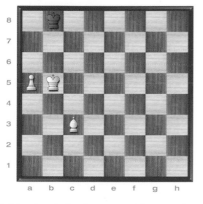

Black's king heads for the corner. The nice thing from Black's point of view is that there was no need to think. It is sufficient to know that a bishop accompanied by a rook pawn (i.e. a pawn on the a-file or h-file) cannot force a win where the defending king reaches the queening square, and where the colour of the queening square differs from the colour of the squares on which the bishop can move. In this position, White has a dark-squared bishop, and the queening square is white. Hence, White cannot win because the black king cannot be forced away from the corner.

3   Kb6   Ka8
4   a6   Kb8
5   Be5+   Ka8
6   Ka5   ...

White's king has to give ground, or it will be stalemate.

Left: Black is facing a pawn onslaught on the queenside and has been pushed on to the defensive. It is not a pleasant situation to be in, but there's no reason to panic. With careful play, Black can hold firm and perhaps even win if White overreaches.

Here is the key to this position. As long as Black plays correctly, keeping the king in front of or alongside White's remaining pawn, any attempt by White to drive it from the corner will result in stalemate. There is no way White can force the pawn through to its queening square. Thus:

6   ...   Ka7
7   Bd4+   Ka8
8   a7   Kb7
9   Kb5   Ka8

Any king move forward now brings about stalemate. The game must end in a draw.

Blocked pawns

As well as liquidating all the pawns, there are positions where having blocked pawns right across the board can also help the defender to escape with a draw.

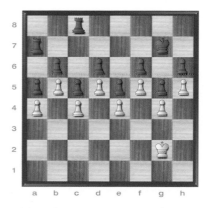

The position above is an extreme but instructive example: White is two rooks down on material. Normally such a deficit would be ruinous, but here White has a safe draw. White simply moves the king around ad infinitum and there is no way that the rooks can force a way through the locked pawn barrier. Notice that it might be different if Black had, say, a light-squared bishop or a knight instead of one of the rooks: such a piece could capture on b5 or d5 to make a breach in the wall and open a file for a rook.

continues on the next page ➡

Opposite bishop endgame

Another scenario that favours the defender is the 'opposite bishop endgame'. Where each side has a bishop (plus pawns), but the bishops move on different-coloured squares, it is often very difficult or impossible for the player with the advantage to force a win.

In this position, with White to play, Black's pawn is only two squares away from the queening square and White's king is a long way from the action. However, White can simply play 1 Bc5 or 1 Bh4. If Black advances the pawn, the bishop captures it and we are left with king and bishop versus king – which we already know is a draw. So long as White's bishop controls the f2 square, there is nothing Black can do to win the game.

Compare that with this position, which is the same except that Black's bishop is on g3 – so we have a same-colour bishop endgame. This is a simple win for Black. If White plays 1 Bc5, Black can use the black bishop to guide the pawn to promotion: 1...Bf4 2 Bg1 Be3 3 Bh2 f2, and the pawn promotes.

If the defending king is well placed, it is possible to defend an opposite-coloured bishop endgame against two (or even more) extra pawns.

White's defensive task is relatively simple. White needs to place the king on e3 and the bishop on f2 and then make moves with the bishop on the e1–h4 diagonal.

Perpetual check

Another useful weapon in the hand of a defender is 'perpetual check', when a player cannot escape from an infinite series of checks. When the player being repeatedly checked gets fed up trying to find a way out, it is normal for the players to agree a draw.

Here White, to play, is a pawn up and seems to have a reasonable chance of winning by promoting one of the far-advanced pawns on b6 and h6. Black's own pawn on e2 is well blockaded by the white king.

1	Rg7+	Kh8

Note that Black moves the king to a square where it will have no further legal moves. This is a clue that Black is hoping for a chance of stalemate.

2	b7?	...

This is a mistake after which Black can force a draw. White should play 2 Rg6, which leaves the king with a legal move (Kh7), thus avoiding stalemate tricks.

2	...	Rb1+!

Black gives up the remaining pawn and embarks on a series of checks.

3	Kxe2	Rb2+
4	Kd3	Rb3+
5	Kc4	Rb4+!

Black is happy to jettison the rook because, if it is taken, it is stalemate. White can run away with the king but Black will keep checking. In fact, the two players (both chess grandmasters) agreed a draw here because they could see that White could never escape the checks. There are a few tricks here that might ensnare a lesser player and it might be worth playing on to see if Black falls for a trick. For example:

6	Kd5	Rd4+??

A big mistake. 6...Rb5+ holds the draw.

7	Kc6	Rd6+

8	Kc7	Rc6+
9	Kb8	...

Now 9...Rc8+ would allow 10 bxc8Q+ to win, while after 9...Rxh6 10 Rd7, White will promote the b-pawn.

Opportunities to bale out for a draw quite frequently occur in the middlegame.

White, to play, is the exchange and a pawn down in material, but has a nice trick to escape with a draw.

1	Nf6+!	gxf6

Black has no choice – or the queen would be lost.

2	Qg4+	Kh8
3	Qh4+	Kg7
4	Qg4+	etc.

A CHESS MASTERPIECE

Playing through games played by masters can be an entertaining way of learning, and probably the most famous chess game of all time is Morphy versus the Duke of Brunswick. (Note that when referring to chess games, the name of the player with White is always placed first – often the two players' names are simply hyphenated.)

Paul Charles Morphy (1837–1884) was a true chess genius, and the best player in the world in the mid-19th century. He was born and lived all his life in New Orleans, but he made a spectacular chess tour of Europe in 1858 and carried all before him.

This game was not really a serious tournament encounter, being played in the Duke of Brunswick's box at the Paris Opera in 1858 during an operatic performance (of Bellini's *Norma*). The Duke (actually an ex-Duke, having been deposed in 1830) was no more than a keen amateur and played in consultation with Count Charles Isouard. They were no match for the world's best player, but the way in which Morphy won was spectacular.

| 1 | e4 | e5 |
| 2 | Nf3 | d6 |

2...d6 is the first move of Philidor's Defence.

| 3 | d4 | Bg4 |

This is definitely not one of the better moves in the position. The problem is that it causes Black to waste time after the coming capture on e5.

| 4 | dxe5 | ... |

Here, the two aristocrats must have noticed that, if 4...dxe5, White could play 5 Qxd8+ Kxd8 and, now that the knight on f3 is no longer pinned, White could simply play 6 Nxe5, winning a pawn. So Black is obliged to capture on f3 first, exchanging the valuable bishop for a knight and leaving the white squares vulnerable as well.

4	...	Bxf3
5	Qxf3	dxe5
6	Bc4	...

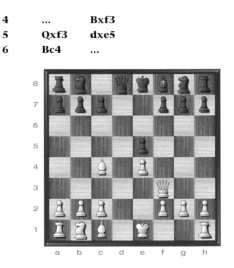

Morphy sets up the rather ungentlemanly threat of Qxf7 mate. Perhaps he was keen to get the game over with and listen to the opera. The most important thing to note here is that White now has two pieces in play whereas Black has none. The plan begun with 3...Bg4 has cost Black valuable time.

| 6 | ... | Nf6 |

Black should really have preferred 6...Qf6 here, as this move allows Morphy to play a double attack.

7   Qb3   ...

Paul Morphy has breached a couple of opening principles already. He has moved his queen out into the middle of the board (admittedly it was a more or less forced recapture) and he now moves the same piece a second time. However, he has created two powerful threats: one is to capture the unprotected b7 pawn and the other is to play Bxf7+, followed by Qe6 mate.

7   ...   Qe7

The two Black players realize they cannot defend both of the threats and play this move to deal with the more serious of the two. Another possibility would be to play a developing move such as 7...Bc5 and let the f7 pawn go after 8 Bxf7+ Kf8. However, Black's position is already critical, whatever he does.

8   Nc3   ...

An interesting choice of move by Morphy. He prefers

development of a piece to the mere capture of a pawn with 8 Qxb7, when Black can effect a queen exchange with 8...Qb4+. One suspects that Morphy was genuinely keen to get the game over with quickly rather than to opt for a queenless middlegame and long, drawn-out endgame. Another possibility would have been to play 8 Bxf7+ when 8...Qxf7 allows 9 Qxb7 and the capture of the rook on a8.

8   ...   c6

Black is more or less obliged to play this to defend the b7 pawn via the queen on e7. Another way to secure the b-pawn is to move it to b6 but, after 8...b6 9 Bg5 and now White is threatening Nd5, so Black has to play 9...c6 anyway. After 8...c6, everything is defended in Black's camp, but there are problems developing the pieces. The bishop is hemmed in on f8 so Black has difficulties in castling, while the knight on b8 cannot go to d7 because White has Qxb7.

9   Bg5   b5

Suddenly it looks like Black may have recovered some ground. Material is level and Black threatens to capture the bishop on c4 with the b5 pawn. The bishop seems to have little choice but to retreat to d3 or e2. But White – the best player in the world at the time – came up with something dramatic.

continues on the next page ➡

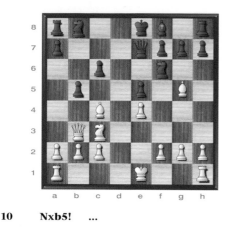

10   Nxb5!   ...

Morphy sacrifices his knight for two pawns. He has also seen that he will get a check with the bishop on the a4–e8 diagonal. Other significant plus-points in his favour are his lead in development (all his minor pieces are in play, whereas Black still has two on their original squares), and the fact that Black's queen is blocking the entry into the game of the f8 bishop. This, in its turn, means that Black is a long way from being able to castle kingside. And, once the pawns on b5 and c6 have disappeared, the king is unlikely to find refuge on the wide-open queenside.

10   ...   cxb5

If Black's objective had been to last as long as possible against Morphy, it might have been better to play 10...Qb4+ and exchange queens. But White would have emerged with two extra pawns after 11 Qxb4 Bxb4+ 12 c3 cxb5 13 Bxb5+ Nbd7 14 cxb4.

MORPHY'S OPPONENT

Karl, Duke of Brunswick (1804–1873) inherited the duchy when he was 11. He ruled until 1830 when he was ousted in favour of his brother Wilhelm. Thereafter he seems to have divided his time between Paris and Geneva (to which city he left his fortune).

---

11   Bxb5+   Nbd7

11...Kd8 is unlikely to last long, since the king is too exposed. White plays 12 0–0–0+ (castling with check) Kc7 13 Rd3, and White is threatening to double rook with 14 Rhd1 or simply play 14 Rc3+.

12   0–0–0   ...

White gets his king to safety and simultaneously sets up the strong threat of Rxd7, which, at the very least, wins the queen. One of the features of this game is the number of times that Morphy plays moves that have a dual purpose.

12   ...   Rd8

Black tries to defend the d7 knight. 12...0–0–0 was not an option for Black because 13 Ba6+ Kc7 14 Qb7 is checkmate. If 12...Qe6, White has 13 Bxf6!, and if 13...Qxb3, 14 Bxd7 is checkmate.

13   Rxd7!   ...

White sacrifices the exchange, which means that he will be a rook for two pawns down in material terms.

13   ...   Rxd7
14   Rd1   ...

White now has all his pieces (except for his king and pawns) pointed in the general direction of Black's king and queen. Although White is a rook down, Black has a rook and bishop tucked away doing nothing on the kingside. This position demonstrates how fundamentally important it is to have all your pieces doing something useful. Black now tries to break the pin on the knight and find a way out for his blocked bishop on f8 and allow a recapture with the knight on d7.

14   ...   Qe6
15   Bxd7+   Nxd7

Now for the denouement. One likes to imagine there was a drum roll coming up from the orchestra pit at this point...

16   Qb8+!!

A stunning queen sacrifice. Black cannot move his king or interpose a piece, but he can capture the queen.

16   ...   Nxb8
17   Rd8 mate

A dazzling display of attacking chess, almost from the beginning of the game to the end. In the final position, White is materially down to the tune of queen and knight for a couple of pawns, but checkmate is the object of the game.

continues on the next page ➲

Pins

The Morphy–Duke of Brunswick game was a good example of the power of the pin in chess.

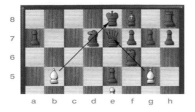

Many of Black's problems stemmed from his inability to shake off the vice-like grip exerted by Morphy's two bishops.

Bishops are often played to squares such as b5 and g5 in order to pin a knight against queen or king. A common way to try and break the pin is to move a pawn to attack the bishop and force it to move away or take the knight. Take or move away? This can often be a tricky decision. Here is an example in the Ruy López Opening, where the bishop moves away and gets into trouble.

| 1 | e4 | e5 | 3 | Bb5 | a6 |
| 2 | Nf3 | Nc6 | 4 | Ba4 | ... |

Typically, the bishop retreats to a4, but 4 Bxc6 is occasionally seen. It has been tried by players as distinguished as Bobby Fischer, so it must be quite a good move.

| 4 | ... | d6 |

A reasonable option for Black, although it brings about a pin of the knight against the black king (sometimes called a 'self-pin'). Now the best move is probably 5 c3,

although 5 0-0 and the delayed capture 5 Bxc6+ are also frequently played.

| 5 | d4 | ... |

This is a little risky, as we shall soon see.

| 5 | ... | b5 | 7 | Nxd4 | exd4 |
| 6 | Bb3 | Nxd4 | 8 | Qxd4? | ... |

A bad mistake. White should play the *intermezzo* move 8 Bd5 before recapturing.

| 8 | ... | c5! | 9 | Qd5 | ... |

At first sight, this position looks rather wonderful for White, who threatens mate in one on f7 and the undefended rook on a8. However, appearances can be deceptive and a nasty shock is in store.

| 9 | ... | Be6 |

With this single move, Black manages to defend against the threat of Qxf7 mate and also protect the rook on a8 (with the queen on d8). But it still looks promising for White after the next move.

| 10 | Qc6+ | Bd7 |
| 11 | Qd5 | ... |

White will have been expecting 11...Be6 when 12 Qc6+ Bd7 13 Qd5, etc, appears to lead to perpetual check. But Black is not interested in a draw.

| 11 | ... | c4! |

Calamity: White's bishop is trapped by the advancing pawn. The best White can do is get two pawns for the loss of the bishop. This opening trap is so old that it is known as the 'Noah's Ark' trap.

The bishop hits back

Sometimes, when the bishop is chased back in this way, it has the last laugh. This example comes from a match between the leading French and British players of the 1830s.

White, to play, wants to break the pin on the knight on f3. White is also a pawn down, having sacrificed a pawn to get an attack going in the opening.

1   g4?   ...

A very natural move, which works in some positions, but unfortunately not in this one.

1   ...   Nxg4+!

Black hits back with a knight sacrifice.

2   hxg4   Qxg4

Far from breaking the pin, White has actually made it worse with the introduction of the queen into the void that has now opened up in front of White's king. If White now moves the f3 knight, Black plays Qh4+ and then takes the queen with the bishop on h5.

| 3 | Be2 | Qf4+ | 5 | Bxf3 | f5! |
| 4 | Kh1 | Bxf3+ | | | |

Black's last move is a clever one. The intention is to play the rook up to f6, which will allow it to move to g6 or h6, where it will intensify the attack against the rather vulnerable white king.

| 6 | Bg2 | Rf6 | 8 | Bh3 | fxe4 |
| 7 | Qd3 | Rh6+ | | | |

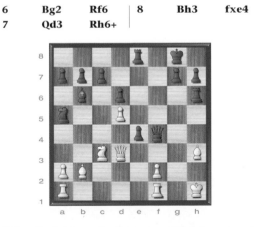

This effectively ends the game. White's queen is attacked and has to give up the defence of the h3 bishop. In fact, White played 9 Nxe4 Rxe4 10 Bc1, and Black played 10...Re3!, which soon led to mate.

KING SAFETY

One of the great attractions of openings such as the Two Knights' Defence and the Giuoco Piano is the chance to attack the king by way of the f2/f7 squares. We have already seen this in the Two Knights' Defence, where White attacks f7 as early as move four. A king can often defend itself by castling.

In the instance above, the threat to f7 is met by playing d5. But, in positions where the bishop has already moved away from its original square, it would be more usual for Black to proceed by simply castling.

For instance, in the Giuoco Piano:

1	e4	e5
2	Nf3	Nc6
3	Bc4	Bc5
4	d3	Nf6
5	Nc3	d6

Some beginners like to continue as follows:

6	Ng5?	0–0

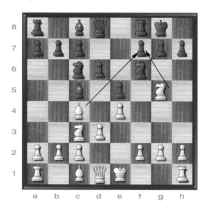

This is a mistaken plan by White. By castling, Black provokes two challengers for the f7 square. If White were to capture with either piece, Black would capture with the rook, e.g. 7 Nxf7 Rxf7 8 Bxf7+ Kxf7. White has given up two minor pieces (3 + 3) for a rook and pawn (5 + 1), so in material terms, it might seem like a fair deal, but in practice, the two pieces will be sorely missed by White as the middlegame struggle begins. Most strong chess players would prefer the two pieces. Of course, if White does not capture on f7, a move or two later Black will chase the knight away with h6 and the whole escapade will just be a waste of time.

Prevention is better than cure

Rather than suffering molestation from pieces that arrive on squares such as g5 or, in the case of White, g4, many players prefer to move a pawn to h6 or h3 to prevent the pieces from ever arriving on the square.

1	e4	e5	4	Nc3	d6
2	Nf3	Nc6	5	h3	...
3	Bc4	Bc5			

White plays h3 in order to prevent an awkward pin such as Bg4, and also to guard against a knight going to g4 and threatening the f2 square.

5   ...   Be6

Since the bishop can no longer go to g4, Black decides to use it to neutralize White's useful bishop on c4.

6   Bxe6   fxe6

Black has accepted the disadvantage of doubled pawns. In compensation, Black has a half-open f-file that may be useful for a later rook attack on White's king.

7	d3	Nf6	9	Qe2	0–0–0
8	Bg5	Qe7	10	0–0	...

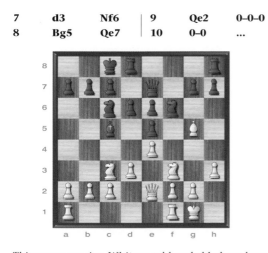

This seems unwise. White would probably have been safer to castle queenside. Now the white king is a potential target for Black's pieces, and the pawn on h3 can eventually be targeted by a pawn advance.

10   ...   h6

This is the prelude to Black's kingside attack. The pawn attacks the bishop and gets ready to support its colleague in the advance to g5.

11	Be3	Bxe3	13	Nb5	...
12	Qxe3	g5			

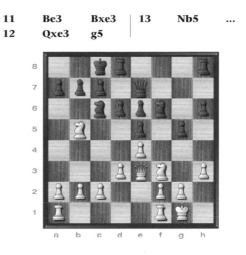

White tries to work up an attack on the opposite side of the board, but Black can counter this easily.

13	...	Kb8	14	a3	...

White is planning something similar to Black's advance on the kingside but it is too slow.

14   ...   g4

Black has completed the first stage of his attack. Whether White captures on g4 with the h3 pawn, or the knight moves away (allowing gxh3), Black has broken up the pawn structure in front of the king.

TRICKS AND TRAPS

Chess is full of tricks and traps, and there are many opening traps into which the unwary may fall. We have already seen the Noah's Ark trap (which costs White a bishop in one line of the Ruy López). Here is another, the 'Blackburne Shilling Gambit', named after British professional player Joseph Blackburne (1841–1924).

| 1 | e4 | e5 | | 3 | Bc4 | Nd4!? |
| 2 | Nf3 | Nc6 | | | | |

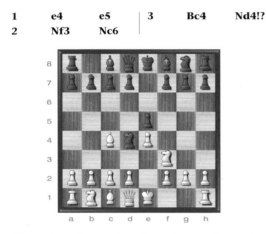

The exclamation mark and question mark are often used in chess notation to denote 'an interesting move'. Here, it really means 'cheeky move'. Play this against an experienced player and they will probably just laugh and say: 'I'm not falling for that!' Nevertheless, many inexperienced chess players continue to take the e5 pawn.

| 4 | Nxe5? | ... |

White's best moves are 4 0-0 or 4 Nxd4, gaining time because Black has moved the knight twice.

| 4 | ... | Qg5! |

Black's queen swings into action attacking the knight on e5 and the pawn on g2. However, White now has a tempting capture on f7, which is attacked by bishop and knight.

| 5 | Nxf7 | ... |

White could defend the double attack with 5 Ng4 but then Black has 5...d5!, attacking the bishop and also discovering a second attack on the knight. Note also that 5 Nf3 runs into 5...Qxg2, with a simultaneous attack on the rook on h1 and the knight on f3. Relatively best is 5 Bxf7+, but White will still have a problem with protecting or relocating the knight on e5 after the black king moves out of check.

| 5 | ... | Qxg2 |

Now White has to move the rook.

| 6 | Rf1 | ... |

If 6 Nxh8 Qxh1+ 7 Bf1 Qxe4+ 8 Be2 Nxc2+, then White will have to take the knight with his queen because 9 Kf1 Qh1 is checkmate.

| 6 | ... | Qxe4+ |

7	Be2	Nf3 mate

The bishop on e2 is pinned by the queen.

Middlegame traps

It is usually only beginners and elementary players who fall for opening traps, but even the most exalted player can occasionally fall for tricks in the middlegame. The following position arose in the first game of the most famous chess match of all time: the 1972 world championship between Boris Spassky and Bobby Fischer.

It was Bobby Fischer's turn as Black. The position is level and most pundits expected a draw to be agreed within the next few moves. Spassky's h-pawn is *en prise* (open to capture), but nobody expected Fischer to take it because it is a familiar trap.

1	...	Bxh2??

Sensation – Fischer takes the pawn. Even amateur players were surprised that the world championship challenger should place his bishop in jeopardy in this way.

2	g3	...

The bishop is now trapped. It is no use playing 2...Bg1 because White plays 3 Ke2 followed by 4 Kf1 and the king will gobble up the incarcerated bishop.

2	...	h5
3	Ke2	h4
4	Kf3	Ke7

Fischer may have overlooked the fact that after 4...h3 5 Kg4 Bg1 6 Kxh3 Bxf2, White can play 7 Bd2!, and the bishop is trapped on f2.

5	Kg2	hxg3
6	fxg3	...

Fischer was now forced to give up his bishop for the pawn on g3. He came close to drawing the game, but eventually lost.

continues on the next page ➔

'Poisoned pawns'

Many traps involve a piece grabbing a pawn on the opposite side of the board and then finding itself cut off behind enemy lines. Here is a classic example of a queen that pays the price for devouring the rather dramatically named 'poisoned pawn'.

Black, to play, is tempted by a pawn on b2, which has been left undefended after White's last move, Be3.

1 ... Qxb2?

The opportunity for the queen to take a pawn on b2 occurs in quite a number of different chess openings, so it is useful to study this closely. Sometimes the queen can get away with it and return with her spoils. This is not the case here.

2 Nb5! ...

This is an equally familiar trap. As well as cutting off couple of escape squares for the queen (a3 and c3), White also threatens Nc7+ forking rook and king.

2 ... Nxd3

Black could try 2...Nba6, but then 2 Bxc5 Bxc5 3 a3 Bd7 4 Qd2 and next move White plays 5 Rfb1 to trap the queen.

3 Qxd3 Bd7
4 Nc7+ and White won.

Sometimes players think they are setting a trap themselves, only to find that the opponent has sprung a much bigger one.

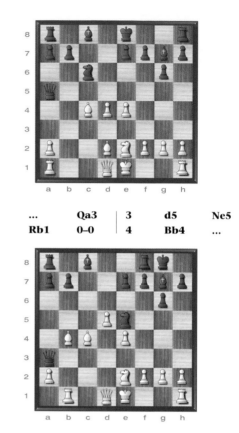

| 1 | ... | Qa3 | 3 | d5 | Ne5 |
| 2 | Rb1 | 0-0 | 4 | Bb4 | ... |

The queen appears to have no escape square. On the face of it, the best that Black can manage is to play 4...Nxc4 5 Bxa3 Nxa3, but that wouldn't save the game.

4 ... Qf3!!

A thunderbolt. If White takes the queen with 5 gxf3, there follows 5...Nxf3+ 6 Kf1 (forced) 6 Bh3 mate.

A picturesque checkmate.

When is a pin not a pin?
Here is an example of an opening trap in the 'Queen's Gambit Declined'.

| 1 | **d4** | **d5** | 2 | **c4** | **e6** |

This very respectable move is the beginning of the Queen's Gambit Declined. It is actually more common than the 'Queen's Gambit Accepted' (2...dxc4).

| 3 | **Nc3** | **Nf6** | 4 | **Bg5** | **Nbd7** |

The move 4...Be7 is seen more often but this is also good, and sets a trap.

| 5 | **cxd5** | ... |

OK, although 5 Nf3 and 5 e3 are more usual here.

| 5 | ... | **exd5** | 6 | **Nxd5??** | ... |

White falls headlong into the elephant trap. Like all the best chess traps, this move looks totally plausible. The knight on f6 is pinned against the queen by the bishop – so why not take the knight?

| 6 | ... | **Nxd5!** |

So Black takes it anyway.

| 7 | **Bxd8** | **Bb4+!** |

Now the penny drops. White is in check and the only legal way to counter it is to interpose the queen.

| 8 | **Qd2** | **Bxd2+** |
| 9 | **Kxd2** | **Kxd8** |

The carnage ends, and the body count shows that White has lost a knight for a pawn.

MAXIMIZE YOUR PIECE POWER: ROOKS

Rooks are the second-most powerful pieces in most chessboard situations, but lose much of their firepower if they are blocked in, particularly behind pawns. They operate best on open files (i.e. files with no pawns) and can be deadly on the seventh rank (the rank on which the opponent's pawns stand in the starting position).

Looking at it from the defence point of view, the best way to defend against a strong rook on an open file is to place one of your own rooks on the same file (as long as it is adequately defended, of course).

In this position, with White to move, the best and most natural move is to grab the open file with the rook.

| 1 | Rd1 | ... |

Black has no easy way to counter White's control of the d-file immediately, but with care it can be defended.

| 1 | ... | Kf8 |

It is not possible to prevent the invasion of the seventh rank with 1...Re7??, because this allows a back-rank mate with 2 Rd8+ Re8 3 Rxe8 mate.

| 2 | Rd7 | ... |

White is now threatening to take the pawn on c7.

| 2 | ... | Re7 |

Black challenges the white rook with his own. After 3 Rd8+ Re8, White is no further forward, having either to exchange rooks or retreat down the d-file. In either case the position is about equal.

If the rook retreats, Black can play the king to e8 and then place the rook on the d-file, as it will be defended by the king. If it were Black to move in the original position opposite, play could proceed thus:

| 1 | ... | Rd8 |

Of course, Black grabs the file while there is the chance.

| 2 | Kf1 | Rd2 | 3 | Rc1 | ... |

The only way to save the c2 pawn.

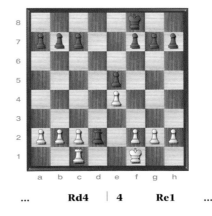

| 3 | ... | Rd4 | 4 | Re1 | ... |

Black could play 4...Rd2, but after 5 Re2, White could hold the balance in the same way as in the first example, when White was to move first.

A partnership of rooks

Two rooks working together on a file or rank can often be an irresistible fighting force.

White has already doubled rooks on the d-file and now seeks to build more pressure.

1 Rd7 Bb6

If Black plays 1...Rxd7 2 Rxd7 Bb6 3 Kf2, now the black rook is tied to the defence of the f7 pawn. White will soon be able to capture the b-pawn with impunity.

2 Kf2 g5
3 Ke2 Kf6

Not the best move, but things are very difficult for Black.

4 R1d6+ ...

4 Rf1+ followed by a capture on f7 is perhaps more effective. Such is the stranglehold exerted by the white rook on d7 that Black can do little but wait for the inevitable. The pawn on b7 is vulnerable, and defending it with the rook on d8 would mean completely surrendering the d-file – not an appealing prospect.

4 ... Kg7
5 Rd2 ...

White has not quite worked out the best way to win yet and plays a 'pass' move. White's advantage of the doubled rooks on the d-file (plus one of them on the seventh) offers the luxury of taking a bit more time.

5 ... Kg6 | **6 Rxb7 Rde8**

Black attacks the pawn on e3, but this is easy to defend.

7 Rd3 f5??

Black cracks under pressure. In practical play (from which this example is taken), it is often enough to establish a dominant position and create maximum problems for the opponent in order to win the game.

8 Rd6+ Rf6 | **9 Bf7+! ...**

White exploits the fact that the f6 rook is pinned, in order to play this fork.

9 ... Kg7
10 Bxe8+ 1–0 (i.e. Black resigned)

MAXIMIZE YOUR PIECE POWER: BISHOPS

Like rooks, bishops also work well when used in tandem and can benefit from plenty of scope along diagonals. As you will see, their effectiveness is not just limited to rapier-like pins and skewers; it can be far more subtle but just as deadly. Keep an eye on your pawn structure, for it can render a single bishop all but useless.

In this example, Black has two bishops against White's bishop and knight. Although in strict material terms, they add up to the same value, the two bishops often confer a practical advantage. In this position, Black also has the advantage that White's pawns are in five groups, compared to Black's three. In particular, the f4 pawn is vulnerable, although it is currently defended by a bishop.

| 1 | ... | Kg7 |

A good plan. Black has kept the king safely in the corner, but the queens and rooks have gone from the board and now is a sensible time to use it actively. It is unlikely to be in too much direct danger from White's bishop and knight.

| 2 | Nf2 | Kf6 |

The black king continues its march up the board, eyeing up the isolated pawn on f4. You may ask what's to stop White from using his king in similar fashion, scuttling across the board to shore up the defences. It sounds sensible enough, but as the game unfolds, keep your eye on Black's two bishops and observe the impenetrable barrier they create. One of them already controls d1 and d3 and stops the white king's approach.

| 3 | Nh3 | Kf5 |

Black's plan is to apply more pressure to the f4 pawn. White has seen this coming and drafted a white knight in to support it further. The snag with this defensive plan is that Black will chase the knight away with the move Kg4 in due course and then gobble up the pawn, so White has to try and block the threat of capture on f4.

| 4 | Ng5 | f6 |
| 5 | Nh7 | ... |

Here, White might have tried a little trick: 5 Ne6, and if 5...Kxe6 6 f5+ Kxf5 7 Bxh6, in the hope that the opposite-coloured bishop endgame might yield a draw.

| 5 | ... | Bg7 |

Now White's knight is virtually a prisoner in the corner. In order to get it out, White has to surrender the defence of the f4 pawn.

6	Bb4	Kxf4
7	Nf8	Kf5
8	Nd7	Ke4
9	Nc5+	Kf3
10	Ne6	Bh6
11	Bd6	f5

The game is not completely over, but it is easy to see that Black has a big advantage: an extra pawn, and control of the important squares on the f-file, which should allow Black's passed f-pawn to promote, or force White to surrender a piece. One important component in Black's advantage was the bishop on e2. Although it did not move, it helped to stop White's king from coming across to aid the defence of the kingside. In this position, Black's two bishops are completely preventing White's king from entering the game.

Say no to bad bishops

It is often important to think about the scope of your bishops before making a pawn move. As far as possible, it is best to arrange your pawns so that they are not all on the same colour square as one of your bishops. Also, when you are trying to restrict the scope of your opponent's bishop, try to occupy the same colour squares with pawns – but always make sure they are readily defensible.

In this position, with White to move, you should definitely not play 1 c4, because it further restricts the scope of the d3 bishop. White, though, does just that.

1   c4?   Kd6

Black could also fix the weakness with 1...c5, but this is more active.

2   b4   c5

Now things are quite difficult for White. The knight will be able to jump around and eventually come to d4, where it could be a nuisance. But the white bishop is hemmed in by its own pawns on c4 and e4.

3   b5   Nc6
4   g3   Nd4

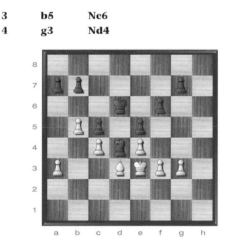

This is a classic example of what chess players call a 'good knight versus bad bishop' position. The move 1 c4 is what is sometimes referred to as a 'positional blunder'. It doesn't lose any material or allow mate (those are called 'tactical blunders'), but it leads White into a horribly passive position where the opponent is causing all the running. By thrusting forward the pawn White has trapped the white-squared bishop behind its own lines, effectively taking it out of the game. Going back to the position before 1 c4: had White played 1 Bc4+, White would have had a perfectly comfortable game, perhaps even a slightly better one.

MAXIMIZE YOUR PIECE POWER: KNIGHTS

Knights don't move along straight lines like bishops and rooks, but their power is also heavily influenced by the pawn structure. If a knight can be located in or near the enemy camp, on a square where it cannot be easily dislodged (particularly by pawns), it can be highly advantageous.

Here, both of Black's bishops are hemmed in, although at least the one on f8 is defending the g7 square. White's single bishop has more scope but it can be blocked effectively in due course. It is White's two knights that hold the key to what follows.

1   Nh5   ...

This was played in the hope that Black would make a weak move that would allow an entry somewhere.

1   ...   f6

This is what White hoped for, but it does block the scope of the white bishop. 1...Ne5 would have been better.

2   Nf4   ...

White spots an entry path into the enemy position via e6. Black will find it hard to evict the knight from there.

2   ...   Ra8?

The best defence was 2...Ne5!. After 3 Nxe5 dxe5, 4 Ne6? would be met by 4...Rxe6!. White cannot capture with the d-pawn without losing the queen. However, 4 Ne2 would still give White the edge because the knight is more valuable than either of Black's bishops.

3   Ne6   ...

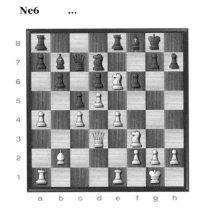

White now has the knight firmly embedded in the heart of the enemy position.

3   ...   Qb8
4   Nh4   Qc8
5   Nf5   ...

In this position, White's knights totally dominate the board. One threat is to capture on f8 and then on d6, which wins at least a pawn. But it might be better to initiate an assault on the king with Qg3. If Black now plays 5...Ne5, White plays 6 Bxe5 dxe5 7 Nxf8 and Black must play 7...Kxf8 because of the threat of 8 Ne7+ forking king and queen. But after 7...Kxf8 8 Nxd6 wins a pawn and the exchange.

Knights like holes

As a defender, it is very important not to let your opponent have 'holes' that knights can jump into. In the following game, Black allowed just that and soon both knights were jumping over White like monkeys.

1	...	f6?

This concedes the e6 square to the d4 knight.

2	b3	Rc8	4	Bxb6	Nxb6
3	Ne6+	Ke8	5	Nxg7+	...

White has netted a pawn.

5	...	Kf7	6	Nd4!	Nc6

If 6...Kxg7 7 Rxe7+ followed by 8 Rxb7 and White will be a comfortable two pawns up.

7	Ngf5	Rc7	9	Nbd6+	Kg6
8	Nb5	Rd7			

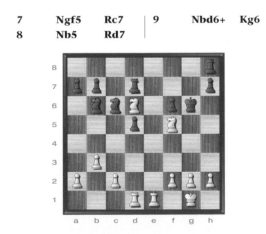

White can now try to weave a mating net.

10	Re3	h5	12	Ne4!	...
11	Rg3+	Kh7			

12	...	Rf8

Black would love to play 12...dxe4, but unfortunately there follows 13 Rxd7+ Nxd7 14 Rg7 mate.

13	Nc5	Rdf7	14	Ne6	...

The white knights relentlessly harass Black's rooks.

14	...	Rg8??

This is a blunder in a hopeless position. Even if Black defended with 14...Re8, White could play 15 Re1 and then play Nf4 to win the h5 pawn.

15	Rxg8	Kxg8
16	Nh6+	...

This move forked the king and rook. Black soon resigned. The key to White's success in this game was free access to squares such as e6 and d6.

EXCHANGING PIECES

Your opponent plays a move that allows you to exchange a piece of the same value or a pawn – what to do? Of course, every specific case must be judged on its merits. The fact is that sometimes it is a good idea to exchange (or 'trade' as North American players call it), and sometimes it isn't.

But there are still a few general principles that can help guide your decision. One is that, if you have a material advantage, you should seek to simplify the position by exchanging pieces (the obverse is, of course, true: if you are down in material, you tend to want to keep the pieces on). The process of exchanging pieces to realize a material advantage is sometimes referred to as 'liquidation'. The idea is that you remove most of the pieces from the board, and with them any prospect that your opponent could generate some sort of tactical come-back. You are effectively trying to transform as fast as possible from middlegame to endgame, which is when the benefit of a material advantage can usually be most easily realized.

As with all general principles, this one has to be treated with the utmost caution. Look, for example, at the following position.

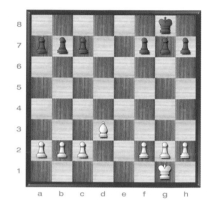

White, to play, is a whole bishop up. Does White want to swap off all the pawns? Absolutely not! If all the pawns are exchanged, checkmate cannot be achieved

with a solitary bishop. It might be satisfactory to swap off two or three pairs of pawns, but certainly not all of them. The basic strategy for White in this position is to use the extra bishop in conjunction with the king (it is high time it came out of hiding on g1) in order to outmanoeuvre the enemy king and win a pawn or two somewhere. Once White is sure of an extra, or a passed, pawn, then it may be time to swap all the other pawns off.

Above, White is a pawn up with very good prospects of winning. Does White want to exchange five pairs of pawns, leaving (say) the extra one on c4? The answer is a qualified 'yes'. If all the pawns except for the one on c4 were suddenly spirited from the board, the position would technically be a draw: the pawn could not be forced through. A good idea here would be to liquidate two pairs of pawns on the queenside, making the c4 pawn into a passed pawn. It can then be used as a decoy as the white king pursues the kingside pawns: a common strategy in king and pawn endgames.

Exchanging can be a useful ploy for reasons other than realizing a material advantage.

In the position bottom left, the material situation is level. But White, to play, has a much better placed king than Black. If the knight on d7 could be removed, then the white king could perhaps advance via c5 or e5, and capture the weak enemy pawns on b7 or f5. The answer is to try and exchange it.

1   Nc5!   ...

If Black accedes, the white king will be one square nearer the b7 pawn. Endgames with only kings and pawns tend to work in favour of the player with what previously had only been a slight edge. The second problem for Black is that, if the knight exchange is avoided, the white knight will take the b7 pawn with impunity. Strong players would consider this position as good as over for Black.

1   ...   Nxc5
2   Kxc5   Kd7
3   Kd5!

Crafty. Black had moved the king in order to defend the b7 pawn, but now the white king doubles back to go after the f5 pawn. It cannot be defended in time.

continues on the next page ➲

Far Left: White takes the bishop on d4, but if Black is able to recapture White's bishop then neither side has gained an advantage. The pieces cancel each other out, so the material balance remains the same.

More on exchanging pieces

A common dilemma occurs in positions where rooks can be exchanged along a file.

In this position, with White to play, 1 Rxd8+ would be quite a serious error. Black would recapture, and White would not be able to challenge Black's control of the d-file. The black rook would come to d2 and harass the white pawns, and White would be put on the defensive. Instead, White should simply hold ground and leave the situation on the d-file unresolved. The same applies if it is Black's move: 1...Rxd1+ would be a serious positional error.

Here, White to play can exchange on d7 with Nxd7, or on c7 with Rxc7. Neither of these exchanges of pieces is a good idea. This natural move, doubling the rooks on the d-file, gets Black back into the game.

1	Nxd7?	Rxd7
2	Rxb5+	Ka6
3	Rc5	Rfd8

Black will regain the pawn previously lost by taking on d4.

If we now go back to the diagram before 1 Nxd7, the thing to notice is how much stronger the knight is than the weak bishop on d7, hemmed in by its own pawns. That is a big clue to the exchange being undesirable. 1 Rxc7+? Kxc7, 2 d5 is better than the 1 Nxd7 variation, but Black may be able to survive. The best move seems to be to avoid exchanges altogether and play 1 d5! when White is threatening to play 2 d6 and force the black rook to exchange on c5, leaving the bishop in peril on the following move.

Another situation where a player may not want to exchange pieces is where the opponent is in a very cramped position. Space on the chessboard is often a very important factor – the more room your pieces have to manoeuvre, the better their scope. By allowing an opponent with a cramped position to exchange pieces, you are allowing the rest of their army more room to manoeuvre.

The diagram at the bottom of the previous page shows just such a situation. Black's bishops, queen and rooks are hopelessly hemmed in by their own pieces, while the knights, though a little more mobile, have few squares to which they can usefully move.

White, to play, can play 1 Nxe5? to exchange a pair of knights, but after 1...Nxe5, Black's cramped position has been partially relieved by the exchange. However, if White plays 1 Nd4!, then the pile-up of black pieces in a confined space leaves Black with problems. Black needs to defend against 2 Ne6 forking queen and rook. The only way to do this is by moving the knight on d7. 1...Nc5 is no good because the knight gets chased back from whence it came by 2 b4!, while 1...Nb8 is a terribly passive move.

In this position, with White to play, it is obvious that the knight is a vastly better piece than the very restricted bishop. However, despite this, it is time to liquidate White's advantage, because White can make the transition into a winning king and pawn endgame.

| 1 | Nxd7! | Kxd7 | 2 | Kf6 | ... |

White is a pawn down but is able to win two pawns right away. Black is now in *zugzwang*, i.e. the compulsion of having to make a move causes Black to give ground.

| 2 | ... | e5 |

The best try. If White were to capture with either the d4 or f4 pawn, Black would at least have a passed pawn which could race down the board.

3	Kxe5	Ke7
4	Kxf5	Kf7
5	Ke5	Ke7
6	f5	...

Zugzwang again. Now Black has to give ground with the black king.

6	...	Kd7
7	f6	Kd8
8	Kd6	...

Now White wins the two remaining black pawns and triumphs easily. This is an example of giving up one advantage (good knight versus bad bishop) in order to simplify the win.

MORE BASIC ENDGAMES

We have already seen how to give checkmate with a single queen or rook left on the chessboard (besides the king), but it is also possible to give checkmate with a pair of bishops or a bishop and knight, as shown by the following basic examples. It's worth taking time to learn the underlying techniques.

This checkmate needs a bit of practice, but an experienced player can probably work it out without having to memorize any particular line of play. With a rook or queen, the idea is to drive the king to the edge of the board, but with the two bishops it is necessary to drive the king into one of the four corner squares. The following shows one example of how to mate with two bishops. Of course, it is not the only way.

1	Bh3	Kf3	4	Kc4	Ke5
2	Kb2	Kf4	5	Bg3+	Ke4
3	Kc3	Ke4			

Black's king has managed to stay in the middle of the board, but, now that the white king has arrived, White starts squeezing Black towards the edge.

6	Bd6	Ke3
7	Bf5	Ke2
8	Kd4	Kf3
9	Kd3	...

It is instructive to see how White cuts off Black's flight path in both directions. This sort of technique takes a little practice, but it will come with time.

9	...	Kf2
10	Bg4	Kf1
11	Ke3	Ke1
12	Bg3+	...

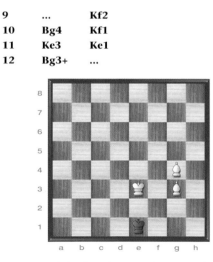

Once the defending king is driven to the edge of the board, the final phase of the process becomes relatively straightforward.

12	...	Kf1
13	Bh3+	Kg1
14	Kf3	Kh1
15	Bf4	...

15 Kf2?? would be a dreadful mistake – stalemate!

15	...	Kg1
16	Kg3	Kh1
17	Bg2+	Kg1
18	Be3 mate	

Mate with bishop and knight

Of the basic checkmates with minimal pieces and without pawns, the textbooks tell us that this is the most difficult. That is true, but it is not so difficult that it cannot be learned. Yes, the bad news is that you have to learn something more or less by heart – the good news is that it is only the last phase of the process that needs to be committed to memory.

The first part of the process is to get the black king to the edge of the board. This can be done with a bit of practice. Starting from the position above:

1	Nb3+	Kd5
2	Kb5	Ke5
3	Kc5	Kf5
4	Kd5	Kg5
5	Be2	Kf5
6	Nd4+	Kf6
7	Bd3	Ke7

8	Ke5	Kf7

At this point, there is something very important to know about this endgame. It is only possible to checkmate the king by driving it to a corner of the same colour as the bishop. Therefore, given that the bishop on d3 moves on white squares in this example, the place we are trying to drive the king to is either h1 or a8. This also influences the plan for the defence. Notice that, having been driven near the edge of the board, the black king now makes a move towards the h8 square – on which it can never be checkmated.

9	Ne6	Ke7
10	Ng5	Kf8
11	Kf6	Kg8

That is the end of the first phase. We have driven the black king to the edge of the board – but to the wrong corner. However, this is all part of the plan. First we drive the king to the wrong corner, and then to the right corner – and then to checkmate.

continues on next page ➔

Now for the final phase of the bishop and knight checkmate. The first thing to do is to study the above position for a while. Remember, we are trying to drive the black king from the wrong corner of the board (marked in red) towards one of the right corners (marked in green). The first part of the final assault is very logical. The black king must be kept out of the black square on h8. The white bishop will never be able to do that because it moves on white squares. So, by Holmesian deduction, it must be the white knight that does it from f7 or g6. So the right move has to be:

12   Nf7!   Kf8

That's it, we've forced the king out of the corner. Now the king must be shifted along the rank, towards execution on a8. So it must be deprived of the g8 square. This is easy.

13   Bh7   ...

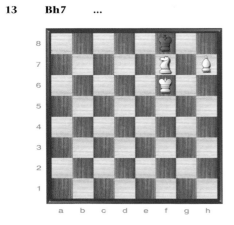

So far, so logical. The bishop move stops the king from returning to g8. Now the king must walk one square further along the rank, towards doom on a8.

13   ...   Ke8 | 14   Ne5   Kd8

Everything is going smoothly. Note that the king could have tried to double-back here with 14...Kf8, but then White plays 15 Nd7+, forcing 15...Ke8 16 Ke6, and then the king is moving in the right direction.

15   Ke6   Kc7

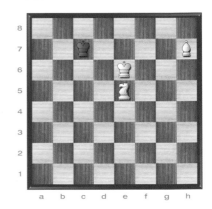

It is at around this point that it becomes necessary to learn a trick or two by heart. It seems as if the black king has escaped its escort at this point and is getting ready for a sprint to a1, another square on which it is immune from checkmate. But the knight and bishop now have a couple of precise moves that stop the king from getting out of the net.

16   Nd7!   Kc6 | 17   Bd3!   ...

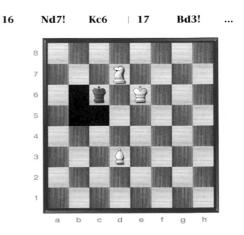

Two deft moves have thrown the net around the black king, stopping it coming to c5, b5 and b6. It can only go to b7 or c7.

| 17 | ... | Kc7 | 18 | Be4! | ... |

This pulls the net tighter. Black now has a choice of only c8 and d8.

| 18 | ... | Kc8 | 19 | Kd6 | Kd8 |

Obviously Black still hankers after one of the wrong-coloured corners, but this can easily be averted.

| 20 | Bg6! | ... |

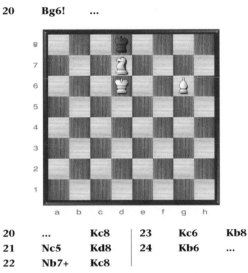

20	...	Kc8	23	Kc6	Kb8
21	Nc5	Kd8	24	Kb6	...
22	Nb7+	Kc8			

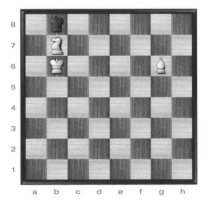

Now the black king is completely boxed in and it becomes quite easy to trap it.

| 24 | ... | Ka8 |

One last try for freedom. 24...Kc8, is rebuffed: 25 Bf5+ Kb8 26 Nc5 reaches the same position in the game.

| 25 | Nc5 | Kb8 |
| 26 | Bf5 | Ka8 |

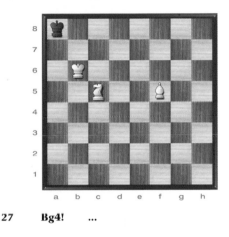

| 27 | Bg4! | ... |

Not 27 Na6?? stalemate. White 'loses' a move (i.e. plays a meaningless move) with the bishop so that Na6 can be played next move with check.

| 27 | ... | Kb8 | 29 | Bf3 mate |
| 28 | Na6+ | Ka8 | | |

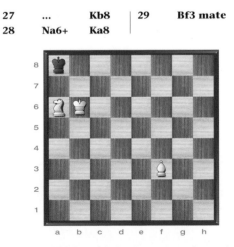

A very satisfying finish. To master the endgame, memorize the sequence between moves 12 to 18.

ENDGAMES: KINGS AND PAWNS

Pawns usually benefit from the support of the king when it comes to the final race through to promotion, but there are situations where they can look after themselves when the king is a long distance away. Usually it's a question of them supporting each other until the king can finally lend a hand.

Here, everything depends on whose turn it is to play. If it is White's turn, White wins, but if it is Black's turn, it is a draw (Black plays 1...Kc6, takes the c-pawn next move and takes the a-pawn soon afterwards). If it is White's turn...

1 a5! ...

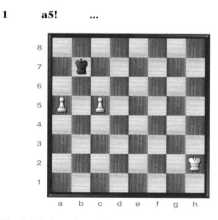

Black is left with a dilemma. If 1...Kc6 is played, then 2 a6! is played and if 1...Ka6 2 c6!. A capture on the following turn would allow the remaining pawn to promote. Let's look at one line:

1	...	Kc6
2	a6!	Kc7

That's a nice try by Black. Now if White plays 3 a7??, Black can play 3...Kb7, capture the pawn and have time to get back to gobble up the c-pawn. However, White doesn't have to move a pawn.

3	Kg3!	Kc6	6	Kd4	Kc7
4	Kf4	Kc7	7	Kd5	...
5	Ke5	Kc6			

Now the win is very easy. It is interesting to see how the two pawns somehow defend each other despite being separated by one file. It is, of course, much easier if the pawns are on adjoining files.

This time it doesn't matter whose turn it is. Black cannot take the a5 pawn because it is defended by the b4 pawn, and Black cannot take the b4 pawn because the a5 pawn could no longer be stopped. In order to win, White simply needs to bring the king over to support the pawns, wait for the king to take a step backwards and then guide one of the pawns home.

Above White is to play but is doomed. When the black king captures f4, having used the h5 pawn as a decoy, it will be two files nearer the kingside and win the race to capture the pawns on a3 and b4 before White captures the black pawns on a6 and b5.

1	Kh4	...

If White sits tight with 1 Kf3, Black plays 1...Kf5 2 Kg3 h4+ 3 Kf3 h3 4 Kg3 h2 and now White has to abandon the defence of the f3 pawn.

1	...	Kf5	3	Kg6	...
2	Kxh5	Kxf4			

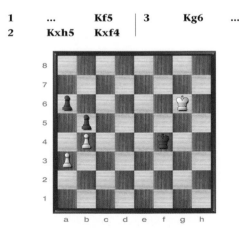

It still looks like White has a chance of doing some damage to the black pawns, but it is an illusion.

3	...	Ke4	6	Kd6	Kb3
4	Kf6	Kd4	7	Kc6	Kxa3
5	Ke6	Kc4	8	Kc5	Ka4!

Now White must abandon the defence of the b4 pawn.

Who dares, loses

This looks dead level, and indeed it is. But the player whose move it is must tread carefully. Let's try White...

1	Kd5??	...

The sub-heading was a big clue. Whoever tries to win the opposing player's pawn will lose this position.

1	...	Kf4!

It is our old friend/enemy, *zugzwang*, again. White must move the king, Black takes the e4 pawn, and duly wins. If it had been Black to move, 1...Kf4?? 2 Kd5!, Black would have to abandon the defence of the e5 pawn and lose.

WINNING A WON POSITION

Chess players are very similar to fishermen in one respect: they are always bemoaning the 'one that got away'. The sentence usually starts with: 'I had a won position but...' – and then follows any one of a vast number of excuses for letting the win slip through their fingers. Complacency is the chess player's worst enemy.

An important general principle and one you can trust absolutely, despite the title of this section, is that there is no such thing in chess as a 'won position'. It's not over until the king has been checkmated. Disaster can strike at any time in the shape of a blunder or a stalemate. Perhaps it is reasonable to say that you have a 'winning position': the present tense implies that there is still some work to do to win. In contrast, the past participle 'won' somehow implies that the work has already been done. Therein lies the fatal delusion.

When your opponent is down to a king, or a few remaining pieces have no legal moves, remind yourself about the possibility of stalemate. It may be closer than you think.

Black is cruising to victory, but notices that White might be threatening perpetual check with Qc5+ etc, so plays...

1   ...   d3??

It must be admitted that it is very natural to play this move, which defends against queen checks on the f1–6a diagonal, but it needlessly squanders a win. A much better alternative would have been 1...Qe1+ 2 Kh2 Qxa5, winning another pawn. After that, Black can move the queen to b6 to defend all the pawns, and then push either the a-pawn or the d-pawn.

2   Qf2!!

A bolt from the blue. If Black plays 2...Qxf2, it is stalemate. However, any other move would cost the queen. So it has to be 2...Qxf2 and the game is drawn. The mistake here was down to Black not bearing in mind the reduced number of pieces that White had at his disposal, and thus not being extra wary about this sort of stalemate trick.

In this position, White has to move the knight on c4. It is a very difficult position for White since Black has a number of advantages. For one thing, the dark-squared bishop on g7 is vastly superior to White's weak bishop on b1. There is the threat of Nf4 in the air (White couldn't take it because of the undefended queen on e2), and there is the possibility of the black queen coming to a3.

1   Na5?   ...

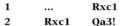

The only move was 1 Nd2, although after 1...Rxc1 2 Rxc1 Nf4 3 Qe1 Nd5 4 Nf1 b4, the black knight will settle on c3 and harass the white position. After the white move, Black has to think about the various advantages of this position and see if they can be translated into a striking chance.

1   ...   Rxc1
2   Rxc1   Qa3!

Black spots a pleasant double attack on the rook and the knight.

3   Qe1   Bb2!

Black exploits the power of the bishop on the long diagonal. Suddenly, White finds that the rook cannot move. If it goes forward up the c-file, Black plays Qxa5!, exploiting the possibility of a back-rank mate with the rook if White captures on a5. If White plays 4 Rd1, Black still plays 4...Qxa5. Let's look at that position.

If White plays 5 Qxa5, the reply is 5...Rxd1+ and mate next move. If 5 Rxd8+, then Black simply replies 5...Qxd8 and remains a knight up on material. So a piece has been lost. After the previous diagram, the game continued:

4   Nc4   bxc4
5   Rxc4   ...

Black has a 'won position'. At such moments, it is all too easy to relax and make a mess of things. The important things to do are: to maintain the same level of concentration as if there were still everything to play for; and to try to find ways to simplify the position so that the win becomes trivial.

5   ...   Qa5!

Black once again exploits the fact that the back rank is exposed to a rook mate. The queen is untouchable.

6	Qf1	Qd5	10	Qe1	Ne4
7	Bc2	Nc5	11	Ra4	Nc3
8	g3	a5	12	Ra3	Be7
9	Qb1	Bf6			

Black will soon be a rook up in material. White resigned.

More winning techniques

The cliché 'and the rest is just a matter of technique' can be found in many chess game annotations, at the point where the writer thinks that the game is as good as won, and that there is no need to make detailed comments about the remaining moves. However, it is not very helpful to readers who have yet to acquire the necessary technique – which simply means 'playing a lot of good moves in succession'. This takes practice and concentration. One problem with chess is that you can play 99 excellent moves, but, if the 100th one is bad, it can cost you the game. The important thing is to maintain even concentration throughout the game, neither relaxing at any point (and playing the first thing that comes into your head), nor agonizing excessively over one move.

Overconfidence is a problem when you have a very good position. You think to yourself: 'I ought to be able to win this' and thereby start to put extra pressure on yourself. Here is an example.

This is undoubtedly a very good position for White, whose turn it is. White is a pawn up, with the opportunity to take a second one (on h7), but Black's king position is rather exposed. However, there is still a lot of material on the board, and some of Black's pieces have attacking possibilities.

1	Bxb7	...

This doesn't compromise White's position, but there were two better moves: 1 Rc3!, which attacks the queen and removes the rook from a square where it might get pinned against the king, and 1 Bxh7, which would have been the next move after 1 Rc3 anyway.

1	...	Qxb7
2	Qe6+	Kf8
3	Nb6?	...

Again, not a total disaster, but far from the best move. 3 Nd4 is much better, with a view to bringing more force to bear against the black king in due course. Notice that, if Black tries to discover an attack on the white queen with, for example, 3...Bxa3, White breaks through the defences with 4 Rxf6+! gxf6 5 Qxf6+ Qf7 6 Qh8+ Qg8 7 Rf3+ Ke7 8 Qf6+ Kd7 9 Nb6+, and White will soon checkmate the black king.

3	...	Rad8

White's advantage has diminished a little. White can no longer deploy the knight on b3 to d4 as before, but White is still a pawn up and generally better placed than Black.

4	Nc4	Qa7

Black pins the rook on e3 against the white king.

5   Ne5??   ...

White plays a rook sacrifice. In some ways it is very clever, but, objectively, it is a complete disaster because Black does not have to accept the sacrifice. White should have been content with the mundane 5 Kh1! which breaks the pin on the rook. After that, White could have claimed an advantage, but, after the move played, is struggling.

5   ...   Bd6!

If Black had accepted the rook sacrifice, Black would have lost: 5...Qxe3+?? 6 Kh1 and now the only way to deal with the threat of Qf7 mate would have been to capture the knight, leaving White with a queen and pawn for rook and knight – and a two-point material advantage.

6   Rxf6+?

White misses a chance of salvation. 6 Ng6+! secures perpetual check after 6...hxg6 7 Rxf6+ gxf6 8 Qxf6+ Kh8 9 Qh6+ and Black can never escape the series of queen checks.

6   ...   gxf6

7   Qxf6+   Kg8
8   Ng4   Bf8!

9   Kh1??   ...

A blunder. White could play 9 Qg5+ Kh8 10 Ne5, etc, and would still be in the game, though struggling.

9   ...   Rd1+

Black concludes the game with a back rank mate.

A CHESS BRILLIANCY

All chess players find chess brilliancies irresistible to read about in books and magazines. The following game is an attractive example of a queen sacrifice followed by a king hunt across the board. It is an unusual example of the power that bishops and knights can wield when attacking an exposed king.

Genuine brilliancies seldom occur in practical chess, and most professional players seek to play the percentages rather than deliberately striving for something aesthetically pleasing.

This game was played in London in 1912. White was Edward Lasker (1885–1981, but not to be confused with the then world champion Emanuel Lasker). Lasker became a US citizen and was a fine player, writer and teacher of the game. Black in this game was Sir George Thomas (1881–1972), an English baronet who won the British Chess Championship in 1923 and 1924. He was even more distinguished as a badminton player, winning the All-England Championships four times, and giving his name to one of the sport's most prestigious trophies.

	Lasker	Thomas
1	d4	f5

This is the first move of the Dutch Defence, which is a bold, counter-attacking defence for Black.

| 2 | e4 | ... |

Offering a pawn sacrifice. This is known as the Staunton Gambit, as it was used by the great English player Howard Staunton as early as 1847.

2	...	fxe4
3	Nc3	Nf6
4	Bg5	e6

These days most players prefer 4...Nc6 in this position. Now White can recapture the pawn.

5	Nxe4	Be7
6	Bxf6	Bxf6
7	Nf3	0–0

| 8 | Bd3 | b6 |

A reasonably balanced position. However, Black's kingside set-up is somewhat lacking in defenders, and White's group of minor pieces are pointing in the general direction of the h7 square.

| 9 | Ne5 | ... |

This leads to a brilliant victory, but objectively, is not the best move. Black should now simply play 9...Bxe5 to remove the attacking knight from the board. After 10 dxe5 Nc6, White has the menacing 11 Qh5, but then 11...Rf5 seems to be perfectly safe for Black. This a further warning against trying to win brilliantly. For every masterpiece you find in an anthology of chess brilliancies, there are probably another thousand flawed concepts that brought only ignominious defeat.

| 9 | ... | Bb7? |
| 10 | Qh5 | Qe7? |

This was Black's chance to stay in the game. 10...Bxe5 seems to keep Black's ship afloat, despite the gale-force wind that seems to be blowing around the h7 square. If now 11 Ng5 h6!, then White has no *coup de grace*.

One imagines Black carefully calculated various White tries in this position. 11 Nxf6+ is quite good, but after 11...gxf6 there is nothing decisive. 11 Ng5 is answered by 11...g6, and Black's position holds. White could even try 11 Nd6, but again 11...g6 12 Nxg6 Qxd6 13 Nxf8 Kxf8 seems reasonably safe for Black. However, Lasker found something unexpected:

11   Qxh7+!! ...

In calculating all the candidate moves by the minor pieces, it was easy for Black to overlook this more drastic blow. Which of us in his shoes would have expected White to unleash such a fiendish sacrifice?

11   ...   Kxh7
12   Nxf6+   ...

Black is in double check, so must move his king. If he plays to h8, the end comes instantly – 13 Ng6 mate. There is only one other move.

12   ...   Kh6
13   Neg4+   Kg5
14   h4+   Kf4
15   g3+   Kf3

The black king has been forced further and further away from the safety of his own camp.

16   Be2+   ...

Not the quickest way to victory (16 0-0 and 16 Kf1 both set up unstoppable mate on the next move with 17 Nh2), but it is perhaps more aesthetically pleasing.

16   ...   Kg2
17   Rh2+   Kg1
18   Kd2 mate

A minor blemish: it would surely have been more piquant to play 18 0-0-0 mate.

RUBINSTEIN'S IMMORTAL GAME

A kiba Rubinstein (1882–1961) never became world chess champion but is universally acknowledged to be one of the finest players who failed to do so. For a number of years between 1907 and 1912, Rubinstein had the best record of any chess player in the world, including Emanuel Lasker. Here is his most famous game.

It is largely unremarkable for the first 19 moves or so, but then explodes into life with a veritable cascade of sacrifices. Rubinstein's opponent in this game, Gersz Rotlewi (1889–1920) was also Polish and a very promising player himself, but, sadly, he died young.

	Rotlewi	Rubinstein
1	d4	d5
2	Nf3	e6
3	e3	c5
4	c4	...

White starts with a Colle Opening, but now chooses to transpose into a Queen's Gambit. It is often possible to transpose from one opening system into another, and chess players often try to keep their opponents guessing in this way.

4	...	Nc6
5	Nc3	Nf6

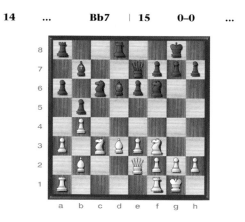

The position is perfectly symmetrical. Notice that neither side has been in a hurry to exchange the pawns in the centre, but now White decides it is time to do so.

6	dxc5	Bxc5	9	Bb2	0–0
7	a3	a6	10	Qd2	...
8	b4	Bd6			

White has not made any tactical mistakes so far, but at the same time one cannot help feeling that he has played a little passively. It is usual for White to try and maintain the initiative in the opening and he has not done so here. Rather than 10 Qd2, White should perhaps play 10 Bd3 and then castle kingside.

10	...	Qe7	13	Bd3	Rd8
11	Bd3	dxc4	14	Qe2	...
12	Bxc4	b5			

White realizes that his Qd2 move was wrong (because of the potential danger coming from the rook on d8) and now relocates the queen to e2. But, in making one unnecessary move with his queen, he has lost time.

14	...	Bb7	15	0–0	...

Note that the position is almost symmetrical again. However, somewhere along the line, Black has got in the useful developing move Rd8, and it is also his move now (whereas it was White's in the original position). Chess players talk about gaining a tempo when they steal a march on the opponent in this way; so here, Black has the advantage of two extra tempi.

15	...	Ne5	18	e4	Rac8
16	Nxe5	Bxe5	19	e5?	...
17	f4	Bc7			

White finally pushes his luck too far. He should play 19 Kh1 or 19 Rac

19   ...   Bb6+ | 20   Kh1   Ng4!

Black unleashes his first threat, which is Qh4 and mate on h2.

21   Be4   ...

21 Qxg4 Rxd3, and Black threatens the knight on c3 and also Rd2, attacking the bishop and the g2 pawn.

21   ...   Qh4
22   g3   ...

This defends the mate threat, but leads to perhaps the greatest sacrificial orgy in chess history.

22   ...   Rxc3!!
23   gxh4   ...

23 Bxb7 Rxg3! 24 Rf3 Rxf3 25 Bxf3 Nf2+ 26 Kg1 Ne4+ wins for Black.

Black has given up his queen for a knight and now has no fewer than three pieces *en prise*. His solution to this problem... is to put a fourth piece *en prise*!

23   ...   Rd2!!

Astounding. White has the pick of four captures, but all of them lead to ruin. For example, 24 Qxg4 Bxe4+ will lose White a rook and a queen to stop mate.

24   Qxd2   Bxe4+
25   Qg2   Rh3!!

At this point, White resigned. There is nothing to be done about the threat of Rxh2 mate. For example, 26 Bd4 Rxh2+ 27 Kg1 Rxg2+ 28 Kh1 Rg3+ 29 Rf3 Bxf3 mate. It's not hard to understand why many consider this game to be Rubinstein's finest moment, nor to appreciate why grandmasters even today still study his games for insight and inspiration. A measure of his greatness is given by the lines named after him in the Sicilian, French and Nimzo-Indian defences.

CHAMPIONS IN ACTION

If you want to improve your chess, there are few better ways of doing so than learning from the masters. The following pages offer examples from play of all the world chess champions. It is instructive to note that each champion has an individual style of play. We begin with the first official world champion, Wilhelm Steinitz.

Wilhelm Steinitz: 1st World Champion (1886–1894)

The first player to be recognized as world champion was Wilhelm Steinitz. Early on, his chess style was mostly based on gambits and tactical play, but he gradually became more positional. This game was played in 1895 at a big tournament in Hastings, UK, against Kurt von Bardeleben, another strong master of that era.

Steinitz	von Bardeleben
1 d5!!	cxd5
2 Nd4	...

The pawn sacrifice 1 d5 clears the square for the knight, which exerts strong pressure on Black's position.

2	...	Kf7	4	Qg4	g6
3	Ne6	Rhc8	5	Ng5+	Ke8

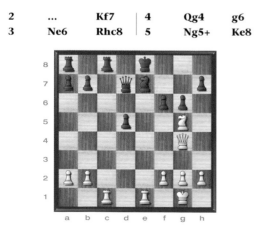

Black seems to have everything defended, but he is in for a shock.

6	Rxe7+!!	Kf8!?

If 6...Qxe7 7 Rxc8+ wins and if 6...Kxe7 7 Re1+ Kd6 8 Qb4+ Rc5 9 Re6+ soon wins.

7	Rf7+!	...

White cannot capture the queen because it would allow a back-rank mate with Rxc1.

7	...	Kg8!	8	Rg7+!	...

The rook is immune to capture from the king because it would allow the queen to be captured with check.

8	...	Kh8	9	Rxh7+!	...

At this point, Steinitz announced to his opponent that he would force checkmate in 11 moves, starting with this one. But von Bardeleben put on his coat and left the tournament room without saying a word. Here is what Steinitz apparently had in mind: 9...Kg8 10 Rg7+ Kh8 11 Qh4+! Kxg7 12 Qh7+ Kf8 13 Qh8+ Ke7 14 Qg7+ Ke8 15 Qg8+ Ke7 16 Qf7+ Kd8 17 Qf8+ Qe8 18 Nf7+ Kd7 19 Qd6 mate.

Emanuel Lasker:
2nd World Champion (1894–1921)

Emanuel Lasker was an academic mathematician and philosopher, and dabbled in other games besides chess, so it was all the more remarkable that he should have managed to dominate chess for so long. His pragmatic approach, despite occasional long breaks from the game, demonstrated a superiority lasting many years.

Lasker was 66 when the following was played in a tournament in Moscow in 1935 – his opponent, Vasja Pirc (1907–1980) was only 28. Lasker was one of the few top players who maintained his chess strength well into his old age.

	Lasker	Pirc
1	e4	c5
2	Nf3	Nc6
3	d4	cxd4
4	Nxd4	Nf6
5	Nc3	d6
6	Be2	e6
7	0–0	a6
8	Be3	Qc7
9	f4	Na5

A fairly standard set-up in the Sicilian Defence. Black's last move intends Nc4, to harass the bishop on e3 and the pawn on b2. However, it wastes a lot of time when Black should really be ensuring the safety of his king.

10	f5	Nc4
11	Bxc4	Qxc4
12	fxe6	fxe6

| 13 | Rxf6! | ... |

Lasker sacrifices the exchange (rook for knight) in order to facilitate his attack on the king.

| 13 | ... | gxf6 | 14 | Qh5+ | Kd8 |

14...Ke7 keeps the queen from entering at f7, but loses to 15 Nf5+! exf5 16 Nd5+ Kd8 17 Bb6+ and White soon mates.

| 15 | Qf7 | ... |

If Black tries to save the rook with 15...Be7, White plays 16 Nf5 and the knight cannot be taken because the queen would be lost.

| 15 | ... | Bd7 | 17 | Qxh8 | Bh6 |
| 16 | Qxf6+ | Kc7 |

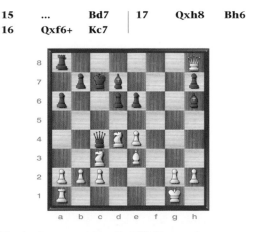

The body count shows that White now has an extra knight and pawn, so Black tries this ingenious trick.

continues on the next page ➔

18   Nxe6+!   ...

Much better than 18 Qxa8 Bxe3+ 19 Kh1 Bxd4 when Black is still in the game.

18	...	Qxe6
19	Qxa8	Bxe3+
20	Kh1	1–0

This game does not end in checkmate, but White has done just enough to ensure that his preponderance of material will win the game.

José Raúl Capablanca:
3rd World Champion (1921–1927)

The Cuban player Capablanca was a child prodigy with a wonderful natural talent for the game. He later turned into something of a playboy, and failed to work hard at the game. But, despite this, he remained one of the best players during the interwar years. His style was generally smooth and positional. Here is an unusual finish, from St Petersburg in 1914, against the great theoretician Aron Nimzowitsch.

Black is a pawn down, but his two rooks have strong pressure against White's queenside.

	Nimzowitsch	Capablanca
1	...	Rb4!

Threatening 2...Bd4, pinning the queen against the king.

| 2 | Qg5 | Bd4+ |
| 3 | Kh1 | Rab8 |

Now Black is putting heavy pressure on the b2 pawn and also threatening the knight on c3. Note also how difficult it is to move the knight to safety. Something has to give. White tries a drastic measure to relieve the pressure.

4	Rxd4	Qxd4
5	Rd1	Qc4
6	h4	Rxb2
7	Qd2	Qc5

Black is now winning comfortably. There is no hurry to finish White off.

8	Re1	Qh5	10	Kg1	Qh5
9	Ra1	Qxh4+	11	a5	...

Nimzowitsch would have been fully aware that the plan of advancing the a-pawn was a forlorn hope. Garry Kasparov described this idea as 'a little joke'.

11	...	Ra8	14	a7	Qc5
12	a6	Qc5+	15	e5	Qxe5
13	Kh1	Qc4	16	Ra4	Qh5+

| 17 | Kg1 | Qc5+ |
| 18 | Kh2 | d5 |

Black is being ultra-cautious: he doesn't want the knight to come to e4 after 18...Rxa7 19 Rxa7 Qxa7.

| 19 | Rh4 | Rxa7 |
| 20 | Nd1 | ... |

And White resigned at last. 20...Qxc2 forces an exchange of queens, and after that it is simple.

Alexander Alekhine: 4th World Champion (1927–1935, 1937–1946)

Alekhine still held the world championship title at his death in 1946, although he had not played a title match since regaining his title from the Dutchman Max Euwe in 1937. He was a forceful attacking player who devoted himself to chess.

Here, he plays White against the leading British player Hugh Alexander (1909–1974).

White has pressure along the long diagonal, but needs to get his kingside pieces into the attack.

| | Alekhine | Alexander |
| 1 | e4! | Nxe4 |

A tricky defence.

| 2 | Qc1 | ... |

2 Bxg7? is not so good because of 2...Nxg5 3 Bxf8 Nxh3+ 4 Kg2 Rxf8 5 Kxh3 Nf6, and Black will win the d-pawn and have a bishop and two pawns for the rook.

| 2 | ... | Nef6 |
| 3 | Bxf5! | ... |

If 3...gxf5 then 4 Nxf5, Black's queen is in a pickle. If 4...Qg6, 5 Ne7! wins it, while if 4...Qf7, 5 Nh6+ wins it. If 4...Qh8, there follows 5 Nh6! Kg7 6 Qg5 mate.

| 3 | ... | Kh8 |
| 4 | Be6 | ... |

Now that the f5 pawn has gone, the white bishop can join in the attack.

4	...	Ba6
5	Rfe1	Ne5
6	f4!	Nd3
7	Rxd3	Bxd3
8	g4	1–0

There is nothing to be done about the g-pawn going to g5, winning the knight and probably more besides.

continues on the next page ➜

Max Euwe: 5th World Champion (1935–1937)

Dutch schoolmaster and academic Max Euwe held the world title for only two years. Yet his achievement in winning it – he was an amateur player – remains one of the great fairytale success stories in chess.

This was the 26th game of Euwe's title-winning match against Alekhine in 1935. It was nicknamed 'the pearl of Zandvoort', after the town in which it was played.

White has two powerful pawns for the exchange.

	Euwe	Alekhine
1	Qe5	Qxe5
2	fxe5	...

Now the two pawns are connected passed pawns.

2	...	Rf5
3	Re1	...

It might have been better to play 3 Rg5 to exchange a pair of rooks.

3	...	h6
4	Nd8	Rf2
5	e6	Rd2
6	Nc6	Re8
7	e7	b5
8	Nd8	Kg7
9	Nb7	Kf6
10	Re6+	Kg5
11	Nd6	Rxe7
12	Ne4+	1–0

A classic example of the power of passed pawns.

Mikhail Botvinnik: 6th World Champion (1948–1957, 1958–1960, 1961–1963)

After Alekhine's death, a tournament was held to fill the vacancy at the top of chess. Mikhail Botvinnik won the five-player competition and became the first of several Soviet world champions. He lost his title twice, to Smyslov and Tal, but, on both occasions, was able to exploit an automatic rematch provision in the rules in order to regain it within 12 months. He was a hard-working player who prepared assiduously for every game he played and was a genius at identifying and exploiting tiny flaws in his closest rivals' games.

In this game he had White against the former world champion Capablanca in a tournament in the Netherlands, in 1938.

White is a pawn down but has powerful pressure against the king with a forceful pin of the knight.

	Botvinnik	Capablanca
1	Ba3!!	...

A superb sacrifice, deflecting the queen away from the defence of the king.

1	...	Qxa3
2	Nh5+!!	...

A second hammer blow. White has worked out he only needs the queen and e6 pawn to finish off the black king.

2	...	gxh5
3	Qg5+	Kf8

| 4 | Qxf6+ | Kg8 |

If instead the king goes to e8, White plays 5 Qf7+ Kd8 6 Qd7 mate.

| 5 | e7 | ... |

White finally stops checking. It is Black's turn to check the white king, but White has calculated that he can eventually escape perpetual check.

5	...	Qc1+	8	Kh4	Qe4+
6	Kf2	Qc2+	9	Kxh5	Qe2+
7	Kg3	Qd3+			

If Black plays 9...Qg6+ 10 Qxg6+ hxg6+ 11 Kxg6, then Black cannot prevent the pawn from promoting and giving checkmate.

| 10 | Kh4 | Qe4+ | 12 | Kh5 | 1-0 |
| 11 | g4 | Qe1+ | | | |

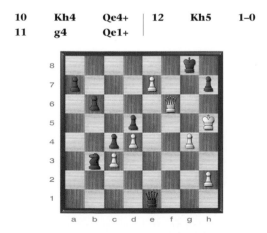

Black cannot prevent the promotion of the pawn (after 12...h6 13 Qg6+ Kh8 14 e8Q+). So he resigned.

Vasily Smyslov: 6th World Champion (1957–1958)

Smyslov had only a brief reign as world champion, but remains one of the great stylists of the chess world. He is famous for his immaculate endgame play. Here, he defeats Mikhail Botvinnik in the 17th match game of the 1957 world championship.

The game was adjourned for the day after five hours' play. Overnight, Botvinnik realized that he could be doing worse here and offered a draw. But Smyslov sensed he could be winning and turned him down.

| | Botvinnik | Smyslov |
| 1 | ... | Kh6 |

This was the 'sealed move'. In other words, Smyslov had not played it on the board, but had written it on a piece of paper and sealed it in an envelope, handing it over to the match official for safe-keeping. By doing this, Botvinnik would not be handed the unfair advantage of extra time in which to analyse the actual position on the board until the resumption.

Black's plan is to win the h-pawn. White cannot defend it adequately because the knight has to cover the advance of the c-pawn.

2	Nc2	Be7	7	Nc2	Bd6
3	Kg3	Kh5	8	Ne1	Kh4
4	Kf3	Kxh4	9	Nc2	Kh3
5	Ne1	g5	10	Na1	Kh2
6	fxg5	Kxg5			

continues on the next page ➔

11	Kf2	...

White is trying to stop the king from infiltrating the position.

11	...	Bg3+	17	Ne1	Bd8
12	Kf3	Bh4	18	Nc2	Bf6
13	Nc2	Kg1	19	a3	Be7
14	Ke2	Kg2	20	b4	a4
15	Na1	Be7	21	Ne1	Bg5
16	Nc2	Kg3	22	Nc2	Bf6

Finally, after long manoeuvring, Black has achieved a *zugzwang*. If 23 Ne1 f4 24 exf4 Bxd4 25 Nd3 Ba7, then White has to give ground.

23	Kd3	Kf2
24	Na1	Bd8
25	Nc2	Bg5
26	b5	...

Otherwise the e3 pawn is lost, and Black's f-pawn will soon promote.

26	...	Bd8	28	Nc2	Ba5
27	Nb4	Bb6	29	Nb4	Ke1

Most players would play on here, but Botvinnik had seen enough and resigned. Either Black's king will sneak along the back row and win that way or (if 30 Kc2 or 30 Kxc3) he will go to e2 and win the e3 pawn.

Mikhail Tal: 8th World Champion (1960–1961)

Latvian star Mikhail Tal had a meteoric career as world champion, dazzling the world with his tactical wizardry at chess. Unfortunately, he paid little heed to his rather serious health problems.

Here, he has Black against Bukhuti Gurgenidze in Moscow, in 1957.

	Gurgenidze	Tal
1	...	Ng4

A casual-looking move that White underestimates. A move such as 2 Nf3 would leave White well placed.

2	h3?	Nxf2!

Tal does not need a second invitation to sacrifice.

| 3 | Kxf2 | Qh4+ | 4 | Kf1 | ... |

4 g3? Bd4+ would be bad: 5 Kg2 Qxh3+ leads to mate.

| 4 | ... | Bd4 |

Threatening mate. The position is now very sharp.

| 5 | Nd1 | Qxh3! |

White cannot take the queen with 6 gxh3 because 6...Bxh3 is mate.

| 6 | Bf3 | Qh2 | 8 | Ndc4 | ... |
| 7 | Ne3 | f5 | | | |

White should probably have tried to run away with 8 Ke2, but it was always hard to work out what was happening when playing Tal. His forte was to make the position as complicated as possible.

| 8 | ... | fxe4 | 9 | Bxe4 | Ba6 |

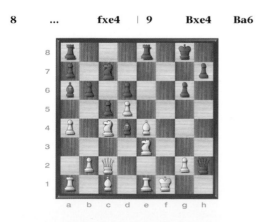

White is still a knight for two pawns up, but his position is probably beyond repair because of the various pins and the exposure of the king.

| 10 | Bf3 | Re5 | 12 | Bd2 | ... |
| 11 | Ra3 | Rae8 | | | |

White could have lasted longer with 12 Rd3.

| 12 | ... | Nxd5! |

Black brings the last attacking piece to bear on things.

| 13 | Bxd5+ | Rxd5 | 14 | Ke2 | ... |

Instead, 14 Nxd5 allows 14...Qg1 mate.

| 14 | ... | Bxe3 | 15 | Rxe3 | Bxc4+ |

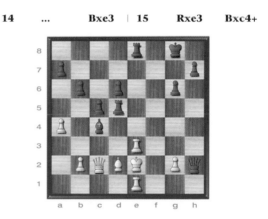

White resigned. If 16 Qxc4 Qxg2+ 17 Kd1 Qxd2 mate, and if 16 Kd1 Rxe3 17 Rxe3 Qg1+ 18 Re1 Qf2 19 Kc1 Bb3! black wins.

Tigran Petosian: 9th World Champion (1963–1969)

Petrosian was a national hero in his native Armenia. He was a cautious and cagey player who avoided risk and tended to draw a lot of games. However, he could be a dangerous tactician on his day and was also a superb match player who finally ended the Botvinnik reign. He was also initially successful against the younger generation represented by Boris Spassky.

continues on the next page ➔

Here is a game from the 1962 world championship qualifying competition, from which Petrosian won the right to play Botvinnik in the final match. Petrosian has White against his old rival Viktor Korchnoi.

White, to play, has a good advantage in terms of development, and he wastes no time in exploiting it.

	Petrosian	Korchnoi
1	b4!	Qe5

If Black plays 1...Qxa3, 2 Nd5! leaves the queen stranded behind enemy lines.

| 2 | f4! | Qb8 |

Once again, Black cannot risk taking a pawn. If 2...Qxe3+, 3 Kh1, then White will play Rf3 next move to trap the queen.

3	Bxf7+!	Kxf7
4	Qb3+	Ke8
5	Nd5	...

Despite his reputation as a complacent player, Petrosian shows that he can play a vigorous and enterprising game here. Having driven Black's queen back into passive defence, he has sacrificed a bishop to open up the king.

5	...	Bd6
6	Ne6	b5
7	Ndc7+	Ke7

7...Bxc7 is best, but after 8 Nxc7+ Kd8 9 Rfd1, Black has not much chance of survival.

| 8 | Nd4 | ... |

Now White threatens the big fork Nc6+, winning the queen.

| 8 | ... | Kf8 |
| 9 | Nxa8 | 1–0 |

After 9...Qxa8 10 Qe6 Be7 11 Nc6, White is winning quite easily.

Boris Spassky: 10th World Champion (1969–72)

Spassky is generally remembered for his part in the famous 1972 world championship match in Reykjavik against Bobby Fischer, but he had been a world-class player for many years previously, after winning the world junior championship in 1955. Before 1972, he had never lost a game to Bobby Fischer and seemed to exercise a psychological advantage over the younger American. His style of play was often described as 'universal': he could play both bold, aggressive chess, or quieter, positional chess. This was Spassky's best game from Reykjavik.

White, to play, had lured Fischer into what is called the 'poisoned pawn' variation, where Black takes the pawn on b2 with the queen. Both players must have prepared this line thoroughly, but Spassky found some more incisive moves.

	Spassky	Fischer
1	Nb1!	...

A surprising return to its original square for the knight.

1	...	Qb4	2	Qe3	...

White avoids the queen exchange and also cuts off the possible return of the black queen to its own camp via b6. White threatens a3 followed by Nc3 to win the queen.

2	...	d5?

Analysts later worked out that Black should have played 2...Ne7, but this move was not so easy to find during the game.

3	exd5	Ne7
4	c4	Nf5
5	Qd3	h4?

Fischer is hoping to play 6...Ng3+! 7 hxg3 hxg3+, followed by a deadly check on the a7–g1 diagonal – but White has a move first.

6	Bg4	Nd6
7	N1d2	f5?
8	a3	Qb6
9	c5	...

Black's position is already beyond repair.

9	...	Qb5
10	Qc3	fxg4
11	a4	h3

Fischer's queen is lost. The surprise is that he doesn't simply resign. The rest of the moves may be passed over in silence.

12	axb5	hxg2+
13	Kxg2	Rh3
14	Qf6	Nf5
15	c6	Bc8
16	dxe6	fxe6
17	Rfe1	Be7
18	Rxe6	1–0

continues on the next page ➔

Bobby Fischer: 11th World Champion (1972–1975)

Bobby Fischer raised the profile of chess by an extraordinary amount when he became world champion in 1972. It gave a huge boost to the game, particularly in places like the UK, where it had always been a minority interest activity. Sadly, Fischer failed to defend his title in 1975 and has not played since, apart from a return match with Spassky in 1992 that had no official status.

Here is Fischer's win against Spassky in the sixth game of the Reykjavik match.

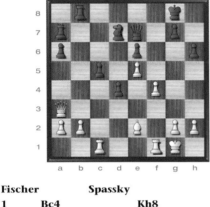

Fischer	Spassky
1	Bc4	Kh8
2	Qh3	...

White uses his queen and bishop to pressurize the e6 pawn.

2	...	Nf8
3	b3	a5
4	f5	...

White plays to open up the f-file for his rooks and create a passed e-pawn.

| 4 | ... | exf5 |
| 5 | Rxf5 | Nh7 |

Setting a trap. If 6 Rf7?? Ng5! forks queen and rook.

| 6 | Rcf1 | Qd8 |

If 6...Ng5 now, White plays 7 Qg3 and then 8 h4 to drive the knight away.

7	Qg3	Re7
8	h4	Rbb7
9	e6	...

Now that Fischer is satisfied that the pawn cannot be attacked by the knight, he moves it to e6. He conducts the attack very calmly and precisely.

| 9 | ... | Rbc7 |

Black has run out of anything constructive to do. If 9...Nf6 10 Rxf6! gxf6 11 Rxf6, then White has too many threats.

10	Qe5	Qe8
11	a4	Qd8
12	R1f2	Qe8
13	R2f3	Qd8
14	Bd3	Qe8
15	Qe4	...

White now decides it is time to launch the final offensive. The threat is Rf8+!, followed by the capture of the knight and Qh7 mate.

15	...	Nf6
16	Rxf6!	gxf6
17	Rxf6	Kg8
18	Bc4	Kh8
19	Qf4	1–0

One impressive aspect of this attack was how unhurried it was. One watching grandmaster compared Fischer's performance to a Mozart symphony.

Anatoly Karpov: 12th World Champion (1975–1985, 1993–1999)

Anatoly Karpov qualified for a world title match with Fischer in 1975, and achieved a bloodless victory when Fischer failed to agree terms to defend his title. However, he then proved his worth by winning a large number of tournaments during the following ten years and also defending his title successfully, twice, against Viktor Korchnoi.

Karpov resembles Capablanca in that he has a huge natural talent for the game and also prefers to play positional (rather than tactical) chess for the most part. In his younger days, he was also known for the remarkable speed of his play, with good moves seemingly coming to him with a minimum of thought.

Here is one of Karpov's wins from his first match with Kasparov in 1984.

Black, to play, should be able to hold this level endgame, but he now makes a tiny slip.

	Karpov	Kasparov
1	...	gxh4?

Nine-hundred and ninety-nine times out of a thousand, White would automatically make the recapture 2 gxh4 here, but Karpov is no ordinary player.

| 2 | Ng2! | ... |

This is a temporary pawn sacrifice with the idea of infiltrating the kingside with his king.

| 2 | ... | hxg3+ |

| 3 | Kxg3 | ... |

White is a pawn down, but he will soon devour the h5 pawn. Equally importantly, he can now move his king into Black's position.

3	...	Ke6
4	Nf4+	Kf5
5	Nxh5	Ke6

Black has to retreat because White threatened to play Ng7, Ne8 and then Nc7 to attack the a6 pawn.

| 6 | Nf4+ | Kd6 | 7 | Kg4 | ... |

Now the king moves up the board.

7	...	Bc2
8	Kh5	Bd1
9	Kg6	Ke7

If 9...Bxf3 10 Kxf6, White will be able to play Ne6, Ng7 and Nf5+ to force the black king to retreat in due course.

10	Nxd5+	Ke6
11	Nc7+	Kd7
12	Nxa6	Bxf3
13	Kxf6	Kd6
14	Kf5	Kd5
15	Kf4	Bh1
16	Ke3	Kc4

continues on the next page ➔

17	Nc5	...

It is rather a long-winded process, but White is gradually establishing a winning endgame.

17	...	Bc6
18	Nd3	Bg2
19	Ne5+	Kc3
20	Ng6	Kc4
21	Ne7	Bb7
22	Nf5	Bg2
23	Nd6+	Kb3
24	Nxb5	Ka4
25	Nd6	1–0

Modern top-level chess can be a war of attrition. Such marathon games as this, even without the added pressure of competing for the crown of world champion, require intense concentration. Both Karpov and Kasparov were blessed in abundance with the ability to stay focused, which undoubtedly accounts for their domination of the game for so long. Though most believe Kasparov to have been the better player, Karpov holds the distinction of being the most successful tournament player of all time.

Garry Kasparov: 13th World Champion (1985–1993, 1993–2000)

Garry Kasparov is widely considered to be the best chess player of all time. Having won his title in a match against Anatoly Karpov, he defended it tenaciously against Karpov and others. His only significant setbacks were lost matches against the computer Deep Blue in 1997 and against Vladimir Kramnik in 2000, which cost him his unofficial (but prestigious) version of the world title. Kasparov is by nature an open, aggressive player but he quickly assimilated the art of positional chess in order to overcome Karpov in the 1980s.

Here, he plays White against Karpov in Spain in 2001, in a game which may yet prove to be the last major clash between the two giants.

Kasparov has stirred up a complex position in order to provoke his rival.

	Kasparov	Karpov
1	h6!	Nxc5

If 1...gxh6 2 Nd6+! there is a twin threat of Qxf7 mate and Bxh6+.

2	Bf4	Kf8

Kasparov thought 2...Qa5+ was better here, but it is very complex.

3	hxg7+	Kxg7
4	0–0–0	...

White gets ready to switch the d1 rook to g1 and then attack the exposed king.

4	...	Kf8
5	Kb1	a6
6	Nc7	Rc8
7	Bxd5	...

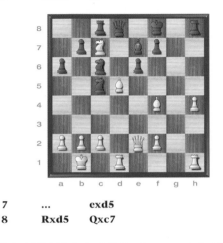

7	...	exd5
8	Rxd5	Qxc7

If 8...Nd7 9 Ne6+ fxe6 10 Qxe6 sets up a lethal finish.

9	Bxc7	Rxc7
10	Rf5	...

Black has three minor pieces for the queen and two pawns. It is resignable.

10	...	Rd7
11	c3	f6
12	Rg1	Nd8
13	Qg4	Ke8
14	Rh5	Rf8
15	Rxc5!	Bxc5
16	Qh5+	1–0

A comprehensive victory that offers a fine example of Kasparov's relentlessly precise technique.

Left: White positions a rook deep in enemy territory, forcing Black on to the defensive. With such a powerful piece in the heart of his position, Black will have to be on the lookout for mating threats and vulnerable material.

COMMON TACTICAL PATTERNS

It is hardly surprising that you have to practise regularly in order to improve at chess, just as you would if learning to play any game, sport or musical instrument. One of the principal benefits of regular practice is pattern recognition. After a while, you will be able to recognize various patterns that have occurred before. One or two of these are already becoming familiar from the pages of this book (e.g. the back-rank mate). This next position will help you spot a few of the most familiar patterns that recur with regularity in games of chess.

Material is level, and the position appears to be fairly balanced, but, in fact, Black (to play) has a way to force a win here. It involves an eight-move combination. Perhaps more surprisingly, if you showed the position to an experienced tournament player (not necessarily a master or grandmaster), you might be surprised to see him or her work it out in a matter of seconds. The reason experienced players can do it so quickly is not because they are brilliant at calculation, nor because they have seen the exact position before, but simply because they can recognize three or four patterns or elements in the position that they have come across before. Try imagining a familiar mating scenario and then quickly see a few moves that can get them to the desired conclusion. Here is the solution:

| 1 | ... | Ng3+! |

The first familiar pattern: the knight fork, with a difference, of course: this would be a winning king and queen fork but for the fact that the h2 pawn will snap the knight off in the next move. So is it a useless pattern here? Not quite: it achieves something by 'forcing' White's reply, which means that Black does not need to worry about what might happen after 2 Kg1.

| 2 | hxg3 | hxg3+ |

This is the next pattern – or perhaps two patterns in one: firstly, the creation of an open file (ideal for exploitation by rooks) and secondly the acquisition of a strong pawn on g3 (useful for imprisoning a king on the back rank, or supporting pieces on f2 and h2). Once an experienced player envisages these two tactical plus points, he or she next seeks a way to exploit the enemy's back-rank weakness, perhaps via the strong points at f2 and (particularly) h2. Using some imagination (something even the best chess-playing computers cannot do – yet), the player will ask themselves the question 'What if I could get my queen to h2?' – and then may see a way to achieve it.

| 3 | Kg1 | Rh1+! |

Black jettisons a rook. The reason why will become clear soon.

| 4 | Kxh1 | Rh8+ |
| 5 | Kg1 | Rh1+! |

Now the other rook is sacrificed the same way.

6	**Kxh1**	**Qh8+**
7	**Kg1**	**...**

If you examine this position with a computer, it may suggest the move 7 Qh5 here. Of course, it doesn't help White's cause at all, because Black takes the queen and wins as before. The reason computers do such things is because they are programmed to stave off checkmate for as long as possible, and this move happens to make the game last a bit longer.

7	**...**	**Qh2+**

There it is – the move that Black envisaged a few moves before. The reason for jettisoning the two rooks was to clear a path for the queen to achieve this objective. This is sometimes referred to as a 'clearance sacrifice'.

Below: White's queen moves in for the kill: Qg7#. Checkmate with the queen on this square, supported either by a pawn or bishop, is one of the common mating patterns used against the castled king.

8	**Kf1**	**Qh1 mate**

The lines show the queen's path to the mating square. An aesthetically beautiful finish, but to an experienced player – almost routine! One reason it is not so difficult to pull off is that all White's moves were forced. In real life, of course, such clear-cut opportunities do not come along all the time – but they do happen once in a while.

THE ENEMY KING'S DEFENCES

It is always worth spending a little time examining the enemy king's defences when it is your turn to move. For example, if you notice undefended squares around the king, or an absence of defensive pieces in the vicinity, it can often indicate that it is a good moment to start a direct attack on the king.

White is to play. An experienced player would note the following plus-points about this position: (a) Black's kingside pawn structure, with the pawn on g6, is a little weak, and could perhaps be exploited if White can establish an unchallenged queen, bishop or knight on f6 or h6; (b) White has three minor pieces to Black's two on the kingside; (c) Black is lagging behind in development (the b8 knight is still on its original square); (d) the white bishop on c4 is usefully placed on the a2–g8 diagonal (although threatening nothing at the moment).

There is only one negative point: the white e4 pawn is currently attacked by two enemy pieces and defended by only one. This last factor can easily be addressed, but such is the preponderance of strategic and tactical plus-points that White should first give serious thought to the possibility of a direct attack on the king. In fact, there is an immediate way to exploit White's development advantage and superior build-up on the kingside.

1   Bxg7   ...

A simple exchange of pieces, but it achieves the objective of removing Black's best kingside defender, the bishop on g7.

| 1 | ... | Kxg7 |
| 2 | Nf5+! | ... |

This knight sacrifice serves to open up the g-file and allow the white queen to land on g5 with check.

| 2 | ... | gxf5 |

If 2...Kg8 3 Qh6 Ne8 (to defend against mate on g7) 4 Ng5 and now 5 Qxh7 cannot be prevented. If 2...Kh8 3 Qh6 Rg8 4 Ng5, then the unstoppable threat is Nxf7 winning the queen. Notice that the well-placed bishop on c4 plays a vital part in this particular line.

| 3 | Qg5+ | Kh8 |
| 4 | Qxf6+ | Kg8 |

The first stage of the assault is over and material equality has been re-established. In visualizing this position, White would note the strength of the bishop on c4 (attacking f7 and covering the possible defensive idea of Ra6), and also the combination Ng5, Qh6 and Qxh7 mate. The two patterns (Bxf7 and Ng5/Qxh7) are both very common and would occur instantly to a strong player, making the next move very easy to find.

| 5 | Ng5 | Qc6 |

If Black's life depended on prolonging the game, the way to do it would be 5...Ra6, but then 6 Bxa6 Nxa6 7 Qxf5 f6 8 Ne6 would win even more material.

6   Bxf7+   1–0

6...Rxf7 7 Qxf7+ Kh8 when 8 Qxh7 and 8 Qf8 are both checkmate.

Here is another example of how to exploit similar weak squares around the king.

White, to move, has fixed a weakness around the black king and it is just a question of how best to exploit it.

1   Bg7!   ...

White might also be tempted to try 1 Bg5, with the idea of playing 2 Qh6 and 3 Qg7 mate. Black has two possible defences, however. One is 1...Bc7 when 2 Qh6 is adequately met by 2...Qf8!, and the other is 1...h5, which prevents the queen from reaching h6.

1   ...   Bc7

This loses immediately, but in fact there is little to be done other than give up a piece on f6 to stop the mate. 1...h5 2 Qg5, and the queen will reach the mating square via h6.

2   Qxh7+!   1–0

Black resigned. This is another clearance sacrifice – the queen gives itself up to clear a path for the rook to give mate – 2...Kxh7 3 Rh4+ Kg8 4 Rh8 mate. Once you have seen a few examples of such attacks, they will become second nature and will be easy to find in your own games.

Computers in Chess

Since the late 20th century, computers have had a profound effect on the way chess is played. With a performance level that is now on a par with world champions, they are formidable opponents to learn from and practise with, and are the means by which people all over the world can play chess with each other on the Internet. There are many affordable versions of chess-playing software, as well as dedicated chess computers, and these have become very popular. However, although computers are capable of winning chess matches against grandmasters, they still have not 'solved' the game. Most players would probably agree that, while computers are useful tools to improve chess strategy, nothing can match the pleasure of a game between human opponents.

Right: For true lovers of chess, the look and feel of a wooden chess set cannot be equalled by anything that appears on a computer screen.

Choosing a Silicon Opponent

Until a few years ago, chess-playing computers were despised by the best players. In 1968, the Scottish chessmaster David Levy made a bet with some computer scientists that no computer would beat him in the following ten years. In 1978, the boast was put to the test and Levy easily defeated the best chess-playing computer of the day. It wasn't until 1989 that a chess-playing program was developed that was strong enough to overcome Levy, and still more years passed before leading grandmasters and world champions began losing to computers with any regularity.

However, things have moved on swiftly in the 21st century, and now it is possible to purchase affordable chess-playing software, for a home computer, that is capable of playing grandmaster-level chess. In terms of playing strength, these programs are vastly stronger that any chess player (other than the world's elite) could possibly need. The main problem in playing against them is the feeling of depression that creeps over you after losing a long succession of games. However, take comfort in the fact that even professional players suffer similar results when they play quick games against computers.

Despite their huge chess-playing strength, these programs are still worth buying, even for beginners. They come with a large range of features. It is possible to set the level of play to suit your own playing strength and enable you to win some games and gauge your rate of improvement. Other facilities of the latest titles include: speech and sound (with supposedly humorous commentary that soon becomes tiresome); 3D-style board designs; training and tuition; hints and advice as you play; games databases (hundreds of thousands of grandmaster games that you can play through and analyse with the help of the computer); and you can add your own games and have the computer analyse and comment on them, although this can sometimes be humiliating.

If you don't own a computer, there is another solution – buying a dedicated chess computer. These vary in style and size: they can be handheld devices (which you can carry in a coat pocket), desktop models (which can be carried in a briefcase), or deluxe models (including a beautiful wooden chess board and pieces, which allow moves to be entered simply by making the move on the board). These are more expensive than the former option. These dedicated computers play strong chess (although not as strong as their PC equivalents) and also come with many other useful facilities, such as teaching modes and handicap levels. Competition chess players tend not to use dedicated chess computers these days, mainly because they prefer to travel with a laptop loaded with chess-playing software, and because dedicated computers don't come with databases or allow you to store your own games or analysis.

The availability of good-quality handheld computers now means that it is possible to load some versions of PC-based chess-playing software on to a gadget that is not much bigger than a mobile phone. This development has caused some disquiet in the chess world, as it means that there is the possibility of cheating if players surreptitiously consult their 'pocket grandmaster' during play.

Above: World chess champion Vladimir Kramnik of Russia contemplates his first move during the final game of his eight-game match against computer software program Deep Fritz, in Bahrain in October 2002. Kramnik and the computer each won two games and four were drawn, making the match score 4–4.

Far left: In the 1950s, a research scientist at Manchester University, UK, set one of the university's computers a chess problem to solve. The computer took 15 minutes to respond but achieved checkmate in two moves.

WHERE TO BUY

♛ ♝ ♞ ♚

Among the top-selling and best-quality chess-playing software titles on the market, the author's favourite is Hiarcs, although several others are equally as good, if not better. The other big names are Fritz, Houdini, Shredder, Junior and the Eastern European program Rybka, which is now very popular among Russian grandmasters. As regards dedicated computers, the Mephisto Exclusive Senator is the top-of-the-range model, with other good ones being Excalibur Grandmaster, Novag Obsidian and Mephisto Master, with excellent software available for Apple and Android devices. Be sure to buy from a specialist chess shop, which can advise you on your exact needs.

PLAYING CHESS ONLINE

Since the millennium there has been a massive boom in people playing chess on the Internet, and also people watching major chess tournaments online.

The advantages

Playing online has some tremendous advantages. You play when you want to play, you can nearly always find an opponent of the right standard, you can play quick games or slow games, you don't have to travel anywhere, you don't have to put up with your opponent's bad breath or repellent manners, and, as long as you are courteous about it, you can stop playing at any time if everyday life intrudes.

The disadvantages

One disadvantage is that not everyone finds it easy to play via a two-dimensional board representation, or to use a mouse. It is also not very sociable (you can 'chat' by typing messages, but sometimes the chat is a little off-putting), you don't always know whether you are playing your opponents or their computer software (yes, people do cheat) and (like other computer-based activities), it is a little addictive and perhaps, if you play too often, bad for the eyesight.

Online or not online?

Some chess players have fallen head over heels in love with Internet chess, whereas others find it completely repellent. Whatever opinions people may hold, there seems little doubt that Internet chess is here to stay, and it will no doubt improve in terms of presentation (which is already very impressive) and facilities.

It is unwise to play on the Internet until you have first had a reasonable amount of experience of playing traditional chess, preferably with someone who can give you a bit of advice and instruction as you develop your skills. Playing online too soon could put you off the game almost before you start.

Even experienced chess players find it quite hard to adjust to chess in two dimensions, and to all the different functions and choices that confront you when first loading up the software. One other negative aspect of chess online is that most online players opt for speed chess, where the players only have a very limited time in which to choose their moves before they are timed out or, as chess players put it, 'lose on time'. Speed chess is fun and has its place, but it is not good for developing good chessboard skills and habits – it is like trying to run before you can walk.

Where to play

Let's assume you have now put in the necessary time practising your game and are sufficiently competent to play online. Which site is best? One of the oldest and most reliable, and with about 30,000 members (of whom you can expect to find 2,000 online at any one time) is the Internet Chess Club (www.chessclub.com). You can have a free trial, become a guest member (which is free) or opt to pay about $35 for six months'

Right: Playing online is very different in several key respects to playing against a 'real' opponent. Primarily, you will have to accustom yourself to playing in two rather than three dimensions.

Above: Garry Kasparov considers his next move against one of 30 junior chess players. The game took place online on his own Internet chess site.

Left: As well as playing online, it is worth investing in a portable chess computer. They can be a great boon, particularly as a way of passing the time on a long journey.

full membership. To play, you download an interface which is fairly intuitive and straightforward to use, and provides you with everything you need to find opponents and play a game.

Other very popular sites include www.chess.com, playchess.com and chess24.com, which all come with very slick features and many other attractive facilities. They have a similar subscription basis and also allow you to watch top pro players in action, both in formal tournaments or simply playing quick games with each other for fun. Some of these sites provide teaching aids and training videos, and it is also possible to engage experienced chess teachers and receive one-to-one tuition via the facilities provided by these websites.

Chess has become a popular spectator sport on the Internet. Most top tournaments now provide facilities to allow chess fans to watch live chess in real time, with high-quality webcasting facilities and entertaining commentators. These attract tens of thousands of chess fans and help give a flavour of top-level grandmaster chess. Often the webcasting facilities are interactive, enabling the spectator to chat with other chess fans or pose questions to the presenters.

KASPAROV AGAINST THE COMPUTER

Most chess players expected that the computer would eventually get the better of humankind when it came to playing chess, but it still came as a shock when, on 11 May 1997 in New York, Garry Kasparov lost the final game of his six-game match against the IBM computer known as Deep Blue, which meant that he had lost the match by 2½–3½. Kasparov had played Deep Blue the previous year, losing the first game but going on to win three of the remaining games and drawing two to triumph 4–2. The 1997 rematch, for which Deep Blue had been significantly upgraded, saw a reversal of fortune. Kasparov won the first game but then lost the second, thereafter becoming obsessed with the notion that the IBM programming team in charge of his silicon opponent (which included a chess grandmaster) had manually interfered with the move selection in that second game.

By the time he sat down for the sixth and final encounter, Kasparov was already a beaten man. He played the last game as if he had forgotten how to play chess. He had the black pieces and played a defence that was unfamiliar to him and totally unsuited to his playing style, and then committed an error on move seven, of which a club player would have been ashamed – and one that was instantly exploited by the computer. From as early as move eight, he was a dead duck and never looked capable of escaping defeat.

It is hard to convey the enormity of what had occurred. Until 1997, Kasparov had scarcely suffered any calamitous results and, whenever he had been under pressure, he had always fought tenaciously and

Below: In 1997 Kasparov lost to the computer Deep Blue. The computer was able to calculate 200 million moves a second, something no person could ever emulate. It came as a shock to the chess community that such a thing could happen, and years passed before Kasparov could get his revenge on the silicon chip.

Above: Garry Kasparov (left) began his first game against the world champion computer chess program Deep Junior in New York on 26 January 2003. In this, his fourth attempt to beat the computer, the match was drawn 3–3.

nearly always achieved his objective. He was unbeaten in match play. He went from all-conquering hero to dispirited zero in the space of eight moves.

What happened to Kasparov?

In truth, 11 May 1997 was not the day when computers became stronger chess players than humans; it was simply the day when Garry Kasparov proved he was a human being. He had allowed his concentration to wander on to what had happened in game two, and had failed to psych himself up for the final game.

It also proved that humans and computers are not really compatible chess opponents. Humans can only maintain a reasonable energy level for a few hours at a time, and need various breaks for food and sleep; whereas computers can go on as long as the electricity supply lasts. Human chess is replete with human emotions and psychology – hope, despair, confidence, disappointment – and the two players can display and decipher elements of body language during play.

Kasparov had always been a grandmaster of psychology as well as chess, with the swagger of a champion boxer as he came to the board, and a number of other mannerisms that had often intimidated other players. His psychological weaponry was completely useless against Deep Blue.

In one important respect, Deep Blue cheated. Its disk banks stored records of every top-level competitive chess game ever played to that date, plus it had access to a huge database of carefully sifted opening moves that had been prepared by grandmasters and tailored for the job of defeating the specific opponent. Of course, Kasparov also had, by human standards, a vast database of opening information too – but in his head. He has a superlative memory for such detail, but no human brain could replicate the perfect memory of a computer. If Kasparov had arrived with his complete chess library and a computer database of his own, he would have been disqualified for making use of notes during the game – one of the rules of the competition.

Thankfully, Kasparov soon recovered, and in 2003 he played a 3–3 drawn match with another computer, called Deep Junior.

BEATING THE SILICON MONSTER

The first thing to say about beating the silicon monster is that it has become a very hard thing to do. Even widely available software titles such as Fritz, Rybka and Chessmaster now play phenomenally strong chess that is good enough to beat grandmasters. The honest truth is that you are unlikely to be able to beat them on their highest levels.

So the first simple piece of advice is don't try to play them on their highest level. Fortunately, the latest PC-based software titles have a whole host of different playing levels, identified by names such as 'Handicap' or 'Friendly', which are cleverly programmed to create a more level playing field between the computer and the human player, while at the same time providing the player with a reasonable challenge. Even experienced players would do well to use these facilities, as losing a long string of games is bad for morale. As well as allowing you to win a few games (this is done in a subtle and not patronizing way), the computer can generate a handicap rating for you, rather like a golf handicap, which you can use to measure your progress.

Right: The latest chess-playing software also gives the player access to online chess-playing sites such as the Internet Chess Club and playchess.com, where it is possible to play against other humans as well as computers.

Below: It is possible to play on the computer with 3D-style display, in which the board and pieces can be moved as if on a three-dimensional chessboard.

Style of play against a computer is very important. Before considering this, it is worth noting that computers do not learn from their mistakes as they play games (i.e. they are not true 'knowledge-based systems', as IT experts would define them). While chess programming techniques have certainly improved over the past 30 years, most of the extra strength of the latest chess-playing software is due to the massive increase in hardware speed that has been achieved with every new generation of the microchip. The computer can sift through millions of different moves in a matter of seconds – obviously far more than the strongest human player could hope to emulate.

Avoid tactical melees

This advantage in calculation speed translates into a phenomenal strength in tactics – in other words, calculation of what happens when the two enemies are at close quarters. No human chess player – even Garry Kasparov – can now rival a good piece of chess software in this aspect of the game. This leads to the next piece

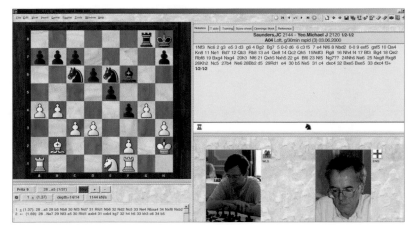

Left: Many expert players now use chess databases to study the game (particularly the opening phase). These often have more than a million games, from the 15th century right up to the present day, as well as photos of thousands of competition players and much other relevant information that enables players to compile dossiers on each other's play.

of fairly obvious advice – avoid complicated tactics. Easier said than done, of course. Even strong grandmasters playing computers occasionally open up the position too readily to a tactical battle, and there is usually only one result possible.

Find a long-range strategy

However, it can be possible to take on the monster in a tactical battle, when the possibility of the tactical denouement can be seen from afar and judged to be in your favour. Computers are not so good at seeing a long way ahead in most positions; this is sometimes referred to as the 'horizon effect'. They usually concentrate on analysing the next few moves to the nth degree, and this is where experience, judgement and pattern recognition can come to the human player's aid.

Keep it simple

Generally speaking, it is a good idea to keep the position simple, with not too much hand-to-hand fighting to be calculated. For this reason, computers tend to play the endgame significantly worse. That said, this deficiency is gradually being eradicated from computer play. Also, when the material on the board is reduced to two or three men each, the computer can benefit from what is known as a 'tablebase'. These reduced-material positions have been exhaustively analysed out by computers, and the absolute best moves recorded on computer databases. If the computer finds that it has the exact position on the board in its database, it will stop calculating its moves in the normal way, and simply look up the right move in its

in-built database. Now that really is cheating, isn't it. If you, the human player, sat down to play a tournament game and consulted an endgame manual during play, you would be disqualified. But that is exactly what some chess-playing programs do.

How not to play

Here's an example of how not to play against a computer. Playing White was a Dutch grandmaster, but he makes the mistake of allowing the position to become tactical quickly. Computers play a different sort of chess from humans (with a heavy emphasis on tactics), which can lead players to adapt their playing style to combat the computer. This can backfire, simply because the human is playing against their natural instincts. Something of the sort is at work here.

	Human	**Fritz SSS (Netherlands 2000)**
1	c4	Nf6
2	Nc3	e5
3	e4	...

This was intended as an 'anti-computer' move, but White does not follow it up accurately.

3	...	Bc5
4	g3	0-0
5	Bg2	Nc6
6	Nge2	d6
7	d3?	...

continues on the next page ➲

Only a tiny error, but it is enough for the computer to start on the offensive. White should play 7 0–0.

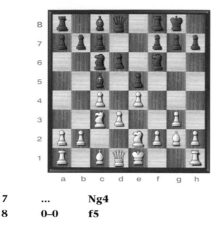

| 7 | ... | Ng4 |
| 8 | 0–0 | f5 |

Black threatens to play fxe4 and attack the f2 pawn with a third piece (the rook on f8).

9	Na4	Nxf2!
10	Rxf2	Bxf2+
11	Kxf2	f4

The main idea behind Black's double capture on f2 was to draw the white king into the line of fire of the black rook on f8, and facilitate Qh4+ (should White play 12 gxf4). But there are a whole host of tactical problems that add up to insurmountable difficulties. For example, Black threatens to play Bg4 followed by Nd4, putting pressure on the e2 knight. The white king cannot move away from the f-file because f3 would fork two pieces. White plays the best move, but it is not good enough.

| 12 | gxf4 | exf4 |
| 13 | Ng1 | ... |

13 Nxf4 g5 loses a piece for two pawns.

13	...	Qh4+
14	Kf1	f3!
15	Nxf3	Qxh2

This position may not look so terrible, but the Dutch grandmaster decided to resign. It is just the sort of position that computers play brilliantly. The computer threatens Bh3 or Nd4, and then the whole White edifice crumbles.

How to beat the computer

Here is the way to win. Another Dutch grandmaster is playing White against the same computer.

	Human	Fritz SSS
1	c4	e5
2	g3	Nf6
3	Bg2	Nc6
4	Nc3	Bb4
5	a3	Bxc3
6	bxc3	0-0
7	e4	a6
8	a4	d6
9	d3	Bg4
10	f3	...

White is playing to keep the position blocked. This is a well-known anti-computer ploy.

10	...	Bd7
11	Ne2	Qc8
12	h3	b6
13	f4	Be6
14	f5	...

Blocking the position. 13...Be6 is poor: it shows that the computer does not understand the position.

14	...	Bd7
15	g4	Ne8
16	Ng3	Qd8
17	g5	Bc8
18	h4	f6
19	Qh5	...

White has a huge attack on the kingside. This is easily visible to the human eye, but the computer does not appreciate the long-term implications of its passivity.

19	...	Na5

20	Ra3	...

Safety first. The threat of Nb3 may have done nothing, but White doesn't want to give the computer the merest hint of counterplay.

20	...	Qe7
21	Nf1	Nc6
22	Ne3	Qd7
23	g6	h6

White had been expecting this attempt to close down the position and that was what his previous knight manoeuvre had been designed to refute.

24	Ng4	Ra7
25	Rg1	1–0

The computer sees what is coming and resigns. White will play Bf3 followed by Bxh6 and it will be over.

Remember that these games were played in 2000. Human brains have not made much progress in the last six or seven years, but computers have. I doubt that this sort of strategy would work as well against current chess programs.

Even today, it is usually a good idea to play for blocked positions against a computer. The fewer the open lines available to the computer's pieces, the less chance that it will be able to exploit its awesome tactical power against you. You can see that the human player in the final position of the above game had a little more space to manoeuvre behind the pawns. This small advantage became a key factor in winning the game.

CHESS TODAY AND TOMORROW

As we continue to progress through the 21st century, chess is played as a professional sport in many countries in the world, and its leading practitioners are known as grandmasters. What does it take to become a grandmaster? How are chess competitions organized? What does the future hold for the game? Who will take over the mantle of Fischer and Kasparov? These are some of the questions examined in this section. One thing is for certain – whatever the future of professional chess, the game will continue to be played and loved by millions of people. There are many types of chess competition, and it is unlike other sports and games – it knows no barriers of distance, incapacity or competence. However busy, remote or disabled the player, there is a way to find a chess opponent.

Right: The knight is symbolic of chess – it makes light of barriers when it moves. In some languages and cultures it is known, more accurately, as 'the horse'.

SO YOU WANT TO BE A GRANDMASTER?

One of the things that many people know about chess, even if they don't play it, is that it is played by people called grandmasters. The word has overtones of wizardry or freemasonry about it, and has done wonders for the image of the game. However, in reality, there is no magic, trickery or secret vows behind the word: a grandmaster is simply someone who has scored sufficiently exalted scores in some top-level chess competitions to be awarded the title by the World Chess Federation (known as FIDE, or Fédération Internationale des Échecs).

The first grandmasters

The title of grandmaster first came into frequent use in chess when Tsar Nicholas II conferred it upon the participants of the 1914 St Petersburg chess tournament. The five players – world champion Emanuel Lasker, future champions José Raúl Capablanca and Alexander Alekhine, plus Siegbert Tarrasch and Frank Marshall – were the leading players of their day and fully deserved the honour. The title continued to be applied unofficially to elite players until the World Chess Federation devised a system for awarding the title shortly after World War II. About 100 players qualified for the title, until the system changed again in the early 1970s and was based on a newly devised rating system. This rating system was based on one that had previously been employed by the United States Chess Federation. International chess ratings are usually called FIDE ratings, or sometimes Elo ratings, after the man who devised the US precursor, Professor Arpad Elo.

The rating system

FIDE Ratings are published every month, with more than 200,000 active chess players worldwide now appearing on the list. Over the course of time, a degree of statistical inflation has crept into the upper levels of the system, making it harder to compare players of different generations. In 1972 Bobby Fischer was the world's top player by a considerable margin with a rating of 2785, while Garry Kasparov peaked at 2851 in 1999. Since 2006 seven more players have exceeded the 2800 barrier. Magnus Carlsen finally broke Kasparov's record in 2013, and reached a peak rating of 2882 in 2014. In order to become a grandmaster, a player must record three tournament performances of 2600 standard, and also achieve a published rating of 2500. To receive a lesser title, international master, a player must achieve three performances of 2450 standard and have a published rating of at least 2400. Titles are conferred for life, although players' ratings tend to decrease after the optimum age for professional chess playing, which is around 30 to 40. The inflationary effect of the rating system has seen a large growth in the number of grandmasters: the figure is now in excess of 1,000. This has had the effect that the title means rather less than it did when the Tsar first conferred it in 1914. In those days, it was confined to a small group of players with genuine world championship aspirations. Today, a player of the calibre of Magnus Carlsen could take on four or five lesser grandmasters in a simultaneous display and defeat them quite easily.

That is not to belittle the achievement of modern grandmasters. It takes a great deal of dedication, hard work and talent to reach grandmaster status. It would be almost impossible to get to that level without starting very young. Most professional players start playing before their teens, and large numbers qualify for the grandmaster title before the age of 20. Given the numbers of players now competing for a limited amount of cash prizes and appearance fees, most do not earn a living that is commensurate with the work they put in. So – do you still want to be a grandmaster?

Right: Frank James Marshall, one of the five original 'grandmasters', and the US Chess Champion from 1909 to 1936. Today's grandmasters, who number in the hundreds, qualify according to the strict rules of the FIDE rating system.

Below: Emanuel Lasker (right) held the title World Champion of chess for a record 27 years, until defeat by Capablanca (left) in 1927. Lasker was noted for his 'psychological' chess playing, which took account of his opponent's style as well as the objective challenges posed by the board.

Left: Tsar Nicholas II of Russia, who presided over the great St Petersburg tournament of 1914 and was the first person to confer the title of 'grandmaster' on leading chess players.

21ST-CENTURY CHAMPIONS

Chess has one phenomenon in common with music and mathematics – the infant prodigy. It is possible to reach a very high level of competence at chess at astonishingly early ages. Paul Morphy, José Raúl Capablanca, Sammy Reshevsky, Bobby Fischer and Judit Polgar were the most famous cases in chess history, but brilliant young players have continued to emerge into the 21st century.

Young grandmasters

Since Bobby Fischer, the age at which a player reaches the grandmaster title has always been used as the yardstick by which a player's achievement has been measured. In some ways this is not an entirely satisfactory yardstick, because there is no doubt that it has become easier to qualify as a grandmaster (or GM) in recent years. Bobby Fischer was 15 years, 6 months old when he became a grandmaster in September 1958, and he did it by qualifying for a world championship decider between eight players who would play off for the right to play the world champion. Effectively, he became a grandmaster by qualifying for the world top nine. In recent years, more than 20 players have qualified for the GM title at a younger age than Fischer, but none of them simultaneously launched themselves into the world elite in quite the same way that Fischer

did. Becoming a GM these days means joining the world's top 1,000. Fischer's was much the greatest achievement and may never be equalled.

However, that is not to disparage the achievements of teenage (and, incredibly, pre-teen) players of recent years. Judit Polgar had the honour of breaking Fischer's age record. She became a GM in 1991 at the age of 15 years, 4 months. Another Hungarian, Peter Leko, broke the 15-year barrier, qualifying as a GM at 14 years, 4 months in 1994. In 1997 the record was broken twice, first by

Above: Magnus Carlsen (right), the current world chess champion, gives a simultaneous display in Spain. The 13-year-old Norwegian played 25 simultaneous games against challengers who ranged from internationally rated adults to children from the Extremadura region. He won 22, drew 2 and lost only 1.

Left: The first child to become a GM, Bobby Fischer from Brooklyn, New York, competing in a tournament at the Manhattan Chess Club, aged 13. Bobby learned to play at the age of 6 and became a GM in 1958, aged 15.

Below left: Top French player Etienne Bacrot took up chess aged 4 and became a grandmaster at the age of 14. He is ranked world no.40 of all active players.

French player Etienne Bacrot, then by Ruslan Ponomariov of Ukraine, before falling to Chinese player Bu Xiangzhi of China in 1999 at the age of 13 years, 10 months. Finally, the current record-holder Sergey Karyakin of Ukraine, qualified as a GM at the age of 12 years, 7 months and 0 days in 2002. His record still stands, but he has not gone on to become world champion. That title is currently held by Magnus Carlsen, who qualified as a GM at the age of 13 years, 4 months in 2004.

Interestingly, one leading contender for the title of 'world's best-ever player' – Garry Kasparov – was a venerable 16 years, 11 months when he became a grandmaster. But this was only because the old Soviet Chess Federation liked to keep its 'secret weapons' to itself. The 14-year-old Garry Kasparov was capable of achieving everything that recent prodigies have achieved.

The next world champion will be...

For the first few years of the 21st century, the way forward for the world championship was problematic, as two different world championship systems were in place. This was finally resolved in 2006 when the two rival champions met, and Vladimir Kramnik of Russia defeated Veselin Topalov of Bulgaria for the undisputed title, ending a 13-year schism.

Kramnik lost his title to Viswanathan Anand of India in 2007, and the Indian player successfully defended his title in 2010 (against Topalov), and 2012 (against Boris Gelfand of Israel). In 2013 he lost the title to 22-year-old Magnus Carlsen of Norway, who retained the title by again defeating Viswanathan Anand in 2014.

As things stand, Magnus Carlsen is both world champion and the world's highest rated player by some margin. Although older rivals such as Hikaru Nakamura of USA and Levon Aronian of Armenia cannot be discounted, Carlsen's replacement as champion is likeliest to come from a yet younger generation. Contenders include Fabiano Caruana of Italy (born in the USA), Anish Giri (Netherlands), Wesley So (USA), plus a number of young players from China, including Hou Yifan, the current women's world champion.

CLOCKS AND THE TIME ELEMENT

For all competition chess, the amount of time you have to think about your moves is strictly regulated. This wasn't always the case. Before the middle of the 19th century, there could be agreed restrictions in the amount of time a player would take to make a move in top-level matches (though it is not clear whether these intervals were monitored in any rigorous way, or whether the agreed financial penalties were ever imposed), but there is no record of time restrictions being imposed in lesser competitions. If opponents were slow to move, you would just have to wait.

Of course, players became frustrated with the slowness of some of their opponents, and the ingenious Victorian mind was set to work to come up with solutions. In the 1860s, a form of double sandglass clock was brought into use: a player would have to make a number of moves before their sandglass ran out and, on moving, set their sandglass to the horizontal while that of their opponent was set to run again.

Eventually, in the 1890s, the modern chess clock came into being: a double clock with, for example, two hours allowed to each player for 40 moves. White's clock would be started with a button or lever and, when the player moved, he or she pressed a button to stop the clock and start the opponent's, and so on. The clock would be set to show four o'clock and, if it reached six o'clock with fewer than 40 moves played, the player would lose the game. For the sake of precision, a small flag was set into each clock face. It would be raised up by the minute hand as it approached the hour, and drop at the exact moment the minute hand reached the hour.

Ever since, tournament chess has involved the use of chess clocks. In recent years, digital chess clocks have been introduced, which have more facilities. One undesirable feature of chess played with

Below: The clock on the left of the back row is an old 1950s model; the two smaller clocks on the right were the most familiar style of clocks from the 1960s to 2000. In recent years the digital model (front, left) has become more popular.

mechanical clocks has been the problem of time trouble. Some players have the habit of thinking too long about their moves, and getting into the situation where they have only a few seconds left but still, for example, 15 moves to play. This can be exciting to watch for spectators. As soon as the player with more time left makes a move, the player in time trouble only has seconds to think of a move and play it.

Many a chess game has been ruined in such situations (which are known as 'time scrambles'). Curiously, 'time trouble' is infectious: very often the player with more time is infected by the panicking of the fast-moving opponent and is the one to make a big mistake. To alleviate this, the makers of digital clocks have introduced an ingenious time setting that works as before (for example, so many hours for so many moves) but also adds on a fixed amount of time (for example, 30 seconds or 1 minute) to a player's

Above: The 1967 World Junior Chess Champion, Julio Kaplan, from Puerto Rico, is seen in play at the 1967/68 Hastings, UK, Christmas tournament. The clock in use is of an older, larger and rather elegant wooden design.

allotment after a move is made. This has the effect that a player never has less time to play one move than the value of the time increment (30 seconds or 1 minute or whatever the increment). Thus, the introduction of digital clocks has largely removed the time trouble element from the game.

Chess clocks are available from specialist chess retailers. They can be used for other two-player board games such as draughts and checkers. Use of a chess clock is not a priority for beginners but, once you have played for a few months, they can be used at home to speed up play, and to get a feel for tournament chess. They are also beneficial if you intend to play Internet chess, since this is nearly always played to specific time limits.

FAST CHESS: RAPIDPLAY AND BLITZ

People who don't know about chess sometimes dismiss it as a 'terribly slow game'. It is true that if you don't play with a clock, it can be, but competition players rarely submit themselves to such torture. Competition chess is always played with a clock – and some competitions can be staggeringly fast. The faster you can play, the more fun it gets.

Competition chess players hardly ever play informal chess without a clock, except when they are engaged in teaching. Assuming the reader of this book to be a beginner, you are not ready for time-limit chess until you have had plenty of practice just moving the pieces around. You don't want to take too long over the moves, but at the same time the presence of an unfamiliar timepiece can be a little off-putting in the early stages of learning chess. When you are fully conversant with the rules, and perhaps are on the point of playing in your first competition, it is time to start playing with a clock. When you first begin to play chess with a clock, it would be a good idea to allow a reasonable time for a game. I would suggest 25 or 30 minutes. This means that each player has 25–30 minutes for all of their moves. If you run out of time, you lose the game – it's as simple as that. If the clock shows you to have run out of time just as you are about to play checkmate, you have lost. Don't believe anyone when they say there is no luck in chess – there is plenty, good and bad. But, also, don't make excuses. The time element is an integral part of the game.

Rapidplay chess

The reason 25 or 30 minutes is best is because this is a commonly used time limit for what are known as rapidplay (or quickplay) tournaments. Typically held on a Saturday or Sunday, they are five- or six-round tournaments held from about 10am to 6pm in the evening.

Below: For the first time in chess history, the 2006 world chess championship was decided by rapidplay games after the 12-game match was tied at 6–6. Vladimir Kramnik (right) went on to defeat Veselin Topalov in a four-game rapidplay decider, thereby becoming the undisputed champion of the world.

Each game takes up to an hour, and is followed by a break of 5–10 minutes while the officials do the pairings, and there might be an hour's break for lunch. It is a good way of getting a tournament played in one day. Even if you lose, you get to play in every round and are paired to play someone on a similar score to yourself. It is one point for a win, half a point for a draw, and zero for a loss. The winner and perhaps second and third place usually receive a cash prize and go home with a sense of achievement. Normally, tournaments are divided up into sections, with beginners and unrated players grouped together. Rapidplay tournaments are almost the ideal entry into the world of competition chess. Consult one of the chess calendars at the back of the book for a list of possible tournaments to enter.

Blitz chess

An even faster form of chess than rapidplay is blitz chess. Typically you have five minutes on your clock to make all the moves in the game. Does that sound ludicrously fast? It is, if you are a beginner. But, after a year of regular practice, your chess reflexes could be ready for some informal blitz chess with a friend. Most competition chess players love playing blitz chess – it is

Top: The European Speed Chess Championship, which took place in 1993 in France. Junior speed chess is played at all levels, and many schools and clubs hold junior speed chess tournaments.

Above: The Estonian supermodel Carmen Kass (b. 1978) is a keen chess player who has been president of the Estonian Chess Federation. Here, left, she is playing a rapidplay game against the 2004 women's world chess champion Antoaneta Stefanova of Bulgaria.

fast and fun, and not too serious. You can chat with your opponent as you play. This is an incentive to practise hard and become good at chess. Blitz is the most fun you can have on a chessboard.

Slow Chess: Correspondence Chess

Not everyone takes to fast chess. Some players prefer to take their time over their moves. Here are a few other impediments to playing conventional club, tournament or even informal chess: you don't live close to anyone else who likes playing chess, or plays at your standard; you are too busy to travel to clubs and tournaments; or you suffer from a disability that means that you cannot easily get to a chess club. The Internet is an answer to some of these problems, but perhaps you don't use (or prefer not to use) the Internet.

Well, the good news is that there is still a way to play chess, even if one or all the above scenarios are true. You can play correspondence chess (or CC, as it is widely known, as opposed to 'over-the-board', or OTB, chess). In correspondence chess, moves can be made by post, telephone, email or fax. It is a very well-established form of chess playing, going back three centuries or more, but only becoming popular in the first half of the 19th century. Hundreds of thousands of CC players enjoy tournaments and compete in championships in this specialized form of the game.

If you join a postal chess club, you are then paired with an opponent, or a number of opponents. It is possible to have several games of postal chess in progress at the same time. The White player starts the game by writing the first move on a chess score sheet and sends it by post to the player playing Black, who posts back a reply. The game continues in the usual way. There are usually time limits (measured in days), so that you normally have to reply to a move within a day or two, and games usually last for a matter of weeks or months.

One significant difference between CC and OTB chess is that when playing CC you are allowed to consult books and computers in playing your moves. Books were always allowed in the past, which meant that players could consult opening manuals at the start of the game, and endgame manuals for the final moves of the game. However, the advent of powerful chess-playing software now means that, if they are so minded, players can simply play moves that the computer suggests, right through the game. Many people regard this as the death-knell of CC but, in fact, things are not so simple in real life. Not every move

that a computer suggests is necessarily the absolute best one, and a good CC player will still exercise his or her own judgement in certain positions. But it cannot be denied that it takes some of the fun out of CC. When you play, you don't really know whether you are playing the opponent or the opponent's computer.

Incidentally, although CC now permits the use of computer software, it is still regarded as unsporting to consult another human for advice. Obviously, it is impossible to police such a rule, and it relies on proper conduct on the part of the players. The good news is that CC players rank well above the average (and their OTB equivalents) in this important respect.

Recently, there has been an explosion of interest in e-mail chess. It works on exactly the same principle, but there is no need for stamps and stationery, and online interfaces make it very easy to keep track of your games.

One word of warning: CC is not really for the absolute beginner. You need some OTB practice before trying correspondence chess. However, once you know the rules and want some practice, it becomes a very attractive option, particularly if you are nervous about your early chess steps being too public. CC allows your entry into (and possible exit from) competition chess to be made very discreetly.

Right: The scoresheet of a correspondence chess game played in 1977. Note that, as well as the moves (in old-fashioned 'descriptive' notation), the players have noted the day on which the move was posted to the opponent

Below: British chess player John Walker posting his latest move to American life prisoner Claude Bloodgood, in 1999. Walker played CC with the notorious inmate for 30 years (although it is said he never won a game). A formidable opponent in more ways than one, Bloodgood, a convicted murderer, was at one point juggling some 2,000 games by correspondence.

Left: When they began playing in 1970, Walker and Bloodgood exchanged moves by post, but the Internet has brought radical changes to the virtual chess world. It is no longer necessary to wait days between moves, and easier to track your progress.

G24
SURREY v BUCKS – WARD HIGGS –
DIVISION 1.   BOARD 3.

White M.J. FRANKLIN   Date 3-11-77   Round
Black J. SAUNDERS   Event

		White	Black		White FEB	Black
NOV.	1	P-Q4	N-KB3	28	if KxN	Q-Q2.
9/9	2	N-KB3	P-KN3	29	P-K4	P-QB4
11/11	3	B-B4	B-N2	30	PxP	if PxP
14/14	4	P-K3	P-Q3	31	Q-Q3	R-Q1
16/16	5	B-B4	O-O	32	QxQ+	if RxQ+
18/18	6	QN-Q2	N-B3	33	K-K3	P-QN4
22/22	7	P-B3	N-Q2	34	R-QB1	P-N5
24/24	8	P-KR4	P-K4	35	N-K2	P-B5
29/29	9	B-KN5	Q-K1	36	N-Q4	PxP
DEC. 1/1	10	P-R5	KPxP	37	if PxP	K-B2
3/5	11	RPxP	RPxP	38	P-B4	R-K2
	12	BPxP	N-N3	39	R-B3	R-K1
8/8	13	B-N3	B-K3	40	N-B3	R-Q1
10/12	14	B-B2	P-R4	41	P-K5	R-Q8
15/16	15	P-R3	P-R5	42	K-K4	R-QR8
21/21	16	N-K4	P-B3	43	N-Q4	R-Q8
24/28	17	B-R6	N-R4	44	P-N4	B-R7
JAN. 4/4	18	N(3)-Q2	BxB	45	R-R3	P-B4+
	19	RxB	K-N2	46	PxP	PxP+
7/9	20	R-R4	R-R1	47	KxP	B-N8+
12/13	21	Q-B3	Q-K2	48	if K-N5	RxN
19/20	22	RxR	RxR.	49	P-B5	K-N2

EXPANDING YOUR HORIZONS

Assuming you have read the book to this point, you will have learned all the rules, gone away and played some practice games, come back and learned a little more about strategy and tactics, and also absorbed a little of the history, background and culture of chess – you are now a knowledgeable chess player. That may be all you want to know about chess – in which case, farewell, reader, go forth and enjoy the game. However, if you now want to raise your chess skills a notch or two further, this chapter supplies you with some advice on what to do next. Chess has a rich cultural heritage, with a vast literature stretching back hundreds of years. This chapter helps you to learn more about what interests you in the world of chess.

Right: You have now learned all the rules and absorbed much about the strategy of the game, plus its history and culture. This is more than enough if you simply want to enjoy a social game with friends. However, if you've decided to take your game further, this chapter helps you get ready for competition chess.

HOW TO TEACH YOURSELF

Unquestionably the best way to teach yourself chess is to practise. There are some wonderful resources available for learning chess at all levels, to supplement the experience of actually playing the game. These are worth using to develop your strategy.

The written word versus software

At one time, there was only one way to teach yourself chess, and that was to read a book. The computer age has lead to the introduction of major alternatives: teaching software, playing software and teaching websites. Before suggesting any specific titles or sources, it is best to consider which aspects of chess need to be studied.

There are several different types of chess book or software title. The book you are currently reading is an introduction to chess, covering the rules, elementary strategy, openings, middlegame and endgame, plus some background on the history, personalities and general culture of the game. You will not be surprised to know that each of these components is itself the subject of many chess books in their own right.

Useful books

Although it is difficult to prove, it has been asserted more than once that more books have been written about chess than all other games and sports combined. This is not hard to believe. Chess has been played in its current form for hundreds of years, and the fact that chess games can be transcribed in notation makes it very compatible with presentation via the written word.

This presents the reader with a problem: what sort of book is best to read? If the goal is to improve as a player from elementary to intermediate (and

Above: The only way to learn how to play chess is by playing, as often as you can. Don't seek out chess 'experts': you'll learn more by playing opponents at your level, or from a parent or elder sibling, who can teach you and enjoy the game at the same time.

Left: A class of girls listens to their teacher Lucy Anness give a lesson on the game of chess at a school in Kent, England, in 1948. Miss Anness was proud to be headmistress of the only girls' school in Britain to teach chess as part of the curriculum.

ultimately further), the following types of book are appropriate in descending order of priority:

• Books teaching middlegame tactics and strategy: look for books that have plenty of examples from the play of amateur or intermediate-level players. Just as it is important to practise against players of a slightly higher standard, it is useful to play through examples taken from ordinary games. When reading such books, it is usually a good idea to set the games and positions up on a board and play through the examples.

• Puzzle books: typically, chess puzzle books have a number of diagrams on each page and invite you to find the next move in a given position. Usually the move will be surprising or spectacular. Working through tactical puzzles is good practice for visualization and just good old-fashioned fun. You don't need a board and pieces to do puzzles, so this makes them useful books to carry when travelling.

• Opening books: there are hundreds of these to choose from, but at this stage you only need a basic overview of available openings and perhaps the rudiments of a repertoire. Small is beautiful.

• A basic book on the endgame might be useful – nothing too heavy.

Books to avoid (for now) are: collections of games, or even instructional books, by famous world champions. These are for more advanced players – and world champions don't write beginners' books. When checking out the credentials of an author, it can be more useful to find out if they have a track record as a teacher rather than a player. Don't be too impressed by the quantity of books they have written.

Computer programs

By all means, play your computer on a friendly level (even one where it evens up the score between you), but don't overdo it. Playing chess in two dimensions can make it hard to adapt to play on a conventional board. Also, always remember that computers play chess in a slightly different way from humans, and you may find human versus human chess difficult to adapt to – though you will also find some humans much easier to beat.

WHERE TO PLAY COMPETITIVE CHESS

In all probability, you will start playing chess against a friend or relative who already 'knows the moves' (as we like to say). This is the best way for most people, unless that person happens to be a high-level competition player. Obviously, it is good to have a strong chess-playing friend from the point of view of learning how to play, but it would probably take too long for you to catch up with him or her in strength so that the games become genuinely competitive. There is only even a point in playing people of approximately the same standard. It may happen that you and your original partner happily go on playing informal chess from now until the end of time. However, for the purposes of this section, let's assume that you decide to take the plunge and involve yourself in the wider world of competition chess.

The first thing to be aware of is that some players at the bottom of the pyramid that represents the world of competition chess are not too far above the beginner level themselves. Someone of average intelligence who practises frequently and does a bit of chess reading can bridge the gap between beginner and low-level competition player in a few months. So there is no

Below: Twenty champion players gathered in 1930 for an international chess tournament in San Remo, Italy. On the left is Hans Kmoch from Austria, and on the right is Karl Ahues from Germany.

Above View of the 1989 Aubervilliers chess tournament in France, with its line-up of playing competitors. In this tournament around 800 competitors played – in some the number of competitors runs into thousands.

need to entertain the notion that everyone at a tournament or in a chess club is some sort of chess-playing genius. Nor are they freaks, geeks or nerds. Men and women, who are rich, poor, young, old, introvert or extrovert can all play chess. Sadly, though, there is a gender bias, with only about 5 per cent of the world's competition players being female. This situation is gradually improving, however.

Your first question is probably: club or tournament? Of course, you can do both in due course. Most reasonably sized towns in the UK and US have chess clubs, which usually meet one night during the week, or afternoon during the weekend, for matches and competitions. You can make contact either by turning up on a club night or contacting a club official. A few addresses are given in the 'Useful List' at the back of this book. Chess clubs always welcome new members and are generally friendly, usually meeting in church halls and community centres, and sometimes at their own premises or in plush rooms in hotels.

As regards tournaments, there are two main types. We have already mentioned rapidplay tournaments, which take place on Saturdays or Sundays, where five or six games are played in the course of one day. Each game lasts no more than one hour. Longer

tournaments can stretch from Friday evening to Sunday afternoon, again with five or six games played, but each individual game can last more than four hours. This may sound gruelling, but there is a tendency for the games of lower-level players to be shorter than that – which means there is time to socialize between games, or perhaps browse a bookstall (chess competitions very often have chess bookstalls) or have a meal or snack. It is usually not expensive to enter tournaments, and many award cash prizes of varying amounts. Your chances of winning might be better than you think – players are grouped together in sections of approximately equal strength, and relative beginners sometimes walk away with decent prizes.

Several chess calendars listing upcoming tournaments can be found on the Internet. A good place for European tournaments is chess-calendar.eu, and for the USA, uschess.org

Chess tournaments are often held in coastal resorts and holiday destinations during the summer, and they can offer an enjoyable way to combine an ordinary holiday with some chess.

PLAYING AT A CHESS CONGRESS

Playing chess at a congress or in a chess club is a little different from playing informal chess with friends, and takes a bit of getting used to at first. That is not to say that informal chess is not played at chess clubs. On your first visit to a club, you will probably be paired to play a few informal games that are not part of any competition and are more a way of breaking the ice – people will be casting an eye over you, to see if you are any good. These games will be much the same as you play with your friends. Some of the rules may be relaxed for the duration.

Bending the rules

The rule that you must move a piece that you have touched or moved may, for example, be waived. If it is just a friendly game and you play a ridiculous move that loses instantly, the polite enquiry 'Can I take that move back?' will probably be answered in the affirmative. You may also notice that other people are playing friendly games and talking incessantly during games, including teasing each other and making derogatory comments about each other's play. In this respect, chess club meetings can differ quite markedly from each other. Some have an atmosphere like a working man's club, with plenty of chat and people drinking alcohol as they play. At others, chess is played in library-like silence as if the result of the world chess championship were at stake.

However, if a formal match or tournament is in progress, the game is played by the rulebook. Silence is observed in the clubroom, even if some of the games being played are not part of the competition. During a competitive match, a request to take a move back would be met by total incredulity.

Team chess

One of the most enjoyable and sociable ways of playing chess is team chess, with clubs developing their own camaraderie. Many clubs run second, third and other subsidiary teams, and players of all standards can find their niche in such line-ups. Club team chess is usually confined to weekday evenings, fitting in with players' work patterns. Team chess is very popular in schools throughout the world. Teams may compete within a school and between schools. In the USA, for example, there are high-school championships.

Tournament chess

Played in line with the formal rules of the game and using chess clocks, you should not ask for any relaxing of the rules when playing in a tournament. An arbiter is present to ensure fair play. However, that does not mean it is unfriendly or unsociable. Between games, players will chat with each other and – if it is not your turn to move – it is perfectly proper to walk around, obtain refreshments, and perhaps chat with a friend (as long as you do not disturb people in play). As well as using the clock, you will be expected to keep score of the moves. This is extremely useful, and you should spend time going through the game afterwards, particularly if you lose. Tournament chess is also played at junior level. Information about tournaments at any level can usually be found on the websites of the many chess federations that exist around the world, such as the US Chess Federation, the English Chess Federation and the Australian Chess Federation.

Most such tournaments take place at the weekend (they are known as weekend congresses), normally over four to six rounds. In most, players are usually divided into a number of sections, according to playing strength. Players play in all five games, and winners are paired against each other.

Below left: Young boys from the Reykjavik Chess Club concentrate on a game. Many schools run chess clubs and members need not be budding Kasparovs to take part in mini-tournaments and inter-school games. While it is widely recognized that chess encourages concentration and mental agility, it can also be a very sociable activity.

Below: There are almost as many players watching as playing in this depiction of a 19th-century French salon. Chess spectators are sometimes called 'kibitzers' – a Yiddish word meaning people who watch (and even offer advice) while others play.

CHESS PROBLEMS AND STUDIES

One branch of the game that beginners sometimes find hard to grasp is the composition of problems and studies. There are several different types of composition, although there are some similarities among all of them. The idea is to compose a chess position where one of the sides has an unusual, hard to find and/or aesthetically pleasing way to win (or sometimes draw) available.

The popularity of chess problems in the 19th century led to several composers becoming famous. Probably the most well-known was the US composer Sam Loyd (1841–1911). He created a great many ingenious and entertaining chess puzzles, including the Excelsior, published in 1861.

Chess problems

The most common type of chess problem has a caption stating: 'Mate in x moves', where x is often 2, 3 or occasionally a larger number. Let's assume x is 2: this means that White is to play and make a remarkable or surprising move and, in reply to any move by Black, will reply with a second move that is checkmate (the second white move could be clever or quite obvious).

Over many years, conventions have grown up around chess problems and, in trying to solve the problem, you can be fairly sure of the following: 1) the first move will not be a major capture (and probably not a capture at all); 2) it won't be a checking move; 3) it will be something quite counter-intuitive in the context of practical chess (e.g. a queen being placed *en prise* to a pawn).

Chess problems often have quite outlandish positions that are unlikely to arise during a normal game. However, they use all the rules of chess and it can be quite useful to work through them. One important point: be sure to check all Black responses very carefully because there is often a surprise resource for Black that makes a nonsense of your proposed solution. Black is simply trying to extend the game beyond White's second move in order to invalidate a proposed solution.

Chess problem composing and solving are two different specialisms and there are chess competitions that test both skills. It is said that comparing the normal playing of chess to problem composition is like comparing prose and poetry: composition is about subjective considerations such as ingenuity, aesthetics, originality and taste. Solving problems involves skills such as visualization and clarity of thought, which play a vital part in chess-playing itself.

Here is a typical example of a chess problem. This particular problem dates from 1880.

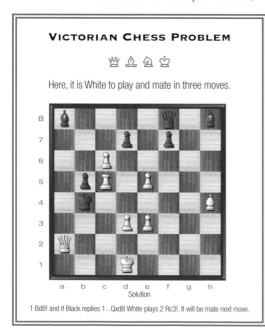

VICTORIAN CHESS PROBLEM

Here, it is White to play and mate in three moves.

Solution

1 Bd8! and if Black replies 1...Qxd8 White plays 2 Rc3!. It will be mate next move.

Mate in Two

The solution is 1 d4! – after that, all Black replies will be answered by checkmate in one move, e.g. 1...bxc4 2 Rxe5 mate, 1...Kxe4 2 Qh1 mate, 1...exd4 2 Qxd4 mate, 1...Qxc5 (don't forget to look at outlandish replies), 2 dxc5 mate, etc.

Chess studies

Studies are composed endgame positions resembling situations that arise in practical chess, with the caption 'win' or 'draw'. The solver is thus challenged to find a winning or drawing line by White (who usually plays first). The 'clever' part of the solution may come at any point of the winning/drawing sequence, or may even be every move of the sequence. As with problems, it must be assumed that the defender finds the very best defence. Here is an example of a study with a difference. White is to win – however, Black moves first and the challenge is to find the best try to avoid the loss. Only then is White tasked to find the way to refute Black's ingenious drawing attempt. The big problem for Black is how to stop White queening the pawn and then routinely winning.

Below: Composed problems are as old as competitive chess, and appeared in many old chess books alongside instruction and advice on how to play the game.

Black's clever starting move is 1...Be8!!. That may look like madness, but 2 fxe8Q is stalemate and if 2 f8Q? Nd7+! forks the king and queen so that, after 3 Nxd7, it is stalemate again. It is no good underpromoting to a rook because the same thing will happen. But after the astonishing 2 fxe8B!! – i.e. pawn takes bishop and promotes to a bishop – Black must make a knight move, and the knight will be lost. White will be left with the technical task of winning with the bishop and the knight – and, having reached a theoretically won position, the study is deemed to be solved.

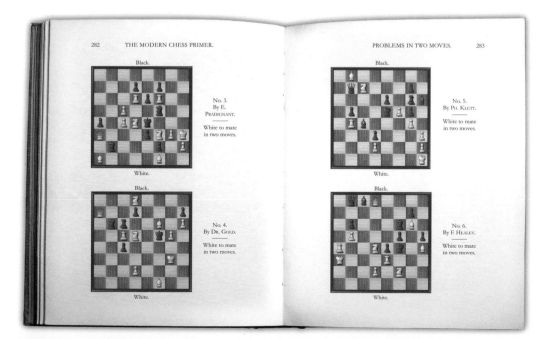

282   THE MODERN CHESS PRIMER.

Black.

No. 3.
By E.
Pradignant.

White to mate
in two moves.

White.

Black.

No. 4.
By Dr. Gold.

White to mate
in two moves.

White.

PROBLEMS IN TWO MOVES.   283

Black.

No. 5.
By Ph. Klett.

White to mate
in two moves.

White.

Black.

No. 6.
By F. Healey.

White to mate
in two moves.

White.

HOW TO
PLAY BRIDGE

A fun and social game combining luck and skill, bridge is played all over the world in bridge clubs, tournaments and championships, from small clubs with only a few tables to the World Championships and Olympiads where hundreds of people play.

STARTING OUT

This section assumes no knowledge of the game and will explain clearly all the basic concepts. You will learn the ranking of the various cards, how to deal and how to "sort out" your cards. Next you will see the meaning of the term "trick" and how the play of the cards progresses. On most deals one of the four suits is chosen as "trumps" and this, too, will be explained. Once you understand the importance of the trump suit and how tricks are scored in the play, the idea of "bidding" will be discussed. By making "'bids", the players decide whether a suit should be made trumps and what the target number of tricks should be for the partnership who bids highest.

Right: Declarer is about to play a contract of 4♠. Before playing a card from dummy he should make a plan.

THE BASICS

Four players take part in a game of bridge and are conventionally known in bridge literature as North, East, South and West. The players in the North and South seats form one partnership and sit opposite one another. They will compete against East and West, who form the other partnership.

For each deal, one of the players is the "dealer". (In a social game, the dealer for the first deal is chosen by a cut of the cards. Thereafter, the deal passes clockwise to the next player. In tournament bridge, the plastic or wooden board containing the cards indicates who is the dealer.) The dealer deals the pack of 52 cards in a clockwise direction, one card at a time. When the whole pack has been dealt, each player will hold a "hand" of 13 cards. It is customary to sort these into suits, with the cards in descending order within a particular suit. For example, you might sort out your hand like this:

♠A Q 9 5 4   ♥A 8 5 3   ♦K 9 4   ♣5

Above: West has five spades to the ace–queen, four hearts to the ace, three diamonds to the king and a singleton club.

You have sorted all the spades to be together. The rank (order of importance) of the cards is: ace (highest), king, queen, jack, 10, 9, 8, 7, 6, 5, 4, 3, 2 (lowest). As you see, the five cards in the spade suit are arranged in descending order of rank, with the ace on the left and the 4 on the right. If someone were to ask you afterwards what hand you held, you would reply

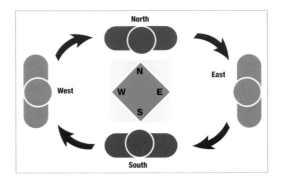

Above: For both the bidding and play, the action takes place in a clockwise direction. If South makes the first call in the auction, for example, West will make the second call. If West later leads to the first trick, the second card will be played by North.

"I had five spades to the ace–queen, four hearts to the ace, three diamonds to the king and a singleton club". A "singleton" is a holding of just one card in a suit; a "doubleton" would be a holding of two cards. When you describe a hand, you cannot be expected to remember the low cards (known as "spot cards") and would usually name only the "picture cards" (aces, kings, queens or jacks) that you held.

So, each of the four players holds a hand of 13 cards. These are held close to the chest, so that the other three players can see only the backs of the cards. The subsequent action consists of two parts: the "bidding" and then the "play" of the cards.

Although the bidding occurs before the play when you are actually engaged in a game of bridge, it is not possible to understand the bidding until you know how the play will go. For that reason the play will be described first here. So that you can understand the basics, if you are new to the game, the idea of tricks and trumps will be addressed first. Later the bidding will be described and a sample complete deal of bridge will give you a general idea of how the game is played.

Above: Bidding sequence. In tournament bridge each player creates a line of all his calls during the auction. Here, the player has made three bids.

What is a trick?

The play of the cards, at bridge, is very similar to that in the old game of whist. It consists of a sequence of "tricks". A trick consists of four cards, one played by each player. The highest card played will "win the trick".

This is a typical trick, with the cards played in a clockwise direction around the table:

West plays first to the trick and chooses to play the

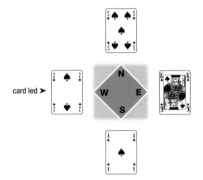

♠2. You might also say that "West leads the ♠2". (You will see later how it is decided who leads to the first trick and to each of the subsequent tricks.) West "leads" the ♠2, then, and North plays the ♠5. East plays the ♠K and South "wins the trick" with the ♠A. He wins the trick because his card is the highest one played in the suit that was led. Remember that the ranking of the cards is: ace (highest), king, queen, jack, 10, 9, 8, 7, 6, 5, 4, 3, 2 (lowest). Because South won the trick, he will lead to the next trick. It will be his choice whether to lead another spade or to play some different suit.

If you hold a card in the suit led, you must

┌───┐

A ROUND OF TRUMPS
♠ ♥ ♦ ♣

The term "round" is similar in meaning to "trick". If declarer plays a "round of trumps", this means that he leads a trump and the other three hands play a card to the trick. If, for example, both defenders hold at least one trump, this round of trumps will draw two trumps from the defenders' hands. For that reason, you might also say "declarer draws a round of trumps". You might also say "declarer draws trumps in three rounds", meaning that he had to lead trumps three times, on three successive tricks, in order to remove all the defenders' trumps.

└───┘

"'follow suit". In other words, if a spade is led you must play a spade if you have one. When you cannot follow suit, you must play a card in a different suit. Unless you play a card from the suit chosen as the "trump suit", your card in a different suit cannot win the trick, however high it is. Suppose the trump suit is spades and South leads the ♣J here:

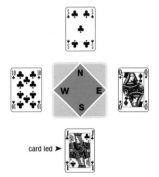

South, who won the previous trick, leads the ♣J. The next two players follow with lower cards in the same suit and East has no clubs left in his hand. He "discards" the ♦Q. South's ♣J wins the trick because it is the highest card in the suit that was led.

What are trumps?

During the bidding, which will be explained in a moment, a suit may be chosen as "trumps". This suit then becomes more powerful than the other three suits. A low trump, such as the two, will defeat even the ace of a different suit. When you have no cards left in the suit that has been led, you can play any card in the trump suit and win the trick with it. Let's assume that spades are trumps and this trick arises:

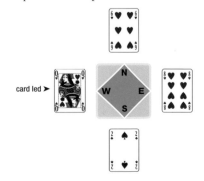

West, who won the previous trick, leads the ♥Q. The next two players follow with lower hearts. South, who has no hearts left, plays the two of trumps. Even though his trump is a lowly two, he wins the trick. Bridge players would say "South trumped with the two" or (more commonly) "South ruffed with the two".

Sometimes two players have no more cards in the suit that was led and both choose to play a trump. In that case the higher trump will win the trick:

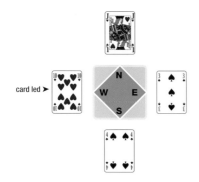

West leads the ♥10 and North beats this with the ♥J. East has no more hearts and attempts to win the trick by ruffing with the ♠3. South "overruffs" with the ♠4. He wins the trick because his card is the higher of the two trumps played.

You can see how useful trumps are. You can use them to prevent the other side from winning tricks with their high cards in other suits. You can also use them to score extra tricks of your own – by ruffing low cards of a non-trump suit, cards that would otherwise not win a trick.

NOTATION FOR CARDS IN BRIDGE

♠ ♥ ♦ ♣

When a suit symbol precedes a number, or a letter that denotes a picture card, this represents a card. It is the accepted shorthand for representing a card in print, perhaps in a bridge book or article or in a newspaper. So, ♠ 3 is short for the card known as the "three of spades". ♦ K is the "king of diamonds". ♠ A J 7 6 is the written form of a spade suit containing four cards: the ace, jack, seven and six.

The bidding

During the bidding each partnership tries to assess how many tricks they will be able to make during the play, also which trump suit they should choose. (The trump suit is the most powerful suit during the play of the cards, remember. Any trump, however low, will win against a card from any other suit). A further option is to play the hand in "no-trumps", in other words without a trump suit.

We will see in a moment how you make a bid. For the moment, let's suppose that the bidding ends with South announcing that he, in conjunction with his partner's hand opposite, can make ten tricks with spades as trumps. The cards are then played and South must attempt to score ten tricks out of the 13 that are available. The other two players, known as the defenders, will try to prevent him from achieving this target.

That is the purpose of the bidding, then. One side, usually the one with the most high cards (aces, kings and queens) between them, will set themselves a target of tricks and choose whether they want a particular suit to become trumps.

What is a bid?

During the "bidding", or "auction", each player may make a "bid" when it is his turn to speak. He may instead choose to "pass". (There are two other possible calls, "double" and "redouble", which will be explained later.)

The first actual bid, as opposed to a pass, is known as the "opening bid". To open the bidding, you need slightly better than an average hand. The strength of a hand consists of two main factors – the quantity of high cards (such as aces and kings) and the length of your suits. A hand with plenty of high cards will obviously offer a good prospect of scoring several tricks when the time comes for the play. So will a hand that contains one or more long suits – seven spades, for example. That is because you can make such a suit trumps and score several tricks with it.

To measure the high-card strength of a hand, a point-count system is used. An ace is worth 4 points, a king 3 points, a queen 2 points and a jack 1 point. As a rough guide, you can open the bidding when you hold at least 12 points. Suppose you are the dealer and therefore have the first chance to bid. Your hand is:

♠A J 9 4   ♥K Q   ♦A K Q 7 5   ♣6 3

You have 19 points (5 in spades, 5 in hearts and 9 in diamonds) and this is easily enough to make an opening bid. You will bid 1♦ (one diamond), since diamonds is your longest suit and at this stage it is therefore your best guess as a satisfactory trump suit.

Above: Since you have a strong hand, you will open the bidding. Your longest suit is diamonds and you will open 1♦.

During the play there will be 13 tricks available. A bid at the one-level says that you think you can score seven tricks with your chosen suit as trumps. In other words, you will make seven tricks and the defenders will make six tricks; you will score more tricks than the other side, but only just. The first six tricks are known as "the book" and your bid says how many extra tricks, over the book, you think you can make in conjunction with your partner's hand opposite. Here your bid of 1♦ means that you think you can make seven tricks with diamonds as trumps. A bid of 2♥ would mean that you thought you could make eight tricks with hearts as trumps. Similarly, a bid of 3NT (three no-trumps) would mean that you thought you could make nine tricks in no-trumps, in other words with no suit as trumps.

Once someone has made an opening bid, the auction continues in a clockwise direction around the table. Each player, when it is his turn, has the chance to pass or bid. If he chooses to bid, he must make a higher bid than the last one that was made. This is why the bidding is also called the "auction". You can make a bid at the same level, here the one-level, provided your suit is ranked higher than the suit bid previously.

This is the ranking order of the five possible "denominations":

NT no-trumps (highest)
♠ spades
♥ hearts
♦ diamonds
♣ clubs (lowest)

So, a bid of 1♥ (one heart) is a higher bid than 1♦ (one diamond) because hearts are ranked above diamonds. Spades and hearts are known as the "major suits"; diamonds and clubs are the "minor suits". If all the possible bids were stretched out from the lowest to the highest, this would be the order: 1♣, 1♦, 1♥, 1♠, 1NT, 2♣, 2♦, 2♥, 2♠, 2NT, etc... 7♣, 7♦, 7♥, 7♠, 7NT.

An opening bid of 1♣ is the lowest possible bid, meaning that you think you can score seven tricks with clubs as trumps. A bid of 7NT is the highest possible bid, meaning that you think you can score 13 tricks (seven plus the "book" of six) with no trump suit.

Look again at the line of bids. Suppose someone, either your partner or an opponent, has already bid 1♠ and you have a hand on which you want to make a bid in clubs. You cannot bid 1♣ because this bid is lower than 1♠. You would have to bid 2♣. (You might also choose to bid 3♣, or some higher bid in clubs, on certain types of hand.)

The auction continues until there are three consecutive passes. The last bid then determines what is known as the "contract". If the last bid was 4♠, for example, the partnership making that bid would then try to make ten tricks (four plus the book of six) with spades as trumps. So, the bidding sets a target number of tricks for one of the partnerships.

NOTATION FOR BIDS
♠ ♥ ♦ ♣

When a suit symbol is placed after a number, this represents a bid (rather than a card). So, 2♥ is short for the bid of "two hearts". This would mean that the bidder thought his partnership could score eight tricks (the book of six, plus two) with hearts as trumps. Similarly, 3NT is short for "three no-trumps". If you read in a bridge article that "West led the ♦6 against 4♠", this would mean that West led the six of diamonds (a card) against four spades (the contract, determined by the final bid in the auction).

The play

It is an unusual aspect of bridge that one player becomes the "declarer" (the player trying to make the number of tricks specified in the contract). Suppose, as in the previous section, that the contract is 4♠. The player who first made a bid in spades becomes the declarer. The player to his left (one of the defenders) will lead the first card of the first trick. This play is known as the "opening lead".

Once the opening lead has been made, declarer's partner lays his entire hand face-up on the table. The hand, known as the "dummy", is arranged in four lines facing towards the declarer, with the trump suit (if any) on the left. Declarer's partner will take no further part in this deal. The declarer will play the cards from the dummy as well as from his own hand.

Above: The dummy is arranged in four vertical lines, one for each suit, with the cards in descending order of rank (highest at the top).

For the rest of the play, the dummy (and its remaining cards) will be visible to declarer and to each of the defenders. Whichever of the four hands wins a particular trick, this will be the hand from which the first card is led to the next trick.

Bidding a game

Even in this basic summary of the game, it is necessary to mention something about the scoring. That is because it has a critical effect on the bidding. If you make the contract determined in the auction you score these points for each trick bid and made:

When ♦ or ♣ are trumps: 20 points for each trick
When ♠ or ♥ are trumps: 30 points for each trick
In no-trumps, 40 points for the first trick and 30 points for each subsequent trick

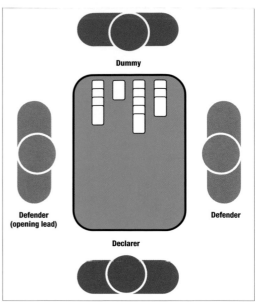

Above: The four players. The defender on declarer's left makes the opening lead and declarer's partner (the dummy) displays his hand face upwards on the table. Declarer plays a card from dummy, the other defender plays a card and declarer completes the trick with one of his cards.

One of the main aims in bridge is to "make a game". To achieve this, you need to score at least 100 points. In no-trumps this can be done by bidding and making the nine-trick contract of 3NT, since 40+30+30 = 100. When the trump suit is spades or hearts (known as the "major suits", remember), you need to bid the ten-trick contract of 4♠ or 4♥, since 4 times 30 is 120. Most difficult is to make a game with diamonds or clubs (known as the "minor suits") as trumps. You would then need to bid 5♦ or 5♣, since 5 times 20 is 100. This will require you to make 11 of the available 13 tricks.

During the auction the partnership that holds the majority of the high cards will have two main decisions to make. They must decide which suit to make trumps, or perhaps to play in no-trumps. They must decide also whether their combined strength merits attempting a "game contract". In very rough terms, since suit lengths are also important, a partnership can make a game contract when they hold 25 of the available 40 high-card points between them. During the bidding they will attempt to discover if this is in fact the case.

A typical hand of bridge

The time has come, in this brief summary of the game, to see a complete hand of bridge (see below).

North, who was the dealer and holds the 19-point hand that we saw earlier, opens 1♦. East has a poor hand and passes. South holds 6 points. To "respond" to an opening bid at the one-level (in other words, to make a bid when your partner has already opened the bidding), you need 6 points or more. South has enough to respond and bids 1♠, suggesting spades as trumps. This is a higher bid than 1♦ because the spade suit is ranked higher than diamonds.

West has a strong club suit and decides to enter the bidding. He cannot bid 1♣, since this would be a lower bid than 1♠. He therefore overcalls 2♣. The word "overcall" means to make a bid after the opponents have already bid. North is pleased that his partner has bid spades because he also holds spade length. This means that spades will make a good trump suit. He plans to "agree spades as trumps" by making a further bid in spades himself. He will have to choose how high to bid in spades – the higher he bids, the stronger the hand he will show.

Since his own hand is very strong, North judges that the partnership can make a game in spades. (As a

FINDING A TRUMP FIT
♠ ♥ ♦ ♣

To make a satisfactory trump fit, you usually need at least eight of the available 13 cards in a particular suit. On this deal North holds four spades and knows, from his partner's 1♠ response, that South holds at least four spades too. The North–South partnership has therefore "found a trump fit". North confirms that spades will be trumps by "raising his partner's suit". Because his hand is so strong he raises it to 4♠, a game contract. If he held a minimum opening bid of around 12 points, he would instead raise to just 2♠.

rough guide, 25 points between the hands will be enough to make a game contract. Here North holds 19 points and expects his partner to hold at least 6 points for his response.) North jumps to 4♠ because this will be worth 120 points and is therefore a game contract.

The next three players pass and the auction is over. The "final contract" is 4♠ and South will be the declarer since he was the first player to bid spades. West, the player to the dealer's left, will make the opening lead.

Right: Bidding game in spades. North's bid of 4♠ is followed by three passes and so becomes the final contract. South will become declarer, since he was the first player to bid spades. West will make the opening lead and the North hand will be laid out as the dummy.

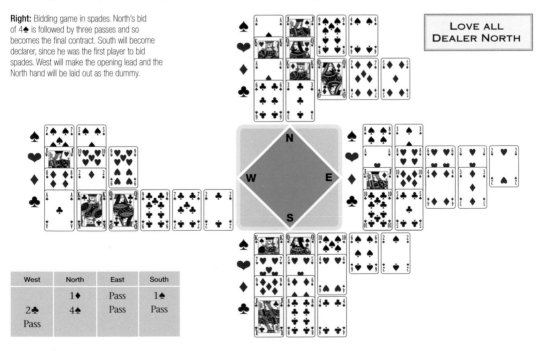

LOVE ALL
DEALER NORTH

West	North	East	South
	1♦	Pass	1♠
2♣	4♠	Pass	Pass
Pass			

We will now see the play of the cards. South, the declarer, must attempt to score ten tricks with spades as trumps. West, the player to declarer's left, makes the "opening lead" of the ♣A. North lays his cards on the table, displaying the dummy. From now on, declarer will play a card from the dummy to each trick as well as a card from his own hand.

Trick 1: The other three players follow with lower clubs and West's ♣A wins the trick.

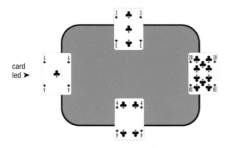

Above: Trick 1. West wins the first trick with the ♣A, the other three players following suit.

Trick 2: Since West won the trick he will lead to the second trick. He leads the ♣K and again the other three players follow with lower clubs. East–West (known as the "defenders") now have two tricks.

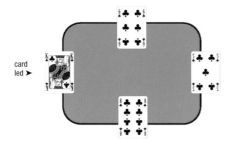

Above: Trick 2. West leads the ♣K, everyone following, and wins the trick.

Trick 3: West leads the ♣Q. Since the dummy has no clubs left, declarer can "ruff in the dummy". If he carelessly ruffs with the ♠4, East (who also has no clubs left) will overruff with the ♠8. That will be three tricks for the defenders and the ♥A would then give them a fourth trick to defeat the contract. Declarer therefore ruffs with the ♠9. He knows that neither defender holds a higher trump than this, so he has prevented an overruff.

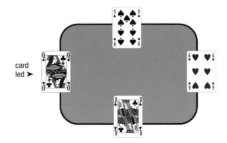

Above: Trick 3. West leads the ♣Q and declarer ruffs with the ♠9. East cannot overruff and discards a heart.

Trick 4: Declarer now starts to "draw trumps". In other words, he will play sufficient rounds of trumps to remove the defenders' trumps. They will not then be able to ruff any of his tricks. Declarer leads dummy's ♠4 to his ♠K and both defenders follow.

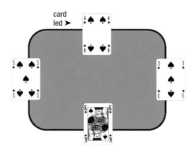

Above: Trick 4. Declarer leads dummy's ♠4 to his ♠K and both defenders follow suit.

Trick 5: Declarer leads the ♠2 to dummy's ♠A and both defenders follow again. Since there were only four trumps missing, he has now drawn trumps.

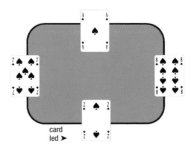

Above: Trick 5. Declarer draws a second round of trumps, everyone following suit.

Tricks 6/7/8: Declarer scores tricks with the ace, king and queen of diamonds. On the third round he has no diamond to play from the South hand and discards one of his hearts. West also "shows out", discarding a club. If the diamond suit had "broken 3–2" (in other words, one defender had held three diamonds and the other had held two), the ♦7 and the ♦5 would have scored two further tricks and declarer would have been able to discard his two remaining hearts.

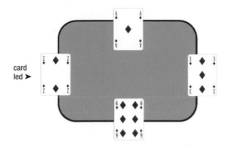

Above: Trick 6. Declarer scores a diamond trick by leading dummy's ace.

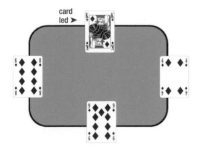

Above: Trick 7. Declarer continues with dummy's ♦K, scoring a second diamond trick.

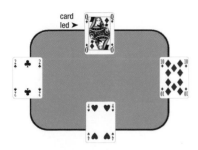

Above: Trick 8: Declarer discards a heart on the dummy's ♦Q and is disappointed to see West show out, throwing a club.

Trick 9: As it is, declarer leads the ♥K and East wins with the ♥A. Declarer has "knocked out" the ♥A, as bridge players say, and "established" the ♥Q as a winning card.

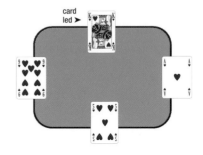

Above: Trick 9: Declarer leads the ♥K to East's ♥A, thereby setting up the ♥Q as a winner.

Trick 10: East leads a heart and the trick is won with dummy's ♥Q.

Above: Trick 10. Declarer wins East's heart return in the dummy.

The last three tricks will be taken with the three trumps remaining in declarer's hand. In total, declarer scored ten tricks: five trump tricks, one club ruff in the dummy, three diamond tricks and one heart trick. He therefore made his game contract of four spades. We will look at scoring in some detail, later in the book. For the moment, we will just say that North–South will score 120 for making four spades and a bonus of 300 for bidding and making a game. That is a score of +420 for North–South. The defenders, East–West will score -420 because the game was made against them. Scorepads (social bridge) and scorecards (competition bridge) have a plus column and a minus column.

The History of Bridge

Contract bridge has existed as a game only since 1925. It evolved over a long period of time, beginning in the early 17th century with the trick-taking game of "whist". In that game, the choice of trump suit was determined by the turn of the dealer's last card. Towards the end of the 19th century, variants known as "bridge whist" and "auction bridge" introduced elements of bidding into the game, to choose the trump suit. In 1925, Harold Vanderbilt proposed some further changes. The most important of these was that a partnership must actually bid a "game contract" to score the bonus points that such a contract attracted. (The same applied to "slam contracts", where a target of 12 or 13 tricks was set.) The new game was called "contract bridge". Millions were drawn to it and all previous similar games were swept aside. The history section contains some exciting deals, played in various world championships. If you are new to the game, you may wish to read the early instructional sections on bidding and play first.

Right: A famous hand held by Charles Goren, who followed a brilliant line of play in the ensuing 6♥ contract.

PREDECESSORS OF THE GAME

Nearly all games and sports develop gradually, sometimes over many decades or even centuries. The same is true of contract bridge (or, more simply, bridge – as it is known today). A hand of bridge consists of a bidding auction followed by the play of the cards. The format of the play, 13 tricks contested by four players in two partnerships, comes directly from the ancient game of whist.

Whist

This game originated in England at the start of the 17th century and was derived from an earlier game, known variously as "ruff and honours", "triumph" or "trump".

There is no bidding in whist and the trump suit is determined by the turn of the dealer's final card. The scoring is simple. The partnership that scores the majority of the tricks is awarded one point for each

Above: Whist in progress. Since the game is whist, rather than bridge, all four players are holding their own cards during the play. (In bridge, one of the hands is displayed face-up, as the dummy.)

trick made in excess of the six-trick "book". If they make nine tricks, for example, they score three points. To win a "game", you had to score nine points in early versions of the game, later increased to ten points.

The earliest works that touched on whist were Charles Cotton's *Compleat Gamester* (1674) and Richard Seymour's *Court Gamester* (1719). However, it was not until 1728 that the rules of whist were formalized. The first book entirely devoted to whist was *Short Treatise on The Game of Whist* (1742) by Edmund Hoyle. The book was such a success that counterfeit copies began to appear. The next major authority on the game was "Cavendish" (Henry Jones). His book *Cavendish on Whist* (1862) sold prodigiously and ran to 30 editions.

Whist was not a game played in high society; it was more of a social pastime in the coffee houses of the day. A writer in the mid-18th century described whist as being "only fit for hunting men and country squires, and not for fine ladies or people of quality". Elsewhere it was described as "the game of the servants' hall".

In many ways the play of the hand at whist was considerably more difficult (or, at any rate, contained more guesswork) than the play in bridge today. There was no bidding to guide the players, of course; neither was any "dummy hand" exposed. Various conventions in the play became established, such as leading the fourth-best card from a strong suit. If you signalled with a high card, followed by a low card, known as a "high-low signal", you showed strong trumps and suggested that your partner should lead a trump when he gained the lead. As in bridge today, a player who had just won his partner's lead with an ace was expected to return the higher of two remaining cards and the original fourth-best from any longer holding.

In the last decade of the 19th century, whist became bogged down with a plethora of conventions in the play of the cards, as well as arguments about which signal should be made from a given card combination. Such intricacies deterred players of moderate ability from playing the game. They were attracted instead by a new and apparently simpler game, known as "bridge whist" – or in those days, "bridge".

Bridge whist

In the game of bridge whist, for the first time, one of the four hands (known as the "dummy", the hand of the declarer's partner) was exposed to view. Also, play in no-trumps was permitted. Another change was that the trump suit was chosen by the dealer or his partner rather than being determined by the last card to be dealt. The scoring was more complicated too, with the trick value depending on which suit was trumps. Spades were the lowest value suit, then clubs, diamonds and hearts. No-trumps was the highest scoring denomination. The trick values were 2, 4, 6, 8, 12 respectively. If the dealer held no great length in the high-scoring heart suit, he was likely to pass the decision on choosing trumps to his partner. Thirty points were required to make game, so 11 tricks in diamonds would produce game (5 times 6), as would ten tricks in hearts (4 times 8) or nine in no-trumps (3 times 12).

Either the dealer or his partner had to choose a trump suit, however weak they both might be. The penalties for failing to make a contract were ferocious – 50 points for every trick by which you fell short (for each "undertrick", as bridge players say). For the first time, the notion of doubling and redoubling became

> ### THE FRUSTRATIONS OF BRIDGE WHIST
> ♠ ♥ ♦ ♣
>
> Bridge whist was played for around 12 years, at the end of the 19th century. You can imagine how infuriating it must have been for a player to pick up ♠3 ♥A K Q J 10 8 2 ♦A K Q 7 ♣A, only to find that the dealer, on his right, would then choose spades as trumps! If the other side held the majority of the spades, as was very likely, they would probably score at least seven tricks. The fine hand, worth a small slam if its owner had the chance to make hearts the trump suit, would therefore come to nothing.

part of the game. So much so, in fact, that bridge whist was regarded as a serious gambling game, much to the horror of its more staid followers.

Below is a typical hand of bridge whist, as described by the great American writer of the time, J. B. Elwell. Note the order of the suits, which is different from that used nowadays for contract bridge. The highest-scoring suit (hearts) was positioned at the bottom of the hand.

Right: A deal of bridge whist. The player called "Z" (nowadays he would be called "South") chooses to play the deal in no-trumps. That is all the bidding that was allowed in this form of the game.

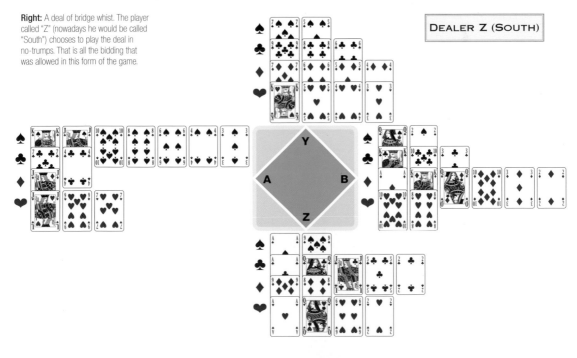

DEALER Z (SOUTH)

The players we now call West and East were referred to as A and B. Similarly, North and South were called Y and Z. Elwell's description begins: *Z deals and makes it "no-trump"*. In other words, the dealer (sitting South, as we know it) exercised his privilege to choose a trump suit or, in this case, to play the hand in no-trumps.

There was no further bidding in bridge whist, so it was West to lead and the play would take place in no-trumps. We are told that West led the ♠10 and declarer won with the ♠A. He played the ace and queen of hearts, both defenders following, and now needed to enter dummy twice to finesse in the club suit. (The term "finesse" means to lead towards a card, hoping that a higher card lies with the defender playing second to the trick. Here declarer leads towards his ♣Q, hoping that East holds the ♣K.)

Cleverly, declarer led the ♥6 (rather than the ♥2) to dummy's ♥K. A finesse of the ♣Q proved successful and declarer was then able to lead his carefully preserved ♥2 to dummy's ♥5 to finesse the ♣J. In this way he made five club tricks, four heart tricks and the ♠A. Elwell concludes: *The dealer wins four odd tricks*. By this strange-sounding phrase, he meant that declarer had scored ten tricks, four tricks over the book. Nowadays, we would say that declarer had scored ten tricks in no-trumps. In contract bridge, North–South would also need to bid to the game-level.

Auction bridge

In both whist and bridge whist, the play of the cards was exactly as it is in contract bridge. The main difference from the game today was that there was no auction before the play started. This was the major innovation of auction bridge, the next stepping stone on our journey. In this version of the game, the dealer could start the auction with a bid in one of the suits or he could opt to pass. Each player in turn could then do the same until one side was unwilling to bid any higher. If the highest bid was, say, three hearts, then hearts became trumps and declarer would have to make at least nine tricks.

The ranking of the denominations changed to that of today, with clubs (lowest), followed by diamonds, hearts, spades and no-trumps (highest). The trick value was 6, 7, 8, 9, 10 respectively and you needed to accumulate 30 points to make a game. As in contract bridge, contracts of 5♣ or 5♦ would suffice for game; so would 4♥ or 4♠. Playing in no-trumps, a contract of 3NT would yield the necessary 30 points.

The first side to score two games was said to have "won the rubber" which attracted a bonus of 250 points. In contract bridge, you need to actually bid a game or slam to receive the appropriate bonus. This was not the case in auction bridge. Even if you won the auction at just 1♠, you would still receive a game bonus if you made 10 tricks and a small slam bonus for 12 tricks.

Left: When several tables of whist are in play at one venue, this is known as a "whist drive". The players change tables every few deals and therefore face several different pairs of opponents. These sociable events were often held in church halls.

To get a flavour of auction bridge, here is a deal described in Denison's *The Play of Auction Hands* (1922). Again, the diagram looks strange to modern eyes because the diamond suit is placed at the bottom of each hand, despite the ranking of the suits being the same as it is today. This was so that the red and black colours of the suits were alternated.

Right: A deal of auction bridge, described by Denison in 1922. More than one player can make a bid but there is no necessity to carry the auction to the game-level in order to score a game bonus.

North opened 1♦ and South responded 1NT. It was natural for him to lay claim to the highest-scoring denomination since his side held the balance of the high cards. There was no reason to bid any higher, because you did not need to bid a game or slam in order to enjoy the bonus that those levels attracted.

West led the ♣J, East winning with the ♣K and returning the suit to dummy's bare ace. Declarer took a successful finesse of the ♥Q and then ran the ♦J. Denison now describes East's clever defence: *East refuses to take the Jack as declarant will then probably place the Queen with West and finesse dummy's 10 on the second round. Then if he has no more diamonds, he cannot make dummy's suit. While holding up the Queen will lose a trick if declarant does not again finesse, it is worth trying on the chance of saving game.*

As you see, if East wins with the ♦Q, declarer will score four diamonds, two hearts, two clubs and the ♠A, making game in no-trumps. If instead declarer falls for East's deceptive play and finesses the ♦10 on the second round of the suit, he will score only one diamond trick and fall short of the nine tricks required.

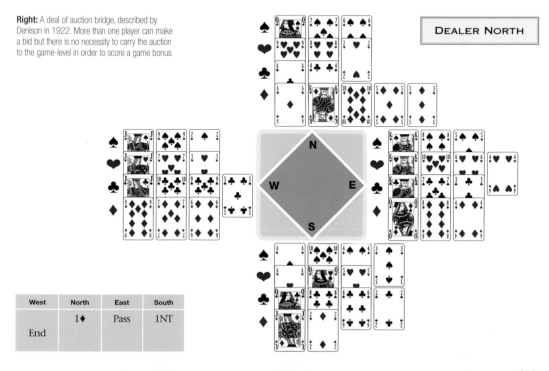

DEALER NORTH

West	North	East	South
	1♦	Pass	1NT
End			

THE ARRIVAL OF CONTRACT BRIDGE

The modern game of contract bridge is the result of changes to the scoring method suggested by Harold Vanderbilt in 1925. The most important of these, which transformed the whole game, was that you could count tricks towards a game or a slam only if you had contracted to score them during the auction.

Above: Harold S. Vanderbilt, the originator of contract bridge. The great grandson of a famous sea captain, he was a brilliant yachtsman and defended the America's Cup successfully in 1930, 1934 and 1938.

The value of each trick bid and made was set at 20 points per trick if trumps were diamonds or clubs and 30 points per trick if trumps were spades or hearts. If you played in no-trumps, you would score 40 for the first trick and 30 for each subsequent trick. Ten tricks (four above the "book") with spades as trumps would be enough for game, but only if you had bid 4♠ during the auction. If you stopped in 2♠ and scored ten tricks, you would score only 60 points (2 times 30) below the line on the score-sheet. The remaining 60, for the two overtricks, would go above the line and would not count towards game.

It is hard to over-emphasize the difference that this made to the game. Much more skill was required in the auction because a partnership had to assess accurately the trick-taking potential of their two hands together. Previously they had only to choose their most profitable trump suit and to outbid the opponents, should they have competed. On many deals there was a considerable risk involved with bidding a game, even more so if you contracted for a slam. That is because you would end with a minus score if you failed to achieve your objective. If you bid 4♠ (contracting for ten tricks) and then made only nine, you would score nothing and your opponents would receive an award for each "undertrick". As all contract bridge players know, it is a very skilful business to assess the combined playing strength of two hands, solely by making bids based on the sight of just one of these hands. This is one of the great attractions of the game.

Vanderbilt also introduced the notion of becoming "vulnerable" after you had won a game, which increased the penalties if you subsequently failed to make a contract. Within a few years, contract bridge had become so popular that it displaced bridge whist and auction bridge almost completely. The term "bridge" became synonymous with "contract bridge". Although there have been some minor changes made to the scoring of contract bridge, the game has remained largely untouched from the 1920s to this day.

Opposite is a typical deal of contract bridge – one that involves bidding by both sides:

CONTRACT BRIDGE SCORING
♠ ♥ ♦ ♣

When you make a part score (a contract below the game level) you score the trick value, plus a bonus of 50. So 2♠ made with an overtrick is worth 3 x 30 + 50, for a total of 140. Games, bid and made, attract a bonus of 300 (non-vulnerable) and 500 (vulnerable), so ten tricks in 4♥ when non-vulnerable gives you 4 x 30 + 300, for a total of 420. Vulnerable, you would score 620. When you bid and make a small slam (12 tricks) you score an additional bonus of 500 (non-vulnerable) and 750 (vulnerable). A vulnerable 6♠ is therefore worth 6 x 30 + 500 + 750 = 1430. A grand slam (13 tricks) attracts a bonus of 1000 (non-vulnerable) and 1500 (vulnerable). 7NT, vulnerable, is worth 2220.

Right: A deal of contract bridge. In order to qualify for a game bonus, North–South have to bid the heart game as well as make it. Note that the auction is competitive, with East–West bidding in spades.

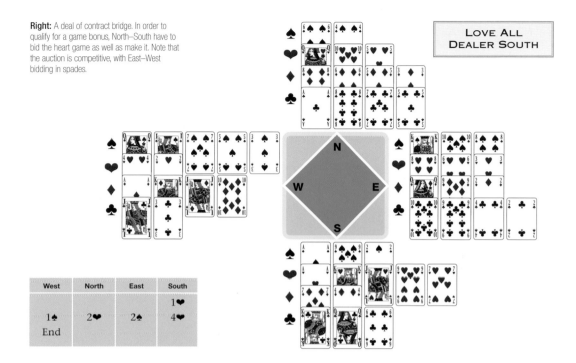

LOVE ALL
DEALER SOUTH

West	North	East	South
			1♥
1♠	2♥	2♠	4♥
End			

South opens 1♥ and West overcalls 1♠. North raises the opener to 2♥, showing heart support and a fairly weak hand. East raises to 2♠, similarly. At auction bridge, South would now bid just 3♥ because there would be no point whatsoever in bidding more. If he happened to score ten tricks, as was likely, he would receive the game bonus even when playing in 3♥. Playing contract bridge, however, South bids 4♥ because he needs at least 100 points below the line to give his side a game. (Here 4 x 30 = 120, enough for game.)

West leads the ♦A against the final contract of 4♥ and East has the chance to "signal", by following with an appropriate spot-card. Because East holds the ♦Q he plays a high card, the ♦9, to encourage a diamond continuation from his partner. West leads the ♦K next, winning the second trick, and plays a third diamond, which declarer ruffs. Declarer can see five trump tricks, three certain club tricks and the ♠A. That is a total of nine tricks. If he draws trumps next, he will need the defenders' clubs to divide 3–3. Dummy's ♣8 would then be worth a trick on the fourth round. Rather than rely on luck, declarer plans to ruff a spade loser in dummy. He delays drawing trumps and leads a low spade from his hand. West wins the trick and leads a fourth round of diamonds,

ruffed by declarer. He can now cash the ♠A, ruff the ♠9 in dummy and draw trumps. Declarer scores ten tricks: five trump tricks, three top winners in clubs, the ♠A and a spade ruff in dummy. He therefore makes his contract of 4♥ exactly and will score 420 points for the non-vulnerable game in a major suit.

PENALTIES FOR GOING DOWN
♠ ♥ ♦ ♣

When you are not vulnerable (you have not yet won a game), each undertrick at contract bridge costs you 50. If the defenders have doubled the contract – see later section on penalty doubles – the penalty is 100 for the first undertrick, 200 each for the next two, and 300 each thereafter. Four down doubled would result in an 800 penalty (100+200+200+300). When you are vulnerable the penalties are more severe, with undoubled undertricks costing 100 each. If you are doubled, the first undertrick costs you 200 and each subsequent undertrick costs 300. So, going four down doubled would now result in an 1100 penalty (200+300+300+300).

275

POPULARIZING THE GAME

Ely Culbertson was born in 1891 in Romania, the son of an American engineer and a Cossack princess. He eventually became the leading authority on contract bridge in America and was largely responsible for making the game popular worldwide. This was no easy task, even in America, because at that time card-playing was regarded as a pastime for the idle and even reckoned by some to be sinful.

Above: Ely Culbertson. The most brilliant self-publicist the game of bridge has ever known. Three of his phenomenally popular bridge books reached the USA's top ten best-seller lists for non-fiction.

Largely self-educated, Culbertson was fluent in Russian, English, French, German, Italian, Spanish and Czech. He also had a fair knowledge of several other languages, including Latin and Greek. His family's considerable fortune had been lost in the Russian Revolution of 1917. Culbertson fled to Paris and earned a living there as a skilful player of several card games.

After World War I, Culbertson moved to New York and he married Josephine Murphy Dillon, a leading bridge teacher, in 1923. He soon realized the business opportunity that the emerging game would offer and attempted to install himself as the country's leading authority. In 1929 he founded the *Bridge World*

magazine and began to publish a string of best-selling books on bridge, which had reached the peak of its popularity in the 1930s. In 1937 alone, *Bridge World* made a profit of over a million dollars, from which Culbertson collected royalties of more than $200,000.

In the Culbertson bidding system the requirements for opening bids and responses were not measured in terms of the point-count system that is familiar today (where an ace is worth 4 points, a king 3 points, a queen 2 points and a jack 1 point). The emphasis was instead on "honour tricks". This was Culbertson's Table of Honour Tricks:

Ace/King	2 honour tricks
Ace/Queen	1½ honour tricks
Ace	1 honour trick
King/Queen	1 honour trick
King/Jack/10	1 honour trick
King/x	1½ honour tricks
Queen/Jack/x	1½ honour tricks
Queen/x and Jack/x	½ honour trick

To open the bidding with one of a suit, you required 2½ honour tricks. For example, you might hold:

♠ A Q 8 6 2   ♥ J 9 2   ♦ K Q 5   ♣ 8 6

This hand contains 1½ honour tricks in spades, 1 honour trick in diamonds and no further honour tricks in hearts and clubs. That is a total of 2½ honour tricks, so the hand would be deemed worth an opening bid of 1♠.

If you held 2½ honour tricks but no suit worth bidding, you could open 1NT. With 5 honour tricks, you would open 2NT.

As a player, Culbertson was one of the leading lights in the 1930s, winning several domestic events including the prestigious Vanderbilt Trophy. He took an international team to England, winning several matches there, and won the Schwab Cup in 1933 and 1934. Opposite is a deal from the 1933 event is shown, along with some of Culbertson's comments.

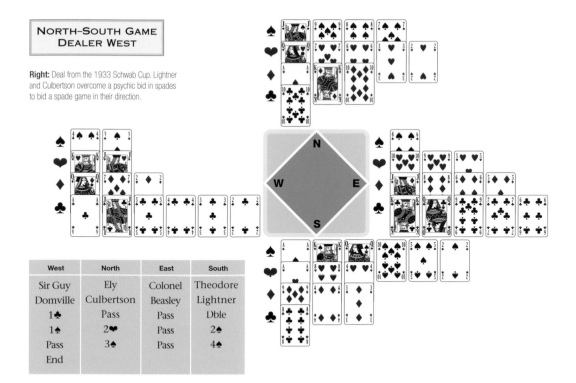

NORTH–SOUTH GAME
DEALER WEST

Right: Deal from the 1933 Schwab Cup. Lightner and Culbertson overcome a psychic bid in spades to bid a spade game in their direction.

West	North	East	South
Sir Guy Domville	Ely Culbertson	Colonel Beasley	Theodore Lightner
1♣	Pass	Pass	Dble
1♠	2♥	Pass	2♠
Pass	3♠	Pass	4♠
End			

Culbertson wrote: *Very interesting bidding. North is vulnerable and an overcall of 1♥ is dangerous against the keen opponent who is quick on the trigger. South precedes his Spade bid by a Take-out Double to show 3 or more Honour tricks. At this stage Sir Guy Domville makes a fine psychic Spade bid (in other words, bidding 1♠ when he did not hold spades in an attempt to mislead the opponents). He fears the opponents might get together on a game in spades. Note that Domville's Spade bid is safe because he has already warned his Partner that his best suit is clubs. Domville's brilliant psychic proves to be a dud. Unfortunately for him, South's Spade suit is too strong. The spade game is bid and made.*

Culbertson's name became synonymous with the game of bridge itself. He transformed a previously elitist game into an entertaining pastime for millions.

JOSEPHINE CULBERTSON
♠ ♥ ♦ ♣

Ely Culbertson's wife, Josephine was a fine player, described in the 1930s as "the modern miracle – the woman who can play on even terms with the best men". She played high-stake set games in partnership with Ely and achieved fame in the Culbertson–Lenz match. Her trend-setting clothes and the chic way in which she wore them drew the attention of the nation's fashion magazines. She and Ely were divorced in 1938 but continued to work as business partners. She died of a stroke three months after Ely's death in 1958.

Above: Josephine married her bridge partner Ely Culbertson in 1923.

THE CULBERTSON–LENZ MATCH

Towards the end of 1931, Culbertson felt that his position at the pinnacle of bridge was being threatened by another authority, Sidney Lenz. In the *Bridge World* magazine, and in several national newspapers, he challenged Lenz (and his chosen partner) to a grand match. This would determine which player's methods were superior and should therefore be adopted by the millions of bridge players in the USA.

Vast numbers of reporters relayed details of the daily play to their newspapers. By today's standards, the quality of the bidding and play was unexceptional. Culbertson and his partner, von Zedtwitz, did however fare well on the deal shown below.

Culbertson, sitting North, suggested a slam with his jump to 2♥ and von Zedtwitz indicated strong heart support with his rebid of 4♥. Aware that his heart suit was of moderate quality, Culbertson then suggested diamonds as an alternative trump suit for the small slam. Von Zedtwitz was happy to accept and the partnership had reached a fine contract.

West led the ♥10 and declarer played low from dummy, capturing East's ♥Q with the ♥K. He could not play for a spade ruff in dummy by conceding a spade trick, since he would then suffer a heart ruff. Von Zedtwitz cashed the ♣K, drew trumps in three rounds and crossed to the ♥A. After throwing a spade on the ♣A, he ruffed a club and crossed to dummy with the ♥J. At this stage West was down to ♠K–8–5 and the ♥9. He was thrown in with a heart and then had to lead away from his ♠K. Declarer therefore made both the ♠A and the ♠Q, scoring the 12 tricks that he needed. It was a fine piece of card play.

Making psychic bids (those that bear little relationship to your hand, such as opening 1♠ with only two spades in your hand) was a large part of the game in those days. On one deal, Jacoby overcalled 1NT on just 5 points, rather than the 16–18 points normally required. Lenz was furious at yet another psychic bid from a partner who had supposedly agreed to decline from such action. "Why do you make such rotten bids?" he cried. "You're having a lot of fun.

Below: A well-bid diamond slam. Culbertson's rebid of 6♦ offers partner a choice of slams and von Zedtwitz leaves it in diamonds.

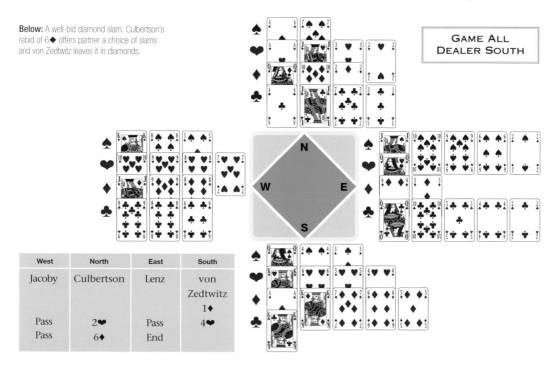

GAME ALL
DEALER SOUTH

West	North	East	South
Jacoby	Culbertson	Lenz	von Zedtwitz
			1♦
Pass	2♥	Pass	4♥
Pass	6♦	End	

Right: An ill advised penalty double. Liggett and Lenz did well to reach the club game and received an extra reward when Mrs Culbertson chose to double.

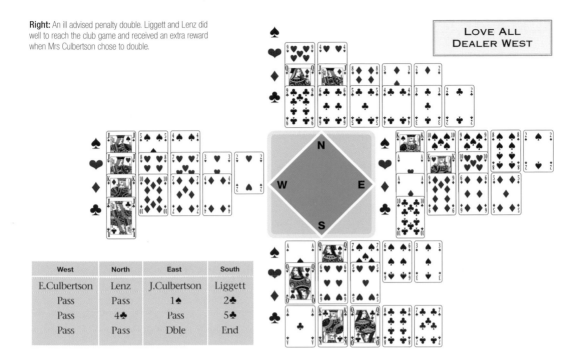

LOVE ALL
DEALER WEST

West	North	East	South
E.Culbertson	Lenz	J.Culbertson	Liggett
Pass	Pass	1♠	2♣
Pass	4♣	Pass	5♣
Pass	Pass	Dble	End

Give me a chance. I can't tell whether you have anything or not when you bid." Jacoby, who had played very well to this point, left the match the following day and was replaced by Winfield Liggett. The newcomer had an early success on this board, which featured an unwise penalty double.

West had passed throughout on the deal shown above and there was no reason for Josephine Culbertson to place him with any values. No one had forced South to bid the club game and he presumably had distributional values (a shapely hand) to make up for the missing two aces and two kings that were in the East hand. Few players would double 5♣ on the East cards nowadays.

When Ely Culbertson led the ♠J, Liggett threw a heart from dummy and won with the ♠Q. He drew trumps in one round and discarded dummy's other heart on the ♠A. He then ruffed three spades and two hearts in the dummy, meanwhile ruffing four diamonds in his hand. When diamonds broke 4–4, dummy's ♦Q became established and declarer made all 13 tricks.

Right: Culbertson-Lenz match. The contestants discuss a deal after the cards have been played.

The Culbertson team, which had at one stage led by over 20,000 aggregate points, eventually won by 8,980 points. As a result of huge publicity for the match in the press, sales of Culbertson's books rocketed. Indeed, two of his books on bidding featured in that year's national non-fiction Top Ten best sellers.

CHARLES GOREN'S INFLUENCE

Charles Goren was born in Philadelphia in 1901 and graduated in law at McGill University, Montreal. While studying there, a girlfriend expressed amusement at his lack of bridge-playing ability. This triggered him to study existing books on the game and he rapidly became a top-class player. In the 1930s the huge success of Ely Culbertson eventually persuaded Goren to abandon the law and pursue a career in bridge.

The strength of a bridge hand had previously been measured in honour tricks (where, for example, an ace–king combination counted as 2 honour tricks). Goren favoured a point-count system developed by Milton Work, where 4 points were counted for an ace, 3 for a king, 2 for a queen and 1 for a jack. In 1936 he wrote his first book, *Winning Bridge Made Easy,* in which he publicized this method. Players found the point-count system easier to use than counting honour tricks. The 4–3–2–1 method is still in universal use today, when most players would scarcely know what an honour trick is.

Goren produced several more best-selling bridge books, also writing a syndicated bridge column that appeared in dozens of newspapers from coast to coast. Between 1959 and 1964, he increased his reputation further with the first successful bridge programme on television – *Championship Bridge with Charles Goren.*

As a player, Goren was a member of the winning American team in the inaugural Bermuda Bowl (open world championship) in 1950. He won 34 national titles, many of them in his famous partnership with Helen Sobel. On eight occasions he won the McKenney Trophy, which is awarded to the player who collects the most master points in each season. (Master points are awarded by national bridge organizations for success in tournaments at all levels. For winning a session at your local club, you might win 30 master points; for winning a national championship the award would be several thousand.) As a result of this regular tournament success, Goren had the highest master point total in America throughout the period 1944–62.

As well as being a top-rank player, Goren was a very successful teacher and lecturer. He enhanced the 4–3–2–1 point-count system to assign extra values for long suits and shortages. Once a trump fit had been found, 5 points were added for a void and 3 for a singleton. Goren also pointed out that there were advantages to be gained from opening in a four-card major suit. Previously it had been common practice to insist on a five-card suit for an opening bid of 1♠ or 1♥. Players debate the benefits of five-card majors and four-card majors to this day. In most parts of the world the pendulum is swinging towards five-card majors.

Left: Charles Goren. His name was synonymous with the game of bridge for many decades in the USA. "Do you play Goren?" players would ask.

Right: A brilliant winner-on-loser play. Goren makes 6♥ by playing a losing club, throwing West on lead, and throwing a winning spade.

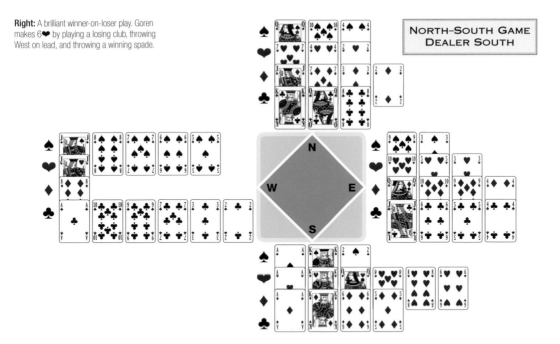

NORTH–SOUTH GAME
DEALER SOUTH

Above is one of Charles Goren's most famous hands. After a bidding sequence that has not survived (neither have the names of the other three players), he arrived in a small slam in hearts.

West decided to lead his singleton jack of trumps. Goren won and drew a second round of trumps. If the trump suit had broken 2–2, he would have led the ♥6 to dummy's ♥7 and played the ♣K, discarding a diamond loser. West would have been welcome to score his ♣A because declarer could subsequently throw his other diamond loser on the established ♣Q.

When trumps broke 3–1, Goren drew East's last trump. All would still be well if the diamond suit produced three tricks. This was an excellent prospect, requiring a 3–2 break, West to hold the ♦Q or East to hold a singleton ♦Q. However, when Goren cashed the two top diamonds West showed out on the second round.

Few players would realize that any hope remained. Goren could see a chance, however, if he could reach dummy twice in order to play clubs. Seeking an extra entry to dummy, he cashed the ♠A and then led the ♠2, finessing the ♠10. When this card won, he led dummy's ♠K, discarding the ♠K from his hand! West won with the ♣A but had only black

cards left. If he played a club, Goren would win with dummy's ♣Q. If instead he played a spade, Goren would win with dummy's ♠Q (which was the point of throwing the ♠K from his hand on the previous trick). Whatever was played by West, declarer would reach the dummy and be able to discard his two losing diamonds.

Did the American maestro gain a big swing when this result was compared with the score at the other table of the match? No, indeed. When the board was replayed, North–South overbid to a contract of 7♥. West made the uninspired lead of the ♣A, ruffed by declarer, and there were now two discards available on the king and queen of clubs.

BIDDING GUIDELINES
♠ ♥ ♦ ♣

A good general guideline is to bid boldly when a game contract is possible but to be more cautious when considering a possible slam. Failure at the slam level causes you to lose the game bonus you would otherwise have won. Be particularly wary of bidding uncertain grand slams, where failure to make the contract will cause you to lose the small slam bonus as well as the game bonus.

BRIDGE CHAMPIONSHIPS

THE BERMUDA BOWL

The first world championship for the Bermuda Bowl was held in 1950. The three invited teams were the USA, Europe and Great Britain. The USA won by a good margin, represented by six players whose names are well known in bridge circles even today: John Crawford, Charles Goren, George Rapee, Howard Schenken, Sidney Silodor and Sam Stayman. The trophy for the winners was presented by the government of Bermuda.

The next six Bermuda Bowls were two-team challenge matches between the USA and the winners of the European Championship. The USA retained the trophy for the next three holdings until Great Britain won in 1955. After a win by France in 1956, there followed a long dominance by Italy, who remained unbeaten until 1970. Their team, known as the Blue Team, included such great names as: Massimo d'Alelio, Walter Avarelli, Giorgio Belladonna, Eugenio Chiaradia, Pietro Forquet, Benito Garozzo and Camillo Pabis-Ticci.

During this period the number of teams was gradually increased. In 1958, the South American champions joined. In 1966 the South Pacific zone sent their champions. In 1979 the Central America and Caribbean Zone winners were admitted, joined in 1981 by the champions of Asia and the Middle East. Also, in 1981, a second European team was admitted.

From 1976 until the present day the Bermuda Bowl has been dominated by the USA. In total, the USA have won the event 16 times, while Italy has won

it 15 times. France has won twice and four teams have won on a single occasion: Great Britain, the Netherlands, Iceland and Brazil. The Bermuda Bowl had begun as an exclusive event, with a gladiatorial atmosphere. Nowadays the character of the championship has changed and around 20 teams take part. They compete in two mini-leagues, with the top four teams from each section advancing to the knock-out quarter-finals. As a result of the advent of other world championships – the Olympiad and the Rosenblum transnational world championship – the Bermuda Bowl is now held only on odd-numbered years.

AN OLYMPIC SPORT
♠ ♥ ♦ ♣

In 2000 the President of the International Olympic Committee, Jacques Rogge, declared that bridge had been accepted as a sport by the Olympic movement. To retain this classification, non-smoking restrictions had to be introduced. Also, players at the two world championships in 2000 were randomly selected for drugs tests. Drugs such as steroids, which carry advantage in track and field events, are of little benefit to bridge players. However, there is a limit on the amount of caffeine that is allowed and bridge players are known for their heavy consumption of coffee! A demonstration bridge event was held at the 2002 Winter Olympics in Salt Lake City.

Right: Unbeaten in the World Championship between 1958 and 1970, the Italian Blue Team are regarded as the most successful team in bridge history.

Above: The Bermuda Bowl. Awarded for the open world championship every two years, it is the ultimate prize in bridge.

The deal below comes from the 1954 Bermuda Bowl, with France facing the USA. In matches of this sort, each deal is played twice (to reduce the luck factor). At one table the USA sat North–South and stopped in 4♠, making 12 tricks after a diamond lead. At the other table France sat North–South and their pair bid to 6♠. If this could be made, France would gain a huge swing. (The scoring for each board is based on the difference between the two results.) West led the ♥2, hoping that his partner could win and deliver a club ruff. Declarer won with the dummy's ♥A and continued with the ace and queen of trumps, the suit breaking 3–2.

The world championship book of that year gives the play only for the first three tricks. Yet it states that the slam went one down. Declarer presumably drew the last trump and then needed to score four club tricks. A low club to the queen is the correct safety play, because it wins against any lie of the suit. Here West would show out on the first round of clubs and East would take the ♣Q with the ♣K. Declarer could then ruff the heart return, cross to the ♣J and finesse the ♣9. After cashing the ♣A, he would cross to the ♦A to discard his potential diamond loser on dummy's fifth club. We can assume that declarer cashed the ace of clubs on the first round, after which there was no way to recover. East would then be assured of two club tricks.

Moving forward to 1965 marks the middle of the period of Italian dominance. Although the Italians were all fine card players it was perhaps their bidding that attracted the greatest admiration.

Right: Declarer misses the safest play. To pick up the 4–0 club break, declarer must refrain from cashing the ace on the first round.

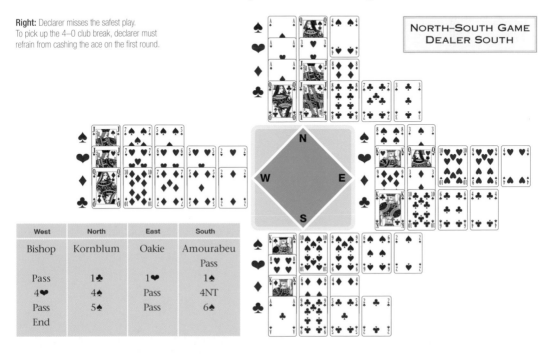

| North–South Game |
| Dealer South |

West	North	East	South
Bishop	Kornblum	Oakie	Amourabeu
			Pass
Pass	1♣	1♥	1♠
4♥	4♠	Pass	4NT
Pass	5♠	Pass	6♠
End			

Right: A brilliantly-bid grand slam. When South bids so strongly, missing three aces, North deduces that his partner's trumps must be solid.

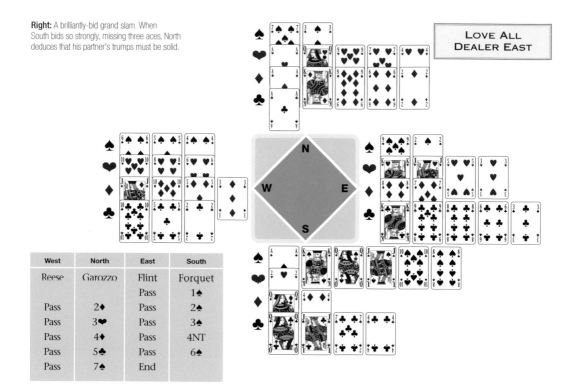

LOVE ALL
DEALER EAST

West	North	East	South
Reese	Garozzo	Flint	Forquet
		Pass	1♠
Pass	2♦	Pass	2♠
Pass	3♥	Pass	3♠
Pass	4♦	Pass	4NT
Pass	5♣	Pass	6♠
Pass	7♠	End	

The deal shown above was played in the 1965 world championship, during the ten-year period when Italy dominated world bridge. Here is a grand slam, bid by the Italians and missed by the British.

On a strong responding hand, it was part of the Italian system to make a canapé response – in other words, to bid the second longest suit first. Although Garozzo's (North) suits were of equal length, this method implied that he would bid diamonds before hearts. Forquet (South) rebid his spades twice and Garozzo then rebid his diamonds, to show 5–5 in these suits. South was too strong to sign off in 4♠, so he made a natural slam try of 4NT. When Garozzo showed a club control with 5♣, he leapt to a small slam in spades. Garozzo had so many controls in the side suits, he could judge South's spades to be solid and therefore raised to the grand slam.

Without a trump lead, declarer can simply ruff two clubs in dummy and discard the remaining club loser on the third round of diamonds. West did lead a trump, however, and now declarer had a little more work to do. After winning the trump lead, Forquet crossed to the ♣A. He re-entered his hand with the ♦Q

Above: Benito Garozzo. Now resident in the USA, Garozzo is thought by many to be the best bridge player of all time.

and led the ♣Q, ruffing with dummy's remaining trump. He then cashed the ♦A and ruffed a diamond, establishing the suit against the 4–2 break. After drawing trumps, he could then claim the remaining tricks. The king and nine of diamonds were good for two club discards and the ♥A would provide the necessary entry to dummy.

At the other table Albert Rose opened 4♠ on the South cards, raised to 6♠ by Harrison Gray. In tournament play the difference in aggregate scores is converted to International Match Points (known as IMPs) according to a standard table. Here the Italians scored 1,510 for their grand slam, the British scoring only 1,010 for an overtrick in the small slam. The difference of 500 gave the Italians a "swing" of 11 IMPs.

We will see next the deal that decided the 1974 Bermuda Bowl. The final, between Italy and North America, was nearing its close when a potential slam deal (shown below) arose.

Forquet bid 4♣ to set clubs as the trump suit. The next two bids (4♦ and 4♠) were cue-bids that showed a control in that side suit. A cue-bid can be made on an ace or a king, also sometimes on a singleton or void. Bianchi won the heart lead with the ace and played a

SCORING IN DUPLICATE MATCHES
♠ ♥ ♦ ♣
To reduce the effect of slam hands, where luck can have a huge effect, the difference in scores (when a hand is played twice in a duplicate match) is reduced by converting it to International Match Points, known as IMPs. For example, a difference of 1,000 points converts to 14 IMPs, while a difference of 500 points converts to 11 IMPs. The relatively small difference of 100 points, meanwhile, is worth a full 3 IMPs.

trump to the ace, West showing out. He then played two rounds of diamonds, throwing his heart loser, and led another trump. East won with the king and returned a third round of trumps. When the king and ace of spades stood up, Bianchi was able to ruff a spade with the ♣J, return to hand with a ruff and draw East's last trump to make the slam.

If East had held only one spade, declarer's intended safety play of a trump to the ace would have misfired. East would then have been able to ruff the second round. The commentators at the time

Right: A slam deal from the 1974 Bermuda Bowl. Bianchi shows that his play of a trump to the ace was safe even against a 4–0 trump break.

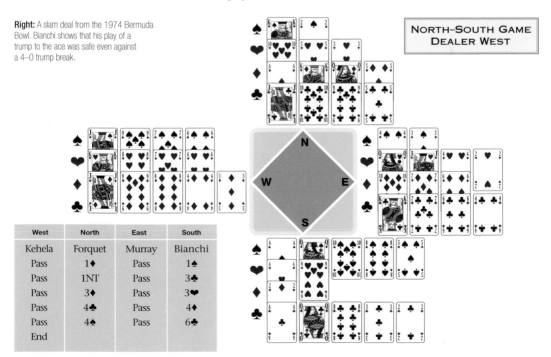

NORTH–SOUTH GAME
DEALER WEST

West	North	East	South
Kehela	Forquet	Murray	Bianchi
Pass	1♦	Pass	1♠
Pass	1NT	Pass	3♣
Pass	3♦	Pass	3♥
Pass	4♣	Pass	4♦
Pass	4♠	Pass	6♣
End			

suggested that it would have been better to discard the heart loser before drawing trumps, and then to run the ♣J. If this lost to the ♣K with West, declarer would be able to draw trumps in two more rounds at worst. He could then ruff one spade loser and discard the other.

The USA's Bob Hamman and Bobby Wolff stopped in 4♠ on these cards. They lost 12 IMPs on the board and the Italians eventually won by 196–166.

In the 1983 Bermuda Bowl, an unfortunate bidding misunderstanding by Belladonna and Garozzo, on the penultimate board of the final against the USA, handed victory to their opponents. Italy led by 8 IMPs with two boards to play and had two seemingly favourable results already obtained in the other room, where play had finished. The fatal board for the Italians in the Open Room is shown below.

Belladonna's 2NT was artificial, showing good spade support and a side-suit singleton. He might make the bid either when seeking a game contract or when he had a slam in mind. The opener was expected to rebid 3♣, after which responder would bid 3♦, 3♥ or 3♠ to show a game-try hand with a diamond, heart or club singleton. With a slam-try hand, opener would rebid at the four-level. Garozzo had opened on a 10-count and attempted to indicate this by rebidding 3♠, not even

asking partner to define his hand further. The bid appeared to confuse Belladonna, who was no doubt exhausted after playing for so many days. The report in USA's *Bridge World* stated that he had interpreted 3♠ as a "trump-asking bid" and that his six-step 4NT response showed his six trumps to the ace–king. He then took 5♦ as a control-showing cue-bid, after which he bid a small slam. Garozzo said instead that 4NT had been Blackwood, asking how many aces his partner held, and Belladonna had suffered from a momentary aberration. Whatever the explanation, the pair who at that time were rated the strongest in the world had given away a world championship by bidding a slam with two aces missing. At the other table the Americans stopped in 5♠, which they duly made.

Moving to more recent times, we will end with a dramatic slam deal from the final of the 2003 Bermuda Bowl, between Italy and the USA. Italy's Giorgio Duboin probably still has nightmares about the board opposite.

After no fewer than nine rounds of bidding, Duboin (South) arrived in 6♠ redoubled. The Americans doubled this contract and the Italians redoubled. (When one partnership has been doubled in a contract and think they can make it nevertheless, they have the right to redouble.)

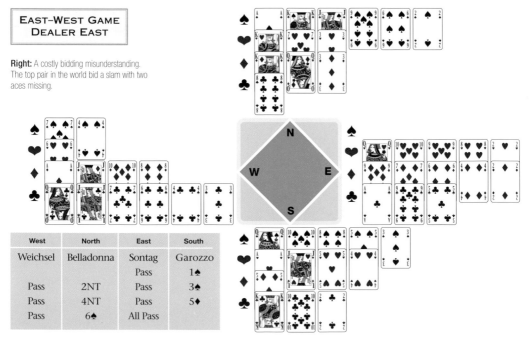

**EAST–WEST GAME
DEALER EAST**

Right: A costly bidding misunderstanding. The top pair in the world bid a slam with two aces missing.

West	North	East	South
Weichsel	Belladonna	Sontag	Garozzo
		Pass	1♠
Pass	2NT	Pass	3♠
Pass	4NT	Pass	5♦
Pass	6♠	All Pass	

Although the ♥K was offside (lying over the ♥A–Q) and the trumps were breaking 4–0, it seemed to the onlookers that there was every chance of landing the contract.

Bob Hamman (West) led the ♦10. Duboin won with dummy's ♦A and led a heart towards his hand without first cashing a top trump from dummy.

> **MAKE SURE IT ADDS UP!**
> ♠ ♥ ♦ ♣
> Eddie Kantar, the American expert and teacher, tells his students: "Count your losers and then count your winners. If the answer does not come to 13, count your cards!"

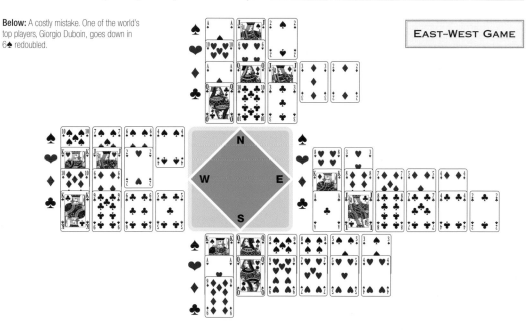

EAST–WEST GAME

The commentators in the auditorium expected him to finesse the ♥Q, but Duboin rose with the ♥A and returned a second round of hearts. Hamman won with the ♥J, East following, and promptly placed the ♥K on the table. Declarer knew that East held no more hearts and had to decide whether to ruff with a low trump or one of dummy's trump honours. Because he had not cashed an early round of trumps, to investigate the situation in that suit, Duboin did not yet know that trumps were breaking 4–0. It was natural for him to ruff the third round of hearts with dummy's ♠J, to avoid an overruff. Imagine his thoughts when he continued with the ♠A and East showed out! West now had to score a trump trick and the redoubled slam went one down.

At the other table the American North–South pair, Jeff Meckstroth and Eric Rodwell had bid 1♠ – 2♦ – 2♥ – 4♠, making 12 tricks. Duboin had therefore lost 12 IMPs where he might have gained 17. The Americans eventually won the final by 303–302!

Above: Giorgio Duboin, photographed in 2007, when he was first ranked as the world's best player. He had won 12 European and world championships.

THE VENICE CUP

The women's world championship, the Venice Cup, was first contested in 1974 and is now held every two years. The USA has a fine record in the event, with no fewer than nine wins. Great Britain and Germany have each won the event twice, with France and the Netherlands recording a single win.

The original holding, in 1974, was a two-team affair. Italy, champions of Europe and the Olympic champions, challenged the USA, and lost by 35 IMPs. Again in 1976 only two teams played: the USA were challenged by Great Britain, European champions. In 1978 the event was brought in line with the Bermuda Bowl, with one team representing each continent: USA, Italy, Argentina, Australia and the Phillipines. Nowadays the entry is much larger, as in the Bermuda Bowl. Twenty-two teams contested the 2005 event.

The deal shown below features an excellent piece of card play by the USA's Carol Sanders, playing South in the very first Venice Cup in 1974. She arrived in 4♠ and appeared at first to have four losers: one heart, two diamonds and one club.

North's 2NT showed a sound raise of spades to the three-level. Had she instead bid 3♠ directly over the double, this would have shown a weak hand with four-card spade support.

The Italian West led a top club against the spade game and switched to ace and another diamond. East won the second diamond with the king and played back a club, ruffed by declarer. All now depended on not losing a heart trick and South knew from West's take-out double that the ♥Q was likely to be offside. She drew trumps, ruffed her diamond loser in dummy and then played her remaining trumps. West had to find one more discard from ♣K and ♥Q–10–7. Whatever she threw, declarer would have her tenth trick. The play was identical at the other table, for a classy flat board.

The narrowest winning margin in any world championship came in the 1999 Venice Cup, with USA facing the Netherlands. With one board to be played, the atmosphere in the VuGraph theatre was electric, as the Dutch led by just 0.5 of an IMP. (The fraction was due to a 2.5 IMP penalty applied on the Americans for finishing five minutes late in one session.) This was the last board of the final:

Right: A well played contract of 4♠. Carol Sanders catches her Italian opponent in a major-suit squeeze.

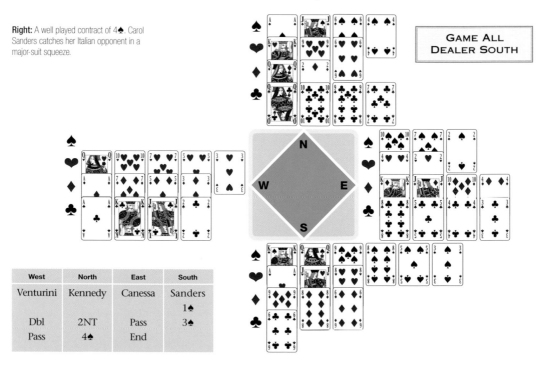

GAME ALL
DEALER SOUTH

West	North	East	South
Venturini	Kennedy	Canessa	Sanders
			1♠
Dbl	2NT	Pass	3♠
Pass	4♠	End	

Right: With only 0.5 IMPs separating USA and Italy, one extra overtrick could decide the championship.

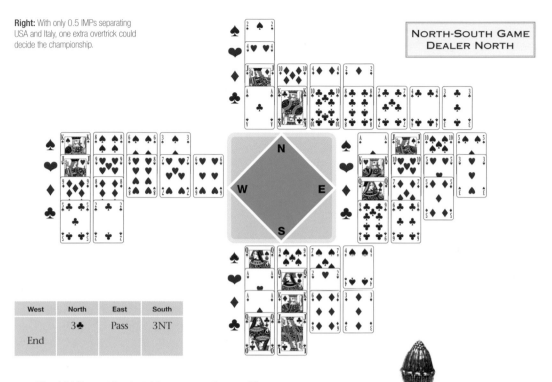

		NORTH-SOUTH GAME
		DEALER NORTH

West	North	East	South
	3♣	Pass	3NT
End			

The bidding at both tables was as shown. The USA declarer, Randi Montin, had already played the deal. A spade lead would have given the defenders the first three tricks, holding declarer to +630. The Netherlands West had led the normal ♥7, however. Declarer had won East's king with the ace, cashed the ♦A and run seven rounds of clubs. When no diamonds were thrown, she declined to risk the diamond finesse and collected +660 for 3NT made with two overtricks. So, if the USA West led a spade, restricting declarer to ten tricks, the USA would gain 1 IMP and win the championship by 0.5 IMPs.

To the anguish of the American spectators watching VuGraph, West led a heart instead of a spade. The Netherlands declarer duly took the same 11 tricks as in the other room, thereby retaining their 0.5 IMP lead and winning the world championship by the narrowest conceivable margin. Had they avoided the earlier penalty for slow play, the Americans would have been world champions instead.

Right: The Venice Cup is awarded for the women's world championship, held every two years. Each team member receives a miniature version of the trophy.

Who would have guessed then that there would be a similarly exciting Venice Cup final only two years later? Germany faced France in the final and with only 16 boards to be played, the French led by a full 46.5 IMPs. The Germans played strongly and were within touch when the board shown below hit the table.

At both tables West opened with a weak two-bid and North doubled for take-out. Both Souths responded 3♦ and there was no more bidding at the other table, where the French declarer scored +130 for ten tricks. Here 3♦ had suggested around 8–10 points

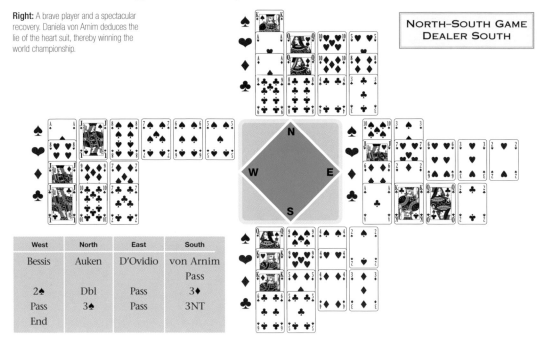

Right: A brave player and a spectacular recovery. Daniela von Arnim deduces the lie of the heart suit, thereby winning the world championship.

	USA TEAMS IN THE VENICE CUP
	♠ ♥ ♦ ♣

By virtue of its number of bridge players, the USA enters two teams for the Venice Cup whereas all other countries may have a maximum of one (if they qualify from their continental championship). In the Venice Cups where two American teams have participated, their second team has in fact won three times and the first team has won once.

NORTH–SOUTH GAME
DEALER SOUTH

West	North	East	South
Bessis	Auken	D'Ovidio	von Arnim
			Pass
2♠	Dbl	Pass	3♦
Pass	3♠	Pass	3NT
End			

(because South would have bid a conventional 2NT to show a hand of 0–7 points). Auken probed with 3♠ and the Germans duly arrived in 3NT.

After an unlikely club lead, the French defenders would have claimed the first five tricks. This would have defeated the contract and given the French team the world championship. West, however, made the natural lead of the ♠7. Dummy's ♠K won the trick and declarer now needed eight red-suit tricks to make her game. She played three rounds of diamonds and East discarded a heart on the third round. All now depended on how von Arnim played the heart suit. West had shown up with nine cards in spades and diamonds to East's four,

so East figured to hold the heart length. East would scarcely discard a heart if she had begun with four cards in the suit, so von Arnim correctly deduced that East must have started with five hearts. She crossed to the ace of hearts and boldly finessed the nine of hearts on the second round. She could then cash the king of hearts and enter dummy with the fourth round of diamonds to score the heart queen.

Germany moved into a 2.5 IMP lead and, when the last board proved to be flat, that was their eventual winning margin. The German women had won the last set 51–2, making it one of the most exciting fight-backs on record.

THE BRIDGE OLYMPIAD

Following the tradition, the Bridge Olympiad is contested every four years, in different locations around the world. The event was first held in 1960, with France winning the open championship and the United Arab Republic the women's championship. Since then, France has won the open event a further three times. Italy has won five times and there are three one-time winners: USA, Poland and Brazil. The USA has had four wins in the women's event, Italy two wins and several countries have enjoyed one win: Great Britain, Sweden, Denmark, Austria and Russia.

Twenty-nine teams contested the first Open Olympiad in 1960, including two from Sweden and no fewer than four from the USA. (The USA Spingold 2 team was packed with big names: Charles Goren, Harold Ogust, Paul Allinger, Lew Mathe, Helen Sobel and Howard Schenken.) Nowadays only one team is permitted from each country. To get a flavour of the 1960 event, we will look at a slam deal from the match between Italy and USA Vanderbilt I.

It was the Italian style of bidding to respond in their second-best suit (here clubs) when they held a strong hand, a method known as "canapé responses".

Chiaradia's 3◆ rebid showed long diamonds and the Italians then wasted little time in reaching a small slam in the suit. The USA West led the ♠A, winning the first trick. He then found the best switch of a heart, forcing the Italian declarer to decide immediately whether to finesse in hearts (before he could see whether he had four club tricks and therefore a discard for his potential heart loser). With little to guide him, Chiaradia eventually decided to finesse the ♥Q and went one down.

At the other table the American declarer, Norman Kay, played in just 5◆ from the North hand. After a spade to the ace and a heart switch, he could not afford to finesse in case he lost a heart trick and a heart ruff. He rose with the ♥A playing safe, and duly made an overtrick when clubs proved to be 3–3.

EUROPEANS ASCENDANT
♠ ♥ ◆ ♣

The European teams have claimed a near monopoly in the Olympiad, restricting the USA to just a single win in the open event in 1988. The USA women's team has won four times.

EAST–WEST GAME
DEALER NORTH

Right: A sharp defence forces the Italian declarer to a critical guess.

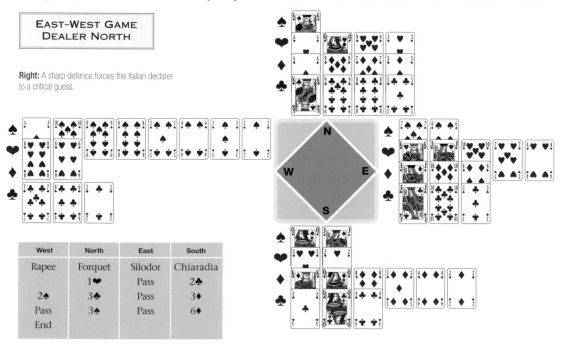

West	North	East	South
Rapee	Forquet	Silodor	Chiaradia
	1♥	Pass	2♣
2♠	3♣	Pass	3◆
Pass	3♠	Pass	6◆
End			

Twenty years later, in the 1980 Olympiad event, France and the USA qualified for the final. The Americans were desperate for their first win in the event but the French, led by Paul Chemla, had other ideas. The deal below received much publicity. Robert Hamman (USA) found himself on lead against a grand slam with two aces in his hand. He had to decide which ace to lead and the fate of the grand slam rested on his choice.

Right: Bob Hamman faces an important decision on which ace to lead against a vulnerable grand slam.

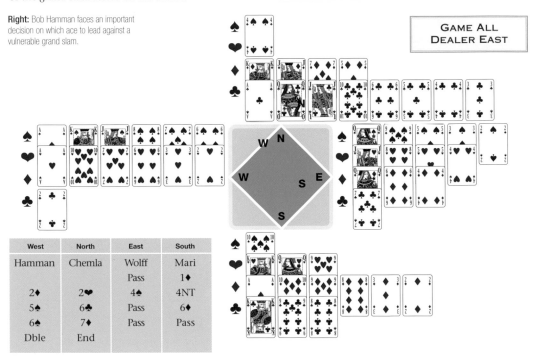

		THE VANDERBILT TROPHY
		♠ ♥ ♦ ♣

Every four years the winners of the Open Olympiad receive the Vanderbilt Trophy. It was presented for the first time at the 1960 Olympiad in Turin, by Harold S. Vanderbilt, to the victorious French team.

GAME ALL
DEALER EAST

West	North	East	South
Hamman	Chemla	Wolff	Mari
		Pass	1♦
2♦	2♥	4♠	4NT
5♠	6♣	Pass	6♦
6♠	7♦	Pass	Pass
Dble	End		

Hamman's 2♦ overcall was a Michaels cue-bid, showing at least five cards in each of the major suits. Chemla's 2♥, also a bid in an opponent's suit, showed strong diamond support. Wolff raised to the game-level in spades and Mari indicated a hand that was suitable for a slam with his bid of 4NT. Hamman attempted to buy the contract at the six-level eventually by bidding only 5♠ for the moment. Chemla showed his second suit of clubs and Mari corrected back to diamonds. Hamman continued with his plan by bidding his spades one more time.

At the other table the auction went no higher. The American North–South pair doubled the French in 6♠ and took the contract one down after a lead of the ♣A. At this table the great French player, Paul Chemla,

aimed for greater things by bidding the grand slam in diamonds. Hamman doubled and all now depended on his choice of opening lead. His partner had raised spades to the four-level and would therefore hold longer spades than hearts. This suggested that the ♥A was more likely to stand up (in other words, not be ruffed). Hamman duly led this card and had to suffer the agony of seeing Mari ruff in the dummy. Knowing that West was long in both major suits and therefore likely to be short in diamonds, Mari cashed the ♦K on the first round. When West showed out, declarer was able to finesse the ♦J, draw trumps and claim the doubled grand slam. The swing was 2,130 aggregate points, which converts to 19 IMPs. France eventually won the match by 131–111.

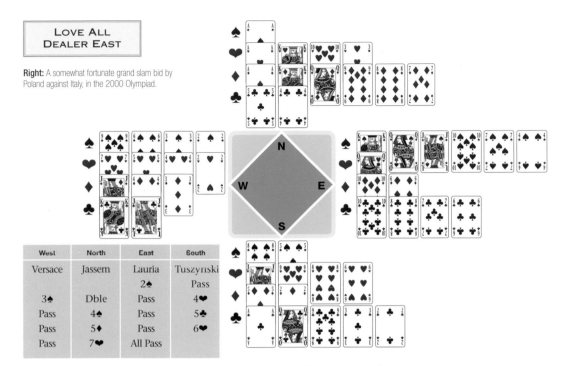

LOVE ALL
DEALER EAST

Right: A somewhat fortunate grand slam bid by Poland against Italy, in the 2000 Olympiad.

West	North	East	South
Versace	Jassem	Lauria	Tuszynski
		2♠	Pass
3♠	Dble	Pass	4♥
Pass	4♠	Pass	5♣
Pass	5♦	Pass	6♥
Pass	7♥	All Pass	

Continuing to sample the great action over the years, we will move forward another two decades. The grand slam shown above arose in the 2000 Open Olympiad with Italy facing Poland.

The Italian East opened with a weak two-bid, raised to the three-level, and Jassem made a take-out double. When partner responded 4♥ North might well have passed (indeed, in the Women's Olympiad, Mildred Breed did pass for the USA). He continued with 4♠ (once trumps have been agreed, hearts here, a bid in a new suit at this level is a "control-showing cue-bid", usually showing the ace of the suit bid). After two further cue-bids, Tuszynski leapt to 6♥. Placing partner with the ♣A and hoping that his hearts were headed by the queen, Jassem raised to 7♥.

Versace, West for Italy, led a trump and East's queen fell under dummy's king. Declarer cashed the ♠A, crossed to the ♥8 and ruffed his last spade with the ♥A. He then overtook the ♥10 with the ♥J, drew trumps and ran dummy's diamond suit to discard the four club losers in his hand. Grand slam made! At the other table the Polish East opened 3♠, raised defensively to 4♠. North doubled and there was no further bidding. The Italians collected only 300, losing 15 IMPs on the board.

Above: The Vanderbilt Trophy. Due to the generous provision made by Harold S. Vanderbilt, each member of the winning team receives a silver replica of the trophy.

BRIDGE ON THE COMPUTER

There are two main ways in which you can play bridge on your computer. You can install a bridge-playing program and then compete against three robot players, whose bids and plays are calculated by the computer. Alternatively, you can join one of several Internet sites that allow you to play bridge with and against human players from around the world. The screen appearance will be similar in both cases. You will click on a bidding table to select your bid and click on one of your cards to select which one to play. These bridge-playing programs fight amongst themselves to determine which can win the world computer bridge championship. Finally, it is now possible (using the free software: Bridge Base Online) to watch many of the world's top tournaments on the Internet. The cards and bids are shown in the same way as when you are playing bridge yourself. International commentators add their comments and analysis so you can follow the passage of play.

Right: Playing bridge on the Internet is popular because you do not have to plan a session in advance. With an hour to spare, you can log on and join a game immediately.

PLAYING BRIDGE AGAINST THE COMPUTER

By using the Internet, you can play with human players from around the world. Alternatively, without needing to access the Internet, you can play bridge on your own computer. Your partner and your opponents will be provided by software that runs on your machine. They will bid and play their cards automatically. The early bridge-playing programs were disappointingly weak, making poor bids and even worse plays. However, they have greatly improved in the last few years and can now give you an entertaining game.

There are many such software packages on the market (including Jack, Q-Plus, Bridge Baron and GIB). The saved screen below reflects the bidding of a hand on GIB. The human player (South) was playing

with three computer-generated players, and the deal came from a supplied library of deals from real tournaments. In this case it was from the 2002 Cap Gemini tournament. The human player decided to double 3♠ at this stage. He led the ♥Q against 3♠ doubled and declarer lost two clubs, a diamond and three trump tricks, going two down for a 500 penalty.

Below: A screen from the GIB computer-playing software, taken at a moment South is about to bid.

USER PROFILES
♠ ♥ ♦ ♣

When becoming a member of an online bridge club, you are invited to create a 'profile' that describes yourself. For example, you may choose to disclose your real name (rather than your screen 'nickname'). You may also declare that you are a novice, an expert or world class.

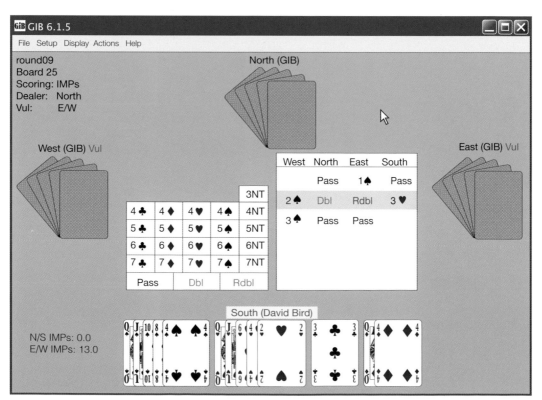

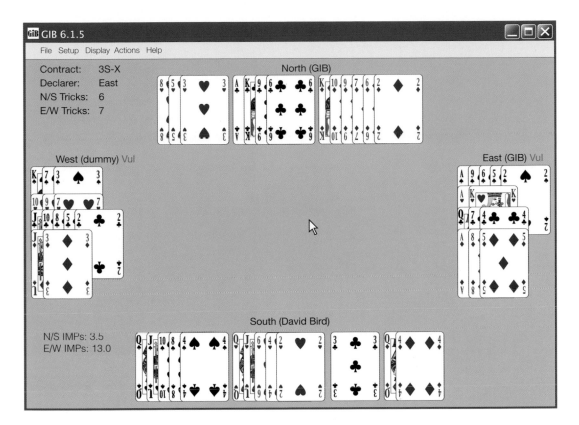

Above: A screen from the GIB computer-playing software, just after completion of the play.

This was the screen at the end of play (above). The score-sheet from the original event reveals that +500 is worth +3.5 International Match Points (IMPs) when compared with the average result. A good bridge-playing package will offer you some means of judging how well you have performed. In other words, you need other scores for a comparison. Either the software can replay the deal, with four computer players, or it can use deals from real tournaments, as we have just seen.

You may wonder how such packages are programmed. GIB decides which card to play by creating several sets of random hands for the two unseen players – hands that match the bidding and the play so far. It then sees which card will produce the best result, by playing each random deal to its conclusion. For example, if playing the ♠9 wins on 15 of the 20 random deals and playing the ♠Q wins on only 12, it will play the ♠9. This is much more effective than trying to program general rules such as 'second hand low'. Indeed, when a super-powered

version of GIB competed against world-class players at a recent world championship, it was placed halfway up the field. This was a phenomenal achievement when you bear in mind how weak bridge-playing programs were in the early days.

North	East	South	West	Contract	Declarer	Result	Score	IMPs
Chagas	Pszczola	Brenner	Kwiecien	3S-X	East	down 3	+800	+9.5
SaelensmindeSacul	Brogeland	Versace	Karwur	3S-X	East	down 2	+500	+3.5
Ravenna	Gawrys	Madala	Jassem	3C-X	West	down 2	+500	+3.5
Westra	Stansby	Leufkens	Gitelman	3S-X	East	down 2	+500	+3.5
GIB 6.1.3	GIB 6.1.3	David Bird	GIB 6.1.3	3S-X	East	down 2	+500	+3.5
Garozzo	Muller	Versace	De Wigs	2H	South	made 3	+140	-5.37
Robson	Auken	Mahmood	Reps	2D	North	made 4	+130	-5.87
Verhees	Gromov	Jansma	Peturin	2D	North	made 4	+130	-5.87
Helness	Weinstein	Helgemo	Garner	2D	North	made 3	+110	-6.37

Click OK to continue to next deal.
click on a line to see the hand record
or select from the menus.

OK

Above: By comparing your own result with those obtained by the players in the original tournament, you can assess how well you fared.

WATCHING BRIDGE ON THE INTERNET

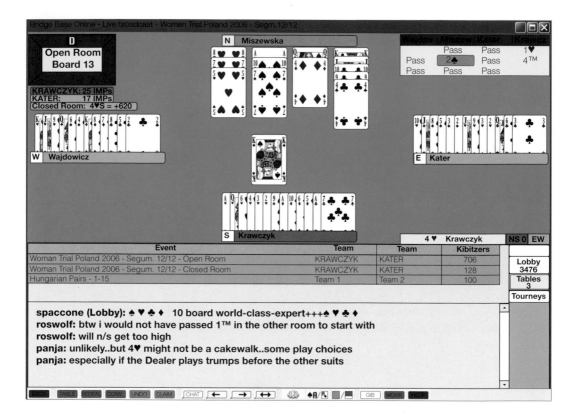

Above: A screen from Bridge Base Online, taken just after the opening lead has been made.

Once upon a time it would cost you a fortune in air fares and hotel bills to watch the world's top bridge tournaments. Not now! The Internet site Bridge Base Online, web address: http://online.bridgebase.com, allows you to watch all the world championships and many big tournaments, internationals and trials absolutely free. You can also play bridge online yourself, on the same site.

The screen capture above shows a live broadcast in progress from the 2006 Women's Trials in Poland. During the auction the bids gradually appear in a bidding table in the centre of the dark green baize. When the auction is over and play begins, the auction is reduced in size and moved to the top-right corner. You can see there that Krawczyk, the South player, opened 1♥ in the third seat. Her partner responded 2♣.

This is shown with a different colour background because it was a conventional bid (Drury, to show a maximum pass with three-card heart support). South then leapt to the heart game and West has just led the ♠K.

As the bidding and the play progress, expert commentators add their thoughts in the grey space at the bottom of the screen. The commentator whose BBO identifier is 'panja' has just expressed the view that declarer may be in trouble if she decides to play trumps straight away. Kibitzers (watchers) are not allowed to add comments to this box. Only the approved expert commentators are 'switched on', as it is called. However, the kibitzers frequently send their questions and views to the commentators, who may then reply within a private conversation.

At the top left, just below the red box, you can see the current score in the match. Krawczyk has 25 IMPs and Kater has 17. Also given is the result from the other room (the Closed Room) for this particular deal. South bid to 4♥ and made ten tricks for a score of +620. If the South player here, in the Open Room, can achieve the same result, it will be a flat board and there will be no swing in International Match Points (IMPs). (In duplicate matches, the aggregate difference between the scores at the two tables is converted into IMPs.)

You can see from the position of the white-arrow cursor that the BBO user who made this screen capture had just clicked on the 'Tables' icon. That is why the three lines shaded in pale green appear. They inform the user that there are three broadcasts currently being transmitted, two from different tables at the Polish Women's Trials and one from the Hungarian pairs championship. As you see, a total of some 934 viewers are logged on. During a major championship such as the Bermuda Bowl, there will be many thousands of viewers.

Finally, look at the icons on the bottom row of the screen. Pressing BACK would take you out of the VuGraph room. You would use this if you perhaps wanted to play bridge on BBO, rather than watch this match. Or you might choose to look through the large record of VuGraph presentations from tournaments over the past few years. Further along is the CHAT button. You would press this if you wanted to ask one of the commentators a question, or talk to a friend of yours who was also watching. A box would then pop up into which you could type your question or comment, also the identity of the person you wanted to talk to.

Further icons allow you to change the appearance of the playing cards or to reduce in size the comment portion of the screen. Pressing the GIB button sets software in motion that will analyze the present hand double-dummy and show which plays will be successful for the current player. Finally, the MOVIE button allows you to see a scorecard of the entire session. You can look back on any deal from the session and remind yourself how the bidding and the play went.

It is a great piece of software. When a big tournament is being shown from, say, China, there might be English commentary from one table and Chinese commentary from the other. Flip to the Chinese table and all the experts' comments would appear in Chinese characters!

Right: To watch or play bridge online, you need to download and install the free Bridge Base Online software, from http://online.bridgebase.com.

PLAYING BRIDGE ON THE INTERNET

Bridge Base Online - Play Bridge!

Play Bridge!
423 Tables   1941 Players

Places to play	Tables	Players
Main Bridge Club	285	1191
Private Bridge Clubs	2	8
Public Bridge Clubs	7	62
Tournaments	74	370
Team Matches	46	275
Play Bridge for money!	9	35

Bridge Base	Help me find a game!
Click to return to the lobby	Take me to a table

rosaherna (Lobby:♥ ♦ ♥ HURRYY ...... ♥LASTTTT ...5..... MINUTES TO REGISTER ♥ we are waiting ♥♥♥ ::
BBO LAND :: indy #547   ♠♥ FAST 10 X 1™ prizes 7$$ - 22$ ♥♥♥
Omei0->Lobby: Substitute players needed for Turney 1110 (#1110 Teams). To play, please enter tourney and click the SUBSTITUTES button
Steve UK 27 (Lobby): ty, not especially nervous, suppose you are?
george332->Lobby: need one at george 332 pls
Omei0->Lobby: Substitute players needed for Tourney 1110 (#1110 Teams). To play, please enter tourney and click the SUBSTITUTES button..

BACK | TABLE | REDEAL | CONV | UNDO | CLAIM | CHAT | ← | → | ↔ | ♠A/♣ | ■/■ | GIB | MOVIE | HELP

The same Internet packages that allow you to watch top-class tournaments will also allow you to play bridge yourself. You can play with a partner and opponents from any part of the world. Each player invokes the software on his own machine and the magic of the Internet allows all the players to see the bids and plays that everyone makes. You might, for example, play with an Australian partner against two opponents from the Netherlands.

The saved screen above shows the various types of bridge game that might be offered. You could choose to play in a friendly, social game. Perhaps you would prefer to play in a teams-of-four or pairs tournament. The software, Bridge Base Online in this illustration, arranges many such tournaments each day. Perhaps you even want to play for money. That is possible too, as with the similar poker sites. Once you have entered a tournament, or joined a social table, the deals appear one at a time on the screen. If it is a

Above: A screen from Bridge Base Online, offering various types of bridge to the user.

social game, you can leave the game at any stage, allowing a new player to take your place. The software will maintain records of all the boards you have played and will provide statistical evaluation of your long-term success (or otherwise!) If this makes you nervous, you can always decline to make your true identity known to other players.

MOMENT OF REALIZATION
♠ ♥ ♦ ♣

Edgar Kaplan, one of the USA's greatest ever players, said: "I decided I was a good bridge player when I found out that people whose names I had heard all my life, people I respected, did the same dumb things that I did."

We are looking at the screen (below) as the East player will see it. Only his own cards are visible at this stage because the bidding is in progress. His partner opened 1NT and he is about to respond 2♦, a transfer bid that shows at least five hearts. He does this by clicking on the '2' (he has already done this, so it is shown in yellow) and then clicking on the diamond symbol just below. To alert the opponents, he has also typed in the meaning of his bid ('transfer') and will mouse-click on the 'Alert' button, so that they are made aware of his conventional bid. Once the auction is completed and the play of the cards begins, declarer and the defenders will click on the card that they wish to play to each trick. Declarer may also CLAIM a contract, to save time. In some types of game, the players are allowed to request an UNDO if they have selected some bid or play erroneously.

As when watching a session, a player can press the MOVIE button, bottom right, to look at the score-sheet. He may then select one of the deals to see again the hands, the bidding and how the play went.

He may also press the CHAT button to type in a message to the other three players at the table. It will appear in the currently empty grey space in the bottom half of the screen.

When you first log on to such a site you are prompted to choose a name by which you will be known as a player. You can choose a representation of your actual name or a fictional name such as 'Cloudy' or 'simpleboi', as we see here. It is up to you whether, in your profile, you give your personal details or prefer to remain anonymous.

One of the advantages of playing online is that you do not have to pre-plan a session or arrange a partner. If you feel like playing bridge for an hour or so, you simply log on and join three other players.

Most players like to play against opponents of a similar standard to themselves. You may therefore see messages on the Home Panel such as 'Two experts needed at table Alan109, please.'

Below: A screen from Bridge Base Online, as seen by East when he is about to make a transfer bid.

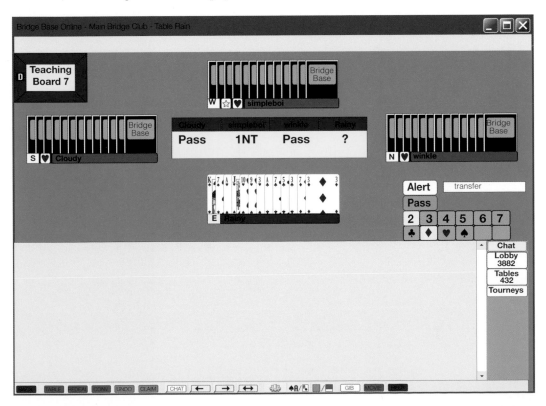

301

BASIC BIDDING

To bid well with your partner, you must each strive to paint a clear picture of your hand as quickly as possible. This section covers various opening bids that begin this process, including one no-trump (1NT) and suit openings at the one-level. You will also see how to respond to such opening bids. The objective for both players will be to make a 'limit bid' as soon as possible, so that partner can add his strength to that shown and calculate whether a game should be bid. The opener's rebid (his second bid) and the responder's rebid come next. Finally it will be explained how such auctions are completed. Strong openings of 2♣ and 2NT will be described, also weak (pre-emptive) openings at both the two-level and the three-level. After a discussion of higher pre-emptive bids, you will see how to bid accurately after the opponents have opened the bidding.

Right: An opening bid of 1NT defines your hand within narrow limits and allows your partner to bid accurately thereafter.

OPENING ONE NO-TRUMP (1NT)

An opening bid of 1NT shows that your hand is balanced. It defines the high-card strength to within a couple of points. The shape will be 4–4–3–2 (in other words: two four-card suits, one three-card suit and one two-card suit), 4–3–3–3 or 5–3–3–2 with a five-card minor. Occasionally some players will venture a 1NT opening with 5–3–3–2 shape and a five-card major. There are two main variations, so far as the number of points is concerned. You can either play a 'strong 1NT' of 15–17 points or a 'weak 1NT' of 12–14 points.

The strong 1NT

A strong 1NT of 15–17 points has a very large following worldwide and that is the method assumed in other chapters of this book. This chapter will look at some examples of both types of 1NT. The first three hands shown below are all prime examples of the strong 1NT:

1

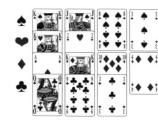

Hand (1) is suitable in every way. It has 16 points (an ace is worth 4 points, a king 3 points, a queen 2 points and a jack 1 point). It also has 4–4–3–2 shape and a 'stopper' in every suit. (A stopper is a card combination, such as K–2 or Q–9–3, that may stop the defenders from scoring several immediate winners in the suit.)

2

You would open 1NT on hand (2) as well. Do not be deterred by the fact that you hold a low doubleton in one of the suits. The problem with opening 1♣ instead is that after a response of 1♠ you would have no satisfactory

rebid (as we will see later, a rebid of 1NT would show 12–14 points).

3

Hand (3) is a strong 1NT that contains a five-card minor. Again you would not open 1♣ instead because this might cause a problem with your rebid. When you play the strong 1NT, look for a different opening bid when you hold 12–14 points and a balanced hand. Suppose you have to choose a bid on this hand:

4

Many players who use the strong 1NT also favour five-card majors (where an opening bid of 1♠ or 1♥ promises at least five cards). This does not cause any problem on (4) because you can open 1♣. If partner responds 1♦ or 1♠, you will rebid 1NT to show 12–14 points.

5

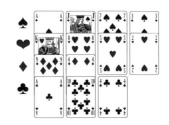

Hand (5) is more difficult. You cannot open a strong 1NT because you are too weak. Neither can you open 1♠ or 1♥ because you do not hold a five-card major. You are therefore forced to open 1♣ on a three-card suit.

6
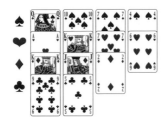

Hand (6) is even more awkward. There are two schools of thought on the best way to treat it. Some players use a method known as 'better minor' and are willing to open 1♦ (as well as 1♣) on a three-card suit. Others prefer an opening bid of 1♦ to promise at least four diamonds and are therefore willing to open 1♣ even when they hold only a doubleton in the suit.

The weak 1NT

Exponents of the weak 1NT favour the bid because hands in the 12–14 point range arise more frequently and they like to open 1NT as often as possible. It is not a clear-cut advantage because when you hold the lower range there is more chance that someone will open in front of you. You would open a weak 1NT on any of these hands:

7
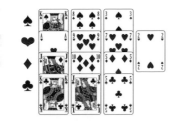

You would be right in thinking that (7) is not much of a hand and is barely worth an opening bid. Although that is true you should think of the weak 1NT as being similar to a pre-emptive bid. By opening 1NT, you could make it much harder for the opponents to bid accurately, should they hold the majority of the points.

8
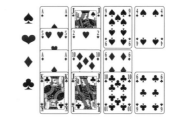

Open a weak 1NT on (8) too. Do not be deterred by the low doubleton in hearts.

9

Hand (9) is an example of a weak 1NT that contains a five-card minor.

When you are playing a weak 1NT and you hold a balanced hand of 15–17 points, you open one of a suit with the intention of rebidding in no-trumps. If you play a five-card major system, you may (as with the strong 1NT) sometimes have to open on a three-card minor suit.

FACING THE CHAMPIONS
♠ ♥ ♦ ♣

Bridge is unique among all games and sports in that it gives you a chance to compete directly against the most famous players in the world. If you enter a big tournament in London, Paris or New York, for example, there is every chance that you and your partner may find yourselves facing a pair of world champions. This could never happen in games like golf or tennis, where expert players compete only against each other.

RESPONDING TO 1NT

When your partner has opened 1NT, you have an excellent picture of his hand and will immediately have a good idea whether the combined hands will produce a part score, a game or a slam. If you are playing a strong 1NT of 15–17 points, you will want to be in game when you hold 10 points or more in the hand opposite. With 17 points upwards, or a strong hand with one or more long suits, your thoughts will turn towards a slam. Sometimes you will be uncertain whether to bid a game or a slam and will therefore seek some way to invite your partner's cooperation.

Responding on a weak hand

On most hands in the range of 0–7 points, you will either want to pass 1NT or to suggest playing at the two-level in a suit where you hold at least five cards. We will see in a moment that a response of 2♣ has a special meaning. These are your options on a weak hand:

Pass	no interest in game and no long suit (except, possibly, clubs)
2♦	no interest in game, at least five diamonds
2♥	no interest in game, at least five hearts
2♠	no interest in game, at least five spades.

These three two-level responses are known as 'weakness take-outs'. Partner will not bid again. A 1NT opening is an example of a 'limit bid', a bid that defines the hand very accurately. It is a sound principle that you should allow partner to control the auction, once you have made a limit bid.

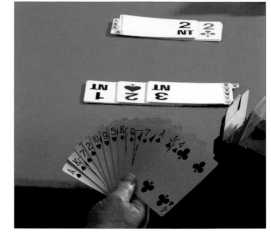

Above: Stayman auction. Partner has invited a game and, with a maximum of 17 points, you accept.

The Stayman convention

When you hold at least enough strength to invite a game (8+ points opposite a strong 1NT), you can bid 2♣ (the Stayman convention) to ask partner if he holds a four-card major. Your objective will be to find a 4–4 major suit fit, allowing you to make that suit trumps. After a start of 1NT – 2♣, the opener rebids as follows:

2♦	"I have no four-card major."
2♥	"I have four hearts (and may also have four spades)."
2♠	"I have four spades."

This is a typical Stayman auction:

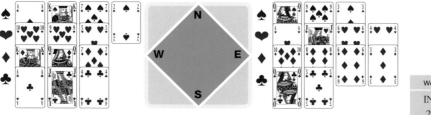

West	East
1NT	2♣
2♠	2NT
3NT	

East bids Stayman to look for a 4–4 heart fit. If West were to rebid 2♥, he would invite a heart game by raising to 3♥. When West instead rebids 2♠, East invites game in no-trumps by bidding 2NT. Since West's hand is in the top half of the 15–17 point range, he bids 3NT.

Inviting a game

When you hold 9 points, or a good 8 points, you can invite game by raising 1NT to 2NT. The opener will accept the invitation when he is in the upper range for his opening bid. On a 15-count he would usually pass. We saw in the previous section that you can also invite a game after partner has responded to your Stayman bid.

Bidding game

When you hold 10 points or more, and therefore want to be in game even opposite a minimum strong 1NT, you can bid a game contract immediately. If you are sure you want to play in no-trumps, you raise 1NT to 3NT. If you hold at least six spades or six hearts, you can bid game in that major. Occasionally you might want to bid game in a minor, but remember that it is usually easier to make nine tricks in no-trumps.

When you have enough for game or slam, and a suit of at least five cards, you can seek trump support by making a forcing bid at the three-level. This is a typical auction:

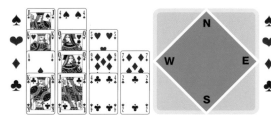
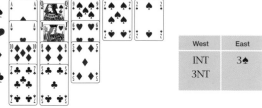

West	East
INT	3♠
3NT	

East's 3♠ shows enough points for game, at least, and a five-card spade suit. Since West has only two spades, he bids 3NT. With three or more spades, he would know that the partnership held at least eight trumps and would bid 4♠ instead.

East has enough points for a game contract but not sufficient to consider a slam. He therefore passes 3NT and that becomes the final contract. If instead he held around 18 points, he would raise 3NT to 6NT.

OPENING ONE OF A SUIT

When your hand is unsuitable for an opening bid of 1NT, either because it is unbalanced or because it is not within the three-point range that you have chosen, you will usually open with a one-bid in one of the four suits. Many people use a bidding system where a five-card suit (or longer) is needed to open 1♥ or 1♠. When their only four-card suit is a major suit, they will therefore be forced to open 1♣ or 1♦ on a three-card suit. The range of an opening one-bid is very wide. You might sometimes open on as few as 10 points with a very good suit. On other occasions you might open a one-bid on as many as 20 points. It is with your second bid (the rebid) that you will define the strength of your hand more closely.

Choosing which four-card suit to bid

When you have no suit of five cards or more, you must choose which four-card suit to open. This choice may be influenced by whether you are playing a five-card major system. Suppose you are playing a strong 1NT and have to open on one of these hands:

1

2

Hand (1) is too strong to open 1NT. You would open 1♦, if playing a five-card major system. Playing a four-card major system, such as Acol, you would open 1♠. Hand (2) is too weak for a strong 1NT. You would open 1♣ in a five-card major system and might do the same in Acol. You would open 1♥ only if your partnership treats the sequence 1♥ – 2♦ – 2NT as showing 12–14 points.

3

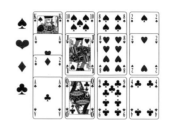

When you hold a hand of 4–4–4–1 shape, such as (3), don't follow any particular 'rule' that you may have heard. Satisfy yourself that you will have a convenient rebid, should partner happen to respond in your short suit. Here you see that you can open 1♣. If partner responds 1♦, which is likely, you can rebid 1♥.

Choosing which five-card suit to bid

When you have two five-card suits, you normally open the higher suit (except when you hold both black suits). Again the choice of suit is based on ensuring a convenient rebid. Suppose you have to choose an opening bid on one of these hands:

4

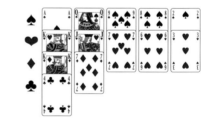

You open 1♠ on hand (4), planning to rebid 2♥. On a weak hand your partner will then be able to give preference to spades at the same level (rebidding 2♠).

5

Similarly, you open 1♥ on (5). If partner responds 1♠ or 1NT, you will rebid 2♣ and again allow partner to return to your first suit at the same level of bidding.

6

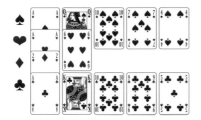

On (6) you would open 1♣, planning to rebid 1♠ and then to bid spades again on the following round (if applicable). However, if the hand was weaker and would not justify so many bids, you might open 1♠, to make certain that partner heard about your five-card spade suit.

COMPUTER DEALT HANDS
♠ ♥ ♦ ♣

From 1970 onwards, tournaments began to use computer-dealt hands. There was an immediate outcry that the deals were much more distributional than normal, with many more voids. Subsequent research showed that the deals were in accordance with the frequencies to be expected mathematically. The problem was that humans tended to deal hands from inadequately shuffled packs. For example, a trick containing four hearts might remain intact in the pack and each player would then receive one heart. This resulted in much more balanced hands being dealt than should be the case.

Opening on a 5–4 hand

When your shape is 5–4 in the two longest suits, it is generally best to open the five-card suit. This is the case even when the five-card suit is quite weak. The important point about choosing a trump suit is the length of the suit. You want to have as many trumps as possible. Look at these three hands:

7

Hand (7) offers no problems at all. You open 1♦, planning to rebid 2♣.

8

On (8) you should open 1♥. If partner responds 2♣ or 2♦, you are not strong enough to rebid 2♠ (we will see in a later section that such a rebid, carrying you past the safety level of two of your longest suit, is a strong bid). You would rebid either 2NT, if that shows 12–14 points in your system, or a simple 2♥.

9

Similarly, on (9), you would open 1♠, planning to rebid 2♠ over a response of 2♥. A rebid of 3♣, carrying you to the three-level would show much greater strength.

Left: Riffle shuffle. In the riffle shuffle, the two halves of the pack are interleaved, by running the thumbs from the bottom of each half to the top.

RESPONDING TO ONE OF A SUIT

Responder has many options facing a one-level opening in a suit. With trump support, he can raise partner's suit. With a balanced hand, he can bid no-trumps at some level. If he follows either of these paths, he will give an accurate picture of how strong his hand is. The higher he bids, in general terms, the stronger he will be. A third option is to respond in a new suit. You will recall that an opening bid at the one-level covers a very wide range, about 10–20 points. Similarly a response in a new suit may be made on 6 points, also on 20 points. The first priority is to find a good trump suit. There will be an opportunity on the second round to show the strength of the two hands.

Raising partner's minor suit

When partner has opened 1♣ or 1♦, it is normal to respond in a four-card major even when you hold good support for partner's suit. That is because game in a major suit needs only ten tricks, whereas game in a minor suit requires 11 tricks. Suppose partner has opened 1♦ and you hold one of these hands:

1

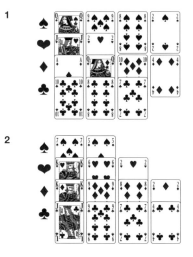

2

On (1) you respond 1♠. Such a change of suit is forcing (in other words, partner must bid again). If partner rebids 2♣, you will give preference to 2♦.

You have no major to bid on (2) and will raise directly to 2♦, showing 6–9 points.

Hand (3) is stronger and you would raise to 3♦, showing 10–11 points.

3

Raising partner's major suit

When partner opens 1♥ or 1♠ and you have a fit, you raise to the level that you expect will be successful opposite a minimum hand. This is a rough guide, opposite a bid of 1♠:

2♠	6–9 points, maybe only three-card support
3♠	10–11 points, at least four-card support
4♠	12–14 points, at least four-card support.

The term 'rough guide' was used because shape is important as well as high-card points. If you hold four-card trump support and a side-suit singleton, partner will be able to score some ruffs in the short-trump hand. The singleton is likely to be valuable and, on average, it is worth 2 or 3 points extra. A void is even more valuable, some authorities assigning it a value of 5 extra points. Suppose partner has opened 1♠ and you hold one of these hands:

4

On (4) you should raise to 2♠, even if you play a four-card major system and partner may hold only four spades. He is likely to hold five spades, even so, and he may well be able to ruff a heart in your hand. Hand (5) contains a valuable singleton in clubs. This elevates the 9 point-count into a raise to 3♠. On hand (6) you are worth a raise to 4♠.

5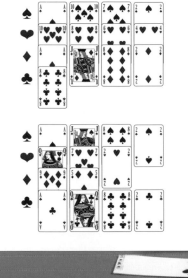

6

Above: With 13 points and a four-card spade fit, responder raises partner's 1♠ opening to 4♠.

Tournament players use various conventional bids to show game-strength hands with good trump support and we will see these in later sections. When such methods are used, a direct raise to 4♠ becomes pre-emptive, showing very good trump support but relatively few points.

JUMPING TO 3NT
♠ ♥ ♦ ♣

When partner opens with a one-bid in a suit, it is not attractive to leap all the way to 3NT. If the opener has a strong hand, you have robbed him of the space to describe it. It is better to make a low-level response in some other suit. If the opener shows a minimum hand, you can bid 3NT then.

Responding in no-trumps

When you respond in no-trumps, you give an accurate account of the number of points that you hold in your hand. A response of 1NT suggests about 6–10 points, 2NT shows 11–12 points and 3NT around 13–15. If you have space to show a four-card major at the one-level you should do that instead of responding in no-trumps.

Suppose partner has opened 1♦ and you hold one of these hands. We will see in a moment that hand (7) is not strong enough for a 2♣ response.

7

Since you have no suit to bid at the one-level, you respond 1NT.

8

Hand (8) is stronger and you would respond 2NT. This is not forcing and partner is allowed to pass if he holds a minimum hand. With 14 or more points, he will advance to a game contract.

9

On (9) there is no hurry to bid no-trumps and you should respond 1♥ in case there is a 4–4 fit in that suit. You should bid 3NT if appropriate on the next round.

When partner has opened 1♥ or 1♠, there is no hurry to respond 2NT or 3NT. You can make a simple response in a minor at the two-level, intending to rebid in no-trumps on the next round. In this way you may find a fit, either in your suit or in the opener's. Suppose partner has opened 1♠ and you hold one of these hands:

10

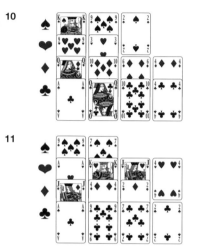

11

Above: With 13 points opposite an opening bid, a game should be bid. To discover more about partner's hand, you respond 2♣.

There are two reasons why you would not respond 2NT on (10). Firstly, you have no guard in hearts. Secondly, there is every reason to think that the hand will play well in spades, where partner is likely to hold a five-card suit (even if you play a four-card major system). You respond 2♣, showing the cheaper of your four-card suits. If the opener bids 2♥ or 2♦ next, you can be sure that he holds five spades

and will invite a game by jumping to 3♠. If you chose to respond 2NT instead, and partner passed on a minimum hand, you would have missed your 5–3 spade fit.

Similarly, on (11) you would not leap straight to 3NT. By doing so, you might miss a 4–4 heart fit. The correct response is 2♣, which leaves space for partner to introduce a four-card heart suit. Note that a response of 2♥ is nearly always based on a five-card heart suit.

Responding in a new suit

You can respond in a new suit at the one-level on 6 points or more. If you hold a five-major suit you can respond on only 5 points. A two-level response requires greater strength, since you will be carrying the bidding higher. In most bidding systems you need around 10 points for such a response.

Suppose partner has opened 1♦ and you must find a response on one of these hands:

12

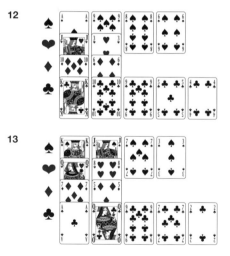

13

There are two reasons why you would not

You respond 1♠ on (12) because you are not strong enough for a two-level response. Also, you do not want to miss a 4–4 fit in spades. Hand (13) contains 12 points and you are therefore worth two bids. On such a hand you should show your longest suit first and then bid your other suit. You respond 2♣, intending to invite game by continuing with 2♠ over partner's 2♦ rebid.

14

When you have two four-card suits, as in (14), you respond in the cheaper suit. Here you respond 1♥. If the opener has four hearts with you, he will raise the hearts. If instead he holds four spades, you have given him the space to rebid 1♠ (which you will raise to 3♠, inviting a game).

When you hold two five-card suits in response, you bid the higher suit first. Suppose partner has opened 1♦ and you hold one of these hands:

15

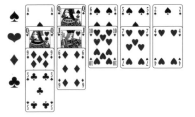

You respond 1♠ on (15). Over a rebid of 2♦ you can bid 2♥ next. Partner will then be able to give preference to spades at the same level, rebidding 2♠.

16

Similarly, you respond 1♥ on (16), intending to continue with 3♣ on the next round.

The jump shift

When you hold a hand that is so strong that you suspect a slam may be possible, you may give a jump response in a new suit (for example 1♥ – 3♣). This is known as a 'jump shift'. Because it uses up so much bidding space, the bid is used only on two types of hands: those that contain a powerful suit and those that contain very strong support for the opener's suit.

Suppose your partner has opened 1♥ and you hold one of these hands:

17

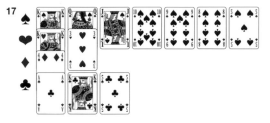

Hand (17) is fine for a jump shift of 2♠. You plan to rebid 3♠ on the next round to let partner know your jump shift was based on a very powerful suit.

18

Hand (18) contains excellent support for partner's hearts and you will begin with a jump shift of 3♣, supporting hearts later.

19

Hand (19) is very strong but it does not belong to either of the categories for a jump shift. You need time to find the best fit and cannot afford to waste space by jumping to 3♦ on the first round. Respond 2♦, intending to continue with a game-forcing 3♣.

OPENING 2♣ AND 2NT

When your hand is so strong that you have enough (or nearly enough) to make game on your own, you cannot afford to open with a one-bid. If your partner held fewer than six points, he might then pass and a game would be missed. There are two opening bids at the two-level that show a very strong hand:

2♣	shows (i) an unbalanced hand of game-going strength or (ii) a balanced hand of at least 23 points
2NT	shows a balanced hand of 20–22 points.

By opening with one of these bids, you ensure that you do not play a game hand at the one-level.

Opening 2♣

An opening bid of 2♣ is the strongest bid that you can make. It is an artificial bid and says nothing whatsoever about your holding in clubs. Partner will usually respond 2♦, to allow you to describe your hand further. If you rebid 2♥, 2♠, 3♣ or 3♦, you are showing your best suit and the bidding must continue to the game-level at least. If instead you rebid 2NT, you indicate a balanced hand of 23–24 points. Your partner is allowed to pass this when he has no more than 1 point in his hand. This is the only time that the bidding may stop short of game after a 2♣ opening.

You would open 2♣ on any of the three hands shown below:

1

Even with a weak hand opposite, you are very likely to make 4♠ on hand (1). If you opened only 1♠ and this was passed out, you would be worried indeed that game had been missed. You open 2♣, intending to rebid 2♠ and the bidding will continue to the game-level at least.

Hand (2) is a balanced 23-count. You will rebid 2NT over 2♦, allowing partner to pass when he holds a valueless hand. If he makes any further bid over 2NT, the bidding must continue to game.

2

Hand (3) is stronger, with 26 points. You will rebid 3NT to make sure that game is reached. Knowing you hold such a strong hand, your partner will often advance to a slam. The range for a 3NT rebid is 25–27. On the rare occasions when you hold a balanced hand of 28–30 points, you will indicate this by rebidding 4NT.

3

OLD FASHIONED TWO BIDS
♠ ♥ ♦ ♣

In the first decades of contract bridge, opening bids of 2♦, 2♥ and 2♠ showed a powerful hand with a strong holding in the suit that had been bid. Hands that would justify such a 'strong two bid' arose infrequently. It was eventually thought preferable to use 'weak two bids', which show a hand of around 6–10 points and a six-card suit. Such hands arise much more frequently. When you do pick up a powerful hand with a long suit, you must either open at the one level or bid 2♣.

Responding to 2♣

On most hands responder will bid 2♦. This keeps the auction low and does not preclude strong bidding thereafter. When responder has a good suit, such as ♥K–Q–J–8–3 and perhaps another good card outside, then a positive response of 2♥ is best. You can also make a positive response in no-trumps (2NT) when you hold a balanced hand of 9 points or more. Usually the two hands will be worth a slam when a positive response is made.

Opening 2NT

You open 2NT with a balanced hand of 20–22 points. It would not be safe to open with a one-bid on such a hand because partner might pass with 4 or 5 points and you would miss a game. These hands are all suitable for a 2NT opening:

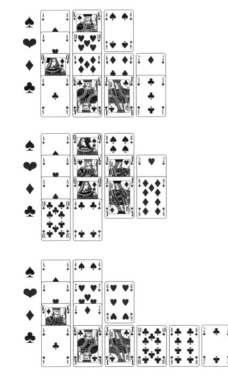

4

5

6

Hand (4) is a typical example, with a stopper in every suit. You may be worried about the clubs on hand (5) but go ahead and open 2NT. You give an excellent description of your hand by doing so. If partner raises to 3NT, the most likely place for his

honours is in clubs (because four of the missing eight picture cards are in that suit). Hand (6) is well worth 2NT too. Only 19 points, but that club suit entitles you to add a point or two. If you opened only 1♣ you might miss a game. Even if partner responded, you would have difficulty in describing such a strong hand.

Responding to 2NT

With fewer than 4 points and no particularly long suit, the responder should pass 2NT. A response of 3♣ is Stayman, asking for a four-card major. Responses of 3♦, 3♥ and 3♠ are game-forcing and show at least a five-card suit. The opener will generally raise the suit when he has three-card support and rebid 3NT otherwise.

BIDDING OPPOSITE A 1NT OVERCALL

♠ ♥ ♦ ♣

So far as is possible, it is a good idea to play the same methods in different circumstances. If you use Stayman and transfers opposite a 1NT opening, it makes good sense to use the same methods opposite a 1NT overcall. The same methods that you use facing a 2NT opening should be used after a start of 2♣ – 2♦ – 2NT, also opposite a natural 2NT overcall.

Above: A typical balanced 26-point hand. You would open 2♣ and rebid 3NT.

THE OPENER'S REBID

A player who has opened with a one-bid in a suit may regard his hand as belonging to one of three categories. Expressed solely in terms of point-count, they are (a) minimum, 12–15 points, (b) medium, 16–18 points and (c) strong 19–20 points. With his first rebid, he will usually specify into which of these classifications his hand falls. That is particularly the case if the responder's first response was a limit bid – either a raise of the opener's suit or a bid in no-trumps. We will look at the opener's rebid in the various situations that may arise.

Responder bid no-trumps

After a start such as 1♠ – 1NT, the opener may pass when he has a minimum hand with only five spades and no other suit of at least four cards. With six or more spades, he may rebid 2♠ on a minimum hand and a non-forcing 3♠ on a medium hand. On the deal below East has only one spade and decides to pass 3♠.

> ## SHOWING A STOPPER
> ♠ ♥ ♦ ♣
>
> Once you have agreed a minor suit as trumps, bids in a new suit (below the level of 3NT) should show a stopper rather than promising a four-card suit. When the bidding starts 1♦ – 3♦ – 3♠, for example, the opener is showing a spade stopper and denying a heart stopper. The responder should bid 3NT when he holds a heart stopper himself.

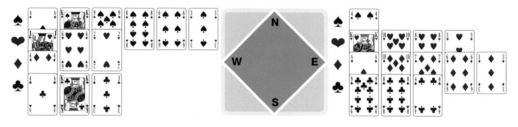

The opener may rebid in a different suit (for example, 1♠ – 1NT – 2♦) on a suit of at least four cards. This is non-forcing, so when the opener sees a chance of game opposite a 1NT response he should consider bidding 2NT, or a game-forcing 3♦ instead.

A rebid of 2♣ would have led nowhere on the West hand shown below. Since West is strong enough to invite a game, but not strong enough to insist on one by rebidding 3♣, he chooses a raise to 2NT. On this occasion, East is happy to raise to 3NT.

West	East
1♠	INT
3♠	

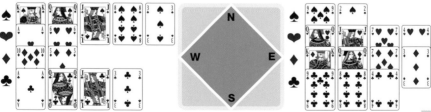

After a start such as 1♠ – 2NT, a rebid of a new suit (such as 3♣) is forcing. A rebid of the opener's suit at the lowest level (3♠) shows a minimum hand and is non-forcing.

West	East
1♠	INT
2NT	3NT

Responder raised the opener's major suit

When the responder raised opener's major suit (1♠ – 2♠), the opener will have a good idea whether a game is possible. If his hand is in the middle range and he cannot make up his mind whether to bid game or not, he will usually bid his second longest suit – a trial bid – to ask whether partner thinks a game is worth bidding. The responder can then see how well his own hand fits with the opener's second-best suit. A shortage opposite this suit will be beneficial.

PRE-EMPTIVE RAISE
♠ ♥ ♦ ♣

After a start such as 1♠ – 2♠, the opener should bid a new suit (a trial bid) to invite a game. When he bids 3♠, this is generally treated as pre-emptive.

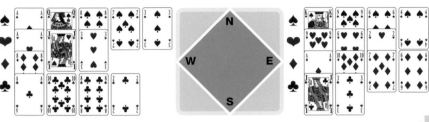

West makes a trial bid in clubs. East accepts the try because he holds a sound 8 points and a ruffing value in West's second longest suit. He expects West to score some club ruffs.

West	East
1♠	2♠
3♣	4♠

Responder raised the opener's minor suit

After a start of 1♦ – 2♦, or 1♦ – 3♦, the most likely game target (if any) will be 3NT. To this aim, a bid in a new suit shows a good stopper in that suit and requests partner to cooperate towards a no-trump contract. This would be a typical auction.

Holding 19 points, West can visualize a game in no-trumps. He can hardly rebid 3NT with only a low doubleton in spades, so he consults his partner with a stopper-showing bid of 2♥. As you see, this does not promise four cards in the suit. Indeed, East is most unlikely to hold four hearts because he responded 2♦ instead of 1♥. East shows his spade stopper, by bidding 2♠, and West is sufficiently emboldened to leap to the no-trump game.

West	East
1♦	2♦
2♥	2♠
3NT	

If East had rebid 3♣ or 3♦ instead, this would deny a spade stopper. Knowing that the spade suit was not stopped, West would rule out a no-trump contract. Game in diamonds might still be possible if East held the ♥A and West would invite a game by bidding 4♣.

The response was one of a suit

When the bidding starts with a bid in two different suits (such as 1♦ – 1♠), neither player has limited his hand; the final contract could be a part score or a grand slam. The opener will now usually limit his hand by making some bid in his own suit or the responder's suit, or by bidding no-trumps. These are the options that limit the opener's hand:

1NT	shows a balanced hand of the opposite range to a 1NT opener (15–17 points when 1NT is 12–14, and 12–14 points when 1NT is 15–17)
2♦	minimum hand with at least five diamonds
2♠	minimum hand with four-card spade support
2NT	18–19 points, balanced hand
3♦	medium hand, 16–18 points and at least 6 diamonds
3♠	medium hand with four-card spade support
3NT	strong hand with long diamonds, expecting to make nine tricks.

The opener may also bid a new suit. The point-count range for such rebids depends on whether the safety level of two of opener's suit has been breached:

2♣	wide range, 12–18 points
2♥	a 'reverse', 17+ points and forcing
3♣	forcing to game.

Both 2♥ and 3♣ carry the bidding past the safety level of 2♦. They therefore show significantly more than a minimum opening bid.

Suppose the bidding starts 1♦ – 1♠ and you hold one of these hands:

1

On (1) you would rebid a wide-range 2♣. You are not strong enough to force to game with 3♣.

2

With hand (2) you would rebid a medium-range 3♦. This is non-forcing but partner can consider advancing to game with 9 points or more.

3
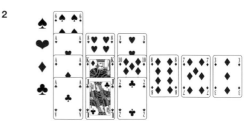

Hand (3) is strong enough for a reverse. You rebid 2♥.

The response was two of a new suit

A two-level response promises at least 10 points. It follows that the opener will want to reach a game contract when his hand is medium range or better. Remember that a medium-range opening hand will contain about 15–17 points. When the responder holds 10 points upwards, the total will be at least 25 points, which is enough for game. All the rebids that show extra strength are forcing to game.

Although a rebid of a new suit below the 'safety level' (for example, 1♠ – 2♣ – 2♥) may be based on a minimum hand, it is convenient to play it as forcing for one round. (This is a fairly recent modification and you would have to discuss it with your partner.)

If you play a weak 1NT, it is normal to play a non-jump 2NT rebid as 15–17 (1♠ – 2♣ – 2NT). Since it is logical to play this as forcing to game, with at least 15 points facing 10, many players are willing to rebid 2NT on 15–19, leaving more space to find a fit. If instead you play a strong 1NT, then most players treat a 2NT rebid as weak (12–14).

These are the possibilities for the opener's rebid after a start of 1♠ – 2♦:

2♥	12–19, forcing for one round
2♠	12–14, minimum hand
2NT	15+ if you play a weak 1NT, 12–14 if you play a strong 1NT
3♣	15+, a 'high reverse', game forcing
3♦	minimum hand with diamond support
3♠	15+, game-forcing with good spades.

Suppose, after a start of 1♠ – 2♦, you have to find a rebid on one of these hands:

4

On (4) you expect to reach game eventually, with 15 points opposite partner's minimum of 10. For the moment, you should bid a simple 2♥, which is forcing for one round. You hope that partner can show support for one of your suits. If not, the most likely game will be 3NT.

5

Since you want to reach game on hand (5) also, you cannot afford to rebid 2♠, which would show a minimum hand. You rebid 3♠ instead, forcing the bidding to the game level. This rebid shows a six-card spade suit, so partner will often raise to 4♠. When he is very short in spades, he may prefer to bid 3NT.

6

Hand (6) is suitable for a raise to 3♦, showing a minimum hand. If partner continues with 3♥, showing good values in hearts, your good stopper in clubs will allow you to bid 3NT. When partner has a strong hand with no heart stopper and cannot bid 3♠ to show spade support, you will have to play in diamonds. The final contract will be 5♦ (or maybe 6♦).

THE RESPONDER'S REBID

By the time three bids have been made – two by opener and one by responder – the auction will have been limited (except in the case where three different suits have been bid). It will often be possible for the responder to announce the final contract or, at any rate, his opinion on what it should be. He will add the strength of his hand to that indicated by the opener. When the opener has shown a minimum hand, the responder will need an opening bid himself to contract for game. When he has around 11 points, he may invite a game. With anything less, he will pass or sign off somewhere.

The opener rebid his own suit

Suppose the bidding started 1♦ – 1♠ – 2♦, the opener showing that he has a minimum hand. The responder may take one of these actions:

Pass	no game ambitions
2♥	showing a second suit (forcing for one round)
2♠	no game ambitions and a six-card spade suit
2NT	balanced, about 11 points, inviting a game
3♣	showing a second suit (game-forcing)
3♦	diamond support, about 11 points, inviting a game
3♠	six spades, about 11 points, inviting a game.

He may also bid any game contract that appears to be a reasonable prospect, in particular 3NT.

The opener rebid 1NT

After a start of 1♦ – 1♠ – 1NT, the opener may take one of these options:

Pass	no game ambitions
2♦/2♥/2♠	no game ambitions
2NT	inviting a game in no-trumps
3♣/3♥	second suit (game-forcing)
3♦	diamond support, inviting a game
3♠	six spades, inviting a game.

Many players use a bid of 2♣ (the 'other minor') as an artificial bid, asking for further information.

The opener showed support

When the opener gave a single raise of the responder's suit (1♦ – 1♥ – 2♥, for example), the responder knows he is facing a minimum opening and will be well placed to announce the final contract. Similarly, after a double raise (such as 1♣ – 1♠ – 3♠), the responder knows that he is facing a medium hand and will advance to game when he is a queen better than a minimum response.

When the raise was in a minor suit, the most likely game contract will be 3NT. Any bid in a new suit will therefore show a stopper.

Left: A typical invitational hand for responder. After a start of 1♦ – 1♠ – 2♣, you would give 'jump preference' to 3♦, inviting partner to proceed to game.

Left: Responder accepts the invitation. After a start of 1♦ – 1♠ – 3♠, you would place partner with a medium hand of around 16 points. With 9 points yourself, rather than a minimum 6, you would raise to 4♠.

In the auction 1♠ – 2♦ – 3♦ – 3♥, the responder shows good heart values and hopes that the opener has a club stopper and can bid 3NT. The opener would have rebid 2♥ if he held four cards in the heart suit, so there would not be much point in responder's 3♥ rebid showing a four-card suit (rather than a stopper).

Three suits have been bid

The most difficult and least limited situation is when three suits have been bid (a start such as 1♦ – 1♠ – 2♣). The opener's range is about 12–18 and the responder must now show his own strength: minimum, game-try, or 'at least game'. These are the responder's options:

Pass	weak and prefers clubs to diamonds
2♦	weak and prefers diamonds
2♥	'fourth suit forcing', see the next section
2♠	weak with long spades
2NT	about 10–12 points, inviting game
3♣	about 10–12 points, club support, inviting game
3♦	about 10–12 points, diamond support, inviting game
3♠	about 10–12 points, six spades, inviting game
Game bids	when the responder knows which game is best.

As you see, there are three actions that are weak. When you hold a near-minimum response, you can pass the opener's rebid when you prefer his second suit to his first. You may also give preference to his first suit at the minimum level or rebid your own suit.

When you are somewhat stronger and wish to invite game, you have four options. You can raise the opener's second suit, give jump preference to his first suit, jump one level in your own suit or bid 2NT.

When you are strong enough to insist on a game, you can either bid such a contract directly or ask for further information to help you to decide which denomination will be best. You do this by bidding the fourth suit (2♥ here). Such a bid is artificial and says nothing whatsoever about the heart suit. The device is in general use around the world and is known as 'fourth suit forcing'.

GIVING PREFERENCE
♠ ♥ ♦ ♣

When the opener has shown two suits (for example, in the auction 1♦ – 1♥ – 2♣), the responder will often want to choose which of them should become trumps. With a weak responding hand he can 'give preference' by passing 2♣ or correcting to 2♦. When responder wants to invite a game, he can instead bid 3♣ or 3♦. Bidding 3♦ is an example of what is known as 'jump preference'.

FOURTH SUIT FORCING

As was mentioned in the previous section, the most wide-ranging start to an auction is when three different suits are bid (for example: 1♦ – 1♠ – 2♣). If the responder now makes any two-level or three-level bid in one of those suits, this will be a limit bid. Sometimes he is strong enough to insist on a game contract, at least, but does not yet know what denomination will be best. In that case the responder must make an artificial bid in the fourth suit – 2♥, here. The meaning is: "I have enough strength for a game contract. Please continue to describe your hand."

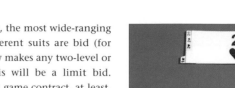

Above: Fourth suit forcing sequence. These bidding cards (from a duplicate game) show that after a start of 1♦ – 1♠ – 2♣, North has rebid a fourth-suit-forcing 2♥.

Bidding the fourth suit to investigate the best game

Let's see some examples of auctions that contain a 'fourth-suit forcing' bid.

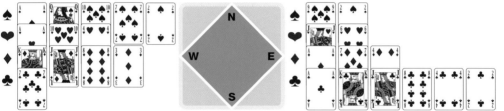

As you see, East's 2♥ bid says nothing whatsoever about his holding in hearts. Indeed, if he held four hearts (or even a good stopper in the suit) he would doubtless have made some bid in no-trumps instead of his fourth-suit bid. Here West has a stopper in the fourth suit, so he rebids 2NT. Remember that the bidding is forced to game, so there is no need whatsoever for West to jump to 3NT. Without the 'fourth-suit forcing' method, East would be stuck for a bid at his second turn. A rebid of 3♣ would be non-forcing. A rebid of 4♣ would be unsatisfactory, since it would carry the bidding past the 3NT level.

West	East
1♠	2♣
2♦	2♥
2NT	3NT

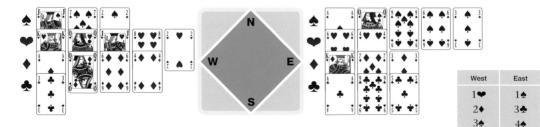

East cannot be certain that 3NT is the right contract, on the second round. He bids a fourth-suit 3♣ instead and is delighted to hear that West has some spade support. If West held one spade and ♣Q–x–x, he would have bid 3NT instead.

West	East
1♥	1♠
2♦	3♣
3♠	4♠

Bidding the fourth suit to make your next bid forcing

Sometimes the responder bids the fourth suit so that he can make his next bid forcing, rather than a limit bid.

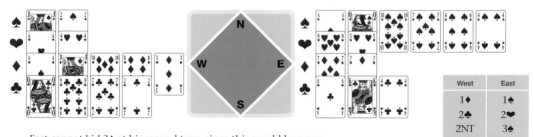

West	East
1♦	1♠
2♣	2♥
2NT	3♠
4♠	

East cannot bid 3♠ at his second turn, since this would be a non-forcing limit bid. He bids a fourth-suit forcing 2♥ instead and then bids 3♠, thereby making this bid forcing. Since West has already bid diamonds and clubs, and shown a heart stopper, he knows that his partner cannot be looking for more than two-card spade support. He is therefore happy to raise to the spade game. With only one spade and a secure heart stopper, he would have bid 3NT instead.

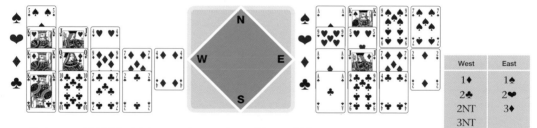

West	East
1♦	1♠
2♣	2♥
2NT	3♦
3NT	

East cannot bid 3♦ at his second turn, since this would be a non-forcing limit bid. As on the previous hand, he bids a fourth-suit forcing 2♥ with the intention of making a forcing diamond bid on the next round. The purpose of showing the diamond fit is to investigate a possible slam in the suit. When West can only bid 3NT on the fourth round, East abandons his thoughts of a slam.

Below: Too strong for a limit bid. After a start of 1♦ – 1♠ – 2♣, you cannot bid 3♠ because this would suggest around 11 points. Instead you must bid a fourth-suit-forcing 2♥, intending to bid a forcing 3♠ on the next round.

USA v USA
♠ ♥ ♦ ♣

The 1977 Bermuda Bowl is unique because the final was contested by two teams from the same country, the USA. Robert Hamman, Bobby Wolff, Billy Eisenberg, Eddie Kantar, Paul Soloway and John Swanson eventually won the trophy, despite being more than 80 IMPs behind at one stage. It was deemed unsatisfactory to have the two American teams meeting in the final. Since then they have been forced to play each other in the semi-final, should they both survive to that stage.

COMPLETING THE AUCTION

When the players have made two bids each, a considerable amount of information has been exchanged. It remains only to put the finishing touches to the auction. When responder's rebid was a limit bid, the opener must assess whether he is strong enough to advance to game. When responder's rebid was a forcing bid in a new suit, the opener will generally be able to give his view of which game will be best.

OPENING LEAD FACE-DOWN
♠ ♥ ♦ ♣

It is recommended practice to make the opening Lead face-down on the table. Your partner then has an opportunity to ask any questions about the opponents' bidding. (He could not ask beforehand, in case his questions affected your choice of lead.) This practice also allows leads that are out of turn to be corrected.

Responder's rebid was a limit bid

Let's see a couple of complete auctions that follow a limited rebid by the responder:

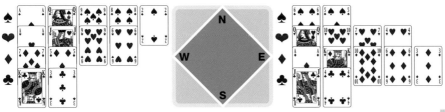

West	East
1♠	2♦
2♥	3♥
4♥	

East's 3♥ was non-forcing, suggesting about 11 points. Since West holds 14 points rather than a minimum 12 points, he decides to bid game. Since there is a big bonus for bidding and making game, most players are fairly adventurous in this area. A game needs to have only a 40 per cent chance of being made for it to be worth bidding.

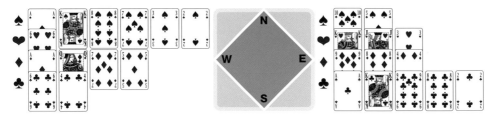

West	East
1♠	2♣
2♦	2NT
3♠	4♠

East's 2NT suggested around 11 points and showed a good stopper in hearts, the unbid suit. Holding six spades, West decided to bid the suit once again. East then judged it best to bid game in that suit. As you see, ten tricks are by no means certain in spades. Nevertheless, it is a contract worth attempting.

Suppose one of West's low spades had been a low heart instead, giving him 5–2–4–2 shape. Since he had already indicated five spades and four diamonds by opening in one suit and rebidding in a lower suit, there would be no reason to bid the spades again. West would rebid 3NT instead.

Responder introduced a new suit

When the responder bids a new suit at the two-level, this is forcing for one round (except when the opener rebid 1NT). Here is a typical auction:

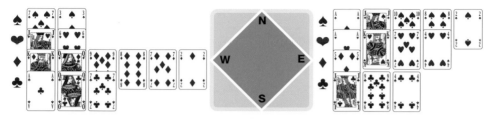

West is happy to bid no-trumps as he has an excellent stopper in clubs, the unbid suit. Since he has a minimum hand he bids only 2NT, which East would sometimes pass. Here East holds 13 points opposite an opening bid, so he raises to 3NT. East has already indicated that he holds five spades and four hearts. If he held four spades and four hearts, he would have responded 1♥ on the first round.

West	East
1♦	1♠
2♦	2♥
2NT	3NT

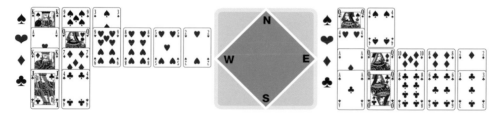

East's bid of 3♣, a new suit at the three-level, is forcing to game. West has a stopper in spades, the unbid suit, so he suggests 3NT as the final contract. East is happy to accept. If West had not held a spade stopper, he would have had to bid his heart suit again (3♥) or give preference to partner's diamonds (3♦).

West	East
1♥	2♦
2♥	3♣
3NT	

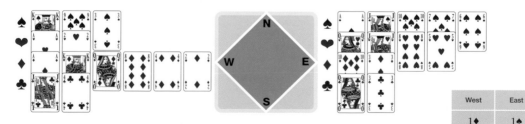

West's rebid of 3♦ is not forcing but it shows a hand in the intermediate range (16–18 points). Since East has 10 points, he has enough for game. He advances with the forcing bid of 3♥ and West gives preference to spades. Game in spades is a sound contract. In 3NT there would have been no stopper in the club suit.

West	East
1♦	1♠
3♦	3♥
3♠	4♠

WEAK TWO-BIDS AND RESPONSES

In the early days of bridge, opening bids of 2♦, 2♥ and 2♠ were forcing and showed a very powerful hand. Such openings arose very infrequently and a new form of two-bid gradually became popular, one that showed a six-card suit and 6–10 points. The classical form of the weak two-bid is based on a good six-card suit. These are all worthy examples:

1

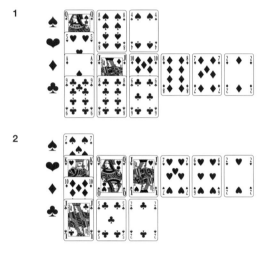

2

3

Most players would open 2♠ on hand (3). Partner will not expect the void club, though, and might pass when he holds enough in the red suits for a game contract to be made.

One of the objects of such openings is to take away the opponents' bidding space when they hold the balance of the points. Some players are therefore willing to open with a weak two-bid on hands that do not fit the classical requirements:

Hand (1) is an obvious 2♦ opening. Hand (2) is a standard 2♥ bid, despite the four-card club suit on the side. However, you would not usually open with a weak two-bid when you held a four-card major on the side.

4

It is tempting to open 2♠ on hand (4), if only to tell your partner that you have a suit that will be worth leading.

5

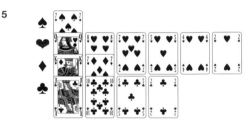

Hand (5) does not contain the recommended 'good suit' but many players would open 2♥, even so, in an attempt to make life awkward for the opponents.

6

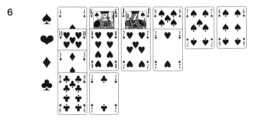

Similarly, some players would open 2♠ on (6), despite holding four cards in the other major. You and your partner can decide whether you want to keep your weak two-bids disciplined or a bit on the wild side!

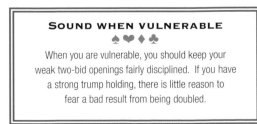

SOUND WHEN VULNERABLE
♠ ♥ ♦ ♣

When you are vulnerable, you should keep your weak two-bid openings fairly disciplined. If you have a strong trump holding, there is little reason to fear a bad result from being doubled.

Responding to a weak two-bid

On most moderate hands, including balanced hands of up to 13 points, you will usually pass. Remember that partner has shown a weak hand. These are the responses available to you when partner has opened 2♥:

2♠	natural and invitational
2NT	relay bid, asking for more information (see below)
3♣/3♦/3♠	natural and forcing
3♥	pre-emptive
game bids	to play.

So, a raise to the three-level is an attempt to increase the pre-emption. The opener is not invited to bid game. When you can see a reasonable chance of game, if partner has values to spare, you normally respond 2NT. This asks the opener to describe his hand further and he will then rebid along the following lines:

3♣	lower-range without two of the three top honours in his suit
3♦	lower-range with two of the three top honours
3♥	upper-range without two of the three top honours
3♠	upper-range with two of the three top honours
3NT	the long suit is headed by the ace-king-queen.

Above: Not enough for game. Many players overbid opposite weak two-bids. Suppose partner opens 2♠ and you hold this hand. You should pass. Indeed, you should be quite glad if partner managed to make eight tricks eventually!

SKIP BID WARNING
♠ ♥ ♦ ♣

When an opponent makes a 'skip bid', in other words a bid that is one or more levels higher than the minimum legal bid in that suit, it may take you a while to decide whether your hand is worth a bid at that level. To avoid giving away information by thinking for a few seconds about bidding and then passing, it is correct etiquette to pretend to think for around eight seconds, whether or not your hand is worthy of such consideration. The opponent should warn you to be ready to pause by saying 'skip bid', or displaying the skip-bid card from the bidding box, before making his jump bid.

This would be a typical auction:

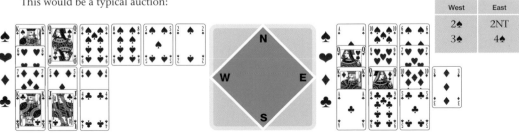

West	East
2♠	2NT
3♠	4♠

With 15 points and three-card support, East decides he will play in game opposite an upper-range opening. He makes the relay bid of 2NT and West's 3♠ response shows that he is upper-range (8–10) and holds two of the three top spade honours. East bids the game and it turns out to be a worthwhile prospect.

WEAK THREE-BIDS AND RESPONSES

An opening bid at the three-level shows a weak hand, usually with a seven-card suit. When you are vulnerable, the suit needs to be fairly strong to offer some safety against a large penalty. Suppose you are dealt one of these hands:

1
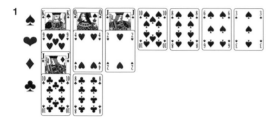

A good guideline for a pre-emptive bid is that you will score many more tricks if you play the contract than you would when defending. Hand (1) fits this requirement admirably. Playing in spades, you are almost certain to score six tricks. Defending a contract by the opponents, you might score none at all; the second round of spades might well be ruffed. So, open 3♠ even when vulnerable. Do not worry that you might go for 800 if you are doubled and partner has nothing. First of all, it will be difficult for the opponents to double you, since a double is nearly always for take-out. Secondly, you will be making life very difficult for the opponents by opening with such a high bid. It is worth taking a small risk to this effect.

2
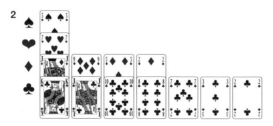

Similarly, you should open 3♣ on hand (2). Don't worry that you might miss a better contract in diamonds. If your partner has good diamonds, the opponents will have a big fit in one of the majors anyway. It is generally advised that you should not pre-empt when your long suit is accompanied by four cards in a major suit. In the first or second seats, when partner may still be strong, it is true that opening 3♦

3

on (3) might cause you to miss a fit in hearts. When you are in the third seat, you should open 3♦ nevertheless. The player on your left is marked with a big hand. Also, if your partner does hold heart length, the opponents will have a great fit in one of the black suits. Don't be one of those players who always find an excuse not to pre-empt.

Above: It is reasonable to open 3♦ on this hand, despite holding four cards in a major suit.

Responding to a three-bid

The purpose of the three-bid is to remove the opponents' bidding space. When it is your partner who holds a good hand, you will have little space to manoeuvre yourselves. The best method is to play that a new suit at the three-level is natural and forcing. Remember, though, that your partner's hand may be very little use to you unless you choose his seven-card suit as trumps.

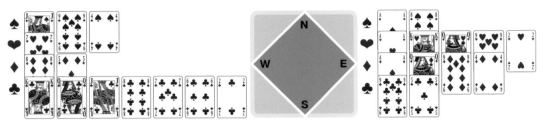

West	East
3♣	3♥
3♠	5♣

East makes a forcing response in hearts and West shows a stopper in spades. It may be tempting for East to bid 3NT now. The contract may make on a good day, but there is every chance that only one club trick will be available. (On the present hands, for example, the defenders will hold up the ♣A for one round.) It may well be better for East to bid game in clubs. The hope is that West's clubs will provide six tricks and that East can add five top winners. Remember that you need a big hand, or a good trump fit, to make game opposite a pre-emptive bid.

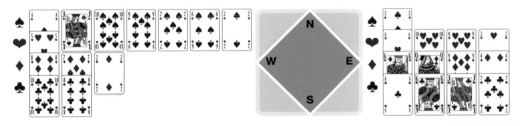

West	East
3♠	4♠

With 17 points, it is reasonable for East to attempt a spade game. Opposite the actual West hand, there is a good chance of losing just two spades and one diamond. Note that it would be very poor to respond 3NT. In all probability, you would score only one spade trick and would finish well short of your target.

The time to respond 3NT to a pre-empt in a major is when you have a good fit for the major and think that nine tricks may be easier to score than ten:

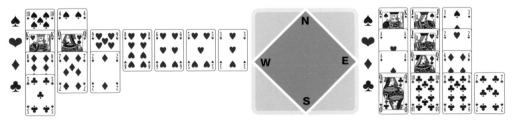

West	East
3♥	3NT

East reckons that nine tricks in no-trumps may be easier than ten in hearts. He hopes to make seven heart tricks and the ♦A. A spade or a diamond opening lead will give him a ninth trick. Even on a club lead you would expect to make 3NT. Playing in 4♥, you would have every chance of four losers in the side suits.

HIGH-LEVEL PRE-EMPTS

We have already looked at weak two-bids and pre-emptive three-bids. To complete the picture, we look now at the Gambling 3NT and at four-level pre-emptive bids. An opening bid of 4♣ can be played as natural, showing clubs and more shape than an opening 3♣ (often an eight-card suit). Another popular treatment is to use 4♣ to show a strong four-level pre-empt in hearts. Similarly, 4♦ shows a strong pre-empt in spades. This method is known as South African Texas.

The Gambling 3NT
The most popular meaning for an opening bid of 3NT is that it shows a solid seven-card minor with no card higher than a queen in the other suits. The responder will pass only when he thinks that 3NT is the best available contract. That will be the case, of course, when the responder holds stoppers in the other three suits. Even when he does not, it may be best to pass and perhaps hope that the weakest suit is not led. This is a typical situation:

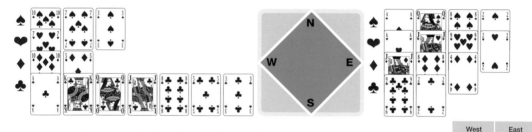

West	East
3NT	Pass

East decides to pass the Gambling 3NT, even though he holds no stopper in the diamond suit. He reasons that a major suit may be led, in which case seven club tricks and two aces will produce the game. Even if a diamond is led, partner may hold a doubleton diamond and a 4–4 break would then limit the defenders to four tricks. On a lucky day West might hold three diamonds. A final reason for passing is that the alternative contract of 4♣ would not yield a game bonus and might not be any easier to make.

When responder does choose to bid 4♣ (or 5♣), this is a request for the opener to pass if his suit is clubs and to correct to 4♦ (or 5♦) if his suit is diamonds. This caters for the case where East holds no minor-suit honour and cannot therefore tell which seven-card suit his partner has.

Responder can count on seven tricks from the opener's solid suit. Therefore, if he is confident that he has the three three-side suits under control and can contribute another five tricks, he will be able to bid a slam.

Right: With a solid seven-card minor suit, and very little outside, you open with a Gambling 3NT.

South African Texas

To distinguish between weak and stronger pre-empts in a major at the four-level, many pairs use 4♣ and 4♦ to show strong pre-empts in hearts and spades, respectively. An opening bid of 4♣, for example, would suggest a one-loser heart suit and an ace outside, or perhaps a solid heart suit and no ace outside.

Suppose you had to find an opening bid on these hands:

1

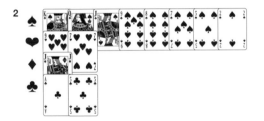

Hand (1) is too strong for 3♠, even when vulnerable, and merits a 4♠ opening.

2

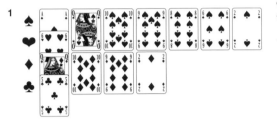

Hand (2) fits exactly the meaning of a 4♦ South African Texas opening. There is only one loser in the 8-card spade suit and an ace is held outside.

3

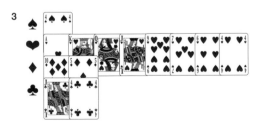

Hand (3) is worth an opening bid of 4♣, since it contains a solid 8-card suit.

The purpose of distinguishing between a strong and a weaker four-level pre-empt is so that the responder can judge whether a slam may be possible. He will have a better idea what to do if an opponent contests the auction with an overcall such as 5♣.

Five-level openings

An opening bid of five of a minor is quite rare and will usually be based on a suit of at least eight cards. With a seven-card suit, particularly opposite an unpassed partner, you would be wary of bypassing a possible game in no-trumps.

Since four of a major is a game contract, an opening bid of 5♥ or 5♠ (also very rare) tells partner you are solid except for the two top trumps. Partner can then raise to a small slam with one top trump and to a grand slam with two top trumps.

1

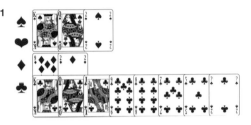

You would open 5♣ on (1). As you see, the hand follows the guidelines for a pre-emptive bid. If you had only two top losers, and a more powerful hand, you would open 1♣ or perhaps an artificial 2♣.

2

On (2) you would open 5♦. Again, your aim is pre-emptive – to make life difficult for the opponents, who will no doubt have a big fit somewhere.

3

Hand (3) illustrates the rare opening of five of a major. You would like partner to raise to 6♥ if he held the ace or king of hearts, to raise to 7♥ with both these cards.

TAKE-OUT DOUBLES AND RESPONSES

In the early days of bridge a double had just one meaning: that you thought the opponents had bid too high and you wanted to double the stakes, thereby increasing the penalty if they failed in their contract. Gradually it was realized that a more useful meaning of a double, particularly at a low level, was to show that you had a good hand but no particularly long suit to bid. This became known as a 'take-out double', because you wanted your partner to take out the double into his longest suit. Nowadays, most doubles at a low level are for take-out.

> ### WHEN PARTNER DOUBLES
> ♠ ♥ ♦ ♣
>
> When partner makes a penalty double (aimed at increasing the penalty when the opponents' contract fails), you are expected to 'leave it in'. In other words, you will pass. The opposite of leaving in a double is to 'take the double out'. In other words, you will make a bid instead of passing. A take-out double from partner explicitly requests you to bid your best suit.

Take-out doubles of a one-bid

This is a typical auction after a take-out double of a one-bid:

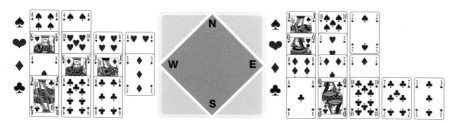

South opens 1♥ and West has the strength for an opening bid, along with a shortage in hearts. He cannot tell which suit will be best as trumps and therefore makes a take-out double.

In responding to the take-out double, East has two duties. The first is to choose a trump suit (or to bid no-trumps). The second is to indicate the strength of his hand. With about 0–7 points, he will bid his best suit at the minimum level. With around 8–11 points, he will jump one level in his best suit. With more than 11 points, the bidding should be forced to game. The responder will either bid a game directly or show his strength with a cue-bid in the opponents' suit (here it would be 2♥).

West	North	East	South
			1♥
Dble	Pass	1♠	End

East has 9 points, so he jumps one level in his best suit. West has a minimum double, with only 12 points, so he passes. If West had 17 points, he would know that he and his partner had 25 points between them. He would bid again, looking for a game contract.

West	North	East	South
			1♠
Dble	Pass	3♣	End

Let's see an example of the cue-bid response:

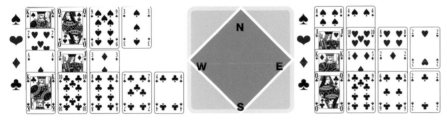

West	North	East	South
			1♦
Dble	Pass	2♦	Pass
2♠	Pass	4♠	End

With 13 points opposite West's take-out double, East wants to reach a game contract in one of the major suits. Rather than guess which one to bid, he shows his strength with a cue-bid in the opponent's suit. The players now bid their suits in ascending order, searching for a trump fit. When West shows four spades, East is happy to choose that suit as trumps.

Take-out doubles on other auctions

Whenever the opponents have bid one or two suits and the bidding is below the game level, a double is for take-out.

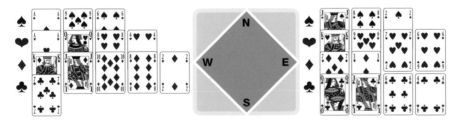

West	North	East	South
	1♥	Pass	2♥
Dble	Pass	3♣	End

West is strong enough to compete at the two-level. Rather than guess which suit to make trumps, he enters the auction with a take-out double. East chooses clubs as trumps and bids them at the minimum level, since he is too weak to look for a game contract.

West	North	East	South
	1♣	Pass	1♠
Dble	2♣	2♥	End

The opponents have bid spades and clubs, so West's take-out double shows hearts and diamonds. When North bids again, East can pass when he has nothing worth bidding. Here he has 7 points and four-card support for partner's indicated heart suit. He rightly competes with 2♥.

OVERCALLS AND RESPONSES

An overcall at the one-level (for example, 1♥ over an opponent's 1♣) shows a good five-card suit. To overcall at the two-level (for example, 2♦ over 1♠), you need a good six-card suit. These are the main purposes of making an overcall:

- you suggest a good opening lead to partner
- you take away the opponents' bidding space
- you can bid to a worthwhile part score or game.

Suppose your right-hand opponent has opened 1♦ and you hold one of these hands:

1

Hand (1) is well worth a 1♠ overcall. You have a good suit, so you are happy to suggest a spade opening lead. You also take away bidding space, preventing your left-hand opponent from responding 1♥.

2

Hand (2) contains a point more but you would be less inclined to overcall. You do not want a heart lead and you will not be taking away any bidding space.

3

On Hand (3) you would bid 2♣, although somewhat hesitantly when vulnerable. You have a very good club suit and are keen for partner to lead it. Also, the overcall will prevent the next player from making a cheap response in one of the major suits. As you see, you can overcall on less strength than would be needed for an opening bid.

The choice between an overcall and a double

Roughly speaking, an overcall tells partner what suit you want to make trumps, whereas a take-out double asks partner to choose trumps. When your hand contains a good five-card major, you will often choose to overcall in that suit, rather than doubling. Suppose your right-hand opponent has opened 1♣ and you hold one of these hands:

4

On (4) you have the values for an opening bid and a shortage in clubs. You are therefore strong enough for a take-out double. However, you are fairly sure that spades will be the best trump suit and should therefore overcall 1♠. If the next player bids 2♣ and two passes follow, you could make a take-out double on the second-round, asking partner to choose a trump suit.

5

It would be dangerous to overcall 1♥ on (5) because partner might pass when you had a game available. So, you should start with a double and then bid hearts on the next round.

6

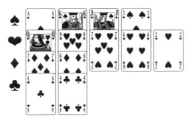

OVERCALL OR DOUBLE?

♠ ♥ ♦ ♣

Make an overcall when you want to suggest a trump suit to partner. Make a take-out double instead when you want partner to choose trumps.

On (6) your five-card heart suit is fairly weak. You cannot be at all sure that hearts will make a better trump suit than spades, so begin with a double, asking partner to choose trumps.

West	North	East	South
	1♠	2♣	Pass
2♥	Pass	3♣	End

Responding to an overcall in a new suit

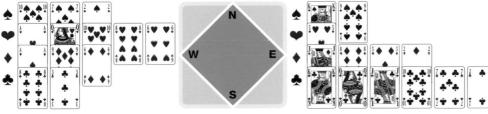

When you bid a new suit in response to an overcall, this should be constructive but non-forcing. In other words, you think that a game may be possible. Do not bid a new suit as a rescue bid, just because you do not like the suit that partner has bid.

With ten points and a good five-card major, West sees the chance of a game if partner has a maximum overcall or a good heart fit. He responds 2♥, non-forcing but constructive. East, on this occasion, has a minimum overcall. If he held two hearts, he might pass. As he has only one heart and a solid club suit, he prefers to bid 3♣.

Raising an overcall

When you have a three-card or four-card fit for partner's overcall, you should raise even on quite a weak hand. Your objective is to remove bidding space from the opponents. If instead you are genuinely interested in game, you can bid the opponent's suit rather than raising directly. Suppose the bidding has started 1♦ – 1♠ – Pass (where your partner has made an overcall of 1♠) and you hold one of the hands opposite.

Raise to 2♠ on (7). There is little chance that your side can make game but the opener probably holds a strong hand and you will make life difficult for him. On (8), with four-card support and a side-suit singleton, you are worth a pre-emptive raise to 3♠.

Hand (9) is a different type entirely. You are genuinely interested in game and should cue-bid 2♦ (bidding the opponent's suit) to show partner that you have a strong hand with a good spade fit.

7

8

9

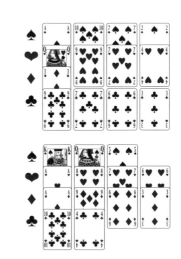

THE REDOUBLE

When your partner's opening bid has been doubled by the opponents, you can redouble to show that your side has the balance of the points and that you are interested in playing for penalties. If instead you bid a new suit over a double, this is generally treated as forcing (a method known as 'ignoring the double'). However, it is popular in the USA for a two-level bid in a new suit, over a double, to be non-forcing.

Suppose the bidding has started 1♦ – Dble and you are sitting in the third seat with one of the hands shown on the right:

Hand (1) is a classic redouble. You hold 11 points and shortage in partner's suit. Some players would redouble on (2) as well, but it is a poor idea. You have no intention of defending 1♥ doubled, should your partner double this bid by the fourth player. It is best to bid a simple and forcing 1♠. You can then develop the auction in the same way that you would have done without the double. Similarly on (3) you do best to bid a forcing 2♣. However, if your method is to play a non-forcing 2♣ over a double, you would have to begin with a redouble.

1

2

3

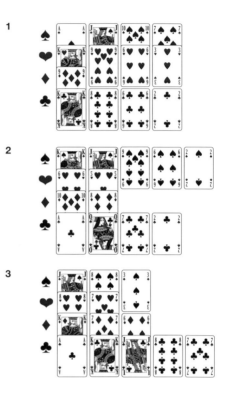

The opener's rebid facing a redouble

It is commonly agreed that if the opener rebids before his partner has had a chance to double the opponents, he is showing a weak hand with some shape.

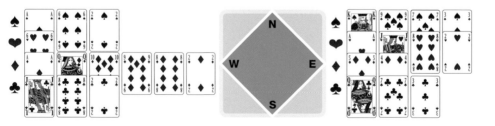

West has a minimum distributional opening bid, with no interest in defending a contract of 1♥ even if it is his partner's intention to double this contract. He announces this by rebidding 2♦ before his partner has even had a chance to double the opponents. Knowing that his partner has a minimum opener, East is not tempted to bid again.

West	North	East	South
1♦	Dble	Rdble	1♥
2♦	End		

If West held a stronger hand with the same shape, he could rebid 3♦ immediately or pass initially and then remove partner's double (if it comes) to diamonds.

Since the redoubler has announced willingness to defend, the opener should double the fourth player's escape freely:

West	North	East	South
1♠	Dble	Rdble	2♦
Dble	End		

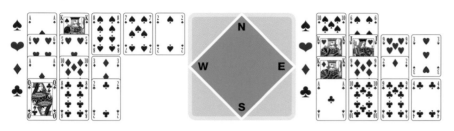

West does not need to wait until he holds four trumps to double. He is unlikely to hold four trumps, in fact, since the redoubler has indicated a willingness to double and is therefore likely to hold at least three diamonds himself.

The SOS redouble

The situation is different when a part score contract (other than 1NT) has been doubled for penalties. Since you will normally get a good result for making a doubled contract, there is no need to use a redouble merely to increase the score even further. Many players use redouble in a conventional way, to ask partner to choose another suit. It is a rescue manoeuvre known as the SOS redouble.

FIVE-SUIT BRIDGE
♠ ♥ ♦ ♣

A game called 'five-suit bridge', played with a 65-card pack, was devised in 1937. The fifth suit, called Royals in England and Eagles in the USA, ranked above no-trumps and was worth 50 points a trick. Since the four hands each contained 16 cards, the 'book' was set at eight tricks and success in a one-level contract therefore required declarer to make nine tricks. The 65th card, originally undealt, was placed face-up and known as the 'widow'. The eventual declarer was allowed to replace any card in his hand with the widow card before play began.

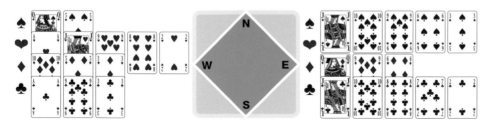

West	North	East	South
			1♦
1♥	Dble	Rdble	Pass
2♣			

North's double of the 1♥ overcall was for penalties. Since East is void in hearts, he decides that the partnership would be better off choosing one of the black suits as trumps. Because the contract is a part score in a suit, his redouble is SOS and asks for rescue into one of the unbid suits. West chooses clubs and North will now have to decide whether to double this contract or to make some other call.

PENALTY DOUBLES

In an earlier section it was mentioned that most low-level doubles are nowadays played for take-out. In this section we will see the main categories of double which are still treated as being for penalties, by most players.

Penalty doubles of 1NT and subsequent rescues

It would not make much sense for a double of 1NT to be for take-out, since no suit has been bid. Indeed, it is standard for a double of a 1NT opening to be for penalties. This is particularly so when the opening is a weak 1NT. (There are some conventional defences to a strong 1NT that include an artificial meaning for a double.) Here is a typical example:

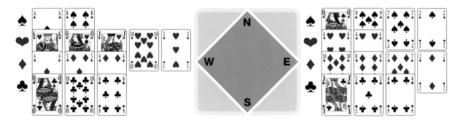

West doubles the 12–14 point 1NT for penalties. He has 16 points, which is more than the maximum count for the weak 1NT. He also has a promising opening lead in the heart suit. East does not hold very much but he has no reason whatsoever to take out his partner's double. Only if he were very weak and held a five-card suit, would he consider removing the penalty double. If North were to attempt an escape to some suit at the two-level and East were to double, this would also be a penalty double.

West	North	East	South
			1NT
Dble	Pass	Pass	Pass

Penalty doubles of an overcall

In traditional bidding, a double of an overcall is for penalties:

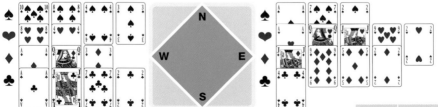

West does not expect 2♣ to be made. Since a game for East–West is uncertain, with 11 points facing an opening bid, he makes a penalty double to suggest defending against 2♣. East has no reason to remove the double.

West	North	East	South
		1♥	2♣
Dble	Pass	Pass	Pass

We will see in a later section that most tournament players now prefer to use a double of an overcall for take-out. This method is known as the 'negative double'.

Penalty doubles of game contracts

When the opponents bid to a game contract and you have an unpleasant surprise for them, such as an unexpected trump holding, you can double them for penalties.

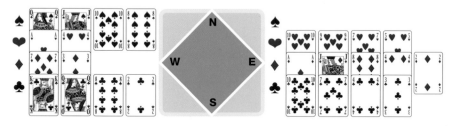

With the trumps breaking badly, the North–South spade game is destined for defeat. Diagnosing this outcome, West inflicts a penalty double.

West	North	East	South
	1♠	Pass	2♣
Pass	3♦	Pass	4♠
Dble	Pass	Pass	Pass

Note that it is not a good idea to double freely bid games just because you hold a lot of points. The opponents knew they were missing these points when they decided to bid the game. They presumably have considerable distributional values to compensate for the lack of points. The time to double is when the opponents' auction is limited and you know that the cards are lying badly for them.

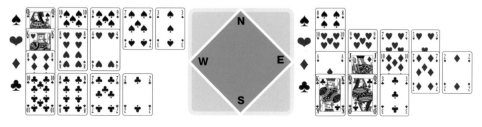

West	North	East	South
	1♦	Pass	1♠
Pass	2♦	Pass	2NT
Pass	3NT	Dble	End

North has shown a minimum-range opening with his 2♦ rebid and South's 2NT indicated around 11 points. North–South have no values to spare and East knows the diamond suit is lying very badly for them and will be impossible to establish. Also, his singleton spade suggests that the spade suit may lie poorly for them. The odds are good that 3NT will go down, possibly two down. East is therefore happy to end the auction with a penalty double.

> ### TAKING OUT A DOUBLE
> ♠ ♥ ♦ ♣
>
> When partner makes a penalty double, it will normally be right for you to pass. This is known as 'leaving in the penalty double'. The alternative action, to make a new bid, is known as 'taking out partner's penalty double'. It can be right only if you have a very shapely hand where you are confident that it will be better to play the contract your way.

BASIC CARD PLAY

Bidding is easily learnt from a book. To play the cards really well, it is sometimes said that you need some innate ability. While that may be true at international level, it is entirely possible to become a good card player simply by acquiring the techniques that are explained in this book. In this section you will see the various types of 'finesse', why it is often right to hold up an ace, and how you should decide whether to draw trumps immediately. You will learn why you should plan a contract right at the beginning, even before you play the first card from dummy. You will see how to take ruffs in the dummy, deciding whether or not to ruff with a high trump, also how to establish a suit, both at no-trumps and in a suit contract.

Right: Holding two ace–queen combinations, the player can visualize the possibility of finessing even before seeing his partner's hand.

THE FINESSE

Suppose you hold the ♦A and the ♦Q, with one of the defenders holding the ♦K. To score a trick with the queen, you will need to lead towards it, hoping that the defender in the second seat holds the king. You will then be able to score the queen at some stage, whether or not the defender chooses to play the king in front of the queen. The play is known as a 'finesse' and the deal below shows three different types of finessing position:

Right: Declarer can avoid a trump loser by finessing against East's king. He has further potential finesses in both the red suits.

West leads the ♣J and you win with dummy's ♣K. In trumps you have the opportunity to 'finesse against the king'. You lead the ♠J from dummy and East follows with the ♠5. You play low from the South hand ('running the jack', as it is called). Because East holds the ♠K, your finesse wins. You lead a second round of trumps to the queen and cash the ace, drawing all the trumps.

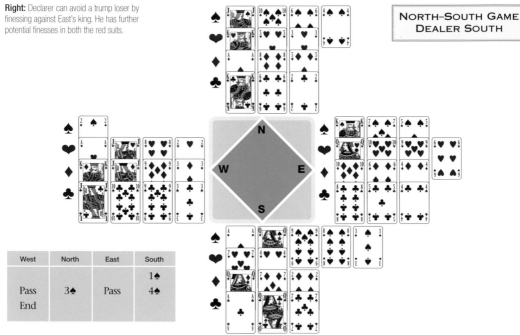

NORTH–SOUTH GAME DEALER SOUTH		

West	North	East	South
			1♠
Pass	3♠	Pass	4♠
End			

card led ▼

Above: A failed finesse. The attempt to score the ♦Q fails because the West holds the ♦K.

Both red suits offer you a further chance to finesse. You cross to the ♦A and lead a diamond towards the queen. If East held the ♦K you would score a trick with the ♦Q, whether or not East decided to rise with the king on the second round. As it happens, West holds the ♦K and the diamond finesse loses. West cashes another diamond winner and exits with a club, which you win in your hand. You have lost two diamond tricks and can afford to lose only one heart trick. You now take your third finesse, leading towards dummy's ♥K. Luck is with you on this occasion. West holds the ♥A and you will lose only one heart trick, whether or not West chooses to rise with the ♥A.

These were all examples of the 'simple finesse', where only one relevant high card was missing in the suit. Next we will see some more complicated finesses, where two or more honours are missing.

The double finesse

When two high cards are missing, you may need to finesse twice in the same suit.

Right: A double finesse. Declarer hopes for three tricks.

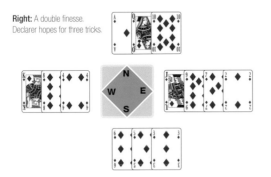

You begin by leading a low diamond to dummy's ten. If West had held both the ◆K and the ◆J this first finesse would have won. You could subsequently return to your hand and finesse the ◆Q, scoring three tricks from the suit. As the cards lie, the first finesse loses and East wins with the ◆J. When you regain the lead, you play a second round of diamonds to the queen. This time you are lucky and the finesse wins. You score two diamond tricks.

Right: A combination finesse. Declarer hopes for two tricks.

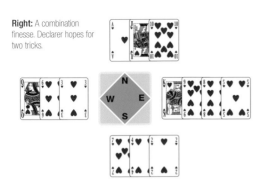

Here you have no chance of making three tricks, but you can make two tricks unless East holds both of the missing honours. A finesse of the ♥J loses to the ♥K but a subsequent finesse of the ♥10 is successful.

ODDS FOR A FINESSE

When you lead towards an ace–queen combination and finesse the queen, the odds of success are 50 per cent. The queen will win when your left-hand opponent holds the king and lose when he does not.

This is a similar position:

Right: A deep finesse. Declarer finesses the ♠9 on the first round.

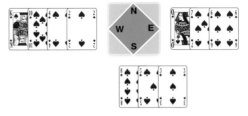

You lead low towards dummy and play the ♠9. This forces the ♠Q from East and you can then finesse against the jack successfully. You will score two tricks from the suit when West holds the king–ten or the queen–ten. The alternative play of finessing the jack on the first round is only half as good, since it will win only against the king–queen with West.

Above: Declarer's deep finesse of the ♠9 loses to the ♠Q. A subsequent finesse of the ♠J may succeed.

The two-way finesse

When you are missing a queen, you sometimes have to guess which defender holds the card.

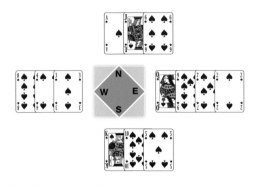

Above: A two-way finesse against a queen.

If you think that West holds the ♠Q you will play the ♠K and then lead a low spade to dummy's jack. If instead you think that East has the missing queen, you will play the ♠A and finesse the ♠10.

Before making such a guess, it is usually best to play the other suits. If you can obtain a count on the hand (determine the shapes of the defenders' hands), you can then play for the queen to be in the longer

Right: A guess finesse. By leading a club early in the play, declarer can apply pressure on the defender in the West seat.

Above: Another two-way finesse. To score two diamond tricks, declarer must guess which defender holds the ♦J.

holding. Suppose, for example, that you discover that East holds four spades to West's three, as in the diagram on the left. The odds will then be 4 to 3 in favour of East holding the missing queen.

The guess finesse

On some deals the success of the contract will depend on you guessing which finesse to take. Look at this deal, where you must score a club trick to bring your total to 12 tricks.

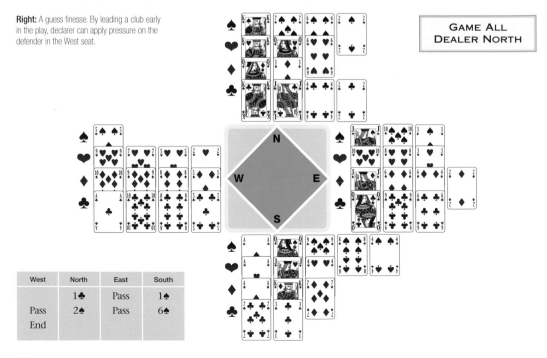

GAME ALL
DEALER NORTH

West	North	East	South
	1♣	Pass	1♠
Pass	2♠	Pass	6♠
End			

West leads the ♦10 against your small slam. All the suits are solid except the club suit. To make the slam, you will eventually have to lead a club towards dummy. When the defenders hold one honour each, you will need to guess which card to play from dummy. When West holds the ♣Q, you will make the slam by playing the ♣J. When West instead holds the ♣A, you will have to rise with dummy's ♣K. This is a 'guess finesse' position.

The best way to play such contracts is to put the defenders under stress. Win the diamond lead with the ♦A and immediately lead the ♣3. It will be a difficult moment for West. For all he knows, you may hold a singleton club (and a possible loser in some other suit). In that case it would be correct for him to rise with the ♣A. Of course, if West does play the ♣A he will save you a guess. The same will be the case if he even pauses for a moment, wondering whether to play the ace. Should West produce a smooth low card, you will be inclined to place the ace with East. In that case your best chance is to finesse the jack of clubs, hoping that West holds the queen.

Suppose instead that you draw trumps and play your winners in the red suits, finally gathering up courage to lead a club. It will then be entirely clear to West that the defenders need two club tricks to beat the contract. It will be much easier for him to produce a smooth low card when he holds the ace.

The ruffing finesse
Suppose you are playing in a spade game with this side suit:

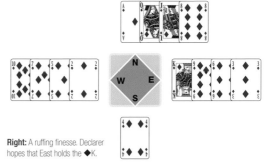

Right: A ruffing finesse. Declarer hopes that East holds the ♦K.

You can play a diamond to the ace and then lead the diamond queen, planning to run the card. East's king is caught in a 'ruffing finesse'. If he plays it on dummy's queen, you will ruff in your hand, setting up dummy's jack and ten. If instead East plays low, the queen of diamonds will score a trick directly. You can then continue with the jack of diamonds, scoring a third diamond trick whether or not East plays the king.

Suppose you held a side suit of ♣K–Q–J–4 opposite a void club in dummy. You could then take a ruffing finesse against the ♣A. You would lead the ♣K, hoping that the defender in second seat held the ♣A. When West chose to cover with the ace, you would ruff in the dummy, setting up two club tricks for yourself.

Right: Declarer takes a ruffing finesse on the second round of diamonds. When East covers the ♦Q with the ♦K, declarer ruffs in his hand.

THE HOLD-UP PLAY

It often happens in a no-trump contract that a defender leads from a five-card suit, finding his partner with three cards there. When declarer holds A–x–x in the suit, he should usually hold up the ace (in other words, refuse to play it) until the third round. One defender will then have no cards in the suit and it will be safe to allow him on lead later in the play. Let's see an example of this important technique:

| NORTH–SOUTH GAME |
| DEALER SOUTH |

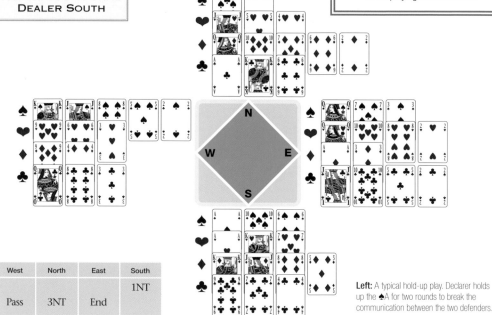

Left: A typical hold-up play. Declarer holds up the ♠A for two rounds to break the communication between the two defenders.

West	North	East	South
			1NT
Pass	3NT	End	

West leads the ♠5 against your contract of 3NT and East plays the ♠Q. You can see what will happen if you win the first (or second) round of spades. You will need to establish the diamond suit to bring your total to nine tricks. When you play a diamond, East will win with the ace and return a spade. The defenders will then score four spade tricks and the ♦A. They will reach the finishing tape before you. They will score five tricks before you have scored nine.

Instead, you should hold up the ♠A until the third round of the suit. East is now a 'safe hand' and you will not mind him gaining the lead. When you play a diamond at Trick 4, good news arrives – it is East who produces the ♦A. Thanks to your hold-up, East has no spade to play. (If he did have a spade left, the suit would have broken 4–4 and would not cause any problem.) You can win whatever other suit East returns and score nine tricks to make the game: four

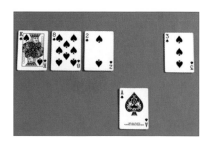

Above: Spade position after the hold-up. You will win the third round of spades, leaving East with no spade to play.

diamonds and five top winners in the other suits. If instead West had held the ◆A, the contract would have gone down however you played.

You should usually hold up an ace for two rounds, unless a switch to some other suit may beat the contract. Even if your stopper is a doubleton ace, it may be worth holding it up until the second round. Suppose West has led the ♥7 against 3NT and you have ♥ 10 8 3 in the dummy opposite ♥ A 4 in your hand. It is still worth holding up the ♥A until the second round. You will then break the defenders' communications when West holds six hearts and East has two. There are three missing spot cards lower than West's ♥7 (the 6, 5 and 2). If West has two of them, he will hold six hearts.

On the next deal, your stopper in the suit that has been led is a king. Once again, you need to hold it up until one of the defenders has no cards left in the suit.

West leads the ♥6 against your contract of 3NT and East wins with the ♥A. When he returns the ♥7, you should hold up the ♥K in order to break the link between the two defenders. You win the third round of hearts and run the ♣Q. The finesse loses, as it happens, but the contract will still be made. Because you held up your ♥K until the third round, East now has no heart to play. If he switches to a diamond, you will rise with the ace and score nine tricks for the contract: four clubs, three spades, one diamond trick and one heart trick.

Right: Holding up a king. Declarer holds up the ♥K on the second round of the suit, to break the communication between the two defenders.

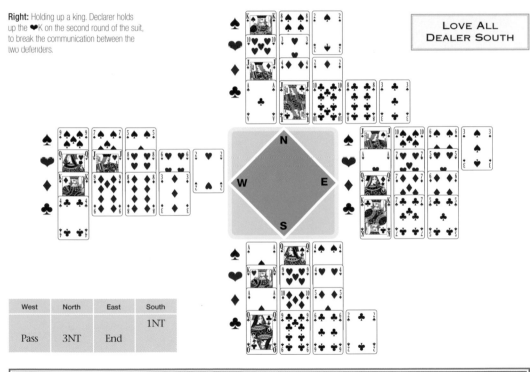

LOVE ALL
DEALER SOUTH

West	North	East	South
			1NT
Pass	3NT	End	

YOUNGEST LIFEMASTER
♠ ♥ ◆ ♣

The record for the youngest player to achieve the rank of Lifemaster is held by Danny Hirschman of Southfield, Michigan, USA. He was 10 years and 2 months old when he accumulated the necessary 300 master points in November 1988. The final fraction of a masterpoint, carrying him past the post, was gained at two o'clock in the morning! Some 20 per cent of the membership of the American Contract Bridge League are ranked as a Lifemaster or higher and they take an average of 20 years playing bridge to reach this level. Danny Hirschman achieved it in only 15 months.

ESTABLISHING A SUIT AT NO-TRUMPS

You bid to 3NT, the opening lead is made and down goes the dummy. You will rarely have nine tricks readily available and may need to establish one or more suits in order to pass the finishing line. Sometimes this involves knocking out high cards. On other occasions you may need to duck a round of suit, thereby absorbing a defensive stopper.

Let's see a couple of deals that involve setting up a long suit in dummy:

Right: Ducking to retain the entry. Declarer ducks a round of diamonds to establish the suit and preserve the entry to dummy.

West leads the ♥Q and you duck the first round, since you are not afraid of a switch to another suit. You win the second round of hearts and see that you have seven tricks on top. If you can score four diamond tricks, this will bring your total to nine. How can you establish the diamond suit? Suppose you play ace, king and another diamond, finding that the suit breaks 3–2. You will establish two extra diamond winners in the dummy but there will be no entry to reach them.

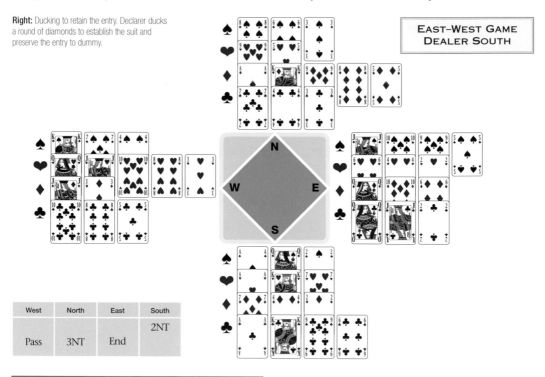

EAST–WEST GAME
DEALER SOUTH

West	North	East	South
			2NT
Pass	3NT	End	

ESTABLISHING A SUIT
♠ ♥ ♦ ♣

To establish, or set up, a suit means to play it until the remaining cards are all good and will each take a trick. For example, if you hold ♦K–Q–J–5 opposite ♦10–9–6–2, you can establish the diamond suit by knocking out the defenders' ♦A. If instead you hold ♣9–5–3 opposite ♣A–8–7–6–2, you can establish the suit by ducking two rounds of clubs, provided the defenders' clubs break 3–2.

Instead, you should duck the first round of diamonds. The defenders are certain to score a diamond trick, so let them win it at a time that is convenient for you. Let's say that East wins the first round of diamonds and clears the heart suit. You lead a diamond to the ace and both defenders follow suit. Because the defenders' diamonds divided 3–2, dummy's diamonds (the king, nine and eight) are good. You will play with the ♦K, followed by the two remaining cards in the diamond suit. Nine tricks and the contract are yours.

Sometimes you duck a round of dummy's long suit as a safety play to guard against a bad break. That's what happens on the next deal:

Right: Ducking as a safety play. Declarer ducks a round of clubs as a safety play against a 4–1 break in the suit.

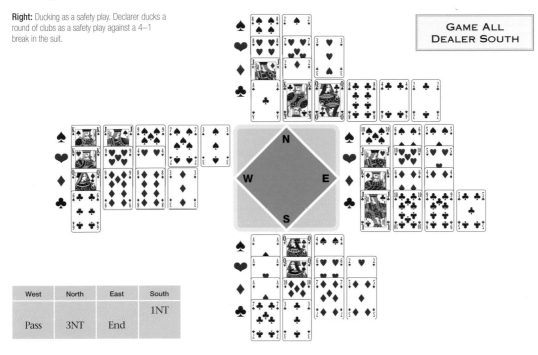

GAME ALL
DEALER SOUTH

West	North	East	South
			1NT
Pass	3NT	End	

West leads the ♠7 against 3NT and you win East's ♠10 with the ♠Q. You have four top tricks outside clubs, so five club tricks would give you the contract. If the defenders' clubs break 3–2, you can play the club suit from the top (beginning with the ace and king) and will score six club tricks. As the cards lie, however, you would go down in your contract. When the 4–1 club break came to light, you would score only three club tricks. No rescue operation would be available in the other suits.

To guard against a 4–1 club break, which happens more than one time in four, you should duck the very first round of clubs. You lead the ♣3 and play the ♣8 from dummy. East wins the trick but the contract is now certain to make. You win East's spade return and cross to dummy's ♣A to run the rest of dummy's club suit. You make five clubs, two spades and the two red aces, bringing your total to nine.

Right: Club position after the duck. Dummy's remaining clubs are ready to run.

This is an example of a 'safety play'. You give up a potential overtrick when the clubs break 3–2. In exchange for that, you make the game when clubs are 4–1. This is good business because an overtrick is worth only 30 while the game is worth 400 or 600 (depending on whether you are vulnerable).

PLANNING A NO-TRUMP CONTRACT

The first step in planning a no-trump contract is to count the top tricks at your disposal. Suppose you are in 3NT and there are seven top tricks. You will then need to plan the safest way to score two more tricks to bring the total to nine. Look at the typical 3NT deal below.

West leads the ♠5 against your game in no-trumps. You have seven top tricks and will therefore need two more tricks to make the game. Since your longest combined suit is clubs, it is natural to look in that direction first. You can create three extra club tricks by knocking out the ace and king of the suit. Next you must check whether it is safe to play on clubs. The defenders will win with their first club honour and clear the spade suit. When you knock out the other club honour, they will score at least three spades. You will lose a minimum of five tricks in the black suits and go down.

Next you see if there is any other possibility of making two extra tricks. You can do so in diamonds, if the suit breaks 3–3 and West holds the ♦Q. It's not a big chance but it is better than the certain defeat awaiting you if you play on clubs. You win the first spade, in one hand or the other, cash the ♦K and finesse the ♦J. The finesse wins and when you cash the ♦A, both defenders follow. You have nine tricks and your game.

Above: Realizing there is insufficient time to set up the club suit, declarer finesses the ♦J instead.

Right: Attacking the right suit. After a spade lead against 3NT, declarer must decide whether to play on diamonds or clubs.

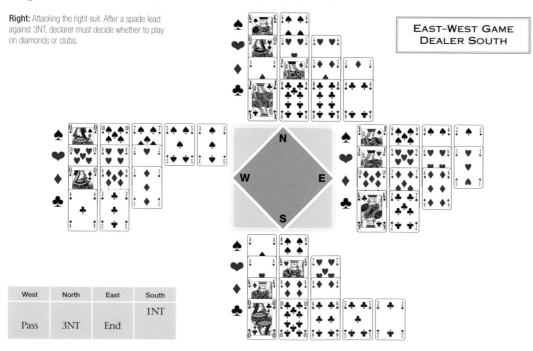

EAST–WEST GAME
DEALER SOUTH

West	North	East	South
			1NT
Pass	3NT	End	

The best plan will often depend on your reading of the opening lead and whether it is from a five-card suit or a four-card suit. Look at the 3NT contract below.

West leads the ♠2 against 3NT and you pause to make a plan. You have six tricks on top and therefore need three more tricks from somewhere. The diamond suit will provide three tricks, once the ace has been knocked out. You must ask yourself whether it is safe to play on diamonds. It is safe provided the spades are breaking 4–4, because the defenders will be able to score only one diamond and three spades. The fourth-best lead of the ♠2 tells you that West does hold only four spades (if the 2 is his fourth best card in the suit, he cannot have a fifth best card!). You therefore win the first trick with the ♠A and play on diamonds. The cards lie as you read them and the game is made.

Suppose that you were playing the same North–South cards and West had led the ♠5 instead of the ♠2. It would then be much more likely that he held five spades, a holding such as ♠Q–J–8–5–3. Fearing that you would lose four spades and the ♦A if you played on diamonds, it would be a more promising line of play to take the heart finesse. When East held the ♥K, you would make the game, scoring the three extra tricks that you needed from the heart suit.

Right: Reading the opening lead. Declarer deduces that the opening lead is from a four-card suit and plays accordingly.

Taking a heart finesse when spades are 4–4, as in the diagram, might lead to defeat. You could lose three spades, the ♥K and the ♦A.

ALWAYS SOMETHING NEW
♠ ♥ ♦ ♣

Film star Omar Sharif explained his fascination with bridge by saying 'Every time you deal the cards there is something new – there is something different.'

Above: Omar Sharif, film star and bridge expert. He learnt bridge by reading an old American bridge book while on a film set in Egypt.

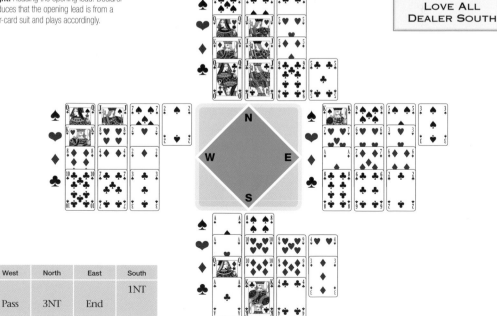

LOVE ALL
DEALER SOUTH

West	North	East	South
			1NT
Pass	3NT	End	

DRAWING TRUMPS

To 'draw trumps' means to play sufficient rounds of the trump suit to remove all the trumps that the defenders hold. When you are playing in a suit contract, the general rule is that you should draw trumps immediately unless there is a good reason to do something else first. The reason to draw trumps is clear – you do not want the defenders to ruff any of your precious winners. If you play a few tricks in the side suits before drawing trumps, there is every chance that you will suffer a ruff.

We will start with a deal where an inexperienced declarer failed to draw trumps and it cost him the contract.

West led the ♦K and declarer won with the ♦A. Seeing a chance to dispose of the diamond loser in the South hand, his next move was to play on the club suit. Disaster! East ruffed the second club and returned a diamond. The defenders still had two aces to come and the contract went one down.

It was unlucky that the club suit broke so badly, yes, but declarer's duty was to ensure the safety of his contract. He should have played a trump at Trick 2,

allowing the defenders to win with the ace and cash a diamond trick. There would then have been only one further loser, a spade. Declarer's third spade could be discarded on dummy's club suit, after all the trumps had been drawn.

Above: After winning the diamond lead, declarer should draw trumps immediately to avoid suffering a ruff.

Right: Paying the price. Declarer fails to draw trumps and goes down in a contract that should have been made.

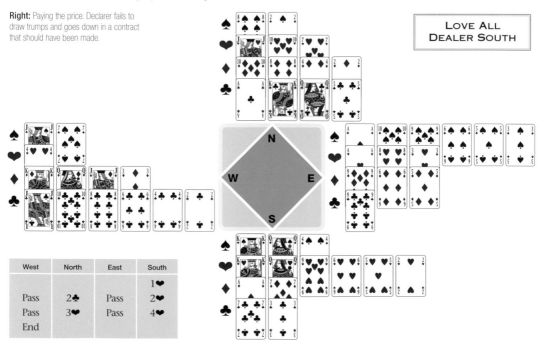

LOVE ALL
DEALER SOUTH

West	North	East	South
			1♥
Pass	2♣	Pass	2♥
Pass	3♥	Pass	4♥
End			

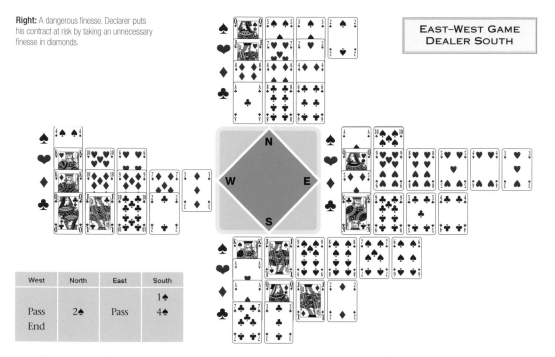

Right: A dangerous finesse. Declarer puts his contract at risk by taking an unnecessary finesse in diamonds.

EAST–WEST GAME
DEALER SOUTH

West	North	East	South
			1♠
Pass	2♠	Pass	4♠
End			

West led the ♣Q and declarer won with the ♣A in dummy. Since he had only one subsequent entry to dummy (the ♠Q) declarer 'took advantage' of the chance to take a diamond finesse. His idea was to repeat a winning finesse later, after crossing to dummy with the ♠Q. It was not his lucky day. The diamond finesse lost to the king and West returned a diamond for his partner to ruff. The trump ace and a further loser in clubs then put the game one down.

Declarer could afford to lose a diamond trick, so there was no reason to avoid drawing trumps immediately and he should have played a trump at Trick 2, minimizing the chance of suffering an adverse ruff. If East rose with the ♠A and switched to the ♦5, declarer could win with the ace and draw the outstanding trump. Playing in this simple fashion, he would lose one trump, one diamond and one club. The game would be made.

EVERYONE SAT NORTH
♠ ♥ ♦ ♣

On the evening of 26 January 2006, a game of bridge was played at one of the most remote locations on the planet, the precise geographic South Pole: 90 degrees South. The weather was sunny, windy and… very cold. Rolf Peterson (USA) partnered Wendy Beeler (USA) representing the South Pole. Their opponents were Chris Dixon (a well-known England international) and Harry Otten (Netherlands). Naturally, because of the location, all four players sat North!

Right: Game at the South Pole. The temperature is -27 degrees C.

TAKING RUFFS IN THE DUMMY

One of the ways of creating extra tricks in a suit contract is to ruff a losing card in a side suit with a trump that would not otherwise have made a trick. Usually this means taking a ruff in the dummy. Suppose you have five solid trumps in your hand and three more trumps in the dummy. You begin with five trump tricks. If you can take one ruff in the dummy, you will score six trump tricks. Take two ruffs there and you will score a total of seven trump tricks. It is good business. Taking a ruff in your own hand, in the long-trump holding, will not bring you an extra trick. It may be useful in some tactical way (helping you to establish a suit in dummy, for example) but it will not create an extra trump trick.

When you need to score a ruff in dummy, it will often be wrong to draw trumps straight away because this would remove dummy's trumps. It is difficult to ruff something when you have no trumps left to ruff with! Look at the deal shown below.

West leads the ♠K and, looking at the South hand, you can see one spade loser, one diamond loser and a possible two losers in clubs. You need

to reduce this total of four losers to three and the best idea is to ruff a club in dummy. You win the spade lead with the ace and must immediately play a club. (It would be foolish to draw trumps, of course, since you would then have no trumps in dummy and could not take a club ruff.) You lead the ♣Q and East wins with the ♣A. When he switches to a trump, you win with the ace, cash the ♣K and ruff a club with dummy's last trump. You then lead a diamond towards your hand, setting up an entry so that you can draw trumps. You will make seven trump tricks, including one ruff in dummy, and three side-suit winners for a total of ten. As it happens, a trump lead would have prevented a ruff and beaten your game.

Suppose next that you have a side suit of four cards in your hand and three cards in the dummy. If the defenders cards break 3–3, the 13th card in the suit will become good after three rounds. If instead the suit breaks 4–2 it may be possible to ruff the fourth round in dummy. Since one of the defenders will be out of the suit by then, you may need to ruff with a high trump.

| GAME ALL |
| DEALER SOUTH |

Right: Taking a ruff before drawing trumps. Declarer delays drawing trumps in order to ruff a club in dummy.

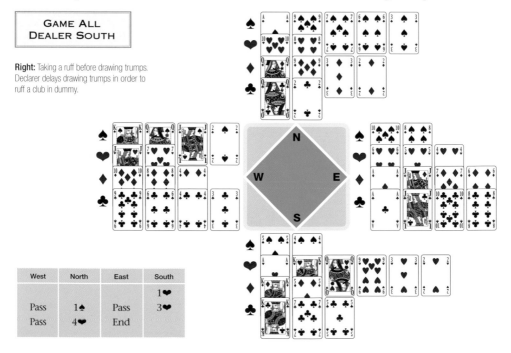

West	North	East	South
			1♥
Pass	1♠	Pass	3♥
Pass	4♥	End	

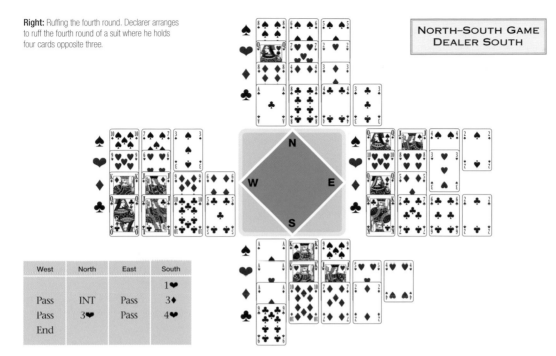

Right: Ruffing the fourth round. Declarer arranges to ruff the fourth round of a suit where he holds four cards opposite three.

NORTH–SOUTH GAME
DEALER SOUTH

West	North	East	South
			1♥
Pass	INT	Pass	3♦
Pass	3♥	Pass	4♥
End			

West leads the ♣Q against your heart game and you win in the dummy. You have one losing spade in your hand and three potential losers in diamonds. All will be well if diamonds divide 3–3. If not, you may be able to ruff the fourth round of diamonds with dummy's ♥Q.

After winning the club lead, you continue with the ace and another diamond. East wins the second round with the ♦Q and switches to a trump. Since you may need to ruff the fourth round of diamonds with the ♥Q, to prevent an overruff, you must win the first round of trumps in your hand. You then concede a third round of diamonds. West wins and plays another trump. Again you win in your hand. You can then ruff the fourth round of diamonds with dummy's queen of trumps. You return to your hand with a spade honour and draw the last trump. The contract is yours. You made six trump tricks (five rounds of trumps and one ruff in the short-trump holding) and four winners in the side suits.

BLIND BRIDGE PLAYERS
♠ ♥ ♦ ♣

Even visually impaired players can play bridge. They use cards with Braille indentations, so that players can identify them by touch. The player on lead announces 'I lead the queen of hearts' and the dummy then calls out all 13 of his cards. From then on, each card is named aloud as it is played by one of the four players. The procedure is the same whether only one player is blind, or all four players are blind.

Right: Braille cards. Look closely and you can see the raised dots.

ESTABLISHING A SUIT BY RUFFING

One of the advantages of playing in a suit contract is that you can use your trumps to establish a long suit. (Remember that 'establish a suit' means to play that suit until the remaining cards are all winners.) By ruffing one or two rounds, until the defenders have no cards left in the suit, you can establish a winner or two. On the next deal it is dummy's club suit that needs to be established.

You reach a small slam in hearts and West leads the ♠Q. You have 7 trump tricks and 4 winners in the side suits – a total of 11. To bring the total to 12 you must establish dummy's club suit. Suppose you win the opening spade lead and draw trumps in three rounds. If clubs were 3–3, you could establish the suit with one ruff and reach the two winners by crossing to the ♦A. Since the clubs are 4–2, you would go down if you played this way.

To establish the clubs against a 4–2 break, you need to ruff two clubs in your hand. This can be done only if you make good use of the ♥Q as an entry to dummy. (An 'entry' is a card that will allow you to cross to one hand or the other. An entry is usually an honour card.

However, you may also use a 'ruffing entry'. In other words, you cross to the other hand by ruffing a card.)

After winning the spade lead, you should cash the ace and king of clubs. You then ruff a club with the ♥9 (ruffing high to avoid an overruff by West) You continue with the ace and queen of trumps, East showing out on the second round, and ruff another club with the ♥10. You can then draw West's last trump with the ♥J, cross to dummy with the ♦A and play the established thirteenth card in clubs, discarding a spade or a diamond. Twelve tricks are yours.

PHYSICAL FITNESS REQUIRED
♠ ♥ ♦ ♣

Playing in major championships, which last for many days, can be an exhausting process. As well as being an expert bridge player, it is important to be physically fit. In the 1985 Venice Cup, Sandra Landy and Sally Horton of Great Britain played 656 hands, more than any open pair in that year's Bermuda Bowl.

Right: Using a trump entry. Declarer uses an entry in the trump suit to establish a side suit despite a 4–2 break.

LOVE ALL
DEALER SOUTH

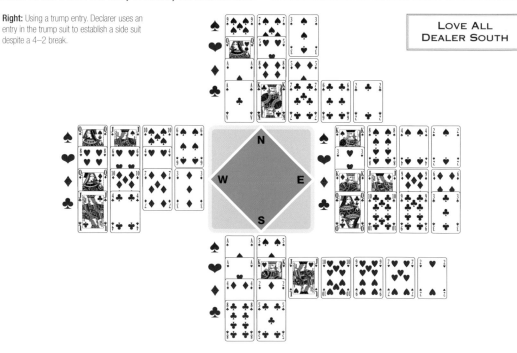

Right: Ducking to preserve an entry. Declarer ducks the first round of the suit to be established, so he can use the ace as an entry on the second round.

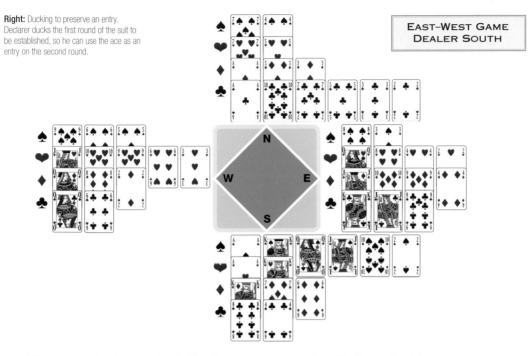

When dummy's side suit is headed by the ace, it will often assist you to duck the first round of the suit. You can then use the ace as an entry on the second round. That's what happens on the deal shown above, where you again need to establish the club suit.

West leads the ♥J against six spades. You must aim to establish dummy's club suit, so that can discard the diamond loser. You win the heart lead and draw trumps in three rounds. If your next move is to play a club to the ace, you will go down. You will not have made full use of the ♣A. Instead you should duck the first round of clubs, playing a low club from both hands. In this way, you will preserve dummy's ♣A as an entry on the second round of clubs.

East wins the first round of clubs and switches to the ♦J. You win with the ♦K, saving dummy's ♦A as a later entry. You cross to the ♣A and ruff a club in your hand. The clubs break 3–2, you are pleased to see, and the club ruff establishes the suit. You can then cross to the ♦A to play one of the good clubs, throwing your diamond loser. The slam is yours.

Sometimes it is worth ducking a round of the suit that you are trying to establish, even when you do not have a certain loser there. By doing so, you can survive an adverse break in the suit.

Look at this diamond position:

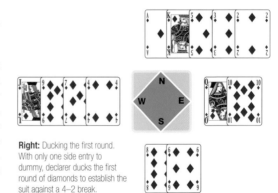

Right: Ducking the first round. With only one side entry to dummy, declarer ducks the first round of diamonds to establish the suit against a 4–2 break.

If you have only one entry to dummy in the other suits, it might well be worth ducking the first round of diamonds. You could then cross to the ♦A on the second round, cash the ♦K and ruff a diamond, establishing the suit even though the defenders' diamonds break 4–2. Suppose instead that you played the ace and king on the first two rounds, proceeding to ruff the third round. You would then need two further entries to the dummy – one to ruff the fourth round and another to reach the established diamond winner.

DISCARDING LOSERS

There are three main methods of disposing of a potential loser in your hand. You have already seen how you can take a finesse or ruff a loser in dummy. The third way to dispose of a loser is to discard it by leading a winner from the dummy. This is know as taking a discard.

Right: Taking a discard. Declarer has an easy discard on the third round of diamonds.

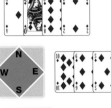

If you need to discard a loser, nothing could be simpler. You play the king, ace and queen of diamonds and throw a loser from your hand on the third round.

Right: Setting up a discard. Declarer establishes the diamond suit to provide a discard.

Sometimes life is more difficult and you must establish a suit before you can take a discard on it.

After a bold auction to a small slam on the deal below, West leads the ♣Q. There is a certain loser in diamonds and declarer must avoid losing a trick in clubs. This can be done only by establishing an extra winner in diamonds, on which the club loser can be discarded.

Declarer wins the club lead with the ace and draws trumps in two rounds with the ace and queen. He must now consider how to play the diamond suit. If the defenders' cards divide 3–3, it will be easy to set up the 13th diamond in dummy. Another possibility is that West holds a doubleton ♦A. By twice leading a low card towards the dummy, declarer can force West to play the ♦A without capturing an honour.

At Trick 4, declarer leads the ♦2 towards dummy. West plays low and the ♦K wins the trick. Declarer re-enters his hand with a heart and leads the ♦4 towards dummy. West has to play the bare ace and declarer is now assured of further tricks for the ♦Q and the ♦J. The last of these winners will provide a discard for his club loser.

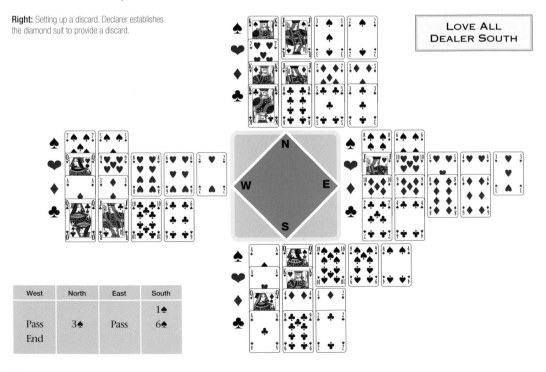

LOVE ALL
DEALER SOUTH

West	North	East	South
			1♠
Pass	3♠	Pass	6♠
End			

Sometimes you must risk taking an otherwise unnecessary finesse, in order to set up a discard for one of your losers. That is the winning line on the deal shown below.

West leads the ♠J against your contract of six hearts. There are two potential losers in the South hand, one in diamonds, the other in clubs. The only real chance of avoiding the diamond loser is a successful finesse of the ♣10. If East holds the ♣J you score two club tricks, whoever is holding the ♣A.

You win the spade lead and draw trumps in two rounds, with the ace and queen. You then play a club to the ten. This forces the ♣A from West. You will win his return, cash the ♣K and re-enter dummy to discard your diamond loser on the ♣Q.

Right: Finessing to establish a discard. Declarer risks an otherwise unnecessary finesse in clubs to set up a diamond discard.

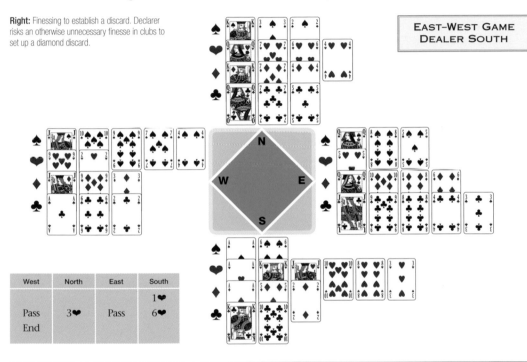

EAST–WEST GAME
DEALER SOUTH

West	North	East	South
			1♥
Pass	3♥	Pass	6♥
End			

THE POPULARITY OF BRIDGE
♠ ♥ ♦ ♣

By the 1950s bridge had become the most popular card game in the world. The USA's President Eisenhower was a regular player, facing expert opposition most Saturday nights. He also attended national tournaments, when possible. Alternative attractions such as television and computer games have caused a slight decline since then. Nevertheless, it is estimated that ten million Americans still play bridge.

Right: Dwight Eisenhower enjoyed bridge as much as golf and was considered an expert player.

PLANNING A SUIT CONTRACT

When you plan a no-trump contract, you count your top tricks and devise the safest plan to increase this to the number of tricks that you need. When you are planning a suit contract, it is usually easier to take a different approach. You consider the potential losers (losing tricks) in the hand with the longer trumps. Suppose you are in 4♠ and you can see five potential losers in your hand. You would then have to make a plan to reduce these five losers to just three. Look at the deal below.

Let's say that you have taken an optimistic view of your hand and bid a small slam in spades. West leads the ♥Q and you must make a plan for the contract. You look at the potential losers in the long-trump hand, South, taking each suit in turn. In spades you have no losers. Nor are there any losers in hearts, since the ace and king cover your two cards there. There are two potential losers in diamonds and one in clubs. You have a total of three potential losers and must reduce them to just one in order to make your ambitious slam.

In general, there are three basic ways in which you can save yourself a loser. You can ruff the loser, discard it, or take a successful finesse in the suit. Here you would plan to take a successful finesse in clubs, to remove the club loser, and to ruff one of the diamond losers. The next stage in making a plan is to decide the best order of play, in particular whether you should draw trumps straightaway. Here it would not be a good idea. Suppose you drew two rounds of trumps with the ace and king. When you subsequently conceded a diamond trick, to prepare for a diamond ruff in dummy, West would win and remove dummy's last trump. You would go down.

So, the plan would be to win the heart lead, in either hand, draw just one round of trumps and then play ace and another diamond. When you regained the lead, you would ruff your last diamond with dummy's ♠Q, draw trumps and eventually take a club finesse. Since West does hold the ♣K, you would make the slam. The contract was roughly a 50 per cent proposition – you would make it when West

Right: Counting the losers. Declarer sees three potential losers in 6♠ and plans to reduce these to just one.

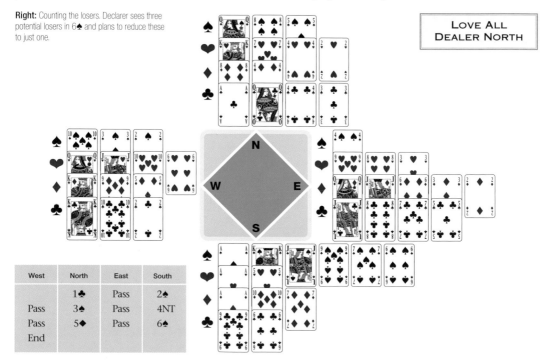

West	North	East	South
	1♣	Pass	2♠
Pass	3♠	Pass	4NT
Pass	5♦	Pass	6♠
End			

held the ♣K and go down when East held that card. Let's see an example of planning a contract where a discard is necessary:

Right: Discarding losers. Declarer begins with three potential losers and plans to discard two of them on dummy's diamond suit.

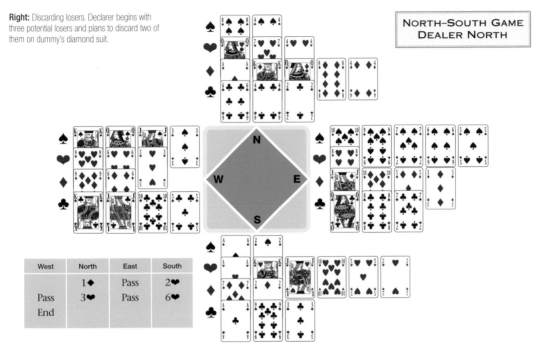

NORTH–SOUTH GAME
DEALER NORTH

West	North	East	South
	1♦	Pass	2♥
Pass	3♥	Pass	6♥
End			

A rough-and-ready auction carries you to six hearts and West leads the ♠K. As always, you look at the potential losers in the long-trump hand, South. You have one loser in spades and two further losers in clubs. There is no possibility of ruffing any of these losers, nor of taking a finesse in those suits. You must rely on discarding two of the three losers on dummy's diamonds.

If the defenders' diamonds break 3–3, you could take three discards on the diamonds and score an overtrick. Since you are only in a small slam, you should concentrate your efforts on planning the best way to score four diamond tricks, discarding two of your three losers. This can be done if the diamond suit breaks no worse than 4–2.

Next you must plan the order of play. The general idea will be to cash the ace and king of diamonds and to ruff a third round of the suit high. The remaining ♦Q–8 will then be good and you will need to reach them with the ♥Q. So, you draw two rounds of trumps with the ace and king. You cannot afford to draw the last trump at this stage, since you are relying on the ♥Q as a later entry to dummy. You cash the two top diamonds and ruff a diamond with the ♥J to avoid an overruff. You then enter dummy with the ♥Q, drawing West's last trump. Finally, you discard your two club losers on the queen and eight of diamonds. Count the tricks that you made: six trump tricks, four diamonds and two black-suit aces.

BRIDGE AIDS YOUR MEMORY
♠ ♥ ♦ ♣

The 2003 *New England Journal of Medicine* recommended bridge as a mentally challenging activity that could restrict memory loss in the aged and slow the onset of Alzheimer's disease. Just as physical exercise will keep your muscles in good shape, so does mental exercise keep the brain working well. 'Using the mind actually causes rewiring of the brain, sprouting new synapses,' said Professor Joseph Coyle.

BASIC DEFENCE

Defence is generally reckoned to be the hardest part of the game. In the early stages of defending a contract, you may be operating partly in the dark. The declarer has the advantage of being able to see his partner's cards (the dummy). Meanwhile, as a defender, you can see only half of the cards that belong to your side.

In this section we will spend some time looking at opening leads – against no-trump contracts, against suit contracts and against slams. We will see also the basic rules for defending in both the second seat and the third seat. (The term 'in the second seat' means that you are the second player to play a card to a particular trick.)

The defenders are allowed to pass information to each other, by signalling with the cards that they play. We will look here at 'attitude signals', where you tell partner whether you like the suit that he has led and would welcome a continuation of that suit. We will see also how to maintain communication between the two defenders' hands.

Right: To some extent you can defend by following general guidelines, such as to lead your fourth-best card and to play high in the third seat. In addition, you must always try to calculate how to beat the opponents' contract.

OPENING LEAD AGAINST NO-TRUMPS

You have two options, when choosing an opening lead against a no-trump contract. You can make an attacking lead, from your own strongest suit, or you can make a passive lead – aiming to avoid giving a trick away. An attacking lead is appropriate on most deals.

To beat a contract of 3NT, you need to score five tricks before the declarer can score nine. The main advantage you have over the declarer is that you can make the first lead and perhaps establish some extra tricks for your side. In general, you should lead your longest and strongest suit. Even if you give away a trick by doing so, you may eventually establish, and then be able to cash, some long cards in the suit.

Suppose the bidding has been 1NT – 3NT and you are on lead with this hand:

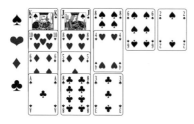

It is obvious to lead a spade. If you are lucky and find partner with the ace or queen of the suit, you will have an excellent chance of beating the contract. Even if partner holds only the ♠10 and your lead allows declarer to score the queen and ace of the suit, all is not lost. You partner may gain the lead early in the play and be able to clear the spades before your entry card, the ♣A, has been removed.

Once you have decided which suit to lead, the choice of card is determined by the following table:

- From a suit headed by a 'sequence' of three touching (i.e. adjacent) honours lead the top card: the ace from A–K–Q, the king from K–Q–J.

- From a suit headed by a 'broken sequence' (such as A–K–J, K–Q–10 or Q–J–9) also lead the top card.

- From a suit headed by an 'interior sequence' lead the middle honour: the jack from K–J–10, the 10 from K–10–9.

- From a three-card suit headed by touching honours, lead the top card: the queen from Q–J–8.

- Otherwise lead your fourth best card from a suit containing one or more honours. Lead the 3 from Q–10–7–3, the 5 from K–J–9–5–2.

- When your suit does not contain an honour, lead the second-best card: the 6 from 8–6–5–3, the 7 from 9–7–6–5–2.

Above: Interior sequence lead. From this hand you would lead the ♥10, the top of an interior sequence.

Above: Second-best from four small. From this hand you would lead the ♠7, the second-best card from a weak suit.

When the opponents have bid some suits

It is generally inadvisable to lead a suit that one of the opponents has bid. Suppose you are sitting West and this has been the auction:

West	North	East	South
			1♥
Pass	2♣	Pass	2NT
Pass	3NT	End	

You have to choose a lead from:

It would be a poor idea to lead a heart and you should choose either a spade or a diamond. It is usually better to lead a major suit rather than a minor. That is because the opponents are more likely to have bid any major suit that they hold (or perhaps sought a fit there with Stayman) than to have bid a minor suit. You should therefore prefer a spade lead to a diamond lead. This is particularly so because your spades here are stronger.

Above: Low from an honour holding. Suppose your partner opened 1♥ and you are now on lead against 3NT. You should lead the ♥4. The old-fashioned lead of the ♥K is too likely to give declarer an extra trick.

Leading partner's suit

When partner has bid a suit, particularly if he has overcalled, you should usually lead that suit even when you are short there. Indeed, his principal reason for making the bid may have been to suggest a good opening lead. Even when partner has not bid, it may be a good idea to lead a short suit when your own hand is very weak and you have little prospect of gaining the lead later. Suppose the bidding has been 1NT – 3NT and you are on lead with this hand:

There is not much prospect of a club lead succeeding. Even if you could establish the suit, you have no high card elsewhere with which to gain the lead. Partner may hold around 12 points, including an entry card or two, so you should try to find his long suit. A three-card holding is a better lead than a doubleton and here you should lead the ♥10.

Above: High from touching honours. After opponents' bidding of 1♥ – 3♥ – 4♥, it is natural to lead a spade. Lead the ♠Q against a suit contract, as someone will surely ruff the third round. (Against no-trumps, you would lead the ♠2 instead.)

DEFENCE IN THE SECOND SEAT

The general rule when defending in the second seat is: 'Second hand plays low'. The reason for this is that it will often cost you a trick to rise with an ace or a king when a low card is led. Look at this diamond position:

Right: Second hand plays low. When South leads the ♦3, West must play low in the second seat or declarer will score three diamond tricks.

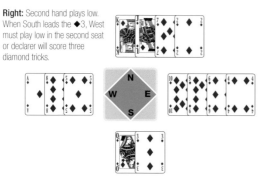

Declarer leads the ♦3 from the South hand. If West plays the ♦A 'on air', as it is called, declarer will make three diamond tricks. If West instead follows the general rule and plays low in the second seat, dummy's king or jack will win but the ace will capture South's queen on the second round. Declarer will score only two diamond tricks. Another reason to play low in that diamond position is that East might hold the ♦Q. By rising with the ♦A, you would save declarer a guess in the suit.

On the deal shown below, declarer can make his slam only by guessing correctly in clubs. West must be careful not to give the club position away.

Sitting West, you lead the ♥10 against 6NT. Declarer has 11 top tricks and needs to establish an extra trick from the club suit. Suppose he wins the heart lead with the ace and immediately leads the ♣3 from his hand. If you rise with the ♣K, or give the position away by thinking of playing it, you will save declarer a guess. If instead you follow smoothly with a low club, declarer will have a difficult guess to make. Because so many defenders would give away the position of the king if they held it, declarer is likely to play the ♣10 from dummy, hoping that you hold the ♣J. After misguessing the clubs, he will have no way to recover.

Right: Second hand plays low. Forcing declarer to guess. When a club is led towards dummy, West must play low smoothly or he will save declarer a critical guess in the suit.

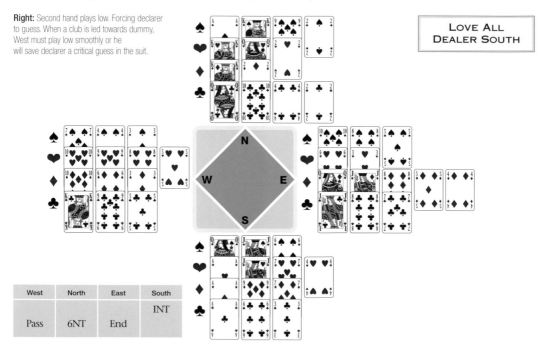

LOVE ALL
DEALER SOUTH

West	North	East	South
			INT
Pass	6NT	End	

Here is another deal where a defender will benefit from following the 'second hand low' rule:

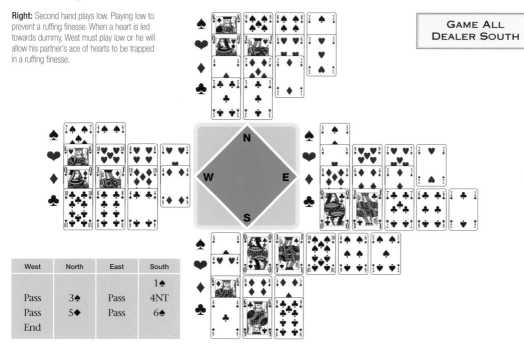

Right: Second hand plays low. Playing low to prevent a ruffing finesse. When a heart is led towards dummy, West must play low or he will allow his partner's ace of hearts to be trapped in a ruffing finesse.

West	North	East	South
			1♠
Pass	3♠	Pass	4NT
Pass	5♦	Pass	6♠
End			

Sitting West, you lead the ♦Q against South's small slam. He wins with dummy's ♦A and East signals with the ♦3, showing no interest in the suit. Declarer draws trumps with the ace and queen and then leads the ♥4 from his hand. If you mistakenly rise with the ♥K, the slam will be made. There are still two entries to dummy in the trump suit. Declarer will use one of these to run the ♥Q through East's ♥A (a play known as a 'ruffing finesse'). If East plays low, declarer will throw his diamond loser. If instead East covers, declarer will ruff and use his remaining trump entry to reach the established ♥J.

When declarer leads the ♥4 from his hand, you should follow the general guideline 'Second hand plays low', playing the ♥5. East will win dummy's ♥Q with the ♥A and declarer will have no way to avoid a further loser on the third round of diamonds. The slam will go one down and South's adventurous bidding will prove costly.

Right: West correctly plays low on the first round of hearts and prevents declarer from setting up a winner in the suit.

OPENING LEAD AGAINST SUIT CONTRACTS

Choosing an opening lead against a no-trump contract is relatively easy. As we saw in an earlier section, you normally lead from your own longest and strongest suit, hoping to set up some long cards. When the contract is in a trump suit, setting up long cards is not a relevant concept because declarer will usually be able to ruff the later rounds of a suit. These are the main types of lead to consider:

- Lead a strong side suit, such as Q–J–10–7 or K–J–8–3,with the aim of setting up some quick winners.
- Lead a short suit, such as 8 or 9–5, aiming to score a ruff.
- Lead a trump, hoping to reduce the number of ruffs that declarer can make.
- Lead a safe suit, such as 9–8–6–5 or 8–4–3, to avoid giving a trick away.

When you have decided to lead a strong side suit, the choice of card is generally dictated by the same table that we saw in the section on leading against no-trumps. You would lead the top honour from a sequence such as K–Q–J–7, fourth-best from K–10–8–5–2 and second-best from a suit with no honour card: 9–7–6–3.

There are two important exceptions, where you would lead differently against a suit contract, compared with no-trumps:

- Do not underlead an ace against a suit contract. To lead from a suit such as A–9–8–2, whether you lead the ace or the 2, is usually a very poor idea. The purpose of an ace is to capture a king or a queen.
- From a four-card or longer suit headed by two touching honours, such as K–Q–8–3 or Q–J–7–6–2, lead the top honour against a suit contract. The third round will normally be ruffed by someone, so make sure that your honours contribute to the first two rounds.

Suppose the bidding has been 1♠ – 4♠ and you have to choose a lead from one of these hands:

1

Lead the ♥5 from (1). You need to find four defensive tricks from somewhere. If you can find partner with the ♥Q or ♥A, you may be able to score some heart tricks.

2

On (2) you should lead the singleton ♦7. When you hold the ace of trumps, there is an extra chance of scoring a ruff because declarer will not be able to draw trumps as soon as he gains the lead.

3

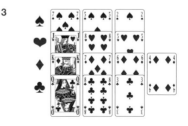

On hand (3) it is unattractive to lead from any of the side suits because your honours there are not accompanied by a high second-best card. It is better to lead from K–J–x–x than from K–10–x–x, better to lead from K–9–x–x than K–8–x–x. When the second-best card is no higher than a 9, there is more chance of giving away a trick by leading the suit than there is of establishing one. So, make the safe lead of a trump on (3).

Leading a trump

As we saw with hand (3) above, you sometimes lead a trump because you have no attractive side-suit lead. There are also a couple of situations where a trump lead stands a good chance of working well. The first is when responder has left the opener in his second suit. After an auction such as 1♠ – 1NT – 2♦, it is likely that responder will have one spade and three or four diamonds. By leading a trump, you may reduce the ruffs that declarer can take.

The other situation is when partner has left in your take-out double of a one-bid. Suppose you double 1♥ and everyone passes. Your partner has indicated long and strong hearts and you should lead a trump, even when you hold only a singleton, to allow him to begin to draw trumps. Except in the situation just mentioned, it is unwise to lead a singleton trump. By doing so, you may damage your partner's four-card holding (such as Q–J–x–x or A–J–x–x), reducing the number of trump tricks that he would otherwise score.

Active or passive?

You will often find yourself having to choose between an active lead (such as attacking in a side-suit of ♦K–J –8–2) and a passive lead such as a trump from ♥6–5–3. In general, you must risk an active lead, hoping to score or set up side-suit tricks, when declarer may otherwise be able to throw his losers away.

Suppose the opponents' bidding is: 1♠ – 2♣ – 2♠ – 4♠ and you are on lead with:

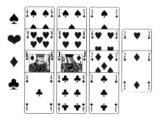

You can visualize a good club suit in the dummy, one that will supply discards once trumps are drawn and the clubs are established. You must make the active lead of the ♦2, hoping to find your partner with the ♦Q or the ♦A. In this way you may score whatever

diamond tricks are your due, before declarer has time to discard his diamond losers on dummy's club suit. When such a lead fails, because declarer holds the ace and queen of diamonds, you will usually find that your lead has given nothing away. Declarer could have discarded his diamond losers anyway.

Suppose next that the opponents' bidding is 1♥ – 2♥ – 4♥ and you are lead with:

A diamond lead is now much less attractive. Your second card is the 10 rather than the jack. Also, there is less reason to think that declarer will be able to discard any diamond losers that he may hold. A diamond lead might be right but in the long run it will pay you to lead a passive trump, aiming not to give a trick away.

> **LEAD AWAY FROM A KING**
> ♠ ♥ ♦ ♣
>
> Don't be afraid to 'lead away from a king'. If the bidding suggests you should be active, leading from such as ♦K–J–8–3 is a promising attack.

DEFENCE IN THE THIRD SEAT

The general rule when defending in the third seat is: 'Third hand plays high'. The reason for this is that you do not want the next player to win the trick cheaply. Even if your card does not win the trick, it will force out a higher one from the opponent on your left. This may promote a trick or two in the suit for the defenders.

Suppose your partner, West, has led the ♦2 in this lay-out:

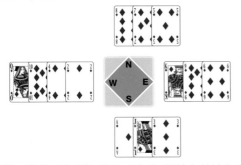

Above: West leads the ♦2 and East must play the ♦K (playing high in the third seat) to prevent declarer scoring a cheap trick with the ♦J.

You play 'third hand high', rising with the ♦K. Declarer wins with the ♦A but will score only one trick in the suit. Your partner's ♦Q–10 are now worth two tricks, sitting over declarer's ♦J. If you had not followed the general guideline, playing a lower card, declarer would have won the first round with the ♦J and scored two tricks from the suit.

The situation is less clear-cut when dummy holds a high card, one that can beat your second-best card:

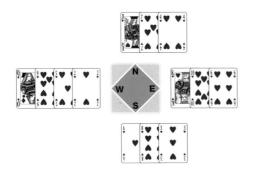

Above: Finessing against the dummy. West leads the ♥2 and East must play the ♥10 to restrict declarer to one trick in the suit.

Suppose West has led the ♥2 against a contract of 4♠. Since it is poor practice to underlead an ace against a suit contract, you can place the ♥A with South. You should therefore play the ♥10 on the first trick, retaining your ♥K to deal with dummy's ♥J later. The ten will force South's ace and he will make only one heart trick. If you play the ♥K instead, declarer will make tricks with both the ace and the jack.

Even if the contract was in no-trumps and West might therefore hold the ♥A, it would still be right to play the ♥10 at Trick 1. If South held ♥Q–8–3, he would be certain to make a trick from the suit anyway. Sometimes in these situations you do have to guess which card will work best. As a general rule, you should play your second-best card if it is the nine or higher.

Above: In the heart position shown on the left, East correctly plays the ♥10 to avoid giving declarer a second heart trick.

DALLAS ACES
♠ ♥ ♦ ♣

The world's first professional bridge team, known as the 'Dallas Aces' and later simply as 'The Aces', was formed in 1968 by financier Ira Corn. His objective was to win the world championship for the USA after a gap of many years. Six players were hired: James Jacoby, Robert Wolff, William Eisenberg, Robert Goldman, Michael Lawrence and Robert Hamman. They were paid a salary and expected to practise for up to 50 hours a week. They won the world championship in 1970 and successfully defended it in 1971.

Right: Breaking the 'third hand high rule'. West leads the ♥8 against 3NT and East will give away the contract if he plays the ♥K, thereby giving declarer three heart tricks.

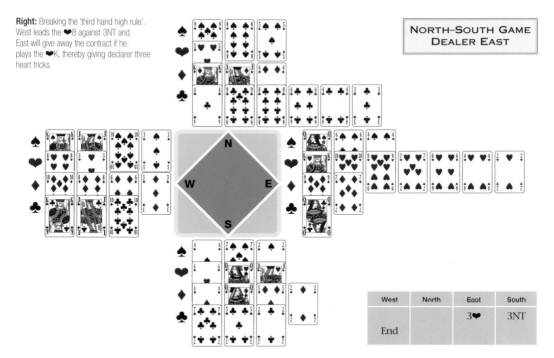

West	North	East	South
		3♥	3NT
End			

There are various situations in which a player should break the 'third hand high' rule. One is when he cannot possibly promote a higher card by playing high, and may give declarer an extra trick by doing so. Look at the deal above.

Sitting East, you open with a pre-emptive three-bid in hearts. South overcalls 3NT and West leads the ♥8. It is clear from the high spot-card lead that declarer holds the ace, queen and jack of hearts. If you play 'third hand high', contributing the ♥K to the first trick, declarer will score three heart tricks. He has six top winners immediately available in the other three suits and will therefore make his contract easily.

The singleton heart in dummy prevents declarer from making three heart tricks under his own steam and you should therefore play a discouraging ♥2 on the first trick. Declarer will win with the ♥Q and duck a club, hoping to establish that suit. You win with the ♣Q and must decide what to do next. Persevering with hearts is no good because declarer will score the nine tricks already mentioned. Instead you should switch to spades. Declarer will hold up the ace of spades until the third round and play ace and another club. West wins the third round of clubs and the 13th spade will then be the setting trick.

LOW SPOT-CARD FROM STRENGTH
♠ ♥ ♦ ♣

When your partner leads a low spot-card he is likely to hold an honour in the suit (unless he is leading a short suit). When he leads a high spot-card, he is denying an honour in the suit. This knowledge will often affect your play in the third suit.

Above: Low from equals in third seat. West leads the ♠2 and dummy plays ♠3. East should play the ♠J (lowest from equals). When this forces South's ♠A, West deduces that East must hold the ♠Q or declarer would have won with that card.

ATTITUDE SIGNALS

When your partner leads a low spot-card to a trick, you will generally have to play 'third hand high' in an attempt to win the trick or to force out a high card from the next hand. The situation is different when your partner leads an honour card, such as the ace or king, or when the trick has been won by the hand on your right. In those cases you can choose from your available spot-cards in the suit to pass a signal to your partner. The traditional method of signalling, when partner has led to the trick, is to play high when you would like a continuation of the suit, low when you would not.

Suppose the contract is 4♠ and your partner, West, has led the ♦A in this lay-out:

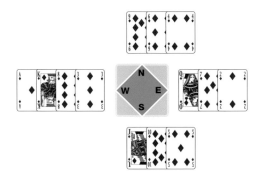

Above: Encouraging signal. West leads the ♦A and East gives an encouraging signal by following with the ♦7.

Sitting East, you play the ♦7 (your highest available spot-card) to show that you like diamonds and would be happy with a continuation of the suit. West will play the ♦K next and then a low diamond to your queen.

FOUR-COLOUR PACK

♠ ♥ ♦ ♣

Players sometimes revoke (fail to follow suit) because they confuse a club spot-card for one in spades, or a heart spot-card for one in diamonds. In an effort to help players to avoid revoking, a four-colour pack was invented. It had orange diamonds and red hearts, blue clubs and black spades.

You would give a 'high to encourage' signal when you held a doubleton too:

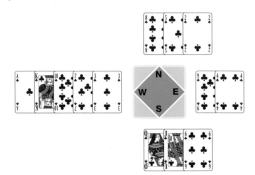

Above: Encouraging from a doubleton. West leads the ♣A and East gives an encouraging signal by following with the ♣9.

West leads the ♣A against a suit contract and you encourage with the ♣9. He cashes the ♣K at Trick 2 and then leads a third round, which you ruff.

SIGNALLING WITH A HIGH CARD

♠ ♥ ♦ ♣

When you decide to signal with a high card, be as clear as possible. To signal encouragement from ♥K–8–6–2, play the ♥8 rather than the ♥6.

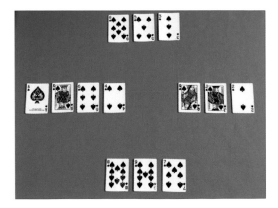

Above: A special signal. West leads the ♠A and dummy plays the ♠3. East should play the ♠Q. This special signal tells partner that both the ♠Q and the ♠J are held. Knowing this, West may decide to lead a low spade to the jack on the second round.

When you do not want a continuation, you signal with your lowest spot-card:

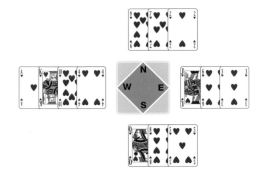

Above: Discouraging signal. West leads the ♥A and East gives a discouraging signal by following with the ♥3.

West leads the ♥A. If he continues with a second round of hearts, he will set up South's ♥Q. You warn him that you do not want a heart continuation by signalling with the ♥3 on the first round. West will then switch to a different suit and declarer will not be given an undeserved heart trick.

Reading an attitude signal

You can only signal with the cards that you have been dealt! If you want to discourage from ♠J–8–7, you will have to play the ♠7 and hope that partner can read that as a low card. Suppose this is the spade lay-out:

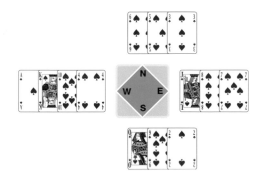

Above: Reading the ♠7. West leads the ♠A and must decide whether his partner's ♠7 is an encouraging or discouraging card.

West leads the ♠A and you signal with the ♠7. If South follows with the ♠2, West should realize that he can see the ♠4 in his own hand, the ♠6–5–3 in dummy and the ♠2 from declarer. So, even though the ♠7 may

seem like a fairly high spot-card, it is in fact the lowest spot-card out and is therefore a discouraging signal. (A cunning declarer might drop the ♠9 on the first round, hiding the ♠2 in the hope that West would read the ♠7 as an encouraging card.)

Similarly, when you want to encourage from ♣K–3–2 you will have to play the ♣3 and hope that partner notices that the ♣2 is missing and that you may therefore be playing your highest spot-card. This may be the club position:

Right: Reading the ♣3. West leads the ♣K and must decide whether his partner's ♣3 is an encouraging or discouraging card.

West leads the club king and dummy wins with the ace. You signal encouragement with the ♣3 and South plays the ♣6. West should take account of the fact that the ♣2 has not yet appeared and you may therefore be signalling encouragement from ♣J–3–2. (It is possible that South is playing deceptively, by hiding the ♣2 from such as ♣J–6–2, but not many players are up to such trickery.)

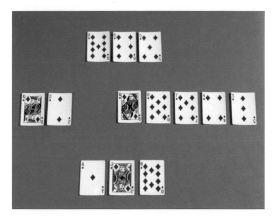

Above: An encouraging signal. West leads a speculative ♦K against a contract of 4♠ and South wins with the ♦A. East should play an encouraging ♦8, to show that he holds the ♦Q. If West can gain the lead with a high trump, he may then cross to the ♦Q for a diamond ruff.

GIVING PARTNER A RUFF

Near the start of a hand, before declarer has had the chance to draw trumps, the defenders may be able to score a ruff or two. This happens most often when the player on lead holds a side-suit singleton. Look at the deal below.

Sitting East, you see partner lead the ◆4. Declarer plays low from dummy and you win with the ◆A, South playing the ◆5. It is fairly obvious that the opening lead is a singleton. First of all, it would not be attractive for West to lead from ◆Q–6–4. Secondly, if declarer held a singleton ◆5, he would probably have played the ◆J from dummy. So, you are going to return a diamond at Trick 2, to give partner a ruff.

Which diamond should you lead? It is a common agreement among good players everywhere that when you give partner a ruff, you should tell him which suit you would like to be returned on the next trick. Here you hold the ♣A and would very much like a club return. You indicate this by leading the ◆2 for the ruff – your lowest diamond asks for a return in the lower remaining side suit, clubs. West ruffs and duly returns a club. You win with the ♣A and give partner a second

diamond ruff to defeat the contract. Suppose you had held the ♥A instead of the ♣A. You would then have led the ◆10 to give partner his ruff. Leading your highest diamond would ask for a return in the higher of the remaining side suits. This is known as 'giving a suit preference signal'.

If you have no particular preference between the other two side suits, you would indicate this by leading a middle card to give partner his ruff.

HOLDING THE ACE IN THIRD SEAT
♠ ♥ ◆ ♣

Suppose partner leads the ♥9 against a spade game and you hold ♥A–10–8–6–2. If the lead is a singleton, it will be right to win immediately and give partner a ruff. If the lead is from a doubleton and partner holds the ace of trumps, it may be better to duck, retaining the ♥A to give partner a ruff later. In general, you should assume a singleton lead, since it is a more attractive proposition for your partner.

Right: Giving a suit preference signal. East wins his partner's singleton diamond lead and must suggest the best return with his choice of card to deliver the ruff.

LOVE ALL
DEALER SOUTH

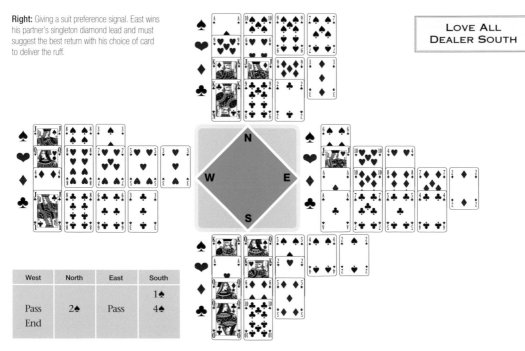

West	North	East	South
			1♠
Pass	2♠	Pass	4♠
End			

On the next deal, West must be alert to the possibility of a ruff and must not allow declarer to draw trumps.

Sitting West, you lead the ♦10. East wins with the ♦A and switches to the ♣9. Declarer plays the ♣J and you win with the ♣K. When you return a club, declarer wins in his hand with the ♣A and leads the ♥3 towards dummy. You must think carefully before playing to this trick.

Since East would not have led the ♣9 from ♣10–9–7, you know that your partner began with a doubleton club. If you play low on the first round of trumps, dummy will win with the ♥10 and a second round of trumps will remove partner's last trump. Instead you must leap in with the ♥A. You can then return a third round of clubs while your partner still has a trump. He ruffs with the ♥5 and the contract goes one down.

Right: Winning the trump ace immediately. When the defenders have the chance of scoring a ruff, they must not allow declarer to slip through a round of trumps.

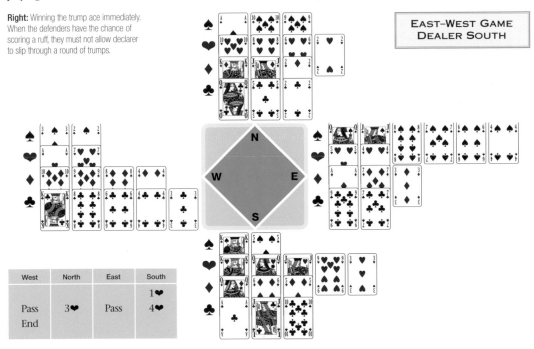

EAST–WEST GAME
DEALER SOUTH

West	North	East	South
			1♥
Pass	3♥	Pass	4♥
End			

PRECISION CLUB SYSTEM
♠ ♥ ♦ ♣

The Precision Club system was invented by C.C.Wei, a ship owner who was born in Shanghai. The system was successfully employed by the Taiwan team in the 1969 and 1970 world championships, also by the Italian team when they won the 1972 Olympiad and the 1973 and 1974 world championships. In Precision, nearly all hands of 16 points or more are opened 1♣. Opening bids of 1♥ and 1♠ promise at least a five-card suit and a response of 1NT is forcing. An opening bid of 2♣ shows 11–15 points and an unbalanced hand containing at least five clubs.

Above: Playing Precision, with 16 points, you would open 1♣.

OPENING LEAD AGAINST A SLAM

A sound general rule is to look for an aggressive lead against a suit slam, and a passive lead against 6NT. Against a grand slam, there is no point in trying to establish a trick with your opening lead. If you were to gain the lead, to cash the established winner, the grand slam would be down anyway! So, always look for a safe lead against a grand slam.

Leading against a small slam in a suit

When declarer is in a contract such as 6♠, he will usually have to lose the lead once during the play. To beat the slam, it will often be vital that you have established a second trick to cash by the time the defenders gain the lead. Look at this typical slam deal.

You are sitting West and must choose a lead. Declarer is likely to have plenty of tricks in spades and diamonds. You must hope that your partner has one high card in these suits and must aim to set up a second winner elsewhere. A club lead is a much better prospect than a heart lead. You hold the king of the suit, so you will only need to find partner with the queen to set up a potential trick there. If you lead a heart instead, you will need to find partner with the king of the suit. But even if partner does hold the ♥K, it may not make a trick if declarer has the ♥A sitting over it. You lead the ♣3, and the slam is doomed. Declarer wins East's queen with the ace, draws trumps and runs the ♦J. When your partner wins with the ♦K, he returns a club and the slam is one down.

One hand proves nothing, you may think, and declarer might easily have held the ace and queen of clubs. It is true, but in that case it is unlikely the slam could be beaten. In the long run it will pay you handsomely to make attacking leads against a small slam in a suit.

CHOOSING A LEAD
♠ ♥ ♦ ♣

Sound advice is to choose an aggressive lead against a small slam in a suit. When leading against 6NT, do the opposite – choosing a safe lead that will give nothing away.

Right: Leading aggressively against a suit slam. West leads the ♣3 against South's suit slam, since this represents the best chance of setting up a defensive trick.

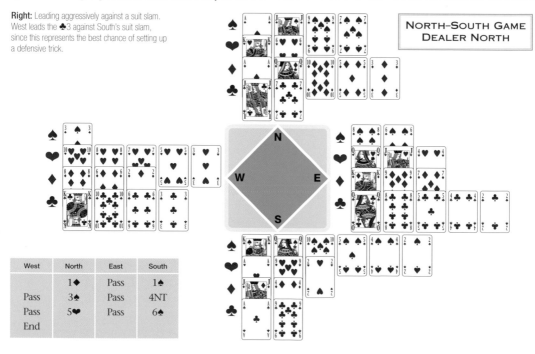

| NORTH–SOUTH GAME |
| DEALER NORTH |

West	North	East	South
	1♦	Pass	1♠
Pass	3♠	Pass	4NT
Pass	5♥	Pass	6♠
End			

Leading against 6NT

In a typical 6NT contract, declarer will have 10 or 11 top tricks at his disposal and will have to seek an extra trick or two to reach his target. You should not make life easy for him by giving away a trick on the opening lead. Leading from something like ♠K–J–8–7–2 is a great idea against 3NT, because you hope to establish several tricks in the suit. It would be a very poor idea against 6NT because declarer is likely to have multiple honours in every suit and would then be certain to score the ♠Q as well as the ♠A. You are West on this typical 6NT contract and must choose a lead:

Right: Choosing a safe lead against 6NT. West leads the ♦7 against 6NT, since leading any other suit would be more likely to give away a trick.

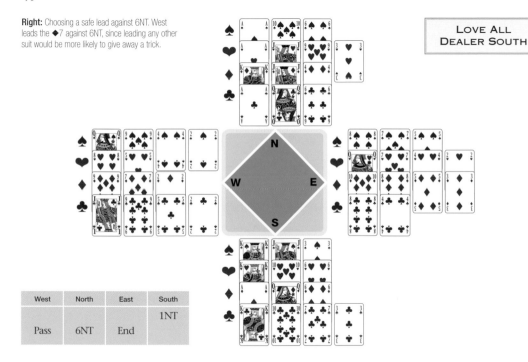

LOVE ALL
DEALER SOUTH

West	North	East	South
			1NT
Pass	6NT	End	

It would be incredibly dangerous to lead a spade or a club. There is every chance that leading from an honour will give away a trick, or save declarer a guess. So, you must choose between ♥8–5 and ♦9–7–3. It is slightly safer to lead from the tripleton. When you have a doubleton, there is more chance that your partner will hold four cards to the queen or jack and you might give away the position. You should lead the ♦7 (second best from a poor suit). Declarer may still make the contract – he may not. At least you will not have handed it to him on a plate.

LEADING AN ACE
♠ ♥ ♦ ♣

Decades ago, players liked to lead an ace against a small slam. Once in a blue moon, partner would hold the king of the suit. He would give an encouraging signal and they would score two quick suits. Leading an ace against a small slam is not a good idea. In general you are much more likely to give declarer an undeserved trick with his king, or two tricks (one undeserved) with the king and queen.

BRIDGE IS GOOD FOR YOU!
♠ ♥ ♦ ♣

In 2000, Professor Marian Diamond of the USA's Berkeley University tested 12 women aged between 70 and 90 as they played bridge for an hour and a half. Blood samples were taken before and after the session. In eight of the women she detected a considerable increase in the levels of key immune system blood cells.

MAINTAINING COMMUNICATIONS

It is often important for the two defenders to keep in touch with each other during the play. In other words, they must take steps to ensure that a defender can reach the hand of his partner, particularly when that player has some winners to cash. To maintain communications effectively, it is necessary that the defenders can read the lie of the suit involved. This can be done by following a standard method when choosing the card to return on the second round.

Look at this typical 3NT deal:

<table>
<tr><td rowspan="2"></td><td colspan="3" align="center">STRATEGIC COMMUNICATIONS
♠ ♥ ♦ ♣</td></tr>
</table>

STRATEGIC COMMUNICATIONS
♠ ♥ ♦ ♣

Suppose your partner leads the ♦3 against 3NT, dummy holds ♦10–8 and you are in third seat with A–Q–6. It can work out well to play the ♦Q. This idea is to force out declarer's ♦K. When you gain the lead subsequently, you can return ace and another diamond. If instead you win the first round with the ♦A, declarer will hold up his ♦K until the third round and defensive communications will be broken.

Right: West maintains communications. Defending 3NT, West must decide whether or not to win with his ♠K on the second round of the suit.

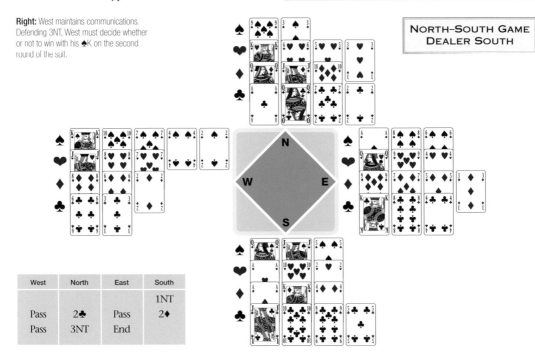

**NORTH–SOUTH GAME
DEALER SOUTH**

West	North	East	South
			1NT
Pass	2♣	Pass	2♦
Pass	3NT	End	

Sitting West, you lead the ♠4. East wins with the ace and returns the ♠8, South playing the queen. Suppose you make the mistake of winning with the king. The contract will then be made, whatever you do next. If you clear the spade suit, declarer will win with the jack and run the ♣J. When your partner wins with the ♣K he will have no spade to return.

With the spades lying as in the diagram, you must hold up the ♠K on the second round, allowing South's ♠Q to win. By doing so, you leave the defenders'

communications intact. When declarer takes a losing club finesse, East can return a third round of spades to your king. You will then cash two more spade winners to defeat the game.

It would not be a good move to duck the second round of spades if South begun with ♠Q–5, so you need to know declarer's spade holding. Your partner will assist you in this regard by following this rule with his return on the second round of the suit you have led:

- with two cards remaining, return the top card
- with three or more cards remaining, return the original fourth-best card.

On the deal we have just seen, East returned the ♠8. This could not possibly be his original fourth-best card, so his holding had to be ♠A 8 6. (South had denied four spades with his Stayman response, so East could not hold a doubleton ♠A–8. Even if the bidding had been 1NT – 3NT, you would have to hope that East had started with three spades.) The right defence was therefore for West to hold up the ♠K on the second round.

Let's see a deal where West should not hold up his honour on the second round:

Right: West reads declarer for a doubleton in the suit led. West needs to know the lie of the heart suit before deciding whether to win the second round of hearts.

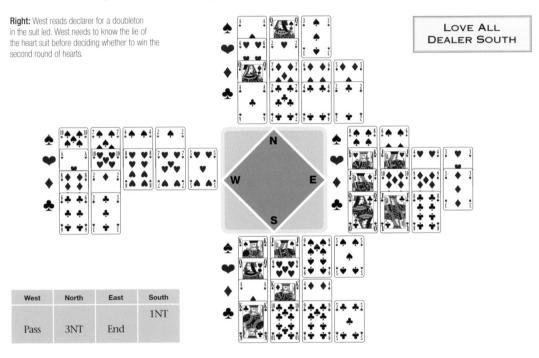

LOVE ALL
DEALER SOUTH

West	North	East	South
			1NT
Pass	3NT	End	

PLAYING IN A 1–1 FIT
♠ ♥ ♦ ♣

In the semi-final of the 1998 Spingold, played in Chicago, Bobby Levin and Steve Weinstein played in a contract of four spades with a trump holding of a singleton ♠7 in declarer's hand and a singleton ♠J in the dummy. Weinstein opened 3♦ and Levin responded with a psychic 3♠ on a hand with five-card diamond support and only one spade. Weinstein raised to 4♠ and the contract went eight down vulnerable for the loss of 800. Had their team-mates also played in 4♠, scoring +650, the loss would have been only 4 IMPs. They actually went one down in 6♠, for an adverse swing of 15 IMPs.

You lead the ♥7 against 3NT and East wins with the ♥K. He returns the ♥3 and declarer plays the ♥Q. You must now decide whether to win with the ♥A or to hold up.

If South started with ♥Q–J–9, you would have to hold up, to preserve communications as on the previous deal. In that case, however, your partner would have started with ♥K–4–3 and would have returned the ♥4. Partner's return of the ♥3 tells you that declarer began with either ♥Q–9 or ♥Q–J–9–4. In neither case can there be any reason to hold up the ♥A. You win with the ♥A, therefore, and continue with the ♥5. South did indeed start with a doubleton heart and the defenders score five heart tricks to beat the game. A misguided hold-up at Trick 2 would have allowed declarer to make the contract.

INTERMEDIATE BIDDING

You should always be reluctant to allow the opponents to choose trumps at a low level, particularly if they have found a trump fit. The first topic in this section on intermediate bidding will be 'balancing', where the player in the pass-out seat bids without the normal values, to prevent the opponents from winning the auction too cheaply. The universally popular transfer responses to 1NT will be described, where you respond in one suit to show length in the next higher suit. Next the important topic of bidding slams is covered, in particular 'control-showing cue-bids', where you bid a suit in which you hold an ace or a king rather than one where you have some length. After a discussion of three types of conventional double – negative, responsive and competitive doubles – the section ends with a discussion on sacrificing, where you bid a contract that you expect to fail. Your aim is to lose fewer points than you would if the opponents were allowed to make their contract instead.

Right: The right-hand opponent opened 1♥. To express this minor two-suiter, overcall 2NT (the Unusual No-trump convention).

BALANCING

When the strength between the two sides is evenly divided, or nearly so, you should be very reluctant to let the opponents choose trumps at a low level. This is particularly the case if they have found a trump fit. When you are in the pass-out seat, you should consider making a call of some sort, even when your own hand is quite weak. The fact that the opponents have stopped low implies that your partner is likely to hold reasonable values. Making such a call, in the pass-out seat, is known as 'balancing' or 'protecting'.

Balancing against a one-bid
Suppose the bidding starts in this fashion:

West	North	East	South
1♥	Pass	Pass	?

and you hold one of these hands in the South seat:

1

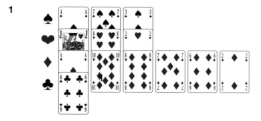

East did not have enough to respond, so your partner may well hold 10 points or so. Rather than allow West to choose trumps, you should overcall 2♦ on (1). You would not be strong enough to overcall 2♦ in the second seat. In the protective seat, however, you are entitled to bid with around a king less than normal. It's the same on (2). An overcall of 1NT would

2

normally show a stronger hand but, in the protective seat, you may bid 1NT on around 11–14 points. If your partner happens to hold 12 points himself, you may be able to make game.

3

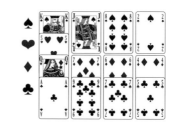

Hand (3) is worth a double. You would be reluctant to double in the second seat, with only 10 points. In the protective seat you can be bolder. Since you may be three points lighter than normal for any action taken in the protective seat, your partner should bid cautiously when advancing towards a possible game.

Balancing against a two-level fit
When the opponents have found a trump fit but stopped at the two-level, the odds are very favourable for balancing. Your side must hold something approaching half the strength in the pack. Since you are both relatively short in the opponents' suit, there is a good chance that you will have a playable fit yourselves somewhere. Suppose the bidding starts

West	North	East	South
1♦	Pass	2♦	Pass
Pass	?		

and you hold one of these hands in the North seat:

1

Compete with 2♥ on (1), rather than let the opponents choose trumps at the two-level. Do not worry that your partner, who is likely to hold around 10 points, will carry you too high. Remembering that you did not overcall 1♥ on the first round, he will realize that you are bidding the combined values of your own hand and his.

2

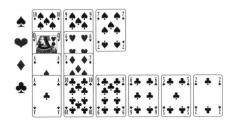

Similarly, you should bid 3♣ on (2). The opponents will often then bid 3♦, which may go down. On hand (3) you should double for take-out.

3

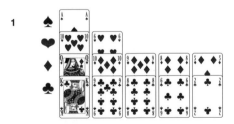

When you hold the minor suits and the opponents have found a fit in a major, you can use 2NT (the Unusual No-trump) to ask partner to choose one of the minor suits.

West	North	East	South
1♥	Pass	2♥	Pass
Pass	?		

Sitting North, you hold one of these hands:

1

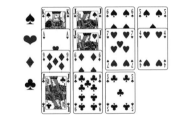

2

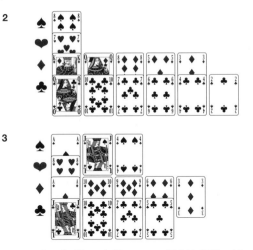

3

On hands (1) and (2) you would bid 2NT, asking partner to choose a minor. On hand (3) you would prefer to double, despite holding only three cards in the other major, spades.

Above: Dangerous to protect. Suppose you hold this hand and the opening 1♦ is followed by two passes. Ask yourself 'Where are the spades?' Your partner did not overcall 1♠ and there is a risk that the opponents may find a spade fit if you bid. It is safer to pass.

HESITATIONS
♠ ♥ ♦ ♣

Many disputes that arise during tournament play involve hesitations. It is perfectly acceptable to think for a while before making a bid or playing a card. You often give away information by doing so, however, particularly if you think for a while and then pass. Your partner must be particularly careful not to take advantage of the information gained.

TRANSFER RESPONSES

Many social players, and nearly all tournament players, use 'transfer responses' when partner has opened 1NT. A response of 2♦ shows at least five hearts and asks the opener to rebid 2♥. A response of 2♥ shows at least five spades and asks the opener to rebid 2♠. There are two big advantages of this method. The first is that the 1NT opener will play any contract in responder's five-card major. His hand will be hidden from view and his honour holdings will be protected from the opening lead. The second advantage is that after a start of 1NT – 2♦ – 2♥, the responder has a second chance to bid. He can continue with a further bid, such as 2NT, 3♦ or 3NT, having already shown five hearts.

Responder may use a transfer response to sign off in his long major. A transfer response does not promise any values at all. You may be very weak, intending to play in your long suit at the two-level. Or you may have a slam in mind. Here the responder has no ambitions:

Above: Oswald Jacoby, who originally conceived the idea of transfer responses in bridge.

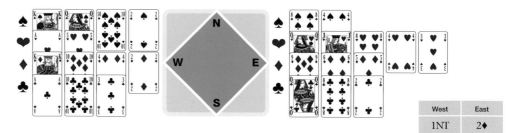

West	East
1NT	2♦
2♥	

West opens a 15–17 point 1NT and East shows five hearts with a transfer response. Since he has no game ambitions, he passes the requested 2♥ rebid.

Because bidding 2♦ forces the opener to rebid 2♥, the responder has a chance to describe his hand further. If he continues with 2NT this will show the values to invite game:

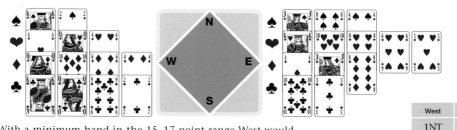

West	East
1NT	2♦
2♥	2NT
4♥	

With a minimum hand in the 15–17 point range West would pass 2NT, or correct to 3♥ with three-card heart support. Since West has 16 points, heart support and a possible ruffing value, he is happy to bid 4♥, accepting the game invitation.

The responder has these options after a start of 1NT – 2♦ – 2♥:

Pass	no game ambitions
2♠	natural and forcing
2NT	inviting a game
3♣/3♦	natural and game-forcing
3♥	inviting a game, at least six hearts
3NT	asking opener to choose between 3NT and 4♥
4♥	to play.

Breaking the transfer

When the opener has four-card trump support and an upper-range hand, he should bid one level higher than normal. This is known as 'breaking the transfer'. Game may now be reached when responder was not quite strong enough to make a try himself:

<aside>
LORD YARBOROUGH
♠ ♥ ♦ ♣

A hand that contains no card higher than a nine is known as a Yarborough. It is so-named after Lord Yarborough, who used to offer players odds of 1,000-to-1 against picking up such a poor hand. The noble lord no doubt knew he was on to a good thing because the true odds against picking up a Yarborough are 1,827-to-1. The odds against two partners picking up a Yarborough simultaneously are 546,000,000-to-1.
</aside>

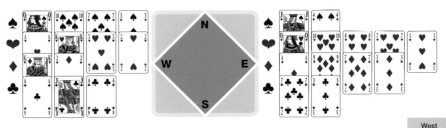

West	East
1NT	2♦
3♥	4♥

With just 7 points and a five-card suit, East would have passed a rebid of 2♥. When partner shows four-card heart support and an upper-range opening, East raises to game.

Transfers opposite a 1NT overcall

When partner has overcalled 1NT, it is a good idea for the responder to use Stayman and transfer bids.

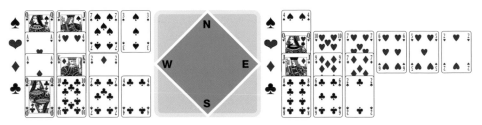

East has a weak hand and seeks sanctuary in his long heart suit.

West	North	East	South
			1♦
1NT	Pass	2♦	Pass
2♥	End		

Transfers opposite a 2NT opening

A similar method is used opposite an opening bid of 2NT. A 3♦ response shows at least five hearts and asks opener to rebid 3♥. A response of 3♥ shows at least five spades and asks opener to rebid 3♠.

CONTROL-SHOWING CUE-BIDS

Suppose you have found a trump fit and have values to spare, so far as a game contract is concerned. You want to tell partner that a slam may be possible and to ask his view on the matter. It is not much use bidding some form of Blackwood. The meaning of a Blackwood bid is: 'I know we have the values for a slam and I just need to check that there are not two aces missing.' No, the only way to invite a slam, without going past the game-level, is to make a control-showing cue-bid. In other words, you bid a new suit (usually at the four-level or higher) after the trump suit has been agreed. This bid shows a control – an ace, king, singleton or void – in the suit that you have bid.

Making a cue-bid with trumps agreed

Suppose the bidding has started like this:

West	North	East	South
1♠	Pass	3♠	Pass
?			

You are sitting West. Partner has agreed spades as trumps and you have to assess slam prospects on the three hands shown below:

1
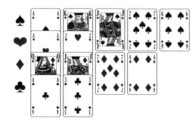

On (1) you can visualize a slam if partner has a diamond control. You make a control-showing cue-bid of 4♣. This passes the message: 'I am strong enough to consider a slam and I have a control in the club suit.' Your partner may now make a cue-bid himself, or perhaps sign off in 4♠. If he were to cue-bid 4♥, that would show a heart control. It would also deny a diamond control, since you show your cheapest control first. You would then sign off in 4♠, knowing that there were two top diamond losers.

2

On (2) you would cue-bid 4♦, meaning: 'I am strong enough to consider a slam and I have a control in diamonds but no control in clubs.' If partner were to cue-bid 4♥, that would show a heart control and also a club control. Without a club control, he would have signed off in 4♠, knowing that there were two top losers in clubs.

3

Hand (3) is not strong enough to suggest a slam, opposite partner's limit raise of 3♠, and you would bid 4♠.

Note that after a start of 1♠ – 2♠, a rebid of 3♣ by the opener would not be a cue-bid. Because the bidding has not yet been forced to game, a bid in a new suit is a game try. A bid in a new suit is a cue-bid only when the auction is already game-forcing.

AVOID THE FIVE-LEVEL
♠ ♥ ♦ ♣

The secret of good slam bidding is to investigate a possible slam while the bidding is still below the game level. When the bidding starts 1♠ – 3♠ – 4♣ (where 4♣ is a control-showing cue-bid), a slam is suggested but the bidding can still stop in 4♠. Ideally, you should play in 4♠ or 6♠. To investigate a slam and then stop in 5♠ is to take an unnecessary risk of going down.

Cue-bidding only with first-round control

The advantage of cue-bidding on both aces and kings, as just described, is that you can diagnose when you have two top losers in a suit. It is a method that was popularized by the great Italian teams of the 1970s. It does mean that you cannot be sure how many aces are held but, of course, you can usually bid Blackwood after making a cue-bid or two, thereby discovering whether there are two aces missing. Nevertheless, some partnerships prefer to make a cue-bid only when they hold a first-round control (the ace or a void). It is something that you must discuss with your partner.

Agreeing a suit by making a cue-bid

On some auctions there is not enough space to explicitly agree partner's suit before making a cue-bid. When a bid at the four-level cannot logically be natural, it will be a cue-bid that agrees the suit last bid by partner. Let's see an example of this:

> ### BLACKWOOD CONVENTION
> ♠ ♥ ♦ ♣
>
> During a slam auction a bid of 4NT is the Blackwood convention, conceived by Easley Blackwood. It asks your partner how many aces he holds and the traditional responses are:
>
> 5♣ with none or four aces
> 5♦ with one ace
> 5♥ with two aces
> 5♠ with three aces

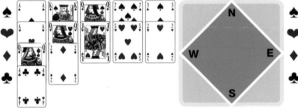

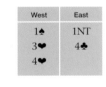

East has a super fit for hearts and indicates this by cue-bidding 4♣ instead of merely raising to 4♥. West has no diamond control, so he signs off in 4♥. Suppose West had held one diamond and two clubs instead. With the diamond suit controlled in his own hand, he would then have been much more interested in a slam. The bidding would have continued to the six-level:

West	East
1♠	1NT
3♥	4♣
4♥	

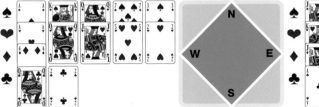

West uses the Blackwood 4NT convention, discovering that partner has one ace. He then bids a small slam in hearts, which is easily made.

You can see from this example how important it can be to show where you hold a control, rather than merely stating how many controls you have. Swap East's minors and he would have cue-bid 4♦ instead of 4♣. West would then know that there were two top losers in clubs and would sign off in game.

West	East
1♠	1NT
3♥	4♣
4NT	
6♥	5♦

BIDDING SLAMS

The foundation of a successful slam auction has nothing to do with Blackwood or control-showing cue-bids. Both players must use the early rounds of the bidding to convey their general playing strength and to look for a trump fit. Only when both these tasks have been completed, and the playing strength for a slam has been confirmed, is it appropriate to check on controls.

The requirements for a slam

Two elements are necessary to make a small slam. You must have the playing strength to make 12 tricks. You also need the controls to prevent the defenders from scoring two tricks.

Look at these two hands:

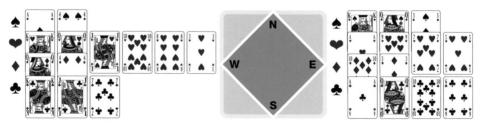

All the aces and all the kings are held, but there is insufficient playing strength for a slam. There are only 10 tricks on top and some luck will be required in the spade suit, even to score 11 tricks.

The next pair of hands contain playing strength in abundance but there is a flaw in the control situation:

An excellent heart fit, with 13 top tricks. Unfortunately no diamond control is held and the defenders will be able to score the first two tricks.

Assessing whether the power for 6NT is present

We will look first at how to assess whether the playing strength for a slam is present. To make 6NT when two balanced hands face each other, you will need 33 points or more. This is comparatively easy to judge. Once your partner has shown his own point-count, you simply add your own to assess the total. Let's see two typical slam auctions in no-trumps.

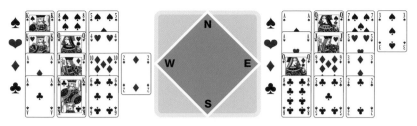

With 13 points opposite 20–22, East can be sure that the combined point total will be at least 33 points. He therefore leaps to 6NT. There are nine top tricks and the slam will be made if South holds the ◆K or the spades split 3–3.

West	East
2NT	6NT

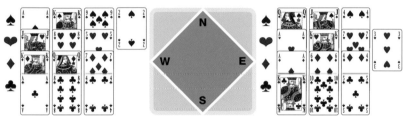

With 17 points facing a partner holding 15–17 points, East is not quite strong enough to jump to 6NT. He invites a slam by raising to 4NT. With a minimum hand for his strong no-trump, West would pass. Here he holds a maximum 17 points and therefore accepts the invitation, bidding 6NT. There are 11 tricks on top and you would seek a 12th by leading towards the ♥J, succeeding when South held the ♥Q or when hearts broke 3–3 (plus some other small chances).

West	East
1NT	4NT
6NT	

Assessing whether the power for a suit slam is present

It is somewhat more difficult to assess whether you have sufficient power to make a slam with a trump suit. High-card points are not so important as playing strength and the quality of the trump suit. In general, you should consider a slam when you have considerably more strength than you would need to raise to game.

There are several situations where the playing strength should be present for a slam, provided you can find a sound trump suit. Suppose the opener has a medium strength hand (16–18 points) and the responder has an opening bid himself. Provided a good trump fit can be found, the values for a slam should be there. The same is true when the responder has made a jump shift (for example 1◆ – 2♠) or when a positive response has been given to a 2♣ opening.

Remember that when partner opens 2♣ and rebids in a suit, he is showing that he has enough strength for a game in his own hand. If you hold an ace in your hand, or a king and a queen, this will often be enough to produce a slam.

Above: Lorenzo Lauria, senior member of the Italian team and winner of five world championships.

Here are some typical auctions investigating a slam contract:

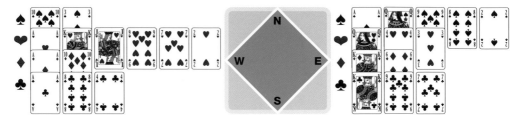

East has considerably more strength than would be needed to raise to 4♥ on the second round. Since he has a control in both the minor suits, he is happy to bid Blackwood. Partner shows three aces and the excellent small slam is reached. (In the later section on Advanced Bidding, we will look at Roman Key-card Blackwood, widely popular in tournament play, where the responses to 4NT identify not only the four aces but also the king and queen of trumps.) Even when a player has made a very strong bid, he may decide to sign off at the game-level when he is minimum for his call.

West	East
1♥	1♠
3♥	4NT
5♠	6♥

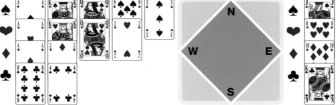

West bids just 4♠ to inform his partner that he has nothing to spare for a 2♣ opening. West has three losers in the minor suits and is confident that East will advance over 4♠ anyway, if he holds something like ◆K and the ♣A.

Let's make the West hand somewhat stronger by adding the ◆K:

West	East
2♣	2◆
2♠	3♠
4♠	

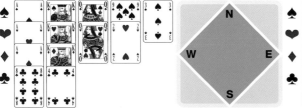

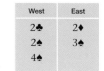

Now West suggests a slam by cue-bidding his diamond control. East is impressed by the fact that West has visualized a slam, despite holding no control in the club suit. He therefore shows his club control, bypassing the 4♠ safety level. This encourages West to jump to a small slam in spades.

West	East
2♣	2◆
2♠	3♠
4◆	5♣
6♠	

You can see that control-showing cue-bids have two purposes. Their main mission is to show a control in one of the side suits. They are used also to indicate a strong hand that is interested in a slam:

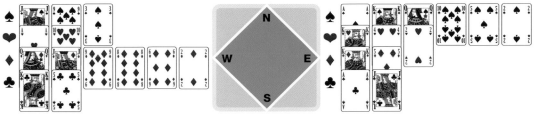

West	East
1♦	2♠
3♠	4♣
4♥	6♠

West has a minimum opening and no top honour in spades, the agreed trump suit. Nevertheless, he should be willing to cue-bid his ♥A because it does not carry the bidding past the next level of the trump suit (here 4♠). As it happens, this information is enough to persuade East to bid a slam. East knows that there cannot be a grand slam available, of course, because West's cue-bid in hearts denies the ♦A.

Play in 6NT when the values are present

When you assess the combined point-count at 33 or more, it is usually wise to play in 6NT rather than in six of a suit. By doing so, you may avoid defeat when the suit that you would otherwise have chosen as trumps happens to break badly:

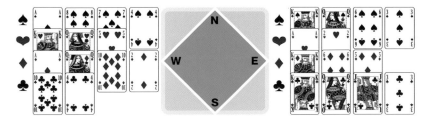

West	East
1NT	6NT

It is not a good idea to seek a spade fit by bidding Stayman on the East hand. The resultant contract of 6♠ will then go down when the spade suit breaks 4–1. Since East knows that 33–35 points are present, he should bid the slam in no-trumps. By doing so, he will also avoid the small chance of an adverse club ruff.

Bidding a grand slam

The general advice about bidding grand slams is that you should do so only when you are confident that 13 tricks are present. Remember that if you fail in a grand slam you lose both the small slam bonus and the game bonus that you would otherwise have accrued. When playing duplicate it is particularly expensive to bid a grand slam and go one down, only to discover that your opponents stopped at the game-level on the same cards. You could then have obtained a big swing by bidding and making a small slam.

NEGATIVE DOUBLES

In rubber bridge, where few conventions are played, the most common type of penalty double is that of an overcall, in an auction such as 1♠ – 2♦ – Dble. In tournament bridge, such doubles are almost universally played for take-out nowadays and are known as 'negative doubles'. The time has come to take a look at this method.

The negative double

When you open with one of a suit and partner doubles an overcall up to the level of 3♠, this is for take-out. Such a double is known as a 'negative double'. (It was originally known as a Sputnik double, since it was conceived around the time of the Russian space satellite of that name.) It suggests that you have no accurate natural bid to make and that you hold one or both of the unbid suits.

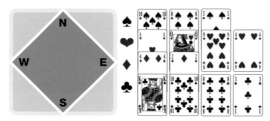

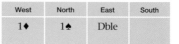

West	North	East	South
1♦	1♠	Dble	

East is strong enough to bid at this level but has no satisfactory natural bid to make. A response of 2♣ would overstate his values. He solves the problem by making a negative double. He strongly suggests four cards in the unbid major and may well have a club suit too. If partner rebids 2♣, 2♦ or 2♥, East will pass on this occasion. If instead he held 11 points or more he would show the additional strength by bidding again.

The higher the auction is, the more values a negative double will show. When the overcall is at the three-level, responder will need almost the values for making game:

Above: The double card. Nowadays a double card is used many more times for take-out than for penalties.

West	North	East	South
1♣	3♠	Dble	

At this level West will quite often pass the double for penalties. That is because it may be easier to score five or six tricks in defence, rather than make a contract at the four-level with no particularly good fit.

Responder has a long suit

When you play negative doubles, the responder has two ways of bidding a new suit. Look at these two sequences, where East holds length in hearts:

1

West	North	East	South
1♠	2♣	Dble	Pass
2♦	Pass	2♥	

2

West	North	East	South
1♠	2♣	2♥	

In sequence (1) responder begins with a negative double and then introduces his long suit on the next round. In (2) he bids his long suit directly instead. It makes good sense to differentiate between these sequences in terms of strength. Most players treat sequence (2) as forcing, showing a strong hand with responder, and sequence (1) as non-forcing. Some players use the sequences the other way round, however, and it is something you should discuss with your partner.

The opener re-opens with a double

When the double of an overcall is played for take-out, responder has to pass when he has a strong holding in the opponent's suit and would like to have doubled for penalties. The penalty will often return to the fold because his partner will re-open with a take-out double most of the time:

Above: Weak with hearts. On this type of hand you will use sequence (1) or (2), according to the methods you have agreed with your partner.

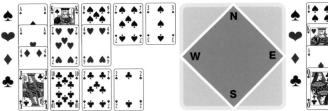

The opponents have stopped at the two-level, so the odds are good from West's point of view that his partner has several points and had to pass because he held length in diamonds. West doubles for take-out, mainly in the hope that partner can pass for penalties. As you see from this example, such a double does not promise any extra values with the opening bidder.

West	North	East	South
1♠	2♦	Pass	Pass
Dble	End		

APPEAL COMMITTEES
♠ ♥ ♦ ♣

When a player does not agree with a ruling that has been given by a director in a major tournament, he has the option of appealing against it. Usually he is required to deposit a sum of money, which will be forfeited if the appeal is deemed to be frivolous. An 'appeal panel' of strong players will then convene to discuss the matter. If you look at the bulletins published on some tournaments, you will find almost as much material on the result of appeals as on the actual deals themselves!

RESPONSIVE AND COMPETITIVE DOUBLES

It is rarely advantageous to double the opponents at a low level when they have found a trump fit. In this section we will look at two situations in which the other side has found a fit and it is therefore best to play a double for take-out instead of for penalties.

The responsive double

When an opening bid has been doubled for take-out and the next player raises to the two- or three-level, a double by the fourth player is also for take-out. It is known as a responsive double.

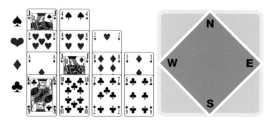

West can tell that his side holds at least half the points in the pack and therefore has no wish to allow the opponents to choose trumps at the two-level. Rather than guess which minor suit to bid, and perhaps end in a 4–3 fit, he makes a responsive double. Since East will almost always hold four spades for his take-out double of 1♥, West would tend to respond in spades if he held four of them. The responsive double on this auction is therefore likely to be based on a hand with the minor suits. Unless East has values to spare, he will rebid 3♣ or 3♦ at his next turn.

Many pairs play responsive doubles up to the level of 3♠ but it is something that you should agree with your partner. As we saw with the negative double, your partner is more likely to pass a double for penalties when the level of bidding is already quite high.

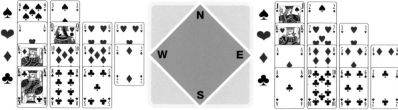

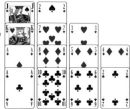

East's responsive double is for take-out but West cannot visualize a game their way, on his minimum double including a doubleton spade. He passes the double for penalties.

<table>
<thead>
<tr><th colspan="4">POSSIBLE CONFUSION
♠ ♥ ♦ ♣</th></tr>
</thead>
<tbody>
<tr><td colspan="4">When the bidding starts 1♦ – Dble – 1♠ – Dble, players are often confused about the meaning of the second double. In standard bidding it is a penalty double, aimed at exposing a possible psychic bid by the third player. Typically, the doubler will hold four spades. With five spades, he would bid 2♠ instead.</td></tr>
</tbody>
</table>

West	North	East	South
	1♥	Dble	2♥
Dble			

West	North	East	South
			1♠
Dble	3♠	Dble	Pass
Pass	Pass		

The competitive double

Similarly, you can double for take-out when your partner has overcalled and the opponents have found a trump fit:

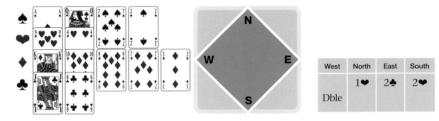

West	North	East	South
	1♥	2♣	2♥
Dble			

West's double is for take-out and is known as a competitive double. It suggests length in the unbid suits, spades and diamonds here, and a tolerance for partner's clubs, probably a doubleton. As before it would rarely be profitable to double for penalties at such a low level, once the opponents have found a trump fit.

Competitive doubles apply up to the level of 3♠, although you must agree this with your partner. As with the responsive double, partner will be more inclined to pass the double, the higher the level of the auction:

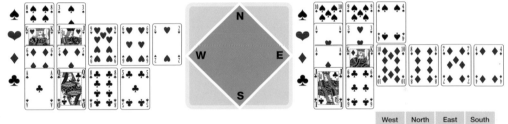

West	North	East	South
	1♠	2♦	3♠
Dble	Pass	Pass	Pass

West's double is for take-out, a competitive double that shows values in hearts and clubs. East has no fit for either of these suits and decides that the best idea is to pass the double for penalties.

THE VALUE OF CONVENTIONS
♠ ♥ ♦ ♣

Three famous Scientists vs Traditionalists matches have been played. One team was allowed to play unlimited conventions while the other could make only natural bids. In 1965, in New York, the Scientists (Roth/Stone, Mitchell/Stayman, Jordan/Robinson) beat the Traditionalists (Murray/Kehela, Becker/Hayden, Mathe/Schleifer) by 53 IMPs over 180 deals. In 1990, in London, the Scientists (Soloway/Goldman, Garozzo/Eisenberg) beat the Traditionalists (Zia/Chagas, Wolff/Forrester) by two sessions to one. In 1992, again in London, the Scientists (Hamman/Wolff, Rodwell/Meckstroth) beat Traditionalists (Chagas/Branco, Forrester/Robson) by 70 IMPs over 128 deals, winning a prize of $50,000.

Above: Jeff Meckstroth of the USA, a multiple world champion.

SACRIFICING

Suppose your opponents bid to 4♥, a contract that is destined to succeed. If they are vulnerable, they will pick up a score of +620. When you and your partner hold a spade fit, it may be worthwhile for you to contest with 4♠. Even if you go two down, this will cost you only 300 when non-vulnerable, or 500 when vulnerable. That is good business already. In addition, the opponents may see fit to bid 5♥. If that contract goes one down, you will have done very well. Bidding a contract that you expect to fail, in the hope that it will cost you less than the opponents' contract, is known as sacrificing.

Sacrificing at the game-level

The most common arena for sacrificing is the game-level. Here is a typical sacrifice deal:

Right: East–West can make 4♥ so it is profitable for North–South to sacrifice in 4♠, where the penalty will be less than the value of a game by the opponents.

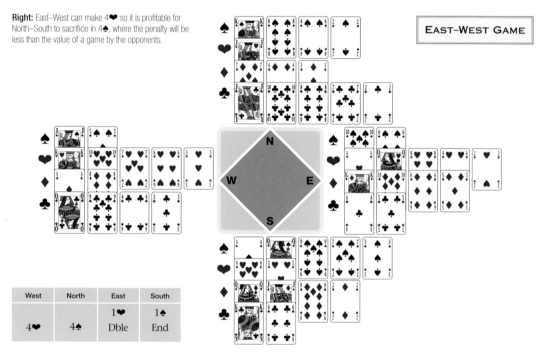

EAST–WEST GAME

West	North	East	South
		1♥	1♠
4♥	4♠	Dble	End

TRUMP ECHO
♠ ♥ ♦ ♣

When defending at no-trumps, or following to a side suit in a suit contract, it is normal to play high–low to show an even number of cards. This is known as a 'count signal'. Somewhat strangely, it is widely agreed that a high–low signal in the trump suit has a quite different meaning. It shows precisely three trumps. Some players have the agreement that such a peter (or echo) also shows that you have the desire to score a ruff somewhere.

East–West bid to a game in hearts, a contract that will easily be made. Non-vulnerable against vulnerable, North decides to sacrifice in 4♠. He does not expect the contract to be made, but there is every chance that the cost will be less than that of the opponents' heart game.

So it proves. East–West are almost certain to find their diamond ruff but the penalty will still be only 300, much less than the 620 that the heart game would have provided. If either East or West had decided to bid 5♥, rather than accept a perhaps inadequate penalty from the spade game, this contract would have been defeated. With two spades in each hand, East-West were deterred from attempting a five-level contract.

The five-level belongs to the opponents

A well-known guideline on sacrificing is that the five-level belongs to the opponents. In other words, if you have pushed the opponents to the five-level, it is rarely advantageous for you to bid five of a higher suit. Take your chance of beating their contract instead. For example, suppose that on the deal we have just seen East–West decided to advance to 5♥. It would be poor tactics for North–South to sacrifice again in 5♠. They should be content to have pushed their opponents to a possibly dangerous level.

Here is another typical sacrifice situation:

Right: When South sacrifices in 5♣, East-West should be wary of advancing to 5♥ and should therefore double.

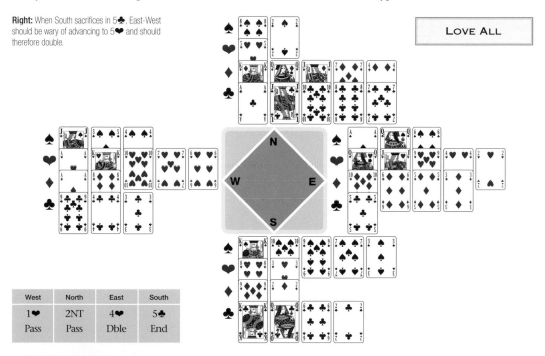

LOVE ALL

West	North	East	South
1♥	2NT	4♥	5♣
Pass	Pass	Dble	End

With the score at Love All, North enters the auction with an Unusual No-trump call to show length in both minor suits. South judges that the heart game is likely to succeed and sacrifices in 5♣. This runs to East, who takes note of the guideline 'the five-level belongs to the opponents'. Since the opponents have chosen to play in clubs, there is no reason for East to place his partner with a singleton diamond. There will be a loser or two in those suits. If the ♠K is missing, it is more likely that South will hold it than North (who has his length in the minor suits). So, East judges well to double. The cards lie well for North–South and the sacrifice goes only one down. Had East–West taken the push to 5♥, they would have gone down instead.

Left: South does not expect to make 5♣ but he expects it to cost less than a heart game made by the opponents.

INTERMEDIATE CARD PLAY

It is time to see some important areas of card play that mainly involve looking at a contract as a whole, rather than considering only one particular suit. First you will see how to maintain communications between declarer's hand and the dummy – when one defender is 'safe' and the other is 'dangerous', you must plan to finesse or duck tricks into the safe hand. The important techniques of reversing the dummy and crossruffing are described next. Then you will see the various ways in which you can prevent the defenders from taking a ruff, also when you should delay drawing trumps because some other task is of higher priority. The idea of safety play is discussed and how you should calculate the best play with an unfamiliar card combination. Finally, you will see how a hold-up play can be useful in a suit contract as well as in no-trumps.

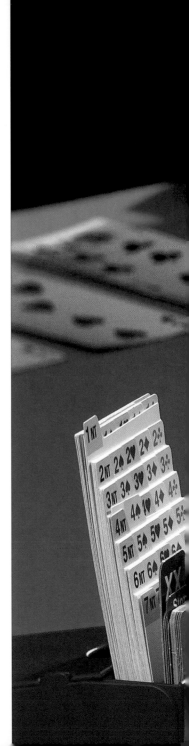

Right: Declarer has won the opening lead and is considering the best line of play. In a suit contract, the presence of a trump suit will offer you more options than in a no-trump contract.

MAINTAINING COMMUNICATIONS

There is little point in creating an extra winner or two in the dummy if you have no entry with which to reach the dummy. An important part of planning a contract is to preserve the entries that you will need to get backwards and forwards between the two hands. The first deal involves two important techniques in this area:

Right: Declarer maintains communication to his diamond winners. Playing in 3NT, South has to employ two different techniques to set up and enjoy the diamond suit.

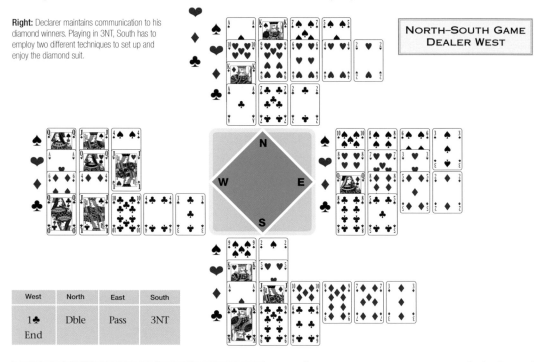

NORTH–SOUTH GAME
DEALER WEST

West	North	East	South
1♣	Dble	Pass	3NT
End			

Hoping that your diamond suit will prove useful, you leap to 3NT on the South cards. The ♣Q is led and you must take some care with the entries to the South hand. The first step (often important) is to win the opening lead in the right hand. Here you must win with dummy's ace of clubs, preserving the club king as a later entry to your hand.

Suppose your next move is to cash the king of diamonds. You are most unlikely to make the contract. The only entry to your hand will be the king of clubs. If you cross to that card and play the ace of diamonds, you will make the contract only when the diamond queen happens to fall doubleton.

Instead, you should overtake the king of diamonds with the ace, thereby gaining an entry to the South hand. You then lead the jack of diamonds, forcing out East's queen. The game cannot then be defeated. The defenders can take at most one diamond and three hearts. When you regain the lead, you will have five diamonds and the two ace–kings in the black suits, giving you a total of nine.

HESITATING WITH A SINGLETON
♠ ♥ ♦ ♣

It is illegal to give false information to the opponents deliberately. For example, suppose you have only one card in the suit that has just been led. It would be illegal to hesitate before playing it, thereby creating the impression that you had a choice of more than one card to play. A similar situation arises when the declarer leads a queen (or jack) from hand and the ace is in dummy. It would be unacceptable to hesitate in second seat when you did not hold a high honour.

Right: Declarer wins with a high card to preserve communications. A spade is led against 3NT and South must win with the ♠A to ensure that the ♠Q is preserved as an entry for dummy's club winners.

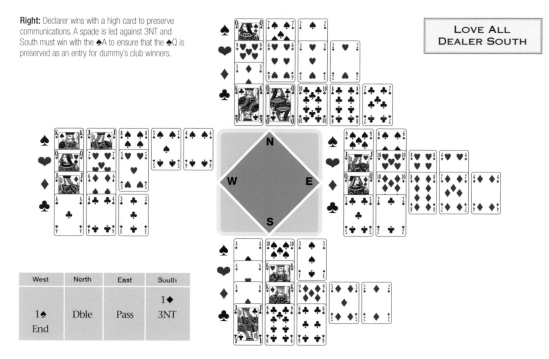

LOVE ALL
DEALER SOUTH

West	North	East	South
			1♦
1♠	Dble	Pass	3NT
End			

North's double on the first round is a "negative double", suggesting length in the unbid suits, hearts and clubs. West leads the ♠5 against the eventual contract of 3NT and, sitting South, you must consider the play carefully. You play low from dummy and East produces the ♠9. It may seem natural to win with the ♠10 but you will go down if you do so. When you play on clubs, West will hold up the ace until the third round. With ♠Q–7 facing ♠A–3 you will not have a spade entry to dummy. You will score only two club tricks and fall one trick short of your target.

To make the contract you must win the first trick with a higher card than is necessary. You capture East's ♠9 with the ace, even though your ♠10 would have been good enough to win the trick. When you play on clubs, West again holds up his ace until the third round. It will do him no good. Whatever suit he chooses to play next, you will be able to win and lead towards the ♠Q, establishing it as an entry for the two good clubs in the dummy. By disposing of the ♠A on the first round, you promote the ♠Q into a potential entry card.

Left: Helen Sobel and Charles Goren of the USA: one of the game's most famous partnerships.

SAFETY PLAYS IN A SINGLE SUIT

The best way to play a suit often depends on how many tricks you need from it. Suppose you have to play this diamond suit:

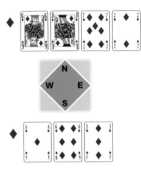

Above: The best play in this diamond suit depends on whether you need four diamond tricks or just three.

If you needed all four tricks from the suit, in order to make the contract, West would have to hold ◆Q–x–x. You would cash the ◆A and finesse the ◆J.

Now suppose that you need only three diamond tricks to make the contract. If you play the suit in the same way (◆A first, then finesse the ◆J), you will make the required three tricks when West holds the ◆Q, when diamonds break 3–3 and when East has a singleton ◆Q. You will fail in your objective when East holds ◆Q–x. When you need only three tricks, you should make the 'safety play' of cashing the king and ace, then leading towards the jack on the third round. You will still make the required three tricks in the three situations just noted. You will succeed also when East holds ◆Q–x.

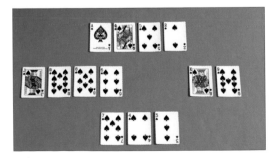

Above: Safety play. Needing only two tricks from the suit, you should duck a round, play the ♠A and then lead towards the ♠Q on the third round.

That's the idea of a safety play, then. You give yourself the maximum possible chance of making the number of tricks that you need. Suppose you are in 6♥ with this trump suit:

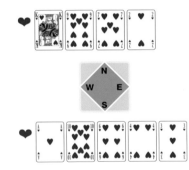

Above: If you can afford one loser in this suit, you must search for a safety play to avoid losing two tricks.

Let's say that there are no losers in the side suits. You are therefore looking for a safety play in the trump suit that will guard against two losers. If you play the ♥A first, you will lose two tricks when East began with ♥Q–J–x–x. Similarly, it is not safe to cash the ♥K first, in case West has all four missing trumps. The safe play is to lead towards dummy and play the ♥9. If West follows and East wins with the queen or jack, the suit must be breaking 3–1 at worst and you will lose only one trump trick. If West shows out on the first trump lead, your finesse of the ♥9 loses to one of East's honours, but you will later finesse the ♥10 to escape for one loser. (It would be just as good to lead towards the South hand on the first round, intending to finesse the ♥10.)

This is another combination that arises frequently:

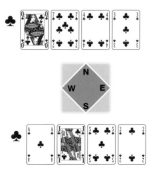

Above: If you need only three club tricks from this combination, you must seek a safety play that gives you the best chance of success.

When you need four club tricks, you play low to the jack in the hope that East holds a doubleton king. The king will then fall under the ace on the second round and dummy's ♣Q–7 will then score the remaining two tricks in the suit.

Suppose instead that you need only three club tricks. The safety play in that case is to cash the ♣A on the first round, thereby avoiding defeat when West holds a singleton ♣K.

We will look at one more suit combination, this time in the context of a complete deal.

West leads the ♥Q against 6♠ and your sole concern is to avoid two trump losers. If you were in the poor contract of 7♠, you would play the ace and king of trumps, hoping that the ♠Q fell. In the more sensible contract of 6♠ you can afford one trump loser. After winning the heart lead, you should cash the ♠A. You then cross to the South hand with a diamond and lead a low trump towards dummy on the second round.

When West follows with a low card, you will finesse dummy's ♠9. If the finesse loses to the ♠10, the suit will be breaking 3–2 and you are home. If instead East shows out, you will lose only one trump trick to West's remaining ♠Q–10.

When West holds ♠Q–10–8–2, as in the diagram, it will do him no good to 'split his honours', playing the ♠10 on the second round. Your ♠9 and ♠J would then be equals against his ♠Q.

Suppose instead that West shows out on the second round of trumps. You then rise with dummy's king and lead towards the jack of trumps. This safety play guards against ♠Q–10–x–x in either defender's hand.

Right: A safety play in the trump suit. To avoid losing two trump tricks to a bad break, declarer must play the suit in a special way.

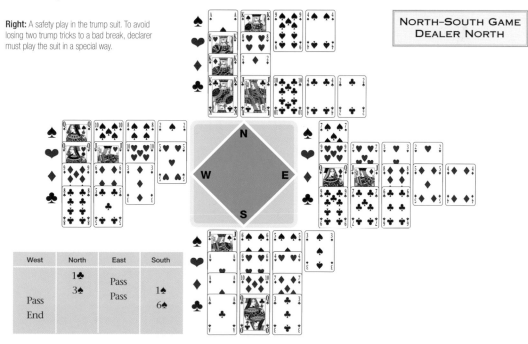

NORTH–SOUTH GAME
DEALER NORTH

West	North	East	South
	1♣		
	3♠	Pass	1♠
Pass		Pass	6♠
End			

FINESSING INTO THE SAFE HAND

It often happens that one defender's hand is 'safe' and the other is 'dangerous'. For example, a defender may be dangerous because he has some winners to cash or can lead through an unprotected king. When you have a choice of finesses to take, you should usually finesse into the safe hand. Even if the finesse happens to fail, it will be the safe defender who gains the lead. The 3NT contract, shown below, is an example of that:

Right: Taking the right finesse first. When you may have to take two finesses (in clubs and diamonds here), it is usually best to finesse first into the safe hand.

West leads the ♠4 and you win East's ♠J with the ♠K. You have eight top tricks and must decide which minor-suit finesse to take.

Suppose you run the ♣J at Trick 2. East will win with the ♣K and return a spade. The defenders will score four spades and one club, putting you one down. It was not a good way to play the contract because the club finesse was 'into the dangerous hand'. If it lost, East would damage you with a spade return.

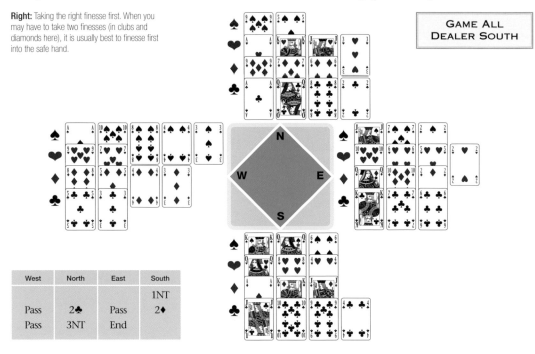

GAME ALL
DEALER SOUTH

West	North	East	South
			1NT
Pass	2♣	Pass	2♦
Pass	3NT	End	

MOST COMMON HAND SHAPE

♠ ♥ ♦ ♣

Although 4–3–3–3 is the flattest possible shape for a bridge hand, it is only the fifth most common shape. Its frequency is 10.5 per cent. The most common shape is 4–4–3–2, which has a frequency of 21.5 per cent. It is followed by hands of 5–3–3–2 shape (15.5 per cent), 5–4–3–1 shape (12.9 per cent) and 5–4–2–2 shape (10.6 per cent).

A better idea is to cross to the ♥J and lead a diamond to the jack. This finesse is 'into the safe hand'. As it happens, the finesse succeeds and the contract is yours.

Suppose the diamond finesse were to lose, though. West could not profitably continue spades from his side of the table. (If he did play a spade, hoping that his partner held the ♠Q, he would give you your ninth trick.) If West played any suit other than a spade, you would win the trick and still be able to take the club finesse. By finessing into the safe hand you give yourself two chances instead of one.

Sometimes you have a two-way finesse for a missing queen. When you can afford to lose a trick in the suit and still emerge with enough tricks for your contract, it makes good sense to finesse into the safe hand. Look at the deal shown below.

West leads the ♥4 against 3NT and East plays the ♥Q. You hold up the ♥A until the third round, aiming to exhaust East of his cards in the suit. There are eight tricks on top and a ninth trick must come from the diamond suit. You can finesse either defender for the missing ♦Q and must decide which way to take the finesse.

You will score an extra trick from the diamond suit, even if the finesse fails. So you can afford the finesse to fail, provided the defenders do not cash enough tricks to beat you.

Right: Finessing into the safe hand. When you have a two-way finesse in a suit (diamonds, here) and can afford to lose a trick, finesse into the safe hand.

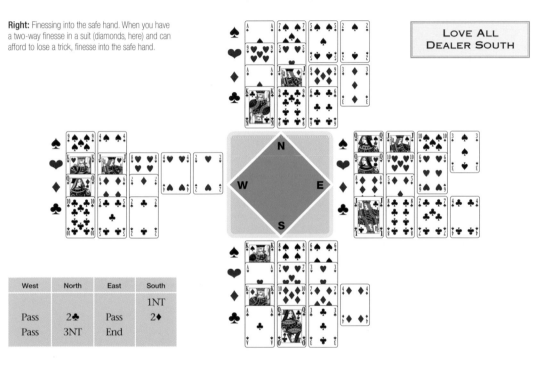

LOVE ALL
DEALER SOUTH

West	North	East	South
			1NT
Pass	2♣	Pass	2♦
Pass	3NT	End	

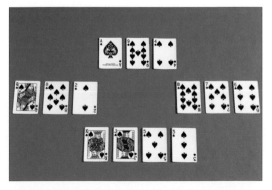

Above: Finessing into the safe hand. Suppose you only need three spade tricks. When West is the danger hand, it makes sense to lead low to the 9, losing a trick to the safe East hand.

Suppose you cross to the ♦A and run the ♦J on the way back, finessing East for the missing queen. This finesse is into the danger hand. If it loses, West will cash two hearts to beat the contract. Instead you should cash the ♦K and lead a low diamond towards dummy, intending to finesse West for the missing ♦Q. If the finesse loses to East, you will still make the contract. East has no hearts left and can do you no damage. (If he did have another heart, the suit would have broken 4–4 and would pose no problem.) As the cards lie in the diagram, the diamond finesse through West will succeed and you will end with an overtrick. The point to remember, though, is that by finessing into the safe hand you would make the contract whether the finesse succeeded or not.

REVERSING THE DUMMY

Suppose you are playing in a spade contract with this trump holding:

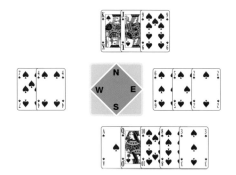

Above: If this is your trump suit, a ruff in the short-trump hand will give you an extra trick and a ruff in the long-trump hand will not.

You begin with five trump tricks and that will be the final number if you draw trumps near the start of the hand. Suppose instead that you take one ruff in the short-trump holding (the dummy). You will then make six trump tricks – five in your hand and one extra trick

Right: A typical dummy reversal. South increases the total number of trump tricks by ruffing three diamonds in the South hand.

from the ruff. If instead you ruffed something in the long trump hand, it would not give you an extra trick. You would still make just five trump tricks.

So, ruffing in the short trump hand gives you an extra trick; ruffing in the long trump hand does not. This is true in general, but if you take so many ruffs in the long trump hand that it becomes the short trump hand you can gain a trump trick. Look back at the spade position above. Take three ruffs in the South hand and you would score six trump tricks – three rounds of trumps in the North hand and three ruffs in the South hand. This is known as 'reversing the dummy'. Let's see an example featuring that very spade holding:

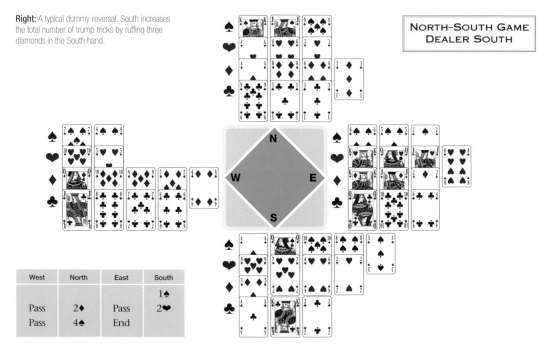

**NORTH–SOUTH GAME
DEALER SOUTH**

West	North	East	South
			1♠
Pass	2♦	Pass	2♥
Pass	4♠	End	

West leads the ♠4 and you see that you have nine tricks on top. Without a trump lead, you could simply have given up two rounds of hearts and played to ruff the fourth round in dummy, if necessary. If you play that way now, though, the defenders will be able to remove dummy's trumps before you can take your heart ruff. A better idea is to reverse the dummy, aiming to ruff all three of dummy's diamond losers in the South hand.

You win the trump lead with the ♠9, cash the ♦A and ruff a diamond. You then play the ace and king of clubs, just in case a defender could discard his clubs as you ruff the diamonds. Returning to dummy with the ♥A, you ruff another diamond with the ♠A. You ruff with such a high trump because you want to lead the ♠10 next to dummy's ♠K. A third diamond ruff with the bare ♠Q gives you the first nine tricks and the ♣J is in the dummy, ready to give you a tenth trick.

It can also be worthwhile ruffing in your hand if this enables you to score the low trumps there. Had you attempted to draw trumps instead, these cards might have been losers.

Let's see a deal that illustrates this technique. Look at the 4♥ contract shown below, where the ace and king of trumps are accompanied by three low trumps.

West leads the ♦Q against your heart game and you win with dummy's ace. Even if trumps are breaking 3–2, you would still need some luck to avoid losing three clubs in addition to one trump. The best way to play the hand is to aim to make all five trumps in your hand (by ruffing three diamonds). Add in the five side-suit winners and that will come to ten. What is more, this line may well succeed when the trumps break 4–1.

Since entries to dummy are not plentiful, you should ruff a diamond at Trick 2. You then cash the ace–king of trumps, revealing that West began with four trumps. You continue with the king, queen and ace of spades, followed by a second diamond ruff. A club to the ace returns the lead to dummy and you ruff dummy's last diamond, both defenders following. Ten tricks are now before you. As you foresaw when you made your plan, you scored five side-suit winners and all five trumps in the South hand.

MAKE A PLAN AT THE START
♠ ♥ ♦ ♣

It is not always right to draw trumps straight away. Always make a plan before starting to play the contract.

Right: Scoring the low trumps. Declarer reverses the dummy in order to make tricks with the low trumps in his hand.

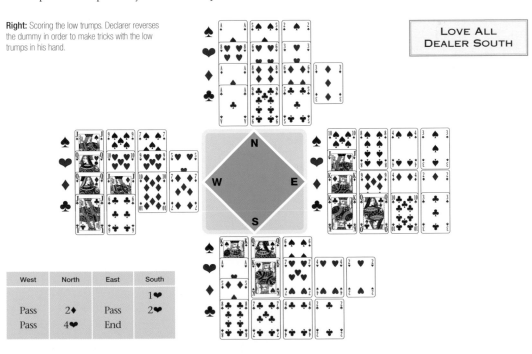

LOVE ALL
DEALER SOUTH

West	North	East	South
			1♥
Pass	2♦	Pass	2♥
Pass	4♥	End	

THE CROSSRUFF

Sometimes you are in a suit contract and both hands contain a singleton or void. In that case the best line of play may be to take several ruffs in each hand, never actually drawing trumps. The 4♠ contract shown below is a good example of this technique, which is known as the 'crossruff':

Right: A typical crossruff. Declarer scores eight trump tricks by ruffing diamonds in dummy and hearts in his hand.

West leads the ◆K against your game in spades. If you begin by drawing trumps, you will be well short of your target. Instead you should aim to make the two side-suit aces along with eight trump tricks. You must score all eight of your trumps separately, by taking ruffs in both hands.

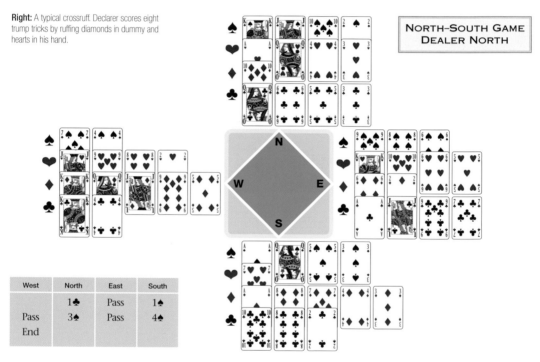

NORTH–SOUTH GAME
DEALER NORTH

West	North	East	South
	1♣	Pass	1♠
Pass	3♠	Pass	4♠
End			

You win the diamond lead with the ace and ruff a diamond with the ♠2. You cash dummy's ♥A and ruff a heart in the South hand, again with a low trump. When you ruff a second diamond East shows out. Since this ruff is with a high trump, East cannot overruff. You ruff a heart with the last low trump in the South hand and the contract is then safe. A diamond ruff, a heart ruff and a fourth diamond ruff, all with high trumps, bring your total to nine tricks and the ace of trumps will make it ten.

The important point to remember is that you take the early ruffs with low trumps, when the risk of an overruff is minimal. Later, you can ruff with high trumps and the defenders are powerless.

On many hands you draw trumps first and then cash your side-suit winners. Since you never draw trumps when playing a crossruff, you should cash your side-suit winners at the beginning of the hand. If you fail to do this, the defenders may discard from those suits while you are crossruffing. They may then be able to ruff your winners. Look at this deal:

Right: Cashing the side-suit winners first. Declarer cashes the two winners in spades before embarking on the crossruff.

North's 4♦ rebid is a splinter bid, showing a sound raise to game in hearts with at most one diamond. South advances to a small slam, via Roman Key-card Blackwood and West leads the ♣5. As declarer, you can count four winners in the side suits. If you can add eight trump tricks, scored on a crossruff, this will bring the total to 12.

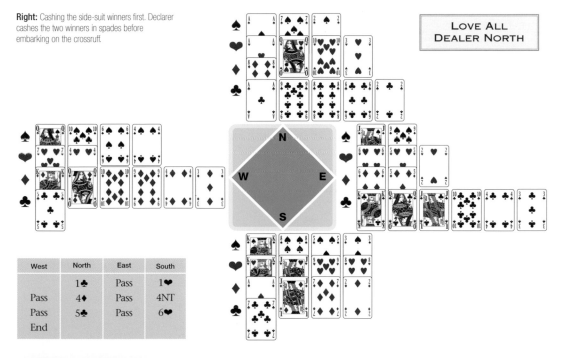

LOVE ALL
DEALER NORTH

West	North	East	South
	1♣	Pass	1♥
Pass	4♦	Pass	4NT
Pass	5♣	Pass	6♥
End			

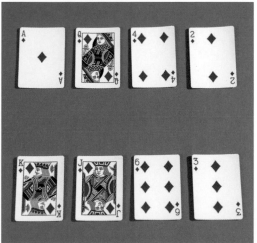

Suppose you embark on the crossruff immediately, ruffing clubs in your hand and diamonds in the dummy. When you take a second diamond ruff in dummy, East will discard one of his spades. It will no longer be possible for you to score two spade tricks, because East can now ruff the second round of the suit. The slam will go down.

To make the contract you must cash the ace and king of spades at the start, before the defenders have had an opportunity to discard any spades. Only then do you start the crossruff. Eight trump tricks will indeed come your way and the slam is made. In addition to the trump tricks, you will score two top spades and the minor-suit aces.

Left: Ruff low first. Suppose this is your trump suit and you need eight trump tricks on a crossruff. You would take the first four ruffs with low trumps. You would then continue with a 'high crossruff', ruffing with the four honours.

AVOIDING A RUFF

The most straightforward way to prevent the defenders from taking a ruff is to draw trumps. When you are missing the king or queen of trumps, you must be wary of taking an unnecessary trump finesse. If the finesse fails, the defender who wins the trick may be able to give his partner a ruff. You will often encounter deals like this:

SUSPICIOUS LEAD

♠ ♥ ♦ ♣

When a defender leads a spot-card in a suit that you or the dummy has bid, you should suspect that it is a singleton and the defender is seeking a ruff.

Right: Avoiding a ruff by refusing a trump finesse. West leads his singleton diamond and declarer will go down if he takes a trump finesse.

**NORTH–SOUTH GAME
DEALER SOUTH**

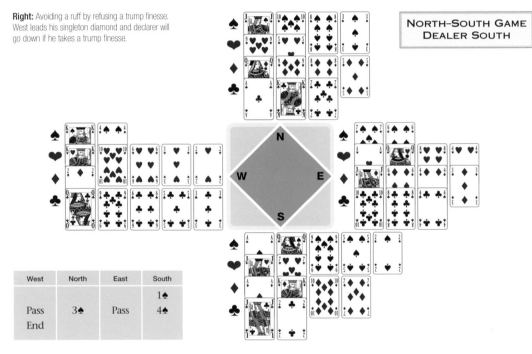

West	North	East	South
			1♠
Pass	3♠	Pass	4♠
End			

West leads the ♦2. You play low from dummy and East plays the ♦J, won with your ace. It could hardly be more obvious that the opening lead is a singleton. Suppose you cross to dummy in clubs and run the ♠J. If the finesse loses, West can cross to his partner's hand with a heart and the ensuing diamond ruff will put the contract one down.

Since you have only two losers in the side suits, you can afford to lose a trump trick. You should therefore play ace and another trump. West wins the second round of trumps with the king and can no longer score a diamond ruff, because he has no trumps left. You will make the contract easily. This is another example of a safety play. You give up your best prospect

of picking up the trumps for no loser in exchange for maximizing your chance of making the contract.

You would make the same sort of play if dummy's trumps were ♠K–8–7–2 and your own trumps were ♠A–J–5–4. Suppose you took your best chance of playing the trumps for no loser, playing the ♠K and then finessing the ♠J. You would run the risk that West could win the second round from ♠Q–9–3 and cross to partner's hand with a heart to receive a diamond ruff.

To avoid such a fate, you would make the safety play of cashing the ace and king of trumps instead. You do not mind losing a trick to the queen of trumps. What you cannot afford is to lose two trump tricks – one to the queen, one to a ruff.

Similarly, when a ruff is threatened you may decide to forgo a finesse in a side suit:

Right: Drawing trumps to avoid an adverse ruff. West leads ace and another heart against 4♠ and declarer must calculate whether to finesse the ♥J.

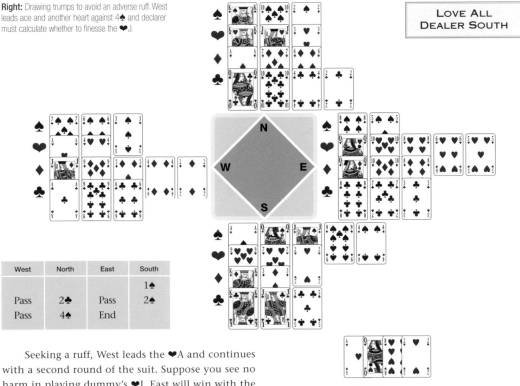

LOVE ALL
DEALER SOUTH

West	North	East	South
			1♠
Pass	2♣	Pass	2♠
Pass	4♠	End	

Seeking a ruff, West leads the ♥A and continues with a second round of the suit. Suppose you see no harm in playing dummy's ♥J. East will win with the ♥Q and give West a heart ruff. You will go one down. Instead you should rise with dummy's ♥K. You can then draw trumps and will make the contract easily, losing just two hearts and one club.

There were two main reasons to play the ♥K at Trick 2. One is that players rarely lead from an ace–queen combination but often try their luck from a doubleton ace. The more compelling reason was that you would risk the contract by finessing the ♥J.

There are many similar positions. Suppose you reach a small slam in clubs, with a heart side suit as shown on the right.

West leads the ♥4 and you have no potential losers outside the heart suit. If you play a low card from dummy, you are running the risk that the opening lead is a singleton. In that case East will win with the ♥K and give partner a ruff. You should play safe for your slam. You rise with the ♥A, draw trumps and give the defenders a heart trick.

Above: When West leads the ♥4 against your small slam in clubs, you must be wary that the lead is a singleton.

A LIKELY SINGLETON
♠ ♥ ♦ ♣

If a player opens with a pre-emptive bid of 3♠ and later leads a spot-card in a different suit, this is very likely to be a singleton, led in the hope of receiving a ruff. Unless his shape is precisely 7–2–2–2, a pre-empter will hold a singleton in his hand.

THE HOLD-UP IN A SUIT CONTRACT

In an earlier section we looked at the very common play of holding up an ace in a no-trump contract. The purpose was to exhaust the holding of one defender. He then became 'safe' and you could afford to lose the lead to him. Exactly the same play – holding up a stopper – can be effective in a suit contract too. Look at the deal shown below.

West leads the ♥K against 4♠. Even if trumps break 3–2, there are four potential losers: one spade, two hearts and one diamond. As declarer, you must seek to discard one of your heart losers on dummy's diamond suit.

Suppose you win the first trick with the ♥A and draw two rounds of trumps. You are over the first hurdle when the trump suit breaks 3–2. You will not make the contract, however. When you play a diamond, East will win with the ♦A and return his remaining heart, allowing West to score two heart tricks and beat the game.

The best chance of making the contract is to duck the first round of hearts. When West continues with a second round of the suit, you win with the ♥A and lead the ♦K. You are now favoured with two strokes of luck. Firstly, it is East who holds the ♦A (if West held the card, he would be able to cash a heart winner). Secondly, East has no heart to play. Your hold-up on the first round of hearts did indeed exhaust his heart holding.

Let's say that East returns a club. You win the trick and play the queen and jack of diamonds, discarding your last heart. You will lose just one trump, one heart and one diamond. The game is yours.

As you may have noted, it would be a mistake to draw two rounds of trumps before leading the ♦K. East could then defeat you with a hold-up play of his own! By ducking the first round of diamonds and winning the second, he would leave you with no entry to reach the established ♦J in the dummy.

On the deal shown at the top of the next page you can diagnose that a hold-up at Trick 1 will work well. The opening lead marks East with the ♥K, so he will not be able to be able to continue the suit without allowing you to score both the the queen and ace.

Right: Holding up an ace in a suit contract. West leads the ♥K against the spade game and declarer must hold up for one round, to break the link between the defenders' hands.

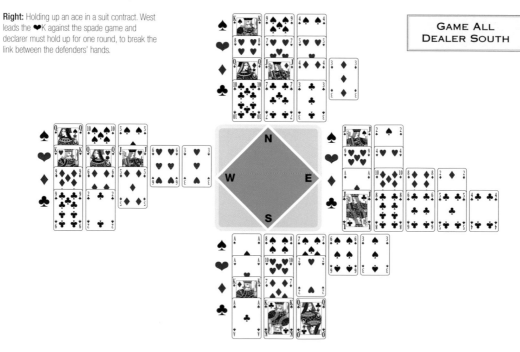

GAME ALL
DEALER SOUTH

Right: Retaining a guard in the suit led. West leads the ♥8 against 4♠ and declarer allows East to win the first trick, diagnosing that he holds the ♥K.

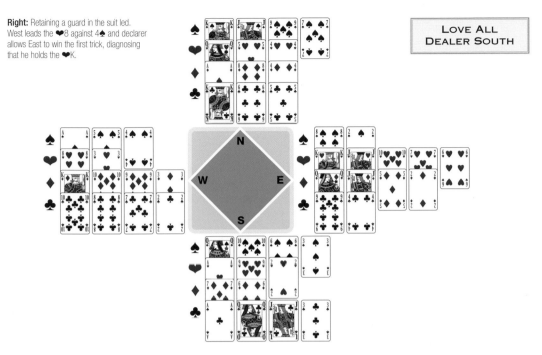

West leads the ♥8 against 4♠. You play low from dummy and East plays the ♥10. You can see four potential losers: one trump, two hearts and one diamond. A heart can be discarded from dummy on the fourth club but the risk is that the defenders will claim their four tricks before you can take a discard.

The first task is to read the likely lie of the heart suit. West would not have led the ♥8 from ♥K–J–10–8, so the lead must be from spot cards, leaving East with the ♥K–J–10. The winning play is therefore to duck the first trick, allowing East's ♥10 to win. He cannot continue the suit safely because you would run a heart return to dummy's queen. (You would then make the contract because, by good fortune, the ace of trumps lies with West, the defender who cannot deliver a heart ruff.)

Let's say that East senses this and switches to a diamond instead. You win with the ace and play a trump. When West takes the ace of trumps and plays another heart, you win with the ace, draw trumps and play four rounds of clubs, discarding dummy's last heart. You will then lose one trump, one heart and one diamond, making your game. Had you won the first round of hearts, the defenders would have scored two tricks in the suit when West won with the ♠A.

WHEN TO DELAY DRAWING TRUMPS

When you are playing in a suit contract, the general rule is that you should draw trumps immediately unless there is a good reason to do something else first. The most common reason for playing a side suit instead is that you need to take a quick discard, or perhaps establish a discard. Look at this deal:

Right: Setting up a discard before drawing trumps. If declarer draws trumps immediately, rather than setting up a discard on the clubs, his 4♠ contract will go down.

West leads the ♦Q against your spade game. There are three aces to be lost, so you cannot afford a further loser in the diamond suit. Suppose you win the opening lead and play a trump immediately. East will win with the ace of trumps and clear the diamond suit. With no way to avoid a diamond loser, you will go one down.

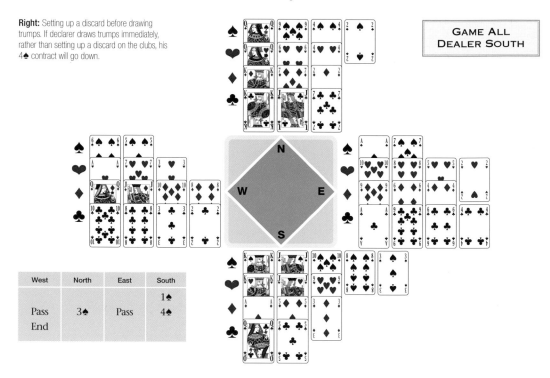

**GAME ALL
DEALER SOUTH**

West	North	East	South
			1♠
Pass	3♠	Pass	4♠
End			

SOMERSET MAUGHAM
♠ ♥ ♦ ♣

William Somerset Maugham said, "If I had my way, I would have children taught bridge as a matter of course, just as they are taught dancing. In the end it will be more useful to them. You can play bridge as long as you can sit up at a table and tell one card from another. In fact, when all else fails — sports, love, ambition — bridge remains a solace and an entertainment."

To make the contract you must delay drawing trumps, setting up a discard on the club suit instead. You win the diamond lead with the ♦A, preserving the ♦K as a later entry to dummy and lead the ♣Q. Let's say that East holds up the ♣A for one round. When you continue with a club to the king, East wins with the ace and returns a diamond. Now you reap the benefit of winning the first round of diamonds in your hand. You win with the ♦K and discard your diamond loser on the established ♣J. You can then play trumps safely and will make the game for the loss of just three aces.

Another reason to delay drawing trumps is when you need to make good use of the trump entries to dummy. This is most often the case when dummy contains a long side suit that you need to establish. That is the situation on the next deal:

Right: Establishing a side suit before drawing trumps. Declarer delays drawing trumps, so he can use the trump ace as an entry to establish dummy's diamond suit.

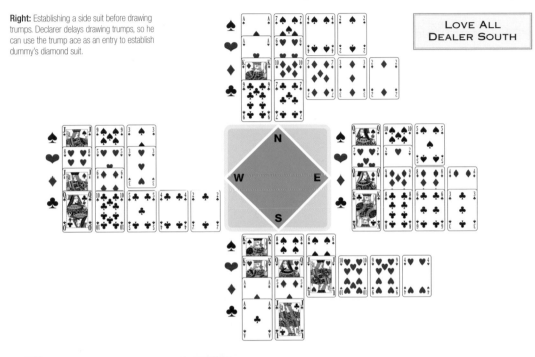

LOVE ALL
DEALER SOUTH

West leads the ♣4 against 6♥ and you win East's ♣K with the ♣A. You have 11 top tricks and must seek to establish at least one extra trick from dummy's diamond suit. Suppose your first move is to draw trumps. You continue with the ace and king of

Above: Declarer sees that he cannot afford to draw trumps straightaway.

diamonds and then ruff a third round of diamonds. All would be well if diamonds divided 3–3. When they break 4–2, as in the diagram, you will go down. You have only one entry left to the dummy (the ♠A) and the diamonds are not yet established.

You need to use the ♥A as an extra entry to the dummy. After winning the club lead, you play the ace and king of diamonds. You ruff a third round of diamonds with the ♥K (to avoid a possible overruff). Next you cross to the ♥A and ruff a diamond with the ♥Q. You can then draw the outstanding trumps and cross to the ♠A to score the established ♦10.

To make such a contract, you must form a plan right at the start. If you make the mistake of drawing trumps first, it will be too late for any planning. You need to establish the diamonds. This will require two ruffs when the defenders' cards divide 4–2, in which case you will need to use the ♥A as an entry to take the second ruff.

DUCKING INTO THE SAFE HAND

To establish a suit, it is often necessary to duck a round – in other words to let the defenders win an early trick in the suit. When one of the defenders is 'safe' and the other is 'dangerous', you must try to duck a trick into the safe hand. Here is a straightforward example of the play:

Right: Establishing a suit by ducking into the safe hand. Declarer holds up the ♠A twice and then sets up the diamond suit by ducking a round into the safe East hand.

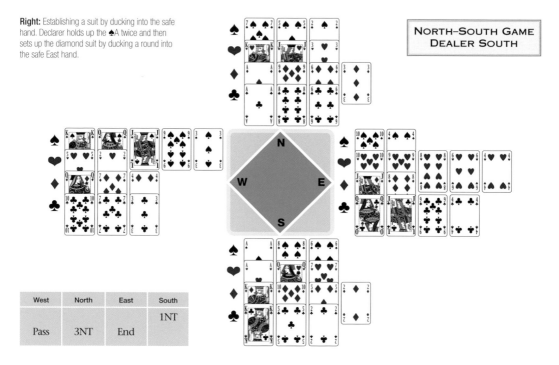

NORTH–SOUTH GAME
DEALER SOUTH

West	North	East	South
			1NT
Pass	3NT	End	

West leads the ♠K against 3NT. Since you are well protected in the other three suits, nothing can be lost by holding up the ♠A until the third round. East discards a heart on the third round of spades. You have eight tricks on top and must try to develop a ninth trick from the diamond suit. This must be done without allowing West to gain the lead.

Suppose you play the ace and king of diamonds and concede a third round of the suit. All would be well if East began with three diamonds. He would win the third round and would have no spade to play. If the cards lie as in the diagram, however, you will go down. West will win the third diamond and cash two spades to put you one down.

You should lead the ♦2 from the South hand and play the ♦9 from dummy. You are ducking the trick into the safe hand. East wins with ♦J and has no spade to play. You win his return in some other suit and cash a total of nine tricks to make the game. Had you played ace, king, and another diamond instead, West would have won the third round of the suit and beaten the contract by cashing two more spade tricks.

Sometimes you duck a round of a suit as a safety play, to guard against a bad break. By ducking into the safe hand, you avoid the risk that the suit will break badly and you would otherwise have to lose a trick to the danger hand. That is the situation on the deal shown opposite.

West leads the ♥4 against 3NT and you win East's ♥Q with the ♥K. (If instead you were to allow the ♥Q to win, East would continue with a second heart and West would hold up his ♥A to maintain communication between the defenders.) You have eight tricks on top and need to develop a ninth trick from the diamonds. If the suit divided 3–3, you would have two extra diamond tricks ready to take, simply by playing the suit from the top. If you play that way here, East will win the fourth diamond and beat you by returning a heart through your ♥J–7. To make the contract even when East holds four diamonds, you need to duck a diamond trick into the safe (West) hand.

At Trick 2 you cross to the ♠A. You then lead the ♦5. When East follows with a low spot-card you cover with the ♦8, ducking a diamond trick into the safe hand. West wins with the ♦10 but cannot continue hearts successfully from his side of the table. If he switches to a club, you will rise with dummy's ♣A. You then play a diamond to the queen and return to dummy with the ♠K to score three more diamond tricks for the contract.

By making this safety play, ducking a round of diamonds, you would score only four diamond tricks instead of five when the suit divided 3–3. The potential loss of an overtrick is a small premium to pay for making the game when diamonds break 4–2.

If East began with ♦J–10–4–2 he would (if awake) play one of his honours on the first round, to prevent you ducking the trick into the safe hand. The contract could not then be made when the heart suit lies as in the diagram.

Right: Ducking into the safe hand in case a suit breaks badly. Declarer ducks a diamond into the safe (West) hand, so that he can establish the suit when the defenders' cards break 4–2.

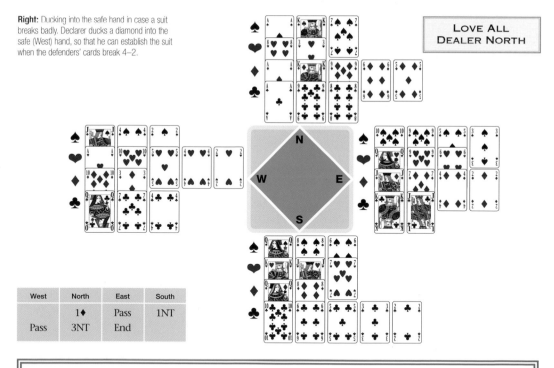

LOVE ALL
DEALER NORTH

West	North	East	South
	1♦	Pass	1NT
Pass	3NT	End	

PUT THE SAFE HAND ON LEAD
♠ ♥ ♦ ♣

Suppose you are in a suit contract, with a side suit of ♦K–8–2 in dummy and a singleton ♦5 in your hand. When West leads the ♦Q, it is obvious that East holds the ♦A. If you think that West could make a damaging play at Trick 2, you should cover with the ♦K, to make sure that East wins the first trick. Otherwise you should duck.

INTERMEDIATE DEFENCE

It is a familiar concept to plan the play of a hand when you are the declarer. It can be just as important to plan the defence of a contract and here you will see how you can do this, both in a suit contract and in no-trumps. You will see also how dangerous it can be to defend too actively by attacking new suits. This is all too likely to give away an unnecessary trick. You need to study all the available evidence before deciding whether to be active or passive with your defence. One of the most difficult areas of defence, contrary to what some players will tell you, is whether to cover an honour card that has been led. You need to make such decisions in advance, so that you do not give information away by thinking about your play when a particular card is led. Finally the important topic of retaining the right cards in defence will be addressed.

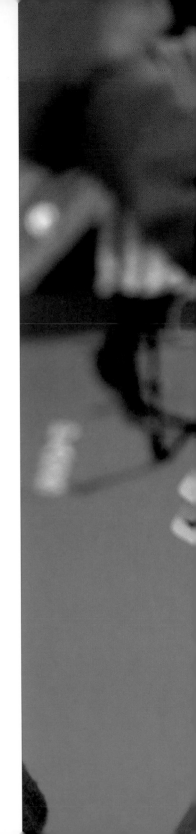

Right: The opponents' bidding will often give you a good idea what the general line of defence should be. The opening lead represents an important part of the defence.

PLANNING THE DEFENCE IN A SUIT CONTRACT

To defend accurately is not easy. You must think clearly and, above all, you must count. You count the tricks available to the defenders and to declarer. You count the points shown by declarer and by your partner. You also count the distribution of the suits, hoping to end with a complete count of the hand. If you think this sounds rather like hard work, you are right. It is the price that has to be paid in order to become a top-class defender.

Counting tricks for the defence

On the following deal, East's defence is dictated by counting the tricks that he can see for the defenders.

Sitting East, you see partner lead the ♣2. You win with the ♣A and pause to plan the defence. It is unlikely that the defence will score any tricks from the major suits. You must therefore hope for four tricks from the minors. You can score three club tricks only if West has led specifically from ♣K–J–2, which is not a big chance. It is more likely that you can score two

club tricks and two diamond tricks. So, you should switch to the ♦2 at Trick 2. As the cards lie, declarer will rise with the ♦K and West will score tricks with the ace and jack of diamonds. The ♣K will then be the setting trick. As you see, a wooden club return at Trick 2 would have allowed the contract to make. West would win with the club king but could not attack diamonds effectively from his side of the table.

The recommended defence might succeed also when declarer held ♦K–J–x. He would then have to guess which diamond honour to play. If he decided to rise with the ♦K, he would again lose four tricks in the minors and go one down.

HELP YOUR PARTNER

♠ ♥ ♦ ♣

An important part of planning a defence is to think how you can help your partner to do the right thing.

Right: Counting the defensive tricks. By counting the tricks available to the defence, East makes the right play on the second trick.

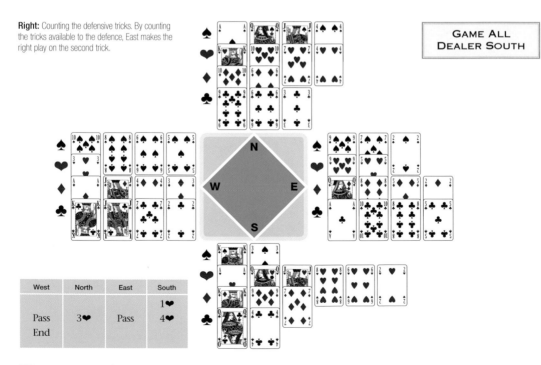

GAME ALL
DEALER SOUTH

West	North	East	South
			1♥
Pass	3♥	Pass	4♥
End			

On the next deal, counting defensive tricks allows East to judge that he should delay giving partner a ruff.

Right: Delaying a defensive ruff. West leads his singleton club against 4♠. By counting the defensive tricks, East calculates that it is not right to give partner a ruff at the second trick.

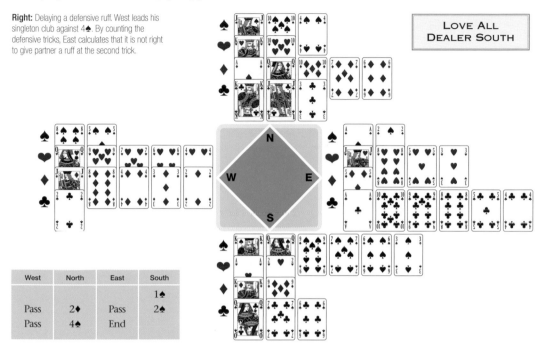

LOVE ALL
DEALER SOUTH

West	North	East	South
			1♠
Pass	2♦	Pass	2♠
Pass	4♠	End	

You hold the East cards. Your partner leads the ♣2 and you win with the ♣A. The odds are high that the opening lead is a singleton. Suppose you return a club immediately, however, giving partner a ruff. You must ask yourself how many tricks the defenders will score. Ace of clubs, a club ruff and the ace of trumps. That is three tricks. If partner started with three trumps, you will be able to give him a second club ruff but that is no certainty. As the cards lie, West will not be able to score a second club ruff and the game will be made.

Instead of returning a club without thought, you should pause to make a plan for the defence. You know that you can give partner the lead with a club ruff. Since you hold the ace of trumps, there is no need to deliver the ruff immediately. To ensure that you score a ruff too, you must switch to your singleton diamond at Trick 2. Declarer wins the trick in the dummy and leads a trump. You rise with the ace of trumps and only now give your partner a club ruff. He returns a diamond, allowing you to ruff, and the game goes one down.

GRANDMASTER
♠ ♥ ♦ ♣

Rixi Markus (1910–92) was the first woman to become a Grandmaster under the World Bridge Federation ranking scheme. Rixi was a tigress at the table but very charming once the game was over. Her most famous partnership was with Fritzi Gordon (1916–92). Together they won two World Pairs Olympiads, a World Teams Olympiad, and eight European championships.

Above: Rixi Markus

Above: Fritzi Gordon

Counting tricks for the declarer

On many deals you can reach the right decision in defence by counting the tricks that are available for declarer. Take the East cards on the deal below.

West leads the ◆Q, which marks declarer with the ◆K. If he holds six solid trumps, he will make the game easily because there is no way that you can

score three quick heart tricks, however the cards lie. You must therefore assume that West holds a trump trick.

Suppose you return the ◆7 at Trick 2, aiming to knock out South's ◆K and establish a diamond trick for the defence. It is quite likely then that declarer will score five trump tricks, four clubs and the ◆K.

Right: Diagnosing a switch by counting declarer's tricks. West leads the ◆Q against the spade game. By counting the number of tricks available to declarer, East sees the need to switch to hearts.

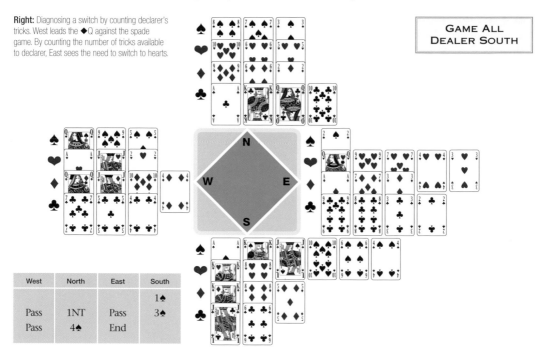

GAME ALL
DEALER SOUTH

West	North	East	South
			1♠
Pass	1NT	Pass	3♠
Pass	4♠	End	

With discards threatened on dummy's clubs, you should switch to the ♥4 at Trick 2, claiming whatever tricks may be available there. As the cards lie, your partner will score two heart tricks and his eventual trump trick will put the game one down.

As you see, a diamond return would have allowed the game to make. Declarer would win with the ◆K, draw two rounds of trumps and turn to the club suit. The diamond loser would be thrown on the third club and one of the heart losers on the fourth club. It would make no difference whether or not West chose to ruff this trick with the ♠Q. Declarer would lose only one trump, one diamond and one heart.

When you can see that declarer has quick discards available, you must switch immediately to the side suit where you may have some quick winners to take.

Here is another deal where you can benefit from counting declarer's tricks. Again you are in the East seat.

West leads the ♣J and declarer plays low from dummy. You must now decide whether to play your ♣A. It may seem attractive to play low, in order to avoid giving declarer two club tricks when he began with ♣Q–x–x. Before doing so, you should check how many tricks declarer will have after such a start to the defence. He will almost certainly have six trump tricks. To this you must add two diamond tricks, once the ♦A is dislodged, one club trick with the queen and one heart trick. That is a total of ten, so you can expect the contract to succeed if you play low at Trick 1.

To beat the contract you need to score the minor-suit aces and two heart tricks. To allow this to happen, you must rise with the ♣A at Trick 1 and then switch

to the ♥J, knocking out one of the dummy's heart stoppers. Declarer has no way to counter such a lively defence. No doubt he will draw trumps and play a diamond towards the dummy. Your partner will rise with the ♦A and play a second round of hearts, giving you two tricks in the suit. The game then goes one down.

You might achieve the same result by counting the possible tricks for the defence. Since there is only one likely trick in the black suits (the ♣A), you will need the ♦A and two heart tricks to beat the contract.

If you watched such a defence in a major championship, you might gasp in amazement. As you see, you can calculate quite logically that it is the only real chance to beat the contract. You must attack the heart suit before the ♦A is removed.

Right: Visualizing the defensive tricks. West leads the ♣J against the spade game and East must count declarer's tricks to diagnose the winning defence.

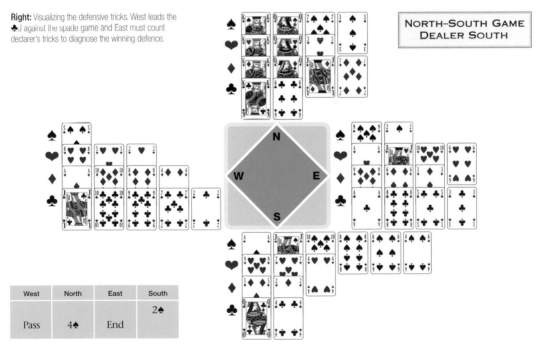

NORTH–SOUTH GAME
DEALER SOUTH

West	North	East	South
			2♠
Pass	4♠	End	

PLANNING THE DEFENCE IN NO-TRUMPS

Defending at no-trumps tends to be easier than in a suit contract. With the elements of ruffing and trump control not present, you can concentrate on communications and on setting up the tricks that you need to beat the contract. When you are sitting over the dummy, the most important decision is often whether to continue partner's suit or to switch elsewhere. By counting declarer's potential tricks, you may find a clear indication of the best chance.

Counting tricks for the declarer

Take the East cards on this deal and see if you would have come to the right 'continue or switch?' decision.

West leads the ♥5 against 3NT and your jack is won by South's ace. Declarer leads the ♣Q at Trick 2, West following with the ♣7. You win with the king and pause for a moment to decide what to do next. Is it possible that your partner led from ♥K–Q–x–x–x and that the heart suit is now ready to run? No, because if declarer had started with ♥A–x–x, he would have held up the ace

for two rounds to exhaust you of your holding in the suit. So, declarer began with ♥A–K–x. (He should have won the first trick with the ♥K, to make this less obvious to you, but not all declarers know that.)

It may seem natural to knock out declarer's last heart stopper, nevertheless. Before doing this, you should count the tricks that would then be at declarer's disposal. He would have three club tricks, two hearts and almost certainly four diamond tricks. That is a total of nine. So, you cannot afford to continue with partner's suit. You must hope to score four quick tricks elsewhere and this can be achieved only in the spade suit. Switch to the ♠Q in the hope that partner holds ♠A–10–x–x. When the cards lie as in the diagram you will beat the contract.

Defenders who follow simple rules such as 'Always return partner's suit' would allow this contract to be made. Good bridge is rarely a question of following this or that rule. In defence, you must think clearly whether a particular defence has a chance of beating the contract.

Right: Counting declarer's tricks. By counting the tricks available to declarer, East diagnoses the right switch when he gains the lead.

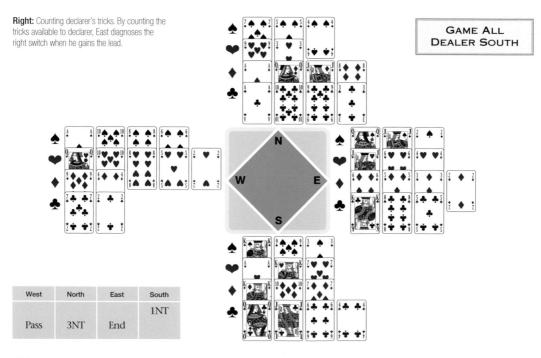

GAME ALL
DEALER SOUTH

West	North	East	South
			1NT
Pass	3NT	End	

Above: When the ♥J is won with the ♥A, the defender places declarer with ♥A–K.

Reading the opening lead

A clever gadget known as 'The Rule of Eleven' will often assist you in reading the lie of the suit that partner has chosen to lead. When partner has made a fourth-best lead from a suit headed by an honour, you subtract the spot-card that he has led from 11. The answer will give you the number of higher cards that are held by the other three hands. Suppose partner has led the ♥6 and the heart suit lies as shown below.

You are sitting East and your ♥Q is won by declarer's ♥K. By applying the Rule of Eleven, you can tell that the North, East and South hands contain

between them five cards higher than the ♥6. (You subtract 6 from 11, getting 5 as the answer.) You can see four of these cards in your own hand and the dummy (the queen, ten nine and seven of the suit). So the ♥K is the only high card that declarer holds in the suit. The defenders' hearts are ready to run. Such knowledge might enable you to rise immediately with an ace in a different suit, switching back to hearts.

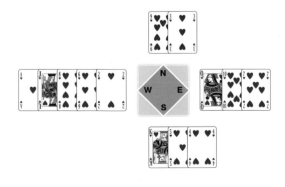

Above: Rule of Eleven.By applying the Rule of Eleven to West's opening lead of the ♥6, East can determine the lie of the heart suit.

COMPUTER CHAMPIONSHIP
♠ ♥ ♦ ♣

The world championship for bridge computer programs has been held annually since 1997. Computers running the rival programs are linked together and they play bridge matches in the same way that human players would, bidding the hands and then playing the resultant contracts.

The Dutch program 'Jack' has won the championship five times. GIB (USA) has won it twice and three programs have won it on one occasion: Bridge Baron (USA), Meadowlark (USA) and Wbridge5 (France). It is a strong selling point for a bridge computer program if its producers can claim that it has defeated all the rival products in the latest world championship.

Let's see a complete deal featuring that heart suit. Take the East cards and plan your defence to this 3NT contract:

Right: Rule of Eleven. West leads the ♥6 to East's ♥Q and South's ♥K. East applies the Rule of Eleven to determine his future defence.

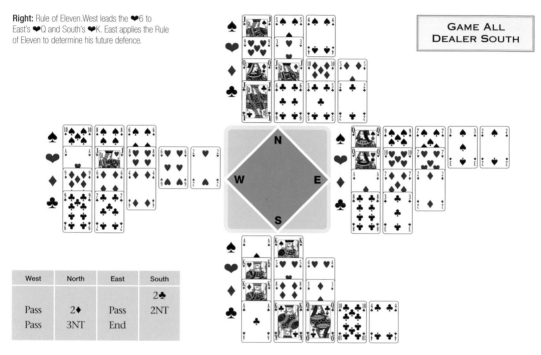

GAME ALL
DEALER SOUTH

West	North	East	South
			2♣
Pass	2♦	Pass	2NT
Pass	3NT	End	

West leads the ♥6 against South's 3NT contract and declarer wins your queen with the king. At Trick 2 he leads the ◆K and you must think carefully how to defend. If you consider the diamond suit in isolation, you might well decide to hold up the ◆A for a round or two, hoping to prevent declarer from enjoying dummy's diamond winners. Such a plan will not work well here, though. If declarer is allowed to make even one diamond trick, he will unveil seven more tricks in the black suits and make his contract.

To beat 3NT, you must win the very first diamond trick and return a heart. How can you be sure that this is the right thing to do? The Rule of Eleven tells you that declarer has no stopper remaining in hearts. There is also a good chance that your partner began with a five-card heart suit because he led the ♥6 and the five, four and two of the suit are missing. Unless declarer began with specifically ♥K-5-4-2, your partner started with at least five hearts and a heart switch will be successful. So, do not follow some

> ### ROUNDED AND POINTED
> ♠ ♥ ♦ ♣
>
> Clubs and spades are known as the 'black suits'; clubs and diamonds are known as the 'minor suits'. What could clubs and hearts be called? Since both symbols are rounded at the top, they became known as the 'rounded suits'. Similarly, diamonds and spades are known as the 'pointed suits'.

general rule about 'holding up an ace to kill the dummy'. Take the ◆A immediately and return the ♥10. Your partner will score four tricks in the suit to defeat the contract.

Sometimes the Rule of Eleven will tell you that partner's lead cannot be a fourth-best card, so he has led his second-best card from a weak suit. In that case it will usually pay you to abandon the suit that has been led and to seek tricks from elsewhere. A high-card lead is a warning that tricks are unavailable from that source.

Right: Diagnosing that the lead is from a weak suit. East calculates that the ♠7 lead must be from a weak suit and defends accordingly, switching to hearts.

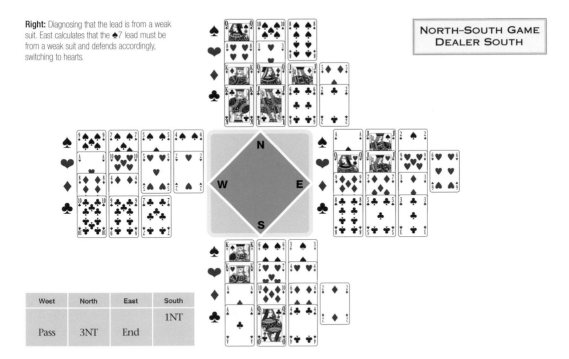

West	North	East	South
			1NT
Pass	3NT	End	

South opens a 15–17 point 1NT and is raised to game. West leads the ♠7 against this contract and the ♠10 is played from dummy. Sitting East, you must decide how to defend. Your first task is to read the lie of the spade suit. If West's spades are headed by the king, you will want to win the first trick with the ♠J and to continue with ace and another spade. You will then score at least four spade tricks, giving the defence a very good start.

Suppose you take the trouble to apply the Rule of Eleven before embarking on this line of defence. If the ♠7 is indeed a fourth-best card, the North, East and South hands will contain four cards in spades that are higher than the seven. In your own hand and the dummy, you can already see five such cards. You can therefore conclude that the ♠7 is not a fourth-best card at all. It must instead be a second-best card from weakness. West will hold either ♠9–7–x or ♠9–7–x–x.

Since there is no prospect for the defence in the spade suit, you should rise with the ♠A at Trick 1. The only chance of scoring several tricks for the defence now lies in the heart suit and you therefore switch to the ♥Q. When the cards lie as in the diagram, this smart defence will be rewarded. You and your partner will score four

heart tricks, putting the 3NT contract one down. If instead you were to play the ♠J on the first trick, declarer would win with the ♠K and quickly add four more tricks in each minor suit to make the contract.

Above: East can see five cards higher than the ♠7. He therefore knows that the lead cannot be fourth-best from strength.

Choosing between Active and Passive Defence

There are many positions where it will cost the defenders to make the first play in a suit. Suppose that, as declarer, you hold ♦J–8–3 in the dummy and ♦Q–6–5 in your hand. If you have to play the suit yourself, and the defenders hold one top honour each, you will probably make no trick at all from the suit. If instead the defenders make the first play in the suit, the defender in the third seat will have to rise with the ace or king. You will then be certain to score a trick with the queen or jack.

When to defend passively

The defenders often have to make an important decision. Do they need to play actively, attacking a new suit to score tricks there? Or will they perhaps do better to play passively, leaving declarer to play the new suit himself? To answer this question, the defenders must try to determine whether declarer, left to his own devices, will be able to discard his potential losers in the key suit. Look at this deal:

Sitting West, and defending the game in hearts, you lead the ♠Q, which declarer wins with the ♠K. He then leads a trump and you rise with the ♥A. The sort of defender who is always 'trying another suit' might well switch to diamonds now. The effect is all too predictable. East would have to rise with the ♦A and declarer would then score a diamond trick, making the contract.

There is no need to play an active defence in this way because it is most unlikely that dummy's club suit can provide a discard of a diamond from the South hand. If declarer held three small diamonds and ♣A–Q doubleton, he would have taken a discard before playing trumps. Nor it is likely that he holds specifically ♣A–Q–J and can take a discard on the fourth round of clubs.

So, as West you do best to exit passively with a spade or a trump. Declarer will eventually have to play the diamond suit himself. He will lose three diamond tricks and go one down.

Right: A passive defence. If West defends too actively here, attacking the diamond suit, he will give away the contract.

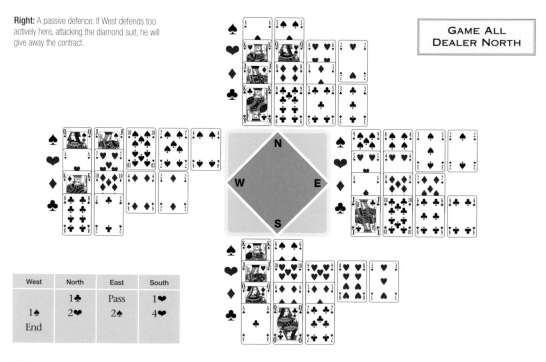

GAME ALL
DEALER NORTH

West	North	East	South
	1♣	Pass	1♥
1♠	2♥	2♠	4♥
End			

When to defend actively

To show the other side of the coin, here is a deal where the defenders do have to play actively. If they fail to do so, declarer will discard his potential losers.

West leads the ◆Q and, sitting East, you win with the ◆A. It is easy to predict what will happen if you exit passively with a trump or another diamond. Declarer will draw trumps and set up dummy's club suit, on which he can discard one or more heart losers.

You need to defend actively, attempting to set up some heart tricks before declarer can take discards on dummy's club suit. So, at Trick 2 you switch to the ♥4, South following with the ♥3. West plays the ♥10 and declarer is doomed to defeat, whether he wins the first or second round of hearts. When he eventually plays on clubs, you will win with the ♣A and cash a total of two hearts, one club and one diamond to beat the contract.

Right: An active defence. East must defend actively on this deal, attacking the heart suit to set up the defenders' winners in good time.

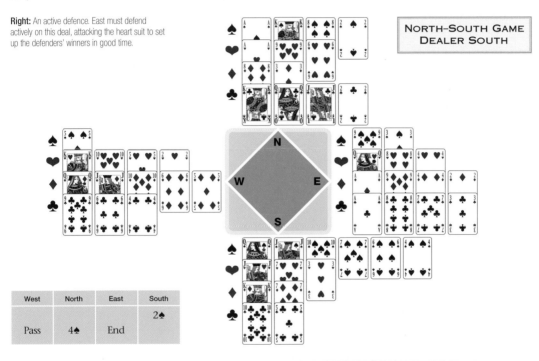

NORTH–SOUTH GAME
DEALER SOUTH

West	North	East	South
			2♠
Pass	4♠	End	

Right: Germany's Daniela von Arnim. In partnership with Sabine Auken-Zenkel, she won the women's world championship in 1995 and 2001.

WHEN TO COVER AN HONOUR WITH AN HONOUR

The advice sometimes given to beginners is 'always cover an honour with an honour'. In other words, if declarer plays an honour from one hand or the other the defender in second seat should cover with a higher honour. There are few hard-and-fast rules in bridge and, indeed, there are many exceptions to this one. Covering will often be a mistake.

Cover to promote a trick

Let us see first how a cover can prove effective. Look at this club position:

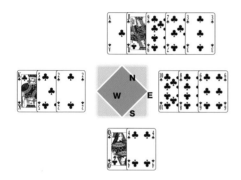

Declarer leads the ♣Q from his hand. If West fails to cover with the king, the queen will be run successfully. Declarer will finesse the ♣J on the next round and end with five club tricks. West should instead 'cover an honour with an honour', playing his ♣K on the ♣Q. Dummy wins with the ♣A but East's ♣10 will now score a trick on the third round. The purpose of covering is clearly illustrated. You cover with the intention of promoting a lesser card, either in your own hand or in partner's.

The situation would be the same, of course, if the ♣Q and the ♣J were swapped. When South led the ♣J, West would cover in the hope of promoting the ♣10 with East. If South happened to hold ♣J–10 or ♣J–10–4, nothing would be lost. All five club tricks would be his, whatever the defence.

Suppose next that the ♣Q–4 were in the dummy, with declarer's club holding hidden from view. It would again be the correct defence to cover the ♣Q with the ♣K.

Do not cover when no promotion is possible

When there is no such prospect of promoting a trick, you should not cover. Suppose declarer is playing in 4♠ or 6♠ with this trump suit:

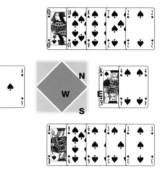

When the ♠Q is led from dummy East should not cover, because there is virtually no chance of promoting a trick by doing so. You can see what would happen if he did cover. West's ♠A would complete a heavily laden first round and declarer would lose only one trump trick. It is also possible that the spade suit lies like this:

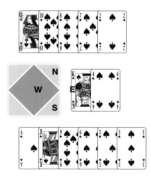

With only two cards missing, declarer has no intention of running the ♠Q. He has led it just in case you hold ♠K–4 in the East seat and are tempted to cover! Provided you follow smoothly with the ♠4, declarer will expect West to hold a singleton ♠K. He will rise with the ♠A and lose a trick in the suit when West shows out.

Do not cover the first of touching honours

When declarer leads one of touching honours, it is usually wrong to cover:

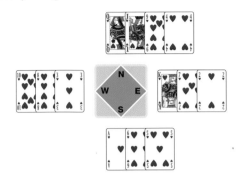

If East covers the ♥Q with the ♥K, declarer will win with the ace and subsequently finesse the ♥9 to score four heart tricks. East should not cover the first of touching honours. The queen is run successfully but declarer cannot then score more than three heart tricks. If he leads the ♥J on the second round, East will cover to promote his partner's ♥10.

It will also cost a trick to cover in this very common position:

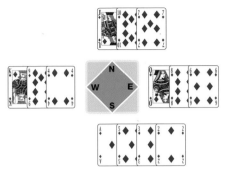

The ♦J is led from dummy. If East makes the mistake of covering with the ♦Q, declarer will win with the ace and lead back towards the ♦10. He will score three diamond tricks instead of the two that were his due. Again, East should not cover the first of touching honours. The ♦J is run to West's ♦K and declarer must now lose a second trick in the suit, however he continues.

JAMES BOND'S SLAM ON 6 POINTS
♠ ♥ ♦ ♣

Perhaps the most famous bridge hand in literature is a version of the Duke of Cumberland's hand, which was used by card cheats for decades. In Ian Fleming's novel, *Moonraker*, James Bond rigs the deck to give villain, Hugo Drax, the East hand shown below:

```
              ♠ 10 9 8 7
              ♥ 6 5 4 3
              ♦ —
              ♣ 7 6 5 3 2
♠ 6 5 4 3 2         N          ♠ A K Q J
♥ 10 9 8 7 2    W       E      ♥ A K Q J
♦ J 10 9            S          ♦ A K
♣ —                            ♣ K J 9
              ♠ —
              ♥ —
              ♦ Q 8 7 6 5 4 3 2
              ♣ A Q 10 8 4
```

Bond, who holds the South hand, is pretending to be drunk. He bids a grand slam in clubs. Drax doubles, scornfully, and Bond redoubles. A large side bet is agreed in addition and the grand slam cannot be defeated! Declarer can establish the diamond suit and pick up East's ♣K–J–9 with two finesses.

Above: With 31 points in his hand, East cannot believe that 7♣ will be made against him.

KEEPING THE RIGHT CARDS

One of the most important aspects of good defence is the ability to keep the right cards when you are forced to make some discards. One good guideline is that you should 'match your length' with any length visible in the dummy. For example, if dummy contains ♠K–Q–8–2, you should not discard a spade from a holding such as ♠J–10–6–3. If declarer has the ♠A, your holding is necessary to guard the fourth round. Even if your partner holds the ♠A, you may still need all your spades to restrict declarer to the minimum number of tricks from the suit.

Matching the dummy's length

Let us see an example of 'matching dummy's length' in the context of the complete deal shown below.

You are sitting East and your partner leads the ♥Q. Declarer allows this card to win, hoping to tighten the end position and cause discarding problems for the defenders later. He wins the next round of hearts with the ♥K and cashes four rounds of clubs, followed by dummy's ♥A. You must now find a discard from ♠10–9–6–2 ♦Q–10–7.

Dummy has four-card spade length and you must retain your four spades, matching dummy's length, to avoid giving a trick away when declarer holds the king and queen of the suit. You may be surprised to hear that your ♦Q–10–7 are virtually worthless. If declarer holds the ♦A–K–J sitting over them, he can finesse in the suit anyway. Otherwise your partner will hold the ♦J and can guard the diamond suit himself. So, throw a diamond and retain your important spade guard. The slam will then go down.

COUNT SIGNALS
♠ ♥ ♦ ♣

One of the important reasons for giving count signals (a high signal to show an even number of cards, a low signal to show an odd number) is to help your partner to decide which cards to retain. If your count signal implies that declarer holds three spades rather than four, for example, partner will not need to keep four spades.

Right: Matching the length in dummy. There are four spades in dummy and East should therefore retain all four spades.

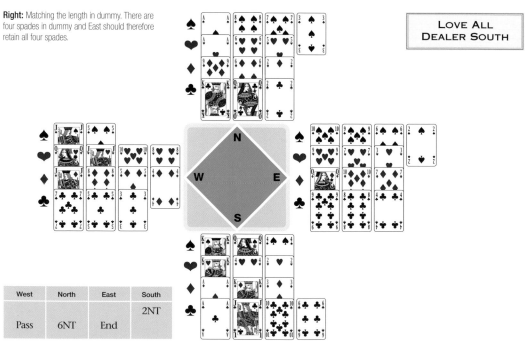

LOVE ALL
DEALER SOUTH

West	North	East	South
			2NT
Pass	6NT	End	

Making deductions from declarer's play

It is often possible to deduce declarer's length in a suit from the way that he has chosen to play the hand. Take the West cards on the deal shown below.

Sitting West, you lead the ♥Q against the spade slam. When this card wins the first trick, you play another heart, South ruffing. Declarer draws two rounds of trumps with the queen and jack. When you show out, throwing a diamond, he continues with three more rounds of trumps. You can safely throw all your hearts. On the last trump you must make one more discard from ♦Q–J–8 and ♣10–9–7–3. If declarer holds ♦A–K–10, you must keep your diamonds. If instead he holds ♣A–K–Q–x, you must keep your clubs. What would your decision be? If declarer did hold ♦A–K–10, he would have ruffed his diamond loser in dummy before drawing three rounds of trumps. So, you should throw a diamond and keep your potential guard in clubs. Declarer will then have no way to avoid a club loser and the slam will go down.

Right: Making a deduction from declarer's play. When declarer draws trumps without first taking a diamond ruff, West can deduce that South holds only two diamonds.

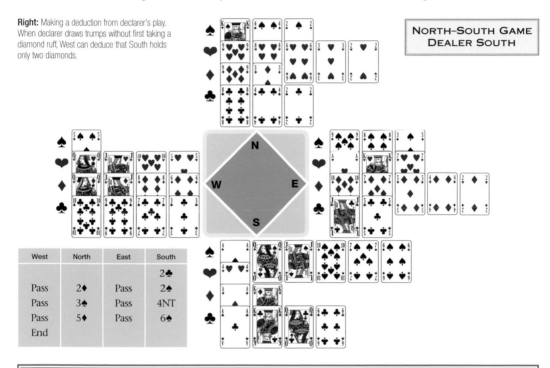

NORTH–SOUTH GAME
DEALER SOUTH

West	North	East	South
			2♣
Pass	2♦	Pass	2♠
Pass	3♠	Pass	4NT
Pass	5♦	Pass	6♠
End			

BRIDGE BOOK COLLECTORS
♠ ♥ ♦ ♣

Since the year 1900 about 8,000 books and pamphlets in the English language have been published on bridge. The most prolific decade was the 1930s, with around 1,400 publications. The world's three biggest bridge-book collections in private hands are owned by Tim Bourke of Canberra, Australia, by Wolf Klewe of Winchester, England and by Gerard Hilte, of Leerdam in the Netherlands.

Right: Tim Bourke of Canberra, Australian bridge expert and owner of one of the world's largest collections of bridge books.

ADVANCED BIDDING

This section looks at some of the most popular bidding conventions from the tournament bridge world. First you will see the Cappelletti defence to 1NT, one of several conventions that allow you to contest the bidding after the opponents have opened 1NT. Next there is a discussion on how you can use bids in the opponents' suit to indicate strong hands in various situations. An important aid to bidding slams is Roman Key-card Blackwood, where you can ask not only about aces but also about the king and queen of trumps. Puppet Stayman allows you to detect a five-card major in the hand of the 2NT (two no-trumps) opener. Splinter bids tell your partner where you hold a shortage, thereby allowing him to judge if the two hands will fit together well. The chapter ends with a discussion of lead-directing doubles, where you double an artificial bid made by an opponent to tell your partner what opening lead you would like against the eventual contract.

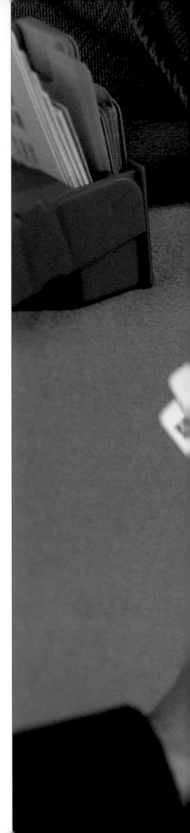

Right: Employing the Cappelletti convention, the player has bid 2♣ to show a long suit somewhere. Partner's 2♦ asks the overcaller to specify which suit it is.

CAPPELLETTI DEFENCE TO 1NT

The scoring table does not reward you very well when you defeat an opposing 1NT contract, particularly when the opponents are non-vulnerable. Whenever you take +50 or +100, defending 1NT, you will usually find that you could have scored at least +110 somewhere, playing the contract yourself. Apart from that, 1NT is a very difficult contract to defend. Declarer will often emerge with seven tricks when, with optimal defence, you could have set the contract. For these reasons, players are keen to contest the bidding when they hear an opposing 1NT bid. There are several conventions available and one of the most popular is the Cappelletti Defence.

Above: The Cappelletti Defence was invented by Michael Cappelletti, who is an expert at both bridge and poker.

The Cappelletti Defence
Both in the second and the fourth seats, these are the possible actions when playing Cappelletti:

Double	a penalty double
2♣	a single-suiter in an undisclosed suit (6–card suit)
2♦	both major suits (at least 5–4)
2♥	hearts and a minor suit (can be 4–5 or 5–4)
2♠	spades and a minor suit (can be 4–5 or 5–4)
2NT	both minor suits (at least 5–5).

Partner shows a single-suiter
When partner bids 2♣, you can pass if you hold six clubs or more, bid 2♦ to ask him to indicate his long suit, or respond in a major with a long holding there. This is a typical sequence:

PART SCORE BONUS
♠ ♥ ♦ ♣

A part score is awarded a 50 bonus at duplicate, so you score +140 (90 + 50) for making a contract of 3♠. On the last deal of a Chicago chukker (a session of four deals), a bonus of 100 is awarded. However, these are not particularly generous assessments. It has been calculated that at rubber bridge a part score is worth 150 at Game all, and 100 at all other scores.

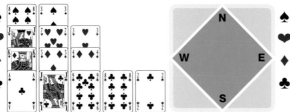

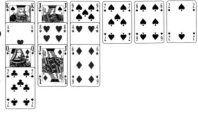

West's clubs are not long and strong enough to pass 2♣, particularly as he holds at least two-card support for whichever suit East may hold. As you can see, there is only a 5–1 fit in clubs, which will make nowhere near such a good trump suit as the 6–2 fit that exists in the spade suit.

To request partner's suit, West responds 2♦. East would pass this with long diamonds, but here he rebids 2♠ and this becomes the final contract.

West	North	East	South
	1NT	2♣	Pass
2♦	Pass	2♠	End

Partner shows both majors or both minors

When partner bids 2♦, showing both majors, you can pass with six diamonds and choose one of the major suits otherwise:

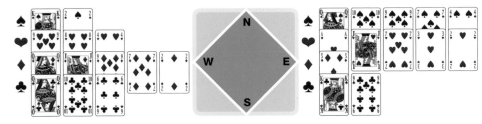

Sitting West, you give preference to hearts. This might sometimes be a 4–3 fit, yes, but that will not be your fault. You cannot always guarantee an 8-card fit somewhere.

Similarly, unless you hold a particularly strong hand, you will merely choose your better minor when partner overcalls 2NT.

West	North	East	South
	1NT	2♦	Pass
2♥	End		

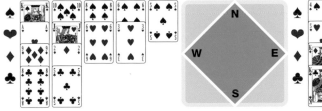

With two doubletons in the minors, there is some chance that you may be doubled. Bid 3♣ first, hoping that you escape a double. If you are doubled in 3♣, you will have to guess whether to try your luck in 3♦ instead.

West	North	East	South
	1NT	2NT	Pass
3♣	End		

Partner bids 2♥ or 2♠

When your partner bids 2♥ or 2♠, showing a major–minor two-suiter, you will often pass. If you wish to discover his minor suit, you respond 2NT:

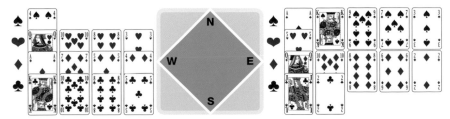

With a certain fit in one of the minors, West responds 2NT to ask East whether he holds diamonds or clubs as his second suit. East rebids 3♦, showing a two-suiter in spades and diamonds, and this bid ends the auction.

West	North	East	South
	1NT	2♠	Pass
2NT	Pass	3♦	End

CUE-BID RAISES

Less experienced players hardly ever make a bid in a suit that has already been bid by the opponents. Since there are only five denominations available (the four suits and no-trumps), this is a big opportunity wasted. Serious bridge players hate to waste any possible call and make very good use of a cue-bid in the opponents' suit. Such a bid will nearly always show a strong hand. When your partner has already bid a suit, a cue-bid shows a strong raise of that suit.

Cue-bid raise of an overcall

When partner has overcalled, as we saw earlier, any direct raise from you is pre-emptive. With a sound raise instead, you cue-bid the opener's suit. Let's see some typical sequences:

Above: With a sound raise of partner's 1♠ overcall, East cue-bids in the opponents' suit.

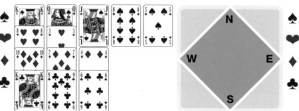

With 12 points and three-card spade support, East is interested in bidding a spade game. He shows his sound high-card raise with a cue-bid of 2♦. West has a minimum overcall and signs off in 2♠. East decides to bid no further, which is just as well because declarer could easily lose five tricks.

When the overcall was made in a minor suit, the purpose of a cue-bid raise will normally be to investigate a possible 3NT contract:

West	North	East	South
			1♦
1♠	Pass	2♦	Pass
2♠	End		

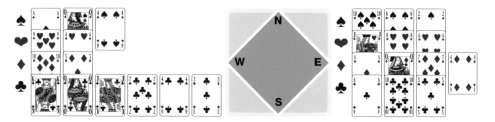

East makes a cue-bid in hearts, the opponents' suit, to show his sound raise in clubs. He hopes that West can rebid 2NT with a heart stopper. West has no reason to be ashamed of his overcall and shows his values in spades.

On some deals this would be enough for East to bid 3NT when he held a heart stopper himself. On this occasion neither player can stop the hearts and there is insufficient playing strength for a minor-suit game. Wisely, they stop in 3♣.

West	North	East	South
			1♥
2♣	Pass	2♥	Pass
2♠	Pass	3♣	End

Cue-bid raise of an opening bid

When your partner's one-bid has been overcalled, you have the opportunity to make use of a cue-bid response. Suppose the bidding has started like this:

West	North	East	South
1♠	2♦	?	

A raise to 2♠ would show three-card support and around 5–9 points. A raise to 3♠ would be pre-emptive, showing 4-card support and around 4–8 points. With a stronger hand including spade support, you would cue-bid 3♦. Suppose you held one of these hands as East:

1

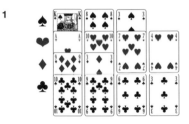

With hand (1) you would raise to 2♠.

2

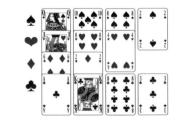

On (2) you would raise pre-emptively to 3♠, shutting out a possible heart fit for the opponents.

3

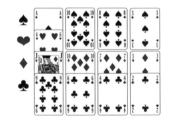

Hand (3) represents a genuine game-try hand in spades, with the values in high-card points. You would therefore cue-bid 3♦. Partner would then sign off in 3♠ when he held a minimum hand and would have passed the normal, uninterrupted sequence of 1♠ – 3♠.

A similar scheme is used when partner has opened 1♣ or 1♦. Suppose partner's 1♦ is overcalled with 1♥ and you hold one of these hands in the third seat:

1

You would raise to 2♦ on (1).

2

With hand (2) you would raise pre-emptively to 3♦, which might well shut out an opposing spade contract.

3

On (3) you cue-bid 2♥, showing a sound raise in diamonds with game ambitions.

ROTH-STONE BIDDING
♠ ♥ ♦ ♣

The Unusual No-trump convention, where 2NT shows a two-suited hand in the lowest unbid suits, was invented by the American Alvin Roth in the 1940s. It was subsequently developed by his partner for many years, Tobias Stone. In the Roth-Stone bidding system, strong opening bids were advocated in the first and second positions. Roth and Stone would often pass 12-point hands.

ROMAN KEY-CARD BLACKWOOD

I n the original version of Blackwood, the responses stated only how many aces were held. When you are aiming for a slam in a suit, the king or queen of trumps can be just as important as an ace. A new version, known as Roman Key-card Blackwood, includes these two cards in the responses. It swept the tournament bridge world like wildfire and the time has come to take a look at it.

5♣	0 or 3 key cards
5♦	1 or 4 key cards
5♥	2 or 5 key cards and no queen of trumps
5♠	2 or 5 key cards and the queen of trumps.

Asking for key cards

When a trump suit has been agreed, either player may bid 4NT (Roman Key-card Blackwood, hereafter shortened to RKCB) to ask how many key cards partner holds. There are five key cards: the four aces and the king of trumps. The table shows the responses.

There is rarely any ambiguity as to whether 0 or 3 key cards are held (or 1 or 4). If the 4NT bidder is uncertain, he may sign off in the expectation that partner will bid again when he holds the more generous allocation. Here is a typical RKCB sequence:

West	East
1♥	1♠
2♣	4NT
5♠	6♠

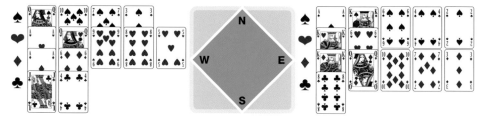

West's 5♠ response shows two key cards (two aces here) and the ♠Q. East is then prepared to bid a small slam.

Let's change West's hand, to give him a 5♣ response:

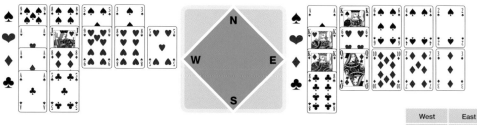

West	East
1♥	1♠
2♣	4NT
5♣	5♠
6♠	

EXCLUSION BLACKWOOD
♠ ♥ ♦ ♣

Exclusion Blackwood is a convention that allows you to ask for key cards even when you have a void in your hand. Instead of using 4NT as the enquiry bid, you jump to the five-level in the suit where you hold the void. In the auction 1♠ – 3♠ – 5♦, for example, the opener would be asking for key cards excluding the ♦A (a card of little value opposite a void).

When East hears the '0 or 3' response, it is possible if unlikely that West has no key cards. Playing safe, East signs off in 5♠. Since West holds three key cards rather than none, he advances to a slam anyway.

Asking for side-suit kings with 5NT

When you bid 4NT and hear how many key cards partner holds, you can continue with 5NT to ask how many side-suit kings he has. You should do this only when all the key cards are present, otherwise there is no chance of a grand slam anyway.

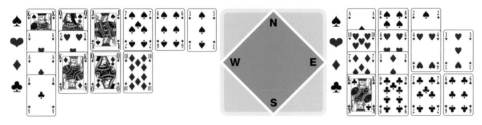

West bids 4NT and hears about the ace of trumps. He is willing to hope for the best in the diamond suit and therefore just needs to know whether a side-suit king is held. East admits to one king (5♣ = 0, 5♦ = 1, 5♥ = 2, 5♠ = 3) and the grand slam is bid.

West	East
2♣	2♦
2♠	3♠
4NT	5♦
5NT	6♦
7♠	

Asking for the trump queen

When your partner's RKCB response is 5♣ or 5♦, he has not told you whether he holds the queen of trumps. You can continue with the cheapest bid not in the trump suit to ask whether the trump queen is held. Responder will sign off without the trump queen. With the queen, he will cue-bid a side-suit king or bid 5NT.

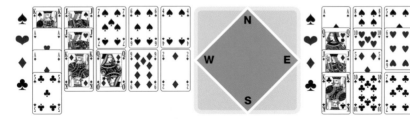

The 5♦ response tells West that an ace is missing. He is still willing to bid the slam, provided East holds the ♠Q. The sign-off in spades denies this card and West lets the bidding die at the five-level. Note that if East holds longer trumps than expected (five trumps rather than four in the present situation) he is entitled to pretend that he holds the trump queen. With ten spades between the two hands, there is a good chance that the defenders' ♠Q will fall on the first or second round. Even if a defender holds ♠Q–x–x, it may be possible to finesse the queen successfully.

West	East
1♠	3♠
4NT	5♦
5♥	5♠

LEAP TO SEVEN
♠ ♥ ♦ ♣

The 5NT bid, asking for side-suit kings, also confirms that all six key-cards are present. Responder is therefore entitled to jump to a grand slam when he has a source of tricks in his hand.

TWO-SUITED OVERCALLS

Hands that contain two five-card suits are inappropriate for a take-out double, since partner is all too likely to respond in the short suit. It is therefore advisable to reserve certain bids to show specifically a two-suited hand. The most popular of these is the Unusual No-trump – a jump overcall of 2NT that shows the lowest two unbid suits. Almost as widely played is the Michaels cue-bid, which shows a two-suiter including any unbid major suit(s).

The Unusual No-trump

When an opponent has opened with one of a suit, a 2NT overcall in the second seat shows a two-suiter in the lowest two unbid suits. Although the point-count does not have to be as high as for an opening bid, the playing strength should be fairly sound because your partner will have to play at the three-level. Here is a typical example of the bid:

Above: With five cards in each minor suit, the player uses the Unusual No-trump convention.

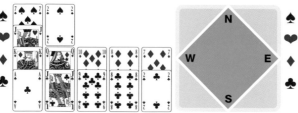 

Although East has 10 points, he realizes that he is a long way from being able to suggest a game contract. He signs off at the three-level in his longer minor suit.

When the 2NT bidder has a very strong hand, he may indicate this by bidding again:

West	North	East	South
			1♠
2NT	Pass	3♣	End

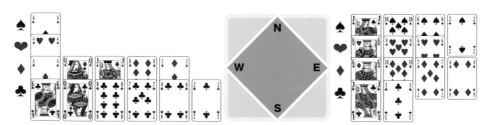

West raises to 4♦, announcing that he is very strong for a 2NT overcall. Although precision is not possible in such situations, East judges that his four-card trump support to the king entitles him to raise to game. This judgement proves sound and the game will probably be made unless the opponents score an immediate club ruff.

In the fourth seat (in an auction such as 1♠ – Pass – Pass – 2NT) the 2NT is normally played as natural, showing around 18–20 points.

West	North	East	South
			1♥
2NT	Pass	3♦	Pass
4♦	Pass	5♦	End

Michaels cue-bids

When an opponent has opened 1♣ or 1♦, a Michaels cue-bid in the same suit (2♣ or 2♦, respectively) shows both major suits. Over an opening of 1♥ or 1♠ a cue-bid in the same suit shows a two-suiter containing the other major and one of the minor suits. Here are some typical sequences:

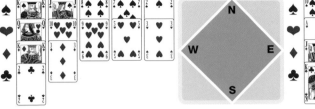 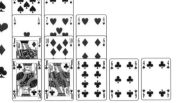

West	North	East	South
			1♦
2♦	Pass	2♥	End

A Michaels cue-bid does not require as much playing strength as an Unusual No-trump bid, because the contract will usually be played one level lower, at the two-level. Here East responds at the minimum level in his better major. If West held 15 points or so, he might suggest a game by raising to 3♥.

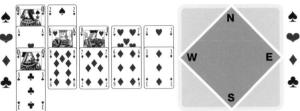 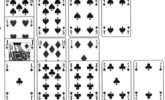

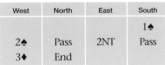

West	North	East	South
			1♠
2♠	Pass	2NT	Pass
3♦	End		

Opposite a major-suit Michael's bid, you may ask for a second suit by bidding 2NT. Here West shows diamonds and East is happy to pass out 3♦.

CONVENTION FORGOTTEN
♠ ♥ ♦ ♣

Even the top experts sometimes forget their conventions. At the 1957 European Championships, Terence Reese and Boris Schapiro were playing that a 4♥ response to 1NT was a transfer bid, showing spades. What is more, they had also agreed that anyone who forgot the method would have to pay a fine of 100 Austrian schillings. On one deal Schapiro did forget the convention, responding 4♥ on a hand with six hearts. When Reese rebid 4♠, Schapiro was nervous of bidding 5♥ in case this was taken as a slam try with spades agreed. Hoping to enlighten his partner, he bid 6♥. This was passed out and the contract was made when the Icelandic opponents failed to cash two aces. 'Don't play the convention any more!' pleaded the rest of the British team. 'No, no, we'll just increase the fine to 200 schillings,' replied Reese.

MICHAELS CUE-BID
♠ ♥ ♦ ♣

In most situations you show a strong hand when you cue-bid the opponents' suit. The Michaels cue-bid is an exception to this general rule and your hand may be quite modest.

PUPPET STAYMAN

When you have a hand with 5–3–3–2 shape and 20–22 points, the only sensible opening bid is 2NT, even when the five-card suit is a major. In order to locate an eight-card fit when responder holds three cards in the suit, many tournament players use a modified form of Stayman opposite 2NT (and 2♣ – 2♦ – 2NT). It is known as Puppet Stayman and asks initially for a five-card major.

Bidding 3♣ to ask for a five-card major

The rebids by the opener after a start of 2NT – 3♣ are:

3♦	'I have at least one 4-card major but no 5-card major.'
3♥	'I have five hearts.'
3♠	'I have five spades.'
3NT	'I have no 4-card or 5-card major.'

Here are some typical sequences:

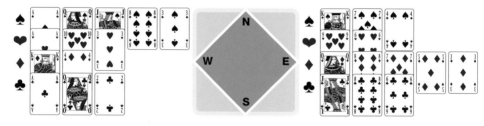

The 5–3 spade fit is discovered and 4♠ proves a better prospect than 3NT, which might fail on a heart lead. If West had bid 3♦ instead, showing at least one four-card major, East would have signed off in 3NT.

West	East
2NT	3♣
3♠	4♠

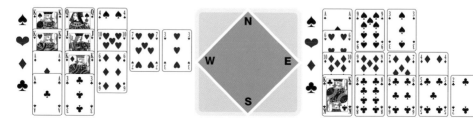

East would be happy to play in a 5–3 spade fit, in case the hearts are underprotected. When West shows five hearts, this fear vanishes and East bids the game in no-trumps. If West had rebid 3NT, denying even a four-card major, East would again play in 3NT since an 11-trick game in a minor suit is unattractive. Opposite a 3♦ rebid, East would have to seek a 4–3 spade fit or take his chances in 3NT.

West	East
2NT	3♣
3♥	3NT

Locating a 4–4 fit

When the bidding has started 2NT – 3♣ – 3♦, there is still enough bidding space to locate any 4–4 fit that may be present. A slightly complicated mechanism is used to ensure that the 2NT opener becomes the declarer. These are the continuations by responder:

3♥	'I have a four-card spade suit.'
3♠	'I have a four-card heart suit.'
4♦	'I have four hearts and four spades.'

As you see, the responder bids three of the major suit that he does not hold. It may seem strange but the 'puppet mechanism', as it is called, works very well. Here are some typical sequences:

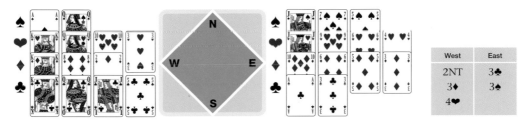

West	East
2NT	3♣
3♦	3♠
4♥	

When West rebids 3♦, saying that he holds at least one four-card major, East bids 3♠ to indicate a four-card heart suit. West duly bids the heart game and his ♦K is protected from the opening lead.

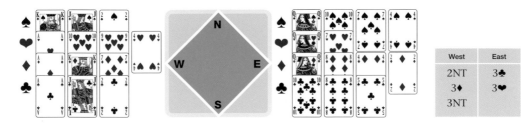

West	East
2NT	3♣
3♦	3♥
3NT	

East bids 3♥ to show a four-card spade suit. No 4–4 fit has come to light and West therefore bids 3NT, which ends the auction.

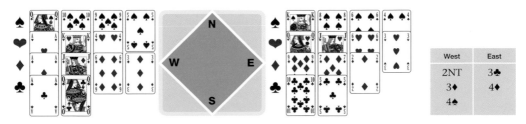

West	East
2NT	3♣
3♦	4♦
4♠	

East shows both four-card majors and West bids game in spades. The strong hand will be hidden from view.

SPLINTER BIDS

When two bridge hands fit well together, the trick-taking potential is greater than you might expect from the number of points held. One aspect of two hands fitting well is that little honour strength in one hand is wasted opposite a shortage. Suppose declarer holds ◆A–8–7–2 and the dummy holds ◆6. That represents an excellent fit. The ace will win the first round and the low cards can be ruffed. Suppose instead that declarer holds ◆K–Q–8–4 opposite a singleton. One point more in the suit, yes, but the fit is very poor. Not only will the first round now be lost, the king and queen may well be worth very little. They could have been ruffed anyway.

A 'splinter bid' shows where you hold a side-suit singleton (or void). Your partner will then be able to assess whether the two hands fit well together. If they do, a slam may be possible. This is the scheme of splinter-bid responses after partner has opened bidding with 1♠:

4♣	shows a sound game raise with at most one club
4♦	shows a sound game raise with at most one diamond
4♥	shows a sound game raise with at most one heart.

A typical splinter bid by responder suggests around 10–14 points. Suppose partner has opened 1♠ and you hold one of these hands:

Above: A splinter bid of 4♣ will allow the opener to judge how well the two hands fit. Your partner can then see if the two hands fit well together.

1

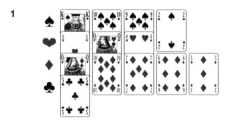

You would respond 4♣ on (1), showing a sound raise to game in spades and at most one club. Similarly, you would respond 4♦ on (2). The values in (3) are not quite sufficient for a game raise and you would respond just 3♠.

Over an opening bid of 1♥, the three splinter bids would be 3♠, 4♣ and 4♦. You may also agree to play splinter bids over an opening bid in a minor suit. Over 1♦, for example, the splinter bids would be 3♥, 3♠ and 4♣.

Let's see a couple of full auctions that involve a splinter bid by responder. In both cases the opener is able to judge whether the two hands fit together well.

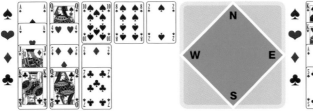

West	East
1♠	4♣
4♠	

West has a respectable opening bid but his ♣K–Q–7 represents a poor fit with partner's announced shortage in the suit. He therefore signs off in game.

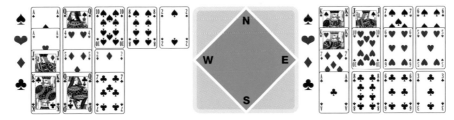

West	East
1♠	4♦
4NT	5♥
6♠	

When East's minor suits are switched, West has only one point wasted opposite the shortage and knows that the hands will fit very well. He bids Roman Key-card Blackwood, hearing of two key cards (the ♠K and the ♣A). He then advances to 6♠, in the reasonable expectation that there will be only one trick to be lost – in diamonds. This does indeed prove to be the case and an excellent slam is made on a combined total of just 27 points.

Splinter bid by the opener

The opener can make a splinter bid, when he has a good fit for responder's suit:

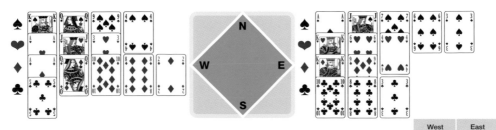

West	East
1♦	1♠
4♣	4NT
5♣	6♠

A rebid of 3♣ by West would have been natural and game-forcing. The higher bid of 4♣ is therefore available as a splinter bid. It shows a sound raise to 4♠ and at most one club. With three low cards in the splinter suit, East diagnoses a fine fit and heads for a small slam.

LEAD-DIRECTING DOUBLES

Even when you hold a poor hand, there are two good reasons to pay attention when the opponents are engaged on some lengthy auction. The first is that you may be able to use the information gained, when the time comes to defend their contract. Another reason is that you may have the chance to double a conventional bid, in order to suggest a good opening lead to your partner.

Doubling a transfer bid or Stayman
When the opponents are playing a strong 1NT, it is normal to play a double of a transfer bid or of a Stayman 2♣ as lead-directing:

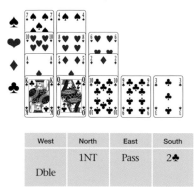

West	North	East	South
	1NT	Pass	2♣
Dble			

West's double of the artificial 2♣ bid suggests a club opening lead. If South had responded 2♦ instead, a transfer bid to show long hearts, West would double when he held strong diamonds.

When North instead has opened with a weak 1NT, it is better to play that a double of Stayman or a transfer bid shows a hand that would have made a

penalty double of 1NT. In other words, a double shows upwards of 15 points and says nothing whatsoever about your holding in the suit artificially bid.

Doubling a fourth-suit bid
When the opponents bid the fourth suit, you will have another chance to double. Do so when you hold strength in the suit and would like partner to lead it.

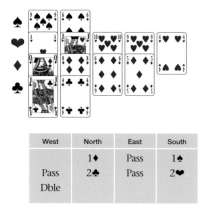

West	North	East	South
	1♦	Pass	1♠
Pass	2♣	Pass	2♥
Dble			

West has good hearts and doubles to suggest a lead of this suit.

Doubling a strength-showing cue-bid
When your partner has overcalled, the next player will sometimes cue-bid in the same suit to show a sound raise. When you would like partner to lead the suit he has bid, because you hold an honour there, you can double the cue-bid.

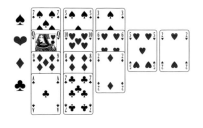

West	North	East	South
	1♠	2♣	3♣
Dble			

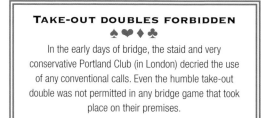

TAKE-OUT DOUBLES FORBIDDEN
♠ ♥ ♦ ♣
In the early days of bridge, the staid and very conservative Portland Club (in London) decried the use of any conventional calls. Even the humble take-out double was not permitted in any bridge game that took place on their premises.

South shows a strong spade raise with his cue-bid in the suit that East has bid. Holding a doubleton ace in partner's suit, you would welcome a club lead. You announce this by doubling the cue-bid. Suppose instead that you had held two or three low cards in clubs. You would then have passed the cue-bid, letting partner know that you had no particular reason to welcome a club lead.

Doubling a Blackwood response or control-showing cue-bid

When an opponent responds to Blackwood, and your partner may be on lead against the eventual slam, you will again have a chance to double.

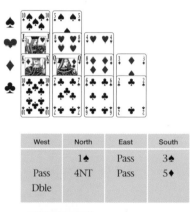

West	North	East	South
	1♠	Pass	3♠
Pass	4NT	Pass	5♦
Dble			

You double the 5♦ response to suggest a diamond lead. Similarly, you can double a control-showing cue-bid.

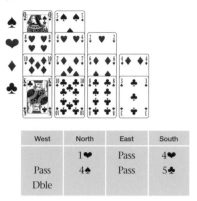

West	North	East	South
	1♥	Pass	4♥
Pass	4♠	Pass	5♣
Dble			

Since South is likely to hold the ♣A, you are willing to double the control-showing cue-bid when holding just the king, sitting over the ace. Such a double is only worthwhile because your partner will be on lead against the eventual heart contract.

If you failed to double 5♣, on the above sequence, partner would be entitled to draw the negative inference that you had no particular liking for a club lead.

Below: Holding the ♣K over South's likely ♣A, you double to suggest a club lead to partner.

ADVANCED CARD PLAY

A skilled declarer looks everywhere for clues as to how he should play the hand. Here you will see how important clues can be drawn from the bidding. The next topics are how to create extra entries to the dummy, and how you can maintain control of the trump suit. You will see also how you can combine two different chances of making a contract, which is nearly always better than relying on just one chance. You will learn how to perform an elimination play, where you force a defender to make the first lead in a suit that you do not want to play yourself. Finally you will see the squeeze, the most famous card play technique in the game.

Right: The defenders have launched a forcing defence and declarer must be careful not to lose trump control.

CLUES FROM THE BIDDING

When you are declarer, one of your tasks is to build a picture of the defenders' hands. The opening lead is usually quite informative. Every time a player shows out of a suit, you move closer to obtaining a complete count on the hand. Another important source of information comes from any bids that the defenders made. In particular, when a defender has shown length in one suit (perhaps with a pre-emptive opening, or an overcall), he is likely to be shorter than his partner in any other suit.

Look at the deal below, where East has made a pre-emptive opening of 3♣, suggesting a weak hand and seven cards in the club suit.

West leads the ♣8 and you win East's ♣10 with the ♣A. Since there are at least three losers in the side suits, the first task is to pick up the trump suit without loss. With nine cards between the hands, you would normally play to drop a missing queen. This is only a 52 per cent chance, compared with 48 per cent for finessing one or other defender for the card.

Right: Length in one suit implies shortage elsewhere. East's pre-emptive opening shows long clubs and he will be correspondingly short in the other three suits.

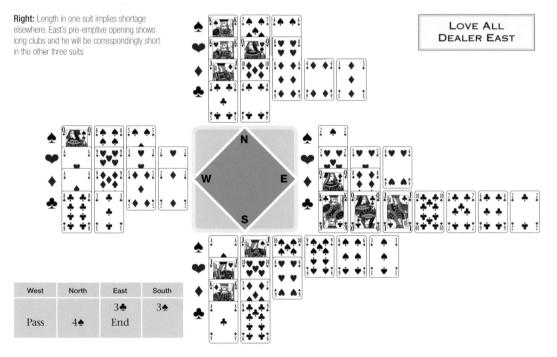

LOVE ALL
DEALER EAST

West	North	East	South
		3♣	3♠
Pass	4♠	End	

BEER CARD
♠ ♥ ♦ ♣

Among youth players, the seven of diamonds is known as the 'beer card'. When declarer makes his contract and scores the final trick with the seven of diamonds, his partner has to buy him a beer. Similarly, if a contract is defeated and a defender scores the last trick with the seven of diamonds, his partner too must buy him a beer. If the contract was doubled or redoubled, the drink order must reflect this.

Once a defender is known to be long in one of the side suits, the odds switch in favour of a finesse.

Here you expect East to hold seven clubs to West's two, so West is likely to hold longer spades than East. (You can see that, in fact, West is longer than East in all three of the suits outside clubs which predominates here.) You should therefore cash the ♠A and then run the ♠J.

This play proves successful and you draw West's last trump with dummy's ♠K. To make the contract, you now have to escape for just one diamond loser.

When the missing diamond honours are split between the two defenders, you will need to guess whether to run the ♦J or to lead towards the ♦K. Again the bidding will give you a big clue as to the lie of the diamond suit. If East held seven clubs to the K–Q–J and an ace, he would probably have rated his hand as too strong for a pre-emptive opening. It is therefore better to play him for the ♦Q. You run the ♦J and this does indeed force the ♦A from West. The contract is yours.

It can be just as important to bear in mind that a defender did not make a bid when he had the chance. On the deal shown below, for example, East did not find a response to his partner's opening bid. Since he would normally have done so when holding 6 points or more, it is reasonable for declarer to infer that he must hold fewer points than this.

> **REMEMBER THE BIDDING**
> ♠ ♥ ♦ ♣
>
> At every stage of playing a contract, make sure that your card-reading for the defenders' hands agrees with any bids that they have made. It should also be consistent with any bids that they have declined to make. For example, suppose that a defender has shown up with 10 points outside hearts and he did not open the bidding. He is unlikely to hold the ♥Q in addition. You should therefore finesse the other defender for the missing queen. The same sort of inference can be drawn when a defender declined to overcall or to make a take-out double.

Right: A deduction from the bidding. Declarer makes a valuable deduction from the fact that East did not respond to his partner's opening bid.

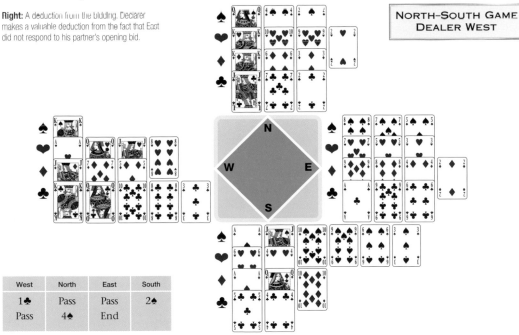

NORTH–SOUTH GAME
DEALER WEST

West	North	East	South
1♣	Pass	Pass	2♠
Pass	4♠	End	

An optimistic auction carries you to a game in spades and West leads the ♣K. East encourages with the ♣9 and West continues with the ♣Q and a third round of clubs to East's ace. You ruff in the South hand and see that you have three certain losers in the side suits. You will therefore need to pick up the trump suit without loss. Normally, with four cards missing, you would finesse East for the ♠K. Think back to the bidding, though. If East held an ace and a king in his hand, he would have responded to West's opening bid. West must therefore hold the ♠K and the only chance of making the contract is that the card is singleton. You play the ♠A from your hand and, as if by magic, the ♠K does indeed fall from the West hand. You draw trumps in two more rounds and concede a trick to West's ♥A, making the game exactly.

CREATING EXTRA ENTRIES

When you are short of entries to the dummy (or to your hand), there are various techniques available to create an extra entry. Some of these involve conceding a trick in a suit that could otherwise have been cashed from the top. Here is an example:

Right: Sacrifice to gain an entry. By giving up a trump trick unnecessarily, declarer conjures an extra entry to dummy.

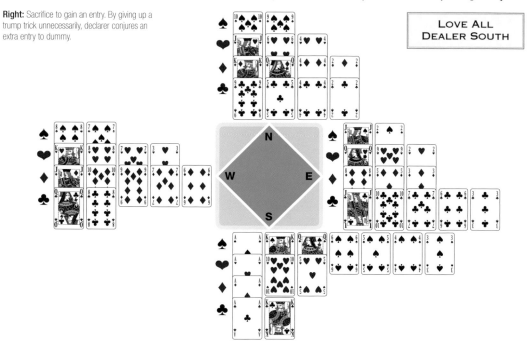

LOVE ALL
DEALER SOUTH

West leads the ♦J against your contract of 6♠ and you win with the ♦A. If you continue with the ace and king of trumps, there will be no way to avoid two subsequent heart losers. You will go one down. Instead you must seek a way to reach dummy's king and queen

---

FOUR ACES MISSING
♠ ♥ ♦ ♣

In the 1971 world championship, the French pair of Roger Trézel and Jean-Louis Stoppa were playing against Brazil when they reached a grand slam (7♥) with no fewer than four aces missing! Trézel had asked for aces, by bidding 4NT, and the 5♣ response showed 0 or 4. He assumed that his partner held four aces, after a strong-sounding bid earlier in the auction, and bid the grand slam. The Brazilians doubled and the grand slam went three down (a void club prevented the cashing of the fourth ace). It was perhaps the most amazing bidding misunderstanding in the history of the world championship.

---

of diamonds. It is easily done in the trump suit. At Trick 2 you should lead a low trump from your hand. Dummy's ♠10 loses to the ♠J and East returns a heart. You rise with the ♥A, cross to the ♠9 and discard your two heart losers on the ♦K–Q. The slam is yours.

You would make the same play (a low trump from your hand) when dummy held only ♠10–2. You would then make the contract when West held the ♠J and dummy's ♠10 could therefore be set up as an entry. In both cases you would give away an unnecessary trick in the trump suit but gain two diamond tricks in return.

(It is interesting to note that a trump lead would have beaten the contract, provided East is alert enough not to play his ♠J on the first trick! Declarer is then given the entry to dummy while the diamond suit is still blocked.)

Right: Overtaking to gain an entry. By overtaking the honour cards in clubs, declarer can create extra entries to the dummy.

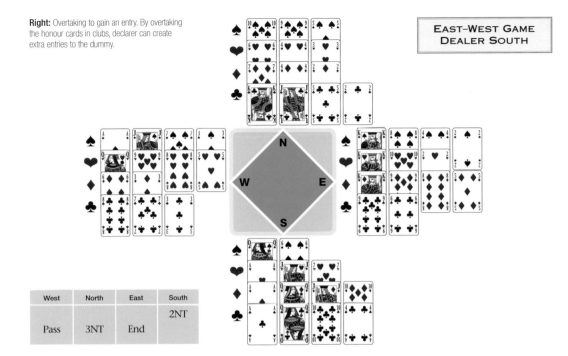

West	North	East	South
			2NT
Pass	3NT	End	

Extra entries may also be conjured by overtaking honour cards. On the deal shown above, you can create three entries to dummy by playing the club suit in clever fashion.

West leads the ♠3 against your no-trump game and the defenders take four spade tricks. You discard two hearts from the South hand and one heart from the dummy. The defenders switch to a heart, dislodging your ace, and you must now try to make four diamond tricks in addition to the four club tricks.

You need East to hold the ♦K, obviously. When he holds four cards to the king, you will need to reach dummy three times in order to take three diamond finesses. You begin by cashing the ♣A, following with dummy's ♣2. On the next round of clubs, you lead the ♣Q, overtaking with dummy's ♣K.

Both defenders follow suit, you are pleased to see, and you play a diamond to the queen, receiving further good news when the finesse wins. You next lead the ♣10, overtaking with dummy's ♣J. A finesse of the ♦J wins and you can now reach dummy for the third time by overtaking your ♣4 with dummy's ♣5.

Note that this play was possible only because you disposed of your queen and ten of clubs under dummy's king and jack. You take a third diamond

finesse, playing low to the ♦10, and the contract is yours. Suppose you were to swap the North and South club holdings, moving the ♣A–Q–10–4 to the dummy. You would then be able to reach dummy no fewer than four times in the club suit (provided the defenders' cards broke 3–2). You could lead the ♣K to the ♣A on the first round, the ♣J to the ♣Q on the second round, the ♣5 to the ♣10 on the third round and finally the ♣2 to the ♣4!

KEEP THE LOWEST TRUMP

♠ ♥ ♦ ♣

Your lowest trump is often an important card that is worth preserving. Suppose your trump holding is ♠6–3–2 in the dummy and ♠A–K–Q–J–10–4 in your hand. If the defenders force you to ruff early in the play, it will often be right to take the ruff with a high trump. By preserving the ♠4, you would give yourself a possible route to the dummy. When the defenders' trumps broke 2–2, you would be able to cross to dummy on the third round of trumps, leading the ♠4 and overtaking with the ♠6.

KEEPING TRUMP CONTROL

When a defender holds four trumps, he will usually lead his strongest side suit. His aim is to force declarer to ruff, thereby eventually causing him to lose trump control. Declarer can sometimes repel this attack by using the short-trump holding, usually in dummy, to absorb the force. Here is an example of this technique:

Right: By using the short-trump holding in the dummy, declarer can avoid being forced in the long-trump holding.

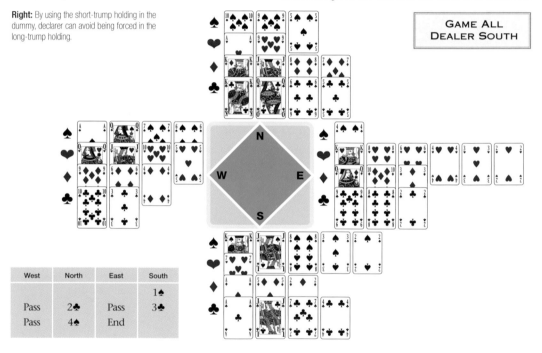

GAME ALL
DEALER SOUTH

West	North	East	South
			1♠
Pass	2♣	Pass	3♣
Pass	4♠	End	

With a chunky four-card trump holding, West embarks on a forcing defence by leading the ♥Q. You win with dummy's ♥A and run the ♠10, West winning with the ♠Q. When West continues with a second round of hearts, you must play carefully. Suppose you ruff in your hand. When you play another trump, West will hold up the ace and East will show out. There will then be no way to make the contract. If you play a third round of trumps, West will win with the ace and force your last trump with another heart. You will then lose three trump tricks and a diamond, going one down.

To survive this hostile attack on your five-card trump holding, you must call for assistance from the dummy's trumps. When West leads a second round of hearts, you should throw a diamond from your hand instead of ruffing. A third round of hearts will cause no problem, because you can ruff in the dummy, thereby preserving your own trump length. It will then be a simple matter to knock out the ace of trumps and ruff the heart continuation in the South hand. You will draw West's last two trumps and claim the remaining tricks.

THE LAST CHANCE
♠ ♥ ♦ ♣

When the famous player Oswald Jacoby reached the age of 80, he tended to make a bid each time it was his turn, whether he had the values or not. Tolerant as his partners were, they eventually asked him why he was bidding so much. 'At my age the bidding may not get round to me again,' he replied.

Above: Oswald Jacoby

On the next deal declarer's play in the trump suit is dictated by the need to use the short trumps in dummy to protect against a forcing defence.

Right: Declarer must give up a trump trick, while dummy's remaining trump will protect him against a continued force in hearts.

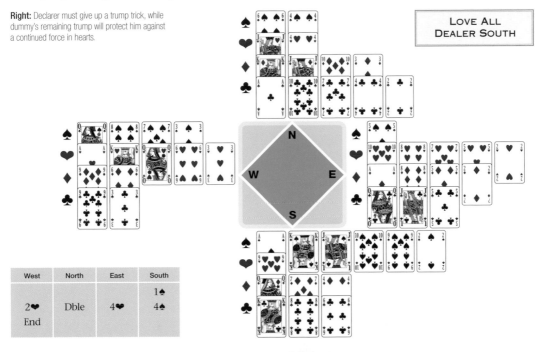

LOVE ALL
DEALER SOUTH

West	North	East	South
			1♠
2♥	Dble	4♥	4♠
End			

North makes a negative double on the first round, suggesting length in the minor suits. West leads the ♥A against the eventual spade game and continues with the ♥K (although a minor-suit switch would in fact work better). You ruff in the South hand and pause to consider your next move. If you play the ace of trumps, you will go down. When you continue with the king and jack of trumps, West will win with the ♠Q and force you with another heart. If you draw West's last trump then, you will have no protection against a heart continuation when you knock out the ♦A. If instead you play on diamonds without drawing the last trump, East will win and force your last trump with a heart, setting up a second trump for West.

To make the contract, you must lead the ♠J at Trick 3, giving up the trump trick that you can afford to lose at a moment that suits you. West wins with the ♠Q but cannot continue hearts effectively because you would be able to ruff in the dummy. When you regain the lead, you will be able to draw trumps and knock out the ♦A, making the contract easily.

Above: The defenders have launched a forcing defence and declarer must be careful not to lose trump control.

ELIMINATION PLAY

Opne of the most important, and frequently occurring, card play techniques is that of elimination play. You begin by eliminating one or more of the side suits (either by removing them from your own hand and the dummy, or by removing them from the defenders' hands). You then throw a defender on lead. He cannot play an eliminated suit, either because he has no cards left in that suit or because it will give you a ruff-and-discard. He will therefore be forced to make the first play in another suit, thereby giving you a trick. Here is a straightforward example of elimination play:

Above: The Aces team that won the 1971 Bermuda Bowl for the USA, defeating France in the final.

Right: A typical elimination play. Declarer does not want to play the diamond suit himself and uses elimination play to force the defenders to play diamonds.

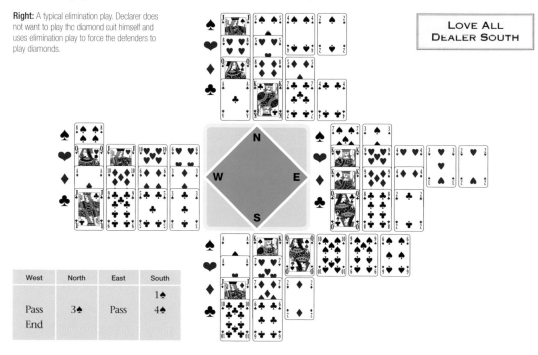

LOVE ALL
DEALER SOUTH

West	North	East	South
			1♠
Pass	3♠	Pass	4♠
End			

West leads the ♥Q against your spade game. You have one loser in the heart suit and three more losers in diamonds, if you have to play the suit yourself. If the defenders had to make the first play in diamonds, however, you would be certain to score a diamond trick. By using elimination play, you can force them to do exactly that. Your plan will be to eliminate the black suits and then exit with a second round of hearts, forcing the defenders to win the trick.

TRUMPS IN BOTH HANDS
♠ ♥ ♦ ♣

An essential requirement for an elimination play end position is that you have at least one trump in both your own hand and the dummy. This means that the defenders cannot return an eliminated suit without giving a ruff-and-discard.

You win the heart lead and draw trumps with the ace and king. Your next task is to eliminate the club suit (so neither defender will be able to play a club when he is thrown in). You play the ace and king of clubs and ruff a club in your hand. You then cross to the ♠J and ruff dummy's last club. These cards remain to be played:

Right: Elimination ending. Declarer exits in hearts, forcing a defender to play a diamond (or give a ruff-and-discard).

The preparation is complete and you now lead the ♥7. It makes no difference which defender wins the trick. A third round of hearts would give you a ruff-and-discard, allowing you to ruff in one hand and discard a diamond loser from the other. The defender who wins the trick will therefore have to play a diamond. You are certain to make a trick with the queen or jack and the game is yours.

Sometimes you can use elimination play to save you from having to guess in a suit. That is the situation here, where you have an apparent guess to make in the heart suit:

West	North	East	South
			1♠
Pass	2♠	Pass	4♠
End			

GAME ALL
DEALER SOUTH

Right: Elimination play to avoid a guess. Declarer uses elimination play to avoid having to guess which defender holds the ♥Q.

Sitting South, you win the ♣Q lead with the ace. When you play two rounds of trumps, you find that East has a trump trick. There are now three certain black-suit losers, so you will need to avoid a further loser in hearts. You could finesse either defender for the missing ♥Q. If you happened to guess wrongly, you would go down.

With the help of elimination play, you can avoid the need to guess in the heart suit. You play the ace and king of diamonds and ruff a diamond. Since diamonds are now eliminated from both your own hand and the dummy, neither defender will be able to play that suit without conceding a ruff-and-discard. These cards remain:

Right: Declarer exits in clubs, forcing a defender to play a heart (or give a ruff-and-discard).

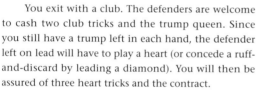

You exit with a club. The defenders are welcome to cash two club tricks and the trump queen. Since you still have a trump left in each hand, the defender left on lead will have to play a heart (or concede a ruff-and-discard by leading a diamond). You will then be assured of three heart tricks and the contract.

Look back at the two deals we have seen. On the first deal, diamonds was your 'problem suit' – the suit that you very much wanted the defenders to play for you. On the second deal, hearts was the problem suit. Sometimes you throw a defender on lead with the first round of the problem suit itself. Look at this deal:

Right: Exiting in the problem suit itself. Declarer hopes to avoid a loser in clubs and performs the elimination play by exiting on the first round of clubs.

**EAST–WEST GAME
DEALER SOUTH**

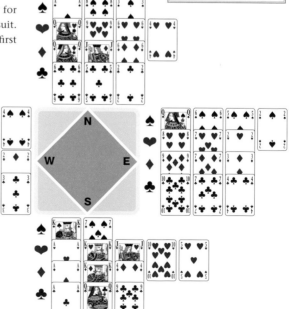

West	North	East	South
			2♣
Pass	2♦	Pass	2♥
Pass	3♥	Pass	4♥
Pass	6♥	End	

You win the ♠J lead in your hand and note that there are two potential losers in the club suit. If you had to play clubs yourself, you would first finesse the ♣9, forcing the king when East held both the jack and ten of the suit. If a finesse of the ♣9 lost to the jack or ten, you would win West's return in a different suit and then finesse the ♣Q. As you see, such a line of play would not succeed here. You would lose two club tricks and go down. To make the contract, you should eliminate spades and diamonds before playing a club to the nine. If West wins with the ten or jack, he will not be able to return a spade or a diamond without conceding a ruff-and-discard. He will be forced to play a club instead.

You draw trumps in three rounds, which still leaves you with at least one trump in both hands (an important requirement of elimination play, so that you could benefit from a ruff-and-discard). You then cash the king and ace of spades and ruff a spade, eliminating that suit from the battlefield. When you continue with three rounds of diamonds, ending in the dummy, the spades and diamonds have been eliminated. The lead is in dummy and these cards remain:

Left: By playing a club to the nine, declarer endplays West. He will have to return a club into the ace–queen tenace or give a ruff-and-discard.

All the preparation work is complete and you lead a club to the nine. West wins with the jack and has no safe return. A club will be into your ace-queen tenace and a diamond will give you a ruff-and-discard. It would do East no good to rise with the ♣10 on the first round of the suit. You would cover with the ♣Q and West would then have to lead into your ♣A–9 tenace when he won the trick.

COMBINING DIFFERENT CHANCES

It is almost always better to combine two chances of making the contract, rather than relying on just one. This may involve taking the second-best chance in one suit because this will allow you to retain the lead and take advantage of your chance in another suit. That is what happens on this deal:

West leads the ♦K against your game in spades. You win with the ace and see four potential losers, one in trumps and three more in the red suits. Looking at the trump suit in isolation, the best chance of avoiding a loser is to cash the ♠K and then to finesse the ♠J. If you follow this line and the finesse loses,

Right: Declarer combines two chances. Declarer takes the second-best chance in the trump suit, so that he can combine the additional chance of discarding the diamond loser.

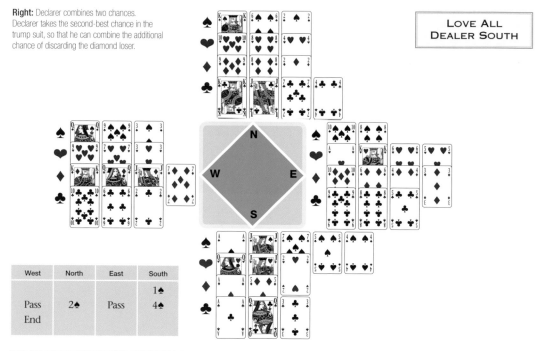

LOVE ALL
DEALER SOUTH

West	North	East	South
			1♠
Pass	2♠	Pass	4♠
End			

LUCK FACTOR REDUCED
♠ ♥ ♦ ♣

It was realized as long ago as 1857, in the days of whist, that the luck factor in card games could be reduced by playing each hand more than once and comparing results. Nowadays, nearly all competitive bridge (both for pairs and teams-of-four) employs this principle and is known as 'duplicate bridge'.

Right: Duplicate bridge. When the deal is over the cards will be returned to the board, ready to be played again at another table.

however, you will go down. When West wins with the ♠Q, the defenders will take one diamond trick and two hearts, beating the game.

A better idea is to begin with the second-best chance in trumps, playing the king and ace. If the ♠Q falls on the second round, which is quite a substantial chance, you will draw the last trump and make an overtrick. If the ♠Q does not fall, you will still be on lead. You will be able to take your second chance – discarding the diamond loser on the fourth round of clubs. With the cards lying as in the diagram you will be successful. West has to follow to three rounds of clubs and you throw the ♦5 on the fourth round of clubs, not caring whether West ruffs or not. You will lose just one trump and two hearts. By following the recommended line you make the contract when the ♠Q falls doubleton or when you can discard your diamond loser. That is a much better combined chance than relying solely on picking up the trump suit with a finesse.

It is sometimes important to combine your two chances in the right order. This is often the case when one chance will require you to lose an early trick in a suit. Look at the 6NT deal shown below, where you have prospects of an extra trick in both spades and hearts. You must seek to combine those chances.

West leads a safe ♦10 against 6NT. There are 11 tricks on top and two apparent chances of scoring a 12th trick. If East holds the ♠K, a finesse of the ♠Q will give you the slam. Another chance is that West holds the ♥Q. In that case a lead towards dummy's ♥J will yield the extra trick.

There is no need to choose between these chances. Provided you tackle the suits in the correct order, you can make the slam when either chance pays off. Suppose you win the diamond lead and finesse the ♠Q immediately. The finesse will lose and it will be too late to tackle the heart suit.

Since you will have to surrender a trick in hearts, even if the ♥Q is favourably placed, you should play that suit first. You win the diamond lead with the queen and lead a low heart towards dummy. Whether or not West chooses to rise with the ♥Q, you will score a third trick in hearts and make the slam. Suppose the cards had lain differently and the ♥J had lost to the ♥Q with East. You would still have been able to take your second chance in spades. That is because you would not need to lose the lead in order to take advantage of the ♠K lying with East. A finesse of the ♠Q would win and you could then cash the ♠A, scoring two tricks from the suit.

Right: Taking finesses in the right order. Declarer combines the chances in hearts and spades by taking the two finesses in the right order.

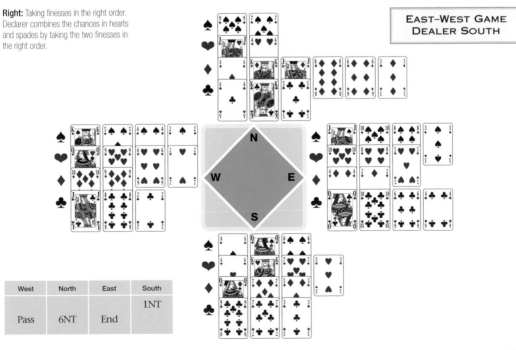

EAST–WEST GAME
DEALER SOUTH

West	North	East	South
			1NT
Pass	6NT	End	

THE THROW-IN

In an earlier section we looked at elimination play, where you threw a defender on lead at a time when both declarer's hand and the dummy still contained at least one trump. Because the defender could not afford to give a ruff-and-discard, he had to lead your problem suit, giving you a trick there. When one of the hands does not contain a trump, or the contract is being played in no-trumps, it is still possible to gain a trick by throwing a defender on lead. The play is then known, simply, as a throw-in. Here is an example:

Right: A typical throw-in play. Declarer makes 3NT by throwing East on lead in clubs when he has no safe return to make.

NORTH–SOUTH GAME
DEALER EAST

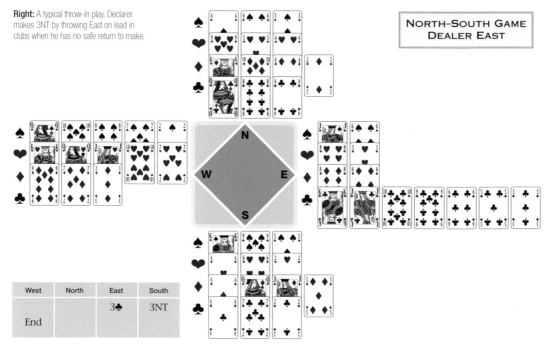

West	North	East	South
		3♣	3NT
End			

West leads the ♥K. You duck the first two rounds of hearts and win the third round, East throwing a club. You have eight top tricks and the only serious chance of a ninth trick is to throw East on lead with a club, forcing him to lead away from the ♣K.

To prepare for a throw-in, you must remove East's possible exit cards in the other suits. You must hope that East has no more than two cards in spades. You begin with four rounds of diamonds and continue with the ace and king of spades. When East follows twice in each suit, as he did in hearts, it is a near certainty that his shape is 2–2–2–7. In that case he will have nothing but clubs left in his hand. You lead the ♣2 from your hand and West does indeed show out. You play the ♣4 from dummy and East wins the trick cheaply. Since all his remaining cards are clubs, he must lead a club from the king. You run this to dummy's ♣Q and nine tricks are yours.

On the next example too, an opening bid by East allows you to be fairly certain of the lie of the cards.

West leads the ♥7 against your no-trump game. East plays the ♥10 and you allow this to win.

Right: Reading the cards after an opening bid. Declarer is able to diagnose a throw-in play on East because of the values shown by his opening bid.

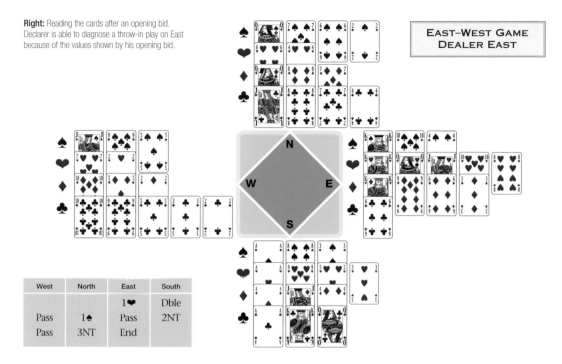

West	North	East	South
		1♥	Dble
Pass	1♠	Pass	2NT
Pass	3NT	End	

You duck the heart continuation and win the third round of the suit, West discarding a club. You have only six tricks on top but the bidding marks East with the ♠K and the ♦K. He will therefore be in trouble when you throw him in.

You cash the ♣A–K–Q and throw East on lead with a heart. He cashes his last heart winner and you discard a spade from your hand. Meanwhile, you have thrown two spades and a diamond from the dummy. These cards remain:

Below: East, who has been thrown in, now has to lead away from one of his remaining kings, giving declarer an extra trick and access to the ♣J in the dummy.

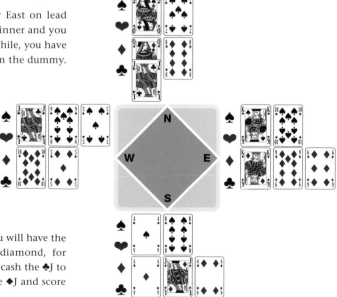

Whichever card East plays next, you will have the remaining tricks. If he plays a low diamond, for example, you will win with the ♦Q and cash the ♣J to throw a spade. You can then finesse the ♦J and score the ♦A at Trick 13.

THE SIMPLE SQUEEZE

Perhaps the most famous play in bridge is the 'squeeze'. A defender who holds a guard on two of declarer's suits is forced to make a critical discard and has to release one of his guards. Here is a straightforward example:

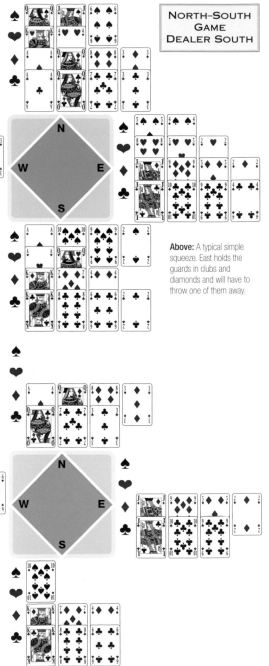

NORTH-SOUTH
GAME
DEALER SOUTH

Above: A typical simple squeeze. East holds the guards in clubs and diamonds and will have to throw one of them away.

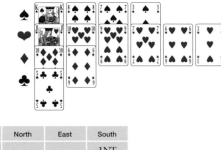

West	North	East	South
			1NT
Pass	6NT	End	

You win the heart lead with the queen, cross to the ♣A and run the ♠Q, losing to the king. You win the heart return and see that you have 11 tricks on top, 12 if the clubs break 3–2 or the diamonds break 3–3. Before testing your luck in the minor suits, you should cash your spade winners. This position will result:

Right: Squeeze ending. When the ♠10 is led, East has to throw away one of his guards.

You cash the ♠10, throwing a club from dummy, and East is squeezed. He will have to throw a diamond or a club, releasing his guard in one of the suits. You will score your 12th trick from whichever suit he throws, making the slam.

An essential part of most squeezes is that you should lose at an early stage the tricks you can afford to lose. In other words, you should lose one trick in a small slam, four tricks in a 3NT contract. If you fail to do this, the defender with the two guards will have a spare card in his hand. He will not be squeezed when you play your last winner in the other suits. Look at this deal.

West leads the ♠10 against 6NT, East playing the ♠Q. Let's suppose first that you win immediately with the ♠A. You will not make the contract. West holds the

guards in both the red suits but he will not be squeezed. When you play four rounds of clubs, West will discard his three remaining cards in spades. You will score only 11 tricks.

Before playing to Trick 1, you should make a plan. You have 11 top tricks and can make a 12th when the diamond suit breaks 3–3, or when the same defender holds at least four diamonds and four hearts. In the latter case you will be able to squeeze the defender, but only if you lose one trick early in the play.

Right: Rectifying the count. Declarer gives up a trick at an early stage, so West will have no spare card to throw later in the play.

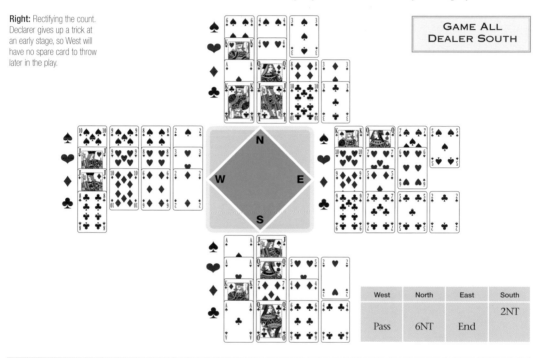

GAME ALL
DEALER SOUTH

West	North	East	South
			2NT
Pass	6NT	End	

BILL GATES
♠ ♥ ♦ ♣

Founder of Microsoft, Bill Gates, says: 'Bridge is a game you can play at any age. If you take it up young, you will have fun playing it for the rest of your life. A lot of games don't have that depth. This one does.' Gates competed in the 2002 world bridge championships in Toronto. In 2006 he partnered former world champion, Sharon Osberg, in the Verona world bridge championships. He told the press that programmers at Microsoft are working on sophisticated computer programs to play bridge.

Left: One of the world's richest men, Bill Gates is now a keen bridge player.

Now to see what happens if you duck the very first trick, allowing East to win with the ♠Q. You win the spade return and cash four rounds of clubs. The tableau to the right shows the position, where one club winner is still to be cashed. Because you ducked a round of spades at Trick 1, West has no card to spare when you lead the ♣Q:

Right: Squeeze ending. When the ♣Q is led, West has to abandon one of his red-suit guards.

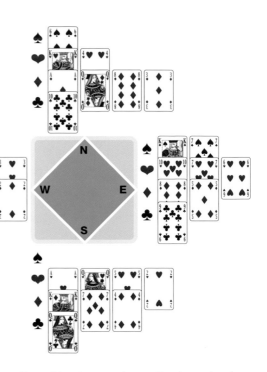

West will have to throw one of his red-suit guards and you will then score your 12th trick from the suit he has abandoned. The action of deliberately losing one or more tricks, to tighten the eventual end position, is known as 'rectifying the count'.

If we strip that end position down to the basics, we can visualize the elements of a simple squeeze. Let's suppose that you cash the king, ace and queen of hearts and the diamond ace and king, before playing the ♣Q. The minimal end position shown below would result:

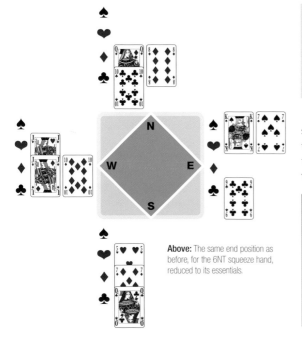

Above: The same end position as before, for the 6NT squeeze hand, reduced to its essentials.

Everything is now clearer. You have the three main elements of a simple squeeze:

- the 'squeeze card' (♣Q), the card that you play to force a critical discard
- a 'one-card threat' (♥5), guarded by West's ♥J
- a 'threat with an entry' (♦Q–8) that lies opposite the squeeze card.

As before, West has no card to spare on the squeeze card (the ♣Q). If he throws a heart, the ♥5 in the South hand will become good. If instead West throws a diamond, you will score the last two tricks with dummy's ♦Q and ♦8.

CHARLES SCHULTZ

♠ ♥ ♦ ♣

The cartoonist Charles Schultz was a keen bridge player and featured bridge in several of his Peanuts cartoons. His Snoopy character is the only 'honorary lifemaster' of the American Contract Bridge League.

So, every time you plan a simple squeeze, you must look for a squeeze card, a one-card threat and a threat with an entry. It is all rather daunting on first acquaintance but after a while you will find it becomes easier. Opportunities for simple squeezes are very frequent and will give you many a tricky contract. Let's see one more example:

Right: The Vienna Coup. Declarer prepares for a heart–club squeeze by playing the ♥A, thereby freeing the ♥Q to act as a threat card against either defender.

NORTH–SOUTH
GAME
DEALER SOUTH

West	North	East	South
			1NT
Pass	6NT	End	

You win the spade lead and run the ♦Q to East's ♦K, winning the diamond return. You have 11 top tricks and can score a 12th if the same defender holds the ♥K and the club guard. Try to visualize the components of the squeeze. The one-card threat will be the ♥Q. The 'threat with an entry' will be dummy's club suit. The squeeze card will be the last spade. After playing dummy's top diamonds, you cash the ♥A to free your ♥Q as a one-card threat. You then play the remaining spades, arriving at the position shown in this tableau:

Below: Squeeze ending. When the ♠J is led, East has to throw one of his guards.

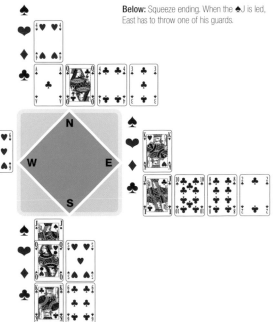

You play the squeeze card (the ♠J), throwing the ♥4 from dummy. East is squeezed and must discard one of his guards. If he throws a club, you will make four club tricks with the king, ace, queen and four of the suit. If instead he throws the ♥K, you will score a trick with the ♥Q.

ADVANCED DEFENCE

Much good play at bridge involves counting. This is particularly true in defence, where you can count declarer's points to allow you to calculate which cards your fellow defender may hold. You will see why it is important to hold up high cards in defence and how to conduct a forcing defence, where you attack declarer's trump holding. When you hold a doubleton honour in defence, it is often right to throw the high card away, rather than risk being end-played with it later. Another important topic is how you can break declarer's communications, in particular by attacking an entry to dummy. Finally the two main ways in which the defenders can promote extra trump tricks for themselves are discussed – the straightforward trump promotion, where a defender is threatening to overruff, and the more spectacular 'uppercut'.

Right: East unblocks the ♠K on his partner's ♠Q lead. If he fails to do so, he will win the second round and be unable to continue the suit.

COUNTING DECLARER'S POINTS

Counting is an important part of the game, for the defenders as well as for declarer. By counting declarer's points and comparing this total with the points indicated in the bidding, the defenders can often tell which line of defence has the best chance.

Ruling out a defence by counting points

Take the East cards on this deal and see how you fare.

Right: Counting points to determine the right defence. East diagnoses the winning defence by counting declarer's points and ruling out a continuation of partner's suit.

<table>
<tr><td colspan="3" style="text-align:center">DEDUCTIONS FROM COUNTING
♠ ♥ ♦ ♣</td></tr>
<tr><td colspan="3">Suppose declarer has indicated 12–14 points in the bidding and has already shown up with 11 points outside the hearts. As a defender, you can deduce that he does not hold the ♥A.</td></tr>
</table>

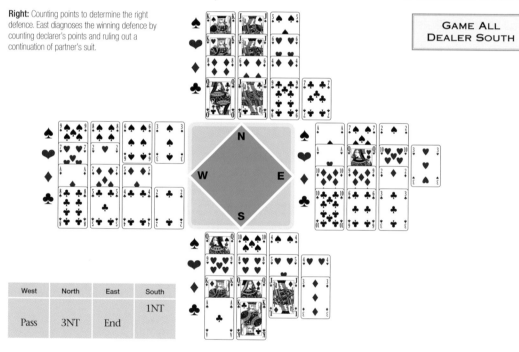

GAME ALL
DEALER SOUTH

West	North	East	South
			1NT
Pass	3NT	End	

South opens with a 15–17 point 1NT and is raised to game. Your partner, West, leads the ♠8 and declarer plays low from dummy. Sitting East, you pause to make a plan for the defence. Your partner would not have led the ♠8 from ♠Q–10–9–8, so the opening lead must be his second-best spade from a weak suit. Declarer is therefore marked with the queen and ten of spades. You win with the ♠A and must decide what to do next.

If you follow the general guideline to 'lead up to weakness in the dummy', switching to the ♦10, declarer will easily make the contract. Before making such a play, you should count the points that are out.

You hold 10 points and there are 11 in the dummy. This leaves only 19 points for the two closed hands, of which South must hold at least 15. So, your partner can hold at most one high card in diamonds. What is more, declarer will have to play on diamonds himself, to stand any chance of scoring nine tricks.

Having worked this out, you should switch to a low heart – into the teeth of dummy's ♥K–J–6. It may seem strange to lead into strength in this way, but see the effect of it. When declarer wins the heart switch and plays a diamond, your partner wins with the ace and plays back a second round of hearts. You score three heart tricks and the game is defeated.

Calculating which useful card partner may hold

By counting declarer's points, you can deduce how many points are left for your partner. Only a good player in the East seat would defeat this 3NT game:

Right: Calculating which useful card partner holds. By counting declarer's points, East determines which useful card it is possible for West to hold.

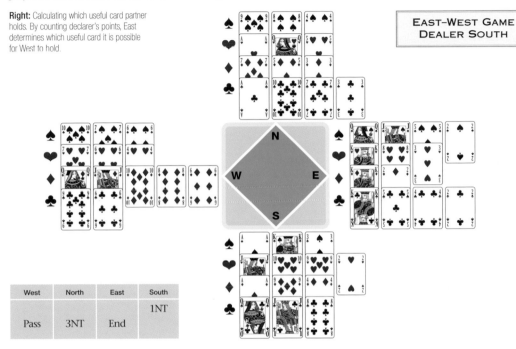

EAST–WEST GAME
DEALER SOUTH

West	North	East	South
			1NT
Pass	3NT	End	

South opens a 15–17 point 1NT and is raised to game. Take the East cards now. West, your partner, leads the ♦Q and you must plan your defence. The first move is clear – you must overtake with the ♦K. Otherwise you risk blocking the suit. Declarer could then win the first trick and run the ♣Q to you, making the contract easily.

Declarer allows ♦K to win, breaking your link with partner's hand in diamonds. Many East players would now return their remaining diamond. It is not a strong defence. You can see 22 points between your hand and the dummy. Declarer is marked with at least 15 points for his 1NT opening, so your partner can hold no honour card outside his ♦Q–J. If you set up his diamonds, he will have no possible card of entry.

Once you have deduced that a diamond return cannot be successful, it is obvious that you should switch to a low spade. If partner holds ♠10–x–x, you will be able to set up two tricks in the suit before your remaining two kings are dislodged. Declarer wins the ♠2 switch with the

♠A and runs the jack of hearts to your king. You clear the spade suit and cash the setting tricks in spades when declarer takes a losing club finesse. If you returned a diamond instead, declarer would win with the ♦A and finesse in clubs. When you won with the ♣K, it would be too late to attack the spade suit. Declarer would win your spade switch and finesse in hearts, setting up enough tricks for the contract while he still held a spade stopper.

CHINESE FINESSE
♠ ♥ ♦ ♣

Suppose you need to avoid a loser with a side suit of ♦Q–9–8–3 opposite ♦A–5. If there is no possibility of an end-play of some sort, you may try the desperate manoeuvre of leading the ♦Q. When the player in the second seat holds something like ♦K–7–2, he may place you with ♦Q–J–10–x and thus decline to cover with the king. This deceptive play is known as a 'Chinese Finesse'.

DEFENSIVE HOLD-UPS IN A SUIT CONTRACT

It is a familiar technique for the defenders to hold up an ace (or even a king), when defending in no-trumps. The same sort of move can work well against a suit contract too. The purpose, as always, will be to interfere with declarer's communications.

Holding up to prevent declarer taking a discard
Take East cards on this deal and see how you get on.

Right: A hold-up to prevent a discard. East holds up the ♦A, to prevent declarer from obtaining a discard on the suit.

COUNT SIGNALS
♠ ♥ ♦ ♣

By showing whether you hold an even or odd number of cards in a suit that declarer is playing (a high card shows 'even', a low card shows 'odd'), you can help your partner to judge when to hold up an ace in defence.

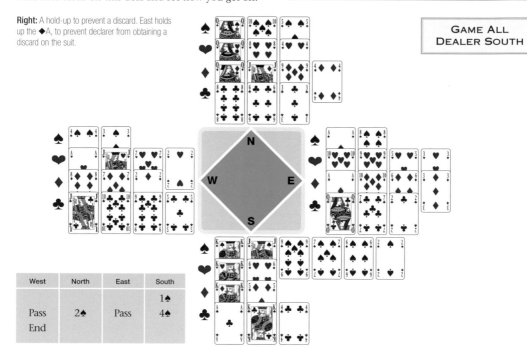

GAME ALL
DEALER SOUTH

West	North	East	South
			1♠
Pass	2♠	Pass	4♠
End			

West leads the ♣J. South wins with the ♣A and plays the ♦K from his hand. Sitting East, you must decide whether to win with the ♦A or to hold up the card. Suppose first that you do win the ace immediately, returning a club. This will be very much to declarer's liking. He will win the club return with the king and cross to dummy with the ♦Q. He can then throw his club loser on the ♦J. He will make the game, losing tricks only to the three aces.

When the ♦K is led, West will give a 'count signal'. A high diamond will indicate an even number of cards in the suit; a low diamond will show an odd number.

Here he will play the ♦2. Sitting East, you can then place West with three diamonds and declarer with two. On that basis you should hold up the ♦A on the first round. You win the second diamond and clear the club suit. Declarer has no quick entry to dummy, to take a discard on the ♦J, and will now go down. When he plays a trump to the queen, you will win with the ace and cash a club winner, followed by a heart to West's ace.

Suppose instead that West held ♦8-7-5-2. He would signal his count with the ♦7 (second highest from four cards). East would then take his ♦A immediately, preventing declarer from scoring the singleton ♦K.

Holding up to prevent declarer taking a finesse

Sometimes a hold-up will keep declarer out of dummy, preventing him from taking a finesse through your hand.

Right: A hold-up to prevent a trump finesse. East holds up the ◆A to prevent declarer from entering dummy with the ◆Q to finesse in trumps.

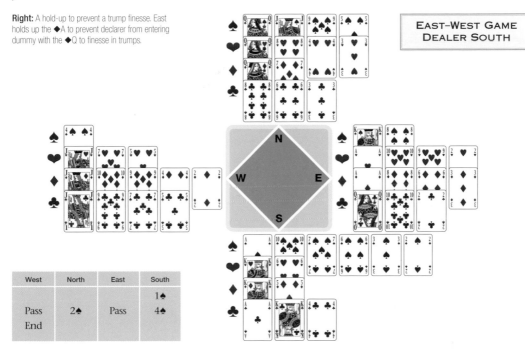

EAST–WEST GAME
DEALER SOUTH

West	North	East	South
			1♠
Pass	2♠	Pass	4♠
End			

West leads the ◆J and declarer plays low from dummy. You must consider your defence from the East seat. If you rise with the ◆A, declarer will unblock the ◆K from his hand and subsequently enter dummy with the ◆Q to finesse against your king of trumps. You should therefore play low at Trick 1. Another reason to play low is that you do not want declarer to score two diamond tricks (throwing a club from dummy on the third round of the suit) if he began with ◆K–x–x.

Declarer wins the first trick with ◆K and immediately leads the ♥K. Your partner follows with the ♥5, his lowest card in the suit showing an odd number of cards in the suit. You must hold up the ♥A, to prevent declarer from crossing to the ♥Q to take a trump finesse. After this bright start to the defence, declarer cannot reach dummy and will not be able to finesse against your ♠K. He will have to cash the ♠A from his hand. He cannot avoid a loser in every suit, as the cards lie, and will go one down.

RULE OF FIFTEEN
♠ ♥ ♦ ♣

When you are short in spades, it is somewhat risky to make a light opening bid in the fourth seat. The defenders may then discover a spade fit and end in a successful part score (or even a game) in that suit, when you could have passed the deal out. Some players use the 'Rule of Fifteen' to decide whether to open: *When the sum of your high-card points and the number of spades in your hand is 15 or more, you should open the bidding.*
Suppose, after three passes, your hand is :
♠3 ♥A–J–9–8–4 ◆K–Q–8–4 ♣Q–10–5.
You have 12 points and only 1 spade. According to the Rule of Fifteen, you should pass rather than opening 1♥. In any of the first three seats this hand would be worth an opening bid. The Rule of Fifteen applies only in the fourth seat.

THE FORCING DEFENCE

When you hold four trumps in defence, it is often best to lead your strongest side suit. Your aim is to force declarer to ruff, thereby weakening his trump holding. If you can end with more trumps than declarer, he will have lost trump control and may well go down.

Playing a forcing defence

West holds four trumps, defending this spade game, and therefore leads from his powerful heart side suit. His ♥K wins the first trick, and he continues with a low heart to East's ♥10.

Right: A typical forcing defence. By continually leading hearts, West forces declarer to lose control of the trump suit.

MULTIPLE MEANING

♠ ♥ ♦ ♣

Many bridge words, such as 'forcing' here, have more than one meaning within the game. A 'forcing bid' is one that partner is not allowed to pass. A 'forcing defence' describes the situation where the defenders force declarer to ruff, in order to weaken his trump holding. Also a defender might play a king, 'forcing out dummy's ace'.

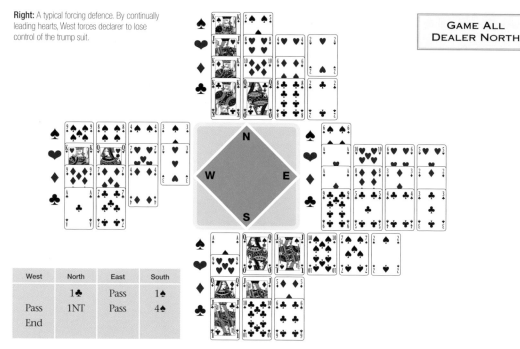

GAME ALL
DEALER NORTH

West	North	East	South
	1♣	Pass	1♠
Pass	1NT	Pass	4♠
End			

Declarer ruffs and now holds five trumps to West's four. He plays two rounds of trumps and discovers the 4–1 break. Suppose he draws West's last two trumps and then plays on clubs. West will win with the ♣A and force declarer's last trump with a third round of hearts. Declarer can score three club tricks, but this will bring his total only to nine tricks. When he eventually plays on diamonds, East will win and the defenders will score a heart trick to beat the contract. The outcome will be exactly the same if declarer plays on clubs before drawing West's last two trumps. Another heart will reduce him to just two trump winners and he will not be able to set up and enjoy a diamond trick.

Even though South began with six trumps to West's four, the force was successful. That is because declarer needed to dislodge two high cards and the defenders would have two more chances to force him.

Holding up the trump ace to maintain the force

Suppose you are conducting a forcing defence and you hold four trumps headed by the ace. You will often have to hold up the ace until the trumps in declarer's shorter holding (usually the dummy's trumps) are exhausted. You can then persist with your force on the longer trump holding. The deal below is an example of this technique:

Right: Taking the trump ace at the right moment. By holding up the ace of trumps, West is able to continue his forcing defence.

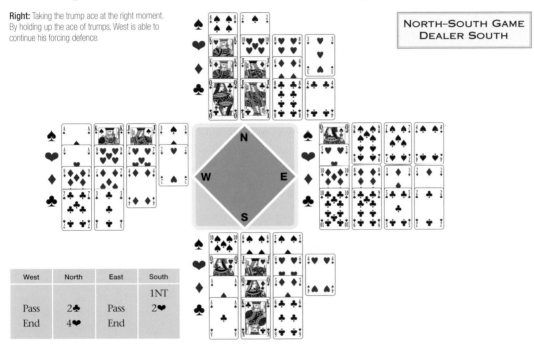

NORTH–SOUTH GAME
DEALER SOUTH

West	North	East	South
			1NT
Pass	2♣	Pass	2♥
End	4♥	End	

Above: Dummy's trumps have been forced once already. West now holds up the ace of trumps twice, planning to win the third round and force out declarer's last trump with another spade.

West leads the ♠A against South's heart game and the defenders play two more rounds of spades, forcing the dummy to ruff. When declarer leads the king of trumps from dummy, the key moment of the hand has been reached. If West makes the mistake of winning this round of trumps, he will not be able to persist with his forcing defence. That's because a fourth round of spades could be ruffed in dummy, in what has now become the shorter trump holding. Instead West should duck not only the first round of trumps but also the second round.

If declarer continues with a third round of trumps, dummy will have no trumps left. West will be able to win with the ♥A and force declarer's last trump with another spade, setting up his ♥9 as the setting trick. Declarer's only alternative is to abandon trumps after two rounds and to turn to the side suits. West will then ruff the third round of clubs, again scoring two trump tricks to beat the game. In the common situation where declarer has four trumps in each hand, you need to attack the trump length in both hands. The idea is to reduce the trump length in one hand, hold up the ace of trumps until that hand has no trumps remaining and then attack the trump length in the other hand.

UNBLOCKING HONOURS IN DEFENCE

Any time that you have a doubleton honour in a side suit, you must consider playing the honour on the first round. Failure to do this can cost you in various ways. You may block your partner's long suit, for example. You may also leave yourself open to an end-play by the declarer.

Unblocking an honour in partner's suit

When you hold a doubleton honour in the suit that partner has led against no-trumps, it is generally right to play it on the first round, even if this is not necessary in an attempt to win the trick. Take the East cards here:

Above: East unblocks the ♠K on his partner's ♠Q lead. If he fails to do so, he will win the second round and be unable to continue the suit.

Right: Unblocking in the suit led. West leads the ♠Q against 3NT and East must play the ♠K to avoid the suit becoming blocked.

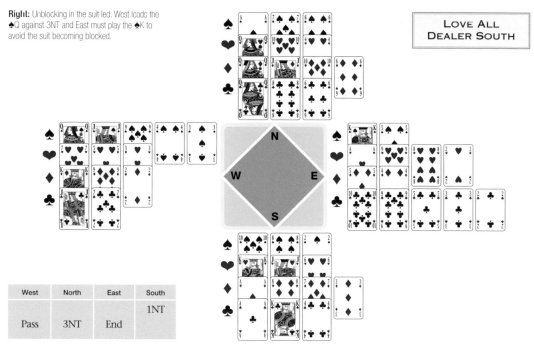

LOVE ALL
DEALER SOUTH

West	North	East	South
			1NT
Pass	3NT	End	

Your partner leads the ♠Q and declarer plays low from the dummy. It is essential you unblock your ♠K on the first round. You then return the ♠5, clearing the suit whether your partner has led from ♠Q–J–10–x–x or ♠Q–J–9–x–x. Declarer must take a diamond finesse at some stage. Your partner will win with the king and cash his spade winners. Four spades, the king of diamonds and the ace of hearts puts the contract two down.

Suppose instead that you fail to unblock, following with the ♠5. Declarer will duck the second round of spades and you will have to win with the bare ♠K. With his spade stopper intact, declarer will easily make the contract.

You would make the same unblocking play of the king if declarer played the ♠A from dummy at Trick 1, or if dummy had held ♠7–6–2.

Unblocking to avoid an end-play

When declarer holds plenty of trumps in both hands, you must be particularly careful not to leave yourself with a bare honour in a side suit. If you do, you may be thrown in with the card and forced to give declarer a ruff-and-discard. Take the West cards here:

Right: Unblocking to avoid an end-play. When declarer plays the ♦A, West must unblock the ♦K to avoid being end-played later.

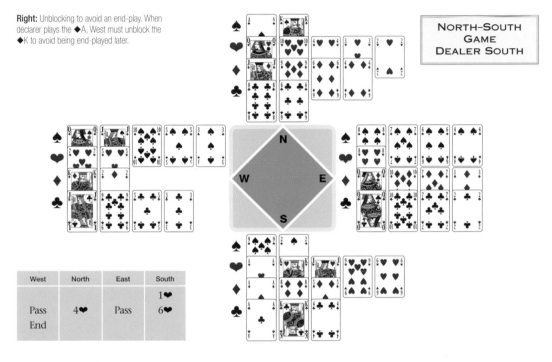

NORTH–SOUTH
GAME
DEALER SOUTH

West	North	East	South
			1♥
Pass	4♥	Pass	6♥
End			

Above: World Grand Master Catherine D'Ovidio, shown on the extreme right of the French national team, has ranked World's top female player.

Sitting West, you lead the ♠Q against the slam. Declarer wins in the dummy, draws trumps in two rounds and cashes the ♦A. Suppose you see no need for special action and follow with the ♦2. Declarer will cash dummy's other spade winner, followed by the two high clubs in his hand and a club ruff. With the black suits eliminated, he will then play a second round of diamonds. You will have to win with the bare ♦K and return a black suit, conceding a ruff-and-discard. Declarer will ruff in the dummy, throwing the last diamond loser from his hand. Sadly for you and your partner, 12 tricks will then be his.

Difficult as it may seem, you must play your ♦K under South's ♦A. Your partner will then be able to win two diamond tricks. If declarer held the ♦Q or the ♦10, he would doubtless have finessed in the suit, rather than cashing the diamond ace.

BREAKING DECLARER'S COMMUNICATIONS

A ttractive as it may be for the defenders to set up extra tricks for themselves, sometimes this has to take second place behind the need to disrupt declarer's communications. Before you automatically 'return partner's suit', you should take a look around and see if you can destroy an important entry to the dummy.

Killing an entry to dummy

Take the East cards here and see how you would defend this 3NT contract. Your partner leads the ♠2 and you win with the ace.

Right: Killing the entry to dummy. East wins the spade lead against 3NT and must switch to hearts to kill the entry to dummy's diamonds.

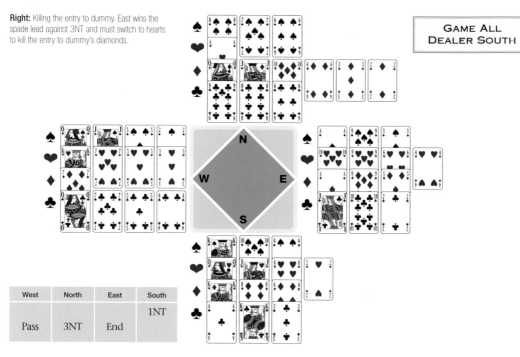

GAME ALL
DEALER SOUTH

West	North	East	South
			1NT
Pass	3NT	End	

Suppose you follow your natural instincts and return the ♠9. Declarer will win with the king and lead the ♦K. It will not do you any good to hold up the diamond ace for a couple of rounds because the ace of hearts is still intact as an entry to dummy. The defenders can score three spades and a diamond but declarer will then score five diamonds and the four top winners in the other three suits, making the no-trump game.

At Trick 2 your top priority, sitting East, is to kill declarer's source of tricks in dummy's diamond suit by removing the heart entry to dummy. You should switch to a heart, won by dummy's ace. The job of cutting declarer off from his diamond winners is only half done. When he plays on diamonds, you must hold up the ace until the third round. Declarer will then make two diamond tricks, rather than five, and will go two down.

The Merrimac Coup

As we have just seen, it is easy enough to dislodge a bare ace from dummy. When the ace is guarded, something more spectacular may be required. Take the East cards here:

Right: A spectacular sacrifice. East notes that dummy's diamonds are threatening and sacrifices his ♠K to remove the ♠A entry to the dummy.

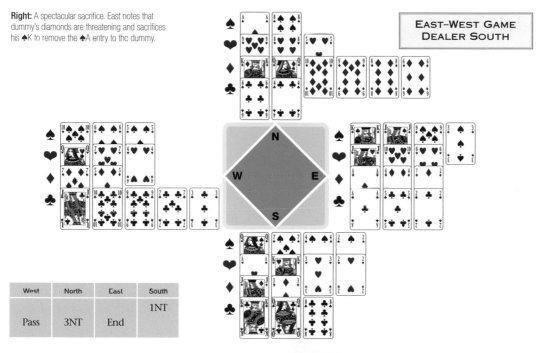

EAST–WEST GAME
DEALER SOUTH

West	North	East	South
			1NT
Pass	3NT	End	

West leads the ♣J and you must plan the defence from the East seat. There are only 18 points missing from the West and South hands. West has already shown the ♣J, so declarer is marked with the ♣K as well as the ♣Q.

If you play low at Trick 1, declarer will win and clear the diamond suit while the ♠A is intact as an entry. He will make the contract with an overtrick, however you defend thereafter. Instead you must rise smartly with the club ace and attack the spade entry to dummy. Switching to a low spade will not be good enough, as the cards lie, because declarer will be able to win with the spade queen. The only winning defence is to switch to the ♠K! Declarer has no answer to this. If he wins with dummy's ace, you will subsequently hold up your ♦A to cut him off from the diamond suit. If instead declarer allows your ♠K to win, you will continue with a low spade, removing dummy's side entry. Either way, the contract will go at least one down.

Above: The Merrimac Coup, a sacrificial play, is named after the deliberate scuttling of the American coal-carrying ship, *Merrimac*, in Santiago Harbour in 1898. The aim was to bottle up the Spanish fleet.

PROMOTING TRUMP TRICKS IN DEFENCE

Few things are more enjoyable in defence than promoting extra trump tricks. You can do this in two different ways. The first is to lead a suit where declarer (or the dummy) is now void and your partner is in a position to overruff. If declarer chooses to ruff low, your partner will indeed overruff. If instead declarer ruffs high, this may promote a trump trick for one or other of the defenders. The second promotion technique is known as the 'uppercut'. A defender ruffs with a high trump, aiming to force declarer to overruff with a higher trump. The intention is to promote some lesser trump in the other defender's hand.

The trump promotion

The deal below shows an example of the basic form of trump promotion where one defender is in a position to overruff the declarer.

East opens with a weak two-bid in spades and South arrives in 4♥. West leads the ♠9 and East wins with the ♠J. He cashes the ♠A and then leads a third round of spades in the hope that this will achieve a trump promotion. If declarer ruffs with the ♥9, West will overruff with the ♥10 and the trump ace will give the defenders a fourth trick for one down. Since declarer knows from the bidding that the spades are breaking 6–2, he may well ruff with the ♥K instead.

All will now depend on West's reaction. If he succumbs to the temptation to overruff with the ♥A, the contract will survive. When declarer regains the lead, he will draw West's remaining two trumps with the queen and jack. West should decline to overruff, discarding a diamond instead. His ♥A–10–4 will then be worth two tricks, sitting over South's ♥Q–J–9–7–2. The third round of spades will have promoted an extra trump trick in the West hand. West will score both the ace and the ten of the suit.

Suppose West had held ♥A–9–4 instead of ♥A–10–4. Again it would be right to decline to overruff. By defending in this way, he would promote a second trump trick when his partner held the ♥10.

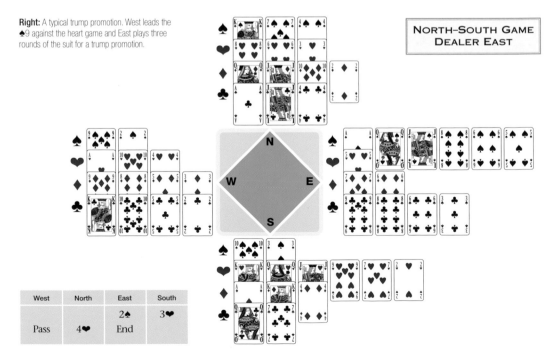

Right: A typical trump promotion. West leads the ♠9 against the heart game and East plays three rounds of the suit for a trump promotion.

NORTH–SOUTH GAME
DEALER EAST

West	North	East	South
		2♠	3♥
Pass	4♥	End	

The uppercut

You can also promote a trump trick by ruffing high when you expect to be overruffed:

Right: An uppercut. East defeats the spade game by administering an uppercut, ruffing with the ♠Q on the fourth round of hearts.

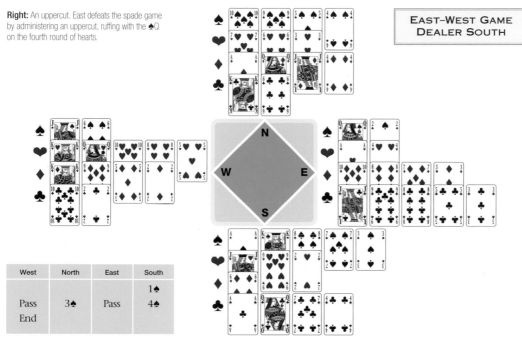

EAST–WEST GAME
DEALER SOUTH

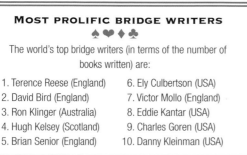

West	North	East	South
			1♠
Pass	3♠	Pass	4♠
End			

West leads the ♥K. If East follows with the ♥4, an overtrick will be made. He will have to win the next heart with the bare ace and that is the last trick that the defenders will take.

Instead, East overtakes with the ♥A and returns the ♥4. West scores the ten and queen of the suit, giving the defenders the first three tricks. On the third round of hearts East discards the ♣3, showing no interest in that suit. With his ♦K sitting under the dummy's ♦A–Q–J, West can see no prospect of a minor-suit trick for the defence. The only chance is to promote a trump trick. West continues with a fourth round of hearts and East ruffs with the ♠Q (a play known as an uppercut). Declarer overruffs with the king or ace and now has to lose a trick to West's ♠J. The game goes one down. The same defence would have been successful if East had started with a singleton ♠Q, or a singleton or doubleton ♠K.

MOST PROLIFIC BRIDGE WRITERS
♠ ♥ ♦ ♣

The world's top bridge writers (in terms of the number of books written) are:

1. Terence Reese (England)
2. David Bird (England)
3. Ron Klinger (Australia)
4. Hugh Kelsey (Scotland)
5. Brian Senior (England)
6. Ely Culbertson (USA)
7. Victor Mollo (England)
8. Eddie Kantar (USA)
9. Charles Goren (USA)
10. Danny Kleinman (USA)

Above: David Bird and Terence Reese, who have written the greatest number of books about bridge.

FAMOUS PLAYERS

Every game or sport has its larger than life characters, who catch the public eye and are remembered for decades. Bridge is no exception. It is largely a game for extroverts and this section pays homage to some of the outstanding figures who have spent their lives gracing the bridge table. Film star Omar Sharif is perhaps the most well-known bridge player in the world. Robert Hamman and Jeff Meckstroth of the USA, Gabriel Chagas of Brazil and Zia Mahmood of Pakistan (now of the USA) are all currently playing at the top level. Maestro Benito Garozzo, star of the fabulous Italian Blue Team, still plays bridge on the Internet. The other three players described in this section are no longer alive – the great player and writer, Terence Reese of England, and two of the finest women players of all time: USA's Helen Sobel and Rixi Markus of Austria (later of England).

Right: Omar Sharif plays a tense game of bridge with some of the world's best players as part of a televised competition in Mayfair, London, in 1970. The opponent on the left is Jonathan Cansino of England.

GABRIEL CHAGAS (BRAZIL)

Gabriel Chagas is by far the most successful bridge player to emerge from South America. Since 1968, he has won the South American championship 22 times and the Brazilian championship 24 times. He has also represented Brazil in more than 40 world championship events. He is one of only eight players ever to have won bridge's Triple Crown: the Olympiad, the Bermuda Bowl and the World Pairs. A company director living in Rio de Janeiro, Chagas speaks eight languages fluently and can communicate well in several others. He is also proficient at tennis, sings and plays the piano.

Here is a brilliant deceptive defence of his, from the 1995 Rio Teams Championship. Chagas was East on the deal shown below. North had promised a four-card major, by using the Stayman convention, and his subsequent 3NT denied four cards in the heart suit. Deducing that there was a 4-4 spade fit, South bid 4♠ over his partner's 3NT.

Right: A brilliant deceptive defence. Chagas disguises his club holding to persuade declarer not to finesse in diamonds.

Following the scheme popular in the USA, West led the ♣2 from his holding of three small cards. Chagas could see 25 points between his own hand and the dummy. South's 1NT bid had promised 15–17 points, so Chagas knew every honour card in declarer's hand. Suppose East wins with the ♣J and switches to a diamond at Trick 2. Declarer will have no alternative but to finesse the ♦J. This will succeed and he will make the game easily. He will draw trumps, play the ♦A and lead a club to the 10. After scoring two club tricks, East would be end-played, forced to lead a heart into dummy's tenace or to concede a ruff-and-discard.

Chagas decided to put up a smoke screen. Pretending that he held ♣A–J doubleton, he cashed the club ace at Trick 2. He then switched to the ♦9. How could declarer possibly take the finesse now? If it lost, West would surely give his partner a club ruff and beat the contract. Barbosa duly rose with the ♦A, drew trumps and took what he assumed was the guaranteed finesse of the ♣10, to set up a discard for his diamond loser. We can only imagine his reaction when the club finesse lost to the ♣Q and Chagas proceeded to cash the ♦K.

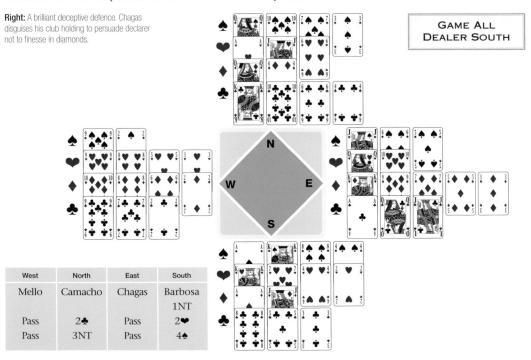

GAME ALL
DEALER SOUTH

West	North	East	South
Mello	Camacho	Chagas	Barbosa
			1NT
Pass	2♣	Pass	2♥
Pass	3NT	Pass	4♠

BENITO GAROZZO (ITALY)

Benito Garozzo was born in Naples in 1927. He learnt to play bridge with some friends during World War II (1939–45). Amazingly he attributes his early fascination with card combinations to Autobridge. (Autobridge was a teaching aid, containing hands set by Culbertson. The player had to slide open small windows in a plastic box to reveal the cards.) By 1954 Garozzo was playing with the top players in Italy and he eventually became a leading light in what was perhaps the greatest bridge team ever – the Italian Blue Team. His list of partners includes many of Italy's finest players. From 1961–72 he played with Pietro Forquet. Then, from 1972 for three years he joined forces with the fiery Giorgio Belladonna. Arturo Franco and Lorenzo Lauria were his next partners, each for a two-year period, and from 1982–5 he rejoined Belladonna. Throughout these years the Blue Team was almost unbeatable. Garozzo won the Bermuda Bowl ten times and the World Teams Olympiad three times. From the time of his first

Above: Garozzo considers his next move.

Bermuda Bowl win in 1961, he never played in a losing team in international competition until 1976, an incomparable record of excellence.

Garozzo rates as his finest performance the closing stages of the 1975 Bermuda Bowl in Bermuda. The Italian team had been forced to withdraw one of their three pairs, after an allegation of passing signals via foot-tapping. The remaining two pairs therefore had to play throughout, which was exhausting. At one stage in the final they were 70 IMPs behind a very strong American team. Amazingly they fought their way back to win.

Here is a fine deceptive play, made by Garozzo during the 1975 Italian Open Teams.

Right: An imaginative deceptive play. By ducking a trick that he could have won, Garozzo misleads the defender and makes an 'impossible' game.

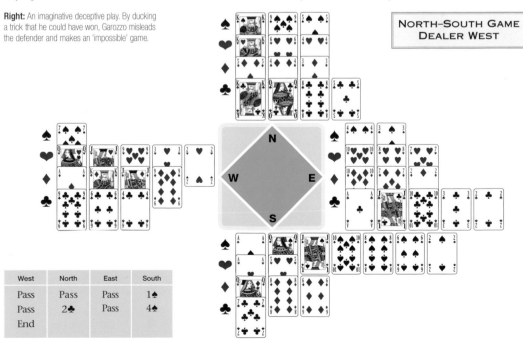

**NORTH–SOUTH GAME
DEALER WEST**

West	North	East	South
Pass	Pass	Pass	1♠
Pass	2♣	Pass	4♠
End			

Most players would open on the West cards nowadays and a surprising number would open on the North cards too. As it was, Garozzo opened 1♠ in the fourth seat and leapt to game in spades when Belladonna responded at the two-level.

West led the ♦K and received a discouraging signal from his partner. He then switched to the ♥Q. Garozzo had a fair idea how the cards must lie. West had indicated the ♦A–K with his opening lead and had also shown at least two points in hearts. If he held the ♣A in addition he would have 13 points, enough to open the bidding. It was therefore certain that East held the ♣A. If declarer played in straightforward fashion, drawing trumps and trying to establish a diamond discard on dummy's clubs, East would win the first round of clubs and sink the contract by switching back to diamonds.

Rather than accept defeat, Garozzo made the brilliant deceptive play of allowing the ♥Q to win! A club switch, followed by a return to diamonds, would now have put the game two down. West naturally assumed that his partner held the ♥A, however. He continued with a second round of hearts and the contract was home. Garozzo unmasked his deception, winning with the ♥A, and then drew trumps in two rounds, ending in the dummy. He discarded his singleton club on the ♥K and led the ♣K for a ruffing finesse. When East covered with the ace, he ruffed in the South hand and returned to dummy with a trump to discard one of his diamonds on the established ♣Q. He had made the seemingly impossible game.

In these days of full-time professional players, it is an interesting reminder of times gone by that Garozzo had another professional 'day job' throughout his great bridge career – he owned a jewellery store in Naples, Italy. He now lives in California, USA, where he plays bridge frequently on the Internet, and is also found at the table with Lea DuPont. In both cases you can be sure that an army of admirers will be following his every move.

ROBERT HAMMAN (USA)

Robert Hamman became the world's top-ranked player in 1985 and retained that status for an amazing 20 years. He has won an unparalleled number of North American titles, the 1988 Olympiad, and the Bermuda Bowl an almost unbelievable nine times (1970, 1971, 1977, 1983, 1985, 1987, 1995, 1999 and 2003). He also won the World Open Pairs championship with Bobby Wolff in 1974. Unlike most of the USA's top players, Hamman achieved all this success while performing an important job outside the game – he was president of SCA Promotions, a prize promotion company.

Hamman joined Ira Corn's Dallas Aces team in 1969, initially partnering Eddie Kantar. He went on to partner Mike Lawrence, Paul Soloway, Billy Eisenberg and Don Krauss, before forming a 25-year-long partnership with Bobby Wolff. His wife, Petra, won the Venice Cup in 2000.

Here is a fine play by Hamman, from USA's win in the final of the 1970 Bermuda Bowl. The Chinese West led the ♠K and Hamman allowed this card to win.

Above: Robert Hamman, playing in the 1973 World Bridge Championship at the Casa Grande Hotel in Guaruja, Brazil. The USA team reached the final but were defeated by Italy.

He took the next round of spades and now had to set up a diamond discard on the club suit. It was not just a question of finding clubs 3–3 with the ace onside, because the defenders might be able to establish their diamond trick before declarer could enjoy his discard.

At Trick 2 Hamman led the ♣7 from his hand. Suppose West were to rise with the ♣A now and switch to a diamond. East's ♦10 would force the ♦A, yes, but declarer could then run the ♦9 to establish a discard for his remaining club loser. West in fact played low on the first round of clubs and Hamman played accurately by passing the trick to East's ♣10. East, who could not attack diamonds successfully from his side of the table, returned another spade. Hamman ruffed and drew trumps with the king and queen. He could then lead a second round of clubs towards the king, setting up the discard that he needed whether West took his ♣A now or on the second round. (If trumps had broken 3–1, the ♥A would have served as an entry to the long clubs.)

As the cards lay, West could have defeated the game with the amazing play of the ♣J on the first round! If declarer wins with dummy's ♣K, West can win the second round of clubs with the ♣A and clear a

Above: The USA win the 1983 Bermuda Bowl in Stockholm. Hamman is shown with team-mates Ron Rubin, Bobby Wolff and Peter Weichsel.

diamond trick. If instead declarer ducks in the dummy, West can switch to a diamond then, with two club tricks guaranteed.

Right: Clever play justifies a bold bid. By ducking the first round of clubs, Hamman avoids a damaging diamond switch.

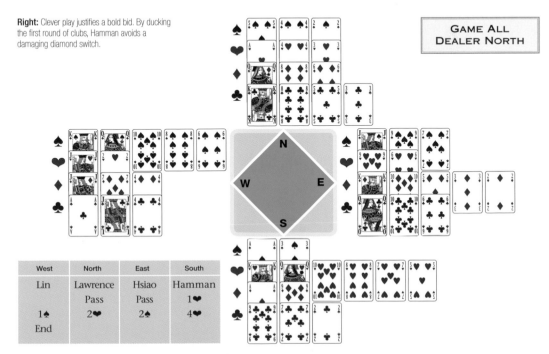

GAME ALL
DEALER NORTH

West	North	East	South
Lin	Lawrence	Hsiao	Hamman
	Pass	Pass	1♥
1♠	2♥	2♠	4♥
End			

ZIA MAHMOOD (PAKISTAN/USA)

Zia is one of the most colourful and skilful players in the game today. If you enter the playing area of a tournament where he is competing, you can easily find his table. It will be the one with the greatest number of spectators (a large proportion of them female). Born into a wealthy family in Pakistan, he represented his home country with great distinction. The highlight was in 1981 when Pakistan exceeded all expectation by reaching the final of the Bermuda Bowl, eventually losing to the USA.

Zia did not learn bridge until he was 25. At that time a beautiful woman invited him to play with her that evening at the local club. 'You do know how to play, don't you?' she said. 'Of course,' Zia replied. He spent the afternoon studying *Five Weeks to Winning Bridge* by Alfred Sheinwold, but was nevertheless exposed as a completely hopeless player in the evening bridge session. Zia soon lost interest in the woman but became addicted to the game of bridge and could not learn quickly enough.

Nowadays Zia has homes in London and New York and represents the USA at bridge. On his first major appearance for an American team he persuaded his team-mates to wear Pakistani costume, to quell any guilt he might have had on switching allegiance. Zia's regular partner is Michael Rosenberg, formerly of Scotland but now also representing the USA. Zia and Rosenberg finished 2nd in the 2002 World Open Pairs in Montreal.

In 1990, in Atlantic City, Zia won the Omar Sharif World Individual Championship, where players are required to partner every other player for one round and a fixed bidding system is played. The event carried a $40,000 first prize. By winning the 2004 World Transnational Teams Championship in Istanbul, Zia acquired the coveted rank of World Grandmaster.

Shown below is a big deal from the semi-final of the 1981 Bermuda Bowl – contested in Port Chester, New York – with Pakistan sitting in the North–South seats and facing Argentina:

**GAME ALL
DEALER SOUTH**

Below: A fine grand slam in the 1981 Bermuda Bowl. Zia establishes the heart suit to dispose of his diamond losers.

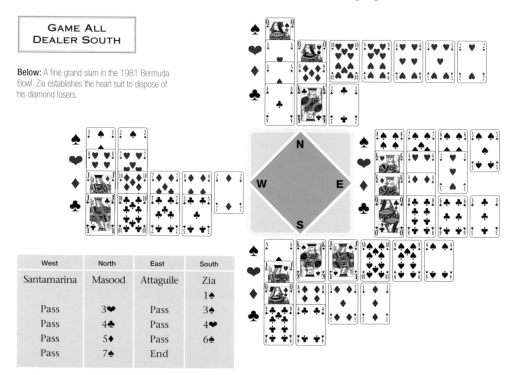

West	North	East	South
Santamarina	Masood	Attaguile	Zia
			1♠
Pass	3♥	Pass	3♠
Pass	4♣	Pass	4♥
Pass	5♦	Pass	6♠
Pass	7♠	End	

led the ♠Q to Trick 2, overtaking in his hand. After drawing trumps in four rounds, he led the ♥J to dummy's ♥A and ruffed a heart. When hearts broke 3–2, he was able to cross to dummy with a club and establish the heart suit with a further ruff. He could then return to the remaining club honour and enjoy the rest of the heart suit, claiming his grand slam. Pakistan went on to defeat Argentina, eventually losing to the USA in the final.

Above: Zia Mahmood is a great advocate of natural bidding, rather than artificial bidding – another reason why he is a favourite with kibitzers.

Zia's leap to 6♠ on the fourth round persuaded Masood that the trump suit would be solid. Trusting that the heart suit could be brought in, he raised to the grand slam. (At the other table, after the same first six bids, the Argentinian South bid only 5♠ and passed his partner's raise to 6♠.)

Zia went on to win the diamond lead with dummy's ace. He knew that to play on hearts immediately, ruffing the second round high, would lead to trouble if the trumps broke 5–1. Zia therefore

Above: Zia lent his strong support to the building of a school, to be known as the World Bridge School, in an earthquake-stricken part of Pakistan.

RIXI MARKUS (AUSTRIA/ENGLAND)

Rixi Markus was born in Austria and represented that country as they won the 1935 and 1936 European women's teams championships, followed by a win in the women's world championship in 1937 in Budapest. Driven to England in the war years, she formed a fearsome partnership with Fritzi Gordon, another émigré Austrian. At the time they were rated by many as the top women's pair in the world. Rixi won another

seven European Championships, now representing Great Britain. In 1962 she and Fritzi won both the World Women's Pairs and the World Mixed Teams, followed in 1964 by a win in the Women's Olympiad in New York. In 1974 the pair again won the World Women's Pairs, by a record margin. Rixi became the first female World Grandmaster. For her services to the game of bridge she was honoured by the Queen with the MBE.

A tiger at the bridge table, Rixi was charming socially and had countless friends around the world. Her bidding was undisciplined and she entered the auction in situations that would terrify a lesser personality. It was in the card play that she excelled.

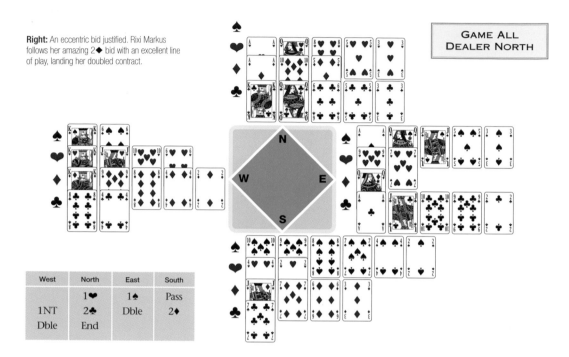

Right: An eccentric bid justified. Rixi Markus follows her amazing 2♦ bid with an excellent line of play, landing her doubled contract.

GAME ALL
DEALER NORTH

West	North	East	South
	1♥	1♠	Pass
1NT	2♣	Dble	2♦
Dble	End		

Above is a typical piece of Rixi action, taken from a rubber bridge game.

Expecting her partner to be void in spades, after the opponents' bidding, Rixi tried her luck in 2♦. West was happy to double this. He led the ♠K, which Rixi ruffed in the dummy. When she continued with the ♣K, East won with the ace and returned the ♦Q to dummy's ace. Some players now might cash the ♣Q, throwing a heart, and then score as many tricks as possible by ruffing hearts in hand and spades on the table.

Rixi realized that this line would bring her only seven tricks. Abandoning her established club trick, she ruffed a low club in her hand. She was then able to take the heart finesse, which was a near certainty on the bidding and the play so far. She then cashed the ♥A, ruffed a heart, ruffed a spade, ruffed a heart and ruffed another spade. In this way she scored two hearts and six trump tricks. She made the doubled contract exactly, without ever scoring her established second trick in clubs.

Right: Fritzi Gordon, long-time partner of Rixi Markus. She won the World Women's Teams in 1964, the World Women's Pairs in 1962 and 1974 and the World Mixed Teams in 1962.

JEFF MECKSTROTH (USA)

Ask any top bridge player nowadays who they rate as the toughest opposition in the world and the likely answer is Jeff Meckstroth and Eric Rodwell of the USA. Meckstroth was a scratch golfer as a teenager. He learnt bridge before going to college, met Rodwell in 1974 and formed a partnership with him the following year. Together they have won almost everything worth winning in bridge – several Reisingers, Vanderbilts and Spingolds (the premier championships in the USA), the Macallan Invitational Pairs in 1995 and 1996, the World Team Olympiad in 1988 and the Bermuda Bowl in 1995, 1999 and 2003.

Meckstroth and Rodwell play a very scientific version of the Precision Club system, one that involves light opening bids. The printed description of their bidding system runs to two or three hundred pages. They are noted for their supreme temperament at the table, despite fiery reputations from their younger days. In 1992 they joined Robert Hamman and Robert Wolff to represent the Scientists against the Naturals in a £50,000 challenge match in London, winning by 70 IMPs.

The deal below features a supremely inventive piece of declarer play by Meckstroth, when facing the world class Norwegians, Geir Helgemo and Tor Helness.

South's 3♣ was a weak response, as the Americans play it. Rodwell rebid 3NT, the contract bid and made at the other table, but Meckstroth took another bid and ended in the apparently doomed club game.

Helness led a diamond and Meckstroth saw that there was little prospect in trying to set up the hearts for a spade discard. When he knocked out the first heart, the defenders would surely switch to spades, establishing a third trick for themselves there. To make life more difficult for his opponents, Meckstroth made the amazing play of the ♦10 from dummy! Helgemo won with the ♦Q and could see no pressing need to switch to hearts. He returned another diamond, on which Meckstroth discarded one of his hearts. The defenders could no longer beat the contract. A heart was played to the queen and ace and a spade switch would not now help the defenders. Declarer was subsequently able to take a ruffing finesse through East's ♥A, setting up a discard for his spade loser.

Below: A brilliantly inventive deceptive play. Jeff Meckstroth surrenders an unnecessary diamond trick, causing the world-class defenders to go wrong.

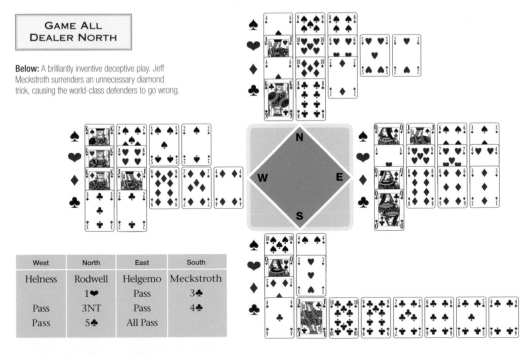

West	North	East	South
Helness	Rodwell	Helgemo	Meckstroth
	1♥	Pass	3♣
Pass	3NT	Pass	4♣
Pass	5♣	All Pass	

TERENCE REESE (ENGLAND)

There can be little doubt that Terence Reese is the greatest bridge writer there has ever been. He wrote 107 titles, which included several genuine masterpieces that were years ahead of their time: *The Expert Game*, *Reese on Play* and *Play Bridge with Reese*. He named various expert techniques, including the Crocodile Coup, the Dentist's Coup, the Vice Squeeze and the Winkle Squeeze. He also wrote eruditely on the Principle of Restricted Choice, which mystifies many players even today.

At his peak, Reese was rated by many as the best bridge player in the world. He formed an outstanding partnership with Boris Schapiro and won four European Championships, the 1955 Bermuda Bowl, the 1962 World Pairs championship and the 1961 World Pair championship (where very difficult hands are set for the players). On the domestic front, he won Britain's Gold Cup eight times and the Master Pairs seven times.

Reese's parents met when they were 'First Gentleman' and 'First Lady' at a whist drive. He learned to play cards before he could read and learnt Auction Bridge at the age of seven. He recounts in his autobiography *Bridge at the Top* how he had to dismount from his chair to sort his cards behind a cushion, 13 being somewhat of a handful.

Reese's career as a player was severely dented by a cheating allegation at the 1965 Bermuda Bowl in Buenos Aires. It was claimed that he and his partner Boris Schapiro had been using finger signals during the bidding, to inform their partner how many hearts they held. The pair was convicted by the World Bridge Federation but later acquitted by a special inquiry set up by the British Bridge League. Although photographs had been taken that showed unusual finger positions by the pair, there was remarkably little evidence from the records of the play of any advantage having been taken of the knowledge supposedly gained. To this day, players will dispute whether any cheating did in fact take place. Be that as it may, the partnership never played again in any international event.

Below: Press photographers await Reese and Schapiro on their return from Buenos Aires. The allegation of finger signalling was news across the world.

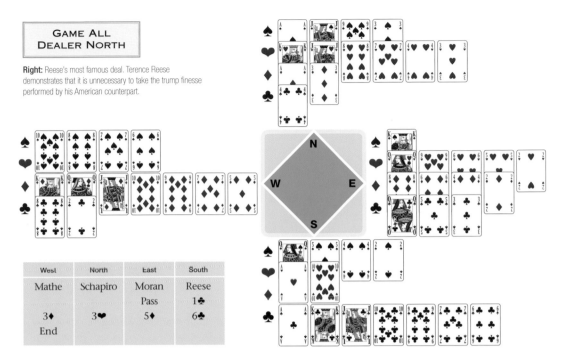

Right: Reese's most famous deal. Terence Reese demonstrates that it is unnecessary to take the trump finesse performed by his American counterpart.

West	North	East	South
Mathe	Schapiro	Moran	Reese
		Pass	1♣
3♦	3♥	5♦	6♣
End			

The slam shown above is perhaps the most famous contract that Reese ever played.

A brief auction carried Reese to a small slam in clubs. West led the ♦9, rather than the normal top honour from a sequence, in the hope that East might win with the ♦A and deliver a heart ruff. Reese ruffed the opening lead and spurned the trump finesse, cashing the ace and king. When the ♣Q did not fall, he needed to set up dummy's heart suit to avoid losing a spade trick.

Reese played the ♥A, West showing out, and continued with a heart to the king and the ♥7, covered and ruffed. He then threw East on lead with the queen of trumps. Whatever card East played next, Reese would have enough entries to dummy to take a ruffing finesse in hearts and eventually enjoy the winners in the suit. He would be able to throw all his potential losers in spades.

At the other table, Rosen (for the USA) reached the same contract. He won the diamond lead with dummy's ace and took a successful trump finesse, making the slam easily. A flat board, yes, but he would have gone down if the trump finesse had lost to a doubleton queen with West. The superior line taken by Reese would be remembered for decades.

PERFECT COMBINATION
♠ ♥ ♦ ♣

Many of the world's top bridge partnerships have consisted of one steady, technical player combined with a more flamboyant partner. A classic example of this was the long-standing partnership of Terence Reese and Boris Schapiro. Reese was a scholarly card-player but a somewhat cautious bidder. Schapiro was less accurate in the play and far more ambitious in the bidding. The pair won many championships, including a record number of Gold Cups.

Above: Boris Schapiro (left) was never afraid of displaying his emotions at the bridge table. His partnership with Terence Reese (right) lasted some 25 years.

OMAR SHARIF (EGYPT)

Omar Sharif, the film actor who first came to public attention playing the role of Ali Ibn Kharish in *Lawrence of Arabia* (1962), has had a life-long fascination with the game of bridge. He captained the team representing the United Arab Republic in the 1964 Bridge Olympiad and by 1968 had formed an attachment with some of the best players in the world. A team known as the Omar Sharif Bridge Circus was formed, containing Delmouly and Yallouze of France, the incomparable Belladonna and Garozzo of Italy and Omar himself. They played a match in London, against England's Flint and Cansino, for the huge stakes (then) of £100 a 100. Sharif's team won handsomely but were generally thought to have had the better of the cards.

In 1975 Sharif's team toured the USA, playing 60-board matches against the champion teams of each region. They were sponsored by Lancia cars and any team that could beat them would win a red Lancia sports car each! The team's PR man, the famous tennis player Nicola Pietrangeli, did not enjoy phoning the sponsors in Rome no fewer than three times, to tell them that they should arrange the shipment of another set of cars.

In his book *Omar Sharif Talks Bridge*, Omar tells this story:

Playing bridge and acting have one thing in common. When you are performing, your heart beats very much faster than normal. When I first started to play with members of the Italian Blue Team, they tended to frown every time I put down the dummy. This put a great strain on my heart. As often as not, all would turn out well in the end and the contract would be made. Meanwhile I had been suffering a thousand deaths, thinking that I made some big mistake in the auction.

After a while I explained gently to them that a man has only one heart. I asked them to take pity on me and not to frown so much. We even arranged a code by which they could let me know how good the final contract was. Members of our team often switched from one language to another during a session and my idea was that if the contract was cold my partner should say '*Merci*' when I put down the dummy. If the contract was touch-and-go and might require some luck or good play, my partner would say '*Thank you.*' Finally, if the contract was hopeless, the response to dummy's appearance would be '*Grazie.*'

In a tournament in Deauville, I was partnering Pietro Forquet. After a very long auction, he arrived in a club grand slam. A trump was led and I put down the dummy.

'*Grazie*,' said Forquet.

'With a splendid dummy like that?' I cried. 'How can it be *Grazie*?'

BUSINESS BEFORE PLEASURE

♠ ♥ ♦ ♣

When asked whether acting or bridge was more important to him, Omar Sharif replied 'Acting is my business – bridge is my passion.'

Left: Omar Sharif shows his hand during the Sunday Times International Bridge Pairs Championships, at the Hyde Park Hotel, London in 1980.

Right: A fine play by Omar Sharif at trick one. By ducking the first round of diamonds, Sharif ensures that his diamond entry cannot be removed.

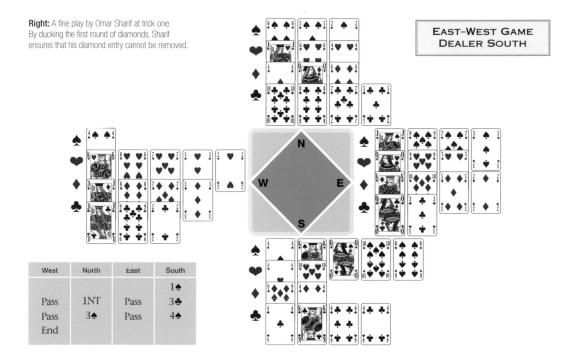

EAST–WEST GAME
DEALER SOUTH

West	North	East	South
			1♠
Pass	1NT	Pass	3♣
Pass	3♠	Pass	4♠
End			

Here is a deal that Omar played well, partnering Paul Chemla in a big tournament in the Deauville casino in France.

West led the ♦3 and Sharif made the excellent play of the ♦6 from dummy. East won but could not continue diamonds into dummy's tenace. He switched to a heart and Sharif won with the ace. When he played the ace and king of trumps, the position in that suit became clear. He crossed to the ♦A and took the marked finesse in trumps. When the clubs came in for only one loser, the game was his. Suppose West had turned up with four trumps to the jack and it was therefore necessary to dispose of the heart loser. Nothing would have been lost by the diamond play at Trick 1. Declarer could finesse the ♦Q on the second round of the suit!

You can see what would happen if declarer was tempted to play the ♦Q on the first trick. East would win with the ♦K and return the suit. When the two top trumps revealed the position in that suit, there would be no entry left to dummy to take a trump finesse.

Several years ago, Sharif underwent a heart triple bypass operation. He gave up playing top-level bridge and now lives a somewhat reclusive life in a Paris hotel. Still, suppose you step into a busy street in London or New York and ask the first passer-by who is the world's most famous bridge player. What answer are you likely to get? 'Omar Sharif, isn't it?'

Above: Actor Omar Sharif at the start of the Macallan International Bridge Pairs Championship in 1997. Sharif joined a line-up of 32 top-class players competing for the trophy, a bottle of The Macallan whisky worth $19,500.

HELEN SOBEL (USA)

There are several claimants for the title 'greatest woman player ever' and the USA's Helen Sobel is certainly among them, having won 33 national championships. She won the McKenney Trophy, for most master points won in a calendar year, on three occasions. Between 1948 and 1964 she was the leading woman in the American Contract Bridge League's all-time master point rankings.

No one meeting a 16-year-old chorus girl in the Marx Brothers' show, *The Coconuts*, would have guessed that they were in the presence of a future great bridge champion. Chico Marx was, in fact, one of the best bridge players in show business. It was from a fellow chorus girl, however, that Sobel learnt the rudiments of bridge. After her first visit to a bridge club, she remarked to a friend, 'You get to know something about trumps, playing pinochle, so I found bridge easy to pick up.'

Sobel herself admitted that in her first couple of years of tournament play, she gained an advantage over any smug male opponents who might have taken her for a dumb blonde and expected soft pickings.

The word soon passed around that the 'tiny blonde who looks like Gertrude Lawrence' played a very tough game indeed.

Her first marriage, at the age of 17, ended in divorce after just three years. It was a second marriage, to bridge expert Al Sobel, that was to change her life. Soon afterwards Ely Culbertson installed her as hostess at the Crockford's Club in New York, while her husband took over the editorship of the magazine *Bridge World*.

In 1937 Sobel was asked by Culbertson to join his team in a world championship event organized by the International Bridge League in Budapest. This was recognition indeed that both she and Josephine Culbertson were rated as the equal of any male player of the day.

Helen Sobel is probably most well known, however, for her enduring partnership with the great Charles Goren. Together they made an incredible team, and represented the USA in the 1957 Bermuda Bowl and the 1960 Olympiad.

Sobel's 33 national titles include the Spingold five times, the Chicago (now the Reisinger) four times and the Vanderbilt twice.

Below: Helen Sobel at the table. Edgar Kaplan, editor of *Bridge World*, said of her 'In my lifetime, she is the only woman bridge player who was considered the best player in the world.'

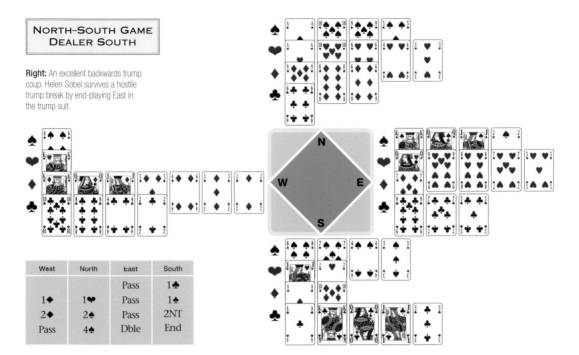

NORTH–SOUTH GAME
DEALER SOUTH

Right: An excellent backwards trump coup. Helen Sobel survives a hostile trump break by end-playing East in the trump suit.

West	North	East	South
		Pass	1♣
1♦	1♥	Pass	1♠
2♦	2♠	Pass	2NT
Pass	4♠	Dble	End

It's time for us to see an example of Sobel's dazzling card play, also her bravery in the bidding. The deal above shows her sitting South during the 1944 Summer Nationals.

Many players of the day would have refused to bid a spade suit of four cards to the eight. Helen Sobel not only bid the spades but continued to 2NT, over a single raise, on a hand that was not much more than a minimum. With a stack of trumps in his hand, East somewhat unwisely doubled the eventual spade game.

Sobel won the ♦K lead with the ♦A and played three rounds of clubs, discarding dummy's two diamond losers. She then led a heart, West's king appearing, and won with the ace in dummy. A second round of hearts was won by East's queen, West discarding a diamond. At this stage the defenders had one trick in the bag and it seemed likely that East would score three more with his ♠K–Q–J–2 poised over dummy's ♠A–10–9–5. See how the play developed, though.

East returned a heart and Sobel ruffed carefully with the ♠7, preventing an overruff from West's ♠6. She continued with a trump to the six, nine and jack. Declarer won the heart return in dummy, throwing the ♣3. She then led another heart, ruffing with the

♠4 in her hand. Trick 11 had been reached and East's last three cards were the ♠K–Q–2. Sobel ran the ♠8 to East's ♠Q and he was forced to lead a trump into dummy's ♠A–10 tenace at Trick 12. It was a splendid example of the technique known as a backward trump coup. If East's double had not alerted declarer to the bad trump break, it is unlikely that the winning line of play would have been found.

It was a source of minor aggravation to Sobel that the question most frequently asked of her, by worshippers of Charles Goren, was: 'What is it like partnering a great player?' Her standard reply was: 'Ask Charlie!'

MAN'S WORLD
♠ ♥ ♦ ♣

In an age where it was almost unheard of for women to compete at world level in open events, Helen Sobel was part of the USA open team that finished second in the World Team Championships in New York, 1957. She also finished fourth representing the USA open team at the 1960 World Team Olympiad, contested in Turin.

GLOSSARY

Chess

algebraic notation Chess notation in which each square of the board is given a unique identifier from a1 to h8, where the letter identifier signifies the file and the number the rank.

attack A move that threatens the advantageous capture of a piece or pawn on the following move, or gives check (q.v.) to the opposing king.

backward pawn A pawn that cannot be defended by another pawn or readily advanced without support from another pawn.

Black The player moving the black chess pieces is usually referred to as 'Black'.

blindfold chess A form of chess where one or both of the players plays without sight of the board and pieces. Moves are communicated verbally.

block To interpose a piece between the opponent's attacking piece and a more valuable piece.

board The chessboard of 64 squares. In the context of a team chess match, games are referred to as boards, e.g. 'board one', 'top board', etc.

castle Or 'castling'. A special combined move involving the king and a rook on the same turn. Note: beginners sometimes refer to the rook as a 'castle' but competition players never do so.

centre The four squares in the middle of the chessboard (in notation: d4, e4, d5, e5).

check A position where the king is attacked, or 'in check', but has means of escaping it. The player making the attack is said to 'give check' or play 'check' or a 'checking move'.

checkmate A position where a king is attacked (or 'in check') and has no legal move to escape the check. A player whose king is thus attacked loses the game. More often simply referred to as 'mate'.

closed position A position where the pieces of both sides have limited scope as the result of pawns blocking most of the lines for manoeuvre.

combination A sequence of moves by one side with a specific tactical purpose (e.g. checkmate or winning a piece).

defend, defence A piece is said to be 'defended' (or 'protected') if its capture can be immediately met by capturing the piece used to take it.

deflecting sacrifice An opposing piece is lured away from the defence of a major piece by the offer of a lesser-value one.

development The process of moving as many pieces into useful positions during the opening phase of the game.

diagonal A line of same-colour squares running obliquely across the board. The lines of squares between opposite right-angles of the chessboard (in chess notation, a1-h8 and h1–a8) are known as the 'long diagonals'.

diagram The two-dimensional representation of a chess position as shown in a chess book or article.

discovered A 'discovered attack' is where a move of a piece effects an attack by another piece of the same colour which had previously been blocked. A 'discovered check' is a move which uncovers an attack by another on the opponent's king.

double check A move that attacks the opponent's king and at the same time discovers (q.v.) an attack by a second piece on the king.

doubled pawns Two or more pawns of the same colour on the same file.

draw A chess game can conclude in a draw, typically where the players agree to do so, or stalemate occurs.

en passant A pawn attacking a square crossed by an opponent's pawn that has advanced two squares on its initial move

may capture the opponent's pawn as though it had only advanced one square. It is said to capture *en passant*.

en prise A piece that may be captured on the opponent's next turn is said to be *en prise* (usually pronounced 'ahn preez').

endgame The phase of a game in which only pawns and a greatly reduced number of other pieces remain on the board, leading to a change of strategy. Not all chess games reach an endgame. Also known as the 'ending'.

exchange Usually refers to the capture of one piece of equivalent value by each of the players on successive moves. For example, White uses a bishop to capture the opponent's bishop, and Black takes the bishop on the following turn.

fianchetto A move by a bishop to an adjacent square in front of the adjoining knight (b2, g2, b7, g7) in the opening phase of the game. A bishop so placed is sometimes referred to as a 'fianchettoed bishop'. From an Italian word meaning 'little flank'.

FIDE Stands for *Fédération Internationale des Échecs*. Also commonly referred to as the World Chess Federation, this organization is responsible for drafting the recognized laws of chess and organizing world championships.

file A column of eight squares between White's side of the board and Black's. In chess notation, the eight files of a chessboard are lettered a to h.

flank the side of the board (normally in reference to the a, b, g and h files)

fork A move that makes a significant or dangerous attack on two or more opposing pieces.

gambit An opening (q.v.) in chess in which a player invites the capture of pieces (or more often pawns) in order to expedite the disposition of the pieces with a view to a quick attack.

grandmaster Title awarded by FIDE (q.v.) to an expert or professional chessplayer who has achieved a number of big scores in major competitions.

intermezzo An intermezzo move (also often referred to as a *zwischenzug* – German for 'in-between move') is a move played in between a sequence of exchanges.

isolated pawn A pawn that cannot be defended or supported by another pawn of its own colour on an adjoining file.

kingside Refers to the side of the board on which the kings stand as the game begins, i.e. the 32 squares on White's right-hand side.

major piece A queen or rook.

match A formal series of games between two opponents, with one point awarded for a win and half a point for a draw. Also refers to a team chess encounter.

mate Short for 'checkmate' (q.v.).

material Describes a player's pieces in terms of their overall values (q.v.). A player with an extra pawn, or a rook versus the opponent's bishop, is said to have a 'material advantage'.

middlegame The phase of a game after opening moves have been made and many of the pieces are deployed in the centre of the board or in close proximity to the enemy forces.

minor piece A bishop or knight.

move The turn to play. References to a number of moves invariably mean 'moves by each player'; thus, 'a game of 30 moves' means 30 moves by White and 30 by Black.

opening The initial moves of the game.

Many standard openings have formal names and are played from memory by experienced players. Note: not all openings are 'gambits' (q.v.).

outpost An outpost is a square on the opponent's half of the board which is easily defensible by pawns but cannot be attacked by enemy pawns.

passed pawn A pawn is referred to as 'passed' if there is no enemy pawn ahead of it on the same file or on adjoining files.

perpetual check A series of checks that do not lead to checkmate but cannot be evaded by the opponent. Normally the game will conclude at this point as an agreed draw or a threefold repetition (q.v.).

piece Loosely used to refer to any chessman; however, in many contexts this term is used more specifically to refer to chessmen *other than* a pawn.

pin A move that attacks an opposing piece which stands in front of a more valuable piece on the same line of attack is said to 'pin' the piece.

position The arrangement of all the pieces on the board at any one time.

problem A composed chess position in which one side can force an outcome (usually checkmate) in the stipulated number of moves. 'Mate in two' means White plays a move, Black replies and then White gives checkmate on the second move.

promotion A pawn that reaches the rank furthest from its starting position is 'promoted' – i.e. removed from the board and replaced by a queen, rook, bishop or knight of the same colour.

queenside Side of the board on which the queens stand as the game begins, i.e. the 32 squares on White's left-hand side.

rank A row of eight squares laterally across the board.

repetition of position *See threefold repetition.*

resign A player who judges that the opponent is ultimately certain to deliver

checkmate can cut the game short by resigning. This is sometimes signified by turning the king on one side, and in tournaments by offering a handshake.

sacrifice A move that deliberately allows a valuable piece to be captured, with a view to achieving checkmate or a long-term advantage.

simultaneous display A chess exhibition in which a strong chessplayer plays games concurrently against a number of opponents. Often abbreviated to 'simul'.

skewer A move that attacks a high-value piece which stands on the same line of attack as a less valuable one behind it (which will be captured when the more valuable piece moves away).

smothered mate Where a knight gives checkmate to an enemy king which is prevented from escape because it is surrounded by its own pieces.

stalemate A position where the player to move cannot move any of the pieces but is not in check. The game ends immediately as a draw.

strategy Long-term planning, often in positions where there are few immediate attacking possibilities.

tactics Short-term calculation, required in complex or combat positions where there are many attacking possibilities.

tempo A move which, for example, involves moving a piece to a square and then back to its previous square to no effect is said to 'lose a tempo'.

threefold repetition Where the same position occurs three times in a game, with the same player to move on each occasion, a player can choose to claim a draw 'by threefold repetition'.

tournament A formal competition in which players meet a number of other competitors in successive rounds. A number of different tournament formats are used for chess, including all-play-all and (less commonly) knock-out.

value, valuable As a rough guide, pieces other than the king are said to have 'relative values' (e.g. queen 9 points, pawn 1 point). Hence a queen is considerably more valuable than a pawn. The king is of infinite value.

White The player moving the white chess pieces is usually referred to as 'White'.

zugzwang A German word meaning 'compulsion to move'. Refers to a position in which the player to move is not in immediate danger but where any move involves spoiling the position in some way. A player in this position is said to be 'in *zugzwang*'.

Bridge

balanced A balanced hand is one containing no singleton or void, usually 4–3–3–3, 4–4–3–2 or 5–3–3–2 shape.

bid An undertaking to take a specific number of tricks, with a chosen trump suit or at no-trumps. A bid of 2♠ (two spades) means you think you can score eight tricks with spades as trumps.

Blackwood A conventional bid of 4NT, asking partner how many aces he holds.

call A term covering any bid, pass, double or redouble.

clear To clear a suit is to drive out all the winners held by the opponents.

combination finesse A finesse where two adjacent cards are missing.

communication The ability to go from hand to hand.

contract The final call determines the contract in which the hand is played – for example, 4♠ doubled.

control A holding that will prevent the opponents from scoring two quick tricks in a suit (ace, king, singleton or void).

convention An agreement between partners to use a bid in an artificial sense.

cross To move from one hand to another.

cue-bid (a) A bid in an opponent's suit, usually to show strength. (b) A bid that shows a control, such as an ace, rather than a suit.

declarer The player who must attempt to make the contract, playing the dummy's cards as well as his own.

defenders The two players who attempt to stop declarer from making his contract.

denomination The chosen trump suit, or no-trumps.

discard The play of a card (not a trump) which does not belong to the suit led.

distribution The pattern of suit lengths in a player's hand (for example, 5–4–3–1).

double A call that increases the penalties if a contract is not made, also the bonuses if it is made.

double finesse A finesse that seeks to entrap two cards, as when you lead to the 10 in an A–Q–10 combination.

double raise A raise that covers two steps – raising 1♥ to 3♥, for example.

doubleton A holding of two cards in a suit.

drop To cause an opposing high card to fall by playing higher cards.

dummy (a) The partner of the declarer. (b) The hand exposed opposite the declarer.

duck To play low, making no attempt to win a trick.

entry A card used to cross from one hand to the other.

establish To set up winners in a suit by removing the opponents' high cards.

finesse An attempt to win a trick with a lesser card in a tenace. You hope that the outstanding higher card lies to the left.

forcing bid A bid that requires your partner to bid again.

forcing defence A style of defence where you attack declarer's trumps by forcing him to ruff.

forcing to game A bid that requires both partners to continue bidding until game is reached.

game To make a game, you must score 100 points below the line.

grand slam A contract to win all 13 tricks.

guard A high card that prevents the opponents from running a suit.

hold up To refuse to part with a high card.

honour card Can be an Ace, king, queen, jack or 10.

insult A bonus awarded to the side that makes a doubled contract.

intervening bid A bid by the side that did not open the bidding.

jump A bid, rebid, raise or response made one or more levels higher than necessary.

key cards The four aces and the king of the agreed trump suit.

knock out To remove a defender's high card.

lead To play the first card to a trick.

limit bid A bid which defines the strength of your hand within narrow limits.

major suit Spades or hearts. A contract of 4♠ or 4♥ will give you a game.

minor suit Diamonds or clubs. A contract of 5♦ or 5♣ will give you a game.

negative double A double of an overcall (for example, 1♣ – 1♠ – Dble) that is intended for take-out.

no bid Call that denotes a pass. (In the USA the word "Pass" is used.)

no-trumps Denomination with no trump suit.

open the bidding To make the first bid (not a pass).

opening lead The first card of the first trick.

overbid A bid that overstates the value of the hand.

overcall The first bid made by the side that did not open the bidding.

overruff To play a higher trump than that of a player who has already ruffed.

overtrick A trick in excess of the contract.

part score A contract below the game level.

pass Call indicating that the player does not want to bid, double or redouble.

penalty Points scored when the opponents' contract has failed.

penalty double A double seeking to increase the penalty when the opponents' contract fails.

point count A method of valuation in which points are assigned to aces, kings, queens and jacks. The most popular scheme is to assign values of 4, 3, 2, 1 respectively.

pre-empt To make a high call on a weak hand with a long suit. The aim is to prevent the opponents from bidding accurately.

preference A bid or pass that indicates to your partner during a game which of the suits you prefer.

protection Bidding in the pass-out seat to prevent the opponents from winning the contract at a low level.

raise To make a higher bid in a suit just bid by your partner.

rebid (a) The second bid made by a player. (b) To bid again a suit that you have already bid.

redouble Either member of a side that has been doubled may redouble. This increases the score if the contract is made, also the penalty if the contract fails.

responder (a) The partner of the opening bidder. (b) The player who responds to any specific call.

reverse A player reverses when he bids at the two-level a suit higher-ranking than his first suit (as in 1♦ – 1♠ – 2♥).

reversing the dummy A form of declarer play where you take several ruffs in the long-trump holding, thereby increasing the total number of trump tricks scored.

revoke To illegally fail to follow suit when you could have done.

ruff To play a trump when a side suit has been led.

sacrifice To bid a contract that you expect to fail, with the aim of conceding a penalty less than the value of the opponents' contract.

sequence A group of consecutive cards, usually honours, such as K–Q–J.

show out To fail to follow suit, having no card of the suit that has been led.

side suit A suit other than the trump suit.

signal The play of a card that passes a message from one defender to another. For example, a high-card signal may encourage a continuation.

sign-off A weak bid designed to end the auction.

single raise Usually a raise from one to two.

singleton A holding of one card in a suit.

slam A contract to make 12 or 13 tricks.

small slam A contract to make 12 tricks.

squeeze A form of dummy play where a defender is forced to discard one of his guards.

Stayman A conventional bid of 2♣ over your partner's 1NT, asking him to bid a four-card major suit.

stopper A high card that will prevent the opponents from running a suit (usually at no-trumps).

support (a) To raise your partner's suit. (b) Trump support is your holding in a suit bid by your partner.

take-out double A double that asks your partner to choose a trump suit (or bid no-trumps), also to indicate how strong his hand is.

tenace Two non-touching high cards, such as A–Q or K–J.

touching honours Two or more honours that are adjacent in rank. For example, the king–queen–jack are three touching honours.

trick A trick consists of four cards, The tricks are played in turn from each of the four hands.

trump A suit, determined in the bidding, which has the power to beat any card in a different suit.

underbid A bid that understates the value of the player's hand.

undertrick The trick or tricks by which the declarer fails to make his contract.

void A holding of no cards in a suit.

VuGraph A method of presenting a bridge game to a large audience. The cards and the bidding are displayed electronically and one or more commentators describe the play to the crowd of watchers.

vulnerable A side that has won a game then becomes vulnerable. Penalties and some bonuses are increased.

USEFUL CONTACTS

CHESS BOOKS AND SOFTWARE
A comprehensive and current list of beginner and elementary chess books and software titles: www.chess.co.uk

USEFUL LINKS
John Saunders's links to chess websites: www.saund.co.uk/chesslinks.html

CHESS CALENDARS
English Chess Federation: www.englishchess.org.uk/event-calendar
Chess Scotland Calendar: www.chessscotland.com/calendar.php
Irish Chess Union Calendar: www.icu.ie/events

CHESS NATIONAL FEDERATIONS
English Chess Federation: www.englishchess.org.uk
Welsh Chess Union: www.welshchessunion.org.uk
Chess Scotland: www.chessscotland.com
Ulster Chess Union: www.ulsterchess.org
Irish Chess Union: www.icu.ie
World Chess Federation: www.fide.com
US Chess Federation: www.uschess.org
Chess Federation of Canada: www.chess.ca
Australian Chess Federation: auschess.org.au
Chess in New Zealand: www.newzealandchess.co.nz

CORRESPONDENCE CHESS
British Correspondence Chess Association: www.bcca.info
National Correspondence Chess Club: www.natcor.org.uk
Chess.com: www.chess.com/echess
Red Hot Pawn: www.redhotpawn.com
International Correspondence Chess Federation: www.iccf.com
US Chess Online: www.uschess.org/content/view/12023/393/
Correspondence Chess League of America: www.chessbyemail.com
Correspondence Chess League of Australia: www.ccla.net.au

CHESS MAGAZINES
Chess (UK) www.chess.co.uk
New in Chess www.newinchess.com
Chess Life www.uschess.org/clo

BRIDGE NATIONAL ASSOCIATIONS
Australian Bridge Federation: www.abf.com.au
American Contract Bridge League: www.acbl.org
Asociación Española de Bridge: www.aebridge.com
Danmarks Bridgeforbund: www.bridge.dk
Nederlandse Bridge Bond: www.bridge.nl
Norwegian Bridge Federation: www.bridgefederation.no/t2.asp
Bridge Federation of India: www.bridge-india.com
German Bridge Federation: www.bridge-verband.de
Contract Bridge Association of Ireland: www.cbai.ie
Canadian Bridge Federation: www.cbf.ca
English Bridge Union: www.ebu.co.uk
Federazione Italiano Gioco Bridge: www.federbridge.it

Fédération Française de Bridge: www.ffbridge.asso.fr
Northern Ireland Bridge Union: www.nibu.co.uk
New Zealand Contract Bridge Association: www.nzcba.co.nz
Polish Bridge Union: www.polbridge.pl
Swedish Bridge: www.svenskbridge.se
World Bridge Federation: www.worldbridge.org

BRIDGE SOFTWARE
Blue Chip Bridge: www.bluechipbridge.co.uk
GIB (Ginsberg's Intelligent Bridgeplayer): www.gibware.com
Bridge Baron: www.greatgameproducts.com
Q-Plus Bridge: www.q-plus.com

LINKS TO BRIDGE WEBSITES
www.bridgelinks.com
www.greatbridgelinks.com

BRIDGE MAGAZINES
Australian Bridge: www.australianbridge.com
Bridge Plus (UK): www.bridge-plus.co.uk
Bridge Magazine (UK): www.bridgeshop.com/magazine.shtml
Bridge Today (online magazine, USA): www.bridgetoday.com
Bridge World (USA): www.bridgeworld.com
Bridge Canada (online magazine): www.cbf.ca/BCanada
International Bridge Press Association bulletin: www.ibpa.com
New Zealand Bridge: www.nzbridge.org.nz

B RIDGE PLAYING ONLINE
Bridge Base Online:
http://online.bridgebase.com
Bridge Club Live:
www.bridgeclublive.com
OK Bridge: www.okbridge.com
Swan Games: www.swangames.com
WorldWinner: www.worldwinner.com

B RIDGE TEACHERS
**American Bridge Teachers
Association:** www.abtahome.com
ACBL bridge teacher locator:
www.acbl.org/learn/findATeacher.html
**English Bridge Union Teachers
Association:**
www.ebu.co.uk/education/ebuta

U SEFUL BRIDGE ADDRESSES
American Contract Bridge League,
2990 Airways Blvd., Memphis, TN
38116-3847, USA
Australian Bridge Federation, PO Box
397, Fyshwick, ACT 2609, Australia

Asociación Española de Bridge,
Juan Hurtado de Mendoza
17, post. 28026-Madrid, Spain
Canadian Bridge Federation,
2719 East Jolly Place, Regina SK,
S4V 0X8, Canada
**Contract Bridge Association
of Ireland,** Templeogue House,
Templeogue Road, Dublin 6W,
Ireland
Deutscher Bridge-Verband, e.V.
Augustinsstr. 9B, 50226 Frechen-
Königsdorf, Germany
English Bridge Union, Broadfields,
Bicester Road, Aylesbury,
HP19 3BG, England
Forbundet Svensk Bridge, Kungsg.
36, 11135, Stockholm, Sweden
Fédération Française de Bridge,
20–21 Quai Carnot-92210
Saint-Cloud, France
Federazione Italiano Gioco Bridge,
Via Ciro Menotti 11, int.C – 20129,
Milan, Italy

Nederlandse Bridge Bond,
Kennedylaan 9, 3533 KH Utrecht,
Netherlands
**New Zealand Contract Bridge
Association,** P.O. Box 7, Carterton,
New Zealand
Norsk Bridgeforbund, Serviceboks 1,
Ulleval Stadion. 0840, Oslo, Norway
Polish Bridge Union biuro Zarzadu
Glownego: 00-019 Warszawa, ul.
Zlota 9/4, Poland

BIBLIOGRAPHY

Averbakh, Yuri, *What You Need
to Know about Endgames* (Caissa
Commerce, 2006)
Basalla, Bob, *Chess in the Movies*
(TPI Wonderworks, 2005)
Brady, Frank, *Bobby Fischer*
(Batsford, 1974)
Chandler, Murray, *How to Beat
Your Dad at Chess*
(Gambit Publications, 1998)
**Chandler, Murray and Milligan,
Helen**, *Chess for Children*
(Gambit Publications, 2004)
Clay, John, *Culbertson: The Man
Who Made Contract Bridge*
(Weidenfeld & Nicolson, 1985)

Clay, John, *Tales from the Bridge Table*
(Hodder & Stoughton, 1998)
Culbertson, Ely, *300 Contract Bridge
Hands* (Bridge World, 1933)
Denison, E.E, *The Play of Auction Hands*
(Lothrop, Lee and Shephard, 1920)
Fox, Mike and James, Richard,
The Even More Complete Chess Addict
(Faber & Faber, 1993)
Golombek, Harry (ed.),
The Encyclopedia of Chess
(Batsford, 1977)
Hamman, Bob and Manley, Brent,
At the Table, My Life and Times
(DBM Publications, 1994)
Hartston, William, *The Guinness
Book of Chess Grandmasters*
(Guinness Publishing, 1996)
Hooper, David and Whyld, Kenneth,
The Oxford Companion to Chess
(Oxford University Press, 1996)
Kasparov, Garry, *Fighting Chess:
My Games and Career*
(Batsford, 1983)
Seirawan, Yasser, *Winning Chess
Strategies* (Everyman Chess, 2003)
Sharif, Omar and Bird, David,
Omar Sharif Talks Bridge
(Finesse Bridge Books, 2004)

Silman, Jeremy, *The Amateur's Mind*
(Siles Press, 1999)
Silman, Jeremy, *How to Reassess Your
Chess* (Siles Press, 2003)
Silman, Jeremy, *The Reassess Your
Chess Workbook* (Siles Press, 2001)
Smith, Marc, *World Class*
(Master Point Press, 1999)
Sunnucks, Anne, *The Encyclopaedia of
Chess* (Robert Hale, 1970)
Ward, Chris, *Improve Your Opening Play*
(Everyman Chess, 2000)
World championship books (American
Contract Bridge League)

Thanks to Tim Bourke for information
on bridge facts and figures. Thanks to
Marc Smith for access to his database
of bridge books.

Index

PICTURE ACKNOWLEDGEMENTS

The publisher would like to thank the following for kindly supplying photographs for this book:
AKG 22 (l), 23; **Alamy** 226, 227 (b); **Ancient Art and Architecture** 49 (b); **Art Archive** 18, 19 (t), 20, 44 (l); **David Bird** 433, 483, 495; **Bridgeman Art Library** 17 (r), 21, 40, 41 (l), 44 (r); **Corbis** 16 (l), 17 (r), 18 (t), 19 (b), 22 (r), 27 (bl), 29 (t), 30 (b), 31, 33, 38 (l), 43 (b), 45 (r), 46 (l), 47, 49 (t), 52, 53 (b), 79, 84, 117, 145, 146, 149, 224, 225, 228, 229, 236, 237, 238, 239, 241, 243 (t), 244, 245 (b), 248, 249, 250, 251, 252, 253, 274, 276, 279 (b), 293b, 351 (t), 359 (b), 496 (b), 497

(b), 484–5; **Chris Dixon** 353 (b); **Corbis** 8 (b); **Empics** 28, 138; **Getty Images** 227 (t), 277 (b), 280, 284 (b), 481 (b), 487 (t); **iStockphoto** 8 (t), 9, 10, 11, 139; **British Chess Magazine** 24, 25, 26, 27 (r), 29, 30, 32, 34, 35, 36, 37, 38 (r), 39, 48, 49 (t), 82, 83, 240, 242, 243 (b), 245 (t); **Mary Evans Picture Library** 270, 272; **The Kobal Collection** 41 (r), 42 (t and c), 43 (t), 496 (t); **PA Photos** 457 (b); **Photos.com** 53 (t); **RNIB** 355 (b); **Jonathan Steinberg** 491; **TopFoto** 46 (r), 494 (b); **World Bridge Federation** 282, 283 (t), 287 (b), 289 (b), 307 (t), 384 (t), 388, 395 (b), 401

(b), 413 (b), 421 (bl), 421 (br), 429 (b), 436 (t), 456 (b), 458 (t), 461 (r), 462 (b), 479 (b), 486 (t), 487 (r), 488 (r), 488 (l), 489 (t), 490 (l), 491 (b), 492 (b), 493 (t), 494 (t), 495 (b), 498 (t), 498 (b).

All other images by Andrew Perris

Every effort has been made to obtain permission to reproduce copyright material, but there may be cases where we have been unable to trace a copyright holder. The publisher will be happy to correct any omissions in future printings.